Dedication

For Charles and Jim

MEDICAL LIBRARY
ASSOCIATION *Guides*

The Medical Library Association
Guide to

Managing Health Care Libraries

SECOND EDITION

Edited by Margaret Moylan Bandy and Rosalind Farnam Dudden

Neal-Schuman Publishers, Inc.
New York   London

Published by Neal-Schuman Publishers, Inc.
100 William St., Suite 2004
New York, NY 10038

Printed and bound in the United States of America.

The paper used in this publication meets the minimum requirements of American National Standard for Information Sciences—Permanence of Paper for Printed Library Materials, ANSI Z39.48-1992.

Library of Congress Cataloging-in-Publication Data

The Medical Library Association guide to managing health care libraries. — 2nd ed. / edited by Margaret Moylan Bandy, Rosalind Farnam Dudden.
    p. cm. — (Medical Library Association guides)
  Rev. ed. of: The Medical Library Association guide to managing health care libraries / Ruth Holst, editor. 2000.
  Includes bibliographical references and index.
  ISBN 978-1-55570-734-7 (alk. paper)
  1. Medical libraries—Administration. 2. Hospital libraries—Administration. 3. Public health—Information services—Management. I. Bandy, Margaret. II. Dudden, Rosalind F. III. Medical Library Association. IV. Title: Guide to managing health care libraries.

Z675.M4 M5 2011
026'.61—dc22

2011000443

Contents

List of Figures

Management in Action

CD-ROM Contents

Chapter 1. Introduction: Libraries in Health Care Settings

Role of Health Sciences Librarians in Patient Safety: MLA Position Statement

Standards for Hospital Libraries 2007

Trends in Hospital Librarianship and Hospital Library Services: 1989 to 2006

Vital Pathways Bibliography 1987–2008

Vital Pathways Brochure. The Hospital Librarian: Your Competitive Edge

Vital Pathways Executive Summary

Chapter 2. The Health Care Environment

2010 Hospital National Patient Safety Goals

Competencies for Lifelong Learning and Professional Success: The Educational Policy Statement of the Medical Library Association

Health Care Reform Resources

Health Literacy Resources

National Action Plan to Improve Health Literacy

Organizations Related to Nursing Education and Certification

Organizations Related to Physician Education and Certification

Resources for Monitoring the Health Care Environment

Chapter 3. Topics in Management

Annual Reports List from AAHSL

Health Sciences + Human Services Library, University of Maryland, Baltimore, 2008–2009 Annual Report

Library Mission and Vision Statements

National Jewish Health 2007 Annual Report

National Jewish Health 2009 Annual Report

Chapter 4. Financial Management

Robert M. Fales Health Sciences Library of the South East Area Health Education Center in Wilmington, NC, Friends of the Libraries Program

Chapter 5. Human Resources Management

Code of Ethics for Health Sciences Librarianship— Medical Library Association

Selected Associations of Interest to Health Care Librarians

Chapter 6. Evaluation and Improvement Management

Data Collection Methodologies Review— NN/LM-OERC

Evaluation Budget Items List

Evaluation Plan Worksheet—NN/LM

Evaluation Report Template

Logic Model Worksheet—NN/LM

MLA Benchmarking Data Collection Worksheet 2007

Resources for Conducting a SWOT Analysis

Taxonomy—Abels-Cogdill Study

University of Wisconsin Extension List of Evaluation Publications

Workbook 4—Needs Assessment

Workbook 5—Quality Improvement

Workbook 6a—Performance Benchmarking

Workbook 6b—Process Benchmarking

Workbook 7a—Library Performance Standards

Workbook 7b—Accreditation Standards

Workbook 8a—Analyzing Studies of Outcomes

Workbook 8b—Using Cost Outcomes

Workbook 8c—Using Logic Model for Outcomes

Chapter 7. Collection Planning Management

Information and Collections Resources

Foreword

In the ten years since the first edition of *The Medical Library Association Guide to Managing Health Care Libraries*, the clinical practice environment for health sciences librarians has changed immeasurably. This second edition is a welcome and much-needed update and expansion of the 2000 edition. While the core mission for health care delivery in the United States remains the same, rapid advances in medical technologies and the pervasive presence of the Internet have changed the way health care is delivered and the way practitioners and recipients of health care services get information.

Health care reform is placing more emphasis on evidence-based practice and comparative effectiveness research. Both of these have implications for medical librarianship. The authors and editors have done an excellent job of expanding the content of the second edition to reflect the new roles that health information professionals can and are playing in the new health care environment. New chapters on "information practice" and "knowledge services" are examples of the way in which the scope of practice for information professionals in hospitals and other health care settings has changed.

While continuing to speak primarily to information professionals in clinical settings, the second edition has more content for practitioners in academic and research settings. Along with the practical "how to do it" content that made the first edition a hands-on reference for practicing librarians, the new edition provides examples of "management in action" to illustrate the basic materials. Further, this edition conveys a new spirit of going beyond the walls of the library and beyond one's comfort zone into the brave new world of health information practice.

Ruth Holst, MSLS, AHIP, FMLA
President, Medical Library Association,
    2010–2011
Senior Editor, *Medical Library Association Guide to Managing Health Care Libraries*,
    First Edition, 2000
Associate Director, National Network of Libraries of Medicine, Greater Midwest Region
Library of the Health Sciences
University of Illinois at Chicago
Chicago, IL

Preface

The *Medical Library Association Guide to Managing Health Care Libraries*, Second Edition, is designed to serve as a comprehensive, practical guide to the processes and programs needed to provide library and information services in health care settings. Increasing financial pressures and radical technological changes have impacted both health care and libraries, necessitating this revision to the acclaimed first edition of this book, edited by Ruth Holst and Sharon A. Phillips more than a decade ago. Librarians in this field are working at the intersection of two volatile and dynamic environments: health care and library and information science.

Health care organizations confront a variety of issues, including:

- The national crisis in health care financing and new health care legislation
- Changing relationships between physicians and hospitals
- Concerns with physician, employee, and patient satisfaction
- Demands by the government and independent agencies for clinical quality and patient safety
- Increasing importance of evidence-based health care
- Advent of the electronic health record
- New roles for nurses and allied health personnel

Librarians have professional challenges that have increased since 2000, including:

- More sophisticated use of information technology
- Expansion and cost of e-journals and e-books
- Trends in scholarly publishing toward open access

- Pressure to be a virtual library with no print resources or customer space
- Changing roles that include more collaboration with work teams
- Involvement in informatics and the electronic health record
- Management mandates to prove the value of professional library services

The Medical Library Association Guide to Managing Health Care Libraries, Second Edition, will help readers meet these demands, preparing them to plan and implement services that deliver information in the best formats to meet the needs of their organization. Health sciences librarians considering a move into management or librarians thinking about entering the health sciences field will find this book a useful guide. The text provides midlevel managers with the latest information in their areas and gives an in-depth picture of the profession. Library directors in hospital or academic medical center settings will find the expertise of the chapter authors a welcome addition to their already extensive knowledge. This book will also be a resource for students in library and information science programs. The book addresses the challenges of managing the technical aspects of the physical and virtual library as well as the services that are essential to meet the information and knowledge needs of customers. Today's electronic environment provides the librarian with a platform to implement systems with the goal of a seamless electronic connection between the customer and the information. To make this happen, the reader will be encouraged to think innovatively and be creatively proactive in dealing with the constant change in information technology both in health care and in libraries. At the same time, the human aspects of library service are covered with information on service desks, meeting the customer outside the walls of the library, embedding the librarian in health care teams, and constant communication with the library customer. The essential task of measuring the value of the library service to health care professionals and administrators will be thoroughly covered.

Organization

This *MLA Guide* has sixteen chapters in three sections. Part I, "Overview," provides essential background information about this rapidly changing field. Chapter 1, "Introduction: Libraries in Health Care Settings," highlights current trends and provides information on essential professional resources. Chapter 2, "The Health Care Environment," covers the who, where, what, how, and when of the health care industry and health care education. This information is critical for anyone planning to enter the field as well as those already engaged in health care library work.

Part II, "Management," contains seven chapters. Chapter 3, "Topics in Management," covers the many roles the library manager needs to play, including leader, planner, and marketer. Chapters 4 and 5 address two core management functions, "Financial Management" and "Human Resources Management." Chapter 6, "Evaluation and Improvement Management," details how we can communicate the value and worth of our programs and how to use appropriate evaluation methods and measurement tools. The early chapters cover how to apply general management skills in a library context; the next set covers library-centric skills. Chapter 7, "Collection Planning Management," addresses the transition for most libraries from a print-only environment to either a digital one or a combination collection. Topics addressed include scholarly communication, format migration, open access, e-portals, metasearch technology, and repositories, as well as selection and deselection, archiving, aggregators, and budget.

Chapter 8, "Collection Technical Management," will help you organize the collection by describing in detail the workings of an integrated library system for control of cataloging, circulation, serials, acquisitions, and an online catalog. New to many librarians is how to manage electronic collections, utilizing e-portals, open URL linking, electronic resource management systems (ERMSs), and journal aggregators. The final challenge in this chapter is a description of working with IT departments. Chapter 9 introduces the library facility as an intellectual

gateway. "Library Space Management" discusses the librarian's roles and responsibilities, whether building a new building or renovating an existing space, covering design trends and basic design principles of new and innovative features in library space.

Part III, "Services," covers an amazing array of topics. Chapter 10 takes a new look at the traditional reference service by examining "On-Site and Web-Based Information Services." On-site services such as desk services, mediated searching, or search consultation services are discussed as well as such web-based services as e-mail, chat, text messaging, "ask a librarian" services, remote access to electronic resources and services, principles of library webpage design, and document delivery services. Chapter 11, "Educational Services," discusses the librarian's role in providing instruction in a coordinated and professional manner. From general user orientation to integrated curriculum programming to database and literature searching education and running a computer lab, the reader will find tips on different kinds of services offered in libraries. Chapter 12 introduces the concept of "Information Practice." The new "information practitioners" will be working with evidence-based medical practice, informatics technology, systematic reviews, meta-analysis guideline development, nursing magnet status, and research projects. The concept of "Knowledge Services" is introduced Chapter 13, helping librarians understand how to manage data, information, knowledge, and understanding. The reader will learn about complexity, systems thinking, and organizational learning and will obtain skills needed to operate in this new arena.

A major specialized service that many health care libraries provide is covered in Chapter 14, "Health Information for Patients and Consumers." Library and management activities such as assessing service needs, funding, staffing, budgeting, and collection development are reviewed from the point of view of this important community service. Librarians are often asked to take on other duties or they see a promotional reason to do so. Chapter 15, "Associated Services," covers some of these services in detail. These include continuing medical education delivery, managing archives, supporting multimedia creation and collections, supporting scholarly communications, and tracking institutional publications. The last chapter, Chapter 16, "Solo Librarians," concerns some of the rewards and challenges of practicing librarianship in a one-person library. Covering planning, staffing, advocacy, and support services, this chapter will give you tips on how to manage in this situation.

Besides technical aspects of library operations, most chapters will include Management in Action case studies.

The accompanying CD-ROM contains a variety of resources to complement the contents of the book and provides live links to the many Internet resources listed in the book. The contents include various MLA policy statements, templates for developing policies and procedures, bibliographies, and evaluation tools. Also included is a copy of each chapter bibliography with clickable links to the web resources.

Throughout the book, the essentials of knowledge and implications for current practice are addressed. Readers will learn the broad issues involved in leading a health care library operation as well as many details that will help them make everyday decisions. The authors challenge library managers to leave the confines of the physical library and meet their customers where they work. The library leader is encouraged to become an active member of the health care team, whether in a hospital or academic setting. Constant attention to customer needs through this kind of interaction will lead to a strong library and information program that will enable the health care library manager to ride the waves of change with skill and grace.

Acknowledgments

The editors want to thank a number of individuals for contributing their knowledge, skills, experience, and encouragement to the completion of this book.

A heartfelt "thank you" to

- Ruth Holst, editor of the first edition of this book, who encouraged us to take on the job of updating and expanding it and was confident that we could do it
- Our chapter authors, who accepted the challenge of updating this classic text and brought to it their enthusiasm and expertise, as well as a willingness to write the book "in the cloud" using web technologies
- Our co-workers, for their support, encouragement, and understanding of our involvement in this endeavor:
  - At Exempla Saint Joseph Hospital:
    - Joyce E. Condon, Reference Librarian
    - Ellen D. Graves, Reference Librarian
    - Darian Ingram, Library Technician
    - Hank Kisner, Video Engineer
    - Tim Rockwood, A-V Technician
  - At National Jewish Health:
    - Shandra Prozko, Information Specialist
    - Barb Griss, Information Specialist
    - Ann Jessen, Library Technician
    - LaVonne Griffie, Library Technician
- Our colleagues, especially Sara Katsh, MA, manager of the AORN Library
- Sandy Wood, our development editor, cheerleader, and mentor in helping us at every stage of editing this book
- Charles Bandy, for providing us with the wonderful Joomla content management system that enabled us to organize and complete this multiauthored book and for his extensive help on organizing and producing the CD-ROM
- Our late parents, who valued education and professional commitment and taught us to do the same:
  - William D. and Catherine E. Moylan
  - George Bronson and Nancy Farnam
- Our life partners Charles Bandy and Jim Mills, whom we can never thank enough for their love and support in this and all of our endeavors

And finally, we thank each other, for over 30 years of friendship and professional collaboration that has culminated in the publication of this book.

I
Overview

**Introduction:
Libraries in
Health Care Settings**

**The Health Care
Environment**

1

Introduction: Libraries in Health Care Settings

Margaret Moylan Bandy *and Rosalind Farnam Dudden*

Health care librarians work in a variety of settings, but all of them are experiencing not only evolutionary change, as was mentioned in the first edition, but also revolutionary change in the health care environment, in technology, and in the expectations of library customers. Whether providing services in clinical care settings, in academic libraries, association libraries, industry libraries, or consumer health libraries, the librarian will need state-of-the-art tools and techniques to meet the demands of this field. Today's library manager needs to continually update the knowledge and skills required to meet customers' needs and changing information-seeking/using habits. Chapters 7 and 8 describe the latest methods of planning and managing modern library collections.

Even something as seemingly simple as reading the literature has changed and it is projected that it will continue to change. Twenty years ago, before electronic journals, physicians, scientists, nurses, and other health care users of the literature would request a literature search of a librarian, get a photocopy from the print collection organized by the library staff, read it, analyze it, and store it in a file cabinet. Today, these same people do their own literature search after some training from the library staff, link to the PDF of an article purchased by the library, using systems developed by the library staff, read it, analyze it, and store it on a computer disk. They can do all of this at their desk without talking to a librarian or coming to the physical library.

Renear and Palmer (2009: 832) ask, "How will scientists work with the literature in 2019?" They believe

> scientists will still read narrative prose, even as text mining and automated processing become common; however, these reading practices will become increasingly strategic, supported by enhanced literature and

ontology-aware tools. As part of the publishing work-flow, scientific terminology will be indexed routinely against rich ontologies. More importantly, formalized assertions, perhaps maintained in specialized "structured abstracts," will provide indexing and browsing tools with computational access to causal and ontological relationships. Hypertext linking will be extensive, generated both automatically and by readers providing commentary on blogs and through shared annotation databases. (Renear and Palmer, 2009: 832)

How will the librarians in 2019 be interacting with this view of the literature? As you will find in many of the chapters in this book, including Chapter 10, health sciences librarians are already interacting with blogs, wikis, work-flow technologies, and indexing and browsing tools. The spirit of innovation and the willingness to get out of the library and meet the customer, as in Chapter 12, will keep the health sciences librarian as an active team member in the transfer of data, information, and knowledge from the physical or virtual page to the mind of the reader.

> **ontology** (n) (computer science) a rigorous and exhaustive organization of some knowledge domain that is usually hierarchical and contains all the relevant entities and their relations; (n) the metaphysical study of the nature of being and existence.

The knowledge environment of individual health care readers as described earlier is changing, as is the system in which they work. As described in Chapter 2, the health care environment in the United States is in the midst of the preliminary stages of reform that it is hoped will some day see all Americans cared for equally. In many countries in the world, this is already happening. As the entire health care system evolves so will the role of information in the system. Health sciences librarianship is international in its scope. Many innovations and evidence-based reports come from outside the United States. In a recent article about future plans for the Norwegian Electronic Health Library (NEHL), the authors describe a system that, by improving its interactive capabilities, will move from a passive knowledge repository to a system "not only for knowledge transfer, but for integrated knowledge management" (Nylenna et al., 2010: 1048). They go on to say that "knowledge is the foundation for high-quality health care. Most efforts to improve quality are linked to knowledge management—i.e., improved creation, organization, diffusion, use, or exploitation of knowledge" (Nylenna et al., 2010: 1048). The new system would "need clarified roles, seamless,

interoperable technology, and a standardized vocabulary. Such systems would provide the infrastructure to deliver knowledge to the user" (Nylenna et al., 2010: 1048). In comparing the need for "clear, clean knowledge" to the need for clear, clean water, Sir Muir Gray (2006: 129) describes a library as being like "a conduit of knowledge, ensuring that the properly formulated information reaches clinicians and patients at a time of need." Chapter 14 specifically addresses serving the information needs of patients.

In the NEHL, what kind of knowledge should then be regarded as clean, clear, and worthy of transporting? It would be evidence-based. "The three Rs of evidence based communication are reliability, relevance, and readability. Such knowledge could be the gold standard, brought from source to user by the conduit" (Nylenna et al., 2010: 1048). In the sidebar, the NEHL's present and future are described further. Librarians, whether in the United States or in other countries, need to be prepared for these kinds of systems. In addition to the technological component of knowledge management, librarians should embrace their emerging role as a facilitator for tacit knowledge sharing as described in Chapter 13. This is a critical factor in successful development of these systems.

> NEHL was based on three concepts: equality, quality, and efficiency. First, provision of health services of equal quality to all groups of the population throughout Norway implies equal access to knowledge within the health system. Second, clinicians need high-quality knowledge based on systematically assessed research evidence, so selected content resources should only be included, with quality more important than quantity. Third, efficient resource allocation and use is crucial in a publicly funded health system, so procurement of licenses and subscriptions would be needed at the national level to increase negotiating power and result in increased content for the same investment. (Nylenna et al., 2010: 1048)

> Use of NEHL to share knowledge and possibly local experiences could generate a mechanism to transform tacit knowledge to explicit knowledge. Additionally, we will consider how to record and share clinical uncertainties in cases where little evidence is available. Integration of our services into local information systems might help knowledge translation. Institutions can now upload and store local information that is also relevant on a national level, so NEHL could become a service that assists knowledge mobilization in the whole health system. NEHL will then help to drive change from passive knowledge transfer to increasingly active and systematic knowledge management. (Nylenna et al., 2010: 1051)

Profiles of Libraries in Health Care Settings

Describing the health care libraries of today has partly been accomplished through surveys, standards, and other initiatives. Whether in hospitals, academic, or other settings, the libraries have advocates in the associations that provide these kinds of description.

Vital Pathways Survey Subcommittee

The first edition of this book summarized a 1990 survey of health care libraries in the United States carried out by the American Hospital Association (AHA) (Wakeley, 1993) and unpublished data from a 1994 membership survey conducted by the Medical Library Association. In 2004 MLA established a Task Force on the Status of Hospital Librarians with the goal of collecting current data, and from that data develop action plans in support of hospital libraries. With the formation by MLA President M. J. Tooey of the Task Force on Vital Pathways for Hospital Librarians in 2005, the 2004 Task Force became the Vital Pathways Survey Subcommittee (VPSS).

The VPSS developed a survey modeled on the 1990 AHA survey and distributed it between September 2005 and October 2006; the survey design and results were published in the *Journal of the Medical Library Association* (Thibodeau and Funk, 2009) and are available on the **accompanying CD-ROM**. The summary conclusions stated the following:

> The status of hospital librarians and libraries is still volatile due to the dynamic nature of the health care and financial environments. While the types and number of services have increased, about a third of the respondents report that staffing has been downsized. However, it appears that a higher percentage of hospital libraries have professional librarians delivering those services than in the past. The change of status report form has shown that closures are continuing, but other pressures are having an impact on the status of libraries, including the loss of MLS staff, changing reporting structures, loss of space and resources, and consolidation within other hospital departments or libraries. (Thibodeau and Funk, 2009: 278)

In response to anecdotal information and at the request of the Vital Pathways Task Force, MLA headquarters also posted a "Change in the Status of a U.S. Hospital Library" form on MLANET (http://www.mlanet.org/resources/vital/status_form.html). The form allows MLA to collect information more quickly than could be done by survey.

The changes reported can be positive or negative, and if requested by the library manager, MLA headquarters will write a letter to the institution's administrator in support of the library. This effort is one of the many resources developed in conjunction with the Vital Pathways Task Force. Additional materials from Vital Pathways are on the **accompanying CD-ROM**.

Health Sciences Library Statistics and Benchmarking

Based on the programs of the Association of Academic Health Sciences Libraries (AAHSL) and other associations, MLA began a program for libraries to compare inputs and outputs across like institutions. The membership of MLA is more varied than AAHSL so it was necessary to make the data gathered in different institutions truly comparable. Definitions of what each measure meant were developed over time. Libraries that participated agreed on the definitions and then started collecting the data in the recommended manner. By using the raw data or using ratios, library managers could see how they compared to others and find specific opportunities for improvement. The comparative figures developed in the surveys of the MLA Benchmarking Network have been used for service comparisons, to establish best practices, for management decisions, or for research projects (Dudden, 2006a; Dudden, 2006b; Health Sciences Library Statistics and Benchmarking, 2007; Dudden, 2007).

Association of Academic Health Sciences Libraries (AAHSL) Statistics

The Association of Academic Health Sciences Libraries (AAHSL) comprises the libraries serving the accredited U.S. and Canadian medical schools belonging to or affiliated with the Association of American Medical Colleges. It includes other related libraries and organizations. The idea for the *Annual Statistics* began with a 1974/1975 national survey conducted by Donald D. Hendricks, director of the University of Texas Health Science Center Library at Dallas, which Hendricks repeated the following year (Shedlock and Byrd, 2003). Since 1978 AAHSL has published annual statistics to provide comparative data on collections, expenditures, personnel and services in medical school libraries in the United States and Canada. The AAHSL *Annual Statistics* are available for purchase to nonmembers through their website (http://www.aahsl.org/mc/page.do?sitePageId=84868).

Standards for Libraries in Health Care Settings

There are three broad types of standards: technical, performance, and accreditation. Performance and accreditation standards are used to measure a whole program. Technical standards are needed for industry and manufacturing so various products can work together, such as the standardization of the size of a light bulb socket so you can buy any brand of bulb. In libraries, technical standards exist for such things as interlibrary loan transactions and cataloging rules and MARC records and now include standards for OpenURL transfer and counting of journal use. While library managers need to be aware of technical standards and be sure products they buy comply with them, most managers are concerned with performance and accreditation.

Performance standards are written for libraries of a certain type usually by the association that supports those libraries, such as the Medical Library Association or the Association of College and Research Libraries. When linked to accreditation programs, surveys are carried out to judge whether or not the standards are met. The result can be that the survey instrument itself becomes controversial, requiring careful training of the surveyor to use the instrument. Rather than be "forced" to comply, some prefer to adopt guidelines, while others who need justification for improvement prefer standards and inspections.

Accreditation standards apply to the institution the library serves. These would be health care educational accreditation standards on all levels and accreditation standards or hospitals and other institutions. Colleges and universities have regional accreditation bodies. Medical schools respond to directives from the Association of American Medical Colleges (AAMC) through the Liaison Committee on Medical Education (LCME). Medical residency training programs are accredited by the Accreditation Council for Graduate Medical Education (ACGME). Nursing education programs are accredited by the National League for Nursing (NLN). Hospitals are accredited by The Joint Commission (TJC). These agencies are important to libraries because they often contain clauses about libraries and information services. Just as important today, they help define the culture of the organization and how that culture could or should use information, information that is often provided by a library. A manager can generate service ideas by looking at library standards from related libraries.

The **Association of College and Research Libraries** (ACRL) has an active program of writing guidelines and standards. Its latest overarching standard, *Standards for Libraries in Higher Education*, was published in 2004 (ACRL College and Research Libraries Task Force, 2004). Other guidelines and standards on their website (http://www.ala.org/ala/mgrps/divs/acrl/standards/index.cfm) include documents for distance learning library services, information literacy competency standards for higher education, and guidelines for media resources in academic libraries.

The **Association of Academic Health Sciences Libraries** (AAHSL) and the Medical Library Association (MLA) produced the report *Challenge to Action* in 1987, which, while not officially a set of standards, has been very helpful in demonstrating to administrators what to expect from an academic health center library (Association of Academic Health Sciences Library Directors. Medical Library Association. Joint Task Force, 1987). Recently AAHSL published the report, *Building on Success: Charting the Future of Knowledge Management within the Academic Health Center* that updates the *Challenge to Action* and introduces all technological, economic, and social changes since 1987 (Association of Academic Health Sciences Libraries, AAHSL Charting the Future Task Force, 2003). The examples of success or suggestions for future collaborations suggest the critical areas in which libraries and librarians provide the most value to the organization.

Standards for Hospital Libraries have been continuously influenced by the library standards of the **Joint Commission on Accreditation of Healthcare Organizations (JCAHO)**, now called **The Joint Commission**. The Hospital Libraries Section (HLS) of Medical Library Association (MLA) and its precursors have a history of publishing standards for hospital libraries that can be traced back to 1953, the most recently updated in 2007. The Joint Commission (TJC) accredits 20,000 health care organizations. TJC has been in existence since 1951 and in 1978 included a hospital library standard, based on work by MLA committees. This action resulted in development of MLA/HLS standards in 1984, 1994, 2002, and 2007.

As libraries move into the fast-changing digital age, evidence of quality and meeting the needs of the user become the hallmark for standards. In her book *Using Benchmarking, Needs Assessment, Quality Improvement, Outcome Measurement, and Library Standards*, Dudden, (2007) includes a chapter that discusses using these standards to help evaluate and manage a library program. This activity is also briefly mentioned in Chapter 6. The

MLA *Standards for Hospital Libraries 2007* (Hospital Libraries Section Standards Committee, 2008) were written again to complement TJC's idea of knowledge-based information (KBI) integration in the health care setting, focusing on functions rather than on a department that provides it. The 2007 standards are included on the **accompanying CD-ROM**. The introduction to the MLA standards is quoted in the sidebar.

MLA's "Standards for Hospital Libraries 2007" have been developed as a guide for hospital administrators, librarians, and accrediting bodies to ensure that hospitals have the resources and services to effectively meet their KBI needs. KBI refers to current expert information, produced externally to the organization, including:

- journals, texts, documents, and databases in print or electronic format;
- benchmarks, best practices, guidelines, and consensus development statements;
- research studies; and
- quality-filtered Internet resources.

KBI is vital to the hospital, in that it supports:

- patient care,
- managerial and strategic decision making,
- performance improvement and patient safety,
- lifelong learning and professional competence of hospital and medical staff,
- patient and family education, and
- research initiatives.

The medical librarian, as a specialized information professional, is uniquely prepared to provide the oversight and management of KBI resources and services to the hospital or health system. The medical librarian brings specialized competencies to the institution, for the selection, organization, dissemination, and integration of KBI resources into the day-to-day operations of the institution. (Hospital Libraries Section Standards Committee, 2008: 163)

Additional Resources for the Library Manager

In addition to standards and benchmarking tools there are a number of agencies and associations that provide tools for effective library services, professional development, and networking opportunities with colleagues. Some of these are briefly listed below and additional information pertinent to specific topics is covered in Chapters 3, 4, and 5.

National Libraries and Professional Associations

National Library of Medicine (NLM) and the National Network of Libraries of Medicine (NN/LM)

Health care librarians are fortunate to have access to the resources and expertise of the National Library of Medicine (http://www.nlm.nih.gov/) and the National Network of Libraries of Medicine (http://www.nnlm.gov). Chapter 10 describes how NLM services and resources are used effectively. Services and resources of the NLM include but are not limited to:

- MEDLINE/PubMed and other scientific databases
- DOCLINE System for Resource Sharing
- MedlinePlus Consumer Health Information
- Preservation and Collection Management
- History of Medicine Resources
- Reference Services
- Grants

The National Network of Libraries of Medicine is divided into eight regions. Under contract to the National Library of Medicine it provides the following:

- Training and Educational Opportunities
- Funding Opportunities
- Consultation Services
- Curricula and Materials for Presentations
- Advocacy and ROI Resources

Medical Library Association (MLA)

The Medical Library Association (http://www.mlanet.org) along with its sections and chapters is the premiere professional association for health sciences librarians. As stated on the website, "MLA provides lifelong educational opportunities, supports a knowledgebase of health information research, and works with a global network of partners to promote the importance of quality information for improved health to the health care community and the public." Some specific resources and services include:

- *Journal of the Medical Library Association*
- Continuing Education Program
- Sections and Special Interest Groups that represent the varied subfields and areas of specialization of the association's membership (http://www.mlanet.org/sections/sections.html)

- Chapters in thirteen regions of the U.S. and Canada (http://www.mlanet.org/chapters/chapters.html)
- Annual and Chapter Meetings
- Books, Pamphlets and Online Publications
- Advocacy Resources
- Grants, Scholarships, and Professional Recognition Awards

MLA frequently addresses national information issues and policies that are relevant to health sciences librarianship. An example is the recent "Role of Health Sciences Librarians in Patient Safety Position Statement" (Bandy, Stemmer Frumento, and Langman, 2009), which is available on the **accompanying CD-ROM**.

Meeting the Challenge for the Next Decade

In the introductory essay to the Vital Pathways Symposium, M. J. Tooey wrote about the challenges facing health care librarians today. Although she was writing specifically about hospital librarians, her words ring true for health care librarians in other settings as well: "Although these are difficult times for all libraries, hospital librarians and libraries seem particularly affected.... [This is] a competitive health care environment that is driven by the bottom line, influenced by real estate hunger, and affected by the belief... that access to health information comes from the Internet and is free" (Tooey, 2009: 268).

One lesson that health care librarians are learning is that the twenty-first-century health care librarian needs to leave the library. This can be a great challenge. The traditional library tasks of selection and organization are still necessary, albeit in a different format. The general management tasks of budgeting, human resources, planning and marketing must still be done. But the customer is no longer stopping by. And when the library customer does come in, they are staring at a screen and not talking to the librarian. How do we choose where we should go?

In her 1983 inaugural address, MLA president Nina W. Matheson exhorted her audience to "Seize the Day" and reminded them that their intellect and talent provide a "potentially powerful engine" (1984: 79). "We must make our libraries and services integral to the information systems of our institutions and we must develop ourselves as professionals to share in the leadership and processes of innovation" (Matheson, 1984: 81). She concluded by saying that it is our vision that will

drive this engine, and quoted the poet Theodore Roethke (1953: 120) to capture this feeling:

> I wake to sleep, and take my waking slow.
> I feel my fate in what I cannot fear.
> I learn by going where I have to go.

What specific steps can we take to engage our vision to meet these challenges? The chapters in this book provide direction. First, we can look at our core values and purpose as a profession. This can be done by reading MLA's or ALA's code of ethics as printed in Chapter 5. MLA's code is also on the **accompanying CD-ROM** (Chapter 5 section). We can discuss our purpose with our colleagues. A group of librarians in Darien, Connecticut, wrote purpose statements following a conference that are "meant to be grand, optimistic, obvious, and thankful to and for our users, communities, and the tireless librarians who work the front lines every day, upholding the purpose of the Library" (Blyberg, Greenhill, and Trainor, 2009). They stated: "The purpose of the Library is to preserve the integrity of civilization." Having stated this, they then explore the role of the librarian and the library and the types of activities that will preserve the library. While from the public library point of view, much is applicable to health care libraries.

Next, we can approach our customers and *ask them what they want*. Lindberg and Humphreys (2005: 1067) state that "everyone craves access to more electronic information, no matter how much is available, but people treasure efficient methods for extracting pertinent information from the fire-hose effect of undifferentiated electronic text (and unwanted commercial offers)". While this great mass of digital information is already here, to help our users to use it efficiently they state that "digital libraries derive much of their value from the selection, organization, analysis, and linking performed by highly skilled human beings aided by increasingly advanced software systems—in other words, digital libraries still need librarians" (Lindberg and Humphreys, 2005: 1069).

Finally, we can monitor trends and appropriately apply them in our settings. Several publications have studied trends and looked to the future. They have been paraphrased in a recent committee report of the Association of College and Research Libraries. While aimed at the academic library, they are applicable to all libraries:

1. Academic library collection growth is driven by patron demand and will include new resource types.
2. Budget challenges will continue and libraries will evolve as a result.

3. Changes in higher education will require that librarians possess diverse skill sets.

4. Demands for accountability and assessment will increase.

5. Digitization of unique library collections will increase and require a larger share of resources.

6. Explosive growth of mobile devices and applications will drive new services.

7. Increased collaboration will expand the role of the library within the institution and beyond.

8. Libraries will continue to lead efforts to develop scholarly communication and intellectual property services.

9. Technology will continue to change services and required skills.

10. The definition of the library will change as physical space is repurposed and virtual space expands. (ACRL Research Planning and Review Committee, 2010: 286–289)

Two documents in particular discuss these trends in some depth. In *No Brief Candle: Reconceiving the Research Library for the 21st Century*, common themes include collaboration between librarians, faculty, and information technology experts to articulate strategies and tactical approaches to a rapidly changing environment. This is a report of a conference held in February 2008, where the Council on Library and Information Resources (CLIR) convened 25 leading librarians, publishers, faculty members, and information technology specialists to consider this question. Participants discussed the challenges and opportunities that libraries are likely to face in the next five to ten years, and how changes in scholarly communication will affect the future library. The report contains eight background essays as well as a summary of the meeting (Council on Library and Information Resources, 2008).

The second document is the National Library of Medicine's (NLM) Long Range Plan, 2006–2016, called *Charting a Course for the 21st Century*. A copy is available on the **accompanying CD-ROM**. The document lays out a strategic vision of what NLM's role will be:

In a world that is increasingly digital, the National Library of Medicine (NLM) already plays a pivotal role in enabling biomedical research, supporting health care and public health, and promoting healthy behavior. By connecting and making the results of research—from scientific data to published literature to patient and consumer health information—readily available, the Library magnifies the positive impact of the country's investment in the creation of new knowledge. In the next ten years, NLM's programs and services will become even more central to scientific discovery, treatment, and prevention. Careful planning and visionary thinking are critical to the pursuit of that future. (National Library of Medicine. 2006: 11)

The NLM Long Range Plan contains four overall goals with recommendations for each:

Goal 1. Seamless, Uninterrupted Access to Expanding Collections of Biomedical Data, Medical Knowledge, and Health Information

Goal 2. Trusted Information Services that Promote Health Literacy and the Reduction of Health Disparities Worldwide

Goal 3. Integrated Biomedical, Clinical, and Public Health Information Systems that Promote Scientific Discovery and Speed the Translation of Research into Practice

Goal 4. A Strong and Diverse Workforce for Biomedical Informatics Research, Systems Development, and Innovative Service Delivery. (National Library of Medicine, 2006: 7–8)

These goals and futuristic ideas affect how physicians and other health care workers will be educated in the future. How will they learn all these new technologies and how will they be able to use them when they start to practice? Stead et al. (2010: 1) propose that "the explosive growth of biomedical complexity calls for a shift in the paradigm of medical decision making from a focus on the power of an individual brain to the collective power of systems of brains. This shift alters professional roles and requires biomedical informatics and information technology (IT) infrastructure." The authors map the informatics competencies needed for future health professionals and summarize the evolving understanding of both beneficial and deleterious effects that informatics-rich environments will have on learning, clinical care, and research. The volume of data the expert will need to integrate for clinical decision making as biomedicine fully exploits structural genetics, functional genomics, proteomics, and other discoveries will increase way beyond what the human mind alone will be able to correlate. Information systems will need to be developed to help inform health care decisions. Librarians need to be part of the teams that develop these systems.

While some librarians are planning new space, others are finding a library space confining and absent of users. The ideas of a "great good place" or the library as a learning commons or hub are discussed in Chapters 9 and 15. If the customers come back, what will they find? Plutchak wants the people in his institution, his customers, to be thinking: "Oh yes, there is that library over there and there are occasions in which I need to go there, but what is really essential to me is the librarian who comes to my space and comes to my lab or my office or my classroom and does their work in whatever space I'm in, and that's what's really important—not that building that happens to be down the street" ("If You're Flexible..." 2005: 24).

The vision of the future described by these institutions and forward-looking individuals will help you develop your own vision for managing your library. The information and resources found in this book are valuable tools for the health care library manager.

Conclusion

The field of librarianship has changed so much in the past ten years since the first edition that the editors carefully considered what to include in the second edition that would still be applicable for the next ten years as well as for today. Many of the chapter authors found that content from the first edition was still very relevant. Due to rapid changes in the field, however, most of the content covers the latest trends. The challenges are constantly shifting and the health care library manager will be prepared to meet them through the knowledge and expertise shared by the chapter authors.

To quote M. J. Tooey, the health care librarian

> is at a critical juncture, where things are not as they were and the future is yet to be defined. Those definitions will most likely come from outside influences and challenges not within a...librarian's control. The response to these influences and challenges is within their control. The most successful...librarians will be closely informed about and aligned with institutional priorities. They will possess creativity and passion for their work, coupled with a willingness to explore new directions and pathways. (Tooey, 2009: 272)

The editors and the chapter authors of this book hope that their efforts will inspire that passion and will provide exciting directions for the future. Seize the day!

References

ACRL College and Research Libraries Task Force. 2004. "Standards for Libraries in Higher Education: The Final, Approved Standard." *College & Research Libraries News* 65, no. 9: 534–543. Accessed July 10, 2010. http://www.ala .org/ala/mgrps/divs/acrl/standards/standardslibraries.cfm.

ACRL Research Planning and Review Committee. 2010. "2010 Top Ten Trends in Academic Libraries; a Review of the Current Literature." *College & Research Libraries News* 71 no. 6 (June): 286–292. Accessed October 10, 2010. http:// crln.acrl.org/content/71/6/286.full.

Association of Academic Health Sciences Libraries, AAHSL Charting the Future Task Force. 2003. *Building on Success: Charting the Future of Knowledge Management within the Academic Health Center*. Association of Academic Health Sciences Libraries. Accessed October 4, 2010. http://www .aahsl.org/mc/page.do?sitePageId=84882. Viewable document at: http://kuscholarworks.ku.edu/dspace/bitstream/ 1808/217/1/Charting_the_Future_viewable.pdf.

Association of Academic Health Sciences Library Directors. Medical Library Association. Joint Task Force. 1987. *Challenge to Action: Planning and Evaluation Guidelines for Academic Health Sciences Libraries*, edited by Erika Love. Chicago, IL: Association of Academic Health Sciences Library Directors, Medical Library Association.

Bandy, Margaret, Katherine R. Stemmer Frumento, and Mary Langman. 2009. "Role of Health Sciences Librarians in Patient Safety Position Statement." Medical Library Association. Accessed November 18, 2010. http://www.mlanet .org/government/positions/patient-safety.html.

Blyberg, John, Kathryn Greenhill, and Cindi Trainor. 2009. "The Darien Statements on the Library and Librarians." Accessed September 1, 2010. http://www.blyberg.net/ 2009/04/03/the-darien-statements-on-the-library-and- librarians/.

Council on Library and Information Resources. 2008. "No Brief Candle: Reconceiving Research Libraries for the 21st Century." Washington, DC: Council on Library and Information Resources. Accessed October 1, 2010. http://www .clir.org/pubs/abstract/pub142abst.html.

Dudden, R. F., K. Corcoran, J. Kaplan, J. Magouirk, D. C. Rand, and B. T. Smith. 2006a. "The Medical Library Association Benchmarking Network: Development and Implementation." *Journal of the Medical Library Association* 94, no. 2 (April): 107–117.

Dudden, R. F., K. Corcoran, J. Kaplan, J. Magouirk, D. C. Rand, and B. T. Smith. 2006b. "The Medical Library Association Benchmarking Network: Results." *Journal of the Medical Library Association* 94, no. 2 (April): 118–129.

Dudden, Rosalind F. 2007. *Using Benchmarking, Needs Assessment, Quality Improvement, Outcome Measurement, and Library Standards: A How-To-Do-It Manual with CD-ROM*. New York: Neal-Schuman.

Health Sciences Library Statistics and Benchmarking. *2007 Benchmarking Survey*. Chicago: Medical Library Association. (Data available to MLA member participants only.) Accessed September 17, 2010. http://www.mlanet.org/ members/benchmark/.

Hospital Libraries Section Standards Committee, Margaret Bandy, Jacqueline Donaldson Doyle, Anne Fladger, Katherine Stemmer Frumento, Linné Girouard, Sheila Hayes, and

Diane Rourke. 2008. "Standards for Hospital Libraries 2007." *Journal of the Medical Library Association* 96, no. 2 (April): 162–169.

"If You're Flexible, Adaptable, and Willing to Take Risks It's a Great Time to Be an Information Professional (Interview with T. Scott Plutchak)." 2005. *Information Outlook* 9, no. 5 (May): 23–28.

Lindberg, Donald A. B., and Betsy L. Humphreys. 2005. "2015—The Future of Medical Libraries." *New England Journal of Medicine* 352, no. 11 (March 17): 1067–1070.

Matheson, Nina W. 1984. "Seize the Day." In "Proceedings of the Eighty-Third Annual Meeting, Medical Library Association, Houston, Texas, May 27–June 2, 1983." *Bulletin of the Medical Library Association* 72, no. 1 (January): 79–81.

Muir Gray, J. A. 2006. "Canadian Clinicians and Patients Need Clean, Clear Knowledge." *CMAJ: Canadian Medical Association Journal* 175, no. 2 (July 18): 129–131.

National Library of Medicine. 2006. *Charting a Course for the 21st Century: NLM's Long Range Plan 2006–2016.* Washington, DC: National Library of Medicine. Accessed October 1, 2010. http://www.nlm.nih.gov/pubs/plan/lrpdocs .html.

Nylenna, Magne, Øystein Eiring, Grete Strand, and John-Arne Røttingen. "Wiring a Nation: Putting Knowledge into Action." 2010. *Lancet* 375, no. 9719 (March 20): 1048–1051.

Renear, Allen H., and Carole L. Palmer. 2009. "Strategic Reading, Ontologies, and the Future of Scientific Publishing." *Science* 325, no. 5942 (August 14): 828–832.

Roethke, Theodore. 1953. *The Waking: Poems 1933–1953.* New York: Doubleday.

Shedlock, James, and Gary D. Byrd. 2003. "The Association of Academic Health Sciences Libraries *Annual Statistics*: A Thematic History." *Journal of the Medical Library Association* 91, no. 2 (April): 178–185.

Stead, William W., John R. Searle, Henry E. Fessler, Jack W. Smith, and Edward H. Shortliffe. 2010. "Biomedical Informatics: Changing What Physicians Need to Know and How They Learn." *Academic Medicine* (August 12): E-pub ahead of print.

Thibodeau, Patricia L, and Carla J. Funk. 2009. "Trends In Hospital Librarianship and Hospital Library Services: 1989 to 2006." *Journal of the Medical Library Association* 97, no. 4 (October): 273–279.

Tooey, M. J. 2009. "A Pathway for Hospital Librarians: Why Is It Vital?" *Journal of the Medical Library Association* 97, no. 4 (October): 268–272.

Wakeley, Patricia J., and Eloise C. Foster. 1993. "A Survey of Health Sciences Libraries in Hospitals: Implications for the 1990s." *Bulletin of the Medical Library Association* 81, no. 2 (April): 123–128.

2

The Health Care Environment

Margaret Moylan Bandy
and Barbara Jahn

The opening statement in the chapter on the health care environment by Eloise C. Foster and Gail L. Warden in the first edition of this book is even more accurate today than it was when the book was published in 2000. "The delivery of health care in the United States is a complex system that is constantly undergoing changes" (Foster and Warden, 2000: 11). They noted the need for health care reform and also the lack of consensus on how health care delivery and payment should be changed. Other significant changes have happened since 2000. The Institute of Medicine report *To Err is Human* (Kohn, Corrigan, and Donaldson, 2000) that set in motion a movement to improve patient safety had just been published. Not surprisingly, in the 2000 edition the phrase "patient safety" appeared once and evidence-based patient care just a few times. The electronic medical record was also mentioned only briefly in the first edition. Since 2000 the numbers of new and influential organizations demanding reports on quality and safety have increased dramatically and quality tools from other industries are being implemented in health care organizations.

The Medical Library Association Educational Policy Statement *Competencies for Lifelong Learning and Professional Success* (available on the **accompanying CD-ROM**) lists understanding "the health sciences and health care environment and the policies, issues, and trends that impact that environment" as the first competency

(Medical Library Association, 2007: 4). Competency elements include the following:

- Current management and business practices
- The parent organization's (academic medical center, hospital, government, corporate, etc.) major policy and program sources
- The health sciences professions
- The clinical care, research, medical education, cultural, ethical, economic, and legal issues and environments
- Various health and health-related organizations (Medical Library Association, 2007)

The goal of this chapter is to help the manager of a library serving health care professionals and consumers understand the complex environment within which the institution and the library functions. Resources to aid the manager in monitoring change are listed on the **accompanying CD-ROM**. The authors will not cover the early history of health care delivery and library development that Foster and Warden ably provided (Foster and Warden, 2000). Logan Ludwig has also written an excellent overview of the health care system (Ludwig, 2008). Rather, the primary focus of this chapter will be on the most significant issues and trends currently impacting the delivery, financing, and regulation of health care in the United States. It is essential that the health care library manager stay abreast of developments in the health care environment that will impact the services that need to be offered. This chapter in some ways is a snapshot in time, but the authors also hope it will help the manager understand the need to constantly stay informed about external pressures and emerging trends in the health care environment.

Health Care Delivery in the United States

Note: Most of the description by Foster and Warden of the types and common organization of hospitals is used verbatim from the first edition of this book; some information has been updated and is cited.

Health care is delivered in a number of different settings, including hospitals, neighborhood clinics, physician offices, other facilities and in the home. As noted by Foster and Warden,

> The hospital is still the predominant institution within the health care delivery system. Hospitals are complex, diverse institutions. . . . They range in size from fewer than 25 beds to more than 1,000 beds. They may be religiously affiliated or nonsectarian. They may have a research mission or be involved in the training of heath care professionals. They may be general or specialized (e.g., psychiatric, children's). They may be independent or part of a health care system or integrated delivery network. But, they share one special characteristic: a patient-care mission. (Foster and Warden, 2000: 14–15)

Hospitals—Classification and Organization

There are a number of ways to classify or categorize hospitals, each focusing attention on a particular characteristic or attribute. In most cases, these characteristics are not mutually exclusive, so that an individual hospital may have several of the characteristics. These classifications are often used to group facilities with similar characteristics.

Classifications

Length of stay: Short-term hospitals, also known as acute care hospitals, are those in which the average length of stay is under 30 days. Patient care institutions where the average length of stay is longer than 30 days are called long-term hospitals. The overwhelming majority of hospitals fall into the short-term category. The average length of stay for most acute care hospitals in the United States in 2008 was 4.6 days (HCUPnet, 2010).

Ownership and control: This classification refers to the types of organizations responsible for establishing policy for the overall operation of hospitals. The four major categories are (1) government, nonfederal; (2) nongovernment, not for profit; (3) investor-owned, for-profit; and (4) government, federal (Wolper, 2004).

Services: Hospitals may be general, offering a variety of services, or special. Special hospitals focus on a particular service or patient category for example, psychiatric, rehabilitation, women's services, children's services, etc.

Level of care: As described in the government document "Improving Health Care" (2004), hospitals are frequently categorized as primary, secondary, tertiary, and quaternary, dependent on the level and complexity of care provided:

- Primary care hospitals offer basic services such as an emergency department and limited intensive care facilities.
- Secondary care hospitals generally offer primary care, general internal medicine, and limited surgical and diagnostic capabilities.
- Tertiary care hospitals provide a full range of basic and sophisticated diagnostic and treatment services, including many specialized services.

■ Quaternary hospitals typically provide services such as advanced trauma care and organ transplantation.

These distinctions, however, are not always clear in practice, as hospitals are not restricted to only offering the services associated with one category (Improving Health Care: A Dose of Competition, 2004).

Most hospitals in the United States are community hospitals. Community hospitals are a good example of the nonexclusivity of the classification schemes. They may be owned by any ownership and control group except the federal government; they may be primary, secondary, tertiary or quaternary care facilities; teaching or non-teaching; urban or rural; independent or part of a health care system. A hospital with one or more accredited educational programs in medicine, nursing, or the allied health professions is considered a teaching hospital.

Organization of Hospitals

Although the diverse nature of hospitals is reflected in their variety of organizational structures, the following basic components are common: governing board, management, medical staff, clinical and ancillary services, nursing, and administrative or support services. These basic components are briefly summarized here.

Governing board: This is a hospital's policy-making body, responsible for the institution's overall operation. Its functions include defining objectives, mandating policies, maintaining the programs and resources necessary to implement policies, and selecting and evaluating the hospital's chief executive officer. The board has ultimate legal responsibility for the operation of the hospital.

Management: Directed by the chief executive officer, the management is accountable for implementing policies and procedures involving the hospital's operations, financial viability, health care delivery capacity, patient safety, patient service, and staff direction, and for monitoring progress to guarantee that policy objectives are met.

Medical staff: The medical staff is an organized group of physicians who contribute actively to the hospital by admitting and caring for patients on a regular basis. It may also include other practitioners, such as dentists, psychologists, or podiatrists. The medical staff governs itself by adhering to written bylaws. A physician cannot practice in the hospital without permission (called a privilege) of the governing board, which also approves the medical staff bylaws. Much of patient care in hospitals is now carried out by "hospitalists." These physicians typically do all their patient care in the hospital and do not have office practices (Jonas, Goldsteen, and Goldsteen, 2007).

Ancillary services: Included in this category are therapeutic or diagnostic services (other than nursing) provided by specific hospital departments, including X-ray and diagnostic imaging, laboratories, anesthesiology, respiratory therapy, electroencephalography, rehabilitative medicine, and pharmacy. Responsibility for some of these departments rests with physicians and for others with professionals from other disciplines.

Nursing service: Nursing is provided to meet patients' physical and psychological needs and to collaborate with patients' physicians in developing and implementing treatment plans. Nurses are functionally responsible to the physicians, providing patient care and being administratively responsible to a designated member of the hospital staff called the Chief Nursing Officer.

Administrative and support services: Administrative services include facilities management, finance, legal, case management, utilization management, human resources, information systems, spiritual care, and the library. Support services include laundry, housekeeping, food service, purchasing, maintenance, central supply, materials management, and security, which support the delivery of clinical patient care.

Ambulatory Care

While hospitals are still the predominant *institutions* for health care delivery, most health care is not delivered to patients occupying hospital beds. "The majority of physician-patient contacts in the United States occur in an ambulatory setting" (Jonas, Goldsteen, and Goldsteen, 2007: 89). There are a variety of ambulatory settings, some within hospitals and others in clinics and office practices of varying sizes.

Hospital Emergency and Outpatient Departments and Clinics

The National Hospital Ambulatory Medical Care Survey (NHAMCS) (http://www.cdc.gov/nchs/ahcd.htm) collects data on the utilization and provision of ambulatory care services in hospital emergency and outpatient departments. Emergency departments are designed to deliver care to individuals who are in life-threatening situations. Emergency departments are regulated by the federal government under the Emergency Medical Treatment & Labor Act (EMTALA) that was enacted by Congress in 1986. "Section 1867 of the Social Security Act imposes specific obligations on Medicare-participating hospitals that offer emergency services to provide a medical screening examination (MSE) when a request is made for examination or treatment for an emergency medical condition (EMC), including active labor, regardless of an individual's ability to pay. Hospitals are then required to provide stabilizing treatment for patients with EMCs. If a hospital is unable to stabilize a patient within its capability, or if the patient requests, an appropriate transfer should be implemented" (Centers for Medicare and Medicaid Services, 2010b).

Outpatient services provided by hospitals may include such things as physical therapy, cardiac and pulmonary rehabilitation, or dietary counseling designed to support patients who have been dismissed from the hospital. Outpatient services may also include diagnostics such as radiology or treatment centers for cancer patients, in addition to other clinics for specific diagnoses.

Hospital-based clinics are usually found in teaching hospitals and are focused on a particular teaching program, such as women's health care clinics for physicians in training for obstetrics and gynecology.

Clinics and Community Health Centers

Various types of clinics provide outpatient services. Clinics can be publicly or privately funded and can provide primary care, specialty care, or a combination. Some clinics are actually health systems, like the Cleveland Clinic or part of a health system, like the Kaiser Permanente clinics. Clinics may be located in urban or rural settings, and also on Indian Reservations.

Clinics that are called Community Health Centers were initially named neighborhood health centers and were created in 1965 as part of the Johnson administration's War on Poverty "to provide health and social services access points in poor and medically underserved communities and to promote community empowerment" (Taylor, 2004: 3). In order to receive federal grant funding, these clinics must meet specific requirements in terms of location—a designated Medically Underserved Area (MUA) or Medically Underserved Population (MUP), services provided, and governance. Community Health Centers must serve all regardless of ability to pay. Community Health Centers are administered by the Health Resources and Services Administration (HRSA), an agency of the U.S. Department of Health and Human Services (DHHS). The 2009 American Recovery and Reinvestment Act provided $2 billion to be invested in Community Health Centers, and in 2010 health care legislation provided $11 billion over five years for Community Health Centers. In 2009, one of every 19 people living in the United States relied on a HRSA-funded clinic for primary care (Recovery Act [ARRA] Community Health Centers, 2010).

Office Practices—Solo and Group

Outpatient medical care by physicians is provided in both solo and group practice settings. Physicians entering the medical profession have a choice of whether to enter private solo practice, join a larger group practice, enter an academic setting, or become an employee of a hospital or other health care organization. The solo practice, practicing without other physician partners, has become less attractive over time to new physicians and is much less common than in previous years. Autonomy is cited as the greatest advantage to practicing as a solo physician. They are characterized by having a small staff and less technology, such as electronic medical records. The physician takes care of all details of administering the practice as well as caring for patients.

Some solo practitioners have entered "boutique" practices, charging a monthly rate for patients to have 24 hours per day, 7 days per week access to their physician. Solo practices are generally at greater financial risk, assuming responsibility for the entire scope of the practice, including compliance with all insurance rules and regulatory compliance issues. Quality of life for the physician may also be impacted.

Group practices, either single or multispecialty, generally consist of two or more physicians practicing together as a group. Group practices have more infrastructure support, financial security, compensation and benefit options for physicians, as well as support for sharing in decision making, collaboration and best practices. Financial risk is spread, and administrative and regulatory compliance is shared. Staff support is generally greater and physician quality of life is less impacted through more shared on-call responsibilities. Other levels of practitioners are commonly utilized in group practices and patients frequently have access to nurse practitioners and physician assistants in this setting. The difference in these models has certainly changed the traditional doctor-patient relationship and the way health care is delivered in the United States (Wolinsky, 1982; Alguire, 2010).

Current Health Care Environment

The health care environment is complex, highly regulated, and constantly changing. It is composed of health care institutions, a variety of health care providers, industry, interest groups representing industries and consumers, and government agencies. Summarizing this environment is difficult, but the following sections highlight some important features.

Health Care Workforce

Health care professionals and other health care workers are most often employed in hospitals, nursing homes, and physician offices. Kovner (2008: 335) points out that "within the health workforce there are hundreds of professionals, subspecialties, and occupations with educational requirements ranging from a high school degree to doctoral and professional degrees." This section of the chapter examines data on the health care workforce, education of some of these professionals, and also trends in deployment of them in hospitals.

State of the U.S. Health Care Workforce

According to the Health Workforce Information Center of the Health Resources and Services Administration, part of the U.S. Department of Health and Human Services, the shortages in the health care workforce have gotten progressively worse:

> Analysts now are projecting a nationwide shortage of almost 100,000 physicians, as many as one million nurses, and 250,000 public health professionals by 2020. Due to the high cost of health insurance and increasingly pervasive staffing shortfalls in the health professions, at least 50 million Americans lack access to the most basic care. A third are children. Targeted workforce studies document and project shortages and other trends that influence the adequacy of the U.S. health care system to meet current and future needs. (HRSA Health Professions, 2010)

Some of the reasons for the predicted shortfall include the aging of the workforce. Also, not enough younger people have been entering the health care professions, some because of unappealing working conditions such as long hours and the stressful environment. There are also shortages of health profession faculty, which limits the number of students that can enroll in programs (Kovner, Knickman, and Jonas, 2008).

The Patient Protection and Affordable Care Act (PPACA) of 2010 discussed later in the chapter includes programs "to support workforce education and training and funding to expand primary care capacity" (Goodson, 2010: 743). However, it will be up to Congress to fund the programs adequately.

Education of Health Care Professionals

Physicians require four years of undergraduate school and four years of medical school. They are also required to complete residency training in a hospital after medical school. Depending on the specialty selected, the training will last three to eight years.

There are 159 medical schools in the United States, 133 of which teach allopathic medicine and award a Doctor of Medicine (MD) degree, and 26 that teach osteopathic medicine and award a Doctor of Osteopathic Medicine (DO) (Health Workforce Information Center, 2010). All states require physicians to be licensed; in addition to the education requirement physicians must pass a licensing examination. Physicians may also choose to be board certified in their specialty, which requires passing an exam at intervals designated by their specialty boards. Physicians' education and training is governed by a number of agencies that accredit the various programs and certifications, as shown in Figure 2.1. This list is also on the **accompanying CD-ROM**.

Nurses receive training in a variety of settings. Prior to the 1970s, most nurses were trained in three-year programs in hospital-based nursing schools. As noted in *Educating Nurses*, "Profound changes in science, technology, patient activism, the market-driven health care environment, and the nature and settings of nursing practice have all radically transformed nursing practice... [and] have enormous implications for nursing education" (Benner, 2010: 1). Currently the Associate Degree in Nursing is the highest degree held by approximately 60 percent of nursing graduates (Benner, 2010).

Figure 2.1. Organizations Related to Physician Education and Certification

Accreditation Council for Graduate Medical Education (ACGME)
http://www.acgme.org

American Board of Medical Specialties (ABMS)
http://www.abms.org

Association for Hospital Medical Education (AHME)
http://www.ahme.org

Association of Academic Health Centers (AAHC)
http://www.aahcdc.org

Association of American Medical Colleges (AAMC)
http://www.aamc.org

Council on Graduate Medical Education (COGME)
http://www.cogme.gov

National Resident Matching Program (NRMP)
http://www.nrmp.org

United States Medical Licensing Examination (USMLE)
http://www.usmle.org

Many nursing organizations now agree that nurses should be educated at the BSN (Bachelor of Science in Nursing) level. The American Organization of Nurse Executives stated:

> The educational preparation of the nurse of the future should be at the baccalaureate level. This educational preparation will prepare the nurse of the future to function as an equal partner, collaborator and manager of the complex patient care journey that is envisioned by AONE. (American Organization of Nurse Executives BSN-Level Nursing Education Resources, 2010)

Advanced nursing degrees include the PhD and the more recent Doctor of Nursing Practice (DNP). The PhD nurse is primarily an educator or researcher. The DNP degree was designed to be a "graduate degree in preparation for advanced nursing practice, including but not limited to the four current roles of the advanced practice nurse" (Donahue, 2011: 281). Within nursing there are over 200 certifications designating levels of practice or specialization. The American Nurses Credentialing Center is the largest credentialing organization for nurses (http://www.nursecredentialing.org/Certification.aspx). Like physicians, nurses must be licensed to practice; the designation RN indicates that the nurse is licensed. A list of organizations related to nursing education and certification is on the **accompanying CD-ROM.**

In addition to physicians and nurses, a number of other health care professionals will be found in health care organizations. The annual *Health Care Careers Directory*, also called the *Health Professions Career and Education Directory*, published by the American Medical Association, includes over 80 health care careers (American Medical Association, 2010) and provides information on programs, educational standards, and the various accrediting organizations. Often called allied health professionals, these individuals include pharmacists, physical and occupational therapists, dieticians, and others.

Collaborative Models in the Delivery of Patient Care

Over the past decade there has been a recognition that patient care is most effectively delivered by teams of providers rather than through the hierarchical model of the past. One model increasingly found in hospitals is shared governance. A nursing shared governance model allows nurses a voice in determining things such as nursing practice and care standards. This model typically consists of several councils, including an oversight council, quality improvement council, education and research, and professional practice council. Often these teams have members from other disciplines. Structures vary according to hospital needs, structure, and nursing functions. Critical to the success of shared governance models is the involvement of staff-level employees, so unit-based councils are formed to address the practice issues in that nursing unit. Successful shared governance models in nursing can assist in recruiting and retaining high-quality nursing professionals. Writers such as Tim Porter O'Grady are calling for an interdisciplinary approach to shared governance that recognizes the importance of teams at the point of care (Porter-O'Grady, 2009).

Interdisciplinary teams in patient care are used to achieve greater employee engagement and improved outcomes in clinical care, patient satisfaction, financial performance, and overall patient safety through an opportunity to participate in decision making. Drinka and Clark defined the Interdisciplinary Health Care Team as

> a group of individuals with diverse training and backgrounds who work together as an identified unit or system. Team members consistently collaborate to solve patient problems that are too complex to be solved by one discipline or many disciplines in sequence... an IHCT creates "formal" and "informal" structures that encourage collaborative problem solving... members determine the team's mission and common goals: work interdependently to define and treat patient problems; and learn to accept and capitalize on disciplinary differences, differential power and overlapping roles. To accomplish these they share leadership that is appropriate to the presenting problem.... (Drinka and Clark, 2000: 6)

Clinical microsystems are one model of interdisciplinary teams. "Clinical microsystems are the small, functional, front-line units that provide most health care to most people. They are the essential building blocks of larger organizations and of the health system. They are the place where patients and providers meet" (Nelson et al., 2002: 473). Health care delivery improvements can be made by improving the work of these front-line clinical and operational units. First developed at Dartmouth-Hitchcock Medical Center, clinical microsystems are in place at many hospitals and medical centers and provide innovation in patient care delivery and improved teamwork on behalf of the patient. Physicians and staff work together to improve the processes of care for the patient and provide care in a coordinated way. These small units are linked to the larger organizational structure, sometimes through an interdisciplinary shared governance structure.

Like the nursing shared governance structure, clinical microsystems have a focus on both patients and staff, and can improve employee engagement through staff participation in design of care on units, decision-making authority and improved relationships among all providers of care in that unit.

A clinical microsystem is a small group of people who work together on a regular basis to provide care to discrete sub-populations of patients. It has clinical and business aims, linked processes, and a shared information environment, and it produces performance outcomes. Microsystems evolve over time and are often embedded in larger organizations. They are complex adaptive systems, and as such they must do the primary work associated with core aims, meet the needs of internal staff, and maintain themselves over time as clinical units. (Nelson et al., 2002: 474)

Health Care Financing

In the United States, health care financing systems involve both government insurance and private plans. Numerous approaches to controlling costs as well as expanding access to care have been developed. Private insurance has primarily been provided by employers. Government payment systems include Medicare, Medicaid, Veterans Administration, and programs that provide health coverage for children.

Payment Systems—Government and Private Insurance

Prior to 1983 and the introduction by Medicare of the prospective payment system, Medicare and private insurance paid hospitals and doctors under a reimbursement model for the cost of a procedure, days in the hospital, and any other services provided. Both Medicare and private payers have tried different approaches to curbing costs, such as managed care. Competition was encouraged and hospitals began to be paid for episodes of hospitalization using a system that involved Diagnosis-Related Groups (DRG). Physicians continue to be paid by a system called fee for service, which pays more for procedures such as those provided by specialists. The complexities of payment systems have forced hospitals and office practices to develop numerous internal systems to manage them.

Health Care Payment Reform— PPACA 2010

The Patient Protection and Affordable Care Act (PPACA) of 2010 was signed into law by President Obama on March 23, 2010. Goals of the new law included providing affordable health insurance coverage to most Americans

Figure 2.2. Health Care Reform Resources

American Nurses Association Health Care Reform Resources
http://www.nursingworld.org/MainMenuCategories/HealthcareandPolicyIssues/HealthSystemReform/HealthCareReformResources.aspx

New England Journal of Medicine Health Care Reform Center
http://healthcarereform.nejm.org/

Kaiser Family Foundation Health Reform
http://healthreform.kff.org/

Commonwealth Fund Health Reform Resources
http://www.commonwealthfund.org/Health-Reform.aspx

U.S. Department of Health & Human Services
http://www.healthcare.gov/

and improving access to primary care. Doherty (2010) has examined issues of access to care, increase in primary care providers, and impact on cost. Because of the complexity of the law, and the various stages of implementation over a period of years, it is impossible to predict how well it will attain the goals set forth in the law. A number of resources available to follow the evolution of health care reform are listed in Figure 2.2. This list is also on the **accompanying CD-ROM**.

Pay for Performance

The Pay for Performance (P4P) program was implemented in 2003 by the Centers for Medicare and Medicaid Services (CMS) to control costs and to improve quality by tying reimbursement to hospitals for outcomes in certain measures established by that agency. Both Medicare and employers were looking for more predictable and better results for patients and lower health care costs. Initially based on a set of ten clinical, evidence based medical practices, the program called for voluntary reporting of results of these measures to CMS by hospitals. The intent was to reward hospitals for providing the right care for patients and to promote better quality care for Medicare beneficiaries. Initially, hospitals received increased payments for reporting results for the ten measures (Lindenauer et al., 2007). CMS then partnered with Premier Inc., an alliance organization owned by not-for-profit hospitals and health care systems (http://www.premier inc.com/quality-safety/tools-services/p4p/index.jsp), to begin another demonstration project that was designed to pay hospitals for improved outcomes in heart attack, heart failure, pneumonia and specific surgeries. Thirty-four measures were selected in all.

Hospitals performing in the top 10 percent are paid a bonus payment. In the third year, hospitals that did not meet the established performance expectations or thresholds were subject to a decrease in reimbursement (Glickman and Peterson, 2009).

Medicare also enacted a rule in October 2008 that essentially eliminated payment to hospitals if certain circumstances or "Never Events" defined by the National Quality Forum (see below) occur while a patient was in the hospital for care. Hospitals will be challenged to have effective systems to meet these requirements.

Medicare has various Pay for Performance initiatives and demonstration projects in place for physician offices, clinic settings and hospitals, all aimed at paying incentives for improved quality of care and reducing the cost of medical care. As part of 2010 health care reform, CMS will expand the Hospital Quality Improvement program, continuing to link Medicare payments to hospitals with their performance on selected measures and care delivery.

Accountable Care Organizations

Another initiative in the 2010 health care reform bill is a provision for Accountable Care Organizations (ACOs). "ACOs are organizations that include physicians, hospitals, and other health care organizations with the legal structure to receive and distribute payments to participating physicians and hospitals to provide care coordination, to invest in infrastructure and redesign care processes, and to reward high-quality and efficient services" (Shortell and Casalino, 2010: 1747). The purpose of ACOs is to lower cost increases while improving health care quality.

As noted by McClellan and colleagues (2010), ACOs can be configured in a variety of ways and it is likely that a number of different models will be tried. ACOs will impact health care financing, the delivery of care, especially primary care, and quality. The list of resources for monitoring the health care environment included on the **accompanying CD-ROM** will be useful in understanding the evolution of ACOs.

Regulation and Accreditation

Many agencies are involved in regulatory activities at the federal level and some at the state level as well. The largest federal agency is the Department of Health and Human Services. In 2006 the department operated more than 300 different programs (Jonas, Goldsteen, and Goldsteen, 2007). In some cases accreditation programs outside the government implement regulatory requirements or stand in the place of the regulatory agency.

Centers for Medicare and Medicaid

The primary regulatory and enforcement agencies for hospitals as well as other health care organizations are the Centers for Medicare and Medicaid (CMS), the federal government agency, and state health departments. These agencies can and do show up unexpectedly to examine or respond to elements of care provision.

CMS publishes its requirements for health care organizations in "Conditions of Participation (CoPs) and Conditions for Coverage (CfCs)" (Centers for Medicare and Medicaid Services, 2010a). Compliance with these requirements is essential for a health care organization to receive payment under Medicare and Medicaid. Furthermore, organizations that don't meet the requirements can have their license to operate suspended or revoked. The areas that CMS reviews include patients' rights, performance improvement, organization of the medical staff and nursing services and requirements for departments in the organization. CMS also administers the Health Insurance Portability and Accountability Act of 1996 (HIPAA, Title II) (Centers for Medicare and Medicaid Services, 2010c). This law required the U.S. Department of Health and Human Services "to establish national standards for electronic health care transactions and national identifiers for providers, health plans, and employers." The Office for Civil Rights enforces other elements of HIPAA that are related to activities in hospitals. They include:

- the HIPAA "Privacy Rule, which protects the privacy of individually identifiable health information;
- the HIPAA Security Rule, which sets national standards for the security of electronic protected health information;
- the confidentiality provisions of the Patient Safety Rule, which protect identifiable information being used to analyze patient safety events and improve patient safety" (Office for Civil Rights, 2010).

Accrediting Organizations

The Balanced Budget Act of 1997 (BBA) and the subsequent Balanced Budget Refinement Act of 1999 (BBRA) gave CMS the authority to establish and oversee a program that allows private, national accreditation organizations to judge or "deem" that a Medicare Advantage organization is compliant with certain Medicare requirements. Six areas are deemable: (1) quality assurance, (2) anti-discrimination, (3) access to services, (4) confidentiality and accuracy of enrollee records, (5) information on advance directives, and (6) provider participation rules. To be approved for deeming authority, an accrediting organization must demonstrate that their program meets or exceeds the Medicare requirements for which they are seeking the authority to deem compliance. (Centers for Medicare and Medicaid Services, 2005).

For hospitals these groups include The Joint Commission (TJC), the Healthcare Facilities Accreditation Program (HFAP) of the American Osteopathic Association (AOA), and Det Norske Veritas (DNV) Healthcare Inc.

- **The Joint Commission** (http://www.joint commission .org): The Joint Commission (formerly called the Joint Commission on the Accreditation of Health Care Organizations or JCAHO) is an independent, voluntary, not-for-profit organization that develops quality standards for hospitals and assesses individual hospitals' compliance with those standards. It is one of the oldest accrediting bodies for health care organizations. Joint Commission accreditation is voluntary, but widely recognized and used by hospitals and other health care agencies. The Joint Commission evaluates and accredits more than 18,000 health care organizations and programs in the United States. Joint Commission patient safety activities are discussed later in the chapter.

- **Healthcare Facilities Accreditation Program** (http://www.hfap.org/): The Healthcare Facilities Accreditation Program (HFAP) of the American Osteopathic Association (AOA) is the accrediting agency for all osteopathic health care facilities.

- **Det Norske Veritas (DNV) Healthcare Inc.** (http://www.dnv.com/industry/healthcare/): Det Norske Veritas (DNV) Healthcare Inc., an organization that certifies and manages risk for many industries, was granted deeming status for hospitals in 2008 (DerGurahian, 2008). Their accreditation program, National Integrated Accreditation for Healthcare Organizations (NIAHO) utilizes the ISO 9001 Quality Management System.

It is likely that other organizations will seek deeming authority from CMS in the coming years. CMS also gives deeming authority to agencies that accredit other types of health care organizations such as clinics, health plans, laboratories, and medical groups.

State Health Departments

State and local governments have played an increasingly more important role in shaping policy and oversight of the health care system, and the overall public health and environment. Involvement initially began with the epidemics of the eighteenth and nineteenth centuries (Altman and Morgan, 1983). State Health Departments today provide oversight and assistance to hospitals, other agencies and health care providers in meeting the needs of health care consumers. The responsibility taken on by state health departments varies widely in the United States, depending on how state and local governments provide for public health. State health departments provide services that include the oversight and regulation of health care facilities and health care workers. They collect data and analyze outcomes, assist in ensuring that health care organizations adhere to standards of care, including the CMS Conditions of Participation, develop policies and standards of care, and ensure that national and state requirements are carried out. State health departments conduct surveys on behalf of the Centers for Medicare and Medicaid to ensure compliance to the quality standards of care (Institute of Medicine, 2003).

Specialty Accreditation Programs

The health care library manager may encounter a number of specialty accreditation programs. These programs may address patient care or research issues.

- **Cancer Care Standards**: The American College of Surgeons Commission on Cancer Standards "have established the foundation and framework for the coordinated, multidisciplinary delivery of cancer care, and the majority of organized cancer care provided in the United States is based on this framework" (American College of Surgeons, 2009). Accreditation teams often visit the hospital library during their surveys.

- **Pharmacy Regulation**: The Food and Drug Administration (FDA) (http://www.fda.gov/) is responsible for protecting the public health by assuring the safety, efficacy, and security of human and veterinary drugs, biological products, medical devices, the nation's food supply, cosmetics, and products that emit radiation. Along with state agencies the FDA regulates hospital pharmacies. In addition, the FDA oversees human subjects research noted below.

- **Laboratory Certification**: The College of American Pathologists (CAP) Laboratory accreditation (http://www.cap.org/apps/cap.portal?_nfpb=true&_page Label=accreditation) process has been granted deemed authority by CMS. The Joint Commission and many state health departments also recognize CAP accreditation in hospital-based laboratories for certification requirements. Standards are considered to be as or more stringent than those agency's regulatory requirements. The inspection process for labs is in-depth and comprehensive, and is conducted by practicing laboratory professionals and physicians. Some labs also apply for ISO 9001:2008 certification which looks at the laboratory management systems and processes.

- **Research Regulations**: A number of laws govern research conducted within organizations. Research with human subjects is under the jurisdiction of the FDA. Organizations that conduct research must establish an Institutional Review Board (IRB). Details on the FDA's research regulations are available at http://www.fda.gov/ScienceResearch/SpecialTopics/ default.htm. Institutions that use laboratory animals for research or instructional purposes must establish an Institutional Animal Care and Use Committee (IACUC). This committee oversees all aspects of the institution's animal care and use program (http:// www.iacuc.org).

Community Health

As mentioned by Foster and Warden (2000), the health care environment has expanded beyond the medical system to include preventive care not only for individuals but also for communities. There are several aspects to this focus. Health care organizations are increasingly aware of the need to appeal to consumers and often offer programs on topics such as alternative treatments and health education. Hospitals are focusing more on customer service and attractive surroundings in order to compete with each other. Drug companies market products directly to the consumer, and hundreds of sources of health information provided by the federal government, voluntary health organizations, and even hospitals are available on the Internet.

Consumer Activism

Health-conscious consumers are demanding more information on medical treatments, nutrition, and environmental issues that relate to health. They are also being asked to take greater charge of their health in order to lower health care costs. Consumer activism can be a challenge to health care providers, especially if some demands are not based on science. One of the biggest signs of consumer activism are the number of advocacy and support groups devoted to specific health issues. Social networking technologies have provided easy access to many groups, and consumers need to be taught how

to evaluate various claims. Chapter 14 provides guidance on this issue.

Voluntary Health Organizations

Voluntary health organizations include groups such as the American Cancer Society and the Alzheimer's Association. These groups engage in advocacy, fundraising, research, education, and support. Often these agencies sponsor community-based screening programs. Members include health care professionals as well as consumers, and guidelines put forth by these agencies can have a significant impact on health care use.

Public Health

It is beyond the scope of this chapter to discuss public health issues in depth. Some important efforts in prevention and health promotion that are part of the DHHS are the following:

- Healthy People (U.S. Department of Health and Human Services, 1991) is a set of health objectives for the nation. The goals were based on the 1979 Surgeon General's Report, *Healthy People,* and *Healthy People 2000: National Health Promotion and Disease Prevention Objectives.* A number of agencies, communities, and business have partnered to implement the goals. Healthy People 2020 objectives are available at http://www.healthypeople .gov/hp2020/Objectives/TopicAreas.aspx (Office of Disease Prevention and Health Promotion, U.S. Department of Health and Human Services, 2010).

- National Environmental Public Health Tracking Network (Centers for Disease Control and Prevention, 2010) is a new program that will attempt to discover the link between the environment and chronic diseases. The Centers for Disease Control and Prevention is currently developing its first report about health and the environment: *A Picture of America: Our Health and Environment.* This report is an introduction to the nation's public health status from an environmental health perspective (http://ephtracking.cdc.gov/showAbout .action).

- Regional Health Administrators (RHA) (http:// www.hhs.gov/ophs/rha/index.html) perform essential functions in the areas of prevention, preparedness, and agency-wide coordination. Prevention efforts include women's health, minority health, family planning, and reproductive health as well as HIV/AIDs prevention. Preparedness involves all areas of hazards and public health emergencies.

The RHA's assist with agency-wide coordination and collaboration across HHS Agencies.

Significant Trends

The authors have chosen to highlight a few significant trends in the current health care environment that health care library managers are or will become involved in. These trends are not mutually exclusive; health literacy and evidence-based health care arc closely related to quality and patient safety. The Electronic Health Record will aid patient safety and the reporting of quality indicators.

Health Literacy

"Health literacy is defined as the degree to which individuals can obtain, process, and understand the basic health information and services they need to make appropriate health decisions" (Nielsen-Bohlman et al., 2004). The problem of low health literacy has been recognized by numerous organizations and federal agencies.

> According to research from the U.S. Department of Education, only 12 percent of English-speaking adults in the United States have proficient health literacy skills. The overwhelming majority of adults have difficulty understanding and using everyday health information that comes from many sources, including the media, web sites, nutrition and medicine labels, and health professionals. (U.S. Department of Education, 2010)

On May 27, 2010, the DHHS released the *National Action Plan to Improve Health Literacy*. The goal of the plan is to engage organizations, professionals, and others in an effort to improve health literacy. "The plan is based on the principles that (1) everyone has the right to health information that helps them make informed decisions and (2) health services should be delivered in ways that are understandable and beneficial to health, longevity, and quality of life" (U.S. Department of Heath and Human Services, 2010). The *National Action Plan to Improve Health Literacy* is on the **accompanying CD-ROM**. Figure 2.3 lists several useful resources related to health literacy. This list is also on the **accompanying CD-ROM**.

Quality and Patient Safety

Over the past several decades both government and non-government entities have encouraged health care organizations, especially hospitals, to adopt quality improvement techniques from other industries. Examples include Total

---

Figure 2.3. Health Literacy Resources

AHRQ Health Literacy and Cultural Competency
http://www.ahrq.gov/browse/hlitix.htm

American Medical Association Health Literacy Resources
http://www.ama-assn.org/ama/pub/about-ama ama-foundation/our-programs/public-health/health-literacy-program.shtml

American Medical Association Manual for Clinicians
http://www.ama-assn.org/ama1/pub/upload/mm/367/healthlitclinicians.pdf

Health Literacy Consulting
http://www.healthliteracy.com/

Medical Library Association Health Information Literacy
http://www.mlanet.org/resources/healthlit/

National Patient Safety Foundation "Ask Me Three"
http://www.npsf.org/askme3/PCHC/

Pfizer Clear Health Communication Initiative, includes the Newest Vital Sign
http://www.pfizerhealthliteracy.com/

The Joint Commission "'What Did the Doctor Say?' Improving Health Literacy to Protect Patient Safety"
http://www.jointcommission.org/nr/rdonlyres/d5248b2e-e7e6-4121-8874-99c7b4888301/0/improving_health_literacy.pdf

---

Quality Management (TQM) and Lean manufacturing methods. In 1986 Donald Berwick and Blanton Godfrey received funding for the National Demonstration Project on Quality Improvement in Health Care. The goal of the project was to see if tools of modern quality improvement such as process flow diagrams could help health care organizations achieve breakthroughs in performance (Kenney, 2008). Berwick, Godfrey, and Roessner (1990) published the results of the 21 projects in *Curing Health Care*.

Shortly thereafter Berwick founded the Institute for Healthcare Improvement (IHI). As one of the most influential organizations devoted to quality improvement and patient safety, IHI has developed a number of Breakthrough Series Collaboratives that focus on specific issues such as reduction in rates of cesarean births. IHI went on to form strategic partnerships with other organizations. Following the Institute of Medicine publications noted below, IHI developed two far-reaching patient safety efforts, the "100,000 Lives Campaign" in 2004 and the "5 Million Lives Campaign" in 2006. Details on these and other IHI initiatives are described at the IHI website (http://www.ihi.org/).

As mentioned earlier, the 1999 Institute of Medicine report *To Err Is Human: Building a Safer Health System* reviewed research that suggested that preventable medical errors kill between 44,000 and 98,000 patients in American hospitals every year. The Institute of Medicine (IOM) is an independent, nonprofit organization that works outside of government to provide unbiased and authoritative advice to decision makers and the public. Established in 1970, the IOM is the health arm of the National Academy of Sciences, which was chartered under President Abraham Lincoln in 1863. Nearly 150 years later, the National Academy of Sciences has expanded into what is collectively known as the National Academies, which comprises the National Academy of Sciences, the National Academy of Engineering, the National Research Council, and the IOM (http://www.iom.edu//About-IOM.aspx).

The 1999 IOM report made recommendations in four areas: create leadership, research, tools and protocols to enhance knowledge of safety issues; identify and learn from errors by creating nationwide mandatory and voluntary error reporting systems; raise safety standards through actions by oversight organizations, professional groups, and health care purchasers; and implement safety systems in health care organizations to enhance safe practices at the delivery level (Larkin, 2009).

The IOM (2001) followed up *To Err Is Human* with the publication *Crossing the Quality Chasm: A New Health System for the 21st Century*. The authors recommended that health care delivery should be based on six key dimensions: safety, timeliness, effectiveness, efficiency, equitability, and patient-centeredness. The authors also made thirteen recommendations in pursuit of these dimensions. More recently the IOM published *Patient Safety: Achieving a New Standard of Care* (Aspden, 2004). This publication focused on the development and adoption of key health care data standards to support both information exchange and the reporting and analysis of patient safety data. The IOM has also examined the nursing environment as it relates to patient safety. *Keeping Patients Safe: Transforming the Work Environment of Nurses* (Page, 2004) and medical residents' workload in *Resident Duty Hours: Enhancing Sleep, Supervision, and Safety* (Ulmer et al., 2009).

Measuring Quality and Patient Safety

Most health care organizations measure and report their quality and patient safety activities using metrics provided by governmental and non-governmental agencies. Some of this reporting is mandatory and some is voluntary. Often an organization may use an internal "report card" to measure progress in quality and patient safety. In addition to this internal reporting, many agencies including states and the federal government use the concept of report cards for public reporting.

- **CMS Measures—Hospital Compare** (http://www.hospitalcompare.hhs.gov/): Medicare currently requires hospitals to report measures that assess compliance with evidence-based therapeutic processes in the areas of acute myocardial infarction (AMI), heart failure (HF), pneumonia (PN) and Surgical Care Improvement Project (SCIP). These performance measures are available publicly on the Medicare website Hospital Compare.

- **AHRQ Patient Safety Indicators** (http://www.qualityindicators.ahrq.gov/psi_overview.htm): Agency for Healthcare Research and Quality (AHRQ) supports research designed to improve the outcomes and quality in health care, reduce its costs, address patient safety and medical errors, and broaden access to effective services. It sponsors, conducts, and disseminates research to help people make more informed decisions and improve the quality of health care services. AHRQ has developed Patient Safety Indicators (PSI) that identify complications that patients experience as a result of exposure to the health care system. Examples include pressure ulcer, postoperative pulmonary embolism, or deep vein thrombosis, and postoperative infections.

- **National Quality Forum** (http://www.qualityforum.org/Home.aspx): The National Quality Forum (NQF) is a nonprofit organization made up of consumer organizations, public and private purchasers, physicians, nurses, hospitals, accrediting and certifying bodies, supporting industries, and health care research and quality improvement organizations The stated mission of NQF is
  - Setting national priorities and goals for performance improvement;
  - Endorsing national consensus standards for measuring and publicly reporting on performance; and
  - Promoting the attainment of national goals through education and outreach programs.

NQF has identified 28 events as occurrences that should never happen in a hospital and can be prevented. They termed them "serious reportable events," or "Never Events." The NQF Never Events are grouped in the following categories:
- Surgical Events
- Product or Device Events

- Patient Protection Events
- Case Management Events
- Environment Events
- Criminal Events

- **The Joint Commission National Patient Safety Goals** (http://www.jointcommission.org/Patient Safety/NationalPatientSafetyGoals/): The Joint Commission has several patient safety initiatives. One of the most important measures now used by hospital and ambulatory facilities is TJC's National Patient Safety Goals (NPSG). First compiled in 2003, compliance with the National Patient Safety Goals is included in the accreditation surveys of hospitals and ambulatory surveys that The Joint Commission conducts. The NPSGs address topics such as medication safety, prevention of infections, communication among caregivers, and many other safety issues. The **CD-ROM accompanying the book** contains a poster of the 2010 Hospital Patient Safety Goals in easy-to-read format.

  The Joint Commission also publishes what are called Sentinel Events. "A sentinel event is an unexpected occurrence involving death or serious physical or psychological injury, or the risk thereof. Serious injury specifically includes loss of limb or function ... Such events are called "sentinel" because they signal the need for immediate investigation and response" (Joint Commission, 2010b). Joint Commission standards include policies on how health care organizations are expected to respond to sentinel events. Examples of sentinel events are wrong-side surgery, suicide, falls, and injury or death due to restraints.

- **Leapfrog Group** (https://leapfrog.medstat.com): The Leapfrog Hospital Survey is comprised of many of the National Quality forum-defined safe practices. The survey was started in 2001 by the Leapfrog Group, which was formed by a large group of employers in 1998, officially becoming a group in 2000. The group was formed in order to use safety data in making health care purchasing decisions.

- **NCQA-HEDIS** (http://www.ncqa.org/tabid/59/Default.aspx): The National Committee for Quality Assurance (NCQA), a private, not-for-profit organization was founded in 1990. NCQA has been successful in driving health care quality improvement in the nation and building consensus among employers, health plans, legislative bodies, providers and patients. HEDIS, The Healthcare Effectiveness Data and Information Set, is the quality measurement tool utilized by the majority of health care plans in the United States to measure performance of a specific set of patient care and service metrics, including chronic disease management. NCQA-HEDIS has been successful in measuring and grading the performance of health plans in the country and increasing awareness and use of evidence based practices and protocols. NCQA's Committee on Performance Measurement develops the standardized HEDIS measures. Performance of health plans on the NCQA-HEDIS measures allows patients, providers and employers to reliably compare health plan performance and make informed purchasing choices ("Health Insurance," 2010).

- **Hospital Quality Alliance** (http://www.hospitalqualityalliance.org/): The HQA is a public organization launched in 2002 as a national collaboration with the intent to make health care quality information readily accessible and useable to the general public. HQA collaborated with the federal government to develop the Hospital Compare website mentioned previously.

Health care organizations may also use data to benchmark their progress in certain areas. For example, a hospital may use a measure called "Lives Saved," which was started by IHI. Premier, Inc. uses a nationally recognized case-mix adjustment methodology to determine a hospital's expected mortality rate. This expected rate reflects the mortality that would be expected to have occurred if the patients a hospital cared for had been treated by the "average" hospitals in the database. Premier's hospital members look at their actual (observed) inpatient mortality compared with the expected mortality derived from the hospitals in the Premier database. These two numbers are used to create a ratio, observed divided by expected, to create a "mortality index" for the hospital (http://www.premierinc.com/).

Quality Designations

A significant trend in the health care quality movement has been the development of a number of designations designed to recognize an organization's achievements in a particular area. Two of the most prestigious are the Baldrige National Quality Program Award and Magnet Recognition Program of the American Nurses Credentialing Center.

- **Baldrige National Quality Program Award**: Leaders in the United States began to understand the importance of improving quality in order to compete successfully in a global market in the mid-1980s. Congress enacted the Malcolm Baldrige National Quality Improvement Act of 1987 and created the Malcolm Baldrige National Quality Award to:
  - Identify and recognize role-model businesses
  - Establish criteria for evaluating improvement efforts
  - Disseminate and share best practices (Baldrige National Quality Program, 2010).

  In 1999 the Baldrige National Quality Program added the health care category. The Baldrige Health Care Criteria for Performance Excellence are used for education and for assessing organizational performance and excellence in seven key areas: Leadership, Strategic Planning, Customer Focus, Measurement/Analysis/Knowledge Management, Workforce Process, Process Management, and Results (Baldrige National Quality Program, 2009). Figure 2.4 explains the criteria in more detail.

- **Magnet Recognition Program**: The Magnet Recognition Program was designed and developed by the American Nurses Credentialing Center (ANCC) in order to recognize those health care organizations providing excellent nursing care and overall excellence in nursing practice and professionalism (American Nurses Credentialing Center, 2010a). First awarded in 1994, the Magnet Recognition Program is intended to:
  - Promote quality in a setting that supports professional practice
  - Identify excellence in the delivery of nursing services to patients/residents
  - Disseminate best practices in nursing services (American Nurses Credentialing Center, 2010a)

  Magnet status is awarded to health care organizations who meet a standard set of criteria measuring the quality of nursing practice. Magnet hospitals are recognized as being able to attract and retain high quality nurses and having other characteristics that make them distinctive in delivering excellent nursing care, involving nurses in decision making and data collection, high nurse satisfaction, and low turnover rates. The "Forces of Magnetism" are "comprised of 5 key components: Transformational Leadership, Structural Empowerment, Exemplary Professional Practice, New Knowledge, Innovation and Improvements, and Empirical Quality Results" (Wolf, Triolo, and Ponte, 2008: 202). Like the Baldrige Award, Magnet Recognition assists organizations in achieving a culture of excellence and continuous

---

Figure 2.4. Baldrige National Quality Award Criteria

Leadership: Examines how senior executives guide the organization and how the organization addresses its responsibilities to the public and practices good citizenship.

Strategic planning: Examines how the organization sets strategic directions and how it determines key action plans.

Customer focus: Examines how the organization determines requirements and expectations of customers and markets; builds relationships with customers; and acquires, satisfies, and retains customers.

Measurement, analysis, and knowledge management: Examines the management, effective use, analysis, and improvement of data and information to support key organization processes and the organization's performance management system.

Workforce focus: Examines how the organization enables its workforce to develop its full potential and how the workforce is aligned with the organization's objectives.

Process management: Examines aspects of how key production/delivery and support processes are designed, managed, and improved.

Results: Examines the organization's performance and improvement in its key business areas: customer satisfaction, financial and marketplace performance, human resources, supplier and partner performance, operational performance, and governance and social responsibility. The category also examines how the organization performs relative to competitors.

Source: National Institute of Standards and Technology (NIST). 2009. "Frequently Asked Questions about the Malcolm Baldrige National Quality Award." NIST, December 8. Accessed September 15, 2010. http://www.nist.gov/public_affairs/factsheet/baldfaqs.cfm.

improvement (American Nurses Credentialing Center, 2010b).

Evidence-Based Health Care and Comparative Effectiveness Research

Evidence-based health care, also called evidence-based medicine and evidence-based practice in nursing began to be defined in the early 1990s (Evidence-Based Medicine Working Group, 1992) and in recent years has become more widely accepted and championed by all areas of health care. Chapters 11 and 12 discuss the steps in the practice of EBHC and the role of the health care librarian in support of EBHC. In terms of the health care environment it is coming even more to the fore in the concept of comparative effectiveness research (CER). The American Recovery and Reinvestment Act of 2009 allocated $1.1 billion to fund CER and charged the Institute of Medicine with defining it and selecting initial priorities (Ratner et al., 2009). As defined by AHRQ "Comparative effectiveness research is designed to inform health-care decisions by providing evidence on the effectiveness, benefits, and harms of different treatment options. The evidence is generated from research studies…" (Agency for Healthcare Research and Quality, 2010). Comparative effectiveness research will have an impact on all areas of health care policy and is likely to be politically charged as well.

> CER is the generation and synthesis of evidence that compares the benefits and harms of alternative methods to prevent, diagnose, treat and monitor a clinical condition, or to improve the delivery of care. The purpose of CER is to assist consumers, clinicians, purchasers, and policy makers to make informed decisions that will improve health care at both the individual and population levels. (Ratner et al., 2009: 29)

Translational Research

A number of recent initiatives have been created due to the demand from clinicians and the public for benefits from scientific and clinical research to be realized much sooner. In 2003 National Institutes of Health (NIH) Director Elias Zerhouni called for an acceleration of medical research (Zerhouni, 2003) in what was called the NIH Roadmap. Translational research is often described as "bench-to-bedside." The NIH Roadmap's goal is to accelerate discovery and translation of new knowledge into effective prevention strategies and new treatments. The roadmap is a 10-year plan that includes three major

themes: new pathways to discovery; developing research teams of the future; and re-engineering the clinical enterprise. As part of the roadmap, Clinical Translational Science Awards (CTSA) have been established. Details about the NIH program are at http://nihroadmap.nih.gov/.

Technology

The recent book *Health Informatics for Medical Librarians* by Ana D. Cleveland and Donald B. Cleveland (2009) provides an excellent introduction to the role of all types of information technologies in health care. This section will touch briefly on several technologies that the health care librarian will need to be familiar with.

Electronic Health Records

Although components of Electronic Health Records have been in various stages of development and adoption for many years, the 2009 passage of the Health Information Technology for Economic and Clinical Health Act (HITECH), part of the American Recovery and Reinvestment Act (ARRA), has accelerated both development and adoption of these systems. HITECH authorized incentive payments through CMS to clinicians in office practices and to hospitals for the use of EHRs. As part of the incentive payment regulations, "HITECH's goal is not adoption alone but 'meaningful use' of EHRs—that is, their use by providers to achieve significant improvements in care. The legislation ties payments specifically to the achievement of advances in health care processes and outcomes" (Blumenthal and Tavenner, 2010: 501). The regulations have defined two major areas of meaningful use. Core objectives cover the basic data elements in an EHR and clinical decision support tools. The second group includes potential tasks that can address such things as medication management, patient education materials and continuity of care.

Meaningful use also includes electronic reporting of data on the quality of care. "Clinicians will have to report data on three core quality measures in 2011 and 2012: blood-pressure level, tobacco status, and adult weight screening and follow-up (or alternates if these do not apply). Clinicians must also choose three other measures from lists of metrics that are ready for incorporation into electronic records" (Blumenthal and Tavenner, 2010: 504).

Another regulation addresses the standards and certification requirements of EHRs. A Final Rule on an initial set of standards, implementation specifications, and certification criteria for adoption by the HHS Secretary was issued on July 13, 2010. EHR developers and purchasers will be looking closely at the requirements for functionality, security, and interoperability of these systems.

The government's Health IT website (http://healthit.hhs .gov/portal/server.pt?open=512&objID=2996&mode=2) provides a great deal of information on these regulations. Information is provided for both health care providers and consumers.

A subset of EHRs is the Personal Health Record that can provide consumers with online access to their medical records. This is an outgrowth of increased consumer demand and the development of web-based technologies that enable it. Some health care providers such as Kaiser Permanente give online access to test results, prescription history, and health information. Third parties such as Microsoft and Google have developed these systems as well. Jones et al. (2010) described the proliferation of products and issues such as standardization of vocabularies, interoperability, and security.

Telehealth

Cleveland and Cleveland (2009: 57) describe the word telehealth as "an inclusive term that implies the use of telecommunication and other information technologies to provide healthcare . . . to distant points" and explore a variety of telehealth applications, many of which have been in use for decades. Telehealth or telemedicine technology is often thought of as primarily a service provided to patients and providers in rural settings, but there are many fairly local environments that also take advantage of these technologies as well. The Veteran's Health Administration has implemented a telehealth system to help patients manage their chronic diseases from home (Chumbler, Haggstrom, and Saleem, 2010). Remote monitoring of patients with heart failure, diabetes, asthma, and other chronic diseases is being addressed with this technology. Telehealth is also being used in education and training (Conde et al., 2010) and has been used for many years in radiology.

As with other health care activities, telehealth is subject to regulation and accreditation. Both The Joint Commission and CMS have requirements but have a different approach to them (UPDATE, 2009) that ultimately will need to be resolved. In addition, states and professional organizations are examining telemedicine standards of care. The promise of improving access to care to underserved communities as well as lowering costs bodes well for an increase in the use of telehealth technologies in the future.

Biotechnology

Biotechnology covers many areas of research. For health care librarians, the work of the National Center for

Biotechnology Information (http://www.ncbi.nlm.nih .gov/guide/) provides a guide for understanding and researching this rapidly developing component of health care. The study of how genes interact with various risk factors in the development of disease is included in the field known as genomics. Genomics touches all health care settings, including research institutions, hospitals, primary care, advocacy organizations, and public health. Other useful resources on genomics include the CDC Office of Public Genomics (http://www.cdc.gov/ genomics/ default.htm) and the National Genomic Research Institute (http://www.genome.gov/). These two resources provide a great deal of information for patients as well as professionals. In addition to the scientific aspects of genomics, public policy and ethical issues are also addressed.

Conclusion

Donald M. Berwick, newly appointed head of CMS, has written, "It is ironic that health care, which occupies nearly one-sixth of the U.S. economy and affects us all, sooner or later . . . remains *terra incognita* for so many of us. It is like the vast black spaces in maps from the Middle Ages. . . . We depend on health care, but in it we feel like strangers" (Kovner, Knickman, and Jonas, 2008: xv). The authors of this chapter hope that some of the mystery of the health care environment that might confront a new or even seasoned library manager has been removed and that this chapter will provide a guide to this complex world of health care.

References

Agency for Healthcare Research and Quality. 2010. "What is Comparative Effectiveness Research?" Accessed August 1. http://www.effectivehealthcare.ahrq.gov/index.cfm/what-is-comparative-effectiveness-research1/.

Alguire, Patrick C. 2010. "Types of Practices." Philadelphia: American College of Physicians (2010). Accessed September 15. http://www.acponline.org/residents_fellows/career_ counseling/types.htm.

Altman, Drew E., and Douglas H. Morgan. 1983. "The Role of State and Local Government in Health." *Health Affairs (Project Hope)* 2, no. 4 (Winter): 7–31.

American College of Surgeons. 2009. "Cancer Program Standards (CPS) 2011." Accessed July 30, 2010. http://www.facs .org/cancer/coc/cps2011.html.

American Medical Association. 2010. *Health Care Careers Directory*. Chicago: American Medical Association.

American Nurses Credentialing Center. 2010a. "Goals of the Program." Accessed September 15. http://www.nursecredentialing.org/Magnet/ProgramOverview/GoalsoftheMagnetProgram.aspx.

American Nurses Credentialing Center. 2010b. "Program Overview." Accessed September 15. http://www.nursecredentialing.org/Magnet/ProgramOverview.aspx.

American Organization of Nurse Executives BSN-Level Nursing Education Resources. 2010. Accessed June 17. http://www.aone.org/aone/resource/practiceandeducation.html.

Aspden, Philip, Institute of Medicine (U.S.), and Committee on Data Standards for Patient Safety. 2004. *Patient Safety: Achieving a New Standard for Care*. Quality chasm series. Washington, DC: National Academies Press.

Baldrige National Quality Program. 2009. *2009–2010 Health Care Criteria for Performance Excellence*. Gaithersburg, MD: National Institute of Standards and Technology.

Baldrige National Quality Program. National Institute of Standards and Technology. 2010. "History." Accessed September 15. http://www.nist.gov/baldrige/about/history.cfm.

Benner, Patricia E., ed. 2010. *Educating Nurses: A Call for Radical Transformation*. 1st ed. San Francisco: Jossey-Bass.

Berwick, Donald M., A. Blanton Godfrey, and Jane Roessner. 1990. *Curing Health Care: New Strategies for Quality Improvement: A Report on the National Demonstration Project on Quality Improvement in Health Care*. The Jossey-Bass Health Series. 1st ed. San Francisco: Jossey-Bass.

Blumenthal, D., and M. Tavenner. 2010. "The 'Meaningful Use' Regulation for Electronic Health Records." *New England Journal of Medicine* 363, no. 6 (August 5): 501–504.

Centers for Disease Control and Prevention. 2010. "National Environmental Public Health Tracking Network." Accessed July 31. http://ephtracking.cdc.gov/showAbout.action.

Centers for Medicare and Medicaid Services. 2005. "Deeming." Accessed July 30, 2010. http://www.cms.gov/Deeming/.

Centers for Medicare and Medicaid Services. 2010a. "Conditions of Participation (CoPs) and Conditions for Coverage (CfCs)." Accessed July 30. http://www.cms.hhs.gov/CFCsAndCoPs/.

Centers for Medicare and Medicaid Services. 2010b. "EMTALA Overview." Accessed July 30. http://www.cms.gov/EMTALA/.

Centers for Medicare and Medicaid Services. 2010c. "HIPAA General Information." Accessed July 30. http://www.cms.gov/HIPAAGenInfo/.

Chumbler, Neale R., David A. Haggstrom, and Jason Saleem. 2010. "Implementation of Health Information Technology in Veterans Health Administration to Support Transformational Change: Telehealth and Personal Health Records." *Medical Care* (April 23): E-pub ahead of print.

Cleveland, Ana D., and Donald B. Cleveland. 2009. *Health Informatics for Medical Librarians*. New York: Neal-Schuman Publishers.

Conde, Jose G., Suvranu De, Richard W. Hall, Edward Johansen, Dwight Meglan, and Grace C. Peng. 2010. "Telehealth Innovations in Health Education and Training." *Telemedicine Journal and e-Health: The Official Journal of the American Telemedicine Association* 16, no. 1 (January–February): 103–106.

DerGurahian, Jean. 2008. "DNV Setting New Standard. Watch Out Joint Commission. There's a New Accreditor in Town, and Some Hospitals Say They're Willing to Give It a Try." *Modern Healthcare* 38, no. 43 (October 27): 6–7, 16.

Doherty, Robert B. 2010. "The Certitudes and Uncertainties of Health Care Reform." *Annals of Internal Medicine* 152, no. 10 (May 18): 679–682.

Donahue, M. Patricia. 2011. *Nursing, the Finest Art: An Illustrated History*. 3rd ed. Maryland Heights, MO: Mosby Elsevier.

Drinka, Theresa J. K., and Philip G. Clark. 2000. *Healthcare Teamwork: Interdisciplinary Practice and Teaching*. Westport, CT: Auburn House.

Evidence-Based Medicine Working Group. 1992. "Evidence-Based Medicine. A New Approach to Teaching the Practice of Medicine." *JAMA: The Journal of the American Medical Association* 268, no. 17 (November 4): 2420–2425.

Foster, Eloise C., and Gail L. Warden. 2000. "The Health Care Environment." In *The Medical Library Association Guide to Managing Health Care Libraries*, edited by Ruth Holst, Sharon A. Phillips, and Karen McNally Bensing, 11–22. New York: Neal-Schuman.

Glickman, Seth W., and Eric D. Peterson. 2009. "Innovative Health Reform Models: Pay-for-performance Initiatives." *The American Journal of Managed Care* 15, no. 10 Suppl (December): S300–S305.

Goodson, John D. 2010. "Patient Protection and Affordable Care Act: Promise and Peril for Primary Care." *Annals of Internal Medicine* 152, no. 11 (June 1): 742–744.

HCUPnet: "Ready-to-use Tables on Commonly Requested Information from HCUP." 2010. Agency for Healthcare Research and Quality. Accessed October 5. http://hcupnet.ahrq.gov/HCUPnet.jsp.

"Health Insurance; How to Pick a Plan in These Changing Times." 2010. *Consumer Reports* 75, no. 11 (November): 17–23.

Health Workforce Information Center. 2010. "Physicians." Accessed July 30. http://www.healthworkforceinfo.org/topics/introduction.php?id=124.

HRSA Health Professions. 2010. "Health Workforce Studies." Health Workforce Information Center. Accessed July 30. http://bhpr.hrsa.gov/healthworkforce/default.htm.

"Improving Health Care: a Dose of Competition. A Report by the Federal Trade Commission and the Department of Justice." 2004. Accessed July 30, 2010. http://www.justice.gov/atr/public/health_care/204694/chapter3.htm.

Institute of Medicine (U.S.). Committee on Assuring the Health of the Public in the 21st Century. 2003. *The Future of the Public's Health in the 21st Century*. Washington, DC: National Academies Press.

Institute of Medicine (U.S.). Committee on Quality of Health Care in America. 2001. *Crossing the Quality Chasm: A New Health System for the 21st Century*. Washington, DC: National Academy Press.

Joint Commission. 2010a. *Hospital Accreditation Standards.* Oakbrook Terrace, IL: Joint Commission Resources.

Joint Commission. 2010b. "Sentinel Events." Accessed July 30. http://www.jointcommission.org/SentinelEvents.

Jonas, Steven, Raymond L. Goldsteen, and Karen Goldsteen. 2007. *An Introduction to the U.S. Health Care System.* New York: Springer Publishing.

Jones, Dixie A., Jean P. Shipman, Daphne A. Plaut, and Catherine R. Selden. 2010. "Characteristics of Personal Health Records: Findings of the Medical Library Association/ National Library of Medicine Joint Electronic Personal Health Record Task Force." *Journal of the Medical Library Association* 98, no. 3 (July): 243–249.

Kenney, Charles. 2008. *The Best Practice: How the New Quality Movement Is Transforming Medicine.* 1st ed. New York: Public Affairs.

Kohn, Linda T., Janet Corrigan, and Molla S. Donaldson. 2000. *To Err Is Human: Building a Safer Health System.* Washington, DC: National Academy Press.

Kovner, Anthony R., James Knickman, and Steven Jonas. 2008. *Jonas and Kovner's Health Care Delivery in the United States.* 9th ed. New York: Springer Publishing.

Larkin, Howard. 2009. "10 Years, 5 Voices, 1 Challenge. 'To Err Is Human' Jump-Started a Movement to Improve Patient Safety. How Far Have We Come? Where Do We Go from Here?" *Hospitals & Health Networks / AHA* 83, no. 10 (October): 24–28.

Lindenauer, Peter K., Denise Remus, Sheila Roman, Michael B. Rothberg, Evan M. Benjamin, Allen Ma, and Dale W. Bratzler. 2007. "Public reporting and pay for performance in hospital quality improvement." *New England Journal of Medicine* 356, no. 5 (February 1): 486–496.

Ludwig, Logan. 2008. "The Health Care Environment." In *Introduction to Health Sciences Librarianship*, edited by M. Sandra Wood, 31–65. Binghamton, NY: The Haworth Information Press.

McClellan, Mark, Aaron N. McKethan, Julie L. Lewis, Joachim Roski, and Elliot S. Fisher. 2010. "A National Strategy to Put Accountable Care into Practice." *Health Affairs (Project Hope)* 29, no. 5 (May): 982–990.

Medical Library Association. 2007. *Competencies for Lifelong Learning and Professional Success: The Educational Policy Statement of the Medical Library Association.* Chicago: MLA. Accessed October 5, 2010. http://www.mlanet.org/ education/policy/.

Nelson, Eugene C., Paul B. Batalden, Thomas P. Huber, Julie J. Mohr, Marjorie M. Godfrey, Linda A. Headrick, and John H. Wasson. 2002. "Microsystems in Health Care: Part 1. Learning from High-Performing Front-Line Clinical Units." *The Joint Commission Journal on Quality Improvement* 28, no. 9 (September): 472–493.

Nielsen-Bohlman, Lynn, Allison M. Panzer, David A. Kindig, and Institute of Medicine. Committee on Health Literacy, eds. 2004. *Health Literacy: A Prescription to End Confusion.* Washington, DC: National Academies Press.

Office for Civil Rights. 2010. "Health Information Privacy. Accessed June 26. http://www.hhs.gov/ocr/privacy/.

Office of Disease Prevention and Health Promotion, U.S. Department of Health and Human Services. 2010. "Public Comment—Healthy People 2020." Accessed July 31. http://www.healthypeople.gov/hp2020/Objectives/Topic Areas.aspx.

Page, Ann, Institute of Medicine (U.S.), and Committee on the Work Environment for Nurses and Patient Safety. 2004. *Keeping Patients Safe: Transforming the Work Environment of Nurses.* Washington, DC: National Academies Press.

Porter-O'Grady, Timothy. 2009. *Interdisciplinary Shared Governance: Integrating Practice, Transforming Health Care.* Sudbury, MA: Jones and Bartlett Publishers.

Ratner, Robert, Jill Eden, D. Wolman, Sheldon Greenfield, Harold Sox, eds. Institute of Medicine. 2009. *Initial National Priorities for Comparative Effectiveness Research.* Washington, DC: National Academies Press.

Recovery Act (ARRA). 2010. "Community Health Centers." Accessed July 30. http://www.hhs.gov/recovery/hrsa/ health centergrants.html.

Shortell, Stephen M., and Lawrence P. Casalino. 2010. "Implementing Qualifications Criteria and Technical Assistance for Accountable Care Organizations." *JAMA: The Journal of the American Medical Association* 303, no. 17 (May 5): 1747–1748.

Taylor, Jessamy. 2004. *The Fundamentals of Community Health Centers: NHPF Background Paper.* Washington, DC: National Health Policy Forum. Accessed December 1, 2010. http://www.nhpf.org/library/background-papers/BP_ CHC_08-31-04.pdf.

Ulmer, Cheryl, Dianne Miller Wolman, Michael M. E. Johns, and Institute of Medicine (U.S.). Committee on Optimizing Graduate Medical Trainee (Resident) Hours and Work Schedules to Improve Patient Safety. 2009. *Resident Duty Hours: Enhancing Sleep, Supervision, and Safety.* Washington, DC: National Academies Press.

United States Department of Health and Human Services. 1991. *Healthy People 2000: National Health Promotion and Disease Prevention Objectives.* Washington, DC: Department of Health and Human Services.

United States Department of Health and Human Services. 2010. *National Action Plan to Improve Health Literacy.* Accessed January 24, 2011. http://www.health.gov/communication/ HLActionPlan/pdf/Health_Literacy_Action_Plan.pdf.

"UPDATE: Comparing Joint Commission and CMS Telemedicine Requirements." 2009. *Joint Commission Perspectives* 29, no. 5 (May): 6–7.

Wolf, Gail, Pamela Triolo, and Patricia Reid Ponte. 2008. "Magnet Recognition Program: The Next Generation." *The Journal of Nursing Administration* 38, no. 4 (April): 200–204.

Wolinsky, Fredric D. 1982. "Why Physicians Choose Different Types of Practice Settings." *Health Services Research* 17, no. 4 (Winter): 399–419.

Wolper, Lawrence F. 2004. *Health Care Administration: Planning, Implementing, and Managing Organized Delivery Systems,* 4th ed. Boston: Jones and Bartlett.

Zerhouni, Elias. 2003. "Medicine. The NIH Roadmap." *Science* 302, no. 5642 (October 3): 63–72.

Further Reading

Barnsteiner, Jane H., Vanetta Cheeks, Wendy H. Palma, Ave Maria Preston, and Mary K. Walton. 2010. "Promoting Evidence-Based Practice and Translational Research." *Nursing Administration Quarterly* 34, no. 3 (July/September): 217–225.

Farberow, Bonne, Valerie Hatton, Cindy Leenknecht, Lee R. Goldberg, Carlton A. Hornung, and Bernardo Reyes. 2008. "Caveat Emptor: The Need for Evidence, Regulation, and Certification of Home Telehealth Systems for the Management of Chronic Conditions." *American Journal of Medical Quality: The Official Journal of the American College of Medical Quality* 23, no. 3 (May–June): 208–214.

Gawande, Atul. 2010. *The Checklist Manifesto: How to Get Things Right.* New York: Metropolitan Books Henry Holt.

Krause, Thomas R., and John H. Hidley, eds. 2009. *Taking the Lead in Patient Safety: How Healthcare Leaders Influence Behavior and Create Culture.* Hoboken, NJ: John Wiley & Sons.

Pronovost, Peter J., and Eric Vohr, eds. 2010. *Safe Patients, Smart Hospitals: How One Doctor's Checklist can Help Us Change Health Care from the Inside Out.* New York: Hudson Street Press.

Reason, James T. 2008. *The Human Contribution: Unsafe Acts, Accidents and Heroic Recoveries.* Farnham, England; Burlington, VT: Ashgate.

Sox, Harold C., and Sheldon Greenfield. 2009. "Comparative Effectiveness Research: A Report From The Institute Of Medicine." *Annals of Internal Medicine* 151, no. 3 (August 4): 203–205.

II

Management

Topics in Management

Financial Management

Human Resources Management

Evaluation and Improvement Management

Collection Planning Management

Collection Technical Management

Library Space Management

3

Topics in Management

Jacqueline Donaldson Doyle and Kay E. Wellik

Libraries of all types are experiencing change faster than ever before, referred to as the "ever-evolving" library. This poses a unique set of challenges to the library leadership as reported in the literature (Matheson, 1995; McClure, 1998; Thibodeau and Funk, 2009; Holst et al., 2009; Maietta and Bullock, 2009; Schachter, 2005). Similarly, the health care environment in the United States, including delivery system and professional education in academic setting, is coping with change, pressures and emerging trends, as covered in Chapter 2. Lucas notes that in order to cope successfully with change, education leaders "have to examine the ways in which they function together" (Lucas, 2000: xv), particularly as members of interdisciplinary teams. Mavrinac (2005: 391) notes there is a need for "transformational change in higher education and academic libraries," and this transformation will be required to meet customer needs in the changing environment that librarians inhabit. This quote from Albert Einstein best captures the state of today's libraries: "Life is like riding a bicycle. To keep your balance, you need to keep moving" (http://www.alberteinsteinsite .com/quotes/einsteinquotes.html). The authors would add the phrase "and never stop learning" to this saying.

The aim of this chapter is to provide an overview of the current state of library administration and management including suggestions and practices to improve library leadership, planning, promotion, and marketing. Recognizing that library management is indeed ever-evolving, the goal is to present a snapshot of today's practice with a nod to today's trends. Topics covered in greater depth in other chapters will be touched on briefly as appropriate. This chapter combines chapters 3 and 4 from the first edition on administrative issues by Holst and Phillips (2000) and on planning and marketing by Salzwedel and Green (2000). These authors are acknowledged with respect and thanks. Much of what was written in the first edition is still viable and core to the librarian's work today. Their work provided the foundation for and is integrated into the current chapter. The section on marketing is predominately as it was in 2000 with updates for language and current technology and trends. The section on planning has been revised to reflect today's ideas.

All subfields of management evolve and change and trends come and go. The changes in the delivery of health care and health education, as reflected in Chapter 2, require adaptation in library management. In the sidebar, the management skills necessary for today's changing

environment are listed. It is noted which chapter covers which skill. This chapter attempts to cover the rest.

The Many Roles of the Library Manager

Librarians based in academic, corporate and clinical settings wear many hats. Besides all the library science skills covered in this book, the library manager does other tasks, including those of staff supervisor, library planner, computer expert, operations manager, copier and printer fixer, reference librarian/database searcher, and more, depending on the size of the library staff. As a department head, the librarian is required to manage what could be viewed as a small business. He or she is expected to manage income and expenses in an efficient and cost-effective manner (see Chapter 4) as well as the duties of managing a staff (see Chapter 5). Some librarians manage related units within the hospital or academic medical center, including continuing medical education, nursing education, archives, information technology/services, audiovisual services, computer labs, and patient or health education (see Chapters 11 and 15). In a recent survey of the literature on the roles of health sciences libraries and librarians in medical education, a list of services performed by health sciences librarians was developed and is shown here in Figure 3.1 (Schwartz et al., 2009: 283). While this may refer to academic librarians, many hospital librarians are now being asked to manage these programs. The list also includes other operations that library managers reported were part of their job. Another list of these types of operations is available in Chapter 15 based on an informal Internet survey. Even if the librarian is not responsible for these areas, formal partnerships or liaisons with these other departments in these same areas can be forged whether in a hospital or academic setting. This activity positions the library manager as a member of management or education teams.

Place of the Library in the Organization's Hierarchy

The position and influence of the library manager can be affected by where the department is placed in the institution. In academic settings, the library may be part of the medical center hierarchy or may report to the main library on the main university campus. The

Section 2 Management of Information Services

From the *Medical Library Association Competencies for Lifelong Learning and Professional Success* (Medical Library Association, 2007).

Leadership in the application of library and information science to the handling of health information resources in complex institutional environments requires specialized knowledge, skill, and understanding of management, including:

- the institution's mission and the specific mission of the information resource center
- institutional functional planning processes
- decision-making strategies
- human resources management and labor relations (see Chapter 4)
- staff development, project and program management and evaluation (see Chapters 4 and 6)
- organizational structure and behavior
- inter-institutional relations
- numerical literacy and computational proficiency (see Chapter 6)
- finance and budgeting, cost analysis and price setting (see Chapter 5)
- skills in fundraising and proposal writing (see Chapter 5)
- public relations and marketing
- facilities planning and space allocation (see Chapter 9)
- oral and written communication
- interpersonal relations

Figure 3.1. List of Services Performed by Health Sciences Librarians

- Provide executive research services for senior hospital administrative staff
- Develop cyber-intelligent search systems or agents that improve search capabilities
- Create new learning tools using, among others, Web 2.0 technology
- Foster lifelong learning by:
  - developing new instructional modalities, such as experiential learning, supporting information literacy, while retaining personalized instruction that is based on an individual learner's unique needs
  - providing classroom-based instruction or education carried out as part of the clinical team
- Develop institution-wide knowledge management programs
- Create management training resources and programs for hospital managers
- Train health care professionals to understand the intrinsic value of information
- Provide knowledge advising and counseling services
- Create new approaches to searching for information, knowledge, wisdom:
  - train expert searchers (i.e., informationists, knowledgists)
  - develop intelligent agents-intelligent search engines
- Deliver enhanced point-of-need delivery systems for library materials
- Provide writing, editorial, and bibliographic assistance
- Conduct ongoing needs assessment and marketing studies

- Serve on institutional committees including institutional review board, strategic planning, patient education, electronic medical record (EMR), etc.
- Contribute to continuing medical education (CME) programs by:
  - managing CME for the hospital or health system
  - serving on the CME committee
- Train health care professionals in cultural competency
- Provide professional education and mentoring of future health sciences librarians
- Collaborate with information systems and technology professionals to:
  - develop in-depth knowledge of networks, system administration, and databases
  - serve on information systems and technology (IST) teams
  - merge some library services with the IST help desk
- Serve as a virtual educator by providing:
  - virtual reference assistance
  - virtual instruction
- Direct, oversee, and maintain hospital operations, such as:
  - archives
  - cancer registry
  - compliance/training
  - computer labs
  - electronic personal health record
  - graphic design
  - HealthStream
  - hospital orientation
  - institutional review board
  - intranet site and/or Internet site as web manager
  - Joint Commission coordination
  - medical photography
  - patient education/ patient TV system
  - telephone system
  - policies, procedures, forms
  - room scheduling
  - telemedicine/telehealth
  - video conferencing
  - visitor's center/ concierge services

Source: Schwartz et al., 2009: 283. Used with permission.

director would then report to a dean or other administrator in the medical center campus to the main university librarian. In hospitals, the librarian can report to a variety of departments. As reported in Chapter 16 on Solo Libraries in Figure 16.1, (Reporting Structure of Health Science Libraries, based on data from the 2007 MLA Benchmarking Survey), 53 percent of librarians in hospitals report to the main administration area or to medical staff, medical director, medical affairs or medical education areas. Other areas include human resources, quality management, information systems or other education areas. Historically, hospital libraries were often administratively under medical records

departments (Holst, 1991: 4), now called health information management, but in 2007 this number was only 3 percent as shown in Figure 16.1. Whatever the reporting pattern or structure, the library manager should take the time to assess the library's perceived value to the organization as reflected by its place in the organization. Sometimes personalities play a role in determining the reporting pattern, which may or may not be advantageous. Opportunities might arise to request a change in reporting structure that would be more advantageous. Also this awareness will help in a transition if the reporting structure is changed due to an overall corporate restructuring.

Another issue is whether the position is a department head or not. A department head has more control over budget and staff and can interact with other members of the management team on a different level. The Standards for Hospital Libraries 2007 (Hospital Libraries Section Standards Committee, 2008) not only recommends the position be a department head but also that it report to senior management as noted in the sidebar.

Standards for Hospital Libraries 2007

STANDARD 1: The library serves as the primary department responsible for developing systems and services to meet the knowledge-based information (KBI) needs of the organization. The library shall have its own budget, and the director, as a department head, shall report to the senior management of the organization. (Hospital Libraries Section Standards Committee, 2008: 163)

Library managers that find themselves in a position that is not a department head might still find it advantageous to take on additional informal or formal leadership responsibilities. These responsibilities might include management or administrative decisions. By doing more management duties, this position description could be changed and perhaps the library could become a department. In most cases, it is advantageous to be classified as such. It is recommended that the library manager in any institution perceive him or herself as an organizational leader, and act in that capacity, whether it is an official designation or not.

The librarian should also be considered as a professional member of the parent organization's faculty or staff. Professionals are usually accorded the degree of flexibility and autonomy that librarians require to fulfill both departmental and professional goals. Professional status employees, e.g., academic professionals in some institutions, may be granted time off to attend conferences without taking personal vacation time. Honea (2000: 3) quotes Drucker when she writes, "The manager's goals are derived from the organization's mission objectives, but the professional's goals and work standards are derived from the goals and standards of professional quality." It could be said that the librarian's direction comes from a higher place than that of the organization itself.

The Librarian as Leader

In this chapter, the descriptors library leader, library administrator, library manager, and library director are used interchangeably since the librarian hired to organize, staff and lead the department is called by these names. These all refer to the person in charge of the library, whether it is a department or division or branch. Other library managers in larger organizations would be the persons who direct a certain function of the library. Whether talking about managing the whole library or the technical functions described elsewhere in the book, managers should aspire to evaluate and improve their leadership skills. Prentice (2004: 102), in the reissue of his classic 1961 *Harvard Business Review* article, describes leadership as "the accomplishment of a goal through the direction of human assistants. The man who successfully marshals his human collaborators to achieve particular ends is a leader. A great leader is one who can do so day after day, year after year, in a wide variety of circumstances." The simplicity of this statement is appealing and still valid today. More recently, Schachter (2005: 10) noted, "The primary function of leadership is to ensure that your staff and the library overall show ongoing success in every endeavor you undertake." She also notes that to be a good leader, "you must first learn what it is to be a good follower" (Schachter, 2007: 40).

In the reissue of his classic 1977 *Harvard Business Review* article, Zaleznik (2004: 74) describes the difference between a leader and a manager as related to the "the concepts they hold, deep in their psyches, of chaos and order." Where managers hold process, stability, and control as valuable, and seek quick solutions to problems, leaders embrace chaos and a lack of structure so they can take advantage of the situation and fully understand existing issues that have created the problem. Librarians need to embrace both concepts. The speed at which the library world is changing mandates that today's librarian see quick solutions and seek a greater level of understanding, simultaneously serving as both leader and manager, changing the hats quite often. See the sidebar for a list of preferred attributes of today's library leader.

The Medical Library Association (MLA) and the Association of Academic Health Science Libraries (AAHSL) offer many opportunities for aspiring leaders to learn leadership skills that will enhance their ability to move into leadership positions. Bedard (2009) provides the introduction to a special issue of the *Journal of Library Administration*, titled "Our Commitment to Building Leaders: Programs for Leadership in Academic and Special Libraries," containing articles that describe several leadership development programs. Aspiring library leaders should peruse this excellent and informative issue. Bunnett et al. (2009) describe the National Library of Medicine/Association of Academic Health Sciences

Skills and Attributes for Today's Library Leaders

- Emotional intelligence
- Flexibility and creativity
- Innovative spirit
- A vision of the library's future
- A deep understanding of the community the library serves
- Self-knowledge
- Passion for the profession
- Ability to leverage change and chaos
- Willingness to take risks
- Intellectually curious
- Optimism combined with realism
- Effective communication skills, oral and written
- Values and results focused
- Customer focused
- Willingness to exemplify desired behaviors for staff
- Enthusiasm for recognizing, valuing and developing staff
- Willingness to collaborate with partners and colleagues

Libraries (NLM/AAHSL) Leadership Fellows Program that has resulted in a valuable mentoring and educational opportunity.

The importance of effective, enthusiastic, clear, and inspiring library internal and external communication cannot be over emphasized. Whether the leader prefers written or in-person methods of communicating with staff, or a combination of the two, the fundamental job is to create a feeling of enthusiasm, competence, and focus so that people are excited about their work and the effect it has on the organization as a whole, as well as the internal functioning of the library. By understanding the mission of the organization and how it is changing, the library leader can anticipate how the library must also change. Successful leaders always share credit with, or give credit to, the library staff that make it possible for the library to be viewed as integral to the organization's success. This is one way the library is evaluated, by its results (see Chapter 6). So it is key that the library leadership and staff communicate those results to administration.

Working in this environment mandates that the library leader learn to work and cope with change, and in some cases become an organizational change agent. Mielke, Singer, and Griffith talk about librarians rarely having time to stop and take a breath, let alone take time to learn how to become a leader or improve leadership skills. In an article aptly titled "Swimming Upstream,"

they note that "demographic, technological, leadership, political, and budget changes can all lead to new models and ways of looking at and being a leader" and that "it's often painful" (Mielke, Singer, and Griffith, 2006: 107). However, there are times the leader must take the time to be the leader and continue to improve one's leadership skills. Leadership skills of connecting, contributing, and collaborating will enable librarians to thrive in an age of chaos and complexity.

The library leader may be part of teams that report the learning-related issues and needs to the administration. He or she may also represent those issues to outside agencies, such as licensing and accrediting organizations like the Liaison Committee on Medical Education (LCME) as discussed in Chapter 15 or The Joint Commission (TJC) as discussed in Chapter 2. The changes in the health care information environment have led to whole new roles for the library leader such as those described it the sidebar.

As the clinical practice environment becomes increasingly technology driven as the result of widespread implementation of electronic medical records, health care professionals will require information management and informatics knowledge and skills to function effectively. In addition to the impact of technology on clinical decision making, professional development activities will also increasingly require knowledge and skill in using many different technological resources. Facilitating the advancement of these skills among health care provider trainees—whether at the undergraduate, graduate, or postgraduate level—will remain an essential role and responsibility of the health sciences librarian. Several accrediting organizations have provided leadership in delineating the role of the librarian in information management education and informatics skill development, including the AOA and the LCME. (Schwartz et al., 2009: 283)

Corporate Culture and Its Impact on the Library

Library planning is heavily influenced, and sometimes dictated, by the procedures of the library's parent organization. In addition, the scope of the librarian's role within a given health care organization is influenced by that organization's corporate or organizational culture. Corporate culture has been defined in a number of different ways. Dowty and Wallace (2010: 57) describe it as "a way of doing business. In this sense its usage refers to how different organizations go about resolving tasks at hand in different ways. More generally, organizational sociologists think of culture as shared understandings that, through subtle and complex expression, regulate social life in organizations."

Each organization has a unique culture that defines and reflects the behavioral norms of the people who work there. Employees, including library faculty, who have worked in a specific organization for many years, follow the often unwritten rules without being aware that they are doing so. Stories told in the organization can be educational for the new library manager. Wines and Hamilton (2009: 441) note that "stories are more powerful as ways of transmitting [and learning] values, confirming identities, and encouraging behavior than mere admonitions or even commands." Corporate culture comes together to create norms by rewarding and recognizing behaviors that are valued by corporate leadership. The reward and recognition practices may be formal and intentional or entirely unintentional. Whatever the case, they will impact the organization's ability to set and achieve its goals.

It is important to understand how an organization's culture affects the way business is conducted and the way individuals relate to one another. Librarians must talk to their peers within the organization and learn as much as they can about the organizational culture. How well the librarian adapts to working within a culture may determine how comfortable he or she is working within the organization and may ultimately determine the success of efforts to manage the library for greatest effectiveness and success.

External Partners, Outreach, and Collaboration

There are multiple reasons for a library leader to seek and create partnerships and collaborations. Reasons can include the need to share resources, either formally or informally, permanently or occasionally. Identified needs can result in formal and ongoing arrangements with other organizations in the form of consortia memberships strictly for the purposes of reducing expenditures or applying for grants. They can include relationships with other libraries within the National Network of Libraries of Medicine (NN/LM) (http://nnlm.gov) or other regional libraries or other regional or state systems. Such relationships can include those with similar or related organizations, e.g., sister libraries within the same health care or university system. New medical

school libraries may find themselves partners because their parent organizations are partners, e.g., with a related medical center or university system. Identifying what is expected of the partnership administratively and financially is necessary.

A library leader may want to identify partners with similar constituencies in order to benchmark, using libraries from the Medical Library Association Benchmarking Network (http://www.mlanet.org/resources/benchmark/). Benchmarking will enable the manager to justify a new budget category by comparing services offered and convincing administration of the need to more effectively compete in the marketplace. More information about the benchmarking process and its value is found in Chapter 6.

Sometimes the librarian may want to initiate the collaboration and sometimes it is mandated by operational agreements. One example of a state-based partnership among education and health care organizations is the Arizona Health Information Network (AZHIN) that was organized to provide "an infrastructure for knowledge-based information to support health care practice and training in Arizona. AZHIN introduces, encourages, and supports widespread use of electronic information by Arizona's health care practitioners." Information about AZHIN and its structure is found at http://azhin.org/.

In addition to identifying partners, the library administrator should also identify opportunities for library outreach. Outreach activities should be based on the library's mission and may be related to those outreach activities encouraged or in some cases mandated by the parent organization's mission. They can also include what some organizations are calling in-reach, or special services offered to specific target audiences within the organization. Some examples of the latter are developing personal or liaison librarian program to, say, the emergency medicine department. Spak and Glover (2007) describe an initiative to medical students where the relationship between librarians and students run the entire time the student is enrolled. Outreach can include identifying opportunities to help one's community through a local nonprofit organization, for example the YMCA or heart association, in health information areas of interest to both organizations. Parker and Kreps (2005) describe and evaluate a range of activities to address the health literacy challenge, including improving written and non-written materials with the goal of improving readability and comprehension by the target audience. The use of many channels of communication is stressed. Cogdill, Ruffin, and Stavri (2007) described the NN/LM's outreach to the public health workforce offering extensive information-oriented education and training, collaboration, evaluations, and meeting public health challenges.

Library Advisory Committees

Many organizations have a library committee to act as an advisory panel to the librarian, providing advice and support as needed. The library committee may be a useful, or even powerful, force for the development of the library. It can provide an essential base of support for library activities by providing evidence that certain library services are needed. The committee may even be able to exert pressure on the administration in support of new library services. It may also function as a group of "representative users," giving the librarian advice on matters of policy, selection of materials, fundraising, and other library issues. According to the MLA 2002 Benchmarking Network Survey, of the 331 hospital libraries reporting, 51 percent had library committees, with the smaller libraries more likely to have one than the larger ones (Dudden et al., 2006: 123).

An alternative view of a committee is that it is "one of the darker corners of library management" (McKeen, 1993: 15). Its actual implementation and success is based on the manager's effective interpersonal relationship skills and organizational politics over which the librarian has little power. Committees may be formal or informal, small or large, diverse or homogeneous, standing or temporary. The committee leader or the organizational culture may require the use of structure, e.g., *Robert's Rules of Order*, or be characterized by informality.

Physicians and other members of the library committee can be influential advocates of funding for library services and capital improvements. Even when the library is financed partially by physicians or other key constituencies represented on the committee, the library committee should not control the budget, except under rare circumstances. These limitations do not lessen the importance of developing an effective relationship with the committee and using it as a support group for the library. They do, however, make it advisable for the librarian to work toward a strong management structure within the library itself, with minimal dependence on the committee for operational decisions. The librarian should also seek support outside the committee, particularly from administrative personnel responsible for decisions that affect the library.

Structure and Composition

The composition of the library committee will depend on the circumstances of the institution, and should be documented in the committee's charge and in library policy statements. In many hospitals it is a medical staff committee and, as such, is subject to the same appointment and operating procedures as other medical staff committees. Whether it is appointed by the medical staff or by the hospital administration, it should be multidisciplinary, representing a variety of different user groups in the hospital. At a minimum, the committee should include representatives from the primary user groups of the library, including physicians, nurses, other health professionals, and administrators. In addition, some organizations include representation from the community at large. Depending on the purpose and scope of the library committee, the chairperson and members may be appointed by the chief medical officer, by an administrator, or by the librarian.

Regardless of how the purpose of the committee is defined, it is important for the librarian to play the major role in setting the agenda and making recommendations to the committee. The librarian has the most extensive library experience and training and, as such, should recommend new services, propose changes in policies and procedures, and provide information to the committee to assist them in making informed decisions. The librarian should also work to increase committee members' understanding of library services issues. See Management in Action 3.1 for a description of a short-term committee and its value in an academic medical library.

MANAGEMENT IN ACTION 3.1

Use of a Library Advisory Committee for Planning

Organization/Library: Academic Medical Center Library

Location: Arizona

Description of Problem/Project: Long-range space planning ad hoc committee

Impact On: Space Planning/Library as Place

People Involved: Library Director, Deputy Director, Building Manager, Information Services Liaison Librarian, faculty and student representatives from all colleges on the health sciences campus, representative from campus "facilities" dept.

Strategies for Success: Library led the process bringing information to the committee members. All faculty and students on the health sciences campus were surveyed insuring wide input. Other library directors met with the committee to ensure a wider perspective.

Barriers Encountered: Some campus leaders outside of the process had preconceived notions of how library space could be used.

(Continued)

MANAGEMENT IN ACTION 3.1 *(Continued)*

Take-Home Points: The committee needed ideas to react to; it could not plan for the library with no starting point. Faculty and students were strong supporters of the library and brought valuable, objective opinions to the table.

Contact Information: Gary Freiburger, Library Director, Arizona Health Sciences Library, Tucson, Arizona. E-mail: garyf@ahsl.arizona.edu

Timeframe: 2009–2010

Roles for the Library Committee

The role of the library committee may depend less on the committee's written charge than on other factors, such as the interests of individual members; the leadership of influential administrators, physicians, or the librarian; or the committee's traditional role. A written charge is necessary both for documentation and for providing guidelines. However, the energy and resourcefulness of committee members usually determine what the committee does and how successful it is. In any case, the librarian should be the key person who provides either official or unofficial leadership or direction.

The committee can serve as the official voice of the customer and can identify problems, trends, or areas of need. It can do this by dealing with customer complaints and comments as they arise or by systematically seeking customer opinion. The librarian should try to be aware of the needs and opinions of all user groups, and the library committee provides a core of individuals who have been specifically charged with this responsibility. Committee members can also help to identify subject area priorities and can provide expertise in recommending new materials for selection.

Another effective role for the library committee is that of advocacy. Committee support of policies can aid in their being accepted by the hospital. Either as individuals or as a group, the committee can present the need for library services to the appropriate administrative funding authority. This "proof of user need" often gives the organization's management assurance that requests are justified. Either the librarian or the committee can conduct a needs analysis to support the committee's recommendations.

Working with the Library Committee

Skill in working with groups of people is essential when dealing with the library committee. Much of the librarian's work with the committee is accomplished outside of formal meetings, particularly keeping the committee informed of library issues and operations. Well in advance of the official presentation of an issue, such as a request for an additional computer workstation, new library space, or a change in online vendors, the librarian should discuss the issue informally with one or two influential members. The purpose of these discussions is to identify potential problem areas and to begin to educate members on the issue. Ideally, by the time the issue appears on the agenda, committee members will already be knowledgeable about it.

In addition to items that require committee action, the agenda should include items for the committee's information. The librarian's skill in choosing and presenting items can increase the committee's understanding of the factors involved in successful library service. The librarian should apply principles of good reporting when preparing such items. Information reported should relate clearly to the committee's needs and interests, and the terminology used should be understandable.

Planning

Managing a medical library in a climate of rapidly changing information technology requires the astute manager to anticipate and then manage (and sometimes advocate for) change. Basic management concepts and the use of strategic planning concepts to allocate resources for the efficient operation of the library and the delivery of high-quality information services are covered in this section. Other chapters include planning for human resources (Chapter 4), fiscal management (Chapter 5), evaluation (Chapter 6), collection management (Chapters 7 and 8), and space or facilities (Chapter 9). As health care organizations face change and unpredictable futures, effective planning plays an important role in the library achieving its purpose of providing information services to meet the needs of its customers. Strategic planning is a tool that allows the library to evolve its products and services in a systematic fashion, taking into account the types of information needed by library users as well as the best way to deliver it.

This section provides an introduction to the strategic planning process by detailing the steps involved in designing and implementing a strategic plan. A well-written strategic plan provides the road map for a team, whether the team is composed of library personnel or staff members from multiple departments. The plan serves as a communication vehicle for members of the organization to help them understand the mission, vision, and future direction of the team, and therefore the organization. A plan is a tool that outlines the action steps needed to achieve the team's goals. The strategic plan will help those not involved in the planning process understand how the service or product addressed by the plan fits into the overall organization. The communication component of a plan is especially important when those outside the planning process control resources vital to the plan's viability

Kerzner (2003: 380) views planning as decision making; it is a "continuous process of making entrepreneurial decisions with an eye to the future.... The alternative to systematic planning is decision making based on history. This generally results in reactive management leading to crisis management, conflict management, and firefighting."

The Planning Process

The planning process is similar to a journey; the steps include identifying the point of departure, the desired destination, and the mode of travel. Planning gives a framework to *what* needs to be accomplished and *how* it will be done. The *what* decisions lead to the establishment of objectives. The *how* decisions lead to methods for accomplishing those objectives, sometimes referred to as action plans or steps. The planning process recognizes, encourages, and measures the value of organized, resource-conscious activity. Each person involved in the plan follows fixed outlined steps to achievement, thereby channeling individual effort into a group effort. The process of planning helps individuals pursue the same end and pull in the same direction.

In many organizations, performance improvement (PI) principles are used to complement the strategic planning process. These principles also may be referred to as continuous improvement (CI), continuous quality improvement (CQI) or total quality management (TQM). The fundamental concepts and techniques of performance improvement complement strategic planning by providing a framework that demands a systematic approach to the steps in providing a product or service. An underlying tenet of the use of PI principles is that work should be viewed as a process. The leader of the planning team will need to assess the appropriateness of using the PI principles and techniques preferred by the institution in conjunction with the overall planning process. For more detailed information about PI principles and techniques, see Chapter 6.

Another tool for planning which is also used for evaluation is called the Logic Model. It can be used for any kind of planning, including strategic. Developed in 1996 by the Kellogg Foundation, it is used by the National Network of Library of Medicine as a tool to plan and evaluate outreach programs. It lists all the parts described in chart form. The Logic Model is described in Chapter 6, and there are resources for its use on the **accompanying CD-ROM**.

Levels of Planning

Planning is often categorized into levels such as strategic, tactical, or operational. Strategic planning usually describes decision making for timeframes of three to five years, tactical or program planning for periods between one and three years, and operational up to one year. From planning day-to-day activities (operational) to organizing a service (tactical), through making decisions regarding the service and staffing mix for the coming three years (strategic), the library's plans must fit into the organization's business scheme. Because strategic planning is generally long range, comprehensive, and detailed, the process for constructing a complete plan consists of an extensive series of steps.

The steps outlined here for strategic planning may apply equally well to the development of a tactical or operational plan. It may not be necessary, however, to repeat every step in the planning process to launch a new service in one functional area of the library. For example, if the library staff has completed a long-range strategic planning process for the library overall, there is no need to write a new mission and vision for the library to plan a new service. Rather, the planning team will want to identify how the new service fits into the library's existing mission and vision.

For tactical and operational planning, many of the planning steps outlined below may be combined or simplified to fit the existing situation. For example, if the library has selected a new electronic license vendor and wants to do a transition plan that will allow for seamless transfer of licenses to the new company, the librarian may only need to follow the implementation steps of the planning process.

It is important that a formal method of planning be applied to all operations within a library: programs, human resources, materials, facilities, and finance. Each subplan must stand on its own, yet fit and support the organization's overall framework. A major challenge, and often one of the most difficult aspects of planning, is for all levels and tasks of the plan to support each other and thereby form a realistic, sound whole.

Strategic Planning

Many health care organizations and their library departments have adopted the formal methodologies of strategic planning to give structure to their planning process. Kuntz notes that "the concept of strategic planning has now become a necessary part of successful library management" (Kuntz et al., 2003: 89). Regardless of the size of the library, it must be recognized as an important information-providing unit for the organization. The librarian should become familiar with some of the basic concepts of strategic planning as a first step in demonstrating to administration that the library is well managed and that the person running the library takes the managerial role seriously. The first step often includes a thorough examination of the services, structures and processes in place (Kuntz et al., 2003). When planning strategically, an organization or department assesses its environment; formulates values, goals, and objectives; and implements the goals and objectives through specific action steps. The strategic planning process introduced in this chapter can be used by library staff for internal department planning as well as by teams of people representing multiple departments as they jointly plan cross-functional projects, such as patient education programs.

Disaster and Service Continuity Planning

Despite forward-looking planning and everyday implementation, problems and challenges arise, sometimes the result of natural or other disasters. To combat the frustration of unforeseen obstacles and circumstances, many organizations perform contingency planning. Sometimes called business or service continuity planning, continuity planning involves identification of all kinds of possible disasters and what resources are needed to continue to offer library service during the time of the calamity. Continuity plans will keep your library up and running through interruptions such as: power failures, IT system crashes, natural disasters, supply chain problems, and more. While developing the plan, the library manager should check with administration to ensure that a library plan for maintaining service in a disaster synchronizes with that of the organization as a whole.

> Even though technology is critical to the delivery of patient care, healthcare business continuity should not be driven solely by IT. Business continuity planning must be an enterprise-wide program driven by senior management. (Rozek and Groth, 2008: 10)

Examples of disasters could include those listed above as well as a sudden decrease in funding, a significant change in upper management, closing of units or of space within a unit. A library may suddenly lose space when a dean or administrator determines there is a better use for a floor or area of the library. Managing an Internet outage is covered in Chapter 8. A major change or enhancement in library service or organization will also force a change of well-laid plans.

Many libraries of all types have disaster plans in place. It is quite possible, however, that they are finished and filed and rarely updated. Librarians who have not experienced a crisis or loss on the magnitude of Hurricane Katrina, a massive tornado, or a flash flood may become complacent or relaxed in their preparedness efforts. A number of articles describe library activities that worked well (Featherstone, Lyon, and Ruffin, 2008; Fleischer and Heppner, 2009; Zach and McKnight, 2010; Shankar, 2008; Clareson and Long, 2006). Hochstein and colleagues describe the extensive plans, resources, and leadership offered by the National Library of Medicine (NLM) to assist libraries to be prepared and to react to disasters, defined as "as serious disruption of the functioning of a community or society" (2008: 3).

NLM has created an excellent and comprehensive website at http://nnlm.gov/ep/, as shown in Figure 3.2 that offers both a preparedness and emergency response plan for NN/LM network members that is constantly updated. A toolkit with a simple ten-step program is included that addresses all types of disaster preparedness, including those mentioned above as well as pandemics, fires and explosions. The ten steps are summarized in Figure 3.3. As this is a priority program of NLM at this time, librarians can contact their regional National Network of Libraries of Medicine (NN/LM) for consultation and advice from experts. The effective library leader should maintain a watch on NLM's site and use it to educate library staff in an ongoing manner. NLM has also created a consumer-focused page about coping with disasters as a part of MedlinePlus (http://www.nlm.nih.gov/medlineplus/copingwithdisasters.html/).

Key Steps of Planning

The planning process usually includes the following parts: prepare for planning; develop the plan; and implement the plan. Each part has its own steps as shown in the sidebar. Every planning process described above, as well as evaluation projects described in Chapter 6, uses these same steps. The manager could spend more effort on some steps than others depending on the planning

Figure 3.2. National Library of Medicine Website on Emergency Preparedness

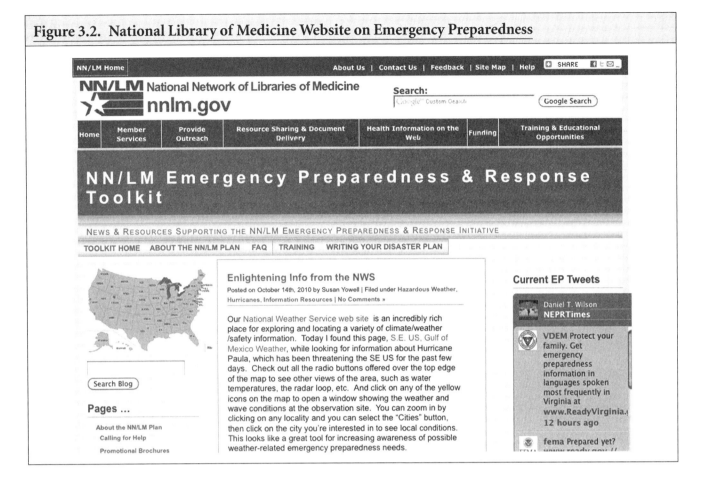

Key Steps of Planning

1. Prepare for planning

- clarify the purpose
- identify key stakeholders
- decide who will develop the plan
- define the constraints
- clarify roles and responsibilities in the process
- outline the communication process

2. Develop the plan

- compose a mission statement and vision statement
- assess the external and internal environments
- assess customers' needs
- set goals
- set objectives

3. Implement the plan

- delineate action steps and timetables
- assign responsibility
- develop contingency plans
- deploy communication strategies
- identify measures to evaluate the plan

Figure 3.3. The NN/LM Ten-Step Approach to Service Continuity Planning

Step 1: Assess risks

Step 2: Protect yourself, your staff, and your patrons

Step 3: Determine your core services

Step 4: Create procedures for remote access to core services

Step 5: Determine your core electronic resources

Step 6: Develop a continuity of access plan for your essential electronic resources

Step 7: Identify your core print collection

Step 8: Identify your unique or highly valued resources

Step 9: Proactively plan for the recovery of your unique and highly valued resources

Step 10: Know how to obtain outside assistance

Source: Taken from current class slides. Accessed September 15, 2010. http://nnlm.gov/ep/10-stepsservice-continuity/.

process. In some cases, a step might be skipped but it is best to note the reason for not doing that step in any report of a planning project. Although time-consuming, following these steps means that every aspect of planning is taken into consideration.

Prepare for Planning

The preparation phase is essential to successful planning. These steps lay the groundwork for the overall planning process. The library manager in conjunction with one or two key advisors accomplishes them in advance of the formal planning process. The chair of the library committee or the administrator who has executive responsibility for the library are examples of key advisors with whom the library manager may want to consult during the preparation phase.

CLARIFY THE PURPOSE OF THE PLAN

Defining the purpose brings everyone to a common understanding of the plan's intent and often clarifies individual and group goals. Each participant in the planning process brings a unique perspective to the table. A clearly stated purpose will help to head off misunderstandings about why the planning team is being brought together and what it is they are expected to accomplish.

IDENTIFY KEY STAKEHOLDERS

A stakeholder is a person or entity that has a share or an interest in a particular program or service. All stakeholders should be identified at the outset of the process. A library's stakeholders include not only users and potential users of the library service, but also library staff members. Siess emphasizes the importance of including library staff and customers when formulating the library strategic plan. A library manager will know when the process implemented "both produces a viable document and through the process of writing the plan, engages the library staff in discussion, sharing, and development of a common idea of what the library is, who it serves, and how each staff member fits into the 'big picture'" (Siess, 2005: 46). The process itself engages staff and enables them to be more creative and involved. Stakeholders have legitimate knowledge and perspectives that can greatly enhance the plan's chances of success. Leaving stakeholders out may cause them to discredit the plan or ignore it. No matter how good the plan may be, if someone feels left out, surprised, or threatened, that person may initiate roadblocks, hoping to cause the plan to falter and fail. The team leader must endeavor to build a collaborative rather than competitive process.

For any plan that affects library operations, library staff members should be considered key stakeholders. Their involvement in the process often translates to greater support for the chosen endeavor, increased consistency of the messages communicated, and commitment to shared goals. If the library team shares in the planning process, they will have a greater investment in successful execution of the plan.

The senior administrator to whom the library manager reports should be considered and/or consulted during the identification of key stakeholders. Although not directly involved with the day-to-day function or service being planned, this person can help to ensure that the plan remains congruent with institutional objectives and can lend support during the budgeting process.

DECIDE WHO WILL DEVELOP THE PLAN

The members of the planning team are usually drawn from those individuals identified as key stakeholders. Forming the planning team is an important first step in getting the plan off the ground. Often groups or teams come together with bits of evidence or a feeling that something is "wrong" and needs fixing. As Lucas (2000: 28) notes, "Change is a team effort." The composition of the team should be determined by the purpose of the planning effort. A strategic plan relating to internal library operations, for example, might include the library manager, the person to whom the library manager reports, and additional members of the library staff as appropriate. A type of plan that crosses departmental boundaries, such as a hospital's information plan, should include the managers of the departments affected. A marketing plan for a library might include two or three library staff members along with a representative of the public relations department.

Assembling the right team can be challenging. A planning team with four to seven members is optimal. Larger groups can be difficult because significant effort will be required to find a meeting time and to provide the resources needed for facilitating consensus. On the other hand, small groups may not contain enough diversity of expertise on the subject. The team must also have the necessary resources and authority to get the plan off the drawing board and implemented. If the plan has financial considerations, someone from financial services needs to be invited to the appropriate planning meetings.

DEFINE THE CONSTRAINTS

Whenever possible, the team leader needs to apprise the team of any budget or human resource constraints at the beginning of the planning process. If the institution has a formal procedure for instituting new services and programs, then the planning team should follow these procedures from the beginning. Effective solutions take constraints into account before implementation rather than after, thus avoiding the problem of wasting the participants' valuable time and energy.

CLARIFY ROLES AND RESPONSIBILITIES IN THE PROCESS

Clearly defined roles and responsibilities often mark the difference between a productive and a nonproductive planning effort. Roles and responsibilities may change as the process progresses. However, answering some of the following questions will help establish order.

- Who serves as chair or team leader?
- Do the roles or responsibilities reside always with a single person, or does the responsibility rotate through all members of the team?
- Who arranges meetings times and rooms?
- Who is responsible for recording minutes?
- Who sends out the agenda and meeting record?
- Who will act as the liaison to groups identified as stakeholders?

OUTLINE THE COMMUNICATION PROCESS

Formal communication mechanisms, such as an agenda, help teams organize and use their time effectively. Quality improvement techniques, such as brainstorming and roundtable discussions, enhance team communication during meetings. Politics or personalities can, at times, detract from the objective sharing of ideas. Tools that allow anonymity may increase unbiased input and acceptance of ideas. The Delphi technique is a data-gathering technique that does not require participants to be face-to-face. Rather it relies on a series of questionnaires and reports containing summarized feedback (Ludwig and Starr, 2005).

The team must also delineate how the plan, and its accompanying changes, will be communicated to others in the organization. As the team works through the process it will be important to identify and notify individuals who need to know of changes. For example, if a plan proposes changes to library policy, the team is responsible for alerting the appropriate administrative body for approval to change policy.

Develop the Plan

Development of the plan itself is, of course, the most critical and time-consuming phase of the planning process. These are the components of the plan that lead to a written document that outlines what will be accomplished as a result of the planning effort.

MISSION AND VISION STATEMENTS

Most health care organizations have a mission statement and many have a service strategy or vision statement. These statements define why the institution exists and communicate the institution's long-term view or vision of itself to those within or outside the organization. Likewise, the library should have mission and vision statements that communicate why the library exists and what its role is within the organization's environment. The library staff often does not have time to write a full featured strategic plan, but if they do anything in the area of planning, they should write a mission and vision statement.

Mission and vision statements are the drivers for most institutional actions. Forsman (1990) discusses the need for incorporating organizational values into the strategic planning process, a point that holds true for any planning effort. He notes that for a library, "values will drive behavior whether they are acknowledged or not. Unless the professional and idealistic values underlying librarianship are set forth, library management and staff may make short-term decisions that lead to long-term failure" (Forsman, 1990: 151).

A mission statement defines the purpose of the library within the organization. It should reflect an understanding of the parent organization's mission statement, without duplicating its content. The mission statement should be realistic enough to take into account the organization's present situation. An example of a hospital library mission statement that connects the library's mission to that of the organization can be found in the sidebar.

Example of a Mission Statement for a Health Care Library

The mission of the Medical Library is to provide high quality information resources and services to customers in an accurate, timely and cost-effective way. Guided by the strategic initiatives of the hospital, as well as professional library standards, the library supports the information needs of the hospital staff as they strive to provide hope, healing and the best care for children and families.

When composing a mission statement, it is important to understand the organizational culture and even use its mission statement as a starting point. Given the library's higher calling, it might be best to begin with its mission, relating it to that of the organization. The "Basics of Developing Mission, Vision and Values Statements" website (http://managementhelp.org/plan_dec/str_plan/stmnts .htm) notes that the mission is a description of the overall purpose of the organization. The same website also provides an introduction to strategic planning. Find more information in Chapter 6 and there are more examples of mission and vision statements in the Chapter 6 section on the **accompanying CD-ROM**.

To complement a mission statement, a vision statement summarizes how the library staff wants the library to be viewed by others within the organization and, perhaps, by the health care community at large. It includes one or more statements that describe an idealized, but achievable, view of the library's service goals and how the library staff will conduct itself to achieve those goals. An example of a library vision statement can be found in the sidebar.

Example of a Hospital Library Vision Statement

The library will:

- Serve as the information center of the hospital
- Be recognized as providing comprehensive, cost-effective and innovative library and information services to its customers
- Be staffed by individuals who are continually improving systems and services by anticipating and exceeding customer needs
- Be a committed participant in the development and implementation of an organization-wide Information Management plan
- Take advantage of technologies as they develop and eliminate distance between products and customers

---

EXTERNAL AND INTERNAL ENVIRONMENT ASSESSMENT

Assessment of the key factors that influence the environment will help the team formulate plans that are realistic and appropriate to their unique situation. This is sometimes called an environmental scan. When evaluating the external environment, the team should gather information about other similar entities and outside influences. For example, a strategic planning team for the library will need to examine the viability of other health-oriented libraries and obtain data regarding the health care industry as well as the medical library field. Economic, political, demographic, social, and technological forces beyond the walls of the library will all have an impact on the library's future direction. See the sidebar for a list of potential examples.

Examples of External Forces That Might Influence a Hospital Library

Economic	Impact of changes in federal reimbursement for medical education on the organization's budget
Political	The level of competition vs. cooperation among hospitals and medical schools in the community
Demographic	Physical distribution of potential library users across the continuum of care and educational structure
Social	Impact of the organization's culture on working styles of employees and staff
Technological	Electronic systems and networks within the organization

---

To create a library strategic plan, the team should examine the internal environment, including a thorough study of the physical surroundings, collections, services, budget, and staff. This analysis should outline the strengths and weaknesses of each of these. Another tool for analysis is called a SWOT analysis. SWOT stands for Strengths, Weaknesses, Opportunities, and Threats. These are listed in a square and analyzed. Find more information in Chapter 6 and on the **accompanying CD-ROM**.

CUSTOMER ASSESSMENT

For planning purposes, knowledge of one's customers is essential. Successful planners try to build customers into the process, striving to identify and satisfy their needs in an organized, resource-efficient manner. Understanding the demographics of library user groups, for example, will allow the planning team to communicate more effectively with them.

Organizational communications vehicles, such as a weekly institutional newsletter, department head meetings, or divisional meetings, provide an opportunity for the library manager to learn about organizational changes. Often these vehicles include information pertinent to the library staff, such as the hire of a new physician or the start-up of a new program that the library staff will want to support. Participating on organization-wide committees is another way for librarians to learn about upcoming activities and programs that may contribute useful information for the planning process. Informal discussions with members of other departments can contribute insight into their goals, resources, and needs. Such knowledge enables the library staff to acquire materials or develop services tailored to the information needs of library users who are part of a new or existing hospital program or a quality improvement strategy.

Established committees, such as the library committee as described previously, provide another appropriate vehicle for surveying customers and assessing their needs. Once rapport is established, the library representative may use individual committee members as a sounding board for proposed projects or as advisors regarding the impact a service or resource may have on an area of the hospital. The committee as a whole may serve as an informal focus group to gather useful ideas. A library committee often contains staunch supporters who become emissaries, carrying back to their departments important information about the library's staff, resources, and services.

To ensure an accurate understanding of customer's needs, the planning team should couple informal methods with a formal assessment program that uses market research techniques. One-on-one interviews, focus groups, or written surveys can contribute valuable details and data about the library's customers. Using these tools within a formal needs assessment process can be effective. Chapter 6 discusses needs assessment as well as some of these tools.

Each methodology has advantages and disadvantages. One-on-one interviews offer the most detailed information, but also require significant time and effort for the staff members conducting the interviews. The advantages of greater depth and breadth of data must be balanced carefully against the disadvantages. Selection of this method is recommended when the team has sufficient time and enough members to conduct the interviews, and when detailed information is needed.

One of the most popular tools is the survey. Crabtree and Crawford (1997: 174) give an excellent, complete, and detailed description of their experience with this methodology and conclude, "the library staff view this survey as one step along a continuous pathway to better service for library clients." Surveys systematically gather information about customers' needs and attitudes. In a more recent study, Perley and colleagues (2007: 173) provide an excellent survey format and reports that she learned "clinicians emphasized the need for 'just in time' information accessible at the point of care. Library nonusers emphasized the need to market library services and resources. Both clinical and nonclinical respondents emphasized the need for information services customized to their professional information needs, preferences, and patterns of use." They also suggest questions for focus groups and telephone interviews.

Well-written surveys are not a simple matter. Teams that plan to gather customer feedback with a survey should seek help from the marketing department or from someone outside the organization who has expertise in the use of surveys. All surveys should be pre-tested using a small group with attributes similar to those of the intended recipients to unearth any ambiguous or misleading questions. The audience for the survey may vary among health care organizations, but should include potential as well as current users. A serious drawback of surveys is the return rate from busy health professionals is frequently low. Figure 3.4 provides a sample of a one-page hospital library survey. Find more comprehensive survey examples in articles by Adams et al. (1994), Crabtree and Crawford (1997), Kennedy (2002), and Hallerberg and Simmons (1997). See Chapter 6 for more information on surveys and questionnaires.

A useful addition to the web for librarians interested in using a survey is the availability of free and low cost survey tools online. "Survey Monkey" (http://www.surveymonkey.com/) and "Zoomerang" (http://www.zoomerang.com/) are some examples. Others are found via one's favorite search engine and will change from day to day. These web-based tools not only help create and distribute the online survey form, but also keep track of data and results, and enable the creation of graphics that will illustrate the results of the survey or questionnaire.

Robbins and Holst (1990) and Higa-Moore et al. (2002) describe the focus group interview technique as a tool for determining users' needs and their perceptions of and satisfaction with the library. A focus group enables the library manager to gather input directly from library customers, which enables the librarian to provide user-centered services and resources. Although recruitment problems exist with the focus group methodology, it is valuable for gathering qualitative comments. Glitz provides an introduction to the focus group methodology, offers many relevant library examples, and analyzes opportunities for the use of this technique (Glitz, 1997).

An Example Use of the Focus Group Technique

The librarian may want to purchase electronic resources in the area of internal medicine but is not sure what types of resources to acquire or how the physician customers will use them in their daily practice. A focus group of physicians and residents could be assembled and asked a number of open-ended questions designed to elicit ideas. General questions about how they use information could be followed with questions about specific types of resources available in the marketplace. Results from the focus group interviews would be used to help select electronic resources that best meet the needs of the target clientele.

Figure 3.4. Questions to Consider Asking in a Library Survey

	Poor	Fair	Good	Very Good	Excellent
1. Please rate the library staff:					
Courtesy					
Helpfulness					
Efficiency					
Knowledge					
Responsiveness					
Technology expertise					
Other, describe:					
2. Please rate the Library's:					
Book collection					
Journal collection					
Media collection					
Ease of locating materials					
3. Please rate the library services:					
Librarian-provided searches					
Library instruction					
Interlibrary loan/document delivery					
Computer lab					
Library webpage					
Library handouts					
Other, describe:					

4. Please describe yourself:
- ○ Student   ○ Physician
- ○ Faculty   ○ Resident or Fellow
- ○ Staff   ○ RN
- ○ Allied health professional— PT, OT, Audiologist, etc.
- ○ Community Member
- ○ Housestaff or Hospitalist
- ○ Pharmacist
- ○ Other: Describe:

5. How can we improve our service to you?

6. What additional *services* would you like us to provide?

7. What additional *resources* would you like us to acquire?

8. Optional:
Name
Department
Contact
Phone/e-mail

SETTING GOALS

Following the environmental and customer assessment steps, the planning team is ready to formulate a set of goals to address problems and opportunities identified during the assessment process. A goal is a broad statement that describes an outcome to be achieved as a result of the planning process.

SETTING OBJECTIVES

Objectives are more specific than goals and are intended to make goals operational. Objectives must be measurable, feasible, and linked in a logical way to one of the goals. Figure 3.5 provides an example of specific objectives linked to a single goal.

Implement the Plan

The plan implementation phase includes steps that assure that the goals identified during the planning process are actually achieved. Everyone has been involved in a planning process at some time that resulted in a beautifully written plan that was placed on a shelf and never touched again. This usually happens because the planning team envisions themselves as the planners and not the doers. Or perhaps, they have good intentions, but because the goals and objectives are never transformed into action steps assigned to specific people, they never get implemented.

Another hazard of a major strategic planning process is that the planning team is exhausted by the time that the planning document is completed and no longer has the energy to carry the plan forward. If this latter situation occurs, it is usually a good idea to wait for a month or two and then review the contents of the plan as a whole. If, upon reflection, the plan is too ambitious or the timing is not right because of other events taking place within the organization, the plan should be scaled down. The list of goals should be reexamined to identify those for which there is enough enthusiasm and sufficient resources to move forward. Any modifications to the plan should be done before the implementation phase if possible.

ACTION STEPS AND TIMETABLES

Once the goals and objectives have been agreed upon, the team will be able to proceed to the development of precise action steps to achieve each objective. Linked to each action step should be a timeline and the name of the person who is responsible for ensuring that the action is completed. For most projects there is a logical order in which the action steps should take place. The

Figure 3.5. Example of a Goal with Several Objectives

Goal 1	Objective
Improve array of e-resources offered by the library	1.1 Identify gaps in collection
	1.2 Identify resources to fill gaps
	1.3 Negotiate and finalize licenses
	1.4 Create online access method, e.g., via OPAC or ERMS
	1.5 Develop and implement training methods to alert customers to new resources, e.g., tutorials, e-mail alerts, webpage postings
	1.6 Monitor and measure usage and cost-per-use
	1.7 Determine value and consider renewal of licenses

actions should be sequenced so that the timelines flow in chronological order. Figure 3.6 includes a set of action plans along with a timetable, responsibility assignments, and measures of success.

ASSIGNING RESPONSIBILITY

Assigning primary responsibility for each action step helps to ensure that someone will be accountable for implementing the plan. Alternatively, each objection could be assigned to a specific person who would then be responsible for ensuring that all the action steps for that objective are achieved. Assignment of accountability for achieving various segments of the plan should be done on the basis of voluntary commitment as much as possible. The success of the plan depends on all participants knowing and accepting who is responsible for each segment of the plan. Being assigned primary responsibility for an action step or objective doesn't mean that the assignee must carry out that step. It simply means that that person is responsible for making sure that it gets done. People with primary responsibility for a segment of the plan should be encouraged to identify other individuals who could provide assistance with a particular action step or objective. For that reason, many planning teams also identify the people who have secondary

Figure 3.6. Example of a Library Action Plan

Objective 3: Improve new array of e-resources offered by the library

Action Steps	Primary Responsibility	Measure of Success	Timetable	Comments
1. Identify collection gaps	J Smith	Create list of subject area gaps and needs	Nov-Dec	Include selected faculty and students in identifying needs; discuss with Library Committee (Lib Comm.)
2. Prioritize needs including costs	S Johnson/Ref Librn and Team	Completed list of needs and costs with rankings	Jan-Feb	Library Leadership Team; share with Lib Comm.
3. Identify resources to fill gaps	B Wood	Brainstorm with ref librarians to identify comprehensive list	Jan-June	Include subject specialists
4. Negotiate and finalize licenses	Admin; Digital Collections Head	Agreed upon and signed licenses/contracts	June-July	Include Finance
5. Create online access method, e.g., via OPAC, including metrics to be collected	Head of Ref + Head of Web Services	Systems that have been tested and are in place in test area	June-July	Include IT/Web Services
6. Develop and implement training methods to alert customers to new resources, e.g., tutorials, e-mail alerts, webpage postings	Instructional Services Team	Curricula and lesson plans are in place and have been presented to focus groups	Jul-Aug	Include Public Services
7. New resources are announced and web access is launched	Lib Admin + Team	Webpages and announcements created	Jul-Aug	Include Ref Librn team
8. Monitor and measure usage and cost-per-use	Reference Team	Monthly reports are run and distributed	Sep-Dec	Ongoing, with annual summary report
9. Determine value and consider renewal of licenses	Admin, head of collections	Reports and analysis developed and shared; decisions made	Dec	

responsibility for each action step or objective as part of the initial plan.

CONTINGENCY PLANS

Problems and challenges will arise. To combat the frustration of unforeseen obstacles in the planning process, many organizations do contingency planning for those steps that are deemed to be most important to the overall success of the plan. Contingency planning involves identification of high-priority steps or objectives that have the greatest risk of failure and then proposing alternative methods for achieving the same results. Identifying potential problem areas before implementation of the plan will reduce the stresses and feelings of failure that result from inevitable midcourse corrections. For high priority objectives, the planning team will want to consider, in advance, what to do if the action steps to achieve this objective do not work.

COMMUNICATION PLAN

Once the goals, objectives, and action steps have been delineated, the plan must be communicated to the other people in the organization who will be affected by the changes described in the planning document. The communication plan is a systematic look at who needs to know what and when. In all probability, the planning group will be smaller than the groups affected by the plan. Those affected by the plan need to know the plan's structure, the anticipated changes to the present situation, and on a personal level will want to know what is expected of them and how their work lives will be altered. Communication of the plan to all affected parties, along with a variety of opportunities to ask questions and provide input, e.g., via a Web 2.0 tool like a Wiki or blog, will enhance acceptance of the plan by those individuals who were not directly involved in the planning process (Rethlefsen et al., 2006; Wilson and Yowell, 2008). The components of the communication plan could include:

- target audience,
- key messages,
- the names of individuals responsible for communicating the messages, and
- the timeframe for communicating the messages.

A complement to traditional strategic planning is scenario planning. Ludwig describes scenario planning as a planning method that takes into account uncertain futures. A number of drivers identified by academic health science library directors include change in scholarly communication, migration of print to electronic publishing, a move from individual to group learning, and more. In addition to engaging library staff to create a set of scenarios from the process, it also provides opportunities for creating unexpected partnerships and alliances. On the possible "down side", it may require more effort to identify and relate to stakeholders, demand more effective teamwork, and result in fewer libraries and less space (Ludwig, Giesecke, and Walton, 2009).

MONITORING AND EVALUATION

The monitoring step is vital to the implementation phase of any planning process. If the plan objectives have been written in measurable terms, then it should be a simple matter to identify when the objective is met. To make it easier to monitor progress toward goals and objectives, many planners find it useful to list the measures of success in a separate section of the plan. Assigning a measure of success to each objective provides a framework for monitoring progress toward achievement of goals. When reviewing the measures of success against the implementation timetable, team members can decide if the objectives, measures, and timeframes are still desirable and achievable. This review process should occur at established time periods throughout the implementation of the plan. By reviewing plan progress from time to time, the team can make midcourse corrections as needed. Chapter 6 goes over various evaluation methods. Use of a Logic Model, as described in Chapter 6, for planning and evaluation of objectives can aid in the overall process of evaluating the success of a plan.

After the establishment of the new product or service that resulted from the planning process, the planning team will want to evaluate the overall effectiveness of the new product or service with respect to the original goals. The same methods described previously to assess the needs of customers at the beginning of the planning process can be used to evaluate the results of the overall process as well. Once the goals, objectives, and action steps have been delineated, the plan must be communicated to other people in the organization who will be affected by the changes.

Marketing, Promotion, and Outreach

A great deal of confusion exists among the terms marketing, public relations, and promotion. Marketing is not synonymous with public relations or library promotion, activities that essentially attempt to create good will for an entity. Promotional strategies involve a generalized effort to advance the cause of the organization or to "sell" a specific product or service. Both of these activities are important to the organization, but they are only two components of marketing. Why must one market? According to Siess (2004: 29), "These days, the library is not the first place people choose to look for information. Your customers have many other choices, from bookstores to document delivery services. Even if an organization wants a library, it may not know that it needs a librarian—a trained information professional." Alford (2009: 272) notes that there is "a prevailing sentiment in libraries that we should not have to promote ourselves, that our value is self-evident." She goes on to say it continues to be important to remind our communities that libraries now offer more than print books and journals and encourages the development of a marketing plan.

Duke and Tucker (2007: 52) define marketing as "communicating to users about what the library has to offer the community." Librarians use every avenue and method to communicate, from word-of-mouth, to the web, to giveaways.

Armstrong and Kotler (2005: 6) define marketing as "a social and managerial process by which individuals and groups obtain what they want through creating value with others." They stress the importance of a customer-centered view that impels the organization to identify the following:

- To whom are we planning to market, also known as market segmentation?
- How satisfied are our customers with our offering?

While many librarians may not consider themselves skilled at marketing, most do see themselves as educators (Bridges, 2005). Marketing is closely tied to education, and as a first step in education is to assess the learner's level, the same goes for marketing. Successful marketing in the health care library environment requires that the librarian understand the library's customers and their perceptions of the library's services and resources. Rather than promoting the products and services that the library staff wants to promote, the library staff should ask the library's primary user groups what products and services would best meet their information needs. To highlight this customer-centered view of marketing, the steps of the marketing planning process will be described and the marketing audit step will be used to further illustrate how marketing plans can be applied to the library.

The Marketing Plan

The marketing plan is a tool and framework that blends principles of strategic planning with principles of marketing. It is thoughtfully developed and tailored for the organization and its setting. It should also be considered a "living" document that may change from year to year and be informed by experience. Many of the steps in the marketing planning process are the same as in the strategic planning process. Powers (1995) suggests that a marketing plan is an effective tool for a special library to define and transmit its image, philosophy, and mission within the organization. She describes a model of marketing planning that involves the following key steps:

1. **Define the organization**: Defining the organization is equivalent to defining the mission and vision of the library along with the major goals and objectives. In this step, the librarian would articulate the business of the library and how it fits into the mission, vision, and goals of the organization overall.

2. **Define external forces, and the competition**: Defining external forces is the same as the external environmental assessment step in the strategic planning process.

3. **Conduct a marketing audit**: Conducting a marketing audit is a systematic analysis and appraisal of the library's operations, characteristics, challenges, and opportunities. Similar to an internal environmental assessment, the marketing audit applies the "Ps" of marketing to library collections and services, meeting customers' demand, costs, direct and indirect, of producing the product or service product, publics, price, place, production, and promotion. Figure 3.7 illustrates how each of the marketing Ps can be applied to the library. A specific example of a library marketing audit is provided in the next section.

4. **Formulate a marketing strategy**: Formulating a marketing strategy is a classic marketing technique that identifies a method to position a product or service to succeed. Possible strategies suggested by Powers (1995) for the special library include
   - market segmentation strategies (offering a new service to existing clients);
   - market development strategies (develop new clients);

Figure 3.7. Application of the Marketing Ps in a Library

Product	Collections and services to customers
Publics	Potential and current customers of the library
Place	Delivery and distribution of products and services, including web-based mechanisms
Production	Providing services customers need/meeting and anticipating demand
Promotion	Means by which customers are made aware of and invited to use products and services
Price	Cost, direct and indirect, of providing products and services. Can also address dollars saved by organization

- market penetration strategies (increased use of services by existing clients);
- diversification strategies (new services to new clients); and
- distribution strategies (new ways of information delivery).

5. **Implement action plans**: Implementing action plans is similar to the action plan steps used in the strategic planning process.

6. **Conduct evaluation**: Conducting evaluations is similar to the evaluation steps used in the strategic planning process.

Marketing Audit

The marketing audit can be used to do an overall assessment of the library's activities or it can be applied to a specific area of need within the library. Figure 3.8 illustrates a marketing audit to outline the readiness and potential options for developing a consumer health library (CHL) within an acute care hospital. The assessment uses the marketing Ps as a framework.

Promotion Strategies

The marketing plan described above provides a systematic method for defining and promoting the mission and philosophy of the library using a planning process. Based on the overall needs assessment of the organization, the library manager develops methods appropriate to the make-up and preferences of the organization. For example, choosing to use paper materials vs. electronic must be determined based on how widespread computer use is across the company. This decision may influence all of the strategies selected for use. Promotion instruments and strategies can be used to advance the library and its services in support of the marketing plan. These strategies often focus on a specific library product or a specific target audience.

Although promotional vehicles may vary from one health care organization to another, there are several approaches and instruments that are used commonly by libraries. The more formal tools include print publications, such as brochures, newsletters, new acquisitions lists, annual reports, and news releases. Using e-mail and other electronic network options, such as Web 2.0 programs, many of these tools can be produced and distributed electronically. In addition, strategies such as special events in the library itself can garner a great deal of positive attention for new services and resources.

Orientations and educational workshops sponsored by the library can also be used to promote library services and resources.

Informal methods rely on taking advantage of opportunities to promote the library. For example, members of the library staff on institutional committees may take advantage of opportunities to promote the library's resources as a support for the committee activities. Department head meetings or employee forums may also afford the opportunity to highlight what's new in the library. Even hallway conversations can be a chance to point out a specific service of the library or alert a colleague about the expertise of a particular library staff member.

Promotion Strategies

- Websites
- Brochures and Fact Sheets
- Newsletters and Acquisition Lists
- Annual Reports
- Visual Displays
- Orientation
- Special Events
- Internal Promotion

Websites

Library websites are a cross between promotion and utilitarian linking to library resources. All of the content of the above listed promotional activities can be present on the library website plus PDF copies of anything developed in print. See Chapter 10 for more information about library websites.

Brochures and Fact Sheets

The brochure is an all-purpose tool intended to give an introduction to or overview of library services and products. The information brochure is particularly useful in promoting the library to a broad audience, including hospital staff members who are not regular customers of the library. The information detailed in the brochure should be information that is not subject to frequent change. Content might include access information such as the library hours, location, phone number, fax number, e-mail address, and web address. In addition, the brochure is a good place to outline the library's services and special collections.

Some libraries use specialized information fact sheets targeted to a specific service or group of users. An information sheet prepared for house officers or residents would contain information different from one prepared

Figure 3.8. Marketing Audit to Determine Feasibility of Establishing a Consumer Health Library (CHL) within a Hospital

Audit	Applicable Questions	Assessment
PRODUCT	<ul><li>What library products and services are currently available to patients, families, and the general public?</li><li>What services and resources are available from other departments in the hospital?</li></ul>	<ul><li>The library currently provides books and periodicals to assist caregivers in providing patient education.</li><li>At least eight patient service departments have small collections of books, pamphlets, and/or videotapes for patients and families.</li><li>Collection access and development for department libraries is coordinated by designated patient educators.</li><li>Reference services are informal or nonexistent.</li></ul>
PUBLICS	<ul><li>Who is likely to use consumer health services and resources?</li></ul>	<ul><li>5,000 inpatients, 10,000 outpatients, and an unknown number of family members visit the hospital yearly.</li><li>Census data indicate that 25,000 people live within 10 miles of hospital.</li><li>Nurses, physicians, therapists, and dietitians would be potential intermediaries for patients and families.</li></ul>
PLACE	<ul><li>Where will the CHL be located?</li><li>How will customers access services and resources?</li><li>When will services be available?</li></ul>	<ul><li>The front lobby would provide good visibility and convenient access for customers.</li><li>The medical library would be most convenient for the library staff, but space limitations are a problem.</li><li>Hours of service and methods of delivery are dependent on location.</li></ul>
PRODUCTION	<ul><li>How will services and resources be selected?</li><li>How will the library staff know if services and resources are meeting the needs of customers?</li></ul>	<ul><li>Appoint an advisory committee to assist with concept development, service design, and initial selection of materials.</li><li>Design method to identify customers' specific needs—current and ongoing.</li></ul>
PROMOTION	<ul><li>How will customers become aware of the CHL?</li><li>What agencies in the community are potential sources of referral?</li></ul>	<ul><li>Develop communication plan:<ul><li>closed circuit television</li><li>on-site brochures</li><li>hospital newsletters</li><li>library and organization websites</li><li>listservs and mailing lists</li></ul></li><li>List public libraries and health-related organizations to be contacted.</li></ul>
PRICE	<ul><li>How will the operating costs of the CHL be covered?</li><li>Will the hospital need to recover some of its costs from the users of the CHL?</li></ul>	<ul><li>Develop budget estimate for lobby location, including staff, capital equipment, and operating expenses.</li><li>Prepare alternative budget for service based out of the medical library.</li><li>Identify local funding sources via hospital foundation.</li><li>Discuss cost-recovery options during budget approval process.</li></ul>

Source: Salzwedel and Green, 2000: 49. Reprinted from Figure 4-7. Used with permission.

for managers. A fact sheet about popular services such as literature searches or interlibrary loan can provide frequently requested information in a succinct way, thereby alleviating the need for library staff members to repeat the same information for every new customer. It also puts the information in writing so that the customer can refer to it later.

Printed tools such as brochures need a professional appearance. The organization's media or public relations department may have a professional artist on staff to assist. Or, if the library's budget permits, other options include the use of a commercial artist or an outside graphics firm willing to take on small design jobs. If the brochure or fact sheet is produced on an in-house desktop publishing system, it may be possible to format the promotional piece in such a way that "changeable" information, such as the names of the library staff members, may be included but revised easily for the next printing.

Another technique is to format webpages so that when printed, they become fact sheets. A two-page webpage on e-journal access can be printed as a double-sided fact sheet. Doing it this way means that the same information is on the web and in print. Since many of the technology-oriented services change so fast, updating the information for staff and customers is easier. You can also e-mail the URL to customers and know that the same information is being provided.

Creating brochures meant to be printed or displayed provides an opportunity for the library to create and utilize a "brand" for itself. Branding can be as easy as consistently adding the library logo or mission statement to all handouts. The image or brand of the library should be carefully considered and created, perhaps within a focus group. Germain (2008: 74) says, "Branding provides the opportunity for libraries to break from the old stereotypical image and present a new robust representation." Print materials lacking a library brand may never reach the intended library audience, will definitely have a lower impact, and is an opportunity not to be missed.

Newsletters and Acquisition Lists

The library may decide to publish a newsletter or new acquisitions list. These tools have the specific communication purpose of alerting a wide audience of current and potential customers about new acquisitions or other items of interest, such as policy changes or special events. Mass distribution is desirable so as to target as many customers as possible. News publications should be sent out on a cyclical schedule so customers come to

expect and look forward to hearing from the library. The goal is to keep library resources and services foremost in customers' minds so that when an information need arises, they will automatically think of the library as the resource of first resort. Using a web newsletter with an e-mail announcement is now an option as well as a news blog.

Whatever the format, a newsletter should include a wide range of topics of interest and can be used as a reflection of library personality. Creating a quality newsletter takes effort. Electronic publishing permits many libraries to produce attractive publications in-house. These can also be converted to PDFs and e-mailed. The content of a newsletter will vary according to the needs of the library and the parent organization.

New acquisitions lists are a popular method for alerting users about new books, journal subscriptions, and electronic resources. A new acquisitions list that opens with a bit of news is a potential substitute for a library newsletter and is generally an easier publication to produce. Arranging the lists by subject allows specific groups to easily locate resources of interest. Many integrated library systems provide a utility that can produce a "newest cataloged" list that can be linked to and made available on the web.

Annual Reports

An annual report is another effective tool for promoting the library. A well-constructed annual report is especially valuable for communication with a small, well-defined target audience: administration. It is an opportunity to present text and data about routine library activities as well as to highlight special achievements of the past year. The annual report should summarize progress toward the goals outlined in the library's strategic plan. It should include statistical data about volumes of key workload indicators, e.g., numbers of literature searches or documents delivered to users. Quality indicators that measure library activity against an organization's quality or productivity indicators, e.g., number of library users per hundred employees, can also be included. Brief descriptions of new services, resources, staff members, or events can help to balance and, in some circumstances, explain the numerical data presented.

In addition, the annual report can serve as a method to communicate changes and trends in library usage. If the library's five-year trend for volume of service transactions is significantly different from that of similar-sized libraries in the community, these comparative data provide useful information about how the library is doing. Portions of the annual report can be used for multiple purposes if desired. For example, a description of new electronic resources launched on the institution's network could be used as a section of the annual report as well as a newsletter column for the local professional librarian's association.

Trends today indicated that the story of the use of resources and services by customers should also be included. Looking at your institution's annual report will show you how important the administrators think these stories are. You can also mimic the format for your report. Examples of several library annual reports can be found on the **accompanying CD-ROM**, including an innovative PDF annual report from the Health Sciences and Human Services Library, University of Maryland, Baltimore. Also available is a list of annual reports from AAHSL.

Visual Displays

Many libraries use bulletin board displays, special collection displays, bookmarks, posters, and table tents to promote awareness of new or existing resources and services. The common link among these promotional tools is that they all provide a simple, attractive, highly visual message for a wide audience. Most displays are theme oriented. For instance, when the organization holds a quality fair and requests posters on quality projects, the library might participate by entering a poster showing the process improvement methodology used to expand access to electronic library resources. The goal of a display is to convey specific information to both current and potential customers in a very visual way. To be effective, it should include lots of color and use graphics to present its message. A well-presented display is a good tool to reinforce the library's professional image. However, displays will generally have limited usefulness since most are constructed for a special event. Posters and table tents are generally less expensive and more flexible than formal displays. They can be positioned in the cafeteria, physician's lounge, lobby, or the library itself to increase contact with target populations. Bookmarks are probably the least expensive way to promote the library and can be produced in quantities that make it possible to hand them out during orientations and at special events. Commercially produced bookmarks, posters, and other materials targeted to library customers can be obtained from library associations and library-oriented vendors to help publicize services and highlight events such as National Medical Librarians Month (NMLM) or National Library Week. Since 1997, October has been designated as National Medical Librarians Month by the Medical Library Association (MLA) to heighten awareness of the

many contributions of medical librarians to the health care team. MLA has a contest for the best NMLM promotion. National Library Week takes place annually during the month of April and promotes the use of all types of libraries—public, school, academic, and special—and provides an opportunity for librarians to make the public aware of the many services available at their local libraries.

Orientation

The goal of orientation is to communicate and promote basic, general information to a diverse population of potential customers. An orientation program or event might in some libraries fall under the purview of the instruction librarian, but often in a small library the library leader does this along with other more general marketing and promotion activities. Library orientations provide an overview and can be prepared for a large, general audience or for small, specialized groups. For example, an overview of library services could be provided during the organization's new employee orientation. Conversely, a tour of the library with an emphasis on nursing resources might be more appropriate for nursing students beginning a rotation at the hospital. Orientations are usually scheduled on a cyclical basis, the frequency of which varies based on the intended audience. An orientation session provides an opportunity to introduce the library's services and resources, as well as to promote an image of the library as a friendly, customer-oriented place.

Holding an orientation session in the library has the obvious advantage of providing an in-person look at the library, as well as the opportunity to demonstrate the resources available. For instance, a small group of nursing students could be shown the area of the library that houses the majority of nursing texts and receive a demonstration of how to search the CINAHL (Cumulative Index to Nursing and Allied Health Literature) database on one of the library's public access computers. If it is not possible to provide an in-person orientation for every potential new customer, the library's webpage or blog is another place to promote the library and its services. A webpage can be updated frequently and has the advantage of being available whenever the customer is ready to seek information about the library.

In general, staff members should think of every new patron as presenting an opportunity to market the library's products and services. Library staff members need to know how to effectively orient customers in five to ten minutes. Although the content of orientation programs will vary according to the individuals being oriented, some topics will probably be appropriate for all library users. Topics would include but not be limited to descriptions of basic library services and policies and procedures such as:

- circulation privileges
- online catalog
- mediated search services
- interlibrary loan or document delivery services
- library hours including after-hours access, location
- list of electronic databases and resources including remote access
- information about educational programs sponsored by the library
- customer-driven methods of providing input to library staff, e.g., Twitter, and other Web 2.0 tools

Several articles are available regarding the use of the latter in marketing and promotions. Word-of-Mouth-Marketing (WOMM) has taken on a whole new meaning and format with the advent of new user-oriented and created websites like Facebook and Twitter. Barber and Wallace describe why WOMM is perfect for libraries: it is affordable and cost-effective, it utilizes what clients think of us, and it is "the most powerful form of communication" (2009: 36). Circle notes the "sea change" (2009: 26) among library managers around the word *marketing*, and itemizes a baker's dozen of trends to watch and use, including Twitter, the importance of value and the value proposition, the online reputation and its management, video marketing, value-added content, mobile marketing, being "green," micromarketing, and maintaining an emotional connection. Circle (2009: 29) suggests the following seven steps to make your marketing stronger:

1. Visit (and learn from) websites of influential organizations.
2. Keep on top of trends (in education and health care).
3. Ask your customers (and potential customers).
4. Use Google analytics on your website.
5. Follow the *Retail Advertising & Marketing Association* (RAMA) (http://www.rama-nrf.org/).
6. Read great blogs (in a variety of disciplines).
7. Convene a marketing task force of key marketers in your area and solicit their help.

Increasingly, orientation or parts of orientation are offered online. One excellent example comes from the Arizona State University Libraries where humor and surprise are effectively used to present what could otherwise be dull (but useful) material (http://libguides.asu.edu/ASULibrariesOrientation).

Special Events

Special events can be an excellent way of promoting the library. One-time or annual events will be geared to reach as many people as possible, including current and potential library customers. Special events take considerable planning, usually revolve around a theme, e.g., National Medical Librarians Month (NMLM), and may involve the use of multiple promotional tools, such as brochures, displays, or posters. In addition, a special event might include refreshments and activities such as quizzes or raffles or contests designed to draw people into the library. Many libraries have developed programs unique to their institutions. For example, an event to honor staff members who have authored books, book chapters, or journal articles is a popular way to draw attention to a very special group of library customers while also drawing attention to the library itself. How to keep a list of staff publications is covered in Chapter 15.

Informal Promotion

Informal techniques of promotion include person-to-person contact and other generalized forms of image building. Library staff members represent the library wherever they go; therefore, it is important to cultivate a professional image. By projecting self-confidence, library personnel inspire confidence in, and curiosity about, the library's services.

Often one of the most daunting tasks for librarians, or other professionals in service roles, is to view self-promotion in a positive light. Librarians and support staff, used to providing services to others, may initially feel uncomfortable making a vigorous case for the library's needs. However, if the library staff can focus on the needs of customers as the driving force for the promotional activity, the occasion becomes a teaching opportunity rather than an exercise in self-promotion.

The library manager, along with the always-prepared "elevator speech," must also have an array of presentations developed in presentation format or modules that can be used quickly and repurposed for special audiences, e.g., nursing administrators, translational science faculty, or administrative assistants. With small modules that can be re-arranged and tailored, the librarian is always prepared for the last minute invitation to speak or fill in for a cancelled or no-show speaker.

Conclusion

Remember the Einstein quote used at the beginning of this chapter: strive to always keep moving and growing and changing, professionally and personally. It is important, as well, to keep the library fresh and new, virtually and physically. Perception is everything and if the library's parent organization views the library as dynamic and current, support and funding is usually available. Library managers should always stay ahead of library clientele by anticipating and fulfilling information needs. Plan to use the best available technology and borrow best practices from colleagues around the country. Plan for evaluation from the beginning so that library administration can measure progress and be ready to justify expenses. Have a good plan in place, one that can be communicated to users and to administration. And, always have that 'elevator speech' prepared as one never knows who might be encountered in the cafeteria or stairwell or even an elevator!

Planning and marketing are as vital to the success of the library as organizing the resources or answering reference questions. Yet, these valuable techniques are often overlooked amid the day-to-day scramble to get all the work done. The difference between having an adequate library service and having a full-service, customer-focused library is usually the extent to which the library staff applies principles of planning and marketing to guide their way.

Planning provides a systematic process for identifying what needs to change in the library and how to change it. Principles of marketing help the librarian assess what products and services the library's customers need and design an organized approach to promoting those products and services. Together, these tools and skills can be used to ensure that the library's services and resources evolve and grow in a purposeful way. The alternative to planning and marketing is usually chaos and crisis management. The choice is up to the librarian.

References

Adams, Deborah L., Nancy Bulgarelli, Karen Tubolino, and Gayle A. Williams. 1994. "Hospital Library Customer Survey: A Needs Assessment Tool." *National Network* 19, no. 2 (November): 4, 24–27. Accessed July 10, 2010. http://www.hls.mlanet.org/newsletter/archives.html.

Alford, Emily. 2009. "Promoting and Marketing E-Resources." *The Serials Librarian* 57, no. 3 (October): 272–277.

Armstrong, Gary, and Philip Kotler. 2005. *Marketing: An Introduction*. 7th ed. Upper Saddle River, NJ: Pearson Prentice Hall.

Barber, Peggy, and Linda Wallace. 2009. "The Power of Word-of-Mouth Marketing." *American Libraries* 40, no. 11 (November): 36–37.

Bedard, Martha. 2009. "Introduction to Our Commitment to Building Leaders: Programs for Leadership in Academic and Special Libraries." *Journal of Library Administration* 49, no. 8 (November–December): 777–779.

Bridges, Jane. 2005. "Marketing the Hospital Library." *Medical Reference Services Quarterly* 24, no. 3 (Fall): 81–92.

Bunnett, Brian, Nancy Allee, Jo Dorsch, Gabriel Rios, and Cindy Stewart. 2009. "The National Library of Medicine/Association of Academic Health Sciences Libraries (NLM/AAHSL) Leadership Fellows Program: A Year in Review." *Journal of Library Administration* 49, no. 8 (November/December): 869–879.

Circle, Alison. 2009. "Marketing Trends to Watch." *Library Journal* 134, no. 16 (October 1): 26–29.

Clareson, Tom, and Jane S. Long. (2006). "Libraries in the Eye of the Storm: Lessons Learned from Hurricane Katrina." *American Libraries* 37, no. 7 (August): 38–41.

Cogdill, Keith W., Angela B. Ruffin, and P. Zoe Stavri. 2007. "The National Network of Libraries of Medicine's Outreach to the Public Health Workforce: 2001–2006." *Journal of the Medical Library Association* 95, no. 3 (July): 310–315.

Crabtree, Anna Beth, and Julia H. Crawford. 1997. "Assessing and Addressing the Library Needs of Health Care Personnel in a Large Regional Hospital." *Bulletin of the Medical Library Association* 85, no. 2 (April): 167–175.

Dowty, Rachel A., and William A. Wallace. 2010. "Implications of Organizational Culture for Supply Chain Disruption and Restoration." *International Journal of Production Economics* 126, no. 1 (July): 57–65.

Dudden, Rosalind F., Kate Corcoran, Janice Kaplan, Jeff Magouirk, Debra C. Rand, and Bernie Todd Smith. 2006. "The Medical Library Association Benchmarking Network: Results." *Journal of the Medical Library Association* 94, no. 2 (April): 118–129.

Duke, Lynda M., and Toni Tucker. 2007. "How to Develop a Marketing Plan for an Academic Library." *Technical Services Quarterly* 25, no. 1: 51–68.

Featherstone, Robin, Becky J. Lyon, and Angela B. Ruffin. 2008. "Library Roles in Disaster Response: An Oral History Project by the National Library of Medicine." *Journal of the Medical Library Association* 96, no. 4 (October): 434–350.

Fleischer, S. Victor, and Mark J. Heppner. 2009. "Disaster Planning for Libraries and Archives: What You Need to Know and How to Do It." *Library and Archival Security* 22, no. 2 (July/December): 125–140.

Forsman, Rick B. 1990. "Incorporating Organizational Values into the Strategic Planning Process." *Journal of Academic Librarianship* 16, no. 3 (July): 150–153.

Germain, Carol Anne. 2008. "A Brand New Way of Looking at Library Marketing." *Public Services Quarterly* 4, no. 1: 73–78.

Glitz, Beryl. 1997. "The Focus Group Technique in Library Research: An Introduction." *Bulletin of the Medical Library Association* 85, no. 4 (October): 385–390.

Hallerberg, Gretchen A., and Paul Simmons. 1997. "Accessing Needs for Published Information." *National Network* 21, no. 3 (February): 25–29. Accessed July 10, 2010. http://www.hls.mlanet.org/newsletter/archives.html.

Higa-Moore, Mori Lou, Brian Bunnett, Helen G. Mayo, and Cynthia A Olney. 2002. "Use of Focus Groups in a Library's Strategic Planning Process." *Journal of the Medical Library Association* 90, no. 1 (January): 86–92.

Hochstein, Colette, Stacey Arnesen, Jeanne Goshorn, and Marti Szcur. 2008. "Selected Resources for Emergency and Disaster Preparedness and Response from the United States National Library of Medicine." *Medical Reference Services Quarterly* 27, no. 1 (Spring): 1–20.

Holst, Ruth, and Sharon A. Phillips. 2000. "Administrative Issues." In *The Medical Library Association Guide to Managing Health Care Libraries*, edited by Ruth Holst and Sharon A. Phillips, 23–35. New York: Neal-Schuman.

Holst, Ruth, Carla J. Funk, Heidi Sue Adams, Margaret Bandy, Catherine Mary Boss, Beth Hill, Claire B. Joseph, and Rosalind K. Lett. 2009. "Vital Pathways for Hospital Librarians: Present and Future Roles." *Journal of the Medical Library Association* 97, no. 4 (October): 285–292.

Holst, Ruth. 1991. "Hospital Libraries in Perspective." *Bulletin of the Medical Library Association* 79, no. 1 (January): 1–9.

Honea, Sion M. 2000. "The Impact of Professionalism on Library Administration." *Journal of Library Administration* 31, no. 1: 1–28.

Hospital Libraries Section Standards Committee, Margaret Bandy, Jacqueline Donaldson Doyle, Anne Fladger, Katherine Stemmer Frumento, Linné Girouard, Sheila Hayes, and Diane Rourke. 2008. "Standards for Hospital Libraries 2007." *Journal of the Medical Library Association* 96, no. 2 (April): 162–169.

Kennedy, Toni. 2002. "Justification for the Library." *Journal of Hospital Librarianship* 2, no. 1: 63–76.

Kerzner, Harold. 2003. *Project Management: A Systems Approach to Planning, Scheduling, and Controlling.* Hoboken, NJ: John Wiley & Sons.

Kuntz, Jennifer, Michele R. Tennant, Ann C. Case, and Faith A. Meakin. 2003. "Staff-Driven Strategic Planning: Learning from the Past, Embracing the Future." *Journal of the Medical Library Association* 91, no. 1 (January): 89–93.

Lucas, Ann F. 2000. *Leading Academic Change: Essential Roles for Department Chairs.* San Francisco: Jossey-Bass.

Ludwig, Logan, and Susan Starr. 2005. "Library as Place: Results of a Delphi Study." *Journal of the Medical Library Association* 93, no. 3 (July): 315–326.

Ludwig, Logan, Joan Giesecke, and Linda Walton. 2009. "Scenario Planning: A Tool for Academic Health Sciences Libraries." *Health Information and Libraries Journal* 27, no. 1 (March): 28–36.

Maietta, Carol, and Sybil H. Bullock. 2009. "A Value-Added Partnership Between a Chief Learning Officer and a Medical Librarian." *Medical Reference Services Quarterly* 28, no. 4 (October-December): 375–384.

Matheson, Nina W. 1995. "The Idea of the Library in the Twenty-First Century." *Bulletin of the Medical Library Association* 83, no. 1 (January): 1–7.

Mavrinac, Mary Ann. 2005. "Transformational Leadership: Peer Mentoring as a Values-Based Learning Process." *portal: Libraries and the Academy* 5, no. 3: 391–404.

McClure, Lucretia W. 1998. "An Essay on Reflection." *Bulletin of the Medical Library Association* 86, no. 2 (April): 251–257.

McKeen, Mike. 1993. "The Library Committee." *Library Review* 42, no. 7: 15–19.

Medical Library Association. 2007. "Competences for Lifelong Learning and Professional Success: the Educational Policy Statement of the Medical Library Association." Chicago: Medical Library Association. Accessed June 10, 2010. http://www.mlanet.org/education/policy/.

Mielke, Linda J., Paula M. Singer, and Gail L. Griffith. 2006. "Swimming Upstream." *Public Library Quarterly* 25, no. 1/2: 105–116.

Parker, Ruth, and Gary L. Kreps. 2005. "Library Outreach: Overcoming Health Literacy Challenges." *Journal of the Medical Library Association* 93, no. 4 (October Supplement): S81–S85.

Perley, Cathy M., Camillia A. Gentry, A. Sue Flemming, and Kristen M. Sens. 2007. "Conducting a User-Centered Information Needs Assessment: The Via Christi Libraries' Experience." *Journal of the Medical Library Association* 95, no. 2: 173–181 and E54–E55.

Powers, Janet E. 1995. "Marketing in the Special Library Environment." *Library Trends* 43, no. 3 (Winter): 478–493.

Prentice, W. C. H. 2004. "Understanding Leadership." *Harvard Business Review* 82, no. 1 (January): 102–109.

Rethlefsen, Melissa L., Nicole C. Engard, Daphine Chang, and Carol Haytko. 2006. "Social Software Libraries and Librarians." *Journal of Hospital Librarianship* 6, no. 4: 29–45.

Robbins, Kathryn, and Ruth Holst. 1990. "Hospital Library Evaluation Using Focus Group Interviews." *Bulletin of the Library Association* 78, no. 3 (July): 311–313.

Rozek, Paul, and Don Groth. 2008. "Business Continuity Planning." *Health Management Technology* 20, no. 3 (March): 10–12.

Salzwedel, Beth A., and Ellen Wilson Green. 2000. "Planning and Marketing." In *The Medical Library Association Guide to Managing Health Care Libraries*, edited by Ruth Holst and Sharon A. Phillips, 37–54. New York: Neal-Schuman.

Schachter, Debbie. 2005. "Leadership Skills for Library Managers." *Information Outlook* 9, no. 1 (January): 10–12.

Schachter, Debbie. 2007. "New Secrets to Success: Change, Leadership, and Expertise. *Information Outlook* 11, no. 10 (October): 40–41.

Schwartz, Diane G., Paul M. Blobaum, Jean P. Shipman, Linda Garr Markwell, and Joanne Gard Marshall. 2009. "The Health Sciences Librarian in Medical Education: A Vital Pathways Project Task Force." *Journal of the Medical Library Association* 97, no. 4 (October):280–284.

Shankar, Kalpana. 2008. "Wind, Water, and Wi-Fi: New Trends in Community Informatics and Disaster Management." *Information Society* 24, no. 2 (April): 116–120.

Siess, Judith A. 2004. "Marketing without Much Money: You Don't Need Big Bucks to Get the Word Out: Here Are (More Than) a Few Ideas." *Information Outlook* 8, no. 10 (October): 29–31.

Siess, Judith A. 2005. "Strategic Planning for Hospital Libraries." *Journal of Hospital Librarianship* 5, no. 4: 37–49.

Spak, Janice, and Janice Glover. 2007. "The Personal Librarian Program: An Evaluation of a Cushing/Whitney Medical Library Outreach Initiative." *Medical Reference Services Quarterly* 26, no. 4 (Winter): 15–25.

Thibodeau, Patricia L., and Carla J. Funk. 2009. "Trends in Hospital Librarianship and Hospital Library Services: 1989–2006." *Journal of the Medical Library Association* 97, no. 4 (October): 273–292.

Wilson, Daniel T., and Susan S. Yowell. 2008. "Resourceful Blogging: Using a Blog for Information Sharing." *Medical Reference Services Quarterly* 27, no. 2 (Summer): 211–220.

Wines, William A., and J. B. Hamilton. 2009. "On Changing Organizational Cultures by Injecting New Ideologies: The Power of Stories." *Journal of Business Ethics* 89, no. 3 (October): 433–447.

Zach, Lisl, and Michelynn McKnight. 2010. "Innovative Services Improvised During Disasters: Evidence-Based Education Modules to Prepare Students and Practitioners for Shifts in Community Information Needs." *Journal of Education for Library and Information Science* 51, no. 2 (Spring): 76–85.

Zaleznik, Abraham. 2004. "Managers and Leaders: Are They Different?" *Harvard Business Review* 82, no. 1 (January): 74–81.

Further Reading

Dive, Brian. 2008. *The Accountable Leader: Developing Effective Leadership through Managerial Accountability*. London and Philadelphia: Kogan Page.

Dowd, Nancy, Mary Evangeliste, and Jonathan Silberman. 2010. *Taking a Bite Out of Marketing*. Chicago: American Library Association.

Dubicki, Elenora. 2007. "Basic Marketing and Promotion Concepts." *The Serials Librarian* 53, no. 3: 5–15.

Fisher, Patricia H., and Marseille M. Pride. 2005. *Blueprint for Your Library Marketing Plan: A Guide to Help You Survive and Thrive*. Chicago: American Library Association.

Goleman, Daniel. 2004. "What Makes a Leader?" *Harvard Business Review* 82 no. 1 (January): 82–91.

Gwyer, Roisin. 2010. "Leading in Difficult Times: What Can We Learn from the Literature?" *New Review of Library Networking* 15, no. 1 (May): 4–15.

Hallmark, Elizabeth Kennedy, Laura Schwartz, and Loriene Roy. 2007. "Developing a Long-Range and Outreach Plan for Your Academic Library." *College and Research Library News* 68, no. 2 (February): 92–95.

Homan, J. Michael. 2010. "Eyes on the Prize: Reflections on the Impact of the Evolving Digital Ecology on the Librarian as Expert Intermediary and Knowledge Coach, 1969–2009." *Journal of the Medical Library Association* 98, no. 1 (January): 49–56.

Mi, Jia, and Frederick Nesta. 2006. "Marketing Library Services to the Net Generation." *Library Management* 27, no. 6/7: 441–422.

Ohio Library Council. 2008. "Marketing the Library." Accessed July 10, 2010. http://www.olc.org/marketing/index.html.

4

Financial Management

Mary Fran Prottsman

Financial Plan

Financial management entails more than tracking expenditures. When used most effectively, the financial plan is an excellent tool for communication as it states the service goals in monetary terms. Librarians should use the financial plan to educate their institutions' senior management about the value of the library's mission and the resources required to achieve the mission. The financial plan should describe the library's anticipated accomplishments; the resources necessary to achieve those accomplishments; the consequences to the organization if the library's goals are not met; and adjustments that must be made along the way as the environment in which the library operates changes. The plan should link the library's services, activities, and output to the organization's mission and vision, emphasizing the ways in which the library assists the organization in meeting its goals. Those who wield the power of financial allocation must view the library as an asset rather than a liability in order to provide continued funding at a level adequate to fully support the library. Libraries do not operate in a vacuum; the librarian must demonstrate clearly the impact that library services have on the organization's bottom line.

> Financial management is a means to achieve proper ends. The user and customer need has to be incorporated in the strategies and policies from which operational and financial goals, aims and objectives will be developed. (Roberts, 2003: 491)

In his article, Joint questions, is it "open access-libraries without walls or librarians without cash?" (Joint, 2008:

63

271) and highlights the uphill struggle to justify present and future funding. Librarians no longer have a service monopoly with the Google generation. It is inherent that we understand our competition, as user behavior impacts on our financial bottom line.

This chapter reviews the components of financial management including budget development, justification, enhancement, evaluation, and monitoring. Budget types, elements, and characteristics are explained. Funding sources including fines, fee for service, grants, gifts, donations, and fundraising activities will be examined.

Budget Development

Libraries do not operate in vacuums. When developing the budget, the librarian must assess the needs of the organization, estimate the costs of providing resources and services to meet these needs and forecast future technological trends and environmental changes.

New programs within the organization may create new user groups or increased demand from existing groups. New technology affords opportunities to offer enhanced services such as more advanced integrated library systems, federated search engines, electronic resource management systems, and mobile applications that enable clients to more easily connect to the information they need. Health care environmental changes and global economic changes invariably affect library funding as well so the librarian must be aware of the challenges and opportunities facing the organization for which the library delivers services.

Needs Assessment and Cost Estimates

The first step in developing the library budget is to determine the goals that the library wishes to accomplish in the coming year and the activities required to achieve these accomplishments. The librarian should review the library's strategic plan, obtain input from staff and clientele, examine service needs, and anticipate technology trends to obtain this information. Chapter 6 on evaluation provides details on conducting a needs assessment program.

Next, the librarian should determine the resources required to support the activities in which the library will be involved by reviewing past expenditures, comparing actual vs. projected spending, and estimating projected increases in the cost of these resources. Increased funding may be required to support new services or the increased use of existing services as well as to meet the demands of inflation. Conversely, the librarian may curtail resources that decline in use or for which funding is no longer available.

Cost projections may be obtained from vendors and the literature. Most book vendors will supply free collection analyses reports of expenditures arranged by time period, subject categories as well as projections for future costs. *Library Journal* publishes an annual periodicals survey in April, which projects future periodicals costs. *Reality Bites: Periodicals Price Survey 2009*, the most recent survey, predicted an average price of $1,401 for a health sciences title in 2010 with 8 to 9 percent increases per year over the past three years (Van Orsdel and Born, 2009). *Library Technology Reports* reviews current technological trends to assist in informed purchases. The January 2009 issue of *Library Technology Reports* offers practical guidelines for making cost-effective technology purchases (Clark and Davis, 2009a; Clark and Davis, 2009b).

Cost-Benefit Analysis

Cost-benefit analysis attempts to justify an activity or purchase by demonstrating that the benefits outweigh the costs. One common type of cost-benefit analysis used by health care librarians is to compare the cost of providing their services with what it would cost the organization to purchase equivalent services elsewhere. (Phillips, 2000: 83)

Another method, particularly useful in clinical settings is to demonstrate cost savings from saving time for highly paid clinical staff.

Cost-benefit analysis assists librarians in determining the best ways in which to provide the required services. One may determine the cost per unit of providing services such as interlibrary loans and document delivery, compare this with alternate service provisions, such as pay-per-use, and determine the most cost-efficient means of providing needed services. *Measuring Your Library's Value: How to Do Cost-Benefit Analysis for Your Public Library* provides basic, clearly defined examples that are applicable to all types of libraries (Elliott et al., 2007). One simple, yet effective means of demonstrating cost-benefit analysis may be achieved by comparing the cost that the library pays for an interlibrary loan to the cost that the patron would pay if interlibrary loan services were not available, as illustrated in Figure 4.1.

The National Network of Libraries of Medicine (NN/LM) MidContinental Region provides online calculators, which assist in demonstrating the value of

Figure 4.1. Interlibrary Loan Cost-Benefit Analysis

Journal Article Costs
January–December 2010

Interlibrary Loans Obtained	ILL Cost *	Commercial Costs **	Cost Avoidance
897	$786	$22,425	$21,639

*Direct costs not including labor.

**Commercial costs are estimated at $25.00 each.

Conclusion: Participation in interlibrary loan arrangements, which include free reciprocal borrowing and NN/LM caps on amounts that libraries may charge, provides reprints of journal articles more cost effectively than paying commercial costs to download articles on the Internet.

libraries and librarians to hospital administrators (http://nnlm.gov/mcr/advocacy/). The Valuing Library Services Calculator (http://nnlm.gov/mcr/evaluation/calculator.html) determines how much it would cost to replace library services on the retail market by calculating the cost to purchase the services provided by the library at a bookstore, through pay-per-view, or from an information broker if the library did not exist. After the librarian plugs numbers into the calculator, the benefit realized by the institution for every dollar budgeted is displayed. The Library Value Calculator (http://nnlm.gov/mcr/evaluation/roi.html) provides benefits realized from utilization of books and journals only, while the Cost Benefit and ROI Calculator for Databases (http://nnlm.gov/mcr/evaluation/dbroi.html) provides the same for databases.

Cost/Use Calculations

Cost per use calculations assist librarians in the annual balancing act of determining which resources require continued funding.

COUNTER (Counting Online Usage of Networked Electronic Resources) was launched in March 2002 to set standards that facilitate recording and reporting of online usage statistics for electronic books, journals, and databases in a consistent, credible, and compatible way (http://www.projectcounter.org/). COUNTER-compliant statistics standardize the metric across multiple platforms enhancing the reliability and usability of the data.

The statistics are offered by major publishers and may be downloaded as Excel spreadsheets and combined with cost data to provide cost per use data. The SUSHI (Standardized Usage Statistics Harvesting Initiative) protocol is the standard the vendors are now using to electronically gather the COUNTER statistics.

In addition to downloading COUNTER-compliant statistics directly from the various publisher websites, librarians will find that aggregators such as Highwire or Ingenta provide COUNTER-compliant statistics. Founded by Stanford University in 1995 to provide online hosting of full-text, peer-reviewed journals for scientific societies and not-for-profit publishers, Highwire consolidates the data for a number of the publishers they host. Once the utilization data has been obtained, the librarian may use a spreadsheet or database to divide the total annual cost of the resource by the total annual use of the resource to determine the cost per use for that particular year. Those resources with the highest cost per use may be examined more closely when determining which resources to renew during subsequent years as illustrated in Figure 4.2. Additional factors, such as impact factors, subject balance, and value to the institution's mission may also be considered.

For a price, vendors provide systems such as Serials Solutions 360 Counter and Swets Stats, which gather and manipulate the data, generating graphical reports of cost per use, titles used least, titles used most heavily, and spreadsheets that the librarian may download for continued review. Pubget.com is also developing a statistical package. The validated data is useful for budget reviews and saves hours of library staff time.

Figure 4.2. Journal Analysis

2010 Journal Analysis (sample of 10 titles)			
Sorted by Cost	**Cost**	**Use**	**Cost/Use**
Circulation	$913	135	$7
American Journal of Clinical Pathology	$723	29	$25
JAMA-Journal of the American Medical Association	$588	232	$3
New England Journal of Medicine	$500	438	$1
American Journal of Clinical Nutrition & Supplement	$499	31	$16
Archives of Pediatrics and Adolescent Medicine	$469	32	$15
Nurse Practitioner	$365	17	$21
Archives of Physical Medicine and Rehabilitation	$324	27	$12
Mayo Clinic Proceedings	$299	58	$5
American Journal of Cardiology	$250	89	$3
American Family Physician	$223	62	$4
Sorted by Use	**Cost**	**Use**	**Cost/Use**
New England Journal of Medicine	$500	438	$1
JAMA-Journal of the American Medical Association	$588	232	$3
Circulation	$913	135	$7
American Journal of Cardiology	$250	89	$3
American Family Physician	$223	62	$4
Mayo Clinic Proceedings	$299	58	$5
Archives of Pediatrics and Adolescent Medicine	$469	32	$15
American Journal of Clinical Nutrition & Supplement	$499	31	$16
American Journal of Clinical Pathology	$723	29	$25
Archives of Physical Medicine and Rehabilitation	$324	27	$12
Nurse Practitioner	$365	17	$21
Sorted by Cost per Use	**Cost**	**Use**	**Cost/Use**
American Journal of Clinical Pathology	$723	29	$25
Nurse Practitioner	$365	17	$21
American Journal of Clinical Nutrition & Supplement	$499	31	$16
Archives of Pediatrics and Adolescent Medicine	$469	32	$15
Archives of Physical Medicine and Rehabilitation	$324	27	$12
Circulation	$913	135	$7
Mayo Clinic Proceedings	$299	58	$5
American Family Physician	$223	62	$4
JAMA-Journal of the American Medical Association	$588	232	$3
American Journal of Cardiology	$250	89	$3
New England Journal of Medicine	$500	438	$1

Budget Justification

Development

> When presenting the budget either orally or in writing, the librarian must consider the audience and translate library jargon into terms that are meaningful to the audience.

Most institutions review the organizational budget annually, requiring departmental presentations of need. Using the same format from year to year maintains consistency with past presentations and enables comparisons to past and future undertakings. The budget review is also a good time to demonstrate the amount of money that the library saves the institutions by comparing the cost of interlibrary loans with commercial document delivery services and by demonstrating the financial advantages of centralized purchase of books and journals for the entire organization. Reports of service delivery costs by clientele group are useful.

Relationships

The librarian should maintain a close working relationship with the organization's financial resources department throughout the year, requesting explanations of terms and procedures that are unclear, and, conversely, explaining the library's requirements as the occasion warrants. The budget review should be a culmination of a relationship that has been maintained through the year.

Anecdotal reports of appreciation such as written comments or paraphrased verbal expressions of support and appreciation of the library's services may be used effectively during the budget review. It is also important to present client support when requesting funds for a major expenditure. Figure 4.3 presents a checklist of items to consider when planning new projects.

Benchmarking Data

MLA benchmarking data can be used during the budget review to demonstrate the position of the library in relation to libraries of similar size and scope and validate the library's resource needs as illustrated in Figure 4.4.

The Association of Academic Health Sciences Libraries publishes the *Annual Statistics of Medical School Libraries in the United States and Canada*, providing comparative statistics for 120 libraries at a cost of $500.00 for non-members. The comparative data include:

- print and electronic collections and databases size and scope;
- expenditures for personnel, collection development, access to external information resources, computing and network systems, and capital improvements;
- revenues from the sale of library services, support provided by affiliated teaching hospitals, gifts, and endowments;
- personnel numbers and types; and
- resource utilization including physical study facilities, the library's website, collections, document delivery services, reference, education, and outreach services.

Budget Components

Types

There are many types of budgetary systems. Often, the parent institution dictates the type of budget used. Many organizations use a combination of techniques.

Line item budgets, also called add-on or historical budgets, are among the most commonly used and list specific revenue sources and expenditure categories. The previous budget is used as a base upon which to make the changes for the next fiscal year in the form of a percentage or a flat dollar amount. Since this system continues the status quo, it generates the least amount of conflict. While it is relatively easy to create and allocate money by adding a percentage that represents normal increases to each line, it is difficult to add lines to the budget for new services or to change a line item. It is also easy for the governing authority to apply across-the-board cuts that have no relationship to the library's actual needs. If line-item budgets are mandated in an institution, defining the line items broadly will increase spending versatility, and supplementing the budget with statistical data will assist in more informed decision making (Hallam and Dalston, 2005).

Zero-based budgets begin every year with no funding and justify all monies required as each program is justified each year. Since zero-based budgets concentrate on whether individual activities are still justified to be funded, it requires a great deal of time to construct and is more likely to be used during a time of fiscal retrenchment. This technique requires the manager to break down expenses into programs, or decision packages. Each decision package includes a brief description and reason for the program and projects how much the program will cost.

Figure 4.3. New Project Planning and Budgeting Checklist

Specific Aim	Why should this project be implemented? What will be improved as a result? Why is the proposed project better than the current way of conducting business?
Facilities Considerations	Describe in detail the electrical, load-bearing, noise, vibration, and ventilation requirements.
Space Considerations	What is the square footage and number of rooms needed? Has suitable space been located? What will be displaced/relocated as a result? How can the current occupants of the space be accommodated?
Personnel Requirements	List all personnel required for the project in full time equivalents (FTEs). Indicate which personnel will come from existing assets and which will need to be hired/assigned. If staff are assigned from existing assets, what will be affected?
Costs	Provide start-up costs, equipment costs, and one-year operating costs. Can this be accomplished within the scope of the library's existing budget? Can award or grant funds be obtained for equipment?
Payback/Cost Savings	Compare the costs above to the current method of performing this function or service. Does the proposed project represent a cost savings? If not, list all other types of benefits (e.g., measurable improvement in quality, improved service/resource accessibility, etc.).
Service Impact	What services will be modified or eliminated if the new project is implemented? Will users in other categories be negatively affected as staff focus on the new service? Will the older method/service be discontinued?
Managed Care	How does this project affect access/prevention/primary care? Does it shorten hospital stays or improve outcome of hospitalization?
Communication	How will the new service be communicated/marketed?
Evaluation/Outcome	Indicate how the project's effectiveness will be evaluated. What type of data will be collected and with whom will the results be shared? How often?

Source: Phillips, 2000: 97. Used with permission.

A zero-based budget identifies alternative service levels and funding options for each program, one option showing funding at the same level and other options showing a decreased funding level and an increased funding level.

Forecast budgets are often used in combination with add-on or zero-based budgeting and involve determining the cost of a particular unit of service and then deciding how many units of service will be provided. Using this technique to forecast an activity such as interlibrary loan, if the cost of providing one interlibrary loan article is estimated to be $10, and 1,000 interlibrary loans are the expected activity level for the year, then $10,000 would need to be budgeted for interlibrary loan for the year. If the volume of interlibrary loan activity is projected to rise to 1,200 interlibrary loans over the next budget year, and if the cost per loan is expected to remain at $10, then $1,200 would need to be budgeted for the next year. Determining the cost per service unit is a key part of successful forecast budgeting, and librarians should gain as much skill as possible in cost-analysis techniques (Phillips, 2000: 94).

Program budgets prescribe not only how funds will be spent but also why they will be spent in this manner. They break down expenditures into particular program or project areas of service such as reference and collection development. Since the focus is on outputs, it is relatively easy to determine which programs are the least cost-effective. Program budgets become a type of performance budget as they closely track output statistics. Program budgets enhance identification of nonproductive programs.

Figure 4.4. Benchmarked Expenditures

	Hospital A	Hospital B	Your Hospital	Variation
Salaries	$66,000	$70,000	$55,000	81%
Supplies	$5,000	$3,000	$4,000	107%
Phone	$2,500	$3,000	$1,000	37%
Databases	$30,000	$45,000	$20,000	56%
Interlibrary Loan	$1,500	$2,000	$750	44%
Books	$10,000	$8,000	$8,000	90%
Journals	$100,000	$95,000	$85,000	87%
Equipment	$2,000	$1,000	$1,800	135%
Training	$3,000	$2,500	$1,000	37%
Total	$220,000	$229,500	$176,550	79%

Performance budgets focus on outcomes, rather than on outputs. It is easy to track the efficiency as well as the cost of each library service. While it takes a great deal of time to implement and has been criticized for emphasizing economy over service, it does tend to meet the need for accountability for outcomes (Linn, 2007).

Planning, programming, and budgeting system (PPBS) is the most common type of program budget and links the planning process with that for budgeting.

This system creates a budget by looking forward rather than looking to the past. One determines the programs' costs and benefits and their comparative importance (Hallam and Dalston, 2005). While doing an excellent job of indicating the cost of providing a service, it does not assess the quality of or need for the service.

Figures 4.5 and 4.6 illustrate the two types of budgets used most often. An example of income and expenditure monitoring systems is shown in Figure 4.7, p. 71.

Figure 4.5. Line Item Budget

FY 11				
Line Item	**Fund Code**	**2010**	**2011**	**Increase**
Salaries	PER	$55,000	$60,000	9%
Supplies	SUP	$4,000	$4,500	13%
Phone	PHO	$1,000	$1,200	20%
Databases	DBO	$20,000	$22,000	10%
Interlibrary Loan	ILL	$750	$850	13%
Books	BKS	$8,000	$8,300	4%
Journals	JLS	$85,000	$90,000	6%
Equipment	EQP	$1,800	$2,000	11%
Training	EDU	$1,000	$1,200	20%
TOTAL		$176,550	$190,050	8%

Figure 4.6. Program Budget

FY 10	Medical Library-Program Budget					
		Collection Resources	Reference	Interlibrary Loan	Administration	Total Budget
PER	Salaries	$10,000	$20,000	$5,000	$20,000	$55,000
SUP	Supplies	$2,000	$500	$500	$1,000	$4,000
PHO	Phone	$200	$200	$200	$400	$1,000
DBO	Databases		$20,000			$20,000
ILL	Interlibrary Loan			$750		$750
BKS	Books	$7,500	$500			$8,000
JLS	Journals	$85,000				$85,000
EQP	Equipment			$1,500	$300	$1,800
EDU	Training	$250	$250		$500	$1,000
TOTAL						$176,550

Characteristics

Clarity, accuracy, and consistency are essential budget characteristics. Define budget elements in terms that will communicate with those who approve the funding. Accuracy is essential to establish trust and validation. Consistency supports trend forecasting over time. Spreadsheets enable one to produce reports that demonstrate: income and expenditure projections, service delivery costs by clientele groups, and cost-center projections. Excel spreadsheets will also facilitate the entire program budget analysis, provide comparative data with previous years, and enable forecasting for future years, including built-in inflation factors. Many integrated library systems contain robust budgeting features that will assist in tracking expenditures as do commercial off-the-shelf products. Hallam and Dalston (2005) offer a selection checklist to assist in purchasing financial management software and provide an excellent source for further reading on capital improvement projects and requests for proposals (RFPs).

The librarian should separate operating and capital activities for reporting purposes. Operating activities recur regularly and can be anticipated from year to year including personnel salaries and benefits; books, journals, databases; integrated library systems and link resolvers; building utilities, cleaning, and maintenance; and IT (information technology) support. Capital expenditures occur irregularly and usually require special fundraising efforts to provide new or remodeled library space or major technology upgrades. Organizations often set cost thresholds for purchases or projects to be considered capital expenses, such as projects in excess of $5,000, and require a higher level of approval.

Librarians should show revenue and expenditures in both operating and capital budgets. Revenue should be broken down by the source of the funding such as organizational appropriations, grant projects, gifts and donations, fines and fees. Expenditures may be grouped in categories with lines representing similar products or services such as:

- personnel costs (salaries, wages, benefits, and professional development);
- general operating costs (office supplies, utilities, communications, building and equipment maintenance);
- contract fees for shared catalogs, document delivery and interlibrary loan costs; and
- collection development costs.

Evaluation and Monitoring

"Awareness of changing circumstances, potential problems, and planning for the next budget cycle must begin almost as soon as the current budget is implemented. Evaluation must be done on a regular basis to make certain that the circumstances, goals, and other environmental information about hospital and library programs remains accurate. This helps to keep library budgets, plans, and spending aligned with the organization's situation and needs. For example, midway through the financial year, the organization may introduce a new program that will create increased demand for library resources in future years" (Phillips, 2000: 77). The librarian should monitor income and expenditures throughout the year, readjusting allocations as necessary. Figure 4.7 is an example of using a spreadsheet to monitor the budget.

Budget Enhancement

The increasingly difficult struggle to keep up with the ever-increasing cost of electronic resources came to a head during the recession of 2009 when the best budgets were those that remained static. Most libraries endured some type of budget reductions, some as much as 40 percent. In response to these difficult economic times and combined pleas from the Association of Research Libraries (ARL) and the International Coalition of Library Consortia (ICOLC), many of the smaller journal publishers held 2010 prices to 2009 levels. Discussion lists and library association meetings shared suggestions for coping with such stringent cuts.

Cooperative Purchases

Consortia offer opportunities to leverage libraries' buying power, provide opportunities for libraries to collaborate on innovative programs, and provide reasonably priced educational opportunities for librarians. They also save on the time required to conduct negotiations and place negotiations in the hands of those who are most experienced in the process. Cooperative collection development, popular in the 1980s when libraries cooperatively purchased periodicals, is undergoing a resurgence today. Examples of viable programs for consortia purchasing include:

The **National Network of Libraries of Medicine (NN/LM) Pacific Southwest Region (PSR)** developed the **E-Licensing Program**, in partnership with the Statewide California Electronic Library Consortium (SCELC) in 2009 to provide consortia licensing opportunities for libraries in hospitals and other health care institutions. NN/LM members in the Pacific Southwest Region from nonprofit organizations are eligible to become SCELC-NN/LM Affiliates; they will then be able to acquire access to electronic resources at reduced rates negotiated by SCELC. Libraries must be in a hospital or other health care institution, be a member of the NN/LM Pacific Southwest Region, and have an IP range. The **Statewide California Electronic Library Consortium (SCELC)** brings together nonprofit academic and research institutions to promote the effective use and dissemination of electronic information to libraries and their users by licensing the electronic resources and educating library staff. Other NN/LM regions may have similar programs.

Amigos Library Services, the largest consortium of libraries in the southwestern United States, has helped its

Figure 4.7. Income and Expenditure Monitoring

FY 10 Jan–Oct				
	Income (Budget)	**On Order**	**Spent**	**Balance**
Salaries	$55,000	0	32000	$23,000
Supplies	$4,000	100	1500	$2,400
Phone	$1,000	0	500	$500
Databases	$20,000	0	15000	$5,000
Interlibrary Loan	$750	75	400	$275
Books	$8,000	566	3000	$4,434
Journals	$85,000	899	80000	$4,101
Equipment	$1,800	0	800	$1,000
Training	$1,000	0	250	$750
TOTAL	$176,550	$1,640	$133,450	$41,460

members obtain affordable services and share library resources and knowledge for more than 30 years. Through membership in Amigos, libraries leverage their buying power, collectively gain access to the latest innovations and services in the library community, and pursue opportunities for continuing professional education.

LYRASIS, created in April 2009 by the merger of SOLINET and joined shortly thereafter by NELINET, is the nation's largest regional membership organization serving libraries. It provides significant cost savings through group purchasing for products from more than 100 vendors, cutting-edge education, preservation and digitization services, and electronic resource licensing. While the primary service area is the Mid-Atlantic, Southwestern, and New England regions, LYRASIS has members throughout the United States and other countries.

Other programs are available at the state and local levels. Funk (2009) recounts the tens of thousands of dollars saved by Katie Wrigley for her 13-hospital system by purchasing Micromedex for all of its members. He mentions state programs such as NOVELNY, which offer access to databases such as Health and Wellness Resource Center and ProQuest Platinum to state residents at no charge.

Vendor Negotiations

Vendors are seeking additional business; librarians are seeking affordable costs.

Librarians may view the confidentiality clause or non-disclosure agreement as an unreasonable gag order while vendors view it as an acceptable way to prevent underbidding by the competition. In spite of these different perspectives, it is in the best interest of each party to negotiate successfully. As stated in "Deal or No Deal," it is important to consider the other side's point of view and communicate clearly (Phillips, 2006).

Librarians can prepare for negotiations by evaluating patrons, products, and pricing. Needs assessment, utilization statistics, and trials assist in determining products that clients most urgently need. Product comparisons may be made by reviewing product literature and websites and discussing pros, cons, and service support with peers. Cost/use studies assist librarians in determining whether the "big" deal is truly a good deal for the library or merely a way for vendors to increase their business and unload little-used titles through bundles. In addition to "big deals," vendors may offer caps on future increases, multiyear purchases at set fees, discounts when librarians

order more than one product, and prepayment discounts. Jan Orick, Director of the Biomedical Library at St. Jude Children's Research Hospital in Memphis, Tennessee, provides insight into the views of vendors and hospital librarians by publishing the results of a questionnaire administered during an MLA chapter meeting in 2003 and provides sample questions for a librarian to consider before entering the negotiation process (Orick, 2004).

Reductions

Some librarians are proponents of cutting visible services as library budgets are reduced so that the cuts are obvious, hoping that the backlash results in restored funding. Mark Funk (2009) coined the term "grumble factor" to describe this process. If there is no backlash, one questions whether the services were essential at all. Others go to great lengths to minimize the impact of budget reductions on their clients. At any rate, services must be examined and prioritized. In some cases, the identification and cancellation of redundant services may enable one to introduce new and more relevant services. Outsourcing operations such as acquisitions and cataloging may be cost-effective.

Dougherty (2009) urges librarians to learn more about the manner in which clients are using library tools and resources so that resources may be deployed most effectively. Some libraries are sharing the cost of the more expensive databases with departments who use them most. Many libraries continue to cancel print journals in favor of online access when it is cost-effective, eliminate print journals that duplicate electronic holdings, use A-to-Z services to identify journal overlaps, refrain from binding print titles that are duplicated by electronic holdings, and cancel multiple copies of subscriptions (see Chapters 7 and 8). Librarians can enhance shared decision making by sharing cost and utilization data with department heads and encouraging them to prioritize journal needs. The Management in Action case study exemplifies the value of this tactic.

Funk (2009) encourages librarians to verify their tiered price quotes against the publisher's website before renewing electronic journals since the vendor's assumption of one's status may not always be correct. Librarians should also compare the prices offered by Amazon.com with those offered by more traditional vendors.

Librarians are also beginning to review the duplication between print and electronic books and to review standing orders, particularly expensive directories. They check utilization statistics before automatically purchasing new

Dealing with Budget Cuts

Location: Rural hospital

Description of Problem/Project: Marilyn Johnson has just been informed that the library's collection budget is being cut 12 percent as part of the medical center's overall strategy in dealing with escalating costs. Marilyn is aware that journal costs inflation is predicted to be 6 percent for the coming year and does not know how she is going to cope with such a drastic decline in financial support.

Impact On: Ability to provide adequate information resources for training and decision-making activities.

People Involved: Medical center employees and physicians.

Strategies for Success: Marilyn needs to obtain input from medical center employees and physicians regarding their preferences for journal subscriptions to increase their buy-in for the decisions that are made. She can download a spreadsheet of her current titles and costs from her periodical vendor and add COUNTER-compliant utilization statistics to develop cost/use information. Marilyn can share this data with department heads and physicians, explaining the sudden budget cuts and asking them to rank the importance of each title.

Barriers Encountered: Possible barriers could be difficulty in reaching community physicians and lack of participation and consensus.

Take-Home Points: Medical center employees and physicians will be more inclined to accept those decisions in which they have had a chance to participate. Marilyn will have the ultimate responsibility for consolidating the responses and using this data in conjunction with other factors such as impact, subject balance, value to the institutional mission and availability elsewhere to reach a final decision.

editions and make the majority of their purchases during vendors' deep discount sales. Some librarians feel that the purchase of electronic books is more cost-effective because they ensure against loss. Those libraries that centralize book and journal orders for the entire institution enable the reduction of unnecessary duplicate orders, enhanced accountability for materials purchase, volume reduction in prices, and enhanced access to all departments as materials are cataloged in the library's online public-access catalogs. Finally, librarians are examining concurrent user seats, feeling that turn-aways are better than no access at all.

Supplemental Funds

Fines and Fee for Service

Whereas institutional support constitutes the major portion of the library's funding, fines and fees for service may also play a role. When deciding whether to charge fines for delinquent materials, the librarian must weigh the negative public relations effects and staff time required against the effects in recovering materials and as a revenue stream. Fee for service includes:

- fees charged for interlibrary loans,
- document delivery,
- searches,
- systematic reviews, and
- copying and printing.

These may be computed on a cost recovery basis or in comparison to the charges made by other local libraries or commercial sources. Net lenders in the interlibrary loan business may want to use their fees for one-time funding or special projects due to uncertainty of the revenue stream's continuation.

Grants and Awards

Grants are an excellent means through which to supplement the library's funding.

While some grants entail a laborious and complex application process, other grant or award application processes are relatively simple and straightforward and can assist libraries with the acquisition of new technology and training.

The **National Network of Libraries of Medicine (NN/LM)** is a primary source of awards for health science libraries. Its mission is to provide all U.S. health professionals equal access to biomedical information thereby enabling them to make informed decisions. The network is administered by the National Library of Medicine (NLM) and consists of eight Regional Medical Libraries (major institutions under contract with the National Library of Medicine), more than 151 Resource Libraries (primarily at medical schools), and 4,196 Primary Access Libraries (primarily at hospitals). The Regional Medical Libraries administer and coordinate services in the network's eight geographical regions. One must be a member of the NN/LM network to obtain awards but membership is free. Full members are health science libraries and health information centers that are regularly staffed, have Internet access and health science collections, provide information services, and participate in DOCLINE. Affiliate members are libraries, information centers, and resource centers that are called upon for health information by their clients, but do not meet the requirements of full members.

The networks offer funding for health information outreach, exhibiting, training, and technology. Technology improvement awards and information access improvement awards range between $1,000 and $5,000, and have been used to purchase equipment to enhance the delivery of information services such as scanners, upgraded dial-up connections to broadband connections, mobile broadband connections, library website enhancements, hardware and software to produce tutorials, Kindle readers to increase electronic services, initial purchase of integrated library systems, and digitization projects. DOCLINE improvement awards have purchased computers to access DOCLINE while technology improvement awards purchase computers for public areas such as clinic waiting rooms, nursing ward stations, and library public service areas. Mobile broadband awards may also provide access to technology normally blocked in many hospitals, such as Google docs and Skype, and to technology which is useful for library collaboration and distance education, such as blogs, wikis, RSS feeds, and social bookmarking, as well as for patron access to surgery videos normally blocked by hospital filters. Promotion events such as author's day, health information kiosks, investigation of smart phone capabilities, podcasting, and software for online subject guides also are funded by these awards. As Figure 4.8 illustrates, the award application process is simple (National Network of Libraries of Medicine, 2009).

Applicants are required to provide quotes for the desired resource and describe their plans for utilization of the award, improved services that will result, a description of the resources to be purchased, intended audience, outcomes, and indicators that will be evaluated to monitor the outcomes, a timeline for completion of the project, and plans for funding ongoing costs upon project completion. A letter of support from the institution's information technology (IT) department confirming the selection of resources and resolution of networking and firewall issues is also required. The award generally lasts 12 months; a summary report of the effectiveness of the award is required at the end of the project. NN/LM staff is available for consultation and assistance with award proposals and writing tips and tutorials and classes for proposal writing are available on the Internet (http://nnlm.gov/funding/support.html). The NN/LM Outreach and Evaluation Resource Center (OERC) offers

publications that assist in planning evaluation for outreach programs with publications on their website, such as *Measuring the Difference: Guide to Planning and Evaluating Health Information Outreach*; *Getting Started with Community-Based Outreach*; *Evaluation in Outreach Project Planning*; and *Collecting and Analyzing Evaluation Data* (http://nnlm.gov/evaluation/guides.html). NN/LM Projects Database (http://nnlm.gov/funding/database .html) describes all projects funded by these awards and can give one ideas of projects to request.

According to Janice Kelly (2008), the Executive Director of the Southeastern/Atlantic (SEA) Region of the National Network of Libraries of Medicine (NN/LM,) the **National Library of Medicine (NLM) Extramural Programs (EP)** is the National Library of Medicine's funding division that funds infrastructure improvements and information management support, research projects, informatics projects, awards for career development and training, and more. Resource awards support improved dissemination of information, and management and use of biomedical information in real settings. They also help health-related organizations use computers and networks to optimize the management of clinical and scientific knowledge for defined audiences. One program provides assistance for the authoring of scholarly works in biomedicine and health. Domestic public or private nonprofit health-related organizations are eligible for the awards.

RePORT Expenditures and Results (RePORTER) (http://report.nih.gov/) has replaced CRISP (Computer Retrieval of Information on Scientific Projects) in supplying information on National Institutes of Health (NIH) research programs. It provides additional query fields, hit lists that can be sorted and downloaded to Excel, NIH funding for each project, and links to PubMed Central, PubMed, and the U.S. Patent & Trademark Office Patent Full Text and Image Database for more information on research results.

The **Institute of Museum and Library Services (IMLS)** (http://www.imls.gov/) provides $5,000 to $150,000 grants awarded for digitization, literacy, service to culturally diverse populations, enhanced integration of open source materials into collections, building institutional repositories (IRs), open source library systems, online patron instruction, improved library services for the elderly, and scholarships for master's and doctoral library education. Sample applications are available on the website.

The **Foundation Center** offers a variety of grants from a number of organizations and provides excellent educational tools for grant-writing with tutorials, full-day classroom training courses, online training courses, books, audio books, guidelines, and sample proposals on

Figure 4.8. National Network of Libraries of Medicine (NN/LM) Award Application

Information Access Improvement Project Award Application, 2010
(http://nnlm.gov/scr/funding/iaip.html)

In addition to the online application, applicants should submit the following to the NN/LM SCR office:

- Letter of support from Institutional Information Technology/Systems Administrator regarding proposed technology to be implemented.

1. **Institution:**	6. **Mailing Address:**
2. **Institution LIBID:**	
3. **Project Manager:**	7. **Telephone:**
4. **Position Title:**	8. **Fax:**
5. **E-mail Address:**	9. **Project Title:**

10. **Summary:** A one-paragraph summary statement of the proposed project.

11. **Describe the target population or audience:**

12. **Explain the need for improving access to Internet-based health information and how this award will assist in this process:**

13. **List your project objectives:**

14. **Describe how you will complete the project objectives (your project plan):**

15. **How will you evaluate your project's effect?** (Applicants should consult the Outreach and Evaluation Resource Center website http://nnlm.gov/evaluation or the NN/LM SCR office when developing needs assessments and/or evaluation plans.)

16. **How will you spend the award?** (Provide a cost breakdown with a justification for each budget line.)

Submit application in electronic format. Additional documentation may be submitted via email or regular mail to the address below:

proposal writing and budgeting. The **Foundation Finder** (http://lnp.fdncenter.org/finder.html) enables one to search for foundations that provide funding.

Grants.gov is the one-stop shopping place to find and apply for government grants (Kelly, 2008). It offers information on applying for grants at all federal agencies, receiving 300,000 submissions in FY 09 and awarding $500 billion annually. User guides, animated tutorials, webcasts, and tutorials assist the potential grantee.

> Librarians may also wish to consult their institution's foundation office for additional opportunities, particularly local ones, and the opportunity to present a coordinated request that could have a better chance of success.

Librarians may stay abreast of current offers by subscribing to the NN/LM RSS feeds, the NIH Guide LISTERV Table of Contents (TOC) information for the current week's issue of the NIH Guide for Grants and Contracts, Grants.gov e-mail notification of new grants postings, ScanGrants (http://www.scangrants.com/) and the Library Grants blog (http://librarygrants.blogspot.com/), which posts grant opportunities specifically for libraries.

Donations

> Displaying the library's donation policy prominently on the library's webpage and through printed flyers displayed prominently in the library will eliminate many of the problems commonly incurred with donations.

Donations can be a blessing or a nuisance depending upon one's point of view and methods of acquiring them. A donation policy, as shown in Figure 4.9, should include the types and ages of the resources one will accept as well as the disposition of the items that the library accepts but cannot use. A disclaimer that explains that one will make no evaluations for tax purposes is also important.

Wish lists of books most urgently needed may be displayed throughout the library in print and on the library's website. Some libraries request donations from staff that are retiring or relocating and find that residents are particularly willing to donate books that they don't want to move. Others request copies of books authored by institutional staff as they congratulate the authors upon their publication. Mary Pat Harnegie reports that Cleveland Clinic libraries have received more than $28,000 worth of books in the past five years that were donated in this manner as a result of institutional policy (Funk, 2009). These donations can be acknowledged by

---

Figure 4.9. Sample Gift Policy

Donate to the Library

The Medical Library gratefully accepts your gifts of new or old books. Books of all types are welcome, including textbooks and leisure reading, hardcovers and paperbacks. We cannot accept gifts of journals, since they usually duplicate existing library holdings and are difficult to redistribute or sell.

Books of scientific or significant historical value, which are not already owned by the library, are added to the collection. Books that are not added are offered for sale at the library's book sale; funds from the sale are used to purchase new books. The library will send you a written acknowledgment, stating the number of volumes given. We cannot provide a detailed inventory, but if you compile a list of the gift items, we will return a verified copy with the letter of acknowledgment. IRS regulations explicitly disallow monetary appraisals by the library.

Please bring your books to the library. We are not able to pick up books and cannot reimburse shipping costs, but if you call in advance, we will provide directions to the library and help to unload the books.

Questions concerning book donations should be directed to Mary Brown, Librarian, mbrown@aka.org or 801-555-2000.

---

the traditional bookplate and also by a note in the online catalog.

Many libraries bring in hundreds or even thousands of dollars annually by selling duplicate, obsolete, and excess books, either in the library or on the Internet. Contracting for a percentage of the sales with a local bookseller who does all the work can be an efficient way to sell on the Internet. Some libraries host annual book sales as special events, while others keep specific shelves set aside for book sale items on a daily basis.

Fundraising

Some institutions have determined that Friends of the Library groups are no longer worth the time and effort expended while other institutions continue to use them successfully to supplement their resources and building programs. Friends of Libraries U.S.A. (FOLUSA) is a nonprofit organization that provides resources, training, consulting, networking, and support groups in libraries of all types. FOLUSA recently merged with the Association of Library Trustees and Advocates (ALTA) to become the Association of Library Trustees, Advocates, Friends and Foundations (ALTAFF), a division of the American Library Association (ALA) (http://folusa.org).

Donna Flake, Library Director of the Robert M. Fales Health Sciences Library of the South East Area Health Education Center in Wilmington, North Carolina, created a Friends program for her library in 2004 and has received $185,000 in additional funds with which to purchase books, journals, furniture, and computers as well as that all-important emotional support for the library. In return, the library gives incentives to Friends members in the form of free copies/prints and interlibrary loans, name recognition at the library entrance and in library publications, and an annual reception. See the **accompanying CD-ROM** for a detailed description of this successful Friends program.

While many may be reluctant to dial for dollars, fundraising can be quite productive if handled appropriately. Auxiliaries and civic organizations such as the Junior League are often eager to assist library campaigns for additional resources and computer hardware, especially that which will be used to develop health literacy and consumer health programs (Falk, 2009). Some believe that the most successful programs focus on the giver's responsibility and benefits rather than the institutions' needs and emphasize the donor's opportunity to shape the future, participate in something larger than one person, and the intrinsic reward for the greater good. Recognition is also an important aspect of fundraising, generally handled with letters of appreciation (Horny, 2009).

Educational Opportunities

A number of inexpensive educational opportunities are available for those librarians who feel the need for additional education in this area. WebJunction, a division of OCLC, provides web-based, self-paced, 1.5-hour courses in the area of budgeting and finance (http://www.webjunction.org/budget-finance). The course, *Basic Budgeting*, covers budget preparation and presentation, forecasting, and analysis while *Financial Management* deals with encumbrances and financial management software. Librarians can also use blogs to learn more about financial management, searching http://blogarama.com and http://blogsearchengine.com to find them. Pat Wagner of Pattern Research, Inc., Denver, Colorado (http://www.pattern.com), teaches a series of management courses, driving her point home with wit and pithy practical examples including "Negotiating Skills" and "Strategic Planning," which were recently offered as a Medical Library Association (MLA) CE course. Wagner often presents on the free SirsiDynix network including

a recent presentation titled "Real Bottom Lines: Myth about Using Business Principles in Libraries."

Conclusion

With the challenging economy and increased competition from commercial resources, financial planning will continue to be of optimal importance to the library's survival. The needs assessment and planning, as covered in Chapters 3 and 6, are essential to good financial management and also serve as key elements of strategic planning for the entire library program. A clearly defined plan of action resonates with busy administrators. Librarians must strive to maintain optimal skills in financial management in order to thrive in today's economic environment.

References

Clark, Laura, and Denise Davis. 2009a. "Tech Budgets Totter." *American Libraries* 40, no. 3 (March): 27.

Clark, Laura, and Denise Davis. 2009b. "The State of Funding for Library Technology in Today's Economy." *Library Technology Reports* 45 no. 1 (January): 1–48.

Dougherty, Richard M. 2009. "Prescription for Financial Recovery." *American Libraries* 40, no. 6/7 (June/July): 50–53.

Elliott, Donald S., Glen E. Holt, Sterling W. Hayden, and Leslie Edmonds Holt. 2007. *Measuring Your Library's Value: How to Do Cost-Benefit Analysis for Your Public Library.* Chicago: American Library Association.

Falk, Steven. 2009. "Asking People for Money: Go for It, But Prepare Well." *Public Management* (March): 91–92.

Funk, Mark. 2009. *Collection Development in Times of Shrinking Budgets.* Invited Presentation at UNYOC. (October 1). Accessed November 4, 2010. http://vimeo.com/7363049.

Hallam, Arlita W., and Teresa R. Dalston. 2005. *Managing Budgets and Finances: A How-To-Do-It Manual For Librarians And Information Professionals.* New York: Neal-Schuman.

Horny, Karen. 2009. "An Unexpected Fundraising Success." *Library Leadership & Management* 23, no. 3 (Summer): 131–132, 149.

Joint, Nicholas. 2008. "It Is Not All Free on the Web: Advocacy for Library Funding in the Digital Age." *Library Review* 57, no. 4 (Winter): 270–275.

Kelly, Janice. 2008. "Getting Funded." *Journal of Hospital Librarianship* 8, no. 4 (Spring): 469–478.

Linn, Mott. 2007. "Budget Systems Used in Allocating Resources to Libraries." *The Bottom Line: Managing Library Finances* 20, no. 1 (January): 20–29.

National Network of Libraries of Medicine. 2009. "Funding." Accessed November 4, 2010. http://www.nnlm.gov/funding.

Orick, Jan T. 2004. "The Business of Negotiating for Hospital Librarians." *Medical Reference Services Quarterly* 23, no. 3 (Fall): 61–69.

Phillips, Kara. 2006. *Deal or No Deal—Licensing and Acquiring Digital Resources: License Negotiations* (November 22) Accessed December 10, 2010. http://www.llrx.com/columns/deal2.htm.

Phillips, Sharon A. 2000. "Financial Management." In *The Medical Library Association Guide to Managing Health Care Libraries*, edited by Ruth Holst and Sharon A. Phillips, 75–103. New York: Neal-Schuman.

Roberts, Stephen A. 2003. "Financial Management of Libraries: Past Trends and Future Prospects." *Library Trends* 51, no. 3 (Winter): 462–493.

Van Orsdel, Lee C., and Kathleen Born. 2009. "Reality Bites: Periodicals Price Survey 2009." *Library Journal* 7, no. 15 (April 15): 36–40. Accessed December 10, 2010. http://www.libraryjournal.com/article/CA6651248.html.

Further Reading

Crawley-Low, Jill V. 2002. "Collection Analysis Techniques Used to Evaluate a Graduate-Level Toxicology Collection." *Journal of the Medical Library Association* 90, no. 3 (July): 310–316.

Harris, Lindsay. 2003. "Sharing the Burden: A Model for Consortium Purchasing for Health Libraries." *Journal of the Medical Library Association* 91, no. 3 (July): 361–364.

Jacobs, Leslie. 2002. "What Is Your Budget Saying About Your Library?" *Information Outlook* 6, no. 6 (June): 6–17. Accessed November 4, 2010. http://www.sla.org/content/Shop/Information/infoonline/2002/jun02/jacobstrouse.cfm.

McKay, Duncan. 2003. *Effective Financial Planning for Library and Information Services*. 2nd ed. London: Europa.

Silverman, Emily. 2008. "Building Your Base: Identifying Library Donors." *The Bottom Line: Managing Library Finances* 21, no. 4 (April): 138–141.

Smith, Stevenson. 2002. *Managerial Accounting for Libraries and Other Not-for-Profit Organizations*. Chicago: American Library Association.

Stembridge, Koren. 2005. "Fundraisers R Us." *American Libraries* 16, no. 3 (March): 38–39.

Wisconsin Department of Public Instruction. 2010. "Developing the Library Budget." Accessed November 4. http://dpi.wi.gov/pld/ae13.html.

5

Human Resources Management

Dixie A. Jones

The author wishes to acknowledge the excellent work of Holly Shipp Buchanan, AHIP, FMLA, who wrote the human resources chapter for the previous edition. The first edition version largely provided the format and inspiration for this version.

The heart and soul of a library is its staff. This chapter will discuss the issues involved in managing the library's most valuable resource—its people. The majority of health care libraries have small staffs but they have many of the same considerations as larger libraries: reporting structure, justification of positions, competitive salaries, alternative forms of staffing to supplement permanent employees, recruiting and hiring, orienting, motivating, evaluating, training, mentoring, dealing with unions, and providing needed services within the confines of allotted full-time equivalents (FTE). The library manager must meet the needs of the staff and must also ensure that the staff is meeting the needs of the library's clientele whether there is just one clerical person or a mixed team of professionals and clerical people. Discussion includes issues related to staffing requirements, as well as hiring, firing, managing and developing staff.

When library staff is referred to in this chapter, the concept includes paid professionals, paid clerical employees, volunteers, paid student workers, full-time as well as part-time personnel, and library school interns, i.e., anyone who works in the library in any capacity. The content here is written for new library managers and/or those who are new to the health care field. Human resource issues are fairly universal, but there are matters which are unique to libraries and in particular to libraries in health care settings.

Nearly all institutions have a Human Resources (HR) Department. The library manager needs to have a good relationship with HR and must be familiar with any HR regulations and procedures. HR staff members can be very helpful with personnel issues, offering guidance about hiring and firing, leave, discipline, and any legalities involved. Most institutions will offer training to their managers on a variety of topics, such as the aforementioned issues, as well as performance appraisal, conflict management, labor relations, and sexual harassment. They will also provide guidance or regulations regarding retention of personnel records (Allegri and Bedard, 2008). In addition to federal and state laws that govern hiring and firing of personnel, each health care institution or system will have its own regulations regarding such matters. The library manager must be conversant with all of these.

Library Personnel/Staffing

Reporting Structure

The reporting structure for the library varies widely among health care institutions. The library manager may report to the medical center's chief executive, to the head of a department such as education or information technology, or to someone at any level between, e.g., the chief of staff or hospital vice president. The Medical Library Association "Standards for Hospital Libraries 2007" (MLA Standards) indicate that a hospital library manager should report to senior management (Hospital Libraries Section Standards Committee, 2008).

Determining Staffing Requirements

Determining the library's staffing requirements in terms of FTE can be accomplished through workload analysis or by applying formulas such as the one in the MLA

Standards (Hospital Libraries Section Standards Committee, 2008). Library management must be proactive in marketing services and publicizing the worth of those services. Justifying FTE after a decision has already been made to downsize will most likely be a lost cause. Health care facilities' library staff members are sometimes asked to take on additional roles, such as managing continuing medical education or managing a hospital website. If these additional duties can be accommodated with existing staff, that is well and good. If not, a case needs to be made to administration that another service will have to be dropped or that additional FTE will be needed in order to absorb the new roles being performed by library staff.

> Once upon a time, "justifying a position" might have meant making a persuasive argument to add another FTE to the library staff. In today's economic climate, it is just as likely to mean making a case for keeping the number of FTEs that the library already has.

Position Mix/Roles

Library staffing is changing. A number of factors contribute to this still-evolving shift in the roles of library staff as well as the knowledge and skills required to fulfill these roles. Recruiting from fields such as education, computer systems, medical informatics and other related fields may be necessary to meet today's staffing needs (Medical Library Association, 2007). The skill mix is changing partly because of technology. More time is spent troubleshooting electronic access issues. More education is being done through web-based tutorials. More library resource users are expecting to be able to access resources on their mobile devices. Grant writing skills are more important than ever, as budgets fail to keep up with rising costs. More demands are being made by various user groups, e.g., nurses in hospitals that are working to achieve Magnet status. Searching for and providing evidence-based literature and appraisal of the literature are important skills to assist clinicians in evidence-based practice. Health literacy issues are also taking more staff time, as librarians serve clinicians who need patient education materials and as librarians directly serve patients who need consumer health information. Position advertisements increasingly require a range of sophisticated skills—not just reference or just cataloging. In some health care organizations, the library staff takes on nontraditional duties, such as managing continuing medical education or the institutional website (see Chapter 15). In small libraries, there may be only one or two people who are responsible for budgeting, ordering, licensing, reference, instruction, clinical reference/rounding, marketing, grant writing, electronic resource management, web maintenance, cataloging, and interlibrary loan.

Position Descriptions

A typical job description answers two questions: what is the job and what education and experience are required?

To answer these questions, the position description (PD) should list the principal duties and the occasional duties: to whom the person in the position answers; the degree of responsibility; who the person in the position supervises (if anyone); any physical, educational, or experience requirements; and the skills or attributes needed to carry out the duties (Stanley, 2008). Position descriptions will change over time as new services evolve and new technologies emerge.

Qualifications for library staff are determined by the institutions. Most health care organizations require library-specific competencies in addition to customer-service competencies and the ability to communicate with people of highly variable literacy levels (Jones, 2008). The library manager can usually work with HR to determine qualifications for a particular position. Ideally, the library manager is a qualified librarian. MLA Standards specify that "A qualified librarian is a person who has earned a master's degree from a program accredited by the American Library Association or its successor accrediting organization or from a master's level program in library and information studies accredited or recognized by the appropriate national body of another country" (Hospital Libraries Section Standards Committee, 2008: 163).

Competencies

In hospital settings, The Joint Commission standards for Human Resources (HR) address competencies. These standards apply to all employees, not just library staff. Competency assessment determines whether staff members have the skills and knowledge to do their jobs. According to The Joint Commission HR standards, this assessment must take place and be documented at least once every three years, although it can be more frequent if required by hospital policy (Joint Commission, 2010).

A number of competencies are common to librarians in all types of institutions. As defined by Cohn and Kelsey (2005: 14), a competency is "the knowledge, skills, attitudes, and values required for successful performance in a job. The demonstration of a competency includes the factors of observation, measurement, training, and learning." The types of competencies are delineated in varying ways by different sources. Basically, core competencies are those which all employees are expected to demonstrate. Personal competencies are those which an individual possesses. Job-specific competencies are those which are required for a particular position within the library. Examples of core competencies are communication skills, service attitude, or resource management. Examples of personal competencies are leadership or networking skills. Job-specific competencies may include knowledge of web-design software, how to use XML, or the searching features of a particular database. Although expert searching skills are still required in many health care organizations, there has been a major shift from mediated searching to teaching constituents how to do their own searching. Competencies in teaching and developing instructional materials are more often required than in the past, when educating users largely consisted of library orientation. See Chapter 11 for more about educational roles of health care organization librarians.

The Special Libraries Association's *Competencies for Information Professionals of the 21st Century* denotes four types of professional competencies (Abels et al., 2003). Following are examples of each type:

A. Managing Information Organizations
Example: "Assesses and communicates the value of the information organization, including information services, products and policies to senior management, key stakeholders and client groups."

B. Managing Information Resources
Example: "Negotiates the purchase and licensing of needed information products and services."

C. Managing Information Services
Example: "Researches, analyzes and synthesizes information into accurate answers or actionable information for clients, and ensures that clients have tools or capabilities to immediately apply these."

D. Applying Information Tools and Technologies
Example: "Applies expertise in databases, indexing, metadata, and information analysis and synthesis to improve information retrieval and use in the organization."

These professional competencies are the ones that are most related to particular job duties.

As noted in *Competencies for Lifelong Learning and Professional Success: The Educational Policy Statement of the*

Medical Library Association, "Individuals cannot achieve mastery of all knowledge and every desirable skill in each competency area, but will emphasize different areas at different points in their careers and in different institutional settings" (Medical Library Association, 2007: 4). See Figure 5.1 for the professional competencies for health sciences librarians as outlined by MLA. They are also included on the **accompanying CD-ROM** in the Chapter 2 section.

In addition to the competency sources mentioned previously, there is a review of competency literature in Dudden's *Using Benchmarking, Needs Assessment, Quality Improvement, Outcome Measurement, and Library Standards*. Dudden (2007) highlights publications that discuss competencies in terms of the future, staff development, those which are specific to hospitals, and more.

Salaries

Support staff may have set salaries, based on their job classifications in the system. Depending on the setting, professional staff may also have set pay scales, such as in federal government libraries. In other settings, there may be a little more leeway in determining salaries. HR can provide assistance regarding regulations and options within the institution for setting salaries. In larger staffed libraries, pay equity is of some importance. Retention may be difficult if longtime employees see new hires coming in at higher salaries. Employees with similar level responsibilities should be compensated comparably. One way to raise salaries, if the institution permits, is by awarding merit pay. For prospective employees, good fringe benefits may make the difference in whether or not the salary is acceptable to them. To stretch salary dollars, the library may be able to work out cost-sharing arrangements with other departments (Allegri, 2008).

Student Workers and Library Interns

If student workers are available, they can be a cost-effective way to accomplish many library tasks. However, as Carol Jenkins (2000; 43) notes, "they may also require considerable on-the-job training, and their commitment is understandably to their academic goals. In general, they do not prove to be as reliable as permanent staff." Certainly, their time on staff is limited, but they can be trained to do shelving, interlibrary loans, circulation work, etc. Another staffing alternative is the library intern. A student in a graduate library and information science program who is interested in gaining experience in a health care library can be a motivated, though admittedly short-term, asset to the staff in accomplishing projects. The library manager should be willing to invest the time to teach the intern; the benefits are often well worth this investment.

Volunteers

Many health care organizations utilize volunteers. Anyone who wishes to provide service on a voluntary basis in the library should go through the organization's usual procedure for becoming a volunteer. Most institutions require a registration process, which may include screening. Volunteers can certainly extend the library's paid staffing, allowing the library to do more within its limited allotment of FTE. The library manager should, however, have the right to tell the voluntary program office "No," regarding anyone who is likely to be more of a detriment than an asset to the work of the library. Health care executives should be made aware that volunteers cannot provide permanent solutions for library understaffing. "Volunteers should not be viewed as a quick fix or as a long-term solution to a library's understaffing problem" (McDiarmid and Auster, 2004: 43).

Most voluntary staff can at least perform tasks such as answering the phone, greeting people at the door, or photocopying. Many have talents and skills that go far beyond these basic duties and can be invaluable. Volunteers do require supervision and feedback regarding their performance, just as paid employees do. They also require training, and customer service should be a part of the training (Todaro and Smith, 2006). Finding ways to recognize volunteers for their time and service is recommended, whether it is a lunch during National Volunteer Week or a certificate of appreciation. Many institutions track volunteer hours and provide formal recognition for milestone numbers.

Recruiting and Hiring

Legal Issues

Hiring practices must comply with federal and state laws, as well as institutional regulations. The primary federal laws are:

- *Title VII of the Civil Rights Act of 1964* prohibits discrimination on the basis of color, race, gender, religion, or national origin
- *Age Discrimination in Employment Act of 1967* prohibits discrimination on the basis of age for those who are age 40 and over

Figure 5.1. Professional Competencies for Health Sciences Librarians

1. Understand the health sciences and health care environment and the policies, issues, and trends that impact that environment including:
   - current management and business practices
   - the parent organization's (academic medical center, hospital, government, corporate, etc.) major policy and program sources
   - the health sciences professions
   - the clinical care, research, medical education, cultural, ethical, economic, and legal issues and environments
   - various health and health-related organizations

2. Know and understand the application of leadership, finance, communication, and management theory and techniques including:
   - understanding the institution's mission and planning processes and the role of the library in the institution
   - forging and maintaining alliances with universities, public libraries, public health services, community-based organizations, and others to meet users' information needs
   - human resources management including recruitment, retention, staff development, and mentoring
   - facilities planning and space allocation
   - budgeting, cost analyses, and fundraising
   - public relations, marketing, and advertising
   - library programs and services administration

3. Understand the principles and practices related to providing information services to meet users' needs including:
   - the information needs of health practitioners, researchers, administrators, educators, students, patients, consumers, and the general public
   - the institution's information policies
   - methods of information delivery and access including consideration of the specific information needs of diverse populations
   - information services management

4. Have the ability to manage health information resources in a broad range of formats including:
   - selection, acquisition, and control of resources including the licensing of resources
   - scholarly publishing, copyright, licensing, privacy, and intellectual property issues
   - conservation, preservation, and archiving of materials in all formats
   - cataloging, classification, abstracting, and thesaurus construction and knowledge representation
   - national and international standards and conventions
   - trends in information formatting, production, packaging, and dissemination

5. Understand and use technology and systems to manage all forms of information including:
   - basic principles of automated systems, data standards, and systems analysis techniques including design and evaluation
   - acquisition, use, and evaluation of information technologies
   - integration of systems and technologies
   - technological solutions for permanent access to electronic information
   - applications in emerging areas of biomedicine, computational biology, and health information, including electronic health care systems and records
   - communications and information infrastructure including the Internet and web

6. Understand curricular design and instruction and have the ability to teach ways to access, organize, and use information including:
   - adult learning theory and cognitive psychology
   - educational needs assessment, analysis, and evaluation
   - instructional methodologies, technologies, and systems design
   - management of education services

7. Understand scientific research methods and have the ability to critically examine and filter research literature from many related disciplines including:
   - using quantitative and qualitative methodologies and techniques and their interpretation
   - locating, organizing, and critically evaluating the research literature
   - using principles of evidence-based practice to support decision making
   - conducting research and reporting and disseminating research findings either individually or in interdisciplinary research teams

Source: Medical Library Association, 2007. *Competencies for Lifelong Learning and Professional Success: The Educational Policy Statement of the Medical Library Association*. Used with permission.

- *Americans with Disabilities Act of 1990* prohibits discrimination against qualified applicants with disabilities
- *Equal Pay Act of 1963* mandates that employers pay equal wages to men and women who perform jobs that are comparable in their required skills and responsibilities with the same working conditions (Stanley, 2008).

Recruiting and Advertising

When planning to hire a library employee, whether for a newly created position or for a vacancy, the recruitment process must be entered into thoughtfully and methodically. When filling a vacancy, one can take the opportunity to amend the responsibilities associated with that job. Library staffing is changing, and one may wish to consider recruiting from a field such as medical informatics or education if doing so will "enhance the library's service role" (Jenkins, 2000: 50). A position description (PD) should be in place in order to effectively advertise the position. Information to include in advertisements includes the PD (or an abbreviated version of it), qualifications for the position, the salary range or a statement regarding salaries, benefits, application deadline, and items to be submitted with the application (Stanley, 2008). Phrases such as "salary commensurate with experience" are really not helpful and can result in a waste of time for both applicants and employers. For professional positions, advertisements may be placed at graduate library programs (for entry-level positions) and in professional organization publications or at their websites. In the health care setting, the Medical Library Association is an organization one may wish to use for advertising. For clerical positions, one may have to advertise within the institution before externally posting the opening. If part of a system, one may wish to advertise within the system before paying for external advertisements. The local newspaper classified ads provide an option that may be less expensive than nationwide advertising if there is likely to be a pool of candidates in the local area. Professional discussion lists provide a medium for widely announcing open positions at no cost. Receipt and processing of applications will probably be the responsibility of the institution's Human Resources department.

Recruitment practices should encourage diversity (Medical Library Association, 2007). Diversity is not just a racial issue; it also involves gender, age, ethnicity, personality type, job type, disabilities, and career stage (Allegri and Bedard, 2008). Diversity-driven workplaces go beyond affirmative action. A diversity-driven work environment should replace affirmative action plans once equity has been successfully implemented (Arthur, 2006). The library manager should be familiar with affirmative action policies at his or her institution.

Interviewing, Checking References, and Evaluating Applicants

One must be aware of any institutional regulations regarding selection of candidates to interview and the interviewing process. Some institutions may require a committee. In small libraries, committee members may include employees from other departments. In large libraries, committee members may include the supervisor of the position, as well as other library staff in that section of the library. After selecting which applicants to interview, the applicants should be notified of the dates and times for the interviews. The candidates should be informed in advance if they will be required to make a presentation, how long they can expect an interview to last, and the type of interview that will be conducted. Providing other pertinent information such as a map or driving directions and where to park is helpful.

An interview may be informal or structured. Some health care institutions are currently using performance-based interviewing, which focuses on asking the candidate to respond to specific scenarios that occur in the workplace. The same questions should be asked of each candidate. One must be careful not to ask questions that are not directly related to the job, such as the interviewee's religious preference or marital status. Indirect questions that force a candidate to provide answers that would reveal this information are also not permissible (Tucker and Mosley, 2008). Even if the interviewer does not ask such a question, the interviewee may volunteer information about marital status, children, or religion. If the applicant provides this information, it should not be written down, the subject should not be pursued any further, and the applicant should be told that this information was not job-related and that the discussion will be returned to the topic of the applicant's qualifications for the position (Arthur, 2006). Answers to questions may be rated numerically according to a predetermined scale, or the interview committee may simply make notes of impressions and responses. A tour of the facility may be conducted. At the conclusion of an interview, the candidate should be thanked and given an idea of when to expect to hear about a decision.

When considering an applicant's qualifications, one may wish to consider talents and abilities, as well as skills. According to Giesecke and McNeil (2010), teaching skills to talented employees is easier than teaching them talents.

The committee will need to review the candidates' responses and evaluate them in terms of the position to be filled. Candidates should be ranked. The committee's first choice will not necessarily accept the position. The candidate may prefer to accept an offer at another institution or, after having interviewed, may feel that the position is not a good fit. With permission from the interviewees, the committee should follow up with the references of the top-ranked candidates. Questions to references should be consistent. Telephone interviews typically provide more candid information than written letters. If the committee does not think that any of the candidates are suitable, Human Resources needs to be contacted about reopening the opportunity to apply for the position. The library manager should not have to accept an inadequate applicant if none of the applicants is satisfactory for the position. All candidates who have been interviewed and do not receive an offer should receive a letter informing them of the decision along with feedback on why they were not selected.

Social networking sites are another source of information about applicants. These sites present new opportunities, as well as dilemmas. Should one check the Facebook page or blog of a job applicant? Should what is posted there affect a hiring decision? Some of the information that is not allowed to be asked in an interview can be found on users' social networking sites. On the other hand, some candidates may have professionally oriented sites to which they voluntarily provide access to showcase their web design skills, educational tools they have created, or projects they have initiated.

Offering the Position

Once a decision is made regarding which candidate to select for a position, the institution's procedures must be followed for making the offer. In some cases, the library manager is the person who contacts the preferred candidate; in other cases, the organization's Human Resources department makes the contact. In addition to notification of the offer, the caller will most likely discuss starting date and other employment details with the candidate (Jenkins, 2000). Once the candidate accepts the position, he or she may have to fulfill requirements such as a background check, drug testing, and/or fingerprinting.

Exiting Process

At the opposite end of the employment spectrum is the exiting process which, of course, may be voluntary or involuntary. If an employee is voluntarily leaving to take another position, to retire, to raise children, or to relocate because of a spouse's job, the process is usually fairly simple and straightforward. There may be problems with accomplishing library tasks because of the vacancy or with being allowed to fill that vacancy, but the exit process itself is not likely to be complicated. HR will be able to advise on needed paperwork and a timeline to accomplish it.

When an employee resigns, conducting an exit interview can provide useful information. The results of the interview might identify problems that cause people to leave (Stanley, 2008). Some institutions require a written exit interview that gives the departing employee a confidential opportunity to explain the reasons for leaving (Jenkins, 2000). Knowing about these problems provides an opportunity to correct them, thereby assisting in employee retention.

Terminating employment because of poor performance is a bit more complex. HR regulations generally require progressive discipline before firing an employee. The person must be given an opportunity to correct performance problems (see the section in this chapter on performance problems).

In some institutions, new employees undergo a probationary period for a specified time. If a new employee exhibits problem behavior, he or she can be fired without going through the usual steps of progressive discipline. In some states, an employee may be fired at any time without specifying a particular reason for doing so. In these "at will" states, it is advantageous not to state why the employee was fired. If no cause is given, the dismissal cannot be legally contested. Library managers should make it their business to find out the laws in their respective states (Tucker and Mosley, 2008).

In times of downsizing, layoffs may occur and can affect health care organization libraries. If layoffs are a possibility, the library manager should prepare a plan in advance for protecting staff if at all possible and for how to continue services if layoffs are mandated. With reduced staff, some services may have to be cut even though customers will expect all the usual services. The library manager will need to inform administration of service reductions necessitated by layoffs.

Staff Management and Relations

One of the fundamentals in library management (or any other kind of management) is treating staff fairly. Another fundamental is practicing the golden rule.

If a library manager treats staff members as he or she would like to be treated, they are likely to be more dedicated and willing to "go the extra mile" when needed. Furthermore, the manager's behavior should serve as a model of what is expected from the library's employees. "Lead by example ... to be truly effective as a manager one must also be an effective leader" (Scroggins, 2004: 311).

Orientation of New Employees

The institution will most likely provide orientation for its new employees. However, the library should provide an in-house orientation to any newly hired library employee. Getting the new staff member off to a good start involves personally welcoming and greeting the employee upon arrival. The new hire's work area should be ready, i.e., clean and neat with equipment and supplies in place. Physically orienting the new staff member to the facility—work area, supply area, restrooms, break area, cafeteria or nearby eateries, the telephone system, entrances and exits, and parking areas is essential, as is introducing the orientee to other staff members and volunteers. Having an orientation checklist can be helpful in ensuring that the new person receives essential information, supplies, and keys. Samples of the types of items to be included on the checklist may be found in Figure 5.2. Human Resources will most likely be the source for information about benefits and institutional regulations. If the employee will be using a computer and the institution requires a user ID and password, expediting the process by providing paperwork ahead of time can prevent delays in getting the employee verified to use the institutional network and any authorized applications such as e-mail, the purchasing system, etc. In a hospital setting, the new employee will be assessed for competencies required by the job and this assessment will be documented (Joint Commission, 2010). The first time a new employee attends a meeting or continuing education course out of town, he or she should be given information about institutional travel regulations.

Communication

Good communication is important for a number of reasons. For a variety of problems that occur in the workplace, analysis will show in many cases that the basic cause of each—regardless of the type of problem—is a breakdown, failure, or lack of communication. When an item needs to be communicated to all library staff, there are multiple ways to deliver the message: posting on a library staff wiki or closed library staff blog; e-mail; circulating print material to each staff member; presenting information in person at a staff meeting; speaking in person to each individual; providing information to supervisors who convey the message to the rest of the staff. For brief items, an e-mail that is sent to all library staff can be very efficient; everyone gets identical information at the same time. However, for more complex communications, a staff meeting might better suit the need, as staff members can ask questions and everyone is present to hear the answers (Jones, 1997).

Figure 5.2. Samples of Items to Include in an Orientation Checklist

Name	
Position	
Supervisor	
Start Date	
Date of Orientation Completion	
Physical Facility (tour)	Restrooms, work area, supplies location, cafeteria, parking, mailroom
Computer System	Login/passwords, e-mail, websites, software
Procedures	Position specific, institution specific
Library Policies	Circulation, interlibrary loan, position-specific policies
Reports/Statistics	Institutional and in-house reports, statistics to be maintained
Institution Policies	Leave/holidays, e-mail use, computer usage, telephone use, parking
Issuance	Identification badge, keys, parking sticker

When something unusual occurs, it is a good idea to be candid with the staff and explain what is happening before rumors and speculation get out of hand. When people don't have enough information, their imaginations begin to fill in the gaps and their guesses are likely to be wilder than the truth.

Being open to communication from the staff can forestall some problems or at least help nip them in the bud before they bloom into something much larger. Having an open-door policy is well worth the interruptions.

Scheduling

In a small library, as health care organization libraries often are, providing coverage for the library's open hours can be a challenge and requires careful planning. Vacations and days adjacent to holidays should be scheduled well in advance. Even lunch hours must be scheduled to ensure that service is available, as lunchtime may be a popular time for the institution's employees to drop by the library. There may also be demand for the library to be open early and/or late for shift employees to be able to use it. To accommodate shift workers and yet stay within the hours allotted, creative scheduling may be required, such as being open in the evenings one or two days a week and early mornings one or two days a week. Twenty-four-hour access is a requirement for some health care organization libraries, but nowadays this requirement can often be met through around-the-clock access to electronic resources.

Ethics

Ethical behavior is an expectation in most professions and health sciences librarianship is no exception. Employees should be aware of ethical principles for dealing with customers, with vendors, and with one another. Many professional organizations have codes of ethics to guide their constituents. For libraries in health care organizations the most pertinent codes, provided in Figures 5.3 and 5.4, are those of the Medical Library Association (2010b) and the American Library Association (2008). For libraries with biocommunications responsibilities, the ethical code of the Health & Science Communications Association (2010) may apply. The MLA code is also found on the **accompanying CD-ROM**.

Creating Teams

To accomplish certain library goals, teams may need to be established. Ideally, these working groups should be large enough to handle their tasks but small enough to effectively interact on a regular basis. The group may be called a committee or a task force or a team but, in any case, it will have a purpose to be achieved through the pooled efforts and individual skills of its members. The purpose of a team may be accomplishing a one-time task such as creating promotional activities for National Medical Librarians Month or an ongoing task such as producing the library newsletter.

When selecting members, those chosen should "have some relationship with the purpose of the team. They should be able to contribute something unique, either by knowing the system under review or having skills the team needs to do the review" (Dudden, 2007: 382).

Teams do not automatically perform well. Dysfunctions described in *Crash Course in Library Supervision* include the following:

- Absence of trust
- Fear of conflict
- Lack of commitment
- Avoidance of accountability
- Inattention to results

Any one of these five problems can prevent a team from working together and accomplishing their goals (Tucker and Mosley, 2008). Team members must each feel that they are respected and that they can offer their opinions. The section that follows on motivating individual employees applies to teams, as well.

> Clearly, many library staff members work in teams already. In the future, library staff will very likely work predominantly in teams with other staff, other information professionals, faculty, and library clientele. Why are teams so important in today's health sciences library? Library work has become more complex, requiring expertise in multiple areas. Teams provide opportunities for increased collaboration among experts from functional areas of the library and, in some cases, will include expertise from outside the library as well. (Jenkins, 2000: 44)

Motivating Staff

> To foster a collaborative, inclusive environment where library staff members are working with one another toward the greater good rather than individually competing with one another for individual success, one must build an atmosphere of trust, mutual respect, and effective, two-way communication.

Staff members' individual strengths should be utilized to accomplish organizational goals and objectives. Differences

---

Figure 5.3. Code of Ethics for Health Sciences Librarianship

Goals and Principles for Ethical Conduct

The health sciences librarian believes that knowledge is the sine qua non of informed decisions in health care, education, and research and the health sciences librarian serves society, clients, and the institution, by working to ensure that informed decisions can be made. The principles of this code are expressed in broad statements to guide ethical decision making. These statements provide a framework; they cannot and do not dictate conduct to cover particular situations.

Society	■ The health sciences librarian promotes access to health information for all and creates and maintains conditions of freedom of inquiry, thought, and expression that facilitate informed health care decisions.
Clients	■ The health sciences librarian works without prejudice to meet the client's information needs. ■ The health sciences librarian respects the privacy of clients and protects the confidentiality of the client relationship. ■ The health sciences librarian ensures that the best available information is provided to the client.
Institution	■ The health sciences librarian provides leadership and expertise in the design, development, and ethical management of knowledge-based information systems that meet the information needs and obligations of the institution.
Profession	■ The health sciences librarian advances and upholds the philosophy and ideals of the profession. ■ The health sciences librarian advocates and advances the knowledge and standards of the profession. ■ The health sciences librarian conducts all professional relationships with courtesy and respect. ■ The health sciences librarian maintains high standards of professional integrity.
Self	■ The health sciences librarian assumes personal responsibility for developing and maintaining professional excellence. ■ The health sciences librarian shall be alert to and adhere to his or her institution's code of ethics and its conflict of interest, disclosure, and gift policies.

Source: Medical Library Association, 2010. Used with permission.

---

among library employees should be celebrated to capitalize on their talents rather than trying to make everyone conform (Jones, 1997). Well-managed diversity results in better problem solving, increased creativity, and innovation. (Giesecke and McNeil, 2010).

Elements necessary to creating this environment include the following:

- Nonthreatening behavior among all staff, i.e., no tolerance of disrespect or of inappropriate humor
- Communicating with everyone, asking for and listening to employee input, informing employees how decisions were made
- Giving credit to others

Help employees to set achievable goals so that they can succeed. Success is a great motivator (Trotta, 2006).

Creating a sense of camaraderie can also be a motivator. Celebrating special occasions such as birthdays and holidays is one way to make staff members feel a part of the whole. However, this cheery environment does not mean that work standards or performance expectations are lower. In fact, if one employee is not pulling his weight, morale may be low for other employees who feel that this situation is unfair. Sometimes, peer pressure can be a motivator for lagging employees to perform up to standard (Tucker and Mosley, 2008). Rewarding employees (see the next section) is another motivational tool.

Rewarding Employees

Monetary rewards are ideal. If the organization has a mechanism for raises based on merit, this is a very good way to use the annual employee evaluation to reward excellent performance. Some institutions may also offer cash bonuses for special contributions that employees have made. If so, participating in such a program is well worth the paperwork involved for library management.

Figure 5.4. Code of Ethics of the American Library Association

As members of the American Library Association, we recognize the importance of codifying and making known to the profession and to the general public the ethical principles that guide the work of librarians, other professionals providing information services, library trustees and library staffs.

Ethical dilemmas occur when values are in conflict. The American Library Association Code of Ethics states the values to which we are committed, and embodies the ethical responsibilities of the profession in this changing information environment.

We significantly influence or control the selection, organization, preservation, and dissemination of information. In a political system grounded in an informed citizenry, we are members of a profession explicitly committed to intellectual freedom and the freedom of access to information. We have a special obligation to ensure the free flow of information and ideas to present and future generations.

The principles of this Code are expressed in broad statements to guide ethical decision making. These statements provide a framework; they cannot and do not dictate conduct to cover particular situations.

   I. We provide the highest level of service to all library users through appropriate and usefully organized resources; equitable service policies; equitable access; and accurate, unbiased, and courteous responses to all requests.

  II. We uphold the principles of intellectual freedom and resist all efforts to censor library resources.

 III. We protect each library user's right to privacy and confidentiality with respect to information sought or received and resources consulted, borrowed, acquired or transmitted.

  IV. We respect intellectual property rights and advocate balance between the interests of information users and rights holders.

   V. We treat co-workers and other colleagues with respect, fairness, and good faith, and advocate conditions of employment that safeguard the rights and welfare of all employees of our institutions.

  VI. We do not advance private interests at the expense of library users, colleagues, or our employing institutions.

 VII. We distinguish between our personal convictions and professional duties and do not allow our personal beliefs to interfere with fair representation of the aims of our institutions or the provision of access to their information resources.

VIII. We strive for excellence in the profession by maintaining and enhancing our own knowledge and skills, by encouraging the professional development of coworkers, and by fostering the aspirations of potential members of the profession.

Source: American Library Association, 2008. Adopted June 28, 1997, by the ALA Council; amended January 22, 2008. Used with permission.

A number of nonmonetary options are available for rewarding library staff members. These rewards may be part of overall institutional recognition programs or just within the library. For example, some health care institutions have an employee of the month program that involves public recognition as well as perquisites, such as a prized parking spot for the month. The recognition might involve having one's picture posted in a prominent location, having one's name prominently displayed, being profiled in an institutional newsletter, and/or a formal presentation from top management. HR may allow rewarding employees with specified periods of time off with pay. Within the library, celebrations may be held for noteworthy achievements or completion of special projects. If the whole staff has been involved in a major effort such as packing up the collection for recarpeting, appreciation may be expressed with a celebratory coffee break or a meal. Rewards may be individualized, such as gift certificates to stores or restaurants that the recipient is known to favor.

One aspect of rewarding employees individually is taking into account their respective generations: veterans/traditionalists, baby boomers, generation X, or generation Y/millennials/nexters. Different age groups may have different perspectives on what they consider a reward (Giesecke and McNeil, 2010).

The library newsletter or website can be used to highlight and publicize the achievements of staff members to the whole institution. Examples of items that might be featured are professional awards, elected offices in associations, publications, speaking engagements, or even quotes from the letters of satisfied customers.

Legal Issues

In addition to the laws mentioned under Recruiting and Hiring, there are legal issues to consider in dealing with employees on a day-to-day basis. The Fair Labor Standards Act (FLSA) "establishes minimum wage, overtime pay, recordkeeping, and youth employment standards affecting employees in the private sector and in Federal, State, and local governments. Covered nonexempt workers are entitled to a minimum wage of not less than $7.25 per hour effective July 24, 2009. Overtime pay at a rate not less than one and one-half times the regular rate of pay is required after 40 hours of work in a workweek" (United States Department of Labor, 2010a). Guidance on determining who is exempt or nonexempt may be found at the United States Department of Labor's *elaws—Fair Labor Standards Act Advisor* (United States Department of Labor, 2010b). In general, salaried and supervisory employees are exempt. In organizations covered by FLSA, one must take care not to ask nonexempt employees to work overtime unless they are paid according to FLSA (Giesecke and McNeil, 2010).

The Family and Medical Leave Act (FMLA) allows an eligible employee to take up to 12 weeks of unpaid leave for conditions as specified in the Act. Basically, an employee may use this type of leave for a serious medical condition for himself or applicable family member or the birth/adoption of a child. For answers to questions about which employers are covered, what makes an employee eligible, and the purposes for which this leave may be taken see *Fact Sheet #28: The Family and Medical Leave Act of 1993* (United States Department of Labor, 2010c). In 2008, FMLA was amended by the National Defense Authorization Act to add specific leave entitlements for military families (United States Department of Labor, 2010d).

To avoid legal problems regarding treatment of employees, the library manager must be aware of any situations that could potentially involve complaints of discrimination or harassment. As mentioned earlier, do not tolerate staff members treating one another with disrespect. As a library manager, treat employees fairly. Communicate clearly to them on matters regarding promotions, merit raises, and evaluations. If anticipating displeasure with a decision, be prepared with documentation to support that decision.

Conflict Management

When bringing the conflicting parties together, do not show favoritism or bias. Ask for the facts and define the problem. Work with the employees to find an acceptable resolution. Put the plan in writing, and then follow up periodically. If necessary, bring in a mediator (Stanley, 2008). A particularly insidious form of conflict is known as mobbing, whereby a co-worker is targeted and shut off from others with the aim of forcing that person out of the organization. "The most important step an organization can take to prevent mobbing is to put in place mechanisms for resolving conflict" (Leiding, 2010: 366).

Even the best-run organizations experience conflicts among staff members at times. If disputes can be managed at an early stage, this intervention can prevent more serious consequences.

Retaining Employees/Preventing Burnout

A manager cannot prevent all good employees from leaving. There will always be legitimate reasons why staff members resign: moving to another institution for a position of higher responsibility, moving to be with a spouse, retiring, leaving the workplace temporarily to rear children or care for an aging parent, etc. However, action can be taken on a regular basis to retain good employees and to prevent their leaving for a reason such as job dissatisfaction. Elsewhere in this chapter, motivation and reward are discussed; these are factors involved in retaining good employees. Preventing burnout is another factor. When employees are unclear about their roles or what is expected of them, they become frustrated. If their workload is too heavy or too difficult for a sustained period, the strain can cause burnout. The library manager has control over these types of factors and should be alert to them in order to correct them and prevent burnout (Jones, 1997).

When losing employees to retirement, one may retain knowledge on the staff by allowing retirees to return periodically through retainer contracts or to continue on a part-time basis. They can enjoy their supplementary income while providing knowledge transfer to younger staff members (McKinlay and Williamson, 2010).

Performance Evaluation

Many employees and supervisors alike dread performance appraisals. Most institutions require some sort of employee evaluation on a scheduled basis. Library managers should keep lines of communication open so that they are aware of the day-to-day performance of library employees not under their direct supervision. The library manager should talk to any employee who seems to be having a problem so that the issue can be corrected as soon as possible, rather than waiting until the end of an evaluation period. Likewise, the manager should praise an employee who has just completed a project or consistently done outstanding work instead of waiting until it is time to complete an appraisal form.

> The most effective kind of evaluation is ongoing, whereby library staff members receive constant feedback about their performance—guidance when they are going astray, praise when they are doing well.

Performance standards should be in place so that employees know what is expected of them. If changes occur, they should be communicated. When it is time for an annual evaluation, the employee's performance is reviewed based on those standards. The organization's procedures must be followed regarding the timeframe and filing of these evaluations. If there have been problems during the year, they should have been addressed at the time they occurred.

Since libraries are dynamic organizations and change is a constant, the performance standards will need to be updated to keep up with changes. The performance evaluation presents an opportunity to update the performance indicators for a position, i.e., to keep up with how the position is evolving. The expectations documented on the performance plan should be measurable and achievable (Brophy, 2006).

Performance Problems

When a problem with employee performance comes to light, it should be addressed as soon as possible. All the facts must be in hand before meeting with the employee. At the meeting, the problem is clearly stated and the employee is asked for his or her perspective on the situation. The library manager ensures that the person has the resources needed to correct the problem and understands what is expected. A plan for improvement should be developed followed up by a meeting at a later date to discuss whether or not the problem has been resolved. If the employee is now meeting expectations, the issue has successfully been addressed. If the problem continues, discipline may be necessary.

Many institutions have procedures in place for employee discipline. These procedures may vary from one organization to another, but they will all involve clearly communicating with the employee and documenting the communication. The employee must know what to expect if behavior does not improve. There will usually be a requirement to document it in writing and to give the employee a copy. Written communication should include a description of the problem, the corrective action needed, the date by which the problem should be corrected, and notification of the employee's right to respond (Tucker and Mosley, 2008). Ideally, the employee's performance will improve with guidance. However, if the problem continues, the library manager must decide if the performance issue is of enough significance to fire the employee. If not, the problem can be noted on formal evaluations and may result in the employee not receiving raises or being considered for promotion.

Communication should continue regarding the need for improvement. If the issue is significant enough to fire the employee, the institution's procedures must be followed regarding the termination process. If an employee is disciplined or threatened with termination, he or she may request union representation if applicable.

If the problem is related to violence in the workplace or theft, there may be an option to place the employee on administrative leave. If so, the employee will need to be informed in writing about the dates of administrative leave and the status of pay during this leave (Tucker and Mosley, 2008).

Performance problems can affect the morale of other library employees. If one employee regularly appears to "get away with" poor performance, such as habitually coming in very late, not producing at the level of other staff members, having lengthy, unaccounted-for disappearances during the workday, or being impolite to clients, this behavior can have a detrimental effect on the whole staff. While counseling of an employee should be done privately, the staff should be able to see that library management is addressing the problem and working to correct it. Management in Action 5.1 is an example of this.

Unions

Labor unions exist in many health care organizations. Except in those institutions where librarians have faculty status and may be members of the American Association of University Professors, health sciences librarians generally do not belong to unions. They usually opt to belong to professional associations that advocate for them, but not as collective bargaining agents. However, library support staff may be members of unions. In

MANAGEMENT IN ACTION 5.1

A Hostile Environment—No Joking Matter

Location: Metropolitan Teaching Hospital

Description of Problem/Project: Janet DuBois has been sending joke e-mails to the library staff excluding the library manager, Bob Smith. Recently, there has been a thread centered around obese people. Tom Julien, an overweight member of the staff, has printed out the e-mails and presented them to the library manager saying that he believes they are offensive and are creating a hostile environment. He wants to know what the library manager is going to do about the situation.

Impact On: Employee morale and ability to work as a team.

People Involved: The employee sending the e-mails and the employee who is offended by the e-mails are the principal players, but the whole staff is involved to an extent and, of course, the manager must address the problem.

Strategies for Success: The first question is whether joke (or any nonbusiness) e-mails are even allowed, offensive or not. If not allowed, the manager can simply send an e-mail to the whole staff reminding them of the policy against using work computers and the institutional e-mail system to send jokes to one another. A reminder may also be verbally offered at a staff meeting where people may ask questions and all are present for the responses. Staff can be reminded that nonadherence to the policy may result in disciplinary action.

If such usage of the e-mail system is allowed within reason as long as people are getting their work done, resolution is more difficult. In this case, the manager needs to speak privately to Janet DuBois to let her know that the jokes she has been sending are offensive to other staff members. Ms. DuBois should be given an opportunity to respond. This response may be that she had no idea she was offending anyone and that she is sorry, or her response may reveal that the complainant had sent jokes himself that disparaged people of her race. In the latter case, the problem is bigger than it originally seemed to be. It requires another conversation with Tom Julien and communication to the whole staff regarding no tolerance for offensive humor. Another action to consider would be some training from Human Resources on what constitutes a hostile work environment.

Strategies involve:

1. determining scope of the problem (whether offense was intended, or whether a history of hostility exists between these two employees);

2. getting both sides of the story;

3. adhering to and enforcing policy;

4. private communication with the offender(s);

5. communication with the whole staff regarding respect for one another and no tolerance of offensive use of humor; and

6. communication that future occurrences will result in disciplinary action. (They could also result in EEO [Equal Employment Opportunity] complaints, which would require arbitration beyond the library.)

Barriers Encountered: Possible barriers to getting to the bottom of the problem and resolving it could include not getting full information about the sequence of the events as perceived by both of the named people.

Take-Home Points: The manager, Bob Smith, should not sweep the problem under the rug, nor should he escalate it. He must maintain a careful balance in highlighting the benefits of respecting one another and working as a team, while making clear that there is no place for humor that can be interpreted as offensive to a particular group of people.

some institutions, even if no library employees are union members, the library manager must be aware of union agreements that affect library operations, such as prior approval of employee surveys.

If any library employees are union members, the library manager must be aware of union regulations that protect these employees.

Staff Safety and Ergonomics

The Occupational Safety and Health Act of 1970 requires that employees be provided with a safe workplace. Library managers are responsible for seeing that the library is free from hazards (Tucker and Mosley, 2008). Staff members should receive training on safe use of library equipment and proper methods of reaching high and low, lifting boxes of books, loading book trucks, etc. When an incident does occur, the manager and supervisors should be aware of institutional regulations for reporting such incidents and seeing that the employee receives proper evaluation and care by occupational health personnel or whomever the institution specifies.

Well-being of library employees is also related to ergonomic conditions. Many health care organizations have experts who can evaluate work areas and make recommendations for improvements that will have healthy effects on employees' eyes, muscles, and joints. Adjustments can often be made rather inexpensively and are worth the investment to prevent eyestrain, back strain, and repetitive motion injuries.

Another aspect of creating a safe environment goes beyond providing a hazard-free facility. Managers must be aware of the potential for workplace violence and educate employees about its prevention as well as what to do when actually threatened. Menacing behavior can originate from a number of sources, whether a disgruntled employee, an unhappy boyfriend or an angry patient. While violence cannot always be prevented, measures can be taken such as conducting careful screening when hiring, teaching employees to be alert to warning signs and training them on the actions to take (or refrain from) when faced with a potentially violent situation (Stanley, 2008).

Staff Development

Continuing Education

Staff members, both clerical and professional, will need training and education from time to time in order to perform their duties and update their skills and knowledge. In hospital settings, The Joint Commission HR standards require ongoing education and training with documentation of that training (Joint Commission, 2010). One of the recommendations from MLA is that employers of health sciences librarians "place a high priority on staff development" (Medical Library Association, 2007: 6). Technologies are constantly changing and usually involve learning curves for those who must employ them.

Training may take a number of forms: in-house and in person by an experienced staff member, an outside trainer brought in to teach staff, an online tutorial, an instruction manual or DVD, or an off-site class. A cost-saving measure used by many institutions is training the trainer. One person attends a class and then comes back and teaches others on the staff what was learned.

Web-based training can also be cost saving. Even if a fee is involved, it may be less expensive than traveling to a training site. Whether someone local can train a staff member depends on the educational need. If training is needed regarding compliance with the Health Insurance Portability and Accountability Act (HIPAA) rule governing the privacy of protected health information, there will most likely be a person or program in the institution who can meet that need. However, if someone needs training on the technical aspects of a particular online catalog system, the employee may have to seek an external source.

Funding should be available for staff development. This funding may be part of the library's budget or the institution's budget. How this funding is allotted can vary from one institution to another. Sometimes, each staff member receives a predetermined amount of dollars for continuing education. In other cases, the library manager may allot funding wherever the training need is greatest.

One method of staff training is to have a staff-development day (Todaro and Smith, 2006). For this type of training, which involves most or all of the staff at once, the focus of the training should be something that affects all library employees, such as customer service or safety.

A common source of library-specific training is the professional organization. For health care libraries, the Medical Library Association (MLA) and its regional chapters both offer formal continuing education courses, as well as educational publications and many informal learning opportunities. Health care library staff members are fortunate that the federal government has established free training through the National Library of Medicine and its regional libraries in the National Network of Libraries of Medicine (NN/LM). The NN/LM regional libraries even have trainers who will travel to institutions and provide MLA-approved continuing education courses at no charge to the institutions or to the individuals enrolling in the courses. The NN/LM regional libraries also offer webinars that individuals can participate in from their desktops. For more general library education needs, organizations such as the American Library Association and the Special Libraries Association offer courses, as do regional, state, and local organizations. Vendors can be another source of training for their particular products. Courses offered by professional associations and the NN/LM usually include continuing education credits.

Some examples of continuing education modalities follow:

- Training within the library taught by an experienced employee
  Example: A librarian on the staff teaches a library technician how to use the library's online catalog system for circulation and tracking overdue items.

- Training within the library by an employee who recently received external training
  Example: An employee who attended a course off-campus on creating online tutorials with a particular software product teaches the other library employees how to use this product.

- An outside trainer brought in to teach the staff
  Example: An instructor from the regional NN/LM comes to the library to train the whole library staff (and other interested people) on writing grant applications.

- Self-directed instruction provided through a manual, an online tutorial, or DVD.
  Example: An employee learns about HIPAA regulations through an online tutorial posted on the institution's intranet.

- A webinar offered to organization members, database subscribers, or the public
  Example: A vendor offers a webinar on the new features of a database to which the library subscribes. Interested employees can access the webinar from their desktops.

- In-person training offered locally by the institution
  Example: Employees attend a safety training course offered to all employees.

- In-person training offered out of town by an organization, university, or vendor
  Example: A library employee takes a continuing education course at a conference sponsored by a professional organization on evidence-based medicine.

- Courses offered for academic credits
  Example: A librarian takes a course from a local university on biostatistics to help with teaching critical appraisal of the literature.

Mentoring/Coaching

Finally, mentoring those new to the profession can acquaint them with aspects of their jobs and further their careers in ways that training and continuing education courses cannot. Mentoring can range from the informal and brief to the highly structured and long-term (Kern, 2004). The library manager may serve as a mentor or may help a new health sciences librarian find a mentor. The Medical Library Association offers a mentoring program that is open to medical librarians who are just beginning their careers, as well as to those who are farther along (http://www.mlanet.org/mentor/index.html#tips). In addition, MLA offers special activities for new members or first-time attendees and pairs them with experienced members when they first attend an MLA meeting. Other organizations offer similar services.

Coaching is often a supervisor's role, paying attention to the needs of the staff member and tailoring the assistance provided in order to achieve desired outcomes. It involves helping employees to learn and to achieve their potential. Both mentors and coaches should lead by example and maintain high ethical standards (Trotta, 2006). A coach should do the following:

- Give advice as necessary.
- Hold back advice when experience would be a better teacher.
- Recognize when individuals have reached a developmental milestone.
- Recognize indirect offers for help.
- Provide encouragement.
- Provide admiration.
- Recognize when performance is not up to par and take appropriate measures.
- Support employees even when performance is at a lower than normal level.
- Help them recognize areas when they may be "stuck."
- Help them by setting limitations and deadlines and sticking to them. (Trotta, 2006: 101)

Professional Associations

Professional organizations, as mentioned in the training section, can be a wonderful resource for continuing education activities. In addition to the formal education courses they offer, these associations provide a number of informal opportunities for professional development through networking. This networking can take place at meetings, in committee tasks, in e-mail discussion lists, and on blogs or other Web 2.0 offerings. The relationships developed through these associations can be invaluable for health care organization librarians who depend on this colleague support. Furthermore, making presentations at association conferences can be a component of professional development. The organizations usually offer publications that also contribute to informal education and provide another venue for sharing of ideas, projects, experiences, and research. Several organizations of interest to health sciences librarians are listed in the appendix at the end of the chapter as well as on the **accompanying CD-ROM**. Regional, state, and local organizations can also offer opportunities for formal and informal development.

A unique professional development program for health sciences librarians is MLA's Academy of Health Information Professionals (AHIP). Membership in AHIP is sometimes mentioned in job ads as a preferred qualification, as it is an indication of professional commitment and achievement of a certain level of knowledge. The academy provides a structure for individualized professional development for health information professionals at all levels of experience (Medical Library Association, 2010a).

Conclusion

While people problems can be most frustrating, successfully and creatively solving these problems can be very rewarding.

Managing a health care organization library's human resources is an essential component of the library's overall administration. Selecting and developing a competent staff will help assure that the library meets and anticipates the needs of its customers. To successfully guide the staff, the library administrator must be ethical and fair, as well as knowledgeable about laws, rules, and human behavior.

References

Abels, Eileen, Rebecca Jones, John Latham, Dee Magnoni, Joanne Gard Marshall, and the Special Committee on Competencies for Special Librarians for the Special Libraries Association Board of Directors. 2003. *Competencies for Information Professionals of the 21st Century*, Revised ed. Special Libraries Association. Accessed July 25, 2010. http://www.sla.org/PDFs/Competencies2003_revised.pdf.

Allegri, Francesca, and Martha Bedard. 2008. "Management in Academic Health Sciences Libraries." In *Introduction to Health Sciences Librarianship*, edited by M. Sandra Wood, 301–340. Binghamton, NY: Haworth Press.

American Library Association. 2008. "Code of Ethics of the American Library Association." Chicago: ALA (Amended 2008). Accessed July 25, 2010. http://www.ala.org/ala/issues advocacy/proethics/codeofethics/codeethics.cfm.

Arthur, Diane. 2006. *Recruiting, Interviewing, Selecting & Orienting New Employees*. 4th ed. New York: AMACOM.

Brophy, Peter. 2006. *Measuring Library Performance: Principles and Techniques*. London: Facet.

Cohn, John M., and Ann L. Kelsey. 2005. *Staffing the Modern Library: A How-To-Do-It Manual*. How-To-Do-It Manuals, no. 137. New York: Neal-Schuman.

Dudden, Rosalind Farnam. 2007. *Using Benchmarking, Needs Assessment, Quality Improvement, Outcome Measurement, and Library Standards: A How-To-Do-It Manual with CD-ROM*. How-To-Do-It Manuals, no. 159. New York: Neal-Schuman.

Giesecke, Joan, and Beth McNeil. 2010. *Fundamentals of Library Supervision*. 2nd ed. Chicago: American Library Association.

Health & Science Communications Association. 2010. "Code of Ethics." Jewett City, CT: HeSCA. Accessed July 1. http://www.hesca.org/?page_id=67.

Hospital Libraries Section Standards Committee, Margaret Bandy, Jacqueline Donaldson Doyle, Anne Fladger, Katherine Stemmer Frumento, Linné Girouard, Sheila Hayes, and Diane Rourke. 2008. "Standards for Hospital Libraries 2007." *Journal of the Medical Library Association* 96, no. 2 (April): 162–169.

Jenkins, Carol. 2000. "Human Resources Management." In *Administration and Management in Health Sciences Libraries*, edited by Rick B. Forsman, 35–73. Vol. 8 of Current Practice in Health Sciences Librarianship. Lanham, MD: Scarecrow Press.

Joint Commission. 2010. *Comprehensive Accreditation Manual for Hospitals (CAMH): The Official Handbook*. Oakbrook Terrace, IL: Joint Commission Resources.

Jones, Dixie A. 1997. "Plays Well with Others, or the Importance of Collegiality within a Reference Unit." *The Reference Librarian* no. 59: 163–175.

Jones, Dixie A. 2008. "Management of and Issues Specific to Hospital Libraries." In *Introduction to Health Sciences Librarianship*, edited by M. Sandra Wood, 341–367. Binghamton, NY: Haworth Press.

Kern, Carol Ritzen. 2004. "Mentoring: A Primer." In *The Librarian's Career Guidebook*, edited by Priscilla K. Shontz, 463–472. Lanham, MD: Scarecrow Press.

Leiding, Reba. 2010. "Mobbing in the Library Workplace: What It Is and How to Prevent It." *College & Research Libraries News* 71, no. 7: 364–366, 384.

McDiarmid, Mary, and Ethel W. Auster. 2004. "Fewer Library Staff and More Volunteers or Vice Versa? Staffing in Ontario Hospital Libraries and Volunteer Use." *Journal of the Canadian Health Libraries Association (JCHLA) / Journal de l'Association des bibliothèques de la santé du Canada (JABSC)* 25: 39–43.

McKinlay, James, and Vicki Williamson. 2010. *The ART of People Management in Libraries: Tips for Managing Your Most Vital Resource*. Oxford, UK: Chandos Publishing.

Medical Library Association. 2007. *Competencies for Lifelong Learning and Professional Success: The Educational Policy Statement of the Medical Library Association.* Chicago: Medical Library Association. Accessed July 25, 2010. http://www.mlanet.org/education/policy/.

Medical Library Association. 2010a. "The Academy of Health Information Professionals." Chicago: Medical Library Association. Accessed July 25. http://www.mlanet.org/academy/.

Medical Library Association. 2010b. "Code of Ethics for Health Sciences Librarianship." Chicago: Medical Library Association. Accessed November 15. http://www.mlanet.org/about/ethics.html.

Scroggins, Cindy. 2004. "Library Management." In *The Librarian's Career Guidebook*, edited by Priscilla K. Shontz, 307–311. Lanham, MD: Scarecrow Press.

Stanley, Mary J. 2008. *Managing Library Employees: A How-To-Do-It Manual.* How-To-Do-It Manuals, no. 161. New York: Neal-Schuman.

Todaro, Julie Beth, and Mark L. Smith. 2006. *Training Library Staff and Volunteers to Provide Extraordinary Customer Service.* New York: Neal-Schuman.

Trotta, Marcia. 2006. *Supervising Staff: A How-To-Do-It Manual for Librarians.* How-To-Do-It Manuals, no. 141. New York: Neal-Schuman.

Tucker, Dennis C., and Shelley Elizabeth Mosley. 2008. *Crash Course in Library Supervision: Meeting the Key Players.* Crash Course Series. Westport, CT: Libraries Unlimited.

United States Department of Labor. 2010a. "Compliance Assistance—Fair Labor Standards Act (FLSA)." Washington, DC: United States Department of Labor. Accessed July 25. http://www.dol.gov/whd/Flsa/index.htm.

United States Department of Labor. 2010b. "elaws—Fair Labor Standards Act Advisor." Washington, DC: United States Department of Labor. Accessed July 25. http://www.dol.gov/elaws/esa/flsa/scope/screen9.asp.

United States Department of Labor. 2010c. "Fact Sheet #28: The Family and Medical Leave Act of 1993." Washington, DC: United States Department of Labor. Accessed July 25. http://www.dol.gov/whd/regs/compliance/whdfs28.pdf.

United States Department of Labor. 2010d. "Fact Sheet #28A: The Family and Medical Leave Act Military Family Leave Entitlements." Washington, DC: United States Department of Labor. Accessed July 25. http://www.dol.gov/whd/regs/compliance/whdfs28a.pdf.

Appendix: Selected Associations of Interest to Health Care Librarians

All of these organizations offer publications to their members, some of which are provided as benefits of membership and others which must be purchased separately.

American Hospital Association (AHA)
One North Franklin
Chicago, IL 60606-3421
(312) 422-3000
http://www.aha.org

> The American Hospital Association (AHA) provides education for health care leaders and is a source of information on health care issues and trends. The AHA is the national organization that represents and serves all types of hospitals, health care networks, and their patients and communities. The AHA Resource Center provides document delivery to libraries.

American Library Association (ALA)
50 E. Huron
Chicago, IL 60611
(800) 545-2433
http://www.ala.org/

> The American Library Association promotes library service and librarianship and has many offerings in a number of areas of interest, such as diversity, library management, ethics, collection development, reference service and literacy. The Office for Human Resource Development & Recruitment (HRDR) is a source of information for guidance on human resource issues.

American Medical Informatics Association (AMIA)
4915 St. Elmo Avenue, Suite 401
Bethesda, MD 20814
Phone: 301-657-1291
http://www.amia.org/

> AMIA is dedicated to promoting the effective organization, analysis, management, and use of information in health care in support of patient care, public health, teaching, research, administration, and related policy. Membership includes a diverse representation of several health-related professions.

Health & Science Communications Association (HeSCA)
39 Wedgewood Drive, Suite A
Jewett City, CT 06351
(860) 376-5915
http://www.hesca.org/

> The mission of HeSCA is to advance an international community of professionals dedicated to promoting excellence in health and science communications through leadership, education, and the application of technology. HeSCA's Libraries and Learning Resources Centers Special Interest Group encourages utilization of print and nonprint education materials, provides training on and assistance with software and nonprint materials, and promotes the informational and educational roles of libraries and learning resource centers.

Medical Library Association (MLA)
65 E. Wacker Place, Suite 1900
Chicago, IL 60601

(312) 419-9094

http://www.mlanet.org/

MLA is the premiere organization for health sciences librarians. MLA provides lifelong educational opportunities, supports a knowledgebase of health information research, and works with a global network of partners to promote the importance of quality information for improved health to the health care community and the public. Many units of MLA are relevant to the interests and work of health care organization librarians, but the most pertinent is the Hospital Libraries Section. The Academy of Health Information Professionals is MLA's peer-reviewed professional development and career recognition program.

Special Libraries Association (SLA)

331 South Patrick Street

Alexandria, VA 22314

(703) 647-4900

http://www.sla.org/

The Special Libraries Association is an international association representing the interests of thousands of information professionals in over eighty countries worldwide. The division of most interest to health sciences librarians is the Biomedical and Life Sciences Division which includes a Medical Section. SLA promotes and strengthens its members through learning, advocacy, and networking initiatives.

6

Evaluation and Improvement Management

Rosalind Farnam Dudden

An essential part of library management is to evaluate library processes and services. Whether the librarian is starting a new library or taking over an existing one, the goal is for the services to meet customer needs and processes to be of the highest quality. They need to be economical, efficient, and effective. The effective library is one that meets the needs of its users in the most cost- and time-efficient way. Strategic planning and planning theory are reviewed in Chapter 3 and will set the library manager on the path to quality, but as part of planning one must build in evaluation and assessment. When discussing measurement, assessment, and evaluation, the end results are to create quality services that have positive outcomes and impacts on the life and work of the customer, and to show the value or benefit or worth of professional library services managed by professional librarians. The terms that are used in this area of study can be misunderstood.

Recommended definitions include these:

- Measurement: The process of ascertaining the extent or dimensions or quantity of something.
- Performance: The doing of something, an activity.
- Evaluation: Assigning merit, value, or worth to the findings. The process of determining whether something is what the evaluator wants it to be.
- Effective: Something that does well what it is supposed to do.
- Assessment: The gathering of meaningful or purposeful data that will provide information that informs, improves, or confirms.
- Value: The importance or preciousness of something, the perception of actual or potential benefit.
- Benefit: The helpful or useful effect that something has.
- Worth: The quality that makes something desirable or valuable or useful.
- Outcome: The consequence, visible or practical result, or effect of an event or activity.
- Impact: The effect or influence of one person, thing, or action, on another.
- Library Outcomes: The eventual result of using library services, the influence the use had, and its significance to the user. (Lee-Thomas and Robson, 2004; Poll, 2003)

Placing some of these words in a sentence shows how they can differ:

The results of *measurement* can be used to *evaluate* the *performance* of a library and thereby determine whether or not it is *effective*. (Calvert, 1994: 17)

Several initiatives, such as the following, will help the librarian set up systems to accomplish meaningful evaluation in the library:

- Communicating value and worth
- Culture of assessment
- Quality improvement and a culture of quality
- Evidence-based library and information practice
- The logic model

After discussing these concepts that help the library manager plan an evaluation program, this chapter includes overviews on planning an evaluation project, choices on what to measure: needs, inputs, quality processes, outputs, quality service, outcomes, and impacts; on methods of evaluation: needs assessment, quality improvement, benchmarking, standards and outcomes; and tools to use in measurement: focus groups, interviews, surveys and observation. Following this, some special considerations will be discussed briefly such as record keeping systems, reporting and communicating, e-measurement, LibQUAL+, return on investment, and other systems of quality management. More details about all of these topics can be found in *Using Benchmarking, Needs Assessment, Quality Improvement, Outcome Measurement, and Library Standards: A How-To-Do-It Manual* (Dudden, 2007), as well as extensive references and web resources.

Communicating Value and Worth

Librarians know that information has value. When an evaluation program has been established in the library, the results should show this value in ways independent of the librarian's judgment. The librarian then needs to learn how to communicate this revealed value. Reporting strategies for communication with upper management are part of any evaluation program. Good communication will bring about collaboration with key members of the institution to build joint ownership over the improvement of the library system.

The word "value" has many meanings, and it is important to understand how it is being used. Nuances can lead to misunderstanding as well as help shape the wording of a communication. Value can refer to an ideal, a quality, a high regard, or a judgment of worth. Definitions for value and benefit, outcome and impact, and library outcomes are listed previously. One type of value is the impact of health care library services on the care of the patient and the outcome of that care. This has been studied and the "results suggest clear evidence of an impact of library services on patient outcomes from both traditional and clinical librarian services" (Weightman and Williamson, 2005: 7). This impact can be expressed as value.

The higher quality traditional library studies suggest effects of impacts of between

- 37 and 97% on general patient care,
- 10–31% on diagnosis,
- 20–51% on choice of tests,
- 27–45% on choice of therapy and
- 10–19% on reduced length of stay (Weightman and Williamson, 2005: 7)

Joanne Gard Marshall has conducted research in many of these areas and gives an overview of the issues in her publication "Determining Our Worth, Communicating Our Value" (Marshall, 2000). Outcomes and impacts in two Marshall studies suggest that information provided by the librarian enabled managers and employees in business and government to do the following:

- Have the ability to proceed
- Make a decision
- Create new opportunity
- Save time
- Save money
- Meet a deadline
- Deal with an emergency
- Improve a policy, procedure or plan
- Lessen conflict
- Save time and resources (Marshall, 1993, 1999, 2000)

These examples are from major studies found in the literature. One strategy of showing value is to be aware of new studies and bring them to the attention of the administration. Using the ideas of experts Urquhart and Hepworth (1995) and Abels, Cogdill, and Zach (2004), Cuddy tied together the ideas from two studies to produce a new study at her library (Cuddy, 2005). Using a value question from the Urquhart critical incident study, Cuddy classified the results using the taxonomy of library and information science contributions in hospital and academic health centers developed in the Abels study. The question is simple enough for anyone to make a comment and the results can also be used as anecdotes in other reports:

> We like to continuously validate and keep records of the contributions that the Health Sciences Library makes to the hospital and/or patient care. Can you please take a moment and write how the information you received helped yourself and ultimately the hospital? (Cuddy, 2005: 447)

Initiatives such as the Medical Library Association's Vital Pathways project can help communicate value statements and data by providing PowerPoint presentations and brochures that can be edited for local use (Medical Library Association, 2006). It adopts the communication technique developed by the Public Library Association's Counting on Results Project called *Numbers You Can Use*, as reported by Steffen, Lance, and Logan (Steffen and Lance, 2002; Steffen, Lance, and Logan, 2002). The method has a three-part focus:

1. Reporting the facts, i.e., statistics from evaluation projects
2. Listing the sources of those facts
3. Telling the library's story using stories and quotes gathered in local outcomes studies

These same three elements can anchor a library annual report. Even if not asked for one, an annual report can inform the administration about the library. There are several examples of annual reports on the **accompanying CD-ROM** in the Chapter 3 section. The purposes of an annual report are as follows:

- Communicate activities and accomplishments from the past year
- Show the administration that the budget is being well spent
- Educate stakeholders about the library
- Recognize users and/or staff
- Serve as a historical record of library activity

A recent report from the United Kingdom recommends a planning pathway for conducting an impact survey of a library service. Techniques such as critical incident questionnaires, brief questionnaires, using independent researchers to reduce bias, personalizing requests, assuring confidentiality, giving small incentives, having prize drawings, and using follow-up reminders are described and recommended (Weightman et al., 2009).

While the concepts of value, worth, and impact are complicated, the library manager is encouraged to always be thinking about value when communicating the results of evaluation projects. Having a library service is no longer viewed as a traditional essential good. When deciding on budgets for a huge enterprise, the decision makers need to know that the library service does add value to their enterprise. If the library manager doesn't tell them, who will?

Culture of Assessment

During library planning, the librarian should consider adopting what is described as a culture of assessment. This is an initiative of the Association of Research Libraries, as described by Hiller, Kyrillidou, and Self (2006), but can be scaled and applied to all types of libraries. A culture of assessment "can only be achieved by creating systems and structures that are based on continuous assessment and evaluation. Libraries and librarians have to create organizational cultures that are customer focused and use assessment systematically" (Lakos, 2004). This approach will help the practicing librarian manage an effective library by:

- establishing a culture of assessment;
- basing decisions on facts, research, and analysis;
- being customer focused;
- having an organizational mission, as well as values, structures, and systems that are performance and learning focused; and
- communicating the library's effectiveness to the administration. (Lakos and Phipps, 2004)

A culture of assessment requires changing the organizational environment of a library and becoming a "learning and listening organization." What the library measures and how the measurement is conducted also changes. The new measures of library effectiveness are not compatible with the structure and culture of traditional internally focused organizations. The library must become "an acting organization—experimenting, seeking new perspectives and new methodologies, and designing new organizational systems that involve, engage, develop, and increase the commitment of staff and partner with customers to design the future they need that includes library values and visions" (Phipps, 2001: 657).

The components of a culture of assessment include two main parts, management and support as shown in the sidebar. While it is not possible to detail all these parts of a culture of assessment, reviewing the literature cited will give the librarian insight into what this important initiative means in the field of assessment and evaluation.

Management:
1. External focus is used for planning
2. Performance measures are a part of organizational planning
3. Leadership is committed and supportive of assessment
4. Value of assessment recognized by staff
5. Relevant data is routinely collected and used

Support:
6. Assessment is supported by computer systems
7. All activities are evaluated
8. Continuous improvement is supported and rewarded
9. Staff is rewarded for the application of new learning
10. Ongoing staff development is provided and supported
11. Critical processes and established measures of success are defined
12. Individuals have customer-focused SMART (Specific, Measurable, Attainable, Realistic, and Timely) goals

Quality Improvement and Organizational Characteristics for Quality Success

The third evaluation initiative, which has been in use since the 1980s under various names, is based on a simple proposition: quality is a result of a finely tuned process. Not so revolutionary today, the search for quality is now part of most institutional cultures. Whether called total quality management (TQM), continuous quality improvement (CQI), quality improvement (QI) or a culture of quality, the program has to do with *when* one measures for quality and *how* one achieves quality. While it shares many organizational characteristics as the culture of assessment, the emphasis is on the search for quality rather than establishing systems of assessment. The two systems compliment each other and could be instituted together. QI was the content of the excellent evaluation chapter in the first edition of this book, some of which is included here (Mein, 2000).

Quality improvement is a philosophy that has transformed industry and health care since the 1980s. The Joint Commission on Accreditation of Healthcare Organizations (JCAHO), now known as The Joint Commission (TJC) (http://www.jointcommission.org), has long supported the quality improvement movement in the health care field by encouraging organizations to review operations from a process perspective rather than a departmental perspective. They encourage studying work processes with the purpose of improving each one and eventually improving the overall delivery of health care.

TJC's philosophy on quality improvement has matured to the point where institutions are expected to document improvements in patient care outcomes and hospital efficiencies gained through the quality improvement programs. The present emphasis of TJC is supporting the development of evidence-based and meaningful performance measures, sound statistical and analytical approaches to data analysis, and the identification of performance improvement and patient safety strategies.

The goal of continuous quality improvement is to study work processes, to make them more effective and more responsive to the needs of the customer. This is a major part of existing library practice in health care settings, where needs assessments and customer satisfaction surveys are common. Quality improvement programs provide health care librarians with powerful tools to accomplish long-held goals by:

- focusing the whole organization on quality;
- placing value on decision making which is driven by data; and
- presenting a crucial need for information about work processes inside the organization as well as the work processes of other organizations for comparative purposes.

The chapter by Mein in the first edition of this book is recommended as an excellent overview of the historical background of the quality movement (Mein, 2000). In studying the various leaders and different names that have been used to describe quality improvement, the major themes or principles remain the same and are listed in the sidebar.

There are many quality programs that the top management might choose to implement based on specific theories, such as Gemba visits, Kaizen, Lean, the Five Ss, the Learning Organization, Six Sigma, or the Balanced Scorecard. All of these programs have the same kinds of organizational characteristics such as described in Figure 6.1. One can find information on these programs on the Internet. The library can be part of the process by providing information not only on the process but also providing information to other managers as they work on their quality projects.

David Orenstein, in his article, "Developing Quality Managers and Quality Management: The Challenge to Leadership in Library Organizations," lists 11 ways to motivate the library to adopt a quality culture, a culture

- *Organization Commitment.* The whole organization, including top administration and every worker, must be committed to continuous improvement of work processes. When quality improvement programs are implemented, organizations develop extensive training programs in quality improvement and in team skills to support the process.

- *Process Focus.* When improving work problems, the focus is on the work process and not on employee performance. The view is that ineffective processes cause problems, not problem employees.

- *Employee Involvement.* Employees are an integral part of the procedure used to change processes. It is considered important to involve employees directly in improvement efforts because they are most familiar with work processes and possess valuable knowledge about how the processes can be improved.

- *Customer Mindedness.* Organizations that are focused on quality improvement go beyond "customer feedback" to involve customers in the design of work processes and services to ensure their needs are met. The definition of customer is also broadened to include internal customers, that is, other departments and individuals within the hospital, as well as external customers, or patients.

- *Learning Organization.* The leadership of quality-focused organizations seeks to establish an environment where new ideas, learning, and innovation are welcomed.

- *Data Driven.* Statistical tools are used throughout the quality improvement process to provide information and analysis based on fact rather than hunches, beliefs, or intuition.

that "considers service issues, people, and challenges as simultaneous and interconnected concerns" (Orenstein, 1999: 44). His insightful article gives many practical tips on how to accomplish these management ideas. The methodology chosen, or that which is chosen by the company, will work well only in a supportive management environment such as the one described by Mein (Mein, 2000) and by Orenstein (Orenstein, 1999). In Figure 6.1, Orenstein's recommendations are placed side-by-side with the corresponding characteristics for quality success discussed here.

Evidence-Based Library and Information Practice

The initiative called evidence-based library and information practice (EBLIP), which also involves critical appraisal of research articles, will help educate the library manager

Figure 6.1. Characteristics for Quality Success

Orenstein's Eleven Ways of Looking at TQM (Orenstein, 1999)	Organizational Characteristics for Quality Success (Mein, 2000: 63–66)
1. Build a shared vision for the library	Mission and vision for the Health Care Organization
2. Put the needs of the customers before the politics of the organization	
3. Build cooperation among all levels of employees	Collaborative approach to problem solving
4. Communicate	
5. Emphasize teamwork	Empowerment of all levels of staff
6. Build trust	
7. Redesign processes and attitudes	
8. Train for quality	Employee education and training
9. Develop leadership skills	Executive leadership of the quality improvement
10. Manage by fact	Information systems available to provide data
11. Motivate staff by making work enjoyable	Reward, recognition and celebration

Source: Dudden, 2007. Used with permission of Rosalind F. Dudden.

on how to manage by fact (Booth and Brice, 2004). Improving the quality of library and information services through research, or searching for the evidence, was one of the main goals of the International Evidence-Based Library and Information Practice (IEBLIP) Conferences. The fifth conference was in 2009 in Stockholm and lists all previous conferences (5th International Evidence-Based Library & Information Practice Conference, 2009). Most of the conferences post the presentations. Evidence-based library and information practice involves applying results from rigorous research studies to professional practice to improve the quality of services to customers. It encourages librarians to read, interpret, and apply their own professional research literature. This may not seem like a new idea, but it gives a name to a professional focus that encourages librarians to look for existing research in their profession and apply it to the management of their library. It is used to support decision making. Whether making policy decisions, fiscal decisions, or programming, service, and staffing decisions, the decision-making process is often based on anecdotal evidence, past practice, and even best guess. EBLIP systematizes the process to achieve more reliable results (*Evidence Based Toolkit for Public Libraries*, 2008).

First used as a term in 1997, evidence-based librarianship grew out of the influence of learning about

evidence-based medicine (EBM). In medical libraries in the 1990s, librarians were being asked to help formulate questions and use effective literature searching to find evidence for medical issues, as discussed in Chapter 12. Librarians in the Research Section of the Medical Library Association suggested these EBM principles could be applied to our own profession. Jonathan Eldredge (2000: 291), one of the leaders in this initiative, explains that EBLIP "seeks to improve library practice by utilizing the best-available evidence combined with a pragmatic perspective developed from working experiences in librarianship." Some of these EBLIP principles follow:

- Improving practice by using evidence
- Using a variety of types of evidence, both quantitative and qualitative
- Rigorous searching for evidence to support decision making
- Valuing diverse authoritative research
- Appreciating all forms of information seeking and knowledge development
- Supporting evidence-based standards and protocols
- Supporting hierarchical levels or grading of evidence (Eldredge, 2000: 291)

Koufogiannakis and Crumley list six areas or domains where librarians will have opportunities to formulate questions to improve their practice:

- Reference/Enquiries—providing service and access to information that meets the needs of library users.
- Education—finding teaching methods and strategies to educate users about library resources and how to improve their research skills.
- Collections—building a high-quality collection of print and electronic materials that is useful, cost-effective and meets the users' needs.
- Management—managing people and resources within an organization.
- Information Access & Retrieval—creating better systems and methods for information retrieval and access.
- Marketing/Promotion—promoting the profession, the library, and its services to both users and non-users. (Koufogiannakis and Crumley, 2002: 113)

All of these evaluation and quality initiatives encourage managers to base their decisions on evidence and not on the way it has always been done. In her paper at the fifth IEBLIP conference, Dalrymple discusses adoption of innovation and the need to put library research and the evidence it produces into the context of the overall organization. She says that evidence isn't enough:

- Evidence alone cannot change practice
- Context is key
- Adapting evidence increases use
- Systems thinking and incentives [are] essential (Dalrymple, 2009: 68)

She concludes with three points:

- Evidence-based practice is a foundation for professional practice.
- Data + insight creates a solid foundation for practice.
- Evidence-based practice can facilitate interdisciplinary discourse and quality improvement. (Dalrymple, 2009: 71)

In these times of extreme technological change, this attitude toward quality through the systematic use of evidence is more important than ever.

The Logic Model

The Logic Model is a tool that helps librarians plan and carry out evaluation projects or any program. It can be considered an initiative because it would be used when planning to evaluate an existing program or when starting a program, project, or grant. It can be adopted as an integral part of all the initiatives previous described here. Started in 1996 by the Kellogg Foundation (W. K. Kellogg Foundation, 2004), the model shows "the logical relationships among the resources that are invested, the activities that take place, and the benefits or changes that result" (University of Wisconsin-Extension, 2005). A Logic Model template from NN/LM is on the **accompanying CD-ROM**, as is a list of all the documents available at the University of Wisconsin-Extension.

> Logic models establish the relationship between an intervention and desired results by describing the theory and assumptions underlying the provision of services. They may also guide the selection of data for monitoring and improving services. A basic logic model identifies the activities; resources or inputs; and output, outcome, and impact measures associated with an intervention or program. (Abels, Cogdill, and Zach, 2004: 50)

Figure 6.2 represents a diagram of the basic parts of a Logic Model. The material is a simplified outline of developing a Logic Model. It is drawn from two major Internet resources for learning about the Logic Model. They contain many examples and forms (National Network of Libraries of Medicine, 2006; University of Wisconsin-Extension, 2005).

When starting to develop a culture of assessment and address quality, it would be too large a task to take on the whole library system. It would be possible by starting small with one program at a time, perhaps a program that presents a problem. Using the theories above and the Logic Model, the librarian and the library staff can start with a system that can be added to and replicated as other programs and services are reviewed or new ones started. First, a Logic Model on the chosen program can be done, followed by another program and then another. Soon, there will be a plan for the whole library with each program analyzed in the same way and the data stored systematically. The planning of a Logic Model can be divided into two parts: (1) determining the problem to be solved and (2) writing or developing the Logic Model.

Determine the Problem to Be Solved

- **Clarify who is asking for the model and why.** Why is activity required? Is evaluation of the program the major requirement? A succinct statement of purpose can be written to discuss with the evaluation team.

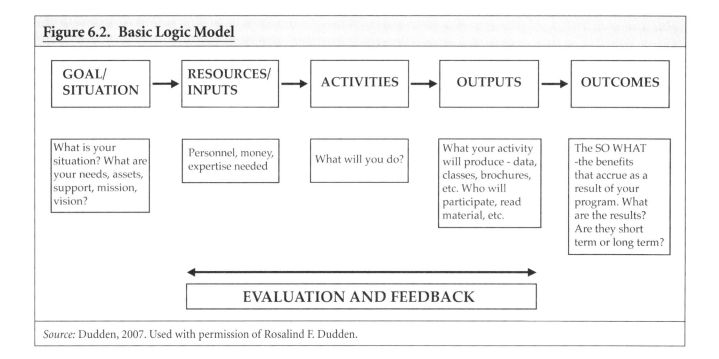

Figure 6.2. Basic Logic Model

GOAL/ SITUATION	→	RESOURCES/ INPUTS	→	ACTIVITIES	→	OUTPUTS	→	OUTCOMES
What is your situation? What are your needs, assets, support, mission, vision?		Personnel, money, expertise needed		What will you do?		What your activity will produce - data, classes, brochures, etc. Who will participate, read material, etc.		The SO WHAT -the benefits that accrue as a result of your program. What are the results? Are they short term or long term?

← **EVALUATION AND FEEDBACK** →

Source: Dudden, 2007. Used with permission of Rosalind F. Dudden.

- **Involve others.** A team can be gathered. This could be library staff members or outside stakeholders, people with an interest, or stake, in the problem.

- **With the team, decide on the scope of the Logic Model.** How will the model be used and by whom? The librarian and the team can discuss and write down the scope of the logic model.

- **Understand the problem, the environment surrounding it, and set priorities by writing a problem statement.** With the team, a SWOT analysis can be developed. See Figure 6.3 for the basic four parts of a SWOT model. Resources for conducting a SWOT analysis can be found on the **accompanying CD-ROM**. Priorities are set for solving the problem.

- **Find out what else has been done to solve this problem by doing a literature search.** Team members can do a literature search and review the literature for possible solutions to the problem defined in the situation statement. The results are

reported back to the team and cited in the problem statement if appropriate.

Outline the problem statement using these five parts.

1. Describe the problem.
2. Ask why it is a problem and what causes it.
3. State whose problem it is.
4. Mention who has a stake in the problem or who cares about it.
5. Mention existing research or studies that describe or address the problem.

The problem statement is written by the team. See an example in the sidebar. It should be kept short (400–500 words or less), and be succinct, avoiding the use of jargon. Others outside the team can be asked to review it for clarity. Priorities are set. Does solving this problem align with the library and/or institutional mission and values? Are the expertise and/or resources to work on this problem available?

Figure 6.3. Basic SWOT Analysis

Strengths: (internal; positive statements about the library)	**Weaknesses:** (internal; what is lacking in the library)
Opportunities: (external; services the library is not providing, perhaps discovered in a needs assessment)	**Threats:** (external; adverse factors in the environment)

Sample Problem Statement

Medical staff and hospital employees need information resources to find the latest treatments and procedures to treat patients. Purchasing these resources department-by-department is chaotic and costly. Book resources can be selected, purchased centrally by a library service, and made available in print and online. The price can be negotiated. By managing the books after purchasing by listing them and their online links in the library catalog, all staff and employees have access to them.

Goal to Solve the Problem

Cost-effectively acquire and manage information resources.

Write or Develop the Logic Model

Write the Outcomes

With the team established and the scope and purpose defined, it is time for part two. The process is to "plan backward, implement forward." Outcomes evaluation and theory are covered in more detail later in this chapter. Outcomes are the "so what" of the program—the difference the program makes, the benefits that accrue because of the program.

There are three kinds of outcomes to consider for the service or program:

1. Short-term outcomes or changes in learning: How would individuals who took advantage of the program have benefited in relation to achievements or changes in skill, knowledge, attitude, behavior, condition, or life status?

2. Medium-term outcomes or changes in action: What would be a change in the actions of the system that would be caused by people participating in the program?

3. Long-term outcomes or changes in conditions: What would be the biggest impacts on the conditions of society or the institution of the changes in the systems that might have been caused by changes in individuals who took advantage of the program?

For example, a program has this goal: "Cost-effectively acquire and manage information resources." Figure 6.4 shows this goal put into a Logic Model grid. The outcomes that could be developed to show that this goal has been reached have been entered into the last column of the grid, i.e., starting at the back.

Work Back Along the Logic Model Grid

The team decides where the library program is going before planning how to do the program or what resources are needed, as in Figure 6.4. There are three columns to the left of the outcomes column in the grid. Fill in these sections for outputs, activities, and resources. Starting on the right, working backward, what outputs would produce the outcome? What activity would bring about the output? What resources in terms of budget and personnel are needed to do that activity? Figure 6.5 demonstrates this backward development. By developing a Logic Model for large or small programs, the librarian and team can get a picture, or a model, of what is happening in the library and how different programs might

Figure 6.4. Sample Logic Model

Goal: Cost effectively acquire and manage information resources.

Resources	Activity	Outputs	Outcomes
Personnel, money, expertise needed	*What you will do*	*What your activity will produce— data, classes, brochures, etc.*	*The SO WHAT-the benefits that accrue as a result of your program*
			Reduce hospital costs by buying shared resources
			Increase value of hospital expenditures by ensuring that ordered materials are received
			Users know that hospital owns title

Source: Adapted from Barnes, Blake, and Kelly, 2006.

Figure 6.5. Sample Logic Model—Fully Filled Out

Goal: Cost effectively acquire and manage information resources

Resources	Activity	Outputs	Outcomes
Personnel, money, expertise needed	*What you will do* ◄	*What your activity will produce— data, classes, brochures, etc.* ◄	*The SO WHAT-the benefits that accrue as a result of your program* ◄
Knowledgeable librarian	Select books and negotiate discounts	Selection list and optimal pricing	Reduce hospital costs by buying shared resources
Budget	Purchase books	Enter PO and ensure access is active	Increase value of hospital expenditures by ensuring that ordered materials are received
Record-keeping system and trained staff	Process books	Catalog records	Users know that hospital owns title

Source: Adapted from Barnes, Blake, and Kelly, 2006.

relate to each other. This allows for better planning, management, communication and evaluation.

Planning an Evaluation Project

In the next parts of this chapter, the nuts and bolts of evaluation will be discussed. But every type of evaluation project flows through the same evaluation steps, no matter what is being measured or what method is being used. Some methods require additional steps but the planning flows in the same way. These steps are often derived from and interact with the Logic Model. Also see information about planning in Chapter 3. Like all projects, an evaluation project needs to have a budget and a final report. Templates for these items can be found on the **accompanying CD-ROM**.

Focus the Evaluation

Just as in developing the Logic Model, the purpose of the evaluation needs to be developed. The evaluation plan should be straightforward and simple: what needs to be known and who needs to know it? The target of the evaluation is determined as well as whether to evaluate the whole program or just part of it. Using the Logic Model developed above as a sample, one place in the model is selected to evaluate. For instance, the activity and output of negotiating discounts and getting optimal pricing could be the focus of the evaluation. Print book wholesalers would be surveyed and their pricing details

compared. The result might enable a change in wholesalers and the librarian then would report the saving to the supervisor, thereby relating the activity to the value of the outcome: reducing hospital costs.

Determine the Resources That Are Available or Needed

The resources needed to carry out the evaluation project are listed. The team can create a responsibility chart listing all the tasks than need to be done and who will be doing them. Which staff members have the time and expertise? The buyers in the purchasing department might be able to help. Using the task list, the team can create a timeline using a Gantt chart. Examples of Gantt charts can be found on the Internet. With some idea of how much time it will take and what purchased resources will be needed, a budget can be calculated to see what the expenses will be. A budget template can be found on the **accompanying CD-ROM**.

Develop the Questions

The team would first review the scope and purpose of the project. What is in the Logic Model that will help shape the questions? The questions are listed and prioritized. Questions outside the focus of the project are eliminated. The number of questions would be limited so as not to overwhelm the respondent. In the previous example, the library manager might limit possible wholesalers to 5 and work with the purchasing department to get bids.

Decide on the Indicators

Indicators are developed using the Indicator Review Worksheet and other resources available online in the University of Wisconsin-Extension web-based course (University of Wisconsin-Extension, 2005).

Questions to ask while filling out the form:

- What will indicate that the outcome (or process) has been achieved?
- What measurement means the outcome happened?

Rate each indicator with these qualities on the form:

- Specific?
- Observable?
- Measurable?
- Useful?
- Practical?
- Adequate?
- Culturally appropriate?

In the case of the survey of book wholesalers, some of the indicators would be the actual discount, delivery time and back orders, shipping costs, and customer service.

Determine a Data Collection Method

The Evaluation Plan Worksheet, as found on the **accompanying CD-ROM**, can be used to help determine a methodology. Before starting, various methodologies could be evaluated to see what are the strengths and weaknesses of different data collection methods in this context. The Data Collection Methodologies Review developed by the NN/LM-OERC is a reference to identify issues, strengths, and weakness in choosing a methodology. This is included on the **accompanying CD-ROM**. In this mini–case study, perhaps a survey and interview might be appropriate.

Analyze the Information

The results are analyzed and determinations and statements about the results are made. Using charts and graphs, the librarian and the evaluation team can look at the quantitative data collected and see what the results are. If it is a qualitative evaluation, it will produce stories and anecdotes. The data are discussed with the team, which comes to a consensus about what the data mean.

Communicate the Findings

With the team, reports are written to various stakeholders using various communication techniques and tools. A report template can be found on the **accompanying CD-ROM**. A communication plan is developed:

- How will results be announced to the stakeholders?
- Who will compile the project reports?
- Who will write the executive summary(s)?
- How will the final information be distributed?

This plan should definitely include plans to publish the results in the professional literature. Given the principles of Evidence-Based Library and Information Practice (EBLIP) mentioned previously, there is a professional obligation to add to the database of the evidence of good library practices.

What to Measure

With the advent of these different philosophies or initiatives now taking place in the evaluation community, people have begun to question what to measure. Traditional measures, such as circulation, gate count, and reference interactions are accused of being meaningless in the Internet age. Often what was measured in libraries was geared toward management of the library and used by the library director and various division heads.

To assure or perhaps prove quality, libraries became involved in the quality improvement trends in the 1980s and 1990s. Library associations such as the Association of Research Libraries (ARL) and the Association of Academic Health Sciences Libraries (AAHSL), started collecting comparative or benchmarking data on library operations. The Medical Library Association (MLA) began a similar benchmarking activity for nonacademic health sciences libraries with surveys in 2002, 2004, and 2007. LibQUAL+ was started in the 1990s to measure service. ARL and other associations have initiatives to measure electronic resource use, such as COUNTER, and determine what those numbers mean.

At the same time librarians are being asked to be more accountable, work hours are being cut. Some of those working on the MLA Benchmarking Network project were charged with contacting potential participants, the majority being hospital librarians. When encouraged to participate, many said they did not have time to report or they did not keep records of what they did. Part of management is communicating with upper management. How can the librarian provide a significant report without any measurements?

But the paradigm shift from the printed word to other media and the impact of the Internet on library operations is unprecedented. Technology has had a major impact, particularly with regard to the integration of all types of information. This integration is industrywide and is reflected in electronic health records, industrywide portals, and federated search engines that aggregate databases. This integration of information sources and services complicates the measurement and evaluation process. There is also a paradigm shift away from the engineering model of management of the 1900s, which was very linear. In this century, the paradigm of management is one of biology, which is one of diffusion, webs, volatility, and adaptability. These paradigms have an impact on how evaluation might be done. The approaches are still somewhat linear but with more circular feedback loops.

User behavior has become more multidimensional, and information resources are used in a multiplicity of ways. Traditional library resources are only one avenue to gain information. Other avenues increasingly involve connecting with experts via e-mail, browsing the Internet, locating blogs and wikis of interest, and sending inquiries to ask-a-services and friend-of-a-friend networks. This complex web of relations provides a richer context for the impact libraries are making. The user doesn't really respond to the linear evaluation model anymore, and the use of the usual linear model of input, activities, output, and outcome is limiting our understanding of a model that is much more cyclical, haphazard, and uncontrolled. This model becomes even more complex when the idea of motion is introduced for both the user and the changing information resources. Such an idea creates a model that looks like a spiral that swirls up and down. It becomes a challenge to tell what is affecting what. As the title of Kyrillidou's article implies, the librarian is no longer looking at the user in the life of the library but needs to look at the library in the life of the user. "This inextricable and complex web of relations provides a richer context for the usefulness of inputs, outputs, quality issues, and the impact libraries are making" (Kyrillidou, 2002: 42).

In this complicated environment, a key responsibility is to communicate to stakeholders what the library does and why it is important. What should be measured to describe a library? Factors that can be measured include needs, inputs, quality processes, outputs, quality of service, outcomes, and impacts. In Figure 6.6, categories of measures are represented in a linear form. This is a simple way to represent this concept but as described above, the process is anything but linear. There is a continuous feedback loop caused by evaluation, where every part of the library is evaluated to ensure maximum effectiveness.

Needs Assessment

How does the library fit into the life of the customer? This can be measured by a needs assessment. The article, "Conducting a User-Centered Information Needs Assessment: The Via Christi Libraries' Experience," by Perley, Gentry, Fleming and Sen, is an example of a needs assessment project in a hospital library (Perley et al., 2007). Used as part of a strategic planning initiative, the assessment allowed the librarians to present to their

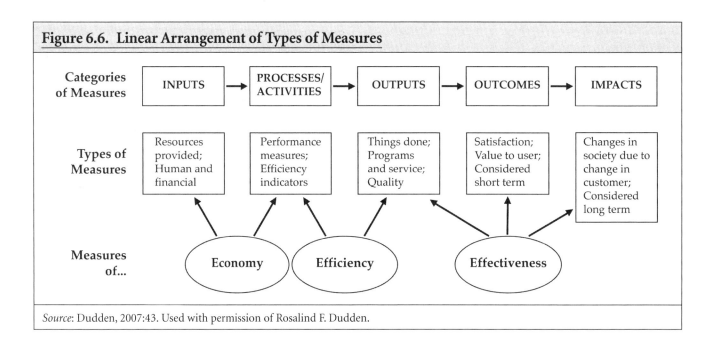

Figure 6.6. Linear Arrangement of Types of Measures

Categories of Measures	INPUTS	PROCESSES/ ACTIVITIES	OUTPUTS	OUTCOMES	IMPACTS
Types of Measures	Resources provided; Human and financial	Performance measures; Efficiency indicators	Things done; Programs and service; Quality	Satisfaction; Value to user; Considered short term	Changes in society due to change in customer; Considered long term
Measures of...	Economy	Efficiency		Effectiveness	

Source: Dudden, 2007:43. Used with permission of Rosalind F. Dudden.

administrators evidence of what the users wanted from a library. The clinicians surveyed emphasized the need for:

- "just in time" information accessible at the point of care;
- information services customized to their professional information needs, preferences, and patterns of use;
- identification of organization-specific information needs; and
- the need for marketing library services and resources as emphasized by library nonusers.

By communicating this information to their administrators, the librarians were able to develop a strategic plan that demonstrated to their administration a forward-looking approach to meeting their customer's needs. Key elements of the strategic plan include:

- a commitment to adapt and expand library information services as warranted by changes in the health care environment;
- development of customized service patterns;
- collaborative initiatives undertaken with key stakeholders across the medical center to meet systemwide goals;
- strengthened communication channels;
- promotion of library services to all entities in the system;
- a plan for the effective utilization and enhancement of financial resources; and
- an outline of the means by which the libraries will demonstrate service value to the Via Christi Regional Medical Center administration. (Perley et al., 2007)

Inputs

What is the size of the staff, budget, space, or collection? How does the library compare to others in benchmarking studies? While comparative benchmarking is often criticized, sometimes management is more familiar with the concept than with other measures. The comparisons answer questions administrators ask because they may not know what else to ask. Using traditional input counts is still an important measure for good management, budgeting, and resource allocation, as well as comparative benchmarking. A list of input and output measures can be found in the electronic appendices A and B (pages e37–42) of Dudden and colleagues, which describes the

results of the MLA Benchmarking Network survey from 2002 (Dudden et al., 2006b). The companion article on the development of the survey gives a description of the reasons for developing the project (Dudden et al., 2006a). The newest list of measures for the 2007 survey is available to MLA members on the MLA website (Medical Library Association, 2010) and on the **accompanying CD-ROM**.

On a more anecdotal level, people often ask the librarian some of these input questions in casual conversation, and it is not in the library's best interest to say, "I don't know." In a casual conversation, someone might ask, "How many e-journals do you have?" Giving just a number does not usually inform the other person. So the manager could say, "350 (or whatever) AND did you know that the process of investigation by our scientists has been fast-tracked by their access to this information at their desktop?" Another answer might be: "1,500 (or whatever) AND did you know that the use of these resources by our high school students at home has increased their ability to have more resources cited in their papers?" In these examples, the library manager is elaborating on the measure collected with outcome or impact statements, as discussed later in this chapter. While the inputs to the library mean very little without explanation, it is still necessary to maintain them.

Quality Processes

The processes and systems of the library need to be measured. This is usually done as part of a quality culture. The principles of total quality management and the various quality improvement techniques can be learned and adapted by librarians to measure and evaluate the library processes. Developing a quality culture has been discussed above. Along with a shared vision and concern for customers' needs, communication, and leadership, managing by fact is critical (Orenstein, 1999).

In some organizations, the whole organization, usually lead by the CEO, adopts a quality program. Some are simple sponsored quality improvement programs, adopting the PDCA (Plan-Do-Check-Act) techniques described below. Other companies adopt programs based on specific theories, such as Gemba visits, Kaizen, Lean, the Five Ss, the Learning Organization, Six Sigma, or the Balanced Scorecard. Searching the Internet for these programs provides a wealth of information. Any of these programs give the library a chance to be part of the process by providing information not only on the process but also to help other managers with information resources as they work on their quality projects.

The movement toward evidence-based librarianship and critical appraisal of research articles as discussed previously will help educate librarians on how to manage by fact. All of these quality programs encourage managers to base their decisions on fact and not on the way it has always been done. In these times of extreme technological change, this attitude toward quality is more important than ever.

Outputs

These measures answer the question, What does the library do? Traditional output measures are used to communicate to stakeholders that tasks were accomplished. There is no indication that they were the right tasks or the best tasks that could have been accomplished with the budget. Almost every library annual report will have these figures because they are expected. Today, in the same report, stories of the outcomes or impacts that the library accomplished are included. Outputs can identify trends. They can lead to staff reassignment or further evaluation of programs that show up or down trends.

Quality Service

Measuring customer service has always been a challenge in library management. LibQUAL+, developed by ARL, is a program for larger libraries that can help libraries measure service quality using a standardized web-based survey. Librarians are trained to administer the survey and interpret the results. Participation often leads to changes in organizational culture and a clearer picture of how the customers see the library. Changes in how the library is marketed can result (LibQUAL+, 2007).

LibQUAL+ seeks to measure three dimensions of library service quality:

1. The library as place (utilitarian space, symbol, refuge)

2. Information control (scope, timeliness, convenience, ease of navigation, modern equipment)

3. Service affect (empathy, responsiveness, assurance, reliability)

Smaller libraries can execute simpler satisfaction surveys using web-based tools such as SurveyMonkey or Zoomerang. Customers can be asked to rate services as to their satisfaction with a service as well as its importance to their work. The results can show the manager areas where improvements can be made and help with prioritizing the services offered in relation to marketing them.

Outcomes

Measuring outcomes started in 1993 with the Government Performance and Results Act (GPRA), which required most federal agencies to develop objective, quantifiable, and measurable goals and to report on their achievements. The influence of this law spread to local governments and other organizations. If a program says it will change the lives of a certain population group, how does it prove it actually did? The Institute for Museum and Library Services (IMLS), which supports library development through federal grants, promotes outcome measurement as part of program development. Their basic definition guides public libraries in efforts to measure outcomes: An outcome is a change in a target audience's skills, attitudes, knowledge, behaviors, status, or life condition brought about by experiencing a program (Institute of Museum and Library Services, 2006).

The IMLS has funded two web-based toolkits to help libraries measure outcomes. *Outcomes Tool Kit 2.0* provides "guidance for going beyond reporting outputs and will help you to discover outcomes, or indicators of impact, of your programs that can be shared with others" (Durrance and Fisher, 2002). Called *Shaping Outcomes*, the other website covers outcomes-based planning and evaluation or OBPE. "OBPE is a systematic way to plan user-centered programs and to measure whether they have achieved their goals. OBPE goes beyond documenting what you did and measures what difference you made in the life of your audience—how has your audience changed?" (Indiana University Purdue University Indianapolis, Institute for Museum and Library Services, and Kryder-Reid, 2006). While these two web courses are geared toward public libraries, all librarians can benefit from reviewing them.

Outcomes and impacts are further removed in time (and perhaps space) for academic and health libraries. The American College and Research Libraries (ACRL) Task Force on Academic Library Outcomes Assessment published their Assessment Report in 1998 that goes over many of the issues. The report lists some possible questions that will need to be answered to respond to the question that the IMLS has posed:

- Is the academic performance of students improved through their contact with the library?

- By using the library, do students improve their chances of having a successful career?

- Are undergraduates who used the library more likely to succeed in graduate school?

- Are students who use the library more likely to lead fuller and more satisfying lives? (Association of College & Research Libraries. American Library Association, 1998)

For health and biomedical libraries, demonstration of program outcomes is a requirement of federal grants. The National Library of Medicine and the National Network of Libraries of Medicine, Pacific Northwest Region, sponsor the Outreach Evaluation Resource Center (OERC) that has created training tools and resources on the Web as well as a continuing education course. Called *Measuring the Difference: Guide to Planning and Evaluating Health Information Outreach*, this course promotes the use of the Logic Model as described earlier (Burroughs and Wood, 2000). Examples of outcomes reported by Joanne G. Marshall's research are listed previously in the section on communicating value and worth (see p. 101).

Impacts

Outcomes are defined as changing the life of the customer. This customer could be a community member, a student, or a business professional. If the library changes enough lives, there might be an impact on the community the library supports. A community member who uses a public library may become more involved in civic actions. A student who uses the library may become a class leader. A business professional who uses the library may contribute more to the company bottom line. The health professional who uses the library may have better or different patient outcomes. To measure this type of impact usually takes a funded study, and several have been published.

In the health professions, Weightman and Williamson (2005: 7) state:

- Research studies suggest professionally led library services have an impact on health outcomes for patients and may lead to time savings for health care professionals.

- Evidence of the impact of professional library services on health outcomes for patients and time savings for health care staff is available and can be used to demonstrate the impact of library services to users, managers, and funding bodies.

- The results suggest clear evidence of an impact of library services on patient outcomes from both traditional and clinical librarian services.

The impacts reported by Weightman and Williamson are listed previously in the section on communicating value and worth (see p. 101).

While most librarians cannot do a major research study, they can do a survey of users and ask an open-ended question such as this:

Can you please take a moment and write how the information you received helped yourself and ultimately the hospital? (Cuddy, 2005: 447).

The result of asking such a question can be significant quotes such as this that can be used in reports:

"The library is critical to my role as a clinical radiologist. Twice within the past month, I have used it to search for a specific clinical diagnosis, resulting in a change of management for the patient, and education for clinician colleagues."

Using published studies and the library's own results, the library manager can present information to administrators about outcomes and value. The librarian can insert locally gathered information based on a small survey to report local outcomes. Telling a specific story or anecdote is very powerful, because that is often what many administrators remember more than the data.

Methods of Evaluation

The chapter so far has been on using evaluations to show value and worth and how to integrate evaluation into the library's management plan. The question then is what evaluation method would be used to evaluate the different parts of the management plan. Since the concepts described above are customer focused, periodic needs assessment should be carried out. Quality improvement techniques or process benchmarking could be used to evaluate processes in the library, the activities that produce the products of the library. Inputs and outputs could be evaluated through comparative benchmarking or trend analysis. Standards could be assessed to see how the library compares to these guidelines. Finally the outcomes or impacts could be assessed through surveys.

The five methods of evaluation reviewed here, needs assessment, quality improvement, benchmarking, standards, and outcomes, are the backbone of evaluation projects. Each one is covered extensively in a chapter in the author's book, *Using Benchmarking, Needs Assessment, Quality Improvement, Outcome Measurement, and Library Standards: A How-To-Do-It Manual* (Dudden, 2007). For each one, there is a workbook delineating the steps to be taken to complete the project. These are available on the **accompanying CD-ROM** of this book, with permission from the author. Here we give a brief overview and a list of the steps.

Needs Assessment

As a management tool, the results of a needs assessment can be used to advocate for more funding or to write a grant. Budgeting and planning can benefit from knowing what users need. The results can be used to explain services to users or to communicate with those with budget or funding authority. A needs assessment is the foundation for evaluating the program of the library as a whole. Doing a needs assessment may be recommended or required by an accrediting body or library association standards. A needs assessment is a systematic process for determining discrepancies between optimal and actual performance of a service (a gap) by reviewing the service needs of customers and stakeholders and then selecting interventions that allow the service to meet those needs in the fastest, most cost effective manner.

In an example from Crabtree's needs assessment (Crabtree and Crawford, 1997), the library staff observed that the actual or real condition is that few allied health staff members use library services. The library's goal was that the optimal or ideal condition would be that a good percentage of allied health staff use the library. What is the "gap" that prevents the allied health staff from using library services? Ask them in a needs assessment.

Some issues about needs assessment follow:

- Be committed to the idea that if a client need is identified, the library system will be prepared to act.

- If a needs assessment is undertaken, users will assume that if an unmet need is identified, library services and systems will be changed to meet that need; watch out for raised expectations.

- One of the guiding rules of needs assessment is that it should be "in context." Questions from other libraries' assessments are not that useful.

- There are various levels of needs assessment: macro- and micro-assessments.

- It is not a user satisfaction survey. It's good to find out if people are satisfied but are they getting what they need?

- If the library doesn't provide what the user needs, they'll find it somewhere else, i.e., the competition? The web?

Conducting a needs assessment has been broken down into 12 steps. Whether the assessment takes four weeks or a year, these 12 steps are followed.

- Prepare for the Project
  - Step 1. Define the purpose or question
  - Step 2. Gather the team: Who is going to do what?
  - Step 3. Identify stakeholders and internal and external factors

- Plan the project and conduct the needs assessment
  - Step 4. Define the goals and objectives
  - Step 5. Determine resources available
  - Step 6. Develop a timeline
  - Step 7. Define the customers
  - Step 8. Gather data from identified sources

- Analyze the data and recommend a plan of action
  - Step 9. Analyze the data
  - Step 10. Make a decision and a plan of action
  - Step 11. Report to administration and evaluate the needs assessment process
  - Step 12. Repeat needs assessment in the future to see if the gap is smaller

Reports of Needs Assessment

Perley, Cathy M., Camillia A. Gentry, A. Sue Fleming, and Kristin M. Sen. 2007. "Conducting a User-Centered Information Needs Assessment: The Via Christi Libraries' Experience." *Journal of the Medical Library Association* 95, no. 2 (April): 173–181, e54–55.

Clougherty, Leo, John W. Forys, and Toby A. Lyles. 1998. "The University of Iowa Libraries' Undergraduate User Needs Assessment." *College & Research Libraries* 59, no. 6 (November): 572–584.

Crabtree, Anna Beth, and Julia H. Crawford. 1997. "Assessing and Addressing the Library Needs of Health Care Personnel in a Large Regional Hospital." *Bulletin of the Medical Library Association* 85, no. 2 (April): 167–175.

Adams, Deborah L., Nancy Bulgarelli, Karen Tubolino, and Gayle A. Williams. 1994. "Hospital Library Customer Survey: A Needs Assessment Tool." *National Network* 19, no. 2 (November): 24–27.

Quality Improvement

Continuous Quality Improvement (QI) works well in the health care industry where the scientific method is widely used and understood. Similar in many ways to the scientific method, the quality improvement process uses statistical methods and data to support decision-making and process improvement. One model that is widely used as a quality improvement procedure in health care is the FOCUS-PDCA Cycle, as shown in Figure 6.7. The FOCUS-PDCA cycle is a method to improve work processes by collecting data, incorporating customer input, pilot testing the proposed process change or improvement, and permanently changing the process.

Find a Process to Improve

In the beginning stages of process improvement, a problem is often being discussed in an attempt to resolve it. Problems are discovered by staff or customers, become known in customer surveys, or are discussed in a department or management meeting. For example, a library manager could decide to improve literature searching because it is a key process in the library and turnaround times are too long.

Organize a Team

Rather than trying to solve the problem alone, the manager who uses QI effectively will convene a team to work on the problem. The requirements for team membership are (1) willingness to participate, (2) ownership of the process under discussion; having a stake in the process, (3) training in process improvement and teamwork. The team may include the manager, who is often the team leader, and often includes a customer (or client) of the process. To continue with the example in the previous paragraph, the library manager and one additional staff member organize a team that includes one or two customers. The customers might be members of the Library Committee or frequent users of the literature search service.

Clarify the Current Process

The team meets on a regular basis to improve the process, using a variety of statistical tools (discussed in the section on statistical tools below), and team meeting skills (discussed in the team meeting skills section below). The current process is studied so the team is sure how the work is currently being done. Customers are interviewed in this step to determine the key quality characteristics (KQC), or which elements of the process they value most. The team also determines the key process variable (KPV), or the key element that most influences the effectiveness of the process. In our example, the team flowcharts the current process and gathers customer feedback regarding the importance of various elements in the process. The team would probably consider turnaround time, number of articles retrieved, and relevance of articles included in the search results as key quality

Figure 6.7. The FOCUS-PDCA Cycle: The Steps to Quality Improvement	
F	Find a Process to Improve.
O	Organize a Team.
C	Clarify the Current Process.
U	Understand the Causes of Process Variation.
S	Select a Process Improvement.
P	Plan the Process Improvement.
D	Do the Process Improvement.
C	Check the Process Improvement.
A	Act to Improve the Process Further or Hold the Gain in Quality.

characteristics. The team decides to select turnaround time as the key process variable, or the most important variable affecting customer satisfaction.

Understand the Causes of Process Variation

In this step, data are gathered about the process to determine what elements are causing variation in the way the work is done. Controlling variation in processes is a major goal of quality improvement and is seen as a way to standardize operations with the goal of improving quality. Understanding the causes of process variation requires the use of statistical tools to complete an analysis of data gathered in the "C" phase. As meetings continue, the team is able to identify and isolate causes that may lead to efficient or inefficient process performance. In our example, the team would measure the turnaround time for searches and explore the elements and circumstances that affect time to complete searches. They could use the Cause-and-Effect diagram to document the causes associated with equipment, people, materials, and methods. They could also measure customer satisfaction with the literature search service.

Select a Process Improvement

After careful study, the team is now ready to select a process to improve. Often, although possible changes to the process under study become obvious during the "C" and "U" steps, the team waits until data are gathered and discussed and consensus is reached on an improvement. In the example we have been working with, the team has identified that an unreliable computer is having a major negative impact on turnaround time, and also that staff scheduling is an issue.

When the FOCUS portion of quality improvement is completed, the PDCA phase begins. This phase is often referred to as the Shewhart cycle, and includes the steps Plan, Do, Check, Act, as shown in Figure 6.8.

Plan a Process Improvement

Planning the improvement is an essential part of the implementation plan. The team formulates procedures, allocates resources, makes implementation and evaluation schedules, designs forms, trains staff, and generally completes all the steps necessary to design the new process and prepare for implementation. The literature search improvement team in our example decides to order new computer equipment and also to redesign the information desk schedule so that there is a clear division of responsibility for literature searches between the two librarians. The team works with Information Technologies to develop requirements for a new computer and then to order it. The team also designs a new schedule for the information desk.

Do the Process Improvement

During this phase of PDCA, the team actually implements the new process. During implementation, careful monitoring ensures that the new procedures are carried out according to design, and no "backsliding" to the old process occurs. The Do step is often a pilot project with a definite time limit. The literature search team decides to

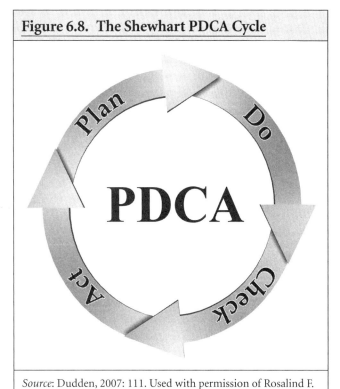

Figure 6.8. The Shewhart PDCA Cycle

Source: Dudden, 2007: 111. Used with permission of Rosalind F. Dudden.

wait until the new computer is installed and then to implement the new information desk schedule for a two-month trial period.

Check the Process Improvement

The Check step in PDCA is the evaluation step. Depending upon the process under study, the evaluation may be an informal discussion including team members and customers of the process, or it may be a full-scale statistical evaluation. This essential step takes place at an interval decided in the Plan phase. The Do phase is allowed to run long enough to gather sufficient data for an evaluation, and the team determines from the data whether the process improvement is working and is truly an improvement. In our example, the literature search team decided to measure literature search turnaround times and customer satisfaction two months after the change is implemented.

Act to Revise the Process or Maintain the Improvement

The Act step is the final part of the PDCA cycle, but it can be a new beginning. As illustrated in Figure 6.8, PDCA is a cycle. When the new process is evaluated, the team has a choice of two courses of action.

If the process improvement is not a success, the team acts to begin the Plan phase again, and uses the experience from the first PDCA cycle to plan a more viable improvement. If the new process is successful, the team still must act to maintain the improvement and ensure that everyone involved in implementing the new process continues to use it effectively. If, for instance, the literature search team were to find that turnaround times and customer satisfaction improved, then they must act to hold the gain or improvement. In other words, they will continue the new process and not slip back into the less-effective process. However, if turnaround time and customer satisfaction are not affected by the process change, the team returns to the "Plan a Process Improvement" phase and determines a new strategy to improve turnaround times for literature searches.

Standards

There are three broad types of standards, technical, performance, and accreditation. Performance and accreditation standards are used for evaluation. Technical standards are needed for industry and manufacturing so various products can work together, such as the standardization of the size of a light bulb socket so any brand of bulb can be purchased. In libraries, technical standards exist for such things as interlibrary loan trans-actions and cataloging rules and MARC records. These standards facilitate the transfer of data between libraries so that they can work together.

Performance standards are written for libraries of a certain type usually by the association that supports those libraries, such as the Medical Library Association or the Association of College and Research Libraries. Some groups write guidelines instead of standards. What is the difference between a standard and a guideline? This debate is still controversial and the politics and semantics of the word have a lot to do with enforcement. Associations tend not to enforce their standards, as this is very costly. When linked to accreditation programs, surveys are carried out to judge whether the standards are met. The result is that the survey instrument itself becomes controversial, requiring careful training of the surveyor to use the instrument. Rather than be "forced" to comply, some prefer to adopt guidelines, while others who need justification for improvement prefer standards and inspections.

Accreditation Standards

Accreditation standards apply to the institution the library serves. For health care libraries this topic is covered in Chapter 2. These types of accreditation standards can be used to identify places where evaluation would be useful to see that the standards are met. Their purpose is to ensure quality. The standards written for hospitals by The Joint Commission (TJC), formerly the Joint Commission on Accreditation of Healthcare Organizations (JCAHO), are the most important to hospital libraries. While these standards are constantly changing, what Dalrymple suggests in 1998 holds true today: "JCAHO stipulates indicators of quality for information management: timeliness and accessibility, accuracy, security and ease of access, use of aggregate and comparative information for improvement, efficiency, collaboration, and sharing" (Dalrymple and Scherrer, 1998: 13). Discussing how the library relates to current TJC standards, while not a formal evaluation, could be a way to discuss library quality, value, and worth with a supervisor and others in the administration.

Performance Standards

Health care libraries in university settings have two sources for standards. The Association of College and Research Libraries (ACRL) has an active program of writing guidelines and standards. Its latest overarching standard, *Standards for Libraries in Higher Education*, was published in 2004 (ACRL College and Research

Libraries Task Force, 2004). Other guidelines and stan-dards on their website include documents for distance learning library services, information literacy competency standards for higher education, and guidelines for media resources in academic libraries (Association of College & Research Libraries, American Library Association, 2005).

The Association of Academic Health Sciences Libraries (AAHSL) and the Medical Library Association (MLA) produced the report, *Challenge to Action* in 1987, which, while not officially a set of standards, has been very helpful in demonstrating to administrators what to expect from an academic health center library (Love, 1986). Recently AAHSL published the report, *Building on Success: Charting the Future of Knowledge Management within the Academic Health Center* that updates the *Challenge to Action* and introduces all technological, economic, and social changes since 1986 (Association of Academic Health Sciences Libraries. AAHSL Charting the Future Task Force, 2003). The examples of success or sugges-tions for future collaborations suggest the critical areas in which libraries and librarians provide the most value to the organization. Under "How should *Charting the Future* be used?" The forward states:

> This report is intended to sensitize decision-makers to the unique strategic and operational roles that the AHC (Academic Health Center) library currently plays and could play in the future of ensuring the success of the institution. It is focused on the areas that can make a significant difference to the bottom line, to faculty and student recruitment and retention, to excellent patient care, to research competitiveness, and to community initiatives. (Association of Academic Health Sciences Libraries. AAHSL Charting the Future Task Force, 2003: 1)

While the AAHLS Report and the ACRL Standards do not seem to relate to the operations of a small special library, reading them can give the librarian ideas about the trends and concerns of these influential libraries. Step-by-step service analogies are not always appropriate but the types of services offered by these libraries will be expected of the special library when these students become practitioners in a few years. Whether in a business library with recent college graduates or a hospital medical library with recently graduated doctors or nurses, these librarians need to keep up with the services provided at the schools and colleges.

As libraries move into the fast-changing digital age, evidence of quality and meeting the needs of the user become the hallmark for standards. The *Standards for Hospital Libraries 2007* work to do that by addressing the role of the librarian (Hospital Libraries Section Stan-dards Committee, 2008: 162):

The standards define the role of the medical librarian and the links between KBI and other functions such as patient care, patient education, performance improvement, and education. In addition, the standards address the development and implementation of the KBI needs assessment and plan, the promotion and publicity of knowledge-based information services, and the physical space and staffing requirements.

Using Standards for Evaluation

Despite controversies, the standards or perhaps guidelines available today can be used for evaluation. They can be used to discuss what a quality library is with a supervisor. Many special libraries and certainly hospital libraries report to supervisors who know very little about how the library is run. They rely on the librarian to teach them the basics and describe a quality service. As Flower states:

> Right from the beginning we must realize that librarians are the only ones who really understand libraries. Or, to put it the other way around, we must begin discussing hospital libraries by grasping the fact that no one we deal with in any hospital will understand much of what we are talking about. They will think they do, but there is an unspoken difference in concept which shadows every discussion of information services between librarians and hospital personnel, at all levels. (Flower, 1978: 296)

Using the standards to educate the administration is a very effective strategy. In her book, the author has reviewed recent standards, including the MLA Standards for hospital libraries 2007 (Hospital Libraries Section Standards Committee, 2008), and devised a workbook that can be used to discuss the programs of the library with the administration by answering specific questions related to each standard. This workbook can be found on the **accompanying CD-ROM**. Each section of the workbook can be related to the plans and programs of a specific library. Baker and Lancaster (1991) are of the opinion that qualitative standards cannot be used for numerical evaluation, and that is true, but qualitative standards do reflect current practices and a point-by-point review of them can demonstrate services and programs that are lacking or that are exemplary. While not a "formal" evaluation, a point-by-point comparison can be made and used to communicate with a supervisor. A review of standards can also help with development of a departmental strategic plan. As it is being written, certain parts can refer to the standards for support.

Benchmarking

Benchmarking is an evaluation tool used to measure quality and is one of several tools that can be used as part of the management philosophy of Total Quality Management (TQM) and Quality Improvement (QI) as discussed above. There is no single best way to address quality. Many of these programs have a positive philosophy about learning new systems and demonstrating a willingness to change. Benefiting the customer is the primary goal of all attempts to measure quality.

What is benchmarking, exactly?

1. A tool to measure and compare a library's performance or work processes with those of other libraries

2. The ongoing comparison and review of a library's own process, product, or service against the best-known similar activity, so that realistic goals can be set and effective strategies can be identified and implemented to work toward their attainment

3. "A continuous, systematic process for evaluating the products, services, and work processes of the organization and comparing it to other organizations that are recognized as representing best practices for the purpose of organizational improvement" (Spendolini, 2000: 9)

Comparing the library operation to others allows the librarian to implement improvements by identifying superior performance and practices. It allows one to identify what *could* or *should* be done. Benchmarking allows the library staff to go beyond their own experience and find innovative activities in other libraries, the kind of activities that may help them survive.

Types of Benchmarking

> Data (performance) benchmarking measures and compares inputs and outputs of a process against a benchmark to assess performance. Process benchmarking analyzes a sequence of activities and compares them with similar functions in best practice organizations. (Henczel, 2002: 12)

There are three types of benchmarking: performance, process, and strategic. A formal benchmarking project can be categorized with two questions (Andersen and Pettersen, 1996). Each question has three answers.

1. What is to be compared?
    a. Overall performance (performance benchmarking)
    b. A process that provides a service to customers (process benchmarking)
    c. An overall look at the library's strategic position (strategic benchmarking)

2. Against what is the library going to be compared?

  a. Internal departments (internal benchmarking)

  b. External organizations, libraries or similar operations (functional benchmarking)

  c. Other organizations that are in direct competition (competitive benchmarking)

When the two questions are compared in the matrix shown in Figure 6.9, there are nine types of benchmarking projects, such as internal-process, external-performance, external-strategic, etc. Each one has different levels of value or relevance to a library operation. Figure 6.9 gives each type a rating as to its value or relevance to libraries. The first decision is to choose a method of benchmarking.

Performance benchmarking compares measures of performance to determine how good an operation is compared to others. It involves measuring inputs and outputs of a process and comparing them with other measurements of the same. Performance benchmarking has many other names, including: comparative, data, metric, or organizational benchmarking. Sometimes performance benchmarking is a limited collaborative exchange of information within a consortium or organization: a "best practices" collaboration.

Process benchmarking compares the methods and practices, or sequence of activities, used to perform a process. It compares the processes with similar functions in partners or peer institutions that are identified as having "best-practices." Called "classic benchmarking" by Todd-Smith and Markwell, this "involves selecting benchmarking partners to compare the steps of a process...to understand why other libraries may do the process faster or better" (Todd-Smith and Markwell, 2002: 86). An example of process benchmarking would be comparing record keeping for an interlibrary loan operation in hopes of having it more streamlined and using less paper.

Strategic benchmarking compares overall strategic choices with others. If usually done as part of a planning process at a company level, it would involve investigating choices and plans made by other companies, usually using public information. On the departmental level, in a library, it might be a systematic review of the literature for trends to see where the profession is heading so the library doesn't get left behind. An example of strategic benchmarking could be that it is noted that larger libraries are purchasing and using federated search programs. Strategically would this service be a good match for the needs of the local library's customers? It could relate to a strategic plan being developing.

The first step is to decide what method of benchmarking is going to be done. The second step is to decide with whom to compare the library's operation. It could be assumed libraries can only benchmark against other libraries but that is not true. There are three choices.

Internal benchmarking compares performance, process or strategies against another department or division in the organization. This is sometimes the easiest to do and could be used to practice the benchmarking process. A support process practiced by all departments such as purchasing or financial record keeping could be compared to see if the systems in place are as efficient as they can be. For instance, comparing how financial information, such as requisitions and vouchers, is handled might streamline the library's own process. Maybe there are electronic means that would cut down on paperwork.

Functional benchmarking, sometimes called **generic benchmarking**, compares the processes or functions that have been chosen to analyze against organizations that have similar processes in the same or a different industry. These organizations are recognized as having state-of-the-art products, services, or processes. Can a library be identified that is considered to be an example of

---

Figure 6.9. Matrix Showing the Value or Relevance (High, Medium, or Low) to a Library Operation When Combining the Types of Benchmarking

		Against whom are you going to compare?		
		Internal	Functional	Competitive
What do you want to compare?	Performance	Low	Medium	High
	Process	Medium	High	Low
	Strategy	Low	Low	Medium

Source: Adapted from Andersen and Pettersen, 1996: 7.

one that uses excellent management principles? Based on the benchmarking library's own operation, is the chosen library more efficient? Process benchmarking is detailed bdlow and choosing partners is described.

Competitive benchmarking compares benchmarking a library's performance against direct competitors selling to the same customer base. This can be done with contacted partners or just shadowing selected partners using public data. This is usually part of a company planning process. Since libraries do not compete with each other by selling a product to the same customer, this is not generally used in libraries. A benchmarking plan could be creative and compare to booksellers or other commercial information providers. As an example, a recent OCLC report compared the daily circulation of all public libraries (5.4 million) to the daily shipments from Amazon (1.5 million) (Online Computer Library Center Inc., 2003).

There are several benefits *and* pitfalls to be aware of when doing a benchmarking project:

- Benefits
  - The strategic goals of the library and organization are supported.
  - Management support will be nurtured.
  - Performance and customer service will be improved.
  - Decision making will be better.
  - Professional and staff relationships will improve.

- Pitfalls
  - Confusing performance and process benchmarking.
  - Choosing cost over quality.
  - Be aware of the resources needed to do the project.
  - Data collection decisions must be collaborative.
  - Changing environments and innovative practices.
  - Identifying partners is difficult.

Performance Benchmarking

Are the measures, inputs or outputs used by the library "good" or conforming to the "best practice" for the library's type? A performance benchmarking project can help assess this. Inputs and outputs from a number of similar libraries can be gathered and compared. This can be time-consuming and in some cases it is hard to find like libraries. Several professional organizations have completed surveys for their members. They collect input measures or parameters of size so like libraries can be found and measures of activities collected so performance can be compared to a group of libraries.

Three associations have conducted this type of survey:

- The Association of Research Libraries (ARL) Statistics & Measurement Program (http://www.arl.org/stats/). Collected since the turn of the century.
- The Association of Academic Health Sciences Libraries (AAHSL) (http://www.aahsl.org/). Collected since 1975 (Byrd and Shedlock, 2003; Shedlock and Byrd, 2003).
- The Medical Library Association (MLA) Benchmarking Network Surveys (members only) (http://mlanet.org/). Collected in 2002, 2004, and 2007 (Dudden et al., 2006a,b).

The surveys collect measures of institutional size, collection numbers, and service output numbers. Participants would use the data to measure their overall performance against others. All are a great service to the participants since, by using these surveys, they did not have to contact other libraries and collect the data themselves. Performance benchmarking can be used to demonstrate that the library's resources or activities are or are not well supported. Performance benchmarking is a simpler activity to do than process benchmarking. It is often used as a wake-up call to a funding body that something is wrong, as in the case of the Kaiser libraries, as described in the sidebar. But performance benchmarking does not give a definite idea or plan about what to improve to gain better quality. It should be considered

Performance Benchmarking Success Story: Kaiser Permanente Libraries of Northern California.

Using the MLA Benchmarking Network 2002 survey, the Northern and Southern California Kaiser Permanente libraries successfully completed such a project (Fulda and Satterthwaite, 2003, 2004). Eleven libraries in the Northern California District compared three items from their budgets: books, journals, and staff, to the median benchmarking data for other libraries of like size. They then submitted a request for additional funding, using as justification the discrepancy they found with the funding for those budget items between the Kaiser libraries and the median for libraries documented in the benchmarking data. The analysis showed that funding of book and journal expenditures and of staff for other libraries as reported in the benchmarking data was significantly higher than the expenditures for these items in the Kaiser library budgets. When requesting a budget increase, the librarians developed scenarios of how additional money would be spent using three different funding levels. The mid-level scenario, which increased funding by one million dollars for the 11 libraries, was subsequently approved.

a first, although major, step in a quality improvement program. It can, however, lead to what has been called the three Ds: disbelief, denial, and despair. First the staff doesn't believe the results of the comparison (how could be we *that* low?). Then the staff might deny the results by claiming that the comparable libraries are not really like the one where they work. Finally, the staff become paralyzed by despair because they don't know how to catch up (Andersen and Pettersen, 1996).

If the staff and administration don't fall victim to the three Ds, they will need to follow up and focus on the processes that contribute to the performance gap. Sometimes all that is needed is to identify the performance difference and use it to the library's benefit through systematic review and open communication. The sidebar provides the steps to follow to do performance benchmarking.

Steps for Performance Benchmarking

1. Identify the measure or measures to be benchmarked and start the planning process.
2. Establish management commitment to the benchmarking process.
3. Plan the Evaluation project by establishing the benchmarking team, defining a budget and setting time lines.
4. Identify, define, and understand the measures to be benchmarked.
5. Use existing surveys or plan to collect data from benchmarking partners.
6. Collect the data from benchmarking partners if needed.
7. Analyze and present the data.
8. Identify areas for improvement and report the results.
9. Continue to conduct benchmarking studies for comparative purposes over time.

Process Benchmarking

As part of an overall evaluation plan that the library staff has developed within the culture of assessment and the emphasis on quality, the librarian and staff might choose to do a process benchmarking project. Perhaps a performance benchmarking project has been done and some activities are comparatively lower than they should be. Perhaps a user survey has been completed and some services received a more negative rating that they should have.

- Could this be because the actual process is inefficient?
- Are the administration and staff willing to change the process?

- Is the process important to the overall library mission and goals?

If any of these questions are answered in the affirmative, a process benchmarking project could be considered.

The actual results of a process benchmarking project are not that useful to other library operations since each project is so specific to the immediate environment. Reports of the data would also have to be detailed to make a local comparison. Therefore, most of the literature on process benchmarking describes an assessment project in general without much detail. One exception is a report from the University of Virginia (White, 2002).

Process benchmarking is "the practice of being humble enough to admit that someone else is better at something and being wise enough to try to learn how to match or even surpass them at it." This quote is attributed on the web to Carla O'Dell, PhD, President of the American Productivity & Quality Center (APQC) (2003). It does get to the heart of the reason to do process benchmarking, and it should describe an attitude needed as the team sets out to accomplish the project. On the web, Sam Walton of Walmart fame is quoted as saying that he spent more time in his competitors' stores than they did. He further states that many of his best ideas came from process benchmarking.

If a library director is about to spend a lot of time measuring and comparing a process, he or she needs to be willing to learn and change. The transfer of the information about the process from the partner to the director is a person-to-person process. Relationships will be built and the library director will need to foster the desire to learn in himself or herself and the staff.

The previous section on performance benchmarking showed a nine-step plan for comparing various activities of the library to others. From that, some areas for further study may have been identified. Or, as part of the library's culture of assessment plans, a customer satisfaction survey may have been done and noted some areas where customers are not satisfied. Perhaps the process for that service could be improved. Process benchmarking could be called for to improve the identified process. The 12 steps involved in process benchmarking are outlined in the sidebar. The APQC predicts each phase will typically divide the project time this way:

- 30 percent: Planning the study
- 50 percent: Collecting information
- 20 percent: Analyzing performance gaps

The decision to do a benchmarking project would be part of an overall strategic or assessment plan. It would

Steps for Process Benchmarking

A. Planning the study: Prebenchmarking

 1. Identify the process to be benchmarked and start.

 2. Establish management commitment to the benchmarking project.

 3. Plan the Evaluation project by establishing the benchmarking team, defining a budget, and setting time lines.

 4. Define and understand the process to be benchmarked.

 5. Identify metrics and collect process data.

 6. Identify, rank, and implement internal process improvements.

 7. Identify and contact benchmarking partners.

B. Collecting and Analyzing Information: Benchmarking in action

 8. Collect process data from benchmarking partners.

 9. Analyze benchmarking partners' process data and compare against internal process

 10. Conduct site visits or interviews, and reanalyze data.

C. Reporting, adapting improvements and monitoring results: Postbenchmarking

 11. Present results, implement improvements, and monitor results.

 12. Continue to conduct benchmarking of this process and recycle the benchmarking process for other areas or processes.

be done in conjunction with supervisors and stakeholders. In her book, the author has devised a workbook laying out tools to use for each of these 12 steps (Dudden, 2007). This workbook can be found on the **accompanying CD-ROM**. Studying the chapter and the references in that book and the references here will be part of the process of learning how to benchmark.

Outcomes

The emphasis on outcomes measurement in libraries could be considered "new." It requires a change of paradigm. As discussed previously, the culture of assessment requires a shift from measuring inputs and outputs to measuring outcomes and impacts on the customer. Management of services has become more customer-focused than process-focused. In this paradigm shift brought on by the age of the Internet, many are asking "What is a library?" These people include librarians as well as those who use libraries and those who fund libraries. Is the library a collection of books, journals, and written materials that is stored

efficiently so they can be retrieved? Then evaluate for efficiency. Is it still true what John Cotton Dana, Denver, Colorado's first city librarian, said in 1889, "the worth of a library is in its use?" If so, report the library's outputs, the number of books circulated, the number of questions answered, how many teenagers attended an after-school technology club, how the library is "used." Is the library a social institution that impacts and changes the lives of the people who use it and the community in which they live or the business where they work? Is the library a tool and not an end in itself, a tool that when used by staff adds value to the bottom line and the vision, mission, and values of the larger organization? Then measure an outcome for the people who use a library service:

- Teenagers who participate in a technology club get better grades in school.

- College students who take information literacy courses write better essays.

- Professional staff who use library services save personal time they can use for other work.

- Physicians order fewer expensive tests after requesting a literature search from the library.

The new paradigm requires us to assess the economic and social value our libraries deliver to our patrons as well as be able to show that use of library services changed the personal, academic, or professional success of an individual.

> It's best to remember that value is priceless, but impacts leave a measurable change in the shape of things.
>
> —Christine Urquhart (2005)

The outcome of the library service may affect the individual who is the customer. The next step is to see what the impact of that person's change has on those around him or her. What is the value of the change and was there a benefit?

- Teenagers who participate in a technology club get better grades in school,
  - AND influence their family at home by talking about technology and maybe the family will start using computers.

- College students who take information literacy courses write better essays,
  - AND when they graduate will do better in business because they have better writing skills.

- Professional staff who use library services save personal time they can use for other work,

- AND with their improved productivity they can contribute more to the company's profits.

- Physicians order fewer expensive tests after requesting a literature search from the library,
  - AND by ordering the more specific test not only save the patient money but perhaps provide better diagnosis and save the patient's life.

These terms, outcome, impact, value and benefit, as defined above, are sometimes used interchangeably but they do have subtle differences. The word chosen needs to means the same thing to all involved in the discussion. As an example, a library program might be shown to have the *outcome* that more parents read to their children in the evening after attending programs at the public library on the importance of the activity. But the *impact* of the change could be that the children do better in school in the early grades. This then has "value" to the community and the family. Or the impact or outcome has "benefit" to the corporation, the community, or the individual.

Impacts and outcomes can be described in pretty dramatic ways. Proving the outcome and impact has generally been left to large, well-funded studies. So the question for this chapter is: What can the practicing librarian in a health care setting do to evaluate or assess the outcomes or impacts of a library service?

A good start is to use the Logic Model described previously. The Logic Model is a planning document that starts with describing the desired outcome, and sometimes impact, and then working backward to delineate the goals and activities that will produce the outcome. Using this planning technique allows the outcomes to be clarified from the beginning. It gives a basis for choosing what to evaluate.

There are some major initiatives to measure outcomes and impacts. Understanding the terminology and who the experts are can help the librarian keep up with new developments. A practicing librarian, even working in a small setting, can accomplish some of these outcomes and impacts measurements.

The first idea is to report outcomes by doing a quantitative survey that counts outcomes. This is based on a funded program, Counting on Results (CoR). The next idea is based on a report in the literature that uses the techniques of another study funded by the Medical Library Association that uses taxonomies to categorize the library's contributions to the institution. Next, by understanding evidenced-based library and information practice and being able to interpret and describe published studies of outcomes resulting from the use of information,

librarians would be able to communicate the results of significant studies to their supervisors. Finally, understanding published studies of cost outcomes could be used to discuss value, benefit, or worth.

To recap:

- Using surveys to count outcomes
- Using taxonomies to categorize contributions to the institution
- Using published studies to describe outcomes using the EBLIP critical appraisal methodology
- Studies of cost outcomes

The Institute of Museum and Library Services (IMLS) (http://www.imls.gov/) manages the Library Services and Technology Act (LSTA) that provides federal funding for libraries across the country (http://www.imls.gov/programs/programs.sht). To assist libraries with the requirements for outcomes measurement, they funded researchers to come up with techniques for outcomes measurement for public libraries. The IMLS describes an outcome as "a benefit to people through achievements or changes in skill, knowledge, attitude, behavior, condition, or life status." One of the programs funded at the Information School, University of Washington and the School of Information, University of Michigan, produced the *Outcomes Toolkit 2.0* that provides "guidance for going beyond reporting outputs and will help you to discover outcomes, or indicators of impact, of your programs that can be shared with others" (Durrance and Fisher, 2002). Another at Indiana University Purdue University Indianapolis, called *Shaping Outcomes*, also included museums (Indiana University Purdue University Indianapolis, Institute for Museum and Library Services, and Kryder-Reid, 2006). Both are programmed learning sites that are free on the web. The principles and techniques set forth can be adapted to any type of library.

In another library-related government effort, the National Library of Medicine (NLM) funded the Outreach Evaluation Resource Center (OERC) located at the National Network of Libraries of Medicine (NN/LM), Pacific Northwest Region, in Seattle, Washington (2006). Public, academic or medical librarians as well as health educators can be funded by NLM or NN/LM to conduct programs to improve access to health information. The OERC provides assistance in developing well-planned evaluation approaches to help target and measure outreach success. They have adopted the Logic Model as the preferred way to measure the outcomes of their funded programs.

Other Kinds of Outcomes Measurements

Using Surveys to Count Outcomes

The IMLS funded program, Counting on Results (CoR), developed a method to survey outcomes and count them. Working with public libraries, they recruited 45 libraries in 20 states to participate in the project. They developed six questionnaires that addressed most of the 13 "service responses" that had been developed in the Public Library Association's book, *The New Planning for Results: A Streamlined Approach* (Nelson and Public Library Association, 2001). These questions were sent out in postcard form for the survey. The postcard surveys are available on the web and the results of this survey are reported online and in print (Colorado State Library Library Research Service and University of Denver College of Education Library and Information Science Program, 2001; Steffen and Lance, 2002; Steffen, Lance, and Logan, 2002). Management in Action 6.1 describes how this approach might be used in a health care library.

By working with a group of libraries, the end result might be more meaningful since a larger group would be surveyed. Like the CoR project, individual library and demographic results could also be reported. With the use of e-mail, a group of like libraries could cooperate and develop some "service response" questions.

Using Taxonomies to Categorize Contributions to the Institution

Much of this discussion about outcomes has been based on the concept that well-planned and evaluated social programs make a difference in peoples' lives. From successes in these individual changes, there are impacts on community and civic life. If public libraries are viewed this way, these methods work well. For special libraries, outcomes of a library service can benefit the individual in somewhat the same way, but the purpose of seeing changes in the individual in the workplace is to have a positive impact on the corporation. How to connect to that outcome and impact is the problem.

MANAGEMENT IN ACTION 6.1

Measure Customers' Needs for Library Space

Location: Metropolitan Hospital

Description of Problem/Project: It has been decided to do a small survey to measure an outcome or benefit to the library's customers. Not many people come into the library any more since they use the library's e-resources at their desk. The library space is in need of minor renovation but before anything is done, it would be good to know what the customers think of the library as a place to benefit them. The library as place is a "service response," part of the mission and a response to the needs of the customers, but how does having that space affect their life and work? Using the IMLS definition of an outcome, how will having a space for customers in the library, or "the library as place," benefit the customers in relation to their "achievements" or changes in their "skill, knowledge, attitude, behavior, condition, or life status?"

Impact On: Library customers, and staff; Library space

People Involved: Library staff and supervisors; Customers

Strategies for Success: The team discovers in the literature that one of Counting on Results's (CoR) six service responses as listed above is "Commons: the library as place." Using the CoR questionnaire on the library as place as a starting point to develop questions for the library's type, a focus group is formed to work on the subject of library as place to help develop questions. For a special or medical library, the library as place questions that could be revised include this list:

- Met a friend or co-worker to work quietly on a project.
- Scanned print journals for new articles.
- Learned about new books.
- Had a quiet comfortable place to think, read, write, or study.
- Took a break with a cup of coffee from the coffee cart.

The Library staff organized a focus group and survey. From the results they instituted some changes in how their space was arranged.

Barriers Encountered: Time it takes to develop the questions and do the survey. Making sure to follow through on changes.

Take-Home Points: Asking customers their opinion is very important. While it takes staff time to do so, it is worth it and gives the library direction for difficult decisions.

Further Readings: Steffen and Lance, 2002; Steffen, Lance, and Logan, 2002; web resource: http://www.lrs.org/CoR.php.

As mentioned in the outcomes section, Theresa Cuddy used the study sponsored by the MLA called *The Value of Library and Information Services in Hospitals and Academic Health Sciences Centers* (http://www.nlanet.org/pdf/research/value_study_final_report.pdf). The first part of the MLA study surveyed librarians and health care administrators to develop a taxonomy of the contributions of library and information services (LIS) in hospitals and academic health sciences centers. By surveying librarians and health care administrators, the authors developed a shared vocabulary or taxonomy to use to enhance communication between libraries and the management of the institution or company they work for (Abels, Cogdill, and Zach, 2002, 2004). In her study, Cuddy gathered a critical incident survey taken over two years. She asked a simple question at the point of service: "We like to continuously validate and keep records of the contributions that the Health Sciences Library makes to the hospital and/or patient care. Can you please take a moment and write how the information you received helped yourself and ultimately the hospital?" (Cuddy, 2005: 447). Cuddy reported her findings by linking the responses to contributions' taxonomy developed in the MLA study. She was also able to demonstrate a table that linked anecdotal statements from the survey. An evaluation using any of the methods outlined in this chapter could be tied to this taxonomy and used to communicate results to the administration by linking the results to the shared vocabulary of the taxonomy as Cuddy did. The taxonomy from the study can be found on the **accompanying CD-ROM** (used with permission).

USING PUBLISHED STUDIES TO DESCRIBE OUTCOMES

Most special libraries work closely with professionals who use published evidence to support their decisions when performing the jobs assigned to them. Why not use published evidence to support the job that libraries and librarians do? Using evidence-based library and information practice (EBLIP) methods of critical appraisal would be one way to present evidence found in the literature to the administration. EBLIP takes its cue from evidence-based medicine (EBM), a movement that teaches health care practitioners to formulate questions and use effective literature searching to find evidence for medical issues. The idea is that, with the explosion of literature in medicine, it takes specific training in search and statistical techniques to find the "best" evidence for a treatment or diagnosis. The proponents of EBLIP believe librarians should change their professional focus from managing by the example of other programs to

managing by applying the results of research studies that show through evidence that service strategies are effective in helping the library customer.

Many studies reported in the library literature are supported by grant funds and done by librarians specializing in evaluation research. While small studies can be done and can be effective, practicing librarians can also report on the large studies others have performed in a way that benefits their own library. While each library is operating in a different context, parallels can be drawn. By locating outcomes-based research in the literature, it can be proposed that these outcomes studies are applicable to the local situation.

The open access journal, *Evidence Based Library and Information Practice*, (http://ejournals.library.ualberta.ca/index.php/EBLIP/index) publishes evidence summaries to review for interesting articles. While these summaries are quite detailed, a form could be devised and articles reported to the librarian's supervisor using the same format each time. The editor, Lindsay Glynn, has devised a critical appraisal checklist (Glynn, 2006) that can be found at the wiki, *Evidence Based Toolkit for Public Libraries* (*Evidence Based Toolkit for Public Libraries*, 2008). Using these tools to learn how to do critical appraisal, a more simplified form might include the following:

- Journal citation
- Copies of interesting tables
- Methodology
- Conclusions
- Results
- Relevance to our situation

STUDIES OF COST OUTCOMES

In special libraries in corporate settings, the approach of using cost and time savings to show the value or worth of the library service to the corporation has been researched and discussed. Using the theories of cost-benefit analysis or return on investment, the studies have been done to describe cost savings in libraries. In their book *Special Libraries: Increasing the Information Edge*, Griffiths and King (1993) take the approach that professionals have a communication pattern and libraries play a role in supporting that communication. They state that: "Professionals who use information extensively and effectively are more successful than those who do not. Increased productivity and improved quality are among the benefits gained. Furthermore, substantially greater benefits are achieved from information provided through organization libraries" (Griffiths and King, 1993: 1).

From the studies they review, Griffiths and King (1993) document that the professionals who make effective use of information and libraries have an "information edge" when it comes to individual, corporate, or societal success.

Using the concepts of the Griffiths and King studies, various value calculators are available on the web. The National Network of Libraries of Medicine (NN/LM), Midcontinental Region, has developed two calculators based on previous work done for public libraries (National Network of Libraries of Medicine [NN/LM] Midcontinental Region, 2008a,b).

The *Valuing Library Services Calculator* determines what a library is worth to its institution. What would it cost to replace the library services on the retail market? First calculate what it would cost to buy library services—at a bookstore, through pay-per-view for articles, from an information broker—if the library was not there. Figures have been input to help, based on the studies, but local calculations can be used. Then input the library budget figures. The total value of library services is shown at the bottom of the worksheet. It is usually an astoundingly large number.

The other, *Cost Benefit and ROI Calculator*, demonstrates cost/benefit analysis and return on investment. These are measures often used by financial managers to gauge the efficiency and effectiveness of their budget policies. How much benefit does the institution receive for every dollar spent by the library? What's the annual return the institution realizes on what is spent on the collection? If the administration is interested in this kind of information, these are very powerful tools. While the numbers generated by these calculators may seem amazing, the studies collated by Griffiths and King were taken from large professional studies and routinely show the same thing. As they state in their final sentence, "It seems abundantly clear that library services pay for themselves by orders of magnitude" (Griffiths and King, 1993: 190).

How to Measure

No matter which evaluation project is planned—needs assessment, quality improvement, use of standards, benchmarking, or outcomes—measurement tools will need to be used. All of the tools mentioned here have extensive resources in print and on the web as well as a more detailed explanation in Chapter 10 of the book *Using Benchmarking, Needs Assessment, Quality Improvement, Outcome Measurement, and Library Standards: A How-To-Do-It Manual* (Dudden, 2007). This overview will give some idea of what these tools are. It is often asked which tool goes with which project. Most of these

tools can be used within any evaluation project. They all need to be planned and budgeted and it is often the time line and budget that determines the tool. According to Johnson (1996) there are two categories of criteria to match the choice of research method to the evaluation plan or questionnaire: meaningfulness and practicality. Meaningfulness includes whether the method is goal-related, able to be interpreted, timely, comparable, or appropriate. Practicality means affordability in terms of intrusiveness, ease and cost. Whatever method is used, approval from an Institutional Review Board for the Protection of Human Subjects or IRB may be needed, as described in the sidebar.

Institutional Review Board

Whenever the evaluation plan involves asking "humans" a question, the program may be doing primary research on human subjects. In a hospital, university, or research setting, these institutions usually have an Institutional Review Board for the Protection of Human Subjects, often known as an IRB. An IRB is a group that has been formally designated to review and monitor biomedical research involving human subjects, in accordance with Food and Drug Administration (FDA) regulations. An IRB has the authority to approve, require modifications in (to secure approval), or disapprove research. This group review ensures protection of the rights and welfare of human research subjects. If the evaluation plan includes a primary data-gathering project of employees using any of these methods, they might be considered "human subjects" and their privacy and other issues may need to be protected. It is best to check to see if a review is necessary so as not to be stopped by regulations in the middle of the project. Of course, the whole point is that the evaluation team and leaders want to know that they are correctly protecting their subjects and the IRB office can advise them on this. Once the data-gathering plans (or research protocols as they might call them) are decided upon, the plans can be presented to the IRB.

Surveys

Considerations for a Survey Project

When most people think of evaluation or assessment, usually the first thing that comes to mind is to go out and take a survey. Surveys can gather information from people about their beliefs, knowledge, opinions, attitudes, and backgrounds. But the team needs to decide, "Is a survey the right method for the current project?" Review the purpose and objectives of the project. Is a survey really going to answer the question?

Ask for help from experts. Be aware that the team may not have the skills necessary to do an extensive survey using statistically valid methods, but it is always appropriate to ask for help from other personnel or colleagues who do. The institution may even have a statistics department. The classic resources for survey development are by Dillman and Salant (Dillman, 2000; Salant and Dillman, 1994).

Develop a Management Plan

The steps it takes to carry out a survey are detailed in Figure 6.10, adapted from Taylor-Powell (Taylor-Powell, Hermann, and University of Wisconsin–Extension. Cooperative Extension Service, 2000). They are detailed for a mail survey or an e-mail survey. Knowing these steps will help the team make a management plan for the survey.

Other considerations are:

- Assigning responsibilities to the project team members

- Scheduling the many tasks involved, perhaps using a Gantt chart

- Budgeting the costs of a survey in terms of labor for development and analysis as well as direct expenses to carry out the survey

Determine a Method of Distribution

This needs to be done before the questionnaire is developed as it will influence what and how many questions are asked. Combining techniques can be appropriate in some situations. This list outlines various ways to administer a survey to attempt to maximize return.

- Surveys can be handed out and completed on the spot, ensuring a good response.

- They can be handed out and collected at a later date.

- The questionnaire can be sent out in the mail.

- A questionnaire can be sent via e-mail and people asked to reply with their answers.

- An online survey software product, such as Survey-Monkey or Zoomerang, can be used.

- The survey questionnaire can be administered in person by appointment as in an interview.

- The questionnaire can be administered by telephone.

Plan the Questionnaire

Now that the purpose and planned method of delivery have been confirmed, it is time to plan the questionnaire, a critical and time-consuming step. The actual details of question writing and pre-testing are covered in

Figure 6.10. Survey Procedure

Mail Survey	Computer Survey on Commercial Site
Complete the planning process	Complete the planning process
Decide if the survey is anonymous or confidential	Decide if the survey is anonymous or confidential
Develop the questionnaire	Develop the questionnaire outline
Pilot test the questionnaire	Input the questionnaire on the commercial site
Develop the cover letter	Pilot test the questionnaire
Develop advance notice material	Develop the introductory e-mail
Develop follow-up postcards	Develop advance notice material
Prepare mailing materials	Develop follow-up e-mails
Do advance notices	Finish the questionnaire
Finish the questionnaire	Do advance notices via e-mail and paper
Send first mailing	Send first e-mail
Track survey responses	Track survey responses
Send Follow-up postcard	Send second e-mail
Send second mailing	Send final e-mail
Send final mailing	Process data
Process data	Analyze and interpret data
Analyze and interpret data	Write reports
Write reports	Communicate findings
Communicate findings	

Source: Adapted from Taylor-Powell, Hermann, and University of Wisconsin–Extension, Cooperative Extension Service, 2000.

the literature or by taking courses (Taylor-Powell, Marshall, and University of Wisconsin–Extension. Cooperative Extension Service, 1998; Lance and Johnson, 1996; Dudden, 2007). These are other issues in questionnaire planning no matter which method of survey distribution is decided on:

- Determine the total population. Sometimes called a "sampling frame," this is a definitive list from which a sample will drawn.
- Determine the sample. Projects rarely have the funds to survey the total population. A correctly chosen sample will allow the results to be generalizable to other situations.
- Plan for quality. These are a few places where the team can check for quality:
  - The actual survey
  - Postprocessing of the survey
  - Planning the analysis
  - Planning to communicate

Focus Groups

Focus groups are a form of qualitative research that can compliment or replace surveys. Focus groups *articulate* people's views, ideas, and opinions, while surveys *quantify* people's opinions. Focus groups are never used to decide on an issue or resolve conflicts, but only to identify opinions. If there is a situation that needs to be resolved, a focus group is not a substitute for a committee that might come up with a plan to solve a problem. Focus groups do not result in action. Focus groups are used in various combinations such as doing a survey and then using a focus group to expand upon problems brought out in the survey or using a focus group to discuss a topic and from this discussion, develop survey questions. Because library customers have varied and strong opinions about information and its uses in their life and work, focus groups can be particularly valuable. Resources by Glitz and Higa-Moore describe in detail how focus groups are used in libraries (Higa-Moore et al., 2002; Glitz, Hamasu, and Sandstrom, 2001; Glitz and Medical Library Association, 1998; Glitz, 1997).

Basically a focus group brings together 6 to 10 people to discuss a topic using a specific set of questions. A moderator is recruited. The person involved in the problem should not lead the group as moderator because he or she might bias the answers. The group usually meets for an hour or two and takes turns answering a preset list of open-ended questions. Another person, the recorder, records the discussion by machine or by hand so long as all participants are informed. The moderator, and/or perhaps the recorder, transcribes the discussion. Then the transcription is analyzed and trends and opinions are coded and pulled out. The responses to each question are analyzed and organized into topics and subtopics. The information is rearranged by these topics so the researcher can see what was said about each issue and suggest from the conversions what the participants consider important. Using a focus group is a form of qualitative evaluation that has its own set of data analysis processes. These include reviewing the comments and categorizing and coding them. The tasks involved in running a focus group are as follows:

- Develop questions or script.
- Decide on a moderator and recorder.
- Recruit participants.
- Meet with group and discuss questions.
- Record discussions.
- Transcribe discussions.
- Code and classify responses.
- Analyze responses.
- Report findings.

Focus groups have some benefits over other data-gathering techniques. They can sometimes be done more quickly than a survey and often using in-house personnel. Librarians often have the skills necessary to conduct focus group research without outside help. Since libraries have so many different types of users, the groups can be segmented by user type, which can often facilitate better discussions. It can be a relatively simple method for getting opinions from users. The open-ended nature of focus groups help identify issues the team might not think to ask about in a survey.

Observation

Sometimes called unobtrusive observation or direct observation, this evaluation technique can be simple if well planned. Watching what goes on is always informative but using observation as an evaluation technique takes a more systematic approach. It requires planning as to what is the purpose, who is being observed, how it will be recorded and analyzed, and how it will be reported.

Observation is useful when direct information is needed or wanted, such as visiting other libraries to see their physical setup. Observation is useful when trying to understand:

- An ongoing behavior, such as circulation or reference
- A situation, such as theft or vandalism
- A process, such as observing manager meetings or training sessions

In a recent article about some of the issues and techniques involved in observation, Baker (2006: 172) states, "Observation is a complex research method because it often requires the researcher to play a number of roles and to use a number of techniques, including her/his five senses, to collect data." Her article describes the types of roles a researcher can assume during an observational study and provides an overview of some of the characteristics unique to observational research, as well as validity and reliability and ethical issues.

Steps in developing an evaluation plan for an observation study include:

- Develop the observation form with checklist.
- Determine how many times the activity or population needs to be observed.
- Determine the time and place where the observation will take place.
- Recruit and train the observers.
- Decide who and how many people are going to be observed.
- Make the observations.
- Analyze and report the results. (Johnson, 1996)

Interviews

Conducting an interview in-person or on the telephone is an alternative method of evaluation. An in-person interview requires that good questions be developed, a time arranged, and an interviewer with good listening skills chosen. Interviewees can be chosen using sampling techniques or through a key informant interview methodology in which a specific set of people are chosen, people who have a knowledgeable perspective on the nature and scope of the problem or question (Higa-Moore et al., 2002). As with all studies, every question on the interview script should have a specific purpose; i.e., What does the evaluation project want to know? Using the principles discussed below in designing questionnaires is essential. Pre-testing is a must. One-on-one interviews can be in person, by phone, online using a web survey or instant messaging, or using a self-recorded audiotape.

Interviewers are the best assets when using the interview method of evaluation. They must be good, trained listeners and observers and not talk too much. It is also best if their age, race, appearance, and social demeanor are similar to the people being interviewed because people tend to speak more candidly to those who look and sound like themselves (Robbins, 1996). If more than one interviewer is used, they need be trained together to make the interviews consistent.

Developing the interview questionnaire follows the same principles of good questionnaire design. As with a paper questionnaire, the interview can be of several types: a standardized, open-ended interview; a guided or structured interview; or an informal, conversational interview. Using interviews instead of paper questionnaires can result in more understanding of an individual's experience and how that experience affected the individual. A bond can develop with the interviewee that may be beneficial in the future, especially with key informant interviews. This method might be chosen when actually hearing the voice of the user appears to be important. Here are the steps in planning to use interviewing as an evaluation tool:

- Determine the purpose of the interview.
- Identify target interview issues.
- Determine the questions to be asked and produce an interview script.
- Determine the method to ask the questions, i.e., in person, on the phone, via e-mail.
- Determine whom to ask or define the sample.
- Pre-test the interview script.
- Select and train the interviewers.
- Prepare interview schedule.
- Obtain written permission at the beginning of each interview.
- Conduct the interviews.
- Code and analyze the notes or tapes.
- Interpret findings.
- Prepare reports.

E-measurement

With the advent of the Internet and electronic resources, measuring electronic resources has become an increasingly complex problem. Initiatives are trying to solve these issues. Most of these measures are technical; the numbers produced are ambiguous in their meaning and other exceptional forces are involved as described in the sidebar.

Assessing the E-library of the Twenty-First Century

"Digital library evaluation is at the crossroads of technology, evaluation, library, and market development. It is challenging disciplinary boundaries and pushing, dissolving, and recreating the boundaries of teaching and learning. Questions of pedagogy, economics, social, and personal development constitute components of a larger picture that the larger National Science Digital Library (NSDL) evaluation process might want to address as it focuses on the educational impact of digital library resources and services. Our project emphasizes the importance of the service delivery aspect of the educational process; we are attempting to measure it in a way that is grounded in users' perceptions" (Cook et al., 2003: 6).

The actual electronic resources and how they work are described in other chapters. Library website development and issues are discussed in Chapter 10. The acquisition of electronic journal and book systems is described in Chapter 7 and their management in Chapter 8. Budgeting for them is covered in Chapter 4. But once all these resources and the library website are available to customers, how are they evaluated?

For the library website, the web-server log can be analyzed to see which pages to support with staff time (Blecic, Fiscella, and Wiberley, 2007). It's not going to be an analysis about whether to have a website but rather how to evaluate its navigation and content (Berger, 2006). For e-journals, there is the COUNTER (Counting Online Usage of Networked Electronic Resources) standard for statistics (http://www.projectcounter.org/). The statistics can be gathered all at once through a system called SUSHI (Standardized Usage Statistics Harvesting Initiative) (http://www.niso.org/workrooms/sushi).

Besides supporting COUNTER and SUSHI, the Association of Research Libraries (ARL) has initiatives to describe the new world of electronic resources. Formerly called the New Measures Initiative (http://www.arl.org/stats/newmeas/), the program has been renamed StatsQUAL (http://www.statsqual.org/). According to the website, as a gateway to the ARL library assessment tools, this initiative attempts to describe the role, character, and impact of physical and digital libraries. Libraries gain access to a number of resources that are used to assess library's effectiveness and contributions to teaching, learning, and research. The five tools are presented as a single interactive framework that integrates and enhances data mining and presentation both within and across institutions. While these programs are available to ARL members and others for a fee, they

influence the culture of evaluation and assessment and set an example of quality. The five tools are:

- ARL Statistics, a series of annual publications that describe the collections, expenditures, staffing, and service activities for ARL member libraries;
- DigiQUAL, a program for modifying and repurposing the existing LibQUAL+ protocol to assess the services provided by digital libraries;
- LibQUAL+, a rigorously tested web-based survey that libraries use to solicit, track, understand, and act upon users' opinions of service quality;
- MINES for Libraries, an online transaction-based survey that collects data on the purpose of the use of electronic resources and the demographics of users; and
- ClimateQUAL, an Organizational Climate and Diversity Assessment which is an assessment of library staff perceptions concerning (a) their library's commitment to the principles of diversity, (b) organizational policies and procedures, and (c) staff attitudes.

Another example is the IMLS-funded **E-Metrics Instructional System** (EMIS) at the Information Use Management Policy Institute and the School of Information Studies at Florida State University (http://emis.ii.fsu.edu/). EMIS was designed to provide library administrators, practitioners, and researchers with a better understanding of the roles and uses of e-metrics. In the context of libraries, e-metrics serve as a means by which to measure the use of electronic services and resources. The EMIS materials and modules provide assistance and continuing education for those seeking to use e-metrics in their library. The EMIS program has an excellent downloadable Electronic Resources & Services Annual Report that can be copied and adapted for the local situation. These initiatives will allow the practicing librarian eventually to be able to measure the new electronic resources available in their library and understand how to communicate the measures to their administrator.

An excellent resource for the study of e-metrics is White and Kamal's (2006) *E-metrics for Library and Information Professionals: How to Use Data for Managing and Evaluating Electronic Resource Collections*. As they say in the introduction, they are trying to "bridge the gap between past [print] collection use management and the emerging solutions for handling virtual collections" (White and Kamal, 2006: xvii). The book is divided into three parts that define e-metrics for libraries, describe the uses for e-metrics, and instruct libraries on methods for creating e-metrics solutions. Librarians with little experience in e-metrics as well as those who already have some data-gathering methods in place can use this resource. This clear guide will be useful for those who wish to begin managing data to support their decisions regarding electronic resources. Using some of the methods outlined will help determine if the library is buying the right resources and getting value for its money.

Conclusion

In these changing, turbulent environments, evaluation is about making decisions and then defending the decisions. Evaluation provides the "evidence" for:

- Development of services and programs
- Improvement of services and programs
- Informed decision making
- Accountability to show others that the services and programs are effective
- Demonstrating value or worth of an information service to the user's life or work

Evaluation allows the librarian to learn to do things better and to do better things. Evaluation projects take many forms, from quality improvement to a statement of value or worth to informed management decisions based on timely, accurate information. Having a culture of assessment improves the likelihood that learning and decision making will be enhanced. The essential ingredients are staff involvement, a customer focus, and a systematic plan. Traditions and politics are powerful forces in virtually every environment and need to be met head on in a systematic way with an evaluation plan.

In response to all these pressures, there is a need to continually examine what a library is today and tomorrow. Many groups are trying to reinvent or reconceptualize the library. Martha Kyrillidou from ARL discusses how libraries have gone from concentrating on the workings of the library to examining the user and seeing how they can use the library and what they need. One new model she quotes is that the "library serves as a physical presence, a memory institution, a learning center, a community resource and an invisible intermediary" (Kyrillidou, 2002: 42). It is through constant evaluation that we will be able to set the course to the new library.

Many initiatives on many levels are addressing these changes. Each initiative has implications for all libraries and needs to be supported across boundaries of association and library type. These initiatives cover different

challenges and work on figuring out how to measure the new information environment, how to explain the new environment to others, how to measure the new political environment, and how to influence the new technical environment. With the help of experts in the field of library and information science evaluation and assessment, we will be able to carry out assessment and evaluation, develop needed services, improve the services we have, make decisions based on the evidence, and demonstrate that our effective library service has value and worth in the life and work of our user.

References

Abels, Eileen G., Keith W. Cogdill, and Lisl Zach. 2002. "The Contributions of Library and Information Services to Hospitals and Academic Health Sciences Centers: A Preliminary Taxonomy." *Journal of the Medical Library Association* 90, no. 3 (July): 276–284.

Abels, Eileen G., Keith W. Cogdill, and Lisl Zach. 2004. "Identifying and Communicating the Contributions of Library and Information Services in Hospitals and Academic Health Sciences Centers." *Journal of the Medical Library Association* 92, no. 1 (January): 46–55.

ACRL College and Research Libraries Task Force. 2004. "Standards for Libraries in Higher Education: The Final, Approved Standard." *College & Research Libraries News* 65, no. 9: 534–543.

American Productivity & Quality Center (APQC). 2003. Houston, TX. Accessed July 10, 2010. http://www.apqc.org/portal/apqc/site?path=root.

Andersen, Bjørn, and Per-Gaute Pettersen. 1996. *The Benchmarking Handbook: Step-by-Step Instructions*. New York: Chapman & Hall.

Association of Academic Health Sciences Libraries. AAHSL Charting the Future Task Force. 2003. "Building on Success: Charting the Future of Knowledge Management Within the Academic Health Center." [Seattle, WA]: Association of Academic Health Sciences Libraries. Accessed October 4, 2010. http://www.aahsl.org/mc/page.do?site PageId=84882. Viewable document at: http://kuscholarworks.ku.edu/dspace/bitstream/1808/217/1/Charting_the_Future_viewable .pdf.

Association of College & Research Libraries. American Library Association. 1998. *Task Force on Academic Library Outcomes Assessment Report*. Accessed July 10, 2010. http://www.ala.org/ala/mgrps/divs/acrl/publications/whitepapers/taskforceacademic.cfm.

Association of College & Research Libraries. American Library Association. 2005. *Standards & Guidelines*. Association of College & Research Libraries. American Library Association. Accessed July 10, 2010. http://www.ala.org/ala/mgrps/divs/acrl/standards/index.cfm.

Baker, Lynda M. 2006. "Observation: A Complex Research Method." *Library Trends* 55, no. 1 (Summer): 171–189.

Baker, Sharon L., and F. Wilfrid Lancaster. 1991. "The Relevance of Standards to the Evaluation of Library Services." In *The Measurement and Evaluation of Library Services*, 2nd ed., edited by Sharon L. Baker and F. Wilfred Lancaster, 321–334. Arlington, VA: Information Resources Press.

Barnes, Susan, Maryanne Blake, and Betsy Kelly. 2006. *Measuring Your Impact: Using Evaluation to Demonstrate Value*. National Network of Libraries of Medicine. Accessed September 15, 2010. http://nnlm.gov/evaluation/workshops/measuring_your_impact/impact-slides.ppt.

Berger, Pam. 2006. "How to Evaluate Websites: For Better or Worse." *Information Searcher* 16, no. 2: 1–10.

Blecic, Deborah D., Joan B. Fiscella, and Stephen E. Wiberley, Jr. 2007. "Measurement of Use of Electronic Resources: Advances in Use Statistics and Innovations in Resource Functionality." *College & Research Libraries* 68, no. 1 (January): 26–44.

Booth, Andrew, and Anne Brice. 2004. *Evidence-Based Practice for Information Professionals: A Handbook*. London: Facet Publishing.

Burroughs, Catherine M., and Fred B. Wood. 2000. *Measuring the Difference: Guide to Planning and Evaluating Health Information Outreach*. Seattle, WA, Bethesda, MD: National Network of Libraries of Medicine Pacific Northwest Region. National Library of Medicine. Accessed July 10, 2010. http://nnlm.gov/evaluation/guide/index.html.

Byrd, Gary D., and James Shedlock. 2003. "The Association of Academic Health Sciences Libraries Annual Statistics: An Exploratory Twenty-Five-Year Trend Analysis." *Journal of the Medical Library Association* 91, no. 2 (April): 186–202.

Calvert, Philip J. 1994. "Library Effectiveness: The Search for a Social Context." *Journal of Librarianship and Information Science* 26, no. 1 (March): 15–21.

Colorado State Library Library Research Service, and University of Denver College of Education Library and Information Science Program. 2001. *Counting on Results*. Accessed July 10, 2010. http://www.lrs.org/CoR.php.

Cook, Colleen, Yvonna Lincoln, Fred Heath, Bruce Thompson, Martha Kyrillidou, and Duane Webster. 2003. *Developing a National Science Digital Library (NSDL) LibQUAL+™ Protocol: An E-service for Assessing the Library of the 21st Century*. Washington, DC, October 12–15. Accessd July 10, 2010. http://www.libqual.org/documents/admin/NSDL_workshop_web1.pdf.

Crabtree, Anna Beth, and Julia H. Crawford. 1997. "Assessing and Addressing the Library Needs of Health Care Personnel in A Large Regional Hospital." *Bulletin of the Medical Library Association* 85, no. 2 (April): 167–175.

Cuddy, Theresa M. 2005. "Value of Hospital Libraries: The Fuld Campus Study." *Journal of the Medical Library Association* 93, no. 4 (October): 446–449.

Dalrymple, Prudence W. 2009. *Applying Evidence to Practice: Gaps, Barriers and Lessons Learned From Healthcare*. Paper read at 5th International Evidence-Based Library & Information Practice Conference, June 29–July 3, 2009, at Stockholm, Sweden. Accessed January 14, 2011. http://blogs.kib.ki.se/eblip5/PDalrymplepresentation.pdf.

Dalrymple, Prudence W., and Carol S. Scherrer. 1998. "Tools for Improvement: A Systematic Analysis and Guide to Accreditation by the JCAHO." *Bulletin of the Medical Library Association* 86, no. 1 (January): 10–16.

Dillman, Don A. 2000. *Mail and Internet Surveys: The Tailored Design Method*. 2nd ed. New York: Wiley.

Dudden, Rosalind F. 2007. *Using Benchmarking, Needs Assessment, Quality Improvement, Outcome Measurement, and Library Standards: A How-To-Do-It Manual with CD-ROM*. New York: Neal-Schuman.

Dudden, Rosalind Farnam, Kate Corcoran, Janice Kaplan, Jeff Magouirk, Debra C. Rand, and Bernie Todd Smith. 2006a. "The Medical Library Association Benchmarking Network: Development and Implementation." *Journal of the Medical Library Association* 94, no. 2 (April): 107–117.

Dudden, Rosalind Farnam, Kate Corcoran, Janice Kaplan, Jeff Magouirk, Debra C. Rand, and Bernie Todd Smith. 2006b. "The Medical Library Association Benchmarking Network: Results." *Journal of the Medical Library Association* 94, no. 2 (April): 118–129.

Durrance, Joan C., and Karen E. Fisher. 2002. *Outcomes Toolkit 2.0*. Ann Arbor, MI, and Seattle, WA: University of Michigan and University of Washington. Accessed July 10, 2010. http://ibec.ischool.washington.edu/static/ibeccat.aspx@subcat=outcome%20toolkit&cat=tools%20and%20 resources.htm.

Eldredge, Jonathan D. 2000. "Evidence-Based Librarianship: An Overview." *Bulletin of the Medical Library Association* 88, no. 4 (October): 289–302.

Evidence Based Toolkit for Public Libraries. 2008. Accessed July 10, 2010. http://ebltoolkit.pbworks.com/.

Fifth International Evidence-Based Library & Information Practice Conference. 2009. Stockholm, Sweden: Karolinska Institutet University Library. Accessed July 10, 2010. http://blogs.kib.ki.se/eblip5/.

Flower, M. A. 1978. "Toward Hospital Library Standards in Canada." *Bulletin of the Medical Library Association* 66, no. 3 (July): 296–301.

Fulda, Pauline O., and Rebecca K. Satterthwaite. 2003. "Proceedings, 102d Annual Meeting Medical Library Association, Inc. Dallas, Texas May 17–23, 2002." *Journal of the Medical Library Association* 91, no. 1 (January): 103–136.

Fulda, Pauline O., and Rebecca K. Satterthwaite. 2004. "Proceedings, 103rd Annual Meeting Medical Library Association, Inc. San Diego, California May 2–7, 2003." *Journal of the Medical Library Association* 92, no. 1 (January): 117–124.

Glitz, Beryl. 1997. "The Focus Group Technique in Library Research: An Introduction." *Bulletin of the Medical Library Association* 85, no. 4 (October): 385–390.

Glitz, Beryl, Clare Hamasu, and Heidi Sandstrom. 2001. "The Focus Group: A Tool for Programme Planning, Assessment and Decision-Making—An American View." *Health Information & Libraries Journal* 18, no. 1 (March): 30–37.

Glitz, Beryl, and Medical Library Association. 1998. *Focus Groups for Libraries and Librarians*. New York: Forbes.

Glynn, Lindsay. 2006. "A Critical Appraisal Tool for Library and Information Research." *Library Hi Tech* 24, no. 3: 387–399.

Griffiths, José-Marie, and Donald Ward King. 1993. *Special Libraries: Increasing the Information Edge*. Washington, DC: Special Libraries Association.

Henczel, Susan. 2002. "Benchmarking—Measuring and Comparing for Continuous Improvement." *Information Outlook* 6, no. 7 (July): 12–20.

Higa-Moore, Mori Lou, Brian Bunnett, Helen G. Mayo, and Cynthia A. Olney. 2002. "Use of Focus Groups in a Library's Strategic Planning Process." *Journal of the Medical Library Association* 90, no. 1 (January): 86–92.

Hiller, Steve, Martha Kyrillidou, and James Self. 2006. "Assessment in North American Research Libraries: A Preliminary Report Card." *Performance Measurement and Metrics* 7, no. 2: 100–106.

Hospital Libraries Section Standards Committee, Margaret Bandy, Jacqueline Donaldson Doyle, Anne Fladger, Katherine Stemmer Frumento, Linne Girouard, Sheila Hayes, and Diane Rourke. 2008. "Standards for Hospital Libraries 2007: Hospital Libraries Section Standards Committee." *Journal of the Medical Library Association* 96, no. 2 (April): 162–169.

Indiana University Purdue University Indianapolis, Institute for Museum and Library Services, and Elizabeth Kryder-Reid. 2006. *Shaping Outcomes: Making a Difference in Museums and Libraries*. Accessed July 10, 2010. http://www.shapingoutcomes.org/course/index.htm.

Institute of Museum and Library Services. 2006. *Outcome Based Evaluation Overview: New Directives, New Directions: Documenting Outcomes in IMLS Grants to Libraries and Museums*. Washington, DC: Institute of Museum and Library Services. Accessed July 10, 2010. http://www.imls.gov/applicants/basics.shtm.

Johnson, Debra Wilcox. 1996. "Choosing an Evaluation Method." In *The TELL IT! Manual: The Complete Program for Evaluating Library Performance*, edited by Douglas L. Zweizig, Debra Wilcox Johnson, Jane Robbins, and American Library Association. Chicago: American Library Association.

Koufogiannakis, Denise, and Ellen T. Crumley. 2002. "Evidence-Based Librarianship." *Féliciter* 48, no. 3: 112–114.

Kyrillidou, Martha. 2002. "From Input and Output Measures to Quality and Outcome Measures, or, from the User in the Life of the Library to the Library in the Life of the User." *Journal of Academic Librarianship* 28, no. 1/2 (January/March): 42–46.

Lakos, Amos. 2004. *Culture of Assessment—Toolkit*. Accessed July 10, 2010. http://lakmau.com/CUtoolkit-1.html.

Lakos, Amos, and Shelley Phipps. 2004. "Creating A Culture of Assessment: A Catalyst for Organizational Change." *Portal* 4, no. 3 (July): 345–361.

Lance, Keith Curry, and Debra Wilcox Johnson. 1996. "Questionnaires." In *The TELL IT! Manual: The Complete Program for Evaluating Library Performance*, edited by Douglas L. Zweizig, Debra Wilcox Johnson, Jane Robbins, and American Library Association. Chicago: American Library Association.

Lee-Thomas, Gwen, and John Robson. 2004. "The Questions of Academic Library Assessment." *Indiana Libraries* 23, no. 1: 6–10.

LibQUAL+. 2007. Washington, DC: Association of Research Libraries. Acessed July 10, 2010. http://www.libqual.org/.

Love, Erica. 1986. "Challenge to Action." *Bulletin of the Medical Library Association* 74, no. 4 (October): 376–379.

Marshall, Joanne Gard. 1993. *The Impact of the Special Library on Corporate Decision-Making*. Washington, DC: Special Libraries Association.

Marshall, Joanne Gard. 1999. "Health Canada Libraries: Past, Present, and Future." In *Practical Information Policies*, edited by Elizabeth Orna. Aldershot, Hampshire, England; Brookfield, VT: Gower.

Marshall, Joanne Gard. 2000. "Determining Our Worth, Communicating Our Value." *Library Journal* 125, no. 19 (November 15): 28–30.

Medical Library Association. 2006. *Vital Pathways for Hospital Librarians*. Chicago: Medical Library Association. Accessed July 10, 2010. http://mlanet.org/resources/vital/index.html.

Medical Library Association. 2010. *MLANET*. Chicago: Medical Library Association. Accessed July 10. http://mlanet.org/.

Mein, Nardina Nameth. 2000. "Quality Improvement." In *The Medical Library Association Guide to Managing Health Care Libraries*, edited by Ruth Holst and Sharon A. Phillips, 55–73. Chicago: Medical Library Association; Neal-Schuman.

National Network of Libraries of Medicine. 2006. *Outreach Evaluation Resource Center (OERC)*. Seattle, WA: National Network of Libraries of Medicine, Pacific Northwest Region. Accessed July 10, 2010. http://nnlm.gov/evaluation/.

National Network of Libraries of Medicine (NN/LM) Midcontinental Region. 2008a. *Valuing Library Services Calculator*. Accessed July 10, 2010. http://nnlm.gov/mcr/evaluation/calculator.html.

National Network of Libraries of Medicine (NN/LM) Midcontinental Region. 2008b. *Cost Benefit and ROI Calculator*. Accessed July 10, 2010. http://nnlm.gov/mcr/evaluation/roi.html.

Nelson, Sandra S., and Public Library Association. 2001. *The New Planning for Results: A Streamlined Approach*. Chicago: American Library Association.

Online Computer Library Center Inc. 2003. *Libraries: How They Stack Up*. Dublin, OH: OCLC Online Computer Library Center Inc. Accessed July 10, 2010. http://digitalarchive.oclc.org/request?id%3Doclcnum%3A53042543.

Orenstein, David I. 1999. "Developing Quality Managers and Quality Management: The Challenge to Leadership in Library Organizations." *Library Administration and Management* 13, no. 1 (Winter): 44–51.

Perley, Cathy M., Camillia A. Gentry, A. Sue Fleming, and Kristin M. Sen. 2007. "Conducting a User-Centered Information Needs Assessment: The Via Christi Libraries' Experience." *Journal of the Medical Library Association* 95, no. 2 (April): 173–181, e54–55.

Phipps, Shelley E. 2001. "Beyond Measuring Service Quality—Learning from the Voices of the Customers, the Staff, the Processes, and the Organization." *Library Trends* 49, no. 4 (Spring): 635–661.

Poll, Roswitha. 2003. "Measuring Impact and Outcome of Libraries." *Performance Measurement and Metrics* 4, no. 1: 5–12.

Robbins, Jane Borsch. 1996. "Interviewing." In *The TELL IT! Manual: The Complete Program for Evaluating Library Performance*, edited by Douglas L. Zweizig, Debra Wilcox Johnson, and Jane Robbins, 161–175. Chicago: American Library Association.

Salant, Priscilla, and Don A. Dillman. 1994. *How to Conduct Your Own Survey*. New York: Wiley.

Shedlock, James, and Gary D. Byrd. 2003. "The Association of Academic Health Sciences Libraries Annual Statistics: A Thematic History." *Journal of the Medical Library Association* 91, no. 2 (April): 178–185.

Spendolini, Michael J. 2000. *The Benchmarking Book*. 2nd ed. New York: AMACOM; McGraw-Hill.

Steffen, Nicolle O., and Keith Curry Lance. 2002. "Who's Doing What: Outcome-Based Evaluation and Demographics in the Counting On Results Project." *Public Libraries* 41, no. 5 (September/October): 271–276, 278–279.

Steffen, Nicolle O., Keith Curry Lance, and Rochelle Logan. 2002. "Time to Tell the Whole Story; Outcome-Based Evaluation and the Counting On Results Project." *Public Libraries* 41, no. 4 (July/August): 222–228.

Taylor-Powell, Ellen, Carol Hermann, and University of Wisconsin–Extension. Cooperative Extension Service. 2000. "Collecting Evaluation Data: Surveys." In *Program Development and Evaluation—10*. Madison, WI: University of Wisconsin–Extension, Cooperative Extension Service. Accessed November 16, 2010. http://www.uwex.edu/ces/pdande/evaluation/evaldocs.html.

Taylor-Powell, Ellen, Mary G. Marshall, and University of Wisconsin–Extension. Cooperative Extension Service.

1998. "Questionnaire Design: Asking Questions with a Purpose." In *Program Development and Evaluation—02*. Madison, WI: University of Wisconsin–Extension, Cooperative Extension Service. Accessed November 16, 2010. http://www.uwex.edu/ces/pdande/evaluation/evaldocs.html.

Todd-Smith, Bernie, and Linda Garr Markwell. 2002. "The Value of Hospital Library Benchmarking: An Overview and Annotated References." *Medical Reference Services Quarterly* 21, no. 3 (Fall): 85–95.

University of Wisconsin–Extension. 2005. *Logic Model*. Madison, WI: University of Wisconsin. Accessed July 10, 2010. http://www.uwex.edu/ces/pdande/evaluation/evallogicmodel.html.

Urquhart, Christine. 2005. "Assessing Impact: Let Us Count the Ways?" *Library + Information Update* 4, no. 12 (December): 26–28.

Urquhart, Christine, and John Hepworth. 1995. "The Value of Information Supplied to Clinicians by Health Libraries: Devising an Outcomes-Based Assessment of the Contribution of Libraries to Clinical Decision-Making." *Health Libraries Review* 12, no. 3 (September): 201–213.

W. K. Kellogg Foundation. 2004. *Logic Model Development Guide*. Battle Creek, MI: W. K. Kellogg Foundation.

Weightman, Alison, Christine Urquhart, Sian Spink, Rhian Thomas, and National Library for Health Library Services Development Group. 2009. "The Value and Impact of Information Provided Through Library Services for Patient Care: Developing Guidance for Best Practice." *Health Information & Libraries Journal* 26, no. 1 (March): 63–71.

Weightman, Alison, and Jane Williamson. 2005. "The Value and Impact of Information Provided through Library Services for Patient Care: A Systematic Review." *Health Information & Libraries Journal* 22, no. 1 (March): 4–25.

White, Andrew C., and Eric Djiva Kamal. 2006. *E-Metrics for Library and Information Professionals: How to Use Data for Managing and Evaluating Electronic Resource Collections*. New York: Neal-Schuman.

White, Lynda S. 2002. "The University of Virginia Library's Experiment with Benchmarking." *Virginia Libraries* 48, no. 4 (October/November/December): 17–25.

7

Collection Planning Management

Craig C. Haynes

"What's important is the knowledge, and most of this knowledge can be contained in a variety of digital formats that are much more efficient than a simple 'box' of physical print. These electronic formats, as well as amazing new levels of interactivity, are just beginning to be created and widely experienced, but their arrival will be the book's biggest leap of evolution since Gutenberg" (Gomez, 2008: 18).

The digitization of data, information, and knowledge has forever changed the fundamental idea of "library" and by extension the meaning and role of library collections and the people who manage them. Individuals no longer need to visit a building or a physical collection in order to access a book, journal, or consult a reference. Because of digitization, collections are now decentralized so that individuals may access a library, a collection or a discreet fact online through a variety of mobile devices wherever and whenever they wish.

Conceptually and politically speaking, digitization has advanced the notion of the freedom of information such that individuals are not only empowered, but inspired to create and share ideas with whomever they choose—often bypassing the traditional, analog protocols for knowledge dissemination and scholarly research. Scientists—who have adopted digitization—expedite the flow of communication, facilitate and encourage collaboration, and as a result, advance and expand human knowledge.

A milestone in the evolution of knowledge transfer, storage, and retrieval emerged with the invention of movable type. Its byproduct, the book, evolved to free knowledge from the confines of a few buildings and from the watchful gaze of a few individuals. Thanks to computer technology, digitization carries on this evolution with amazing speed and in spectacular fashion to once and for all free information from the confines of whatever benign constructs may still exist to confine it—including libraries!

For the time being, certain *principles* of collection management and development remain. On the other hand, certain *practices* of collection management and development have not only changed (or been eliminated), but new roles for collections specialists and library managers have emerged. For example, new roles and changing practices have developed in the realm of acquisitions and certain related public services. In an age when the bulk of collections are now licensed and leased as opposed to purchased and processed, acquisitions talk and activities are now focused around matters such as licensing language, rights and responsibilities, remote access, ERMS (electronic resource management systems) and content integration, just to name a few. Collection practices and public services that have diminished or been eliminated include activities such as serials binding, stack maintenance, and photocopy services.

Current research and casual observation confirms that many health care libraries (hospital and academic), STM (scientific, technical, and medical) publishers, and users (faculty, clinicians, students, researchers, and patients) are, to one degree or another, in a *transition*. They are acquiring, accessing, preserving, producing, creating, and consuming knowledge—sometimes in print *or* electronic formats, and at other times in print *and* electronic formats.

For health care libraries, this transitional environment is reflected in the status of the library's extant but *decreasing* print volumes, particularly serials, and the library's *increasing* electronic collections (Hogan, 2001; Dunlap, 2008; Zambare et al., 2009). There may also be, in this transitional state, redundancy or duplication of library book and journal holdings, such that both electronic *and* print formats may exist in the same collection for the same titles.

For STM publishers, this transitional period is reflected in a production model that for the most part continues to publish print content, but which may also provide an electronic version, i.e., a .pdf (portable document format) of the print. Some publishers have endeavored to provide an authentic electronic journal experience complete with value-added media features and content unavailable in either the print or the electronic facsimile version. However, for these publishers (mostly nonsociety), this dual format production model is not desirable and for some, not sustainable (Johnson and Luther, 2008). Moreover, the shift in the nature of scholarly communication and the increasing pressure and influence of open access (OA), is forcing a

"showdown" and for some publishers, serious business choices.

Users are also in a transition, interacting daily with knowledge in both an electronic and hard copy format. While clearly embracing the accessibility and added value provided by electronic content (Macewan, 1999), even the most ardent digerati prefers a printed hard copy of an article for analysis and research from time to time. It has been observed that convenience or ease of access plays a role in this process and sometimes the personal print subscription *is* the convenient format for the user (Tenopir, King, and Bush, 2004).

Yet, even though for many health care libraries a hybrid status does exist (and may continue to exist for a while), for other libraries, *a clear tipping point has been reached* (Hogan, 2001; Zhang and Haslam, 2005; Prabha, 2007; Johnson and Luther, 2007; Dunlap, 2008). Whether hastened by certain or perceived inevitability or by economic exigency, these institutions have migrated substantial serial holdings to digital or are gradually migrating to digital whenever possible, confident of one thing: in the context of budget and space planning, maintaining *both* print and electronic formats is not a sustainable collections management policy. Collection growth is of particular interest to hospital libraries, where space is continually in short supply and where access to medical references is increasingly desired and now technically and contextually more effective at the *point of care* and within the electronic health record (EHR).

This chapter is divided into three major sections: (1) Transitions, transformations, and trends; (2) Principles and best practices; and (3) Collections. The first section attempts to bring together some of the current developments in health sciences collection management activities and thinking. While primarily for the library manager who may also have responsibility for collection development (e.g., the hospital librarian), there is relevance for the academic health sciences librarian also, who may be one among a team of librarians, but who may have sole responsibility for the strategic direction of collections overall. Of course, there must be the recognition that one size does not fit all and after having fully considered the various trends, transformations and transitions, library managers and collections specialists must ultimately make decisions based on their institution's unique mission, clients, and budget.

The second section will highlight certain practices of collection development as they have changed and developed in the digital world. Certain principles of the practice have not changed and reference to these enduring principles will be made as appropriate. Though this section will be particularly helpful to the novice manager, such managers are advised to consult resources that go into greater depth. There are classic and new health care library science textbooks available providing detailed information, instruction, and discussion for the novice manager or collections specialist, such as Richards and Eakin's (1997) *Collection Development and Assessment in Health Sciences Libraries*; or the recently updated edition of the venerable *Introduction to Reference Sources in the Health Sciences*, edited by Huber, Boorkman, and Blackwell (2008). M. Sandra Wood's (editor) 2008 monograph, *Introduction to Health Sciences Librarianship*, is another fine resource for the novice or individual in a single staffed health care library, providing in-depth, fundamental collection development instruction and guidance. The full citations for these works and other collection management and information resources can be found on the **accompanying CD-ROM**. The third section, Collections, will discuss the various traditional components and emerging formats of the twenty-first-century health care library collection as a whole.

Transitions, Transformations, and Trends

Scholarly Communication

The Internet (and more recently open access—OA) has forever changed scholarly communication and biomedical research protocol and practice. With the ability of scientists to exchange ideas, data, and research findings instantaneously not only via e-mail, but in real time via chat or video (e.g., Skype), the Internet has enabled an unprecedented level of scholarly collaboration—cutting across culture, geographical borders, and transcending the spatial boundaries of place and time. No longer confined to the next monthly or quarterly issue of a particularly prestigious, peer-reviewed journal nor to attendance at an annual conference, scientists and clinicians now have virtually total access to one another and to each other's data, ideas, and discussions. They can use wikis, blogs, chat, RSS (Really Simple Syndication) and other social networking applications that are fully enabled by an impressive array of wireless, mobile devices.

Moreover, research shows that many scientific scholars—themselves pioneers in creating new digital scholarly communication channels—have not only adopted and embraced digital content, formats, and forums, but have indicated (through use patterns) that they *prefer* the

digital at times even to the exclusion of certain, relevant print-only research (Vaughn, 2003).

Such immediacy of knowledge transfer and scholarly communications practice has added yet another layer of competencies and complexity to what was already a very challenging arena for library managers. Competencies such as copyright, fair use, and digital rights management are now joined by issues such as open access, digital repositories, and the relatively new National Institutes of Health (NIH)-funded biomedical research publication requirement.

Organizational development of scholarly communications is a collaborative endeavor. At many universities and academic health sciences institutions, the library has taken the lead on the issue, sponsoring scholarly communications forums across disciplines, creating websites, blogs, online tutorials, and providing classes on topics such as copyright, research methods, federal research publication requirements, and open access (see also Chapter 15). Two examples of institutional scholarly communications resources created by the library include the blog *Scholarly Communications@Duke* (http://library .duke.edu/blogs/schol comm/) and the *Scholarly Communications Portal* of the Bernard Becker Medical Library, Washington University in St. Louis, School of Medicine (http://becker.wustl .edu/services/scholarly/index.html).

Hospital libraries have similar endeavors for clinicians and clinical faculty through specific support services such as assistance with manuscript preparation and guidance for submission of NIH-funded research to PubMed Central. The National Network of Libraries of Medicine (NN/LM) has created a scholarly communications resource titled, *Scholarly Communication: Issues for Health Sciences Libraries in Clinical Settings* (http://nnlm .gov/rsdd/ejournals/nonacad.html), which specifically targets smaller libraries and provides an excellent introduction and guidance to hospital librarians regarding this activity. The Association of Research Libraries (ARL) has created the website, *Developing a Scholarly Communications Program in Your Library* (http://www .arl.org/sc/institute/fair/scprog/index.shtml), which provides a graduated, step approach for the development of a scholarly communications program. The Association for College and Research Libraries (ACRL) has developed the *Scholarly Communications Toolkit* (http://acrl.ala .org/scholcomm/), which is another helpful and practical resource.

Librarians should be eager to collaborate and engage on this topic in order to ensure compliance with federal law, and to facilitate the efficient dissemination, preservation, and continuity of knowledge transfer not only at their own institutions, but also on behalf of the wider scholarly and clinical research communities around the world. Library managers or collections specialists should be prepared to articulate the importance of this issue and their role to their administrators and their constituents. In addition, they should be knowledgeable and consistently participate in the larger effort to educate and inform their academic or hospital community about the important changes in the environment of scholarly communications principles and practices. In doing so, librarians will add value to themselves, their library, and their organization. To summarize:

- The revolution in scholarly communications has changed how research is created, discovered, shared, collected, preserved and disseminated.

- Library managers should play an active and collaborative role to bring awareness and participation by their constituents on this issue, by creating and leading educational outreach efforts, providing educational programs and resources of support—which will foster adoption and compliance across the organization.

Collections Redefined and Collection Services Revisited

Digital libraries have become a complex interactive and interdependent network of resources, user services, social technology interactions, databases, virtual meetings, gateways, real time online instruction opportunities and content management systems. (Dunlap, 2008: 135)

In the age of digitization, what constitutes library collections? In what has become a highly decentralized, "Google-ized" environment, the boundaries blur as users of all levels seamlessly (and at times subconsciously) integrate data, information and research in a variety of formats—books, printed journals, electronic articles, blogs, podcasts, websites, wikis, and mash-ups. While some observers may make an eloquent distinction between digital libraries and digital collections, such a distinction is of little value to the vast majority of users who only care that they have access whenever and wherever they need and want it. As a result, Sennyey, Ross, and Mills (2009), in their exploration of the future of academic libraries, question whether materials so easily accessible over the Web and so seamlessly integrated by users should be "collected" at all.

It is estimated that about 60 percent of the universe of some 20,000 active, peer-reviewed journals are available

in electronic format (Crow, 2006). Surely, this percentage will only increase. The "big deal" licenses negotiated with the large STM (scientific, technical, and medical) publishers, e.g., Elsevier, Wiley, Springer, provide access to thousands of journals, which places many health care libraries in the enviable position of once again being able to provide access to content "just in case" and the opportunity for the serendipity of research and discovery of new content "just in time."

Electronic books have some catching-up to do, but they are not far behind—again providing unprecedented access to thousands of medical texts and reference volumes that could never have been provided through the purchase of multiple print copies nor satisfy user demand or convenience. The *Google Books Library Project* (http://books.google.com), which has the rather ambitious, self-imposed mandate of creating the most comprehensive, searchable catalog of *all* books in *all* languages, will provide even more access to books online—millions of them. There are currently thousands of medical books available through Google Books—some limited view, some providing snippets, and others in full view.

Smartphones with their increasing medical apps and content libraries have replaced hard copy pocket versions of certain core medical handbooks and texts, especially for early adopters such as medical students and residents. At the 2010 HIMSS Conference (Health Information Management Systems Society), keynote speaker Dan Hesse, CEO of SprintNextel, stated that over the next two years 80 percent of clinicians will use smartphones in the course of their work (Hesse, 2010). Smartphones have also become the platform of choice for knowledge-based medical reference. Skyscape's library of more than 300 medical texts, handbooks, drug references, and medical calculators available for Apple iPhone, the Black-Berry, and Android OS devices is only the beginning of an explosion. Skyscape offers group and institutional pricing for their entire line of mobile device content.

E-readers such as Amazon Kindle, Sony Reader, Apple iPad, and Barnes and Noble NOOK are gaining in use, functionality, and features. Libraries with ebrary (acquired by Proquest in 2011), NetLibrary (acquired by EBSCO Publishing in 2010), and other aggregated electronic book subscription licenses may be able to provide these collections or perhaps selected books, or chapters from these collections, on dedicated *Reserve* e-readers—enabling the creation of course-customized e-readers or even e-readers with multiple course reserve materials on them—all available for check-out by students or for download to the user's personal e-reader.

Yale University, with access to over one million e-books via e-brary, NetLibrary, and other vendors, tested e-reader and smartphone access to their e-book content and discovered that 84 percent of their e-book collections could be accessed directly with the Apple iPod Touch or iPhone. Tests with Amazon Kindle and the Sony Reader yielded a lower percentage of access and also required additional technical work (Thomas, 2009). However, with the introduction of the Apple iPad and other such improved e-reader devices, these relatively minor technical impediments will be overcome, as manufacturers and publishers further develop, define, and adopt standards.

North Carolina State University recently began providing to students no-cost, online access to a physics course textbook. The cost to the library for this collection service license was $1,500. Students pay $45 for a hard copy if they want it. While the debate continues regarding whether the library should be the default payee for this service, such activity represents a digital variation on a very traditional practice in which students often check the library for course textbooks before purchasing in order to lower their college costs. Providing online access to textbooks at no cost to students creates enormous goodwill. Moreover, the modest, upfront digital licensing fee saves the library processing, replacement, and re-shelving costs of print copies.

Of course, e-readers, like laptops and other mobile devices supported by the library, will require an infrastructure (e.g., e-readers require electrical recharging). Yet the short-term one-time investment in infrastructure for e-readers may yield some long-term savings in print collection materials overhead such as cataloging and storage. Palm Beach Community College (PBCC) circulates the Amazon Kindle e-reader as it does a regular monograph (http://pbcc.libguides.com/kindle). For PBCC, such use of e-readers expands the collection without expanding the need for more space.

eBooks.com (http://www.ebooks.com), an online consumer bookstore, has an impressive library of scores of standard medical reference books and texts (e.g., *Fishman's Pulmonary Diseases and Disorders*, the Lange Series: *Current Medical Diagnosis and Treatment*, etc.) available for various portable devices such as computers, smartphones, and e-book readers. In addition eBook.com launched *eb20*, a web-based application that allows users to view the downloaded book anywhere an internet connection and web browser is available. YBP, a Baker & Taylor company, and one of the largest book jobbers in the world, provides electronic book selection, approval, and purchase right alongside the hard copy book selections in their Gobi ordering system for institutional customers.

These and other emerging electronic book activities evince a new direction. While print books may still be published and purchased, it is clear their role in future collection development activities may be limited (Shedlock and Walton, 2006). Library managers should consider the numerous implications of electronic book development and the impact on a variety of library collections management services. In addition to user services, space allocation, staffing, and materials processing are a few of the other significant implications to be evaluated. Points to remember include:

- Defining the library collection just got more complicated. The lines are blurred as various content formats are acquired through ubiquitous search engines.

- Collections services will exploit technological opportunities such as e-reader reserves. As a result collection development will become more collaborative as users interact with digital libraries across various library service points.

- Digital content has changed the role of collections in defining the physical library. As a result, library managers will need to regularly market and communicate to users, administrators, and other stakeholders the continuing, evolving (though essential) infrastructure needed to support digital collections. For other relevant issues surrounding the physical library, see Chapter 9.

Format Migration

The role of the printed journal in the institutional marketplace faces a steep decline in the coming 5 to 10 years. Print journals will exist mainly to address specialized needs, users, or business opportunities. Financial imperatives will draw libraries first—and ultimately publishers also—toward a tipping point where it no longer makes sense to subscribe to or publish printed versions of most journals. (Johnson and Luther, 2007: 4)

If Johnson and Luther are correct, there are many unanswered questions for libraries and publishers. First and foremost, will migration from print to e-only provide some or any economic benefit? For libraries, some have suggested that such migration will merely shift the same collections budget concerns—for example, the upward spiral of annual price increases—from subscription costs to licensing fees. Second, how will libraries know when to make the migration? Are there any guidelines to determine when the tipping point has been reached?

The jury may still be out for some library managers on these and other questions as adjustments are made to collection development policies, strategies, and budgets. Likewise, publishers are making adjustments to their products and business models also. In the ARL publication, *The E-only Tipping Point for Journals*, Richard K. Johnson and Judy Luther (2007) provide a thorough treatment of various institutional issues and aspects regarding format migration. Johnson and Luther indicate that the elimination of certain associated costs of print journal management, such as cataloging, check-in, claiming, binding, and storing, may provide some savings. However, they also point out that these savings may be one-time only.

In addition, as publishers find their way regarding their product line, viable production methods, and pricing models for content, it may only be a matter of time before libraries find themselves right back where they started, but with the added potential of being no better off, and possibly, worse. It could well be that a decision to adopt an electronic-only collection by libraries and publishers may at some point mean there will be no print available as a "back-up" plan, resulting in e-only as the only means of access. Subsequently, libraries may not have a choice or any options for access. Thus, any cost savings realized now by libraries as a result of canceling print may be eroded over time as licensing fees annually escalate, trapping institutional subscribers into an inescapable situation.

Open access (OA) could stave off or delay such a dire outcome. Yet, as PLoS (Public Library of Science) participants have recently discovered, publication fees (the fees authors or their parent institutions pay to publish in PLoS journals) can increase as well. OA is not a business model—OA is about unfettered access. Publishing, whether open or for-profit, is not free; it costs and some entity—authors, for-profit and not-for-profit institutions, or governments—will have to pay (see following text for more details on OA).

Moreover, the staff time needed in the e-only economy for license negotiation, troubleshooting access problems, facilitating participation in consortia activities to acquire and maintain licenses and vendor relations is not insignificant (Johnson and Luther, 2007). Thus, libraries willing to make the commitment to electronic only should have no doubts or illusions: There may or may not be long-term savings associated with format migration. There may or may not be additional staffing costs with format migration. If it is any consolation, however, librarians can take some comfort in knowing that the real winners in this endeavor are the individuals they have always sought to serve—library users.

MANAGEMENT IN ACTION 7.1

Reorganizing Workflow to Match User Needs

Location: Academic Medical Center

Description of Problem/Project: Collection content from print to electronic had dramatically changed user behavior and access, yet the library's technical and customer services work flows and staffing had not changed.

Impact On: Technical services personnel and ultimately users.

People Involved: Library administration, technical services staff members, and consultants.

Strategies for Success: Employing the use of outside consultants provided objectivity in supplying data and tools for reorganization/change among a group of seasoned technical services workers. Collaboration with the library's campus colleagues provided a larger forum and discussion for change across the library system. Communication with users at all levels regarding the recommended changes encouraged personnel involved.

Barriers Encountered: The notion of "change" for long-term, veteran staff can be disconcerting. In this case, continuous communication assuaged much of the anxiety normally associated with reorganization. While the technical services unit has been reorganized with new roles and work flows, a method for communicating these new work flows throughout the library is still evolving. Developing clear documentation should diminish any major problems on this front, however.

Take-Home Points:

- Recognition of the impact on personnel and work flow in the move from a print-centric to an electronic-centric collection cannot be underestimated and should be analyzed and addressed sooner rather than later.
- Communication and collaboration with all stakeholders is essential—internal and external users all will be impacted either directly or indirectly.

Contact Information: Daniel Dollar, Head of Collection Development and Management, Harvey Cushing/John Hay Whitney Medical Library, Yale University, New Haven, Connecticut. E-mail: Daniel.dollar@yale.edu (Dollar et al., 2007).

Nevertheless, while the majority of medical libraries, publishers, and users have fully embraced digital collections to one degree or another, print still exists and is still being produced, maintained, and consumed (Johnson and Luther, 2008). As a result, some librarians are a little hesitant to adopt an e-only position, citing concerns for preservation and perpetual access. These librarians have hit the pause button and are taking a bit of a "wait and see" stance.

Fortunately, though, the larger library community (e.g., the National Library of Medicine, professional associations, and other dedicated not-for-profit library entities) are also very concerned about preservation and perpetual access and are not only exploring but deploying various strategies and methods to mitigate these and other concerns associated with format migration. One solution is the third party, trusted digital archive projects such as JSTOR (short for journal storage, http://www.jstor.org); Portico (http://www.portico.org); and Stanford University's LOCKSS (Lots of Copies Keeps Stuff Safe, http://lockss.stanford.edu/lockss/Home). On the local level, the concern for preservation and access to local knowledge and artifacts is being addressed through the creation of institutional repositories (IRs) and digital asset management systems (DAMSs).

Another strategy to mitigate the concern for perpetual access and preservation is the practice of shared print. At institutions such as the University of California, a print copy of each licensed electronic journal title is provided to the university. This print copy is held as the university's single, shared copy, owned forever and held in perpetuity at a shared storage facility for all campuses whenever needed. Of course, this practice is effective as long as publishers continue to provide automatic delivery of the hard copy or via print on demand (University of California Libraries Collection Development Committee, 2009).

The other backup for health sciences libraries is, of course, the National Library of Medicine (NLM) and the National Network of Libraries of Medicine. As the world's largest biomedical library and network of medical libraries, NLM is the de facto holding library for all biomedical research on the earth. Access to NLM's print archive, and the collections of the network libraries via the DOCLINE system, provides the most comprehensive and efficient document delivery method in the world (see Chapter 10 for details). NLM recently introduced an international journal donation program (http://www.nlm.nih.gov/news/journal_donation09.html) in order to fill any gaps in its collections by allowing libraries around the world to contribute to its already massive print holdings. Realizing that many libraries will be discarding print volumes as they migrate to electronic only, NLM wants to ensure that a complete print archive of every biomedical research journal in the world is always available.

However, reliance on a print archive is effective only if publishers continue to produce it, and alas, there are no guarantees. Yet, publishers may continue to do so on demand for institutional subscribers and if the price is right.

It is estimated that around 40 percent of the 20,000 peer-reviewed journals in publication is available only in hard copy. Many of these publishers are small concerns and provide access to fewer than three to four titles, and often only one title. As with some libraries resorting to third-party solutions for preservation concerns, so too it may be that small publishers "outsource" their digitizing concerns as their print content becomes less accessible and less competitive with the ready access of their electronic competitors. Highwire Press (http://highwire.stanford.edu) is focused on society publishing and provides support in the digital environment to not-for-profit organizations wishing to go digital and remain relevant in scholarly communications. Experts agree that it really is only a matter of time before every journal is available in at least an electronic version and a little more time before every scholarly journal is e-only.

For the library manager, knowing when to retain print is as important as knowing when to jettison it. Johnson and Luther's (2007) table, based on responses from a variety of ARL member institutions, provides a guide for making this critical collection development decision (see Figure 7.1).

Currently, print and digital content co-exist together in many libraries. However, some libraries have reached a tipping-point and have migrated some or all of their serial holdings to *electronic only* access whenever certain criteria exist, such as a trusted digital archive. Other points to consider:

- Economic benefits may be realized for libraries migrating exclusively to electronic only. However, these benefits may be short lived as publishers and other electronic content providers determine different product lines and pricing models.

- Open access, though not a business model, could mitigate rapid price increases by publishers as they sort-out what makes sense economically for them and their subscribers.

- Trusted digital archives, shared print, publisher print on demand, and the National Library of Medicine's archiving efforts should allay any lingering concerns by library managers regarding preservation and perpetual access.

Open Access

Libraries will increasingly switch to OA sources, leading to libraries gaining a more prominent role in scholarly research. Libraries will need to move from being passive to active players in the scholarly communication chain. (Oppenheim, 2008: 588)

Figure 7.1. When Do Libraries Retain Print?

When do libraries retain print?

Following are examples of criteria for retaining subscriptions to the print versions of journals that were cited by a number of research libraries:

Demand

- Strong faculty demand for retention of print.
- Print is being used.
- Print is needed to support local curriculum or research.

Price

- The cost/benefit of print is superior.
- The subscription model is still based on print.

Function

- Print offers better features (e.g., browsing or current awareness).
- Poor interface design in the electronic version.
- Quality of images or graphics is demonstrably poorer in the electronic journal.
- Print has significant artifactual or aesthetic value.
- Electronic does not meet needs of users.
- Electronic access has unacceptable limits on use (e.g., simultaneous users, physical location).

Long-Term Electronic Availability

- There is no credible contractual guarantee of continued access to the subscribed electronic volumes in case of future cancellation or in the event the publisher fails.

- There is no evidence of the publisher's commitment to long-term digital preservation of the journal (e.g., journal is not in a trusted digital repository).
- Electronic is available only in aggregator packages and library cannot control if a title drops out (considered unstable).

Print Retention Responsibility

- Library has a consortial or other responsibility to retain a print archive of the journal title or the subject area to which it belongs.
- Resource sharing requirements indicate the need for print.
- Library has a "premier collection" in the field.

Timeliness and Reliability

- There is a delay between publication of the print and availability of online content.
- The provider of the electronic journal is unreliable.

Content

- The content of the print version differs from that of the electronic (e.g., the print contains significantly more material than the electronic; mastheads, letters, conference announcements, etc., are not maintained historically).
- The electronic is not the primary publication venue (e.g., it does not provide at least as much or more content than the print).

Source: Johnson and Luther, 2007. Used with permission.

Open access (OA)—the free availability and unrestricted use of scholarly research—shall not cease. While there are certain, formidable barriers to the adoption of universal OA publishing and protocols, the infrastructure and groundswell of support from governments, publishers, and the academic research community all but ensures OA is here to stay. *The Bethesda Statement on Open Access Publishing* created principles for libraries to consider as they seek to promote OA at their institutions (see the sidebar).

Statement of the Libraries & Publishers Working Group

We believe that open access will be an essential component of scientific publishing in the future and that works reporting the results of current scientific research should be as openly accessible and freely useable as possible. Libraries and publishers should make every effort to hasten this transition in a fashion that does not disrupt the orderly dissemination of scientific information.

Libraries propose to:

1. Develop and support mechanisms to make the transition to open access publishing and to provide examples of these mechanisms to the community.
2. In our education and outreach activities, give high priority to teaching our users about the benefits of open access publishing and open access journals.
3. List and highlight open access journals in our catalogs and other relevant databases.

(*Bethesda Statement on Open Access Publishing*. June 20, 2003. Accessed September 24, 2010. http://www.earlham.edu/~peters/fos/bethesda.htm.)

While funding is very tight for most libraries these days, as print subscriptions are canceled, an initial, one-time savings may be realized and could provide "seed" money for funding or cost-sharing of such OA publishing fees by various departments within the organization. For examples of this funding approach, see Cornell University Library's *Open Access Publication Fund* (http://www.library.cornell.edu/compact/coap.html) or visit the University of Oregon Libraries website on this issue (http://libweb.uoregon.edu/scis/sc/oaps.html). Libraries should also encourage researchers to include such fees and costs for OA publishing in their grant and research proposals.

PubMed is an example of the integration of both licensed and OA journals. Citation results routinely provide icon links to "free" articles alongside an institutional or publisher icon or LinkOut. Other OA databases, which could be catalogued from the library's online catalog or listed separately at a library's open access resources page, include the Directory of Open Access Journals (http://www.doaj.org). DOAJ currently provides access to over 2000, peer-reviewed OA journals, hundreds of which are searchable at the citation level and arranged by discipline. Google Scholar (http://scholar.google.com) also indexes OA journals and will provide locally licensed article links also.

Online catalog access to electronic OA serials ensures users will have a reliable access point to OA titles. Many electronic resource management systems (ERMSs) list OA journals (see Chapter 8 for details on these systems). Users may not know to go directly to DOAJ, or Google Scholar, but they may know the library online catalog or ERMS as the one reliable source of access for most of their journal needs. Such local access also provides an opportunity to talk about open access and other scholarly communications issues with interested faculty and administrators.

Electronic Books

In the book, *Print is Dead*, author Jeff Gomez reminds readers that futuristic scenarios often do not come to fruition and if they do, it usually is not within the timeframe that prognosticators originally declare. The electronic book is one example of this. In the late 1990s electronic books or e-books "were not only going to change everything but they were going to replace everything ... printed books and the ink-on-paper experience were rapidly on their way out, and digital delivery and consumption would soon be commonplace" (Gomez, 2008: 116–117). As we now know, ten years later, printed

books including medical books are still very much a part of the educational landscape and the user experience of learning, training, reference, and entertainment. Nonetheless, there have been significant changes among STM book publishers, aggregators, and book jobbers in the past decade.

Most health sciences librarians who purchase monographs are aware of the practice of providing electronic book versions along with the print. Nursing book publishers, in particular, often provide a CD-ROM version in the hard copy of the book's cover. Moreover, some medical book publishers provide a single-user license for the online or web-based version of the book. While this practice may continue, it is apparent that, as with serials, cover-to-cover digitization of STM books (old and new), aggregated into large specialty packages and offered by the big STM publishing companies may be the preferred production platform.

Print on demand provides promise not only as an access platform, but also as an alternate preservation and perpetual access model. Over the last few years, the STM super-aggregators—Wiley, Springer, and Elsevier—have focused on electronic books as never before and now provide diverse product formats for various types of mobile devices.

Currently, ebrary has a collection of more than 5,000 health sciences (medicine, nursing, allied health) book titles. NetLibrary features *Doody's Core Titles* and provides over 800 medical titles and 400 nursing titles. SpringerLink's electronic book package includes over 2,000 books in medicine and the biomedical sciences.

Searchable libraries of core medical texts are incredibly useful, particularly in the clinical training environment for medical students and residents. In this environment, the efficiency of access afforded by electronic texts and medical references facilitates learning and significantly enhances the training experience. For libraries, electronic books are economical as well, allowing simultaneous access by countless users to core materials at a fraction of the cost of doing so in print.

A la carte selection, provided by some publishers, allows for the creation of e-book collections customized to the library's primary users, programs and needs. While *a la carte* and specialty collections may initially be a little more expensive, over time the increased value and utilization counter balance this, as the library is now able to provide greater access to materials that are truly used. Moreover, electronic books are continuously updated by some publishers, as opposed to the annual new editions in print, which can become outdated a few months after publication. Multiple print copy purchasing was never a sustainable strategy for core medical texts and popular review manuals, which often are lost or vandalized. With electronic versions, users are better served and so is the library's budget and mission.

However, like serials, there are several management considerations regarding e-book materials and collections—considerations such as selection, deselection of print copies, licensing negotiations for aggregated packages, cataloging, and technical troubleshooting, just to name a few. In addition, it should be noted that the current quality of some e-book search interfaces can be a bit clunky and unintuitive to navigate. While this varies from publisher to publisher, improvement of and integration with other online content applications and services needs development. As a result, user support and training may also be a cost point to consider. For a listing of some of the current e-book publishers, aggregators, and vendors, consult the **accompanying CD-ROM**.

E-portals and Metasearch Technology

In an attempt to tame the proliferation of biomedical resources and knowledge in the digital world, many collection specialists have collaborated with electronic services librarians and outreach and instruction librarians to develop various types of information portals—many of which are a combination of digital content as well as discovery/finding aids and tools.

Sometimes referred to as electronic portals or e-Portals, these websites—often maintained by the library or hospital IT department through content management systems (CMSs)—provide a one-stop shop and single point of entry to a finite universe of online resources and services for busy clinicians, trainees, and researchers. Often, clinical users and to a certain extent, clinical project scientists do not want the entire universe of information. Rather, because of time constraints, their needs are more immediate. Having ready access to a few relevant resources is better than complex access to many resources.

Point-of-care resources is the class of electronic medical content that includes databases containing regularly updated, filtered, review-type articles, based on the latest available science or evidence. Point-of-care resources may also include drug information, and common medical procedures with video clips and image files. For nurses, point of care includes patient education or before- and after-care instructions. In order to accommodate various clinical users, facilitate access, and increase awareness of available resources, some health care libraries have deployed a few key technologies and features within their e-portals.

One feature of health care library e-Portals is to provide various page views based on user status. For example, clinical research faculty (e.g., project scientists) may have one view of resources that focuses on research-oriented databases, such as Thomson's Web of Science with access to citation analysis databases. Patient care providers and trainees (physicians, nurses, residents), may have a different tab or page view with links to point of care resources such as eMedicine, Dynamed, or FirstConsult.

Another technology or feature of health care library e-portals is the federated search or metasearch, which allows simultaneous searching across a group of user-selected resources. Some metasearch engines de-duplicate results and may also provide a relevancy ranking of the search retrieval. There are a number of third-party federated search vendors currently in the market. WebFeat (http://www.webfeat.org) and DeepWeb Technologies (http://www.deepwebtech.com) are two such companies. For a fee, these vendors will provide the set-up, technical work, and maintenance. They will maintain and update the list of resource APIs (application program interfaces) and other scripts, programming code or technical changes associated with the content provider.

Some libraries have developed their own metasearch application and in-house maintenance team (see Stanford University's Lane Medical Library—Clinical Portal, http://lane.stanford.edu/portals/clinical.html). A complex endeavor of this type requires a seamless collaboration between hospital or campus IT and the library, plus an ongoing financial commitment to maintaining and developing this service.

As point-of-care resources proliferate, library managers and collections specialists, particularly in academic settings, will be encouraged to provide access to as many of these resources as possible. Some library managers have allocated a set amount of dollars for these resources and others have partnered with various hospital departments at the institution in order to provide the resources users most request. Selection, funding, and evaluation of point of care resources should be a collaborative process, particularly when tough choices have to be made in difficult economic times. Though it may be challenging to do so, clinicians should be a part of the selection and evaluation process, especially if integration of this content into the electronic health record is being considered.

Knowledge Integration

The adoption of the electronic health record (EHR) is increasing across the country. With the passage of the

HITECH Act (Health Information Technology for Economic and Clinical Health), passed by the U.S. Congress on January 16, 2009, the government is providing 20 billion dollars in reimbursement to health care organizations, practices, and clinics that deploy EHRs and other health information technology (HIT), provided such deployments are in compliance with the rules and regulations set forth for *meaningful use* and certification (http://healthit.hhs.gov).

This is a special issue and challenge particularly for medical center and hospital libraries. However, as the reform, overhaul, and updating of medical school curriculums develops, academic health sciences libraries will face similar challenges and issues. Learning management systems (LMSs) also endeavor to integrate licensed library content, such as electronic medical textbooks and course specific journal articles, into the online school of medicine curriculum. Knowledge integration in either or both of these environments requires collaboration between the library, publishers, and medical school curriculum committees and/or EHR implementation teams and hospital IT.

One aspect of integration involves facilitating use of existing licenses and content. In some cases, extending licenses to encompass these new environments (EHRs and LMSs) may require license renegotiations with the publisher. In these cases, there is the potential for additional licensing fees. Library managers should be prepared to thoroughly research this issue not only with content providers but with EHR or LMS vendors also. Such research will bring compliance with copyright and the existing license agreements and the payment of additional licensing fees, if required or appropriate.

With respect to the EHR environment, the knowledge integration application known as the Infobutton is supported by many medical publishers. The Infobutton provides contextually sensitive retrievals from selected licensed resources and medical references within the EHR. Jim Cimino, MD, formerly at Columbia Presbyterian Medical Center and currently at NIH, created the Infobutton. A few years later, the Infobutton protocol was developed by HL-7—Health Level 7, an ANSI standards development group.

Research studies regarding Infobutton use have shown that Infobuttons are an important adjunct in providing quality health care and have the potential to increase patient safety, decrease medical error, and lower health care costs. IMO (Intelligent Medical Objects) uses a slightly different approach to EHR knowledge integration. Similar to the Infobutton, IMO's iHealth search interface provides the same contextual medical reference linkouts, but does so from a menu of resources based on user status, e.g., physician, nurse, pharmacist.

In addition, iHealth employs a variety of controlled vocabularies (e.g., MeSH, CPT, SNOMED CT, ICD-9, etc.) to ensure a deep level of relevancy in the retrieval. Whichever approach and technology is used, as the gatekeeper for knowledge-based systems, the librarian must facilitate this activity and bring together the appropriate stakeholders to continuously select, review, and evaluate EHR knowledge integration and the resources available for such integration.

EHRs and LMSs are critical environments from which to extend access to costly electronic resources. Such activity is well within the library manager's purview and is another opportunity for the library to add value to their mission and that of their institution.

Institutional Repositories

Repositories are being deployed in a variety of environments and contexts. "The many repository platforms available today are changing the nature of scholarly communication" (Texas Digital Library, 2010).

Various institutions and organizations are reestablishing their role not only as publishers, but as stewards and preservationists of locally generated and produced knowledge and research; and they are doing so through the creation of institutional repositories (IRs). Spurred on by the open access movement, institutions have decided that the research, and knowledge generated by their own people must not only be preserved, but controlled. Both in terms of local access, of course, but also in terms of access and availability within the larger national and international scholarly and research communities.

Institutions undertaking this endeavor now realize that they need not rely on an outside entity (e.g., for-profit publisher) or a foreign business model to determine the destiny of the content they have paid faculty, researchers, and others to produce for the public good. An excellent background resource on institutional repositories is *Building Digital Libraries* (Reese and Banerjee, 2008). As one of the "how-to-do-it" manuals from Neal-Schuman Publishers, Reese and Banerjee step users through myriad elements and details of the decision-making, planning, and execution processes. They discuss the philosophical, practical, and technical aspects from beginning to end. This endeavor will require coordination and collaboration by the librarian among various technical and diverse user groups across the organization. If successful, the development and facilitation of an IR by the library manager will bring lasting value to the institution, the library, and the larger scholarly community around the world.

Principles and Best Practices

> As licensing replaces purchasing, and the business practices of software companies replace those of publishers, access to information on demand supersedes collection building, and cooperative acquisitions supplement local collection development. (Pettijohn and Neville, 2003: 20)

In the age of digitization, the health sciences library collection is like an evolving, living organism—interdependent, decentralized, costly, no cost, local, and international—it is all of these things at the same time. The availability of open access journals through PubMed, Freemedical journals.com, the Directory of Open Access Journals, Google Scholar and other websites has significantly influenced serials collection development for many health care libraries.

Similarly, free monograph websites such as Google Books, FreeMedicalBooks4doctors.com, and, for personal registrants, MerckMedicus, have also provided alternatives for users and for libraries caught in the upward spiral of rising materials cost, and the downward spiral of institutional funding. Library managers or collections specialists are challenged to sort out what makes sense for their institution on the local level, of course, but they must also keep an eye on the larger context and interconnectedness of collections on the whole. Such a broad view in the midst of rapid change creates exciting and daunting development and oversight issues. Yet, there are some enduring collection management principles, elements, and tools that can help tame the task and provide some stability.

The extent to which libraries decide to rely on no cost, open access resources shall be determined separately and in the context of each library's users, organizational mission, and priorities. However, such access raises interesting questions and discussion.

For example, in the face of open access to factual information on the web that was once located in expensive, multivolume directories, should the library continue to purchase the print? Directories for grants, physicians, organizations of various types, educational institutions—all of this type of factual information is now a Google search away. Statistics, data sets, guides, biographical sources, and sophisticated geographic information system (GIS) tools are thoroughly and expertly covered by a website somewhere and available to the user almost instantaneously and often at no cost.

Therefore, should the library invest precious, finite financial resources in acquiring these types of materials in print when the evidence increasingly demonstrates that users prefer the online versions? Again, these are choices each library manager or collections specialist will have to make based on the enduring principles and best practices of collection development and the rather individual needs of their health care library, institution, and constituents.

Vision

Having a vision for the collections management program is foundational to planning and continuous development. Part aspiration and part practical, the collections management vision is crafted in the context of the library's vision, mission, and goals, which are influenced by the institution's vision, mission, and goals. In the age of digitization, collaboration, and integration, the library's collections vision should set a tone for how knowledge-based resources and content should be managed, not only in the library, but across the organization. If the library does not do so, which department within the organization will? The library and librarians—the good stewards of knowledge—are historically and professionally qualified to serve as authorities from which the institution's ethos and attitudes toward knowledge management on the whole should take its cues. If crafted in the context of the organization's mission and goals, the library's collections vision should position it at the hub of a strategic activity for the organization and serve not only the library, but the institution now and into the future.

Environmental Assessment

Another enduring element for collections management in the digital age is assessment. Having a clear understanding of the library's and the institution's programmatic and business challenges requires an ongoing vigilance and awareness. Whether the institution is thinking about adding a new program in bioinformatics or deploying an electronic medical record, the library manager or collections specialist should be in regular consultation with supervisors, administrators, and users, and be able to translate the impact of various institutional initiatives into collections management terms and if appropriate into plans and actions.

Collection Development Policies

Collection development policies are supposed to serve as a map for both the library manager or collections specialist and the library's user community. On the internal side, the purpose of such policies and documentation is to add a level of specificity and focus as well as limits or boundaries. On the external side—though it is doubtful any user has ever looked at these policies—the purpose is to provide a justification for what and why a library collects, withdraws, licenses, or digitizes certain content. Such policies set known parameters and can use formulas that over time will change and shape a collection based on institutional programs and priorities. Collections policies are still relevant. However, in the digital age, certain elements of said policies clearly need some revision.

For example, yesterday's detailed collections development policy with its levels of collection and format support may no longer be applicable today. Statements on the breadth and depth of a library's serials collection in a particular field become rather moot in the face of the mega journal packages that provide access to thousands of journals across a much wider range of specialties and subspecialties—offering users local access to online content the library could never have imagined or provided in print.

For this reason, some libraries have abandoned collection development policies per se, but have instead articulated guidelines for specific collections management activities such as migration from print to digital or detailed guidelines and processes for cancellation of print subscriptions. The University of the Fraser Valley has articulated a policy on migration from print to digital and the circumstances and criteria under which such migration will occur (http://www.ufv.ca/library/services_policies/migration.htm).

Key areas to cover in a collection development policy:

- **Scope**—some statement or guideline outlining the overall purpose of the collections of the library and the parameters of support, e.g., primary clientele served. Flexibility is important and should acknowledge that these programs will most likely change over time as the university/business enterprise/hospital/institution/system changes.

- **Subject coverage**—while this list will also change over time, there will most certainly be a core of subjects that will remain constant.

- **Formats**—given the pervasive role of electronic content and the continuing, yet diminishing role of print, it may or may not be necessary to spell out much in this section beyond a statement indicating the library's support for any and all formats that support the education, research, and/or patient care activities of the organization.

- **Gifts/donations**—state institutions must be particularly sensitive to this area of the collections. Often, donors do not understand the restrictions placed on state-sponsored entities and may be mystified by the library's lack of outreach. Also, at a time of decreasing space and a migration away from print, a statement explicating the library's position on print donations can be an appropriate public relations step. See The University of Maryland Health Sciences Library's collection development policy as an example of a comprehensive collections management statement (http://www.hshsl.umaryland.edu/general/about/policies/coll dev.html).

Selection and Deselection

Selection of information resources is at the heart of collection development. It is an acquired skill of experience and knowledge and is inextricably tied to the vision, mission, and goals of both the library and the parent institution. With money as one formidable limit, selection can be especially challenging in tough economic environments, and sometimes unattractive choices must be made. For example, serials cancellation projects can be particularly difficult. Yet, the outcome of such projects may result in a leaner, more focused collection customized to the library's local constituencies.

In addition, while some institutions have economic leverage to purchase or cost share in the large, mega-journal packages offered by the major publishers, such may not be the case for a smaller library and organization; nor does it make financial or collection development sense for a smaller library to license 100 electronic journals when one will do. In such cases, the library manager should consider negotiating single title electronic licensing.

Schools, hospitals, and other health care entities with library services are undergoing rapid change. Government health care policies and medical education accreditation agencies influence curriculums, training programs, and patient care. For instance, consider how the relatively recent emphasis in training and patient care on evidence-based practice (EBP) and quality filtering has put the spotlight directly on the library's resources in support of EBP. The proliferation of point-of-care databases and their integration into the electronic health record, as discussed above, provides *just-in-time* access for both patient care and training activities and is an essential component in the EBP work flow and process.

Selection of point-of-care resources is an important activity. In the face of rising costs for these resources, product proliferation and variation among products, a thorough evaluation is warranted. The South Central Chapter (SCC) of MLA (Medical Library Association) developed a detailed point-of-care evaluation and selection tool a few years ago; it was updated in 2006 (http://ils.mdacc.tmc.edu/papers.html). Librarians can use this spreadsheet to facilitate their own specific point-of-care resources selection and evaluation process and compare strengths, weaknesses, and differences of potentially new products and licenses. Though challenging, involving a select and varied group of users in the evaluation process (physicians, nurses, medical students, residents, pharmacists, and administrators) is critical.

For monographs and serials, selection tools currently available include *Doody's Core Titles* and *Doody's Review Service* (http://www.Doody.com). The Brandon-Hill lists, formerly the gold standard for core book and journal titles, are no longer updated. Because selection is a collaborative endeavor, feedback from faculty, residents, medical students, and research scientists should be continuously encouraged in order to determine whether existing collections are meeting current needs. Nonetheless, one benefit of the decentralized and digitized online environment of research, education, and patient care is that it has relieved much of the pressure to provide local access to everything. If a librarian is no longer getting specific requests for certain serials titles or books, it may be that users have found support from other, most likely, electronic sources. Such activity could enable the enhancement of and focus on materials that are not free or readily available online, but which may be needed locally. Selection of materials of this type add value to the collection and the institution when licensed in this more strategic manner.

Duplication is an important element of selection. Does it make sense to provide both printed and electronic copies of a monograph or serial and if so, when? Moreover, duplication is inextricably tied to the question of how a manager or collections specialist knows or determines when the time has come to discontinue print subscriptions and rely on electronic only. For certain small- to medium-sized libraries, print in various resources is still quite popular, even though an electronic version is available and provided. Furthermore, some libraries maintain a print *browsing collection* of high impact journals as part of the *library as place* philosophy and outreach. However, though libraries have always provided resources in a variety of formats, and for various philosophical and management reasons, in difficult economic times choices must be made regarding the sustainability of such activities. Ultimately, whether to provide one format only or both of a particular journal or monograph will be determined by each library manager

or collections specialist in the context of the mission, dynamic programs, collection policy, users, and budget of the organization.

In an effort to assist library managers and collection specialists in the process of knowing what to withdraw and when, the nonprofit group Ithaka S + R has developed the *Print Collections Decision-Support Tool*, version 1.1. This tool, available for download, is based on the research and work that culminated in the report *What to Withdraw: Print Collections Management in the Wake of Digitization* by Roger Schonfeld and Ross Housewright (2009).

Keeping the collection current and relevant, particularly in a clinical setting, is critical to quality care and, subsequently, risk management. A collections development policy regarding deselection can provide some guidance and specificity. Generally speaking, hospital libraries should keep print monograph editions under five to seven years of age, depending on the subject. A strength of electronic texts and monographs is that some are continuously updated, e.g., *Harrison's Internal Medicine, Harrison's Online* (McGraw-Hill Publishers).

As bound print serial collections are deselected in preference for the online, the librarian should seek avenues for providing these bound journals to sources that can distribute them wherever they might be needed. PROJECT C.U.R.E. (http://www.projectcure.org) is a nonprofit organization that accepts current journals and monographs (usually within 10 years of publication). The previously mentioned NLM Journal Donation Program has specific runs and titles it is collecting.

Archiving

When it became clear that electronic journals were quickly becoming the preferred format, librarians immediately raised the issues of preservation, perpetual rights, and archives. In the analog era, libraries owned the content once purchased through subscription services. However, in the digital era, owning is not the business model of choice for many publishers. Rather, for publishers, licensing the content for a specified time has become the prevailing business model. Thus, when the library's license expires, access to not only current content but content accumulated since the start of the agreement may expire as well. These are troubling matters for libraries, yet very common.

In their role as fiduciaries for access to all knowledge throughout all time, librarians have created some solutions. Sometimes, licensing agreements for content from publishers will include a *perpetual rights access clause* granting institutional licensees access in perpetuity, similar to the access enjoyed in the analog world. In other arrangements, some publishers make the digital back files available for a one-time purchase. Other models for preservation and access include electronic archiving initiatives and services such as Portico, LOCKSS, and JSTOR, mentioned previously. Participation in these services is fee-based. Fees are often tiered based on the institution's size and mission.

Assessment

Assessment of collections and particularly of collection use has always been an important element in the continuous development and prudent allocation of acquisition dollars. Improved resource and vendor management reports have further refined this activity and can assist librarians with providing the resources that are truly utilized by their immediate constituency.

In addition to the management tools and reports from publishers, the library community and various standards development organizations have also developed protocols for the assessment of resources. For example, COUNTER (Counting Online Usage of Networked Electronic Resources), and SUSHI (Standardized Usage Statistics Harvesting Initiative), a NISO standard, provide publishers and electronic resource producers with clear guidelines on the criteria and elements for inclusion in management reports in order that collections specialists and library managers may compare apples with apples and oranges with oranges.

Many of the major publishers—Elsevier, Micromedex, Springer, Wiley, and others—provide or are endeavoring to provide COUNTER-compliant usage statistics. Librarians should actively lobby their publishers to adopt and adhere to these standards. In addition, the circulation modules in ILS (integrated library system) applications are also becoming more useful in the development of assessment tools (see Management in Action 7.2). Monograph analysis capabilities that allow or include evaluation by subject specialty and subspecialty as well as user status and date of publication is very critical to making sure, particularly in hospital and clinical collections, that the most current monographs are available and used. Book jobbers such as Yankee Book Peddler-YBP (a Baker & Taylor company) provide librarians with customized management reports that allow analysis by a variety of parameters, e.g., expenditure by subject or call number.

The quality of the library's collections was once defined by the depth and breadth of locally available materials. Quality also often meant the number of volumes on the

shelves or the range and number of special collections housed. However, in the age of digitization, when access over ownership is far more important, and when even special collections are being digitized and made available to scholars around the world, the old volume counting metric as a descriptor for quality is neither meaningful nor useful. Perhaps, the new metric for quality of collections should be based on the number of licenses held and/or the number of access points provided and format types supported. See Chapter 6 for more on e-metrics.

Aggregators

One of the fortunate outcomes of the digitization of knowledge has been the economies of scale realized by the large STM publishers. As a result, these publishers are able to provide hundreds of electronic versions of their print serials titles. A university, academic medical center, or health care consortium is able to license not one title from a publisher, but scores of titles at a cost that may be less than the same number of titles would have been in print. Nonetheless, even if the cost is more, the access is greatly enhanced, thus making the additional financial commitment a tremendous added value.

However, pricing for electronic journals and books is a moving target. Library managers or collections specialists should negotiate based on their unique institutional preferences and needs. There are as many pricing models as there are publishers. Many observers agree that pricing models for electronic content is a real concern. Publishers say that they have not yet experienced a cost savings in the transport from print to electronic. They explain that while they may no longer have to print on paper, produce color figures and gels, and mail issues to subscribers, there are still significant production costs such as editing and programming, as well as conversion costs and the ongoing management cost of maintaining digital archives in perpetuity. These tasks, they say, must still be accomplished and while some costs are about the same, other costs are slightly higher.

Presently, some publishers, not willing to cannibalize their personal subscriber base, print hard copies and produce an electronic version. This activity is particularly prevalent among the smaller society publishers whose subscribers often receive a print copy of the society journal as a member benefit. Much remains to be sorted out and determined by publishers and in the end, a true savings may accrue. Whether this savings will be passed along to subscribers is an open question. A possible scenario might be that in the face of diminishing personal print subscriptions, if publishers decide to continue them, institutional subscribers will most likely subsidize them. Thus, as the move to electronic becomes more pervasive, annual increases for institutional subscribers/licensees—comparable to what was paid for the print—is entirely probable. But again, for institutional subscribers, the added value is access. Moreover, certain publishers are providing true electronic versions of journals complete with media clips, 3-D graphs, charts, feeds, and integrated video discussions with researchers—features, they may contend, that will justify the cost increases. Refer to Chapter 8 in this text for more discussion on issues related to electronic resources licensing.

Budget

Is there a formula for determining a collections budget? Should parameters regarding expenditures based on various formats or subjects be articulated? The collections budget is one part of the library's overall budget, thus for more detail regarding how this part might fit into the whole, refer to Chapter 4 of this text for more discussion regarding organizational budget preparation and analysis. As previously stated, pricing among publishers for electronic serials content is still a work in progress. Some publishers have shifted from print plus electronic pricing to electronic plus print so that now there is a premium on the hard copy! Perhaps, within the parameters of the allocation the librarian receives for collections, parsing out percentages by format, discipline, or program is a reasonable method. Allowing for annual increases is essential. Yet, without an increase in this allocation that keeps pace with the publisher's annual increases, inflation, and fluctuating currencies, librarians are challenged to strategize in order to simply maintain status quo and adding new content carries with it the discussion of what to cut in order to provide it.

According to the most recent EBSCO pricing information for 2011, the subscription vendor expected "the overall effective publisher price increases for academic and academic/medical libraries for 2011 (before currency impact) to be in the range of 4 to 6 percent" (EBSCO Information Services, 2010: 3). In terms of determining a reasonable budget, "eventually, electronic resources represent a larger and larger slice of the materials budget pie" (Pettijohn and Neville, 2003: 22). Each library must determine the value of this shift and seek methods and opportunities for savings. Internal collaborative funding, though sometimes an administrative headache, can relieve the library's burden and also inform users and administrators regarding the high cost of providing online content. For example, some libraries cost-share with the pharmacy department or pharmacy school when funding online drug information resources. The cost for these decidedly patient care resources makes for a compelling, cost-share argument with hospital administrators because they understand that such resources enhance clinical competency and reduce medical error.

Local or regional consortiums are another method for reducing the cost of online content. The Pacific Southwest Region of the National Network of Libraries of Medicine (NN/LM/PSR) recently launched an electronic licensing program targeted to hospital libraries (http://nnlm.gov/psr/services/e_license/program.html). Another possible opportunity to lower materials and service costs for certain health care libraries might be the relatively new regional cooperative, Lyrasis (http://www.lyrasis.org/), a collaboration and merger of PALINET,

SOLINET, NELINET, and BCR, forming the nation's largest regional membership serving libraries. While the health sciences content offerings and vendors are rather limited right now (Thomson-Reuters, Springer, and a few others), these offerings could increase if health care libraries express sufficient interest in participating.

Collections

Reference

The experience and research evidence regarding reference collections in health care libraries is clear—reference collections are diminishing in use and size (Clemmons and Clemmons, 2005). Online medical reference content that is authoritative, current, and free via various mobile devices has virtually eliminated the need for clinical staff to physically visit the reference collection in the library. Dictionaries, directories, atlases, almanacs, handbooks, coding and accreditation manuals, drug information, and formularies are now available to users online whenever and wherever they need them.

In the analog days before Google, Bing, Cuil, AskJeeves, and all of the other search engines now available to answer quick research-type questions, the "ready reference" print collection, usually comprised of dictionaries, guides, handbooks, and various directories from organizations such as American Hospital Association (AHA), American Medical Association (AMA), and American Psychological Association (APA), populated a location near the reference desk and were handy to the reference librarian for responding to both in-person and telephone queries. However, recent research and survey data indicate that the majority of reference desks are no longer besieged with in-person ready-reference questions or quick queries coming-in over the telephone (Fernandes, 2008). While it is true that these questions still emerge—mostly in virtual reference chat and IMs (instant messages) (Dee, 2005)—the majority of medical reference questions are self-answered via Google or from the proliferating online medical content such as eMedicine or the Merck Manual of Dx & Rx, which are freely available.

Therefore, the need for a segregated section of print resources, e.g., handbooks, directories, dictionaries, etc., for reference or ready reference may no longer be useful, practical, or economical. Nonetheless, the decision to eliminate or transfer reference resources from print to digital, like serials, must be made in the context of the institution's users, financial resources, and mission.

Special Collections

History of Medicine and Organizational Archives

There are a number of health care libraries that maintain both medical history and organizational archives (for more on managing archives, see Chapter 15). These collections are invaluable, unique, and often, in their analog form, difficult to manage and make available for scholarly consultation and use. However, with the advent of digitization, and the development of local institutional repositories (IRs), these collections can now be made available to a wider community for research and discovery. Many academic health sciences libraries affiliated with universities or as a part of a larger library system have transferred biomedical research papers and other unique medical history monographs and artifacts to their central special collections and/or archives libraries on campus, which is an excellent alternative to maintaining these unique collections within the biomedical library. The collections specialist or library manager will most likely become a conduit for the transfer of these unique collections, but should rely on the experts within special collections for any subsequent conversion and management activities associated with such materials. In smaller libraries, the library manager might find assistance from the nearest academic library or through the regional cooperative.

Consumer Health

For many health care libraries, part of the mission, in addition to supporting education, research, and patient care, is patient education. Typically referred to as consumer health in libraries, some health information technology professionals also use the term "participatory health" as a descriptor as well. Within the clinical setting, it is important to draw a distinction between patient education and consumer health. Most hospitals provide inpatient and outpatient clients with before- and after-care instructions for a variety of hospital procedures and conditions. Often these patient education documents are specific to the institution and are maintained, updated, and reviewed by the institution's Patient Education Department. In some settings, the library is called upon to assist with management of these numerous documents, which can proliferate and become an administrative challenge to maintain.

However, these documents are not normally accessed or housed by the library. Instead, some health care libraries provide more generic patient education information in the form of magazines (e.g., MedlinePlus, Harvard Heart Letter, etc.) and books geared to consumers. Some libraries provide various association and government health and human services brochures (e.g., the Medical Library Association's Medspeak series, http://www.mlanet.org/resources/medspeak/). Such materials add to the overall mission not only of the institution, but they contribute to the function of the physical library and support the broader institutional mission of health literacy.

Though many users are finding answers to their medical questions online, others are visiting health care libraries to get authoritative information and assistance. For the average patient with limited medical knowledge, this trend will most likely continue as the online landscape of health information continues to become more daunting to filter and decipher. Thus, maintaining a collection of consumer health books, brochures, magazines and perhaps even an online presence (website) for patients seeking quick answers can be a smart marketing move for the library because it has the potential to provide value as an institutional outreach opportunity in the community, attract new patients, and satisfy accreditation standards. See Chapter 14 for more on consumer health libraries and collection development resources.

Popular Reading

As the twenty-first-century digital health care library moves inexorably toward transformation from print to digital, the collections specialist or library manager would be wise to consider that while users are definitely pleased with access to scholarly information in a digital format, a segment of users may possess a love for the printed page. Even the most computer literate among scientists and clinicians appreciates and uses hard copy books—books of all types, including novels, pictorials, nonfiction, current events, and biographies. Moreover, popular reading materials and their availability from the health care library helps to define the *library as place* and as a hub for a variety of intellectual and social activities including reading and collaboration.

While the librarian may not want to permanently collect or purchase popular fiction or nonfiction, there are leasing plans that allow libraries to provide this service at a reasonable cost and low maintenance. Baker and Taylor, and McNaughton are two providers of leased, shelf-ready book collections. Popular materials may also be provided through donations as well.

Web Resources and Search Engines

New technologies such as robots and artificial intelligence-enabled searching are at hand. Web developers and programmers are seeking ways to make the web smart and specifically, more knowledgeable, more contextual, and more efficient. Currently, the semantic web—a concept and technology created by the Father of the web, Tim Berners-Lee—is showing some promise. It is precisely the task of "understanding" the context of user queries and returning relevant retrievals that the semantic web hopes to accomplish. For more on this web development direction, see "A Roadmap to the Semantic Web" (http://www.w3.org/DesignIssues/Semantic.html). A preview of this merger of Web 2.0 and the semantic web is available in a tool called HealthMash (http://www.healthmash.com). Healthmash is billed as the "Revolutionary Health Knowledge Base and Semantic Search Engine."

In the meantime, making sense of the web for users by libraries in the form of "indexing" or providing catalogued records or lists of web resources is complicated and expensive. Intuitive, customizable finding aids, content management systems (CMSs) and other simple interfaces provide a measure of help. Links to resources from the online catalog is another helpful user aid. However, beyond this, unless the resource is a particularly unique or exceptional resource, the library should exercise restraint and focus on promoting its licensed resources. Attempts to organize health websites has been tried and failed before. That failure was due in large part to the ephemeral nature of content on the web and maintenance costs. Moreover, the idea of imposing an infrastructure based on old technology to a new technology does not work. Google and its subsets, e.g., Google Scholar, may be the best "catalog" and "finding aid" available for now or at least until the semantic (intelligent) web or some iteration of it is fully realized.

Google and Google Scholar, Microsoft's Bing and Cuil, though not perfect, do provide a measure of access and relevant retrievals that satisfies most users. Perhaps a standard for determining whether to provide access to free or open access web resources is PubMed. As the world's leading biomedical indexing and abstracting resource, PubMed is without peer, and thus health care libraries should not think twice about providing access through the library's website or catalog to resources that are similar in quality, value, and scope. It is a unique biomedical resource. In fact, the NCBI Entrez databases (http://www.ncbi.nlm.nih.gov/guide/) are a good starting point from which to develop a core of open access, authoritative resources.

Data Sets

A number of important, no-cost electronic sources exist for data sets and statistics. The CDC's National

Center for Health Statistics (http://www.cdc.gov/nchs/) and NLM's National Information Center on Health Services Research and Health Care Technology (http://www.nlm.nih.gov/nichsr/) are core repositories. Another notable website is Partners in Public Information Access for the Public Health Workforce (http://phpartners.org/), a collaboration among government agencies, health sciences libraries, and public health organizations.

Regarding development and retrieval systems for local data sets, managers will need to determine whether limited human resources can be extended to this endeavor or whether outsourcing or collaboration with other institutions (perhaps through grant acquisition), makes more sense.

Media

Digitization has provided additional formats for research and discovery, education and training, collaboration and caring. Radiographic images, once confined to the viewbox, are now viewable on the iPhone, and transmitted to primary care physicians over the network in a matter of seconds. These data, 3-D models, pictures, slides, graphs, charts, and tables are all digital objects that have meaning. As such, they represent knowledge, which requires adequate descriptors, if they are to be specifically retrieved, and adequate storage if they are to be specifically referenced in the future. Such activity represents an opportunity for the library to take a leading role. As librarians seek new roles to maximize their value to the institution, media coordinator/facilitator/administrator may be a good one to explore. For more on the roles for librarians in media collections, see Chapter 15.

Conclusion

The digitization of data, information, and knowledge has irrevocably changed collections management in health care libraries worldwide. Fortuitously, librarians are both participants in and witnesses to an historic and evolutionary event. As good stewards, library managers must lead with all due deliberation and clarity. However, as witnesses, they may also stand back in awe and reflect on an event that is, in the minds of many, tantamount to the invention of movable type and the printing of the first book. Through it all, it may be helpful for librarians to remember that, "what's important, is the knowledge" (Gomez, 2008: 18).

References

Clemmons, Nancy W., and Susan L. Clemmons. 2005. "Five Years Later: Medical Reference in the 21st Century." *Medical Reference Services Quarterly* 24, no. 1 (Spring): 1–18.

Crow, Raym. 2006. *Publishing Cooperatives: An Alternative for Society Publishers. A SPARC Discussion Paper*. Washington, DC: Sparc Publications. Accessed September 26, 2010. http://www.arl.org/sparc/bm~doc/Cooperatives_v1.pdf.

Dee, Cheryl. 2005. "Digital Reference Service: Trends in Academic Health Science Libraries." *Medical Reference Services Quarterly* 24, no. 1 (Spring): 19–27.

Dollar, Daniel M., John Gallagher, Janis Glover, Regina Kenny Marone, and Cynthia Crooker. 2007. "Realizing What's Essential: A Case Study on Integrating Electronic Journal Management into a Print-centric Technical Services Department." *Journal of the Medical Library Association* 95, no. 2 (April): 147–155.

Dunlap, Isaac Hunter. 2008. "Going Digital: The Transformation of Scholarly Communication and Academic Libraries." *Policy Futures in Education* 6, no. 1: 132–141.

EBSCO Information Services. 2010. *Serials Price Projections for 2011*. Accessed September 25. http://www2.ebsco.com/en-us/Documents/customer/SerialsPriceProjection Report-2011.pdf.

Fernandes, Maria Isabel. 2008. "Ready Reference Collections: Thoughts on Trends." *Community & Junior College Libraries* 14, no. 3: 201–210.

Gomez, Jeff. 2008. *Print is Dead: Books in Our Digital Age*. New York: Macmillan.

Hesse, Dan. 2010. "Remarks at Healthcare Information Management Systems Society 2010." (March 1, 2010). Accessed September 24. http://newsroom.sprint.com/article_display.cfm?article_id=1492.

Hogan, Tom. 2001. "Drexel University Moves Aggressively from Print to Electronic Access for Journals." *Computers in Libraries* 21, no. 5 (May): 22–26.

Huber, Jeffrey T., Jo Anne Boorkman, and Jean Blackwell, eds. 2008. *Introduction to Reference Sources in the Health Sciences*. New York: Neal-Schuman.

Ithaka S + R. 2010. *Print Collections Decision-Support Tool*, version 1.1. Accessed September 12. http://www.ithaka.org/ithaka-s-r/research/what-to-withdraw/print-collections-decision-support-tool.

Johnson, Richard K., and Judy Luther. 2007. *The E-only Tipping Point for Journals: What's Ahead in the Print to Electronic Transition Zone*. Washington, DC: The Association of Research Libraries. Accessed September 25, 2010. http://www.arl.org/bm~doc/Electronic_Transition.pdf.

Johnson, Richard K., and Judy Luther. 2008. "Are Journal Publishers Trapped in the Dual-Media Transition Zone?" *ARL: A Bimonthly Report* 257 (April): 1–6.

Kraemer, Alfred, and Michael Markwith. 2000. "Integrating Vendor Supplied Management Reports for Serials Evaluation:

The Medical College of Wisconsin Experience." *Acquisitions Librarian* 12, no. 24: 65–75.

Macewan, Bonnie. 1999. "Understanding Users' Needs and Making Collections Choices." *Library Collections, Acquisitions, & Technical Services* 23, no. 3: 315–320.

Oppenheim, Charles. 2008. "Electronic Scholarly Publishing and Open Access." *Journal of Information Science* 34, no. 4: 577–590.

Pettijohn, Patricia, and Tina Neville. 2003. "Collection Development for Virtual Libraries." In *Building a Virtual Library*, edited by Ardis Hanson and Bruce Lubotsky Levin, 20–36. Hershey, PA: Information Science Publishing.

Prabha, Chandra. 2007. "Shifting from Print to Electronic Journals in ARL University Libraries." *Serials Review* 33, no. 1: 4–13.

Reese, Terry, and Kyle Banerjee. 2008. *Building Digital Libraries: A How-To-Do-It Manual.* New York: Neal-Schuman.

Richards, Daniel T., and Dottie Eakin. 1997. *Collection Development and Assessment in Health Sciences Libraries.* Chicago; Lanham, MD: Medical Library Association; Scarecrow Press.

Schonfeld, Roger C., and Ross Housewright. 2009. *What to Withdraw? Print Collections Management in the Wake of Digitization.* New York: Ithaka S + R. Accessed July 9, 2010. http://www.ithaka.org/ithaka-s-r/research/what-to-withdraw/what-to-withdraw-print-collections-management-in-the-wake-of-digitization/.

Sennyey, Pongracz, Lyman Ross, and Caroline Mills. 2009. "Exploring the Future of Academic Libraries. A Definitional Approach." *The Journal of Academic Librarianship* 35, no. 3: 252–259.

Shedlock, James, and Linda Walton. 2006. "Developing a Virtual Community for Health Sciences Library Book Selection: *Doody's Core Titles.*" *Journal of the Medical Library Association* 94, no. 1 (January): 61–66.

Tenopir, Carol, Donald W. King, and Amy Bush. 2004. "Medical Faculty's Use of Print and Electronic Journals: Changes Over Time and in Comparison with Scientists." *Journal of the Medical Library Association* 92, no. 2: 233–241.

Texas Digital Library. 2010. "Open Repositories." Austin: University of Texas. Accessed October 8. http://openrepositories.org.

Thomas, Lisa Carlucci. 2009. "Mobile Access to E-Books at Yale." Presented at 2009 LITA National Forum (October 2009). Accessed September 26, 2010. http://www.slideshare.net/lisacarlucci/mobile-access-to-ebooks-at-yale.

University of California Libraries Collection Development Committee. 2009. "The University of California Library Collection: Content for the 21st Century and Beyond." Accessed July 16, 2010. http://libraries.universityofcalifornia.edu/cdc/uc_collection_concept_paper_endorsed_ULs_2009.08.13.pdf.

Vaughn, K. T. L. 2003. "Changing Use Patterns of Print Journals in the Digital Age: Impacts of Electronic Equivalents on Print Chemistry Journal Use." *Journal of the American*

Society for Information Science and Technology* 54, no. 12: 1149–1152.

Wood, M. Sandra. 2008. *Introduction to Health Sciences Librarianship.* New York: Routledge.

Zambare, Aparna, Anne Marie Casey, John Fierst, David Ginsburg, Judith O'Dell, and Timothy Peters. 2009. "Assuring Access: One Library's Journey from Print to Electronic Only Subscriptions." *Serials Review* 35, no. 2: 70–74.

Zhang, Xiaoyin, and Michaelyn Haslam. 2005. "Movement toward a Predominantly Electronic Journal Collection." *Library Hi Tech* 23, no. 1: 82–89.

Further Reading

Bogdanski, Elizabeth L. 2006. "Serials Preservation at a Crossroads." *Serials Review* 32, no. 2: 70–72.

Buckland, Michael K. 2007. "The Digital Difference." *Journal of Library Administration* 46, no. 2: 87–100.

Burrows, Suzetta. 2006. "A Review of Electronic Journal Acquisition, Management, and Use in Health Sciences Libraries." *Journal of the Medical Library Association* 94, no. 1 (January): 67–74.

Carrigan, Esther, Mori Lou Higa, and Rajia Tobia. 2008. "Monographic and Digital Resource Collection Development." In *Introduction to Health Sciences Librarianship*, edited by M. Sandra Wood, 97–126. New York: Routledge.

Coleman, Mary Sue. 2006. "Google, the Khmer Rouge, and the Public Good." Washington, DC: Association of American Publishers, Professional Scholarly Publishing Division. (February 6, 2006). Accessed July 9, 2010. http://video.google.com/videoplay?docid=-4153939245642517135#docid=7138472796546564990.

Conference on Open Access to Knowledge in the Sciences and Humanities. 2003. "Berlin Declaration on Open Access to Knowledge in the Sciences and Humanities." (October 20–22). Accessed June 26, 2010. http://oa.mpg.dehttp://oa.mpg.de/lang/en-uk/berlin-prozess/berliner-erklarung/.

Cooper, Mindy M. 2007. "The Importance of Gathering Print and Electronic Journal Use Data: Getting a Clear Picture." *Serials Review* 33, no. 3 (July): 172–174.

Coyle, Karen. 2006. "Managing Technology." *The Journal of Academic Librarianship* 32, no. 2: 205–207.

Craig, Daza Fox, and Paula Meise Strain. 1980. "Analysis of Collection Development at the National Library of Medicine." *Bulletin of the Medical Library Association* 68, no. 2 (April): 197–206.

De Groote, Sandra L., and Josephine L. Dorsch. 2001. "Online Journals: Impact on Print Journal Usage." *Bulletin of the Medical Library Association* 89, no.4 (October): 372–378.

DeShazo, Kristina. 2009. "Serials Spoken Here: The 2009 Acquisitions Institute at Timberline Lodge." *Serials Review* 35, no. 4: 296–298.

Eddy, Sean R. 2009. "Open Revolution." *PLoS Biology* 7, no. 3: 0431–0432.

Fenner, Audrey, ed. 2006. *Integrating Print and Digital Resources in Library Collections*. Binghamton, NY: Haworth Press.

Hanson, Ardis, and Bruce Lubotsky Levin. 2003. *Building a Virtual Library*. Hershey, PA: Information Science Publishing.

King, Donald W., Peter B. Boyce, Carol Hansen Montgomery, and Carol Tenopir. 2003. "Library Economic Metrics: Examples of the Comparison of Electronic and Print Journal Collections and Collections Services." *Library Trends* 51, no. 3 (Winter): 376–400.

Kirschner, Ann. 2009. "Reading Dickens Four Ways." *The Chronicle of Higher Education* (June 2): 1–5.

Kolowich, Steve. 2009. "Libraries of the Future." *Inside Higher Education* (September 24). Accessed September 26, 2010. http://www.insidehighered.com/news/2009/09/24/libraries.

Kubilius, Ramune K., and Linda J. Walton. 2005. "Seize the E-journal: Models for Archiving Symposium: Report." *Journal of the Medical Library Association* 93, no.1 (January): 126–129.

Landesman, Margaret. 2005. "Getting It Right—The Evolution of Reference Collections." *The Reference Librarian* 44, no. 91/2: 5–22.

Liu, Ziming. 2006. "Print vs. Electronic Resources: A Study of User Perceptions, Preferences and Use." *Information Processing and Management* 42: 583–592.

Lynch, Clifford. 2009. "A Changing Society, Changing Scholarly Practices, and the New Landscape of Scholarly Communication." Atlanta: Georgia Tech, March 6. Accessed July 9, 2010. http://presentations.dlpe.gatech.edu/proed/stream/support/usg_030609/.

———. 2003. "Digital Library Opportunities." *The Journal of Academic Librarianship* 29, no.5 (September): 286–289.

———. 2003. Institutional Repositories: Essential Infrastructure for Scholarship in the Digital Age." *portal: Libraries and the Academy* 3, no. 2: 327–336.

Montgomery, Carol Hansen. 2002. "Comparing Library and User Related Costs of Print and Electronic Journal Collections." *D-Lib Magazine* 8, no. 10 (October): 1–14.

Nicholas, David, Paul Huntington, Hamid R. Jamali, and Anthony Watkinson. 2006. "The Information Seeking Behaviour of the Users of Digital Scholarly Journals." *Information Processing and Management* 42: 1345–1365.

Parry, Marc. 2009. "After Losing Users in Catalogs, Libraries Find Better Search Software." *Education Digest: Essential Readings Condensed for Quick Review* 75, no. 6: 54–57.

Pengelley, Nicholas. 2006. "Reaping the Digital Dividend: Is It Time to Take the Great Leap?" *International Journal of Legal Information* 34, no. 3 (Winter): 512–525.

Robbins, Sarah, Cheryl McCain, and Laurie Scrivener. 2006. "The Changing Format of Reference Collections: Are Research Libraries Favoring Electronic Access Over Print?" *The Acquisitions Librarian* 18, no. 35/36: 75–95.

Rowlands, Ian, and David Nicholas. 2008. "Understanding Information Behaviour: How Do Students and Faculty Find Books?" *Journal of Academic Librarianship* 34, no. 1: 3–15.

Sathe, Nila A., Jenifer L. Grady, and Nunzia B. Giuse. 2002. "Print versus Electronic Journals: A Preliminary Investigation into the Effect of Journal Format on Research Processes." *Journal of the Medical Library Association* 90, no. 2 (April): 235–243.

Shearer, Barbara S., and Suzanne P. Nagy. 2003. "Developing an Academic Medical Library Core Journal Collection in the (almost) Post-print Era: The Florida State University College of Medicine Medical Library Experience." *Journal of the Medical Library Association* 91, no. 3 (July): 292–302.

Tedd, Lucy A. 2009. "Open Access Publishing and Institutional Repositories: An Overview." Paper presented at the 7th International CALIBER-2009, Puducherry, India: Pondicherry University, February 25–27. Accessed July 9, 2010. http://ir.inflibnet.ac.in/dxml/handle/1944/1094.

Tenopir, Carol, Donald W. King, Peter B. Boyce, Matt Grayson, and Keri-Lynn Paulson. 2005. "Relying on Electronic Journals: Reading Patterns of Astronomers." *Journal of the American Society for Information Science and Technology* 56, no. 8: 786–802.

Thompson, Laurie L., and Mori Lou Higa. 2008. "Journal Collection Development: Challenges, Issues, and Strategies." In *Introduction to Health Sciences Librarianship*, edited by M. Sandra Wood, 69–96. New York: Routledge.

8

Collection Technical Management

Gretchen Hallerberg, Michelle Kraft, Marlene Englander, and Marian Simonson

Technology has advanced collection management practices significantly since the publication of the first edition of the *MLA Guide to Managing Health Care Libraries* in 2000. In the first edition, management decisions revolved around effective cataloging and circulation practices and the physical organization of library materials. Integrated library systems were mostly the purview of large libraries. Smaller health care libraries were in the early stages of implementing automated catalogs and circulation as sources for MARC records; personal computers and library software became more affordable (Granath, Englander, and Hallerberg, 2000).

Ten years later, integrated library systems are much more sophisticated and now offer features such as text messaging, RSS feeds, and access from mobile devices.

These new features, plus improvements to the earlier generations of ILS software, allow libraries to connect personally with their customers and provide library materials that reflect customer usage and demand. This chapter discusses the automated components that feed into current collection management practices. Differences can exist between larger academic and smaller hospital libraries in how technology is applied. Where important, these differences are explained.

Technology by its very nature is always changing, so new ideas, software, and trends will be highlighted throughout this chapter under the heading "Innovations." Some of these ideas may never be mainstreamed, but it is important that librarians are aware of alternative solutions as they adapt technology to their own collection management practices.

Integrated Library Systems

The integrated library system (ILS) is software used by library staff for ordering, cataloging, and managing library materials. The ILS software consists of modules for each of these functions and may be loaded locally on the library's hardware or may be web-based. Some modules are designed for library staff use, some for the public, and both library staff and the public share a few. Larger libraries may use one system of several interconnected software modules, while smaller hospitals may use several different programs and resources to re-create the functions that a larger, more expensive system performs.

Selecting an ILS is a key management decision for any library. The process begins with identifying the reasons why an ILS is necessary. Often these include:

- Library users require a system that provides efficient and timely access to library resources.

- Library staff requires a system to automate their job responsibilities to increase productivity.

- Membership in a library consortium requires using a specific ILS.

- The library's current system is outdated and cannot scale to meet current expectations and demand.

- Technical support for the current ILS is poor.

There are many articles on choosing an ILS in the library literature. A good starting point, especially for smaller libraries, is an article by Creissen (2008) that provides step-by-step details, a project plan, and a great checklist in the appendix. For a broader perspective, read the article by Kinner and Rigda (2009) on the evolution and current status of the ILS. Libraries often write a request for proposal (RFP) as part of the bidding process for large investments, such as an ILS. An RFP is usually written as a systematically structured document that outlines the goals, functions, implementation, time lines, and financial components of a project. Multiple vendors receive the RFP, review it, and prepare their own responses if they are interested in accepting the library as a client (Calvert and Read, 2006).

Larger libraries can usually justify the purchase of an ILS and have enough staff for support and maintenance. Smaller libraries, however, should consider sharing an ILS to offset costs and support. For example, a web-based ILS that is hosted by the vendor doesn't require locally installed hardware or software, or local IT staff to support it.

ILS components and configuration vary with the ILS vendor and the needs of the individual library. Some ILSs, such as Innovative Interfaces Inc., require the library to purchase separate modules, while others, such as CyberTools for Libraries, come with almost all of the modules included. Although the authors are most familiar with these two products, libraries need to investigate other vendors as part of the discovery process. Two excellent resources for lists of ILS vendors are the annual *Computers in Libraries Buying Guide* (O'Donnell, 2010) and Marshall Breeding's (2009, 2010) annual column in *Library Journal* in the "Automation Marketplace."

Libraries choose their integrated library systems based on their needs to automate some or all of the following functions:

- Cataloging
- Online catalog
- Circulation
- Acquisitions
- Serials
- Electronic Resource Management

Each function has its own work flow and set of management reports. Decisions made in cataloging, for example, can affect outcomes in circulation, serials, or acquisitions. The integrated nature of the system points out the importance of designing effective work flows and measuring their results. The relative utility of these reports is directly related to the data present in each of these modules. For example, the University of Colorado at Boulder used reports generated from their integrated library system to make collection management decisions on canceling resources due to budget cuts as well as developing remote storage strategies (Knievel, Wicht, and Connaway, 2004).

Management in Action 8.1 illustrates how four libraries in the Cleveland Clinic Health System imple-

---

Innovations in ILS Technology

- It is all about the user experience. Make the ILS interactive by incorporating Web 2.0 features.

- Integrate digital documents with the online catalog using digital object management systems (DOMS).

- Investigate an ILS built on open source software (OSS) for systems with more flexibility and lower cost.

- Customize the ILS by sharing software from different systems that are built on interoperability (Kinner and Rigda, 2009; Dougherty, 2009).

MANAGEMENT IN ACTION 8.1

Selecting and Implementing an ILS: Case Study for Smaller Libraries

Description of Project: Four community hospital libraries in the same health system had separate card catalogs in addition to maintaining a union catalog. This process was labor intensive and the card catalog was not used by library patrons. The librarians needed more efficient methods to catalog their collections, collate circulation statistics, and compile holdings lists for residency and educational programs. This was the impetus to seek out a low-cost yet effective ILS specializing in small hospital library systems.

Impact: The ILS streamlined the usual cataloging and circulation duties as well as provided more options to collect usage statistics for the librarians. The ILS also allowed the collection to be visible to users outside of the library—in their offices or on the hospital floors.

People Involved: Librarians at each of the four hospitals were the primary people involved with implementing the ILS. One hospital also recruited two graduate students in Library Science for the project. ILS support worked closely with each librarian to add records and provide training on the use and maintenance of the system.

Strategies for Success: The overall success of the project depended on selecting the right ILS. In this case, the ILS specialized in medical libraries and received excellent reviews for their support. Next, accurate holdings information was entered using MARCIVE downloads, original cataloging, copy cataloging, and SERHOLD information. The third component was online training since no ILS is easy to use out of the box. Moving from a card catalog to an online system created quite a learning curve for the librarians. The final component was advanced planning as a group to decide the policies, locations, barcodes, and procedures before the ILS is implemented. The ILS vendor provided a helpful worksheet that guided the librarians through many of these issues.

Barriers Encountered: Cost, time, and technology were the major barriers that the librarians faced. While the ILS was inexpensive compared to other products on the market, it is difficult to obtain any extra money as budgets are held flat or reduced. One of the libraries received a grant while the other three libraries were able to get extra funding from administration or used a portion of their book budget.

The entire process of selecting an ILS, planning, and converting the card records to online records takes a lot of time. Librarians who used MARCIVE for record conversion or enlisted the help of detail-oriented volunteers and library students were able to move through the process faster. Technical hurdles such as understanding the basics of MARC and learning the fundamental components of the system required a week of online training for each of the librarians. Even after training the librarians encountered some difficulties with the system, which were quickly solved by ILS support.

Take-Home Points:

- Plan ahead for funding, time, and finding volunteers.
- Graduate LIS students are a great volunteer workforce.
- Consider finding a grant to help with the implementation costs.
- Seek out the best product for your budget and needs.
- When selecting an ILS, choose the system with a great support team even if it is a bit more expensive. If cost is a major factor, choose a product that doesn't have as many features but still provides excellent support.

mented the CyberTools ILS starting in 2005. A fifth library joined the group in 2010.

Automated Cataloging

The cataloging module of an ILS is usually the first to be implemented since the other modules require the cataloging record for their functions. Cataloging identifies material or electronic resources in the library by creating a record for it in the cataloging module. Bibliographic records no longer describe just the print material physically located in the library, but have expanded to electronic resources such as e-books, e-journals, and e-databases. The cataloging staff enhances the records to show holdings information such as the number of copies, location of the item in the library, and its circulation status or availability.

Although library staff members can generate cataloging information by using the work itself (original cataloging), authoritative sources such as the Library of Congress (LC) and the National Library of Medicine (NLM) prepare cataloging copy and make it available to libraries. Cataloging modules import MARC records from bibliographic authorities such as OCLC or LocatorPlus using a standard called Z39.50. For further information on this standard, visit the Library of Congress website (http://www.loc.gov/z3950/agency/).

Three key points about cataloging are:

1. Bibliographic records imported into the catalog should be full MARC records.
2. The ILS must also be capable of exporting full MARC records.
3. Adhering to the MARC standard will make future decisions on joining consortium or moving to a new ILS much easier.

OCLC requires libraries to become members and contribute their cataloging to the shared union catalog for an annual fee. Libraries become OCLC members by participating in statewide consortia. In Ohio libraries join OhioNET, and similar organizations exist in other states. Libraries that can't afford OCLC now have another alternative called SkyRiver. SkyRiver is being developed by Innovative Interfaces to compete directly with OCLC for a lower price (Breeding and Hadro, 2009). A free alternative, especially useful for smaller libraries, is LocatorPlus, the online catalog for the NLM collections (http://www.locatorplus.gov).

The librarian may use cataloging copy as is or make modifications to meet specific needs. Most health sciences libraries in the United States use the National Library of Medicine (NLM) Classification System (http://www.nlm.nih.gov/class). This publication is available on the website as a PDF but is fully searchable on the Internet as well. A copy of a poster listing the various NLM classes is on the **accompanying CD-ROM**. A few use the Library of Congress (LC) Classification System or create their own system to meet the needs of specialized collections. Smaller hospital libraries may also consider outsourcing cataloging. This topic, addressed by St. James (2005), includes pros and cons for outsourcing and ideas for best practices.

Subject analysis is essential for locating library materials, along with consistency in the application of these headings. Subject headings should reflect the content of an item as broadly or as narrowly as the item itself requires. The cataloger must also consider the needs of the library's users. In large libraries, subject headings are further divided by subheadings to guide users to specific topics. Libraries with smaller collections may decide not to use subheadings at all so that it is easier for users to browse by subject. The NLM's Medical Subject Headings (MeSH) is an appropriate choice for hospital and other health sciences libraries. MeSH is the subject thesaurus for PubMed, searchable from the dropdown menu by

the searchbox. For catalogers, it is accessible online at http://www.nlm.nih.gov/mesh/meshhome.html. Its controlled vocabulary allows successful retrieval of information, regardless of the format.

While it is important to have the correct MeSH terms, it is equally important to include alternative titles and entry points to help customers find items in the online catalog. The health sciences literature is filled with acronyms, initialisms, and popular names for texts such as *The Red Book* or *NEJM*. These are examples of terms to include in social tagging or added entry and note fields. Staff in other departments, such as collection development, rely on consistently applied MeSH terms and call numbers for subject analysis, just as users rely upon added entry keywords and notes to more effectively retrieve material.

Social tagging allows the records to be found in ways other than the predefined subject headings that are often unfamiliar to library patrons. Libraries that have an ILS that supports tagging reported positive usage results with library patrons. Both Michigan State University and Glasgow University Library in Scotland reported that users were able to find materials that they were unable to find prior to their implementation of Encore, the Innovative Interfaces social tagging module (Sanders, 2008). Smaller libraries or systems using an ILS without a social tagging module can apply these same principles using the notes and added entry fields.

The integrity of the cataloging and classification procedures has a profound effect on user success in accessing information in the library's collection. The library should maintain a cataloging manual which documents policies and procedures. This manual will help ensure consistency in cataloging decisions as electronic resources change cataloging practices and library staff work flows. According to Perkins (2009: 220), "the cataloging role in the library is becoming less about description and subject analysis, and more about data management." Each library needs to establish its own best practices to maintain quality cataloging records when faced with adding large numbers of bibliographic records from electronic resource packages.

If a library is a member of a consortium with a shared or union catalog, local cataloging practices must agree with the policies and procedures of the consortium. Submitting catalog records with specific standards is often the first step in joining a consortium. The standards ensure that the union catalog functions as a whole instead of a disjointed set of holdings records.

The ILS can provide reports to help catalogers check the integrity of the catalog. The types of reports will vary

Collection Technical Management

according to the ILS; larger systems may offer more reporting features while smaller ones may offer only a few. For example, Figure 8.1 shows the variety of heading reports in Innovative's Millennium Cataloging module. Innovative Interfaces, Inc. also has a statistics generator that lets library staff design custom reports on cataloging activity. Figure 8.2 is a sample report on the number of items cataloged according to the NLM classification schedule. This report is helpful to collection development staff as well as providing statistics by the number of records and copies cataloged during a specific time period. If an ILS does not provide a necessary report, ask the vendor to add the report or offer suggestions on how to approximate the data.

Automated Circulation

After cataloging, circulation is usually the second module of an ILS that is implemented since it is vital for managing the library's borrowing and lending functions.

Innovations in Cataloging

Anglo-American Cataloguing Rules (*AACR* and *AACR2*) has been the standard for descriptive cataloging for 43 years. This is being supplanted by *Resource Description and Access* (*RDA*). According to their website:

> RDA is the new cataloging standard that will replace Anglo-American Cataloging Rules, 2nd edition in 2009. RDA goes beyond earlier cataloging codes in that it provides guidelines on cataloging digital resources and a stronger emphasis on helping users find, identify, select, and obtain the information they want. RDA also supports clustering of bibliographic records to show relationships between works and their creators. This important new feature makes users more aware of a work's different editions, translations, or physical formats. (Joint Steering Committee for Development of RDA, 2010)

The *RDA* website has information on this standard along with information on how to transition from *AACR2* to *RDA*. The principals involved in the project also have a toolkit for this transition available for subscription (http://www.rdatoolkit.org/home).

Figure 8.1. Headings Reports in Millennium Cataloging

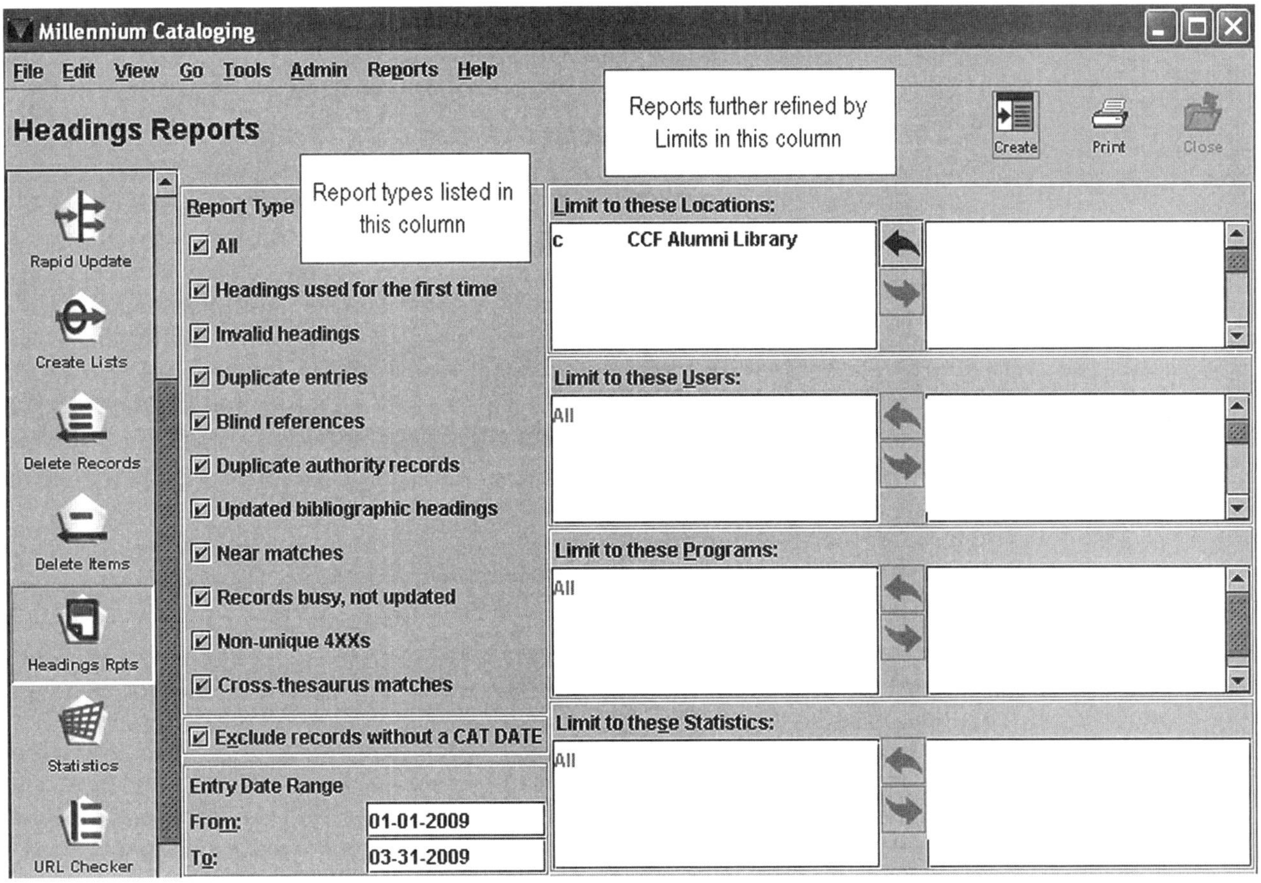

Source: Used with permission.

Figure 8.2. Statistical Reports from Millennium Cataloging

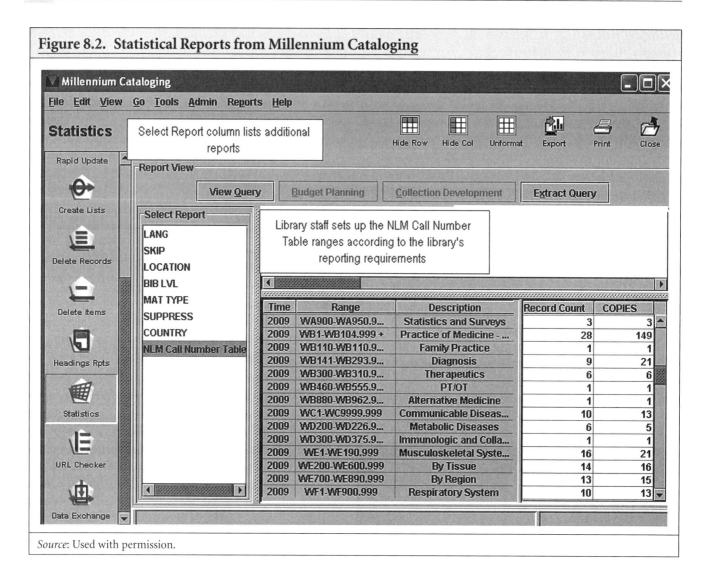

Source: Used with permission.

The first step in automating circulation involves creating a customer database. Library staff creates records for each customer either by typing the information or uploading a file from Human Resources or Admissions. The fields in a circulation record usually contain address and phone information, but other important fields to consider are job categories, departments, termination dates, and borrowing privileges. A unique field is required to identify each customer. Consider using an existing identifier, such as an employee badge number, that is readily available from HR and is familiar to the customer. Social Security numbers are no longer acceptable. If employee badge numbers are not available, barcodes can be assigned to each patron's circulation record and affixed to the ID badge, given that this is approved by the institution.

The second step in automating circulation occurs in cataloging when each item in the library's physical collection is assigned a unique identifier, such as a barcode, as part of physical processing. Automated circulation then ties both pieces together by tracking the circulation status of items by customers. It is important that the data needed to track usage and run collection analysis reports are present in the circulation records from the outset. Most ILSs automatically count check-outs, check-

Portable Barcode Readers for Circulation Functions

Portable barcode readers are hand-held devices that interface with an ILS for various circulation functions such as recording in-house usage, taking inventory, or recording check-ins and check-outs when the ILS is down. Staff can use the reader throughout the library, such as scanning items in the library's photocopy room or re-shelving area for in-house usage statistics or in the stacks for inventory. The reader captures the barcodes in a transaction file that library staff transfer to the ILS.

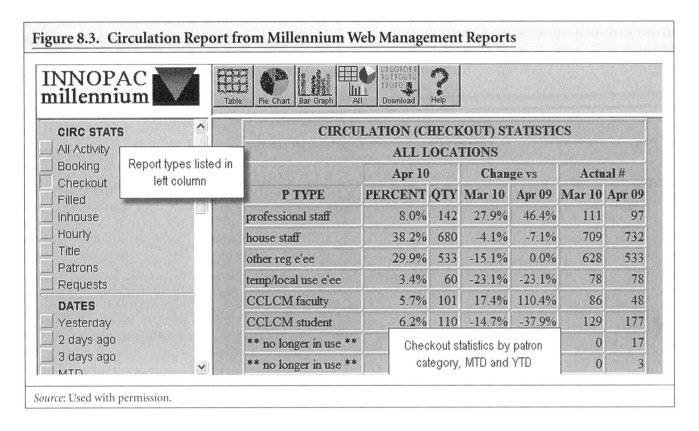

Figure 8.3. Circulation Report from Millennium Web Management Reports

P TYPE	Apr 10 PERCENT	QTY	Change vs Mar 10	Apr 09	Actual # Mar 10	Apr 09
professional staff	8.0%	142	27.9%	46.4%	111	97
house staff	38.2%	680	-4.1%	-7.1%	709	732
other reg e'ee	29.9%	533	-15.1%	0.0%	628	533
temp/local use e'ee	3.4%	60	-23.1%	-23.1%	78	78
CCLCM faculty	5.7%	101	17.4%	110.4%	86	48
CCLCM student	6.2%	110	-14.7%	-37.9%	129	177
** no longer in use **					0	17
** no longer in use **					0	3

Source: Used with permission.

ins, and renewals in both customer and cataloging records. Once an item is no longer checked out to a customer, the system should delete the specific circulation activity from the customer record. III's Millennium circulation, for example, records historic statistics such as total checkouts and renewals by customer but not specific titles. Figure 8.3 shows a snapshot of current circulation activity by type of borrower using Innovative's Millennium Web Management Reports.

In addition, many ILSs have a feature to record in-house usage that tracks how materials are used in the library. When coupled with borrowing statistics, library staff has a complete picture of what is being used in the physical collection. These reports are helpful to both circulation and collection development staff.

Libraries that participate in a lending consortium often share the same ILS. For example, all libraries in OhioLINK, a consortium of 88 college and university libraries and the State Library of Ohio at this writing, use Innovative Interfaces, Inc. Library users search their local catalogs first for materials to borrow. If an item is not available locally, the customer searches the central OhioLINK catalog and places a request to send the item to their local library. The INN-Reach module is the system behind this shared resource-sharing. The customer's circulation record shows the request and is updated as the item moves through the system. When the item arrives at the local library, a notice is automatically emailed showing that the item is available for pick-up.

Lending and borrowing reports for the consortium are based on this circulation data. The consortial borrowing reports list the material users are requesting from outside libraries, whereas the lending reports show material borrowed by outside libraries. Analysis of consortial borrowing will pinpoint areas of the local collection that may need more resources if the subject is in scope for the local collection.

Other features of automated circulation include:

- Managing overdue materials by sending courtesy, overdue, and billing notices;

- Setting up and collecting fines; and

- Creating and managing a hold shelf of material requested by library customers.

In addition to traditional circulation activities, some systems have a software function called API (Application Program Interface). This feature shares the circulation data with other software such as proxy services that authenticate library users for off-campus access to resources. Another example ties the library users' ability to place interlibrary loans or document delivery requests to their circulation records. Only users with records in "good standing" can submit requests using the ILLiad software. Each library interprets "good standing" according to their policies on overdue fines, status, or other parameters.

Up to this point, the discussion has centered on circulation from the library staff viewpoint, but library customers can also use automated features for self-service. Systems now allow customers to view their records, renew materials, and check the status of requested materials online. Some libraries are also using self-service stations to let users check-out and desensitize library materials themselves. These self-service stations are usually in addition to the traditional circulation desk.

Innovations in Circulation

Radio-frequency identification (RFID) is relatively new technology for circulation in which RFID tags replace barcodes as item identifiers. The system reads the RFID tags and desensitizes the material without having library staff handle each item individually. This technology is still expensive and most useful in libraries with large circulation workloads (Breeding, 2008a).

Automated Serials

The serials module was originally used to manage the library's print journal collection through the check-in, claiming, and binding processes. Its functionality is based on the bibliographic record created in cataloging. For print journals, library staff set up a check-in record with an expected arrival date for each issue. As the issue arrives, it is checked in. When all the issues for an entire volume have been received, the bindery function identifies which titles can be sent to the bindery. When a journal issue is late, library staff use the claiming function to identify these titles and send the claims electronically to the journal vendor for fulfillment. Users can see the entire check-in history plus expected receipt of future issues in the online catalog along with bindery and claims information for each journal title.

Libraries began migrating serials from print to online starting in the early 2000s. Larger libraries with the staff and technology to embrace online were the early adopters. This trend continues today but now touches all libraries. The primary issues driving this evolution are serials budgets, space, and user preferences.

- Serials budgets have not kept pace with inflation, consequently libraries cannot afford to purchase the same journal titles in both print and online. By canceling trailing print, libraries save on both budgets and space (Chadwell, 2009).

- Space is problematic for many libraries as collections grow. One way to economize is to drop print titles that users can access online. Publishers are also digitizing older journals and selling these archives as one-time purchases. Libraries can then discard the old print to free up shelf space.

- Users prefer immediate access to journals at their desktops instead of using print journals in the library. Health care practitioners and researchers, under pressure with workloads, now depend on online access to improve their efficiency.

Several excellent papers by Petsche (2008), Ohler and McKiernan (2006), Rosati (2006), and Bardyn and Young (2007) provide details on how academic and hospital libraries have managed this transition from print to online. These guidelines will help libraries assess their own collections and develop their individual migration strategies. Haynes discusses this transition in format from the perspective of digital libraries in Chapter 7.

Now that serials are primarily online, librarians must assess their need for a serials module, especially if the module's work flow is geared toward print. If the serials module cannot accommodate online work flows, staff will need to investigate other management tools, such as A–Z lists or Electronic Resource Management systems (ERMS), which have been developed specifically for e-resources. More information on these tools is available in the Managing Electronic Collections section of this chapter.

Online work flows usually require different processes and skills. Tobia and Hunnicut (2008) examine how several libraries in the South Central chapter of the Medical Library Association managed the print to electronic transition by changing staffing levels and job responsibilities. Dollar et al. (2007) provide further details by describing the reorganization of the technical services department at Yale's Cushing/Whitney Medical Library. The reorganization resulted in new online work flows geared to electronic resources using link resolvers, the online catalog, ERMS, and standard Office software. Libraries of all sizes can adapt ideas from these articles as they develop their own plans for managing their online resources. Depending on the library's cataloging policy, online serials often have a bibliographic record in the online catalog. The 856/956 MARC field in the cataloging record displays the URL to access full-text content from the online catalog. Often, imported cataloging records contain outdated or generic URLs in these fields so staff must verify the accuracy of these links. For libraries with large electronic journal collections, this can be very time-consuming. This is where the use of A–Z lists and ERMSs come into play.

No discussion of e-journals is complete without addressing usage statistics. The ILS does not track usage of e-resources directly. Publishers use a standard measure called the COUNTER protocol that allows comparisons between similar resources when tracking e-journal usage (COUNTER, 2008). Library staff may download these statistics manually (formatted as Excel, XML, or tab-delimited files) or set these up as automated e-mails directly from the publishers. This method of obtaining usage statistics is labor-intensive, but a relatively new protocol, called SUSHI, automates the downloading of usage statistics from the publisher into the ILS (National Information Standards Organization, 2010). SUSHI imports the usage statistics into the ERMS and links it to the e-journal's order record so that cost per use can be calculated automatically. Hospital libraries without an ERMS can create their own cost per usage data by importing their statistics into Excel spreadsheets or database software such as Access or FileMaker Pro. For further discussion of SUSHI and COUNTER, consult Chapters 4, 6, and 7.

Cost per use is calculated by dividing the annual cost of the journal by the number of times articles have been downloaded from it in a year. Collection management librarians often use this calculation as the basis for deciding whether to renew or cancel a journal. The cost per use for a subscription is also compared to the cost of obtaining the article through interlibrary loan. When interlibrary loan costs are greater than subscription costs, it is more cost-effective to subscribe to the title. Libraries will find that cost per use of a title generally decreases over time if the title is popular with users. Libraries can subscribe to journals that are not held by many libraries. In these cases, interlibrary loan revenues can support the subscription costs for these titles. Chapter 4 provides further information on cost/benefit analyses and cost per use calculations.

Online Catalog

The online catalog is the web-based interface used by the public to search for materials in the library's collection. Formerly called an online public access catalog or OPAC and replacing the traditional card catalog, these catalogs revolutionized the customer's access to bibliographic information. Access to library resources consists of both bibliographic and physical access. Bibliographic access presents the cataloging information (author, title, and subject headings) as searchable indexes in the online catalog. Library customers search the catalog to see if the library has the item they need. If the item is in the collection, the users check the full record for the call number to locate the item on the shelves, the holdings information to see if the item is available for check out, and the URL to connect to it electronically.

In addition to the usual search fields of author, title, and subject, many libraries are now using keyword searches as the default search for the online catalog. Even with this change, some libraries have found that the traditional online catalog is nearing the end of its useful life as the popularity of Google, Amazon, and online retail websites has changed user behavior and expectations.

What are the characteristics of these new online catalogs? Librarians, especially members of the Digital Library Federation (DLF), are discussing and researching this question in papers, meetings, e-mails, and blogs. The DLF formed a group called the ILS Discovery Interface Task Force in 2007 that developed a series of recommendations on how to integrate the traditional ILS with a discovery interface. The Task Force recommendations can be found at http://diglib.org/architectures/ilsdi/. Ockerbloom (2009: 13), the chair of the Task Force, describes the process as follows:

- Finding relevant resources (discovery)
- Acquiring them (delivery)
- Managing their usage (patron services)

Emanuel and Kern (2009: 118–119) describe the "nextgen" catalogs as more of a "search experience rather than locating a specific item." Data in the catalog includes local bibliographic records and external websites with information supplementing the local record. Keyword searching is the default interface, which picks up the Google and Amazon-like trend. The searching process matches user behavior by "searching first and refining later." These broad concepts are put into practice by specific systems such as LibraryThing, PennTags, Encore, AquaBrowser, and Blacklight, to name a few (Sadler, 2009; Webb and Nero, 2009; Parry, 2010).

Whether a library uses a discovery layer interface or a traditional online catalog, the ILS should offer a series of collection management reports to analyze user behavior when searching the online catalog. Figure 8.4 from Innovative's Millennium Web Management Reports shows the number of searches in each index during a 10-day period. To further refine the report, staff clicks on any of the indexes (keyword, author, title, subject, etc.) to show the actual terms typed by the customer in alphabetic order or in order of frequency. A third option shows the terms for which there were no results. All these

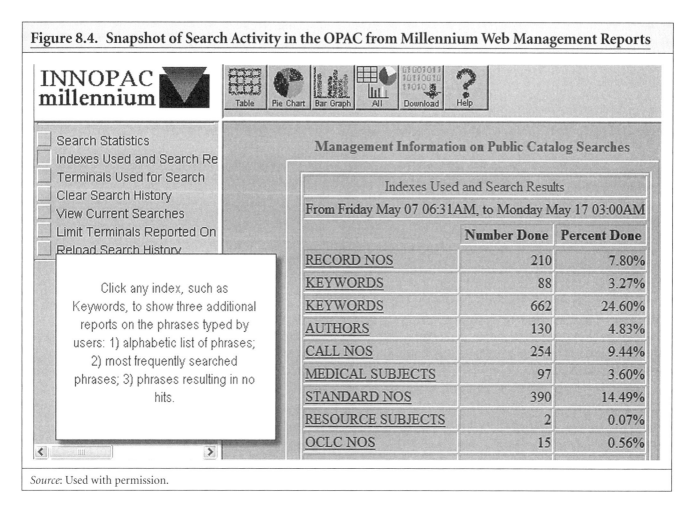

Figure 8.4. Snapshot of Search Activity in the OPAC from Millennium Web Management Reports

Source: Used with permission.

reports provide insights to collection management staff to determine what customers are searching for and if they found material that matches their search requests in the collection.

Before concluding the discussion of ILS components, it is important to emphasize the necessity for a robust reporting or administrative module. Some ILSs incorporate reporting as part of the features of each component, whereas others may provide a separate application. System-generated and customized reports provide the foundations on which to justify system use, support, and expansion. For example, Innovative's Millennium Web Management Reports module analyzes user behavior, circulation activity, collection characteristics, fund reports in acquisitions, and consortia usage. Reports designed specifically for collection development librarians include:

- analysis of the age of the collection;
- summary of the number of items in the collection by year and call number;
- circulation per subject category; and
- cost per circulation.

Customized queries and crosstab reports are additional features. Once a query or report is created, library staff can save it for future use which is especially helpful when generating monthly statistics. Systems used by smaller libraries may not share the same robust reporting features. In these cases, librarians determine the statistics they need and collect the data in spreadsheets. For additional information on reporting, refer to Dudden's discussion on the culture of assessment and evaluation projects in Chapter 6.

Managing Electronic Collections

Managing electronic collections is a broad topic covering e-journal access systems, open URL linking, electronic resource management systems (ERMSs), and journal aggregators. These tools have gained popularity as the serials world has changed from print to electronic formats and as the volume of e-resources increases, especially through consortia purchases. Many of these management tools bypass the ILS allowing libraries to choose the products that provide the right balance of features and price for their needs. This is especially helpful for smaller libraries with more limited budgets.

E-journal Access Systems

The simplest type of e-journal access system is the A–Z list provided by vendors such as EBSCO Information Services, Serials Solutions, Inc., and SFX. The A–Z list aggregates all the library's e-journals into one alphabetical list with links to the full-text content from various providers or publishers. The A–Z list vendor creates a comprehensive database, or knowledge base, of e-journal titles with information such as the publisher, e-journal collection packages, URLs, start and end dates, and embargoes. This knowledgebase is the core of the A–Z list from which library staff select the titles owned by the individual library. To further enhance the A–Z list, many libraries upload their print journal holdings to provide users with a single, comprehensive list of serials to search. All three vendors also offer the ability to add e-books to the A–Z list.

There are several advantages to implementing an A–Z list instead of creating a local HTML list or database. These include:

- time savings and accuracy in setting up the A–Z list;
- efficiency in maintaining the A–Z list;
- enhanced search functions; and
- usage reports.

To create the A–Z list using one of the three major vendors, staff tags the library's holdings using the vendor's web-based management tool. Tagging is as simple as clicking a check box to indicate ownership of a title. Since many e-journals are part of collections, the vendors organize their databases by publishers, e-journal collections, and titles. Identifying e-journals in a package is one check mark instead of searching for and tagging each individual title in the package. The time-savings associated with this feature alone is considerable.

Since the vendors maintain and update the URLs from these diverse publishers, library staff is freed from checking the accuracy of links and updating URLs as they change. In addition to providing accurate URLs, the vendors maintain coverage information such as the beginning or ending dates of a title and embargoes. Embargoes occur frequently for e-journals with some free content. For example, a one-year embargo means that articles published more than one year ago are free; articles published in the past twelve months are not free and require a paid subscription.

If a library wishes to catalog its e-journals in addition to using the A–Z list, the vendors can also provide MARC records for batch loading to the online catalog. All of these features, plus more, are covered by the annual subscription cost, which is usually based on the number of resources being managed or the hospital's bed size. Smaller libraries may find that the functionality of the A–Z list more than meets the needs of staff and users and may decide to forego entering serials into the online catalog, especially if the library does not bind or check-in journal issues.

Editing functions are part of the A–Z service too, so that libraries can customize holdings information or add notes at the title, package, or publisher level. For example, a standard subscription to the *Journal of Clinical Oncology* online starts coverage with 1999. When a library purchases the archive, staff customizes the start date to 1983. Libraries without the archive stay with the default date of 1999.

Assigning notes is a great way to communicate special functions or service issues to library users. For example, journals that do not allow remote access can have a note stating that it is not available off campus. If the library temporarily loses access to e-journals in a publisher's package, it is easy to assign a note to this effect at the package level that displays for each title. Follow the three C's (clear, concise, and consistent wording) when assigning notes or modifying holdings. This practice helps library users navigate the A–Z list and understand any embargo periods, access issues, or other holdings changes.

Before moving on, it is important to note that some vendors have a 24-hour delay before updating the A–Z list with changes made by library staff. Since many health sciences libraries are under pressure to provide quick, if not immediate, access to information, library staff needs to be aware of this possible limitation when evaluating A–Z vendors.

From the customers' perspective, the A–Z list is easy to use and understand. Many libraries place a link to this service on the library's home page for easy access. If the search feature is not on the home page, it is often just one click away. To search the A–Z list, users type the journal title or partial title and click the search button. In addition to searching by title, users can often search by publisher, ISSN, or subject. Results can be limited to titles that begin with, contain, or are exact matches to the terms entered in the search box. Sometimes users need to browse, especially if looking for e-journals in a certain subject. If this is the case, users can usually browse by title, subject, or e-journal provider. These features may vary by vendor, so libraries need to select the features that are most important to staff and users.

Figure 8.5. Search Screen for EBSCO's A–Z List

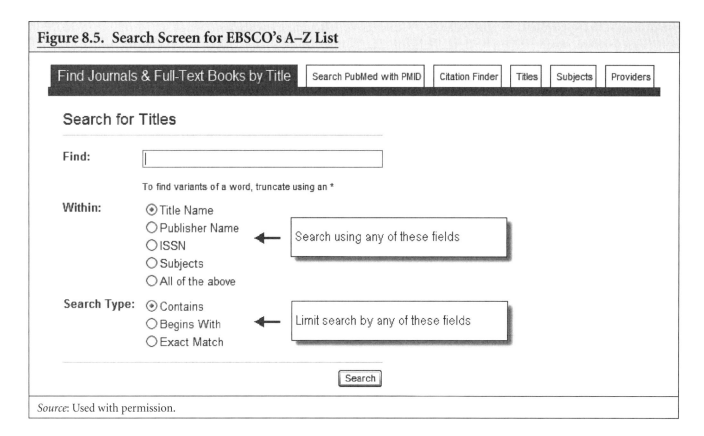

Source: Used with permission.

Figure 8.5 shows the initial search screen for EBSCO's A–Z list. Notice the multiple search parameters. A locally developed A–Z list would require considerable time and programming skills to accomplish similar results.

Figure 8.6 displays the results when a user types "JAMA" in the search box. This example shows the use of customized holdings, notes, and information on print journals. Compare this to the multiple screens users

Figure 8.6. EBSCO A–Z Search Results with Notes and Customized Holdings

Find Journals & Full-Text Books by Title | Search PubMed with PMID | Citation Finder | **Titles** | Subjects | Providers | About This Site

Return to full title list | Refine Search

Find: [   ] Search Advanced search

Titles where title name contains 'jama': 3
Page list: 1. "JAMA" to "JAMA: Journal of the American " ▾ page: ▸1

JAMA
Journal Shelves **Your Access: 1965 to present**   Print journal uploaded from a .csv file

JAMA: Journal of the American Medical Association
American Medical Association 1883 to present **Your Access: 1989 to present** Full text from 1989–1995 works for SOME, not all articles.

Example of Customized Holdings   Example of Customized Notes

Source: Used with permission.

must navigate and understand when using the online catalog and it is easy to see why they prefer searching an A–Z list.

A–Z list vendors provide reports to help library staff analyze e-journal usage independent of COUNTER reports. Examples of some reports include:

- number and length of search sessions;
- top 10 keywords, titles, or subjects searched; and
- counts of the number of times users accessed journal titles, packages, publishers, or resources.

Reports can be tailored by date; filtered by IP address; or downloaded for further manipulation in Excel. This diverse reporting structure provides collection management staff with multiple opportunities to analyze how e-journals are being used.

To complement the usage reports, the A–Z list vendors provide management reports on changes made to the library's holdings and an overlap analysis report. The overlap analysis helps collection development librarians optimize their e-journal selections and allocate their budget economically. Given its considerable advantages, libraries of all sizes should seriously consider implementing this tool.

Open URL Linking

Open URL systems are usually called link resolvers. Their purpose is to link sources of information to targets using ANSI standard Z39.88. Information sources are generally bibliographic citations from research databases, such as Ovid MEDLINE or EBSCO's CINAHL, or references at the end of chapters in full-text databases such as McGraw-Hill's AccessMedicine or UpToDate. Targets are the items that are being linked to and can include any of the following:

- Electronic journals
- Electronic books
- Online catalogs
- Interlibrary loan or document delivery forms, such as ILLiad
- Search engines, such as Google Scholar (Wikipedia contributors, 2010b)

Link resolvers are available from many different vendors; most are fee-based, but some are open source. The Open URL Wikipedia article cited above provides a comprehensive list of these vendors with links to their specific products. Three frequently used fee-based products are EBSCO's LinkSource, ExLibris' SFX, and Serials Solution's 360Link. PubMed provides its own linking services through the use of LinkOut and Outside Tool. This section covers the use of conventional link resolvers first, followed by a discussion of PubMed's services in order to explain the differences between these products and to help staff select the best solutions for their libraries.

The most common application of Open URL is direct linking from a search result in a research database to the full text of the article. After the full text is retrieved, the user returns to the search session to continue reviewing the rest of their results. This same concept applies when linking from database citations to e-books, the library's online catalog, interlibrary loan request forms, or search engines.

The Open URL link resolver builds on the A–Z list. Once a library's A–Z list is set up, it is relatively simple to implement Open URL linking. The vendor provides a base URL for the library and the link resolver creates a query using metadata from the citation. The link resolver interprets this string of data and connects directly to the full-text citation. This process is commonly called Open URL mapping.

The second step in implementing a link resolver is to activate this feature in the databases, online catalog, interlibrary loan request system, and search engines used by the library by working with the vendors' respective support staffs. Each system has its own requirements for setting up the link resolver and establishing the correct mapping algorithms.

This is where the flexibility of Open URL linking shines. Library staff can approach the implementation process in a step-wise fashion according to their staffing levels and time schedules. The following scenario can serve as a guide to the process.

- The first information resources to activate with Open URL are the most popular databases for health sciences libraries, such as MEDLINE, CINAHL, PsycINFO, Web of Science, and Scopus. This gives immediate results to the library's users by connecting them to the full-text article as they conduct their research.

- The next step is to activate the library's interlibrary loan/document delivery request system, if the library has such a system. This provides library users with the opportunity to request an article or book that is not available in their own library's collections.

- The third step is to provide a link to the library's online catalog from the link resolver so that users can see if the resource they want is available in the print collection. Establishing links to the online catalog also serves as an alternate access point if the Open URL links fail.

- Finally, library staff can set up Open URL in search engines and references in e-book collections.

Open URL link resolvers are accurate most of the time; however, e-publications ahead of print, supplements, and issues with special numbering can cause the link to fail. The reason for failure is that these types of publications may have alphabetic characters in the volume, issue, or page numbers, or that some information, such as page numbers, is missing. The mapping algorithm does not know how to interpret the citation when it encounters these exceptions to the usual data format.

Subscription costs for an Open URL link resolver are considerably more than the cost of the A–Z list. This cost may be prohibitive for smaller libraries; however PubMed's LinkOut easily fills this gap. Even if the library already subscribes to a fee-based link resolver, staff should consider implementing PubMed's LinkOut as a supplementary tool. This is especially true if the link resolver, such as Serials Solutions 360Link, can update LinkOut information.

LinkOut is free and displays library holdings of print and electronic journals when viewing PubMed search results in the abstract view. To set up LinkOut, library staff requests an account from LinkOut/NCBI staff. Once staff has the library's user ID and password, they can identify their e-journals by using the Library Submission Utility. For complete instructions, please refer to the LinkOut Help documentation at their website (http://www.ncbi.nlm.nih.gov/bookshelf/br.fcgi?book=help linkout). If LinkOut is activated, customers can browse their search results; link to a full-text journal article to print or save; and then return to browsing the rest of their search results.

Library staff can set up print holdings to display in PubMed by activating LinkOut-SERHOLD. If a library doesn't participate in SERHOLD, staff can upload a file of print holdings. Last, libraries that have a link resolver can register that link resolver using PubMed's Outside Tool. PubMed provides a very helpful table that compares the features of LinkOut, LinkOut Local, and Outside Tool at the following website under the section, "Before Registering" (http://www.ncbi.nlm.nih.gov/bookshelf/br.fcgi?book=helplinkout&part=lib).

To identify the library's holdings when searching PubMed or other NCBI databases, library staff provide icons for full-text and print holdings. If a library doesn't

have customized icons, generic ones are available from LinkOut. The full-text or print icon appears in abstract view when users are reviewing search results, but only if a library subscribes to the journal title and year of the citation. If a library has activated Outside Tool, however, the Outside Tool icon appears in every citation.

Libraries that subscribe to link resolvers debate whether it is necessary to implement LinkOut if Outside Tool has been set up. In the authors' opinion, LinkOut provides one-click access to the full text when searching PubMed. Using Outside Tool, however, requires multiple clicks that open several windows before the customer finally gets to the full text. Each new click and window presents an opportunity for failure. One-click access to full text streamlines the searching process and is important to busy professionals.

Open URL linkers provide usage reports on the titles, publishers, and databases accessed by the library's users. This data, complemented by usage data from the A–Z list, offer a snapshot of linking activity and is a useful addendum to COUNTER reports from journal publishers. Libraries that have activated PubMed's Linkout can also obtain usage statistics by journal title. An example of these statistics is shown in Figure 8.7.

An Open URL linker is the ultimate tool in providing information to library users on their desktops. Its implementation fosters increased usage of e-journals making them even more cost-effective by decreasing the journal's cost per use ratio. Once established, both library staff and users quickly adapt to its convenience and consider it one of the library's essential services.

Innovations in Open URL Linking

The KBART (Knowledge Bases and Related Tools) Working Group represents participants (content providers, link resolver vendors, and libraries) in all aspects of Open URL data. The group published its first set of best practice guidelines in January 2010 that discusses metadata standards for formatting and exchange. When link resolvers and content providers standardize on KBART best practices, librarians can transfer Open URL data between other link resolvers or ERMSs without re-keying data. When evaluating Open URL vendors, be sure to check if their data is compliant with KBART best practices (http://www.uksg.org/kbart).

Electronic Resource Management Systems

Electronic resource management systems (ERMSs) are relatively new library technology. Innovative Interfaces Inc. was the first vendor to introduce an ERMS in 2002.

Figure 8.7. Sample Usage Statistics from PubMed's LinkOut

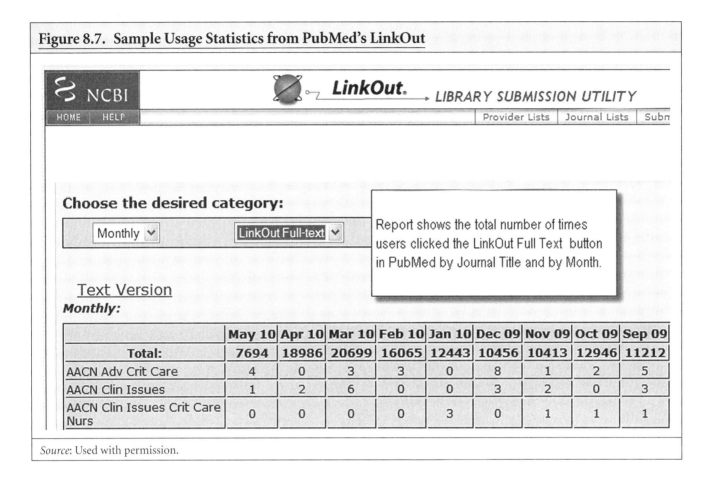

	May 10	Apr 10	Mar 10	Feb 10	Jan 10	Dec 09	Nov 09	Oct 09	Sep 09
Total:	7694	18986	20699	16065	12443	10456	10413	12946	11212
AACN Adv Crit Care	4	0	3	3	0	8	1	2	5
AACN Clin Issues	1	2	6	0	0	3	2	0	3
AACN Clin Issues Crit Care Nurs	0	0	0	0	3	0	1	1	1

Source: Used with permission.

Since its introduction, numerous vendors now offer ERMS modules, either as a separate component of an ILS or as a stand-alone product. For example, Innovative's ERMS is fully integrated into its ILS whereas EBSCO and Serials Solutions offer web-based products that are integrated with the A–Z list.

An ERMS is a library staff management tool that tracks the numerous processes or work flows involved in the lifecycle of electronic resources. It is the bridge that collects ordering, usage, financial, and administrative information about e-resources in one location. ERMS vendors populate the system with a knowledgebase. Each e-resource has a separate record that includes information such as journal title or database name, publisher, provider, type of resource, format, content description, URL, and subject headings. Additional features include mapping e-resource licenses, maintaining contact information, and storing usage data. Vendors such as EBSCO and Serials Solutions use the library's existing knowledgebase for their A–Z list or link resolver to populate the ERMS. Journal vendors such as EBSCO and Swets can populate the knowledgebase with the library's current subscriptions. Collins (2008) reviews nine vendors of current ERMSs based on a survey she conducted and is an excellent

starting point to examine ERMS functions and work flows. Breeding (2008b) shows how the ERMS manages staff work flows using the following timeline:

- **New e-resource to evaluate**: The ERMS may have an existing record in the knowledgebase that provides background information on the product.

- **Trial**: The ERMS record has fields to record the trial start and end date, plus fields for internal notes or messages that display for the library users.

- **Negotiations**: Before discussing licensing and financial terms of a new resource, library staff can check the ERMS to see what other products are already licensed from this publisher. Staff can then negotiate for similar or more favorable terms. Staff can also review the terms offered by similar products from other publishers and use this as a negotiating tool.

- **Licensing**: One of the main features of an ERMS is to track licensing information for an e-resource such as the type of license, perpetual access, interlibrary loan terms, and accessibility off campus. Many can display the terms of the license to users as well as storing the entire license in the ERMS.

- **Acquisition**: Once the library decides to add a resource, the acquisitions work flow occurs in the acquisitions module. If the ERMS is integrated with the ILS, the ordering, receiving, and payment details can be displayed in the ERMS.

- **Administration and Management**: Library staff stores the administrative information about e-resources in the ERMS such as subscriber numbers, administrative login IDs and passwords, registration and activation dates, and the URL for usage statistics. Contact information for sales and tech support are also linked to the ERMS record.

- **Renewal**: Library staff record the start date and end date of each resource's subscription. The system supports tickler files that e-mail reminders about renewals and other upcoming events to library staff. Some vendors have systems that support SUSHI, which means that usage statistics for SUSHI-compliant e-resources are automatically obtained from the publisher and stored in the ERMS. Library staff can then generate cost/use reports automatically. If the ERMS supports SUSHI, usage statistics for non-SUSHI compliant resources can usually be imported manually.

Reports are an important component of the ERMS given the amount of money libraries spend on electronic resources today. As mentioned above, cost/use reports provide valuable data for ongoing collection management decisions. In addition to cost/use for specific e-resources, some systems provide further analyses such as cost/use by subject or provider across time. Title overlap analysis reports help staff compare e-journals from multiple publishers to eliminate unnecessary duplication. In an ILS, staff refreshes data in the ERMS by uploading e-journal records from A–Z lists. The system generates reports that compare pre-existing content with the newly uploaded data to identify titles or resources that may require clean-up efforts from staff.

Although an ERMS is primarily a staff function, many libraries incorporate the ERMS into the online catalog so that users can search for e-resources by title or subject. To implement this feature, ILS support adds searchable fields for e-resource titles and subjects to the online catalog. Some libraries display the e-resources titles and subjects as alphabetic lists on the library's website. This is a considerable time-saver since staff do not need to maintain this data as HTML pages. As staff updates records in the ERMS, changes are live immediately and don't need to be updated a second time on the webpage.

An ERMS is a costly investment for libraries, especially smaller libraries. Staff has to evaluate whether the benefits offered by an ERMS are worth the cost in dollars and staff time. Libraries with large e-collections are the ones who will benefit the most from an ERMS. Smaller libraries can continue tracking their resources with spreadsheets or databases, or can incorporate Web 2.0 technology to mimic some of the functionality of an ERMS. Murray (2008) discusses these Web 2.0 alternatives to ERMSs such as blogs, Google Docs, wikis, widgets, RSS, and mashups and is worthwhile reading for libraries without the budget or staff to implement an ERMS.

No discussion of an ERMS is complete without addressing the issue of standards. Currently, there is a lack of unifying standards for ERMSs that make it difficult for library staff to maintain the data and share it with other systems. Vendors are also frustrated because it is difficult to develop systems without underlying standards. Library staff investigating ERMSs need to check if the following standards are available in the products they are researching:

- SUSHI (Standardized Usage Statistics Harvesting Initiative)
- ONIX (Online Information Exchange)
- ONIX-PL (ONIX for Publications Licenses)
- SOH (Serials Online Holdings)

Even with the availability of standards, library staff may decide that it isn't necessary to incorporate them into their ERMS workflows (Collins, 2008).

Once library staff has implemented an ERMS, considerable work remains in keeping the data refreshed. ERMS maintenance is time-consuming and involves reviewing and changing how staff accomplishes their current jobs. Without this review, staff can be trapped into maintaining multiple systems, thereby defeating the purpose of the ERMS. In real life, librarians find that ERMSs still lack certain functionality revolving around issues of flexibility and interoperability as discussed by Collins (2008) and Grogg (2008). Here are Grogg's comments on the future of ERMSs:

> In theory, ERMs are a winner. Much like other successful technological innovations, such as the Open URL, ERMs are the best type of tool because they can solve very real needs. Yet, in practice, we have discovered that ERMs do not immediately solve all the problems as we expected. In theory and practice the future of the ERM system remains to be seen. (Grogg, 2008: 89)

Other librarians share a different viewpoint, although they acknowledge the issues raised by Grogg. Tijerina and King (2008) present responses received to their question about the future of electronic resource management systems from four electronic resources and collection management librarians and one ERMS vendor. All five agree that ERMSs are here to stay and offer ideas on how they will evolve in the future.

Innovations in ERMSs

ERMS data standards and their mapping to CORE, SUSHI, and ONIX-PL are under review by the National Information Standards Organization (NISO), which is expected to publish its report in 2010. The report will recommend best practices for interoperability between the various standards and will highlight areas for future development. The hope is that ERMS vendors will adopt these best practices when developing their products so that uploading licensing data, usage statistics, and financial information into ERMS can be automated (ERM Data Standards and Best Practices Review Working Group, 2010).

Journal Aggregators

Journal aggregators have been part of the e-journal landscape for many years. The aggregators typically centralize e-journal management functions such as maintaining institutional IP addresses and obtaining usage reports for the electronic journals they provide. Library staff set up administrative accounts so that the aggregator can email monthly usage statistics or alerts when subscriptions are about to expire. Examples of aggregators that fall into this category include Highwire Press, Ingenta, MetaPress, and ScienceDirect. These aggregators may have e-journals from many publishers, such as Highwire, or have e-journals from a single publisher, such as ScienceDirect. Some also provide hosting services by publishing e-journals for societies or publishers, such as Ingenta and MetaPress.

Another type of aggregator provides full-text access as part of a database subscription; examples of database aggregators include EBSCOhost, ProQuest, and MD Consult. The database subscription with full-text access is often much less expensive than providing full-text content directly from the publisher. Without these databases, libraries would subscribe to just a fraction of the titles offered by the aggregator. By utilizing their services, libraries save money, offer an expanded selection of e-journals, and streamline access to the literature for users. The downside of database aggregators is the reliability of their content, embargoes, and lack of access to e-publications ahead of print. Libraries should not rely on data-

base aggregators to provide access to critical e-journals since the content is rarely as current or reliable as subscribing directly from the publisher (Watson, 2003).

Journal vendors such as EBSCO and Swets also provide aggregation services by managing most of the electronic journal renewal process from beginning to end. The library's customer service representative handles most of the administrative details of an e-journal such as obtaining price quotes, gathering licensing information, and activating the e-journal at the publisher's site. If the library also subscribes to the vendor's A–Z list, the customer service representative can work with A–Z list support to populate the library's print and online holdings in A–Z. Management of the e-journal work flow is a valuable service for libraries that are in the process of transitioning to electronic journals or for libraries with limited staff time.

Collection Management: Acquisitions

Acquisitions is the process by which material selected for the collection is ordered. Most ILSs have acquisitions modules; some vendors include acquisitions as part of the initial purchase of the ILS while others charge separately for this module. Larger health sciences libraries implement acquisitions to streamline the ordering, receiving, and invoicing work flows. Smaller libraries, on the other hand, may handle the acquisitions process using locally created spreadsheets, purchase orders submitted to supply chain management, or reports generated by book vendors or publishers. Haynes, in Chapter 7, describes the conceptual process of acquisitions by distinguishing between the principles of collection management, which have not changed, and the practices of collection management, which have undergone significant changes. The driving force behind these changes is that most electronic resources are licensed as ongoing subscriptions instead of one-time purchases.

A synergistic relationship exists between acquisitions and collection development workflows. Collection development staff start the purchasing process by analyzing collection usage, conducting needs assessments, and consulting with health care professionals at their institutions. With this data, selectors choose material to purchase within their allocated budgets. Acquisitions staff take over the workflow at this point and manage the ordering, receiving, and invoicing of the material selected by collection development staff.

Acquisitions Outside of the Library

Departments or divisions outside of the library can purchase electronic resources that are used throughout the institution as well. Library staff can collaborate with the department to administer the resource for them by capitalizing on the librarians' unique skills in:

- negotiating licenses,
- publicizing the resources on the library's website,
- managing usage statistics, and
- troubleshooting access issues.

This is a win-win situation for the library; its e-resources are expanded without expenditures from its own budget and the library fosters goodwill with the department. If the department decides to cancel the resource, the library is in a great position to decide if the e-resource should be added to the library's collection.

Order Processes

The library's order process is generally determined by institutional policies regarding purchasing. The most flexible ordering procedure is when the library acts as its own purchasing agent and bypasses the institution's supply chain management department. This is where having an acquisitions component in the ILS is especially helpful. If orders need to go through Purchasing or Supply Chain Management, as is often the case in hospital libraries, the library must follow the institution's directives. In these cases, staff can still choose to use an acquisitions module or can rely on spreadsheets or purchase orders to track materials on order.

Setting up the acquisitions module requires some forethought so that staff can generate financial reports to support future purchases. Large libraries usually divide their collections budget into several funds according to subject or material format. Acquisitions staff create these funds and assign annual allocations so that collection specialists can track purchases over time. In addition to tracking funds, acquisitions staff develop procedures to track purchases by format type. Pomerantz and White (2009) analyze this process at Adelphi University where staff changed the acquisitions process to accommodate shifts in collection formats.

Smaller libraries are not faced with such complexity; they frequently have a line item in their budget for each type of material: print books, journals (online and print), electronic databases, and media. Health sciences libraries of any size often have endowment or gift funds that can be used for special purposes to supplement the regular budget. With these special funds, the principal remains untouched and selectors spend the interest generated by the account.

Funds are allocated at the beginning of the budget cycle, whether it is a calendar or academic year. Fund amounts decrease as items are ordered or encumbered. As items are received, the encumbered amounts become expenses. Selectors track the balances in their accounts as they place orders throughout the year. Their goal is to spend the entire budget without going over budget. The ILS automatically updates fund balances as orders are placed and alerts library staff when the fund reaches a pre-defined minimum. To further keep accurate fund balances, staff create reports to identify outstanding orders or cancelled titles for follow-up with the supplier. Chapter 4 provides further information on the library's finances and budgeting for acquisitions.

Once the administrative functions, such as fund codes, format codes, and fund allocations, have been determined, the actual order process begins with library staff creating order records manually or importing order data from the supplier. In most systems, order records are tied to a brief bibliographic record consisting of title, ISSN, or ISBN information. Acquisitions and cataloging staff work together on procedures to create the brief bibliographic record. Once an item is received, cataloging staff imports a MARC record for the item that updates the brief bibliographic record. Libraries differ on their policies regarding the display of items on order. Some display the material on order in the online catalog and let users put holds on these items before they are even received. Other libraries choose to suppress this information until the items are received, cataloged, and ready for use.

The last step in acquisitions is processing the invoice and submitting it for payment. Some ILSs can be integrated with the financial systems of the parent institution so that invoices are transferred electronically to accounts payable.

Given the complexity of acquisitions, it is important that the ILS has a robust reporting feature. For example, Innovative Interfaces Inc. has crosstab reports showing the number of items in a library's collection by both material type and subject as shown in Figure 8.8. The acquisitions reports track collection management decisions that will support future purchases and requests for funding increases.

Vendors

Vendors of health sciences texts, journals, and media fall into several categories:

Figure 8.8. Sample Millennium Acquisitions Report

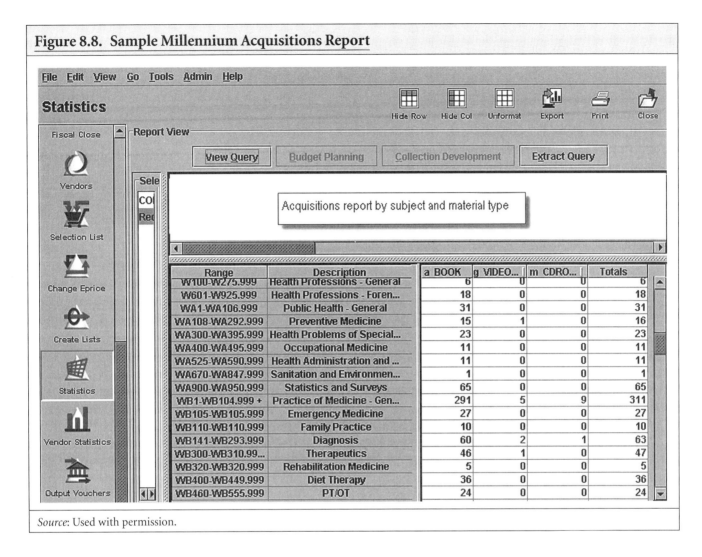

Source: Used with permission.

- Distributors stock items from many different publishers.
- Publishers stock only the items published by that company.
- Out-of-print vendors specialize in items that are difficult to find and may include rare books.
- Consortia can use distributors that track purchases across multiple libraries.

Although distributors supply items from many publishers, they usually stock just one type of material. For example, book distributors handle books, CD-ROMs, or other media, but usually do not handle journals and vice versa. This means that librarians frequently work with various suppliers to order the material for the collections. To simplify the ordering process, library staff should use book and journal vendors specializing in the health sciences. Vendors differ considerably, so spend time finding one that offers the best combination of services and price. Selecting a vendor on price alone is

not advisable if it doesn't offer services to enhance the order process.

Most of these distributors offer collection management services, especially for books. Setting up a customized subject profile or approval plan is a very useful tool so that the distributor can notify library staff periodically when books have been published that match the profile. Some libraries view their approval plan online and select the titles for shipment from this list. Others set up approval plans whereby the distributor ships all recently published books matching the profile for examination. Books that don't meet a library's needs are then returned.

Acquisitions staff can set up standing orders to automatically ship the book titles and series that are essential to the library's collection. This saves staff time and ensures that the library has the most current editions and the complete series of these titles.

Other services provided by vendors include MARC records for purchased material and shipping books to third-party technical services contractors for processing and cataloging. When the books finally arrive at the library, they are ready for shelving. Vendors also track the library's purchases and supply reports on trends in health sciences publishing. Both are useful collection management tools for library staff.

Another excellent source for collection development information for books and software is a web-based subscription to *Doody's Review Service* (http://www.doody .com), for larger libraries, or *Doody's Core Titles in the Health Sciences* (http://www.doody.com/dct/), for libraries with smaller budgets. Experts rate newly published books and software using a standardized scale and publish the reviews online. The site is searchable by subject, title, Doody's ratings, and other parameters. *Doody's Core Titles in the Health Sciences* is published annually as a basic or premium package. For further information, consult Doody's website (http://www .doody.com). Book distributors frequently include Doody's ratings in descriptions of books available for purchase.

Electronic collections of books, journals, and databases are frequently available through consortia. Subscription costs via consortia are generally less expensive due to large scale acquisitions. Consortia purchasing can simplify the ordering and payment process too. For bibliographic and full-text databases not available via consortia, library staff work with individual publishers to order the product.

A significant proportion of the library's budget today is spent on databases and electronic resources as compared to print materials. To make sure that the database meets the needs of library staff and users, vendors frequently offer free 30-day trials. Often, 30 days is not enough time to evaluate an electronic resource, so don't hesitate to ask the vendor for 60- or 90-day trials. If vendors balk at extended trials for free, staff can consider asking for an extended trial with a nominal payment. This is useful when the electronic resource under consideration supports a major project such as integration with the electronic medical record. To preserve good customer relations with library users and vendors, make sure that funds are available to subscribe to the resource before setting up a trial.

Similar to books, journals also have vendors who simplify the ordering process for serials by handling the details of ordering, paying, and claiming missing issues from many publishers. For e-journals, these vendors offer services such as registering e-access for titles, providing license information to staff, and contacting publishers to resolve access problems. This is especially useful at the beginning and end of each calendar year when subscriptions usually expire.

Licensing

With the transition from print to electronic resources, library staff are shifting their acquisitions from purchasing to leasing material for their collections. Licenses now govern the use of electronic content. These are legal documents crafted by the publisher that spell out the terms and conditions under which the electronic content is provided to the library. The license also lists the publisher's responsibilities to provide timely access to the content.

Most publishers have a standard contract that is sent to the library. In preparation for reviewing the contract, librarians should create a checklist of requirements that need to be present in the license. Librarians review the contract to make sure that the license details do not conflict with the library's or institution's policies and that the license matches their checklist of requirements. If any prerequisites are not present, librarians add these as amendments to the license. At a minimum, check the following definitions and conditions to ensure compliance: geographic site, definition of users, off-campus access, interlibrary lending, early termination penalties, and perpetual access.

Once the license represents the needs of the library, staff usually sends the document to the institution's legal department for final approval. Any amendments added to the license require negotiation between the library and the publisher before the license can be signed.

Harris (2009: xvii–xviii), in her book *Licensing Digital Content: A Practical Guide for Librarians*, begins with the following "Quick Starter Tips for a Successful Agreement":

1. Avoid oral licenses.
2. Before reading any license agreement offered to you, write down on a blank piece of paper the "must-haves" for this license arrangement.
3. Understand your obligations.
4. Cover all issues.
5. Avoid legal language.
6. Use consistent words and terms.
7. Each license agreement is unique.
8. Be creative, patient, and flexible.
9. Know when to walk away.

Once licenses are accepted by all parties, library staff develop policies on tracking this information and displaying licensing terms for its users. An ERMS simplifies this process because the system lets staff map the contract details; some also store the legal document digitally. If the ERMS has a web-based component that displays to the public or is integrated with the online catalog, library users can view the license terms governing the use of these e-resources. These terms usually include the types of users allowed access to the material, the locations licensed for the product, and off-campus accessibility of the resource.

E-journals play a significant role in licensing because of the sheer number of e-journals managed by library staff. If the titles are not purchased through consortia or database aggregators, librarians need to negotiate a separate license for each title. Journal vendors, such as EBSCO and Swets, provide services to manage this process each step of the way. Each year at renewal time, library staff creates a profile describing the institution to publishers and submits it to their customer service representative. The profile includes the institution's organizational structure, IP addresses, locations, description, and user demographics so that the journal vendor can accurately and consistently explain the organization to the publisher.

The journal vendor works with the library staff as a team to negotiate the price and is invaluable in negotiating site licenses for institutions with complex organizational structures, such as multisite access. Once the price is negotiated, the journal vendor or publisher sends the license for approval. Many vendors now list license details by journal title in their online systems for purchasing, claiming, and managing serials so that library staff can track details before ordering. This system may be sufficient for smaller libraries without ERMSs.

Despite the best efforts of library staff and journal vendors, e-journals may stop working. The quickest way to restore online access is for library staff to contact their vendor's customer service representative. The journal vendors are better positioned to navigate the publisher's bureaucracy and to answer questions regarding payment,

which is the most frequent reason for losing access in the first place.

Working with IT Departments

Library Roles within the IT Environment

The successful operation of the library is intrinsically tied to the information technology (IT) infrastructure at each institution. Library staff needs IT to configure and troubleshoot their desktop computers or network issues. Most library staff functions are performed using software, be it ILS modules or standard office computing software. Electronic library resources rely on IT for the institution's network structure, bandwidth capabilities, and websites.

At least three common relationships can exist between the library and IT. These include:

1. The library and IT are two separate departments within the institution. Library staff rely on the institution's IT for all computing related functions.

2. The library has its own IT staff to manage library resources. Library IT personnel interface with the institution's IT staff as needed.

3. The library is a department under IT.

The keys to setting up and maintaining a successful relationship between library and IT staff are understanding and communication using the language of IT. Information technology uses a precise vocabulary to describe technical standards and functions. It is the language of computer science and engineering.

In the article "The Art of Talking Tech: Strategies for Effective Communication with Information Technology Departments," Ennis (2009: 211–212) compares communicating with IT departments to traveling to foreign countries: "When traveling to a foreign country it is customary to learn a few choice phrases, check out local laws and customs, get familiar with the currency, and even buy a map or two to find one's way around the locale."

IT has its own rules, language, and customs so it behooves librarians to learn some of these things to better facilitate communication. A cheat sheet containing information necessary for communicating with IT staff is extremely handy.

Cowen and Edson (2002: 5) write, "'Institutional' needs often conflict with 'departmental' needs; given

Innovations in Licensing

SERU: A Shared Electronic Resource Understanding is an alternative to licensing agreements in which libraries and publishers agree to follow the "Statements of Common Understandings for Subscribing to Electronic Resources" and copyright law instead of relying on individual license agreements. Acceptance of SERU as a standard would simplify the entire licensing process for library staff and publishers (NISO SERU Working Group, 2008). If institutional policies permit, librarians should consider asking journal publishers if they participate in SERU before undertaking the license approval process to save considerable time for all parties.

IT Cheat Sheet for Librarians

Typical items to include on the librarian's IT cheat sheet:

- Model and configuration of library public computers
- Model and configuration of library staff computers
- Version numbers of library-specific programs as well as "Office" and Internet browsers
- Institutional IP ranges
- Phone numbers and e-mails for IT and library software support
- Information on previous or repeat problems and steps taken to resolve them.

---

limited resources, priorities are generally given to institutional or multi- departmental needs at the expense of single departments. Right or wrong, library needs are frequently seen as departmental." While many librarians believe they are serving the needs of the institution, they must do an effective job of selling that relationship to the IT department. Knowing the way IT communicates as well as the organization's technical needs and protocols only increases the chances that IT views the library's projects as more than a departmental project. Since library resources are important tools for health care, research and education, library staff must pay special attention to IT policies regarding patient information, local data storage, backups, proxy access, and intellectual property. Whenever possible, try to meet and greet the players in IT who control access to the library's resources. Discuss new services using the network with IT as part of the planning and evaluation process to ensure smooth implementation. Successful interaction between the library and IT is a win-win situation. Users have seamless access to electronic resources, library staff functions are optimized, and IT is mindful of the library's requirements when planning changes to the existing infrastructure.

IP Addresses

IP stands for Internet Protocol and an IP address is required for communication across a network. It is a number represented by the following notation, xxx.xxx.xxx.xxx, where each xxx refers to a number between 0–255 separated by periods (dots). This unique number identifies a device, usually a computer, printer, or server, on the institution's network and on the Internet. Many vendors of electronic resources utilize IP addresses to enable access to an electronic resource at a specific location. IP validation allows all users coming from approved IP addresses to access the resource while simultaneously blocking users outside the approved range of numbers.

IP addresses are categorized into Class A, B, or C networks depending on the number of addresses. Class A networks contain the largest number of possible addresses, with a possible 16,777,216 unique IP addresses. Class B networks have a possible 65,536 addresses and Class C networks can have 256 IP addresses. The institution applies for either a Class A, B, or C group of IP addresses from a regional Internet registry (Wikipedia contributors, 2010a).

Class A, B, or C groups of IP addresses are divided into subnetworks, called subnets for short. A subnet is a group of computers that share the same IP addresses for routing data. It is possible that several subnets are assigned to the same department, such as the library. This occurs when there is more than one wiring closet or router transferring data between the library's computers and the institution's backbone.

The smallest component of IP is the single IP address. This can be assigned as a static or dynamic address. A static (or reserved) IP means that the device attached to the network is identified by a single IP address that never changes. To get a static IP, IT support gets the MAC address of the device and asks the IP administrator to assign a specific IP address to the physical device. The MAC address is a unique group of letters and numbers assigned to the physical device's network card or NIC. A static address is assigned only when a specific service requires it. Most computers are assigned a dynamic address by the network, often using a DHCP (Dynamic Host Configuration Protocol) server.

As a network continues to grow, it is possible to run out of IP addresses. In order to prevent this, institutions have adopted private addresses, which are also called local internal addresses or 10.xxx.xxx.xxx (10 dot) addresses. The private addresses are assigned to devices on the institution's network, but are not visible on the Internet. While each device has a unique private address, many devices can share the same external IP address when they exit the institutional network to the Internet. This is called Network Address Translation or NAT.

A firewall is a network security mechanism that usually blocks external IP addresses from entering the institution's private internal network. Hospitals frequently have several firewalls to prevent access to patient health information. If a firewall perceives a security risk, the IP address of the source is blocked by the firewall (Wikipedia contributors, 2010a).

Library staff needs to know the institution's IP addresses for the registration of electronic journals and resources. In addition, they need to know the physical locations covered by the network, especially for compliance with licenses. When an electronic resource suddenly stops working, one of the first items to check is whether an institution's IP addresses have changed or the vendor has mistyped the address on their end. Another trouble-shooting tip is to check with IT if the firewall has suddenly blocked access to a particular website in error. When placing service requests with IT, library staff must know if a specific resource requires a static IP to save time and frustration for both parties.

Public and Staff Computers

Public computers in the library allow walk-up use of its resources by providing access to the online catalog and links to the library's collection of electronic resources. The online catalog is part of the library's webpages on the intranet or Internet. There is a fine balance between enabling access to library resources and maintaining standard configurations of the library's computers. IT staff are instrumental in configuring public computers with the security measures required to lock down the settings while retaining flexibility in their use.

When the library's public computers are not locked down, users will change software and printer settings and may download potentially harmful software. As Huang (2007: 16) writes, "You can have 100 patrons working 100 desktops and things may seem hunky-dory, but it only takes a single breach to rapidly compromise the other 99 computers, their users, plus a host of behind-the-scene networks and servers." His comments emphasize the importance of balancing security with an open system.

Software programs are available to prohibit changes. Computers on a network can also be configured using network tools, such as group policies. If the library has multiple public access computers, it is especially helpful to use a group policy to configure them. A group policy allows IT staff to create the configuration once and then copy it to all other computers. The specific lock-down mechanisms are generally controlled by IT staff. Most often hospital IT departments will have their own methods to control access or secure computers, however some of their methods may not be compatible with library-specific programs or even the library's ethos on accessibility. Librarians familiar with other methods of computer security can present these ideas to IT to create a policy that balances the security needs of IT and the openness of the library.

Library staff computers may also require configuration and lock-down procedures to ensure a standard and stable computing environment. IT is generally unfamiliar with library systems so it is especially helpful to have knowledgeable library staff that can explain and guide IT on library-specific applications. Depending on institutional policies, library systems staff frequently have the computing rights to manage library software at the institutional and library staff desktop level, freeing up IT to focus on the network infrastructure.

TechSoup for Libraries (2008) is an excellent online resource for librarians to learn more about computer security and to share information and methods to keep public access computers secure. Their "cookbook" titled "Joy of Computing—Planning for Success" is dedicated to providing librarians with ideas, tips, resources, and techniques on keeping library technology running properly.

Mobile Devices

Library resources are now being accessed by mobile devices, such as smartphones, which have replaced PDAs. The most popular platforms are the iPhone, the BlackBerry, and, more recently, the Droid. Kang (2010) from the *Washington Post* reports in her blog that Internet use from mobile devices accounts for 20 percent of Internet use from all wireless devices. Similarly, smartphone sales will surpass desktop pc sales by 2012. Bringing library resources to the mobile device is the ultimate in convenience for many library users. This can be done either through the mobile web or through the use of applications commonly known as apps.

There are several things to consider when evaluating and selecting mobile-friendly resources for an online collection. The first should be the library's website. The library's website needs to be optimized to work with and display on mobile devices. Often this means having two library websites, one for computer browsers and one for mobile devices. This process can be as simple or as complicated as time, personnel skills, and institutional platform requirements allow.

A simple method is to have a link to the mobile-friendly website at the top of the traditional library website to redirect users. Some easy ways to make a website mobile-friendly are to limit the use of images and optimize font size. Single columns of information with few paragraphs are ideal. Because most phones do not support Flash, the mobile site should not have links built around any Flash applications. Web designers and programmers have written several guides on designing for the mobile web. These guides plus others will help librarians stay current with the most recent technical and aesthetic mobile web design trends (Fling, 2009; Mehta, 2008).

Even though library resources are becoming mobile-friendly, this remains an area that will see tremendous growth. Librarians should note which databases, electronic books and journals are optimized for or available to mobile devices. If libraries have to choose between two very similar databases, librarians may want to select the one that is mobile-friendly over the one that is not. While many libraries offer remote access to resources, the ability to access them on a mobile device further increases their availability to library users. Mobile devices now allow users to take the library with them wherever they go.

Another important component to a good mobile library platform is resource usage. While many libraries collect usage data from vendors, often these vendors report overall usage and do not report whether an item is used internally, externally, or through a mobile device. Installing link analysis programs such as Google Analytics can provide information on which resources and URLs are being clicked on and used and which are not. Certain resources may see low usage from the traditional library website but high usage from the mobile site and vice versa. This information is not only extremely handy to have in the redesign of the library's mobile site but is useful should any particular resource vendor decide to charge for mobile access. In addition to usage statistics, librarians should survey their users to see which resources are needed on mobile devices. These surveys make it easier for librarians to discover new resources that are of interest to users.

Apps are applications created to work on specific mobile devices. Some apps require access to either a WiFi or phone data connection to work while others will work "offline." Smartphones and apps are a relatively new and evolving technology. Apps can be free or require payment before downloading. Currently the smartphone and app market is centered on individuals; therefore group or institutional purchases of specific apps may be difficult or cost-prohibitive. However, some medical library vendors have created apps that work in conjunction with their paid institutional subscription to their database or website. Fully investigate how these apps are distributed, and whether there are any charges beyond the regular institutional subscription associated with their usage.

Libraries must be aware of the users' needs as well as their institution's initiatives involving mobile platforms and devices. Various electronic medical record (EMR) programs already have a mobile-friendly component. The hospital's specific EMR program and security protocols may dictate which mobile devices are used within the institution and library. As the EMR becomes more

available on mobile devices, library users' searching and information behaviors will change. They will rely less on desktop computers and rely more on mobile devices because they are easily accessible and usable at the patient's bedside. It is important for librarians to be aware of this when thinking about the selection of mobile-friendly resources for health professionals at the point of care. While it is tempting to select only professional resources, doctors and nurses will also have the need to show patients pictures, videos, and consumer information related to their condition at the bedside as well. Therefore, librarians must evaluate consumer health information resources that are suitable for online mobile devices.

Innovations in Mobile Devices

Apple released its iPad, a tablet pc for the web, e-mail, photos, music, and apps in April 2010. The iPad uses the same operating system as the iPhone and is quickly being copied by other computer vendors. iBooks for the iPad has been very well received for its ease of use. At this writing, it is too soon to see its application in health sciences libraries, but librarians should be on the lookout for iPad apps and e-books by the time this book is published.

Internet Outage Disaster Plan

In this era of electronic resources, an Internet outage of any kind disrupts library operations, services, and resources for staff and customers. Since the nature and length of an outage can vary, advance planning for all types of outages is crucial. Internet outages may include any of the following:

- It may be localized to a building on campus.
- It may occur at the institution's Internet Service Provider (ISP) and affects the entire institution.
- It may occur at an ISP several states away effectively blocking access to resources that need to be routed through the affected ISP.
- It may be even more widespread in the case of electric power outages affecting multiple states.
- It may be wires cut by construction nearby that takes several days to repair.

Both public and technical services staff need to develop plans to cope with Internet outages. According to Norton (2008: 6), in "Nuts and Bolts of Writing a Disaster Plan," "a good plan should address four areas: prevention, planning, response and recovery." The National Network of Libraries of Medicine (NN/LM) has developed a website called the "NN/NLM Emergency Preparedness and Response Toolkit" to help librarians create their own disaster plan. The website includes sample disaster plans as well as phone numbers and contact information to places that can help provide services in the event of an emergency (National Library of Medicine, 2010). In addition to the resources mentioned above, library staff will also want to consult with their institution's disaster planning teams, work with the IT department to address issues concerning the library's locally owned resources, data, and hardware, and consult with their database and e-journal vendors to address data and hardware issues related to external resources.

Loss of access to the intranet, Internet, or both will affect library services so librarians should know which resources are intranet-based versus Internet-based. If the intranet is operational (institution's network and web services are available) but the Internet is down, library staff can usually access documents created by Word, Excel, Access, or any other programs loaded and saved on a local pc or server. For example, an ILS residing on a local server would not be affected by an Internet outage as long as the intranet is live; however access to all Internet resources stored at sites external to the library and its institution would not available. Conversely, if the intranet goes down and the Internet is available, external resources will be available but resources housed on the local server will be inaccessible. Librarians and users will need to use Google or other search engines to find information on the Internet if the library's webpages are down. Printing may also be affected depending on how printers are configured throughout the institution.

As the proportion of library collections shifts primarily toward e-resources, collection management staff need to maintain a core set of print resources for the library in the event that intranet or Internet services are disrupted. The library's noncirculating reference collection is such an example. In addition, staff may wish to identify a group of core journals that are to be maintained in print whether or not they are available electronically. If the library's ILS is unavailable due to an interruption in online access, many basic library services such as searching the online catalog and circulating materials will be affected. If the catalog is down, develop a cheat sheet with medical subjects and their general call numbers to help users find the proper shelves for books on a specific topic. Librarians will also need to determine whether they are willing to circulate materials while the ILS is offline and if so, what information should be collected. Having a backup plan to check out materials and register library users on paper forms is one option.

In any case, interlibrary loan services can be maintained using fax or the mail. Libraries should have emergency contacts in other parts of the country who can supply critical materials in case of local or semi-local Internet outages.

In the event of electrical failure, both the intranet and Internet are shut down as well as computers, lights, copy machines, fax machines, etc. This situation is much more serious and library staff must rely on phones and in-house material to answer critical information needs. Continue staffing the library to answer phones and in-person questions and consider enlisting the help of nearby hospital libraries, academic health sciences libraries, or the NN/LM resource libraries to help provide research services or document delivery.

During a power failure, hospital generators provide power to essential areas of the hospital. Electrical outlets connected to the generators will provide power so hospital librarians may be able to provide limited online services during a power outage if their library has any of these emergency electrical outlets. The emergency outlets may be a different color than a regular outlet. Be sure to check with the hospital's facilities engineering department to see if any emergency outlets are located in the library. Librarians who have at least one emergency electrical outlet should plug their fax machine into it so they can receive search results and documents from other local libraries or from libraries in the NN/LM disaster plan network.

Hospital librarians can also plug a laptop with a wireless air card into an emergency electrical outlet to access Internet resources not affected by the Internet outage. Wireless cards can be purchased from many phone companies and require a monthly subscription fee. Librarians reluctant to pay a monthly service fee for unexpected power failures might want to investigate companies who provide "on demand" wireless activation for people who have a deactivated air card. One such company, Event Radio Rentals, will activate service for Sprint or Verizon air card owners within 24 hours and require a minimum rental of three days. Depending on the number and location of red electrical outlets, librarians may also connect a printer to an emergency outlet and configure it to work with the laptop.

A well-developed disaster plan enables library staff to provide a range of services in the event of intranet, Internet, and electrical outages of varying duration. It is especially important to plan for failures lasting longer than a few hours since library operations will be severely disrupted. After the outage is over, it is important to review the plan and the library's response to the outage.

As Fichter (2005: 53) notes, "coping with disaster doesn't end when the intranet is back online." She suggests a debriefing meeting to discuss and evaluate the effectiveness of the library's response.

Conclusion

Library automation using an ILS was implemented in larger libraries in the not-so-distant past. Now, libraries of all sizes have automated many of their functions so that staff can work efficiently and effectively. ILSs come in many flavors and price points so evaluation and testing are important when selecting a system for the library.

With automation comes the ability to track the usage of library materials. The usage statistics can be manipulated to answer questions, such as which department uses a specific resource the most, which group of library users rely on off-campus access to resources, which constituency borrows the most interlibrary loans and the list goes on. Many ILSs have standard reports that are part of the system. Others offer the capability to develop custom reports to get at very specific aspects of usage. This wealth of information about user behavior helps library staff acquire collections that fulfill users' information requests as never before.

A consequence of automation is that librarians become masters of change management. Technological advances develop new ILSs, network structures, and communication mechanisms. Wireless in the library, smartphone apps, texting, RSS feeds, blogs, wikis, and Internet 2.0 are some examples. Library staffing levels, budgetary expenditures on hardware, software, and collections, and library services are direct reflections of technology. Libraries now, and in the future, will not only need to cope with change, but will need to plan for it as well.

Final Thoughts

"The accelerating pace of information is placing a great amount of responsibility on library managers as they must prepare for their library to live in a perpetual 'beta-state.' There is no definitive end point when all software or hardware will be unaltered" (Kenefick and Werner, 2008: 466).

"It's not all electronic. The idea of the library as a physical place still resonates with users. A strong electronic presence complements the physical library" (Kenefick and Werner, 2008: 467).

References

Bardyn, Tania P., and Caroline S. Young. 2007. "Migration to an Electronic Journal Collection in a Hospital Library: Implications for Reference Service." *Medical Reference Services Quarterly* 26, no. 4 (Winter): 27–44.

Breeding, Marshall. 2008a. "Circulation Technologies from Past to Future." *Computers in Libraries* 28, no. 2 (February): 19–21.

Breeding, Marshall. 2008b. "Helping You Buy Electronic Resource Management Systems." *Computers in Libraries* 28, no. 7 (July/August): 6–8, 10, 12-14, 16–18, 94, 96.

Breeding, Marshall. 2009. "Investing in the Future." *Library Journal* 134, no. 6 (April 1): 26–32.

Breeding, Marshall. 2010. "New Models, Core Systems." *Library Journal* 135, no. 6 (April 1): 22–44, 26–28, 30–32, 34–36.

Breeding, Marshall, and Josh Hadro. 2009. "SkyRiver Sparks Cataloging Competition." *Library Journal* 134, no. 18: 16.

Calvert, Philip, and Marion Read. 2006. "RFPs: A Necessary Evil or Indispensable Tool?" *Electronic Library* 24, no. 5: 649–661.

Chadwell, Faye A. 2009. "What's Next for Collection Management and Managers?" *Collection Management* 34, no. 1: 3–18.

Collins, Maria. 2008. "Electronic Resource Management Systems (ERMS) Review." *Serials Review* 34, no. 4 (December): 267–299.

COUNTER. 2008. "COUNTER Code of Practice for Journals and Databases, Release 3." United Kingdom: COUNTER. Accessed April 23, 2010. http://www.projectcounter.org/code_practice.html.

Cowen, Janet L., and Jerry Edson. 2002. "Best Practice in Library/Information Technology Collaboration." *Journal of Hospital Librarianship* 2, no. 4: 1–15.

Creissen, Sally. 2008. "Library Management Systems: Finding the One for You." *Legal Information Management* 8, no. 2: 117–122.

Dollar, Daniel M., John Gallagher, Janis Glover, Regina Kenny Marone, and Cynthia Crooker. 2007. "Realizing What's Essential: A Case Study on Integrating Electronic Journal Management into a Print-Centric Technical Services Department." *Journal of the Medical Library Association* 95, no. 2 (April): 147–155.

Dougherty, William C. 2009. "Managing Technology: Integrated Library Systems: Where are they Going? Where are we Going?" *Journal of Academic Librarianship* 35, no. 5 (September): 482–485.

Emanuel, Jenny, and M. Kathleen Kern. 2009. "Next Generation Catalogs: What Do They Do And Why Should We Care?" *Reference & User Services Quarterly* 49, no. 2 (Winter): 117–120.

Ennis, Lisa A. 2009. "The Art of Talking Tech: Strategies for Effective Communication with Information Technology Departments." *Journal of Hospital Librarianship* 9, no. 2: 210–217.

ERM Data Standards and Best Practices Review Working Group. 2010. "ERM Data Standards and Best Practices Review." Baltimore, MD: National Information Standards Organization. Accessed May 11. http://www.niso.org/work rooms/ermreview#resources.

Fichter, Darlene. 2005. "Planning for the Unexpected." *Online* 29, no. 2 (March/April): 51–53.

Fling, Brian. 2009. *Mobile Design and Development*. Sebastopol, CA: O'Reilly Media Inc.

Granath, Kimberley M., Marlene S. Englander, and Gretchen A. Hallerberg. 2000. "Access to Library Resources." In *The Medical Library Association Guide to Managing Health Care Libraries*, edited by Ruth Holst and Sharon A. Phillips, 261–287. New York: Neal-Schuman.

Grogg, Jill E. 2008. "Electronic Resource Management Systems in Practice." *Journal of Electronic Resources Librarianship* 20, no. 2: 86–89.

Harris, Lesley Ellen. 2009. *Licensing Digital Content: A Practical Guide for Librarians*, 2nd ed. Chicago: American Library Association.

Huang, Phil. 2007. "How You Can Protect Public Access Computers and Their Users." *Computers in Libraries* 27, no. 5 (May): 16–20.

Joint Steering Committee for Development of RDA. 2010. "RDA: Resource Description and Access." Chicago: American Library Association; joint publication with the Canadian Library Association and Facet Publishing. Accessed September 15. http://www.rda-jsc.org/rda.html.

Kang, Cecelia. 2010. "Mobile Internet Exploding, Online Ads about to Take Off, Says Analyst Mary Meeker." *Washington Post* (June 8, 2010). Accessed June 14. http://voices .washington post.com/posttech/2010/06/mobile_internet_ exploding_onli.html.

Kenefick, Colleen, and Susan E. Werner. 2008. "Moving Towards Library 3.0: Taking Management Basics into the Future." *Journal of Hospital Librarianship* 8, no. 4: 464–468.

Kinner, Laura, and Christine Rigda. 2009. "The Integrated Library System: From Daring to Dinosaur?" *Journal of Library Administration* 49, no. 4 (June): 401–417.

Knievel, Jennifer, Heather Wicht, and Lynn Silipigni Connaway. 2004. "Collection Analysis using Circulation, ILL, and Collection Data." *Against the Grain* 16, no. 6 (December): 24–26.

Mehta, Nirav. 2008. *Mobile Web Development*. Birmingham, UK: Packt Publishing.

Murray, Adam. 2008. "Electronic Resource Management 2.0: Using Web 2.0 Technologies as Cost-Effective Alternatives to an Electronic Resource Management System." *Journal of Electronic Resources Librarianship* 20, no. 3: 156–168.

National Information Standards Organization. 2010. "Standardized Usage Statistics Harvesting Initiative (SUSHI)." Baltimore, MD: National Information Standards Organization (October 29, 2007). Accessed November 5. http://www .niso.org/workrooms/sushi/.

National Library of Medicine. 2010. "NN/LM Emergency Preparedness & Response Toolkit." Bethesda, MD: National Library of Medicine, February 2. Accessed April 23. http:// nnlm.gov/ep/.

NISO SERU Working Group. 2008. *SERU: A Shared Electronic Resource Understanding*. Baltimore, MD: National Information Standards Organization, NISO RP-7-2008.

Norton, Judith. 2008. "Nuts and Bolts of Writing a Disaster Plan." *OLA Quarterly* 14, no. 4: 6–10.

Ockerbloom, John M. 2009. "Open Discovery of Library Resources: The Digital Library Federation's ILS-Discovery Interface Recommendations." Library Systems and Interoperability: Breaking Down Silos (NISO Webinar), June 10. Accessed April 23, 2010. http://works.bepress.com/john _mark_ockerbloom/11.

O'Donnell, Owen. 2010. *Computers in Libraries Buyer's Guide*. Medford, NJ: Information Today, Inc. Accessed November 29. http://bg.computersinlibraries.com.

Ohler, Lila A., and Gerry McKiernan. 2006. "The Keys to Successful Change Management for Serials." *Serials Librarian* 51, no. 1 (September): 37–71.

Parry, Marc. 2010. "After Losing Users in Catalogs, Libraries Find Better Search Software." *Education Digest* 75, no. 6: 54–57.

Perkins, Heather. 2009. "The Effect that Electronic Collections has on Cataloging." *Journal of Hospital Librarianship* 9, no. 2: 218–220.

Petsche, Kevin F. 2008. "Migrating from a Print to Online Periodical Collection." *Indiana Libraries* 27, no. 2: 30–32.

Pomerantz, Sarah, and Andrew White. 2009. "Re-Modeling ILS Acquisitions Data to Financially Transition from Print to Digital Formats." *Library Collections, Acquisitions, & Technical Services* 33, no. 1 (March): 42–49.

Rosati, Karen Thompson. 2006. "The Decline of Print: Ten Years of Print Serial use in a Small Academic Medical Library." *Acquisitions Librarian* 18, no. 35/36: 107–117.

Sadler, Elizabeth. 2009. "Project Blacklight: A Next Generation Library Catalog at a First Generation University." *Library Hi Tech* 27, no. 1: 57–67.

Sanders, Dinah. 2008. "Tag—You're It!" *American Libraries* 39, no. 11: 52–54.

St. James, Memory. 2005. "Small Libraries and the Outsourcing of Technical Services." *PNLA Quarterly* 69, no. 3 (Spring): 7–9.

TechSoup for Libraries. 2008. "Joy of Computing—Planning for Success." San Francisco, CA: TechSoup Global (November 4, 2008). Accessed April 29, 2010. http://www.techsoupfor libraries.org/?q=cookbooks/planning-for-success.

Tijerina, Bonnie, and Douglas King. 2008. "What Is the Future of Electronic Resource Management Systems?" *Journal of Electronic Resources Librarianship* 20, no. 3: 147–155.

Tobia, Rajia C., and Susan C. Hunnicutt. 2008. "Print Journals in the Electronic Library: What is Happening to Them?" *Journal of Electronic Resources in Medical Libraries* 5, no. 2: 161–170.

Watson, Paula D. 2003. "Sources for E-Journals." *Library Technology Reports* 39, no. 2 (March/April): 6–27.

Webb, Paula L., and Muriel D. Nero. 2009. "OPACs in the Clouds." *Computers in Libraries* 29, no. 9 (October): 18–22.

Wikipedia contributors. 2010a. "IP Address." *Wikipedia, The Free Encyclopedia.* Accessed October 1. http://en.wikipedia .org/wiki/Ip_address.

Wikipedia contributors. 2010b. "OpenURL." *Wikipedia, The Free Encyclopedia.* Accessed October 1. http://en.wikipedia .org/wiki/OpenURL.

Further Reading

Breeding, Marshall. 2007. "Next-Generation Flavor in Integrated Online Catalogs." *Library Technology Reports* 43, no. 4 (July): 38–41.

Caudle, Dana M., and Cecilia M. Schmitz. 2007. "Web Access to Electronic Journals and Databases in ARL Libraries." *Journal of Web Librarianship* 1, no. 1: 3.

Clark, Carla. 2009. "Shifting Sands: The Changing Landscape of Managing Electronic Resources." *Louisiana Libraries* 71, no. 3 (Winter): 19–20.

Collins, Maria. 2005. "The Effects of E-Journal Management Tools and Services on Serials Cataloging." *Serials Review* 31, no. 4 (December): 291–297.

"Encore: Innovative's New Discovery Services Platform." 2007. *Public Libraries* 46, no. 6 (November): 69.

Furner, Jonathan. 2008. "User Tagging of Library Resources: Toward a Framework for System Evaluation." *International Cataloging & Bibliographic Control* 37, no. 3: 47–51.

Griffis, Patrick, and Cyrus Ford. 2009. "Enhancing OPAC Records for Discovery." *Information Technology & Libraries* 28, no. 4 (December): 191–193.

Harris, Lesley Ellen. 2009. *Licensing Digital Content: A Practical Guide for Librarians.* 2nd ed. Chicago: American Library Association.

Higa, Mori Lou. 2008. "Integration of Web 2.0 and Electronic Journals." *Journal of Electronic Resources in Medical Libraries* 5, no. 1: 55–64.

Hulseberg, Anna, and Sarah Monson. 2009. "Strategic Planning for Electronic Resources Management: A Case Study at Gustavus Adolphus College." *Journal of Electronic Resources Librarianship* 21, no. 2: 163–171.

Hurd, Sandy, Katharina Klemperer, Linda Miller, and Paul Moeller. 2008. "Tumbling Dice: Publishers, Aggregators, and ERM." *Serials Librarian* 54, no. 1/2 (May): 171–178.

Lawson, Karen G. 2009. "Mining Social Tagging Data for Enhanced Subject Access for Readers and Researchers." *Journal of Academic Librarianship* 35, no. 6 (November): 574–582.

Lingle, Virginia A., and Cynthia K. Robinson. 2009. "Conversion of an Academic Health Sciences Library to a Near-Total Electronic Library: Part 1." *Journal of Electronic Resources in Medical Libraries* 6, no. 3 (July-September): 193–210.

Lingle, Virginia A., and Cynthia K. Robinson. 2009. "Conversion of an Academic Health Sciences Library to a Near-Total Electronic Library: Part 2." *Journal of Electronic Resources in Medical Libraries* 6, no. 4 (October-December): 279–293.

Ruth, Lisa Boxill. 2008. "License Mapping for ERM Systems: Existing Practices and Initiatives for Support." *Serials Review* 34, no. 2 (June): 137–143.

Samsundar, Devica Ramjit. 2007. "Integrating E-Resources into an Online Catalog: The Hospital Library Experience." *Journal of Electronic Resources in Medical Libraries* 4, no. 1: 87–99.

Schwartz, Candy. 2008. "Thesauri and Facets and Tags, Oh My! A Look at Three Decades in Subject Analysis." *Library Trends* 56, no. 4: 830–842.

Singer, Ross. 2008. "In Search of a Really 'Next Generation' Catalog." *Journal of Electronic Resources Librarianship* 20, no. 3: 139–142.

Tenopir, Carol. 2010. "E-Access Changes Everything." *Library Journal* 135, no. 1: 26.

Westall, Sandra. 2000. "Evolution of the INNOPAC Managing Resources with Statistics and Reports." *Acquisitions Librarian* 12, no. 24: 117–123.

"When Servers Crash: Disaster Planning in the Digital Age." 2008. *Visual Resources Association Bulletin* 35, no. 1 (Spring): 49–57.

"Z39.50." 2010. Washington, D.C.: Network Development and MARC Standards Office, Library of Congress (August 2009). Accessed April 23. http://www.loc.gov/z3950/agency/.

9

Library Space Management

Elizabeth Connor

A newly renovated or constructed library facility can support and promote the clinical, teaching, and research missions of the institution through flexible, innovative, and inspirational use of space. A forward-thinking team of librarians, building consultants, architects, engineers, and contractors can work together to design an intellectual haven that expands the community of satisfied, knowledgeable, and successful clinicians, learners, and teachers. Well-designed library space has the potential of increasing workplace productivity, academic achievement, and research output. Library renovation/building projects have been known to result in "positive effects...on university life immediately following completion" (Mash, 2008: 168).

Library as Intellectual Gateway

Effective facility design can establish and build the library's collegial relationships within its organization and throughout the community, and emphasize the library as an active partner and leader in a variety of teaching and learning activities, as well as management and clinical care. The challenge is to frame a concept of a welcoming and inspiring place that focuses on people, access, collaborative learning, and technologies not yet developed. Libraries can serve as transformational spaces for collaborative teaching and learning by providing areas that support and enhance such activities. Emphases on thinking, reflecting, connecting, creating, and disseminating require flexible and visible space. It is human nature to imagine the future in terms of present day needs, but past forecasts have both underestimated and overestimated aspects of library operations and services (Leslie, 1999).

A facility design either fits into an existing culture of collaborative research or helps position the library for the future. While librarians may develop progressive views of the library's role in teaching, learning, and clinical care, sometimes library constituents have basic views of the library as a warehouse and study space, and it may take many months or years of ongoing dialogue to understand what existing clientele need and expect, and what future generations of teachers and learners deserve and expect. Other times, librarians and library supporters alike seek a bigger or fresher shoebox in which to place existing materials and services. Renovation/construction plans are unique opportunities to reimagine library programs.

Sometimes, examples outside of health care are helpful to re-imagine existing library programs, examples such as those described by Demas and Scherer (2002). One mentioned is the Gould Library Athenaeum at Carleton College in Northfield, Minnesota that was designed as a place to create knowledge. With the intention of "bringing together people from different disciplines for intellectual discourse, Athenæum events celebrate the world of books, the life of the mind, scholarly and scientific pursuits, and the arts and letters" (Carleton College, Gould Library, 2008).

In medical settings, the opportunity to create knowledge within library space may relate to colocating visual realization, immersion, or simulation activities. Newer library facilities have emphasized collaborative activities with clinicians, researchers, instructors, and students rather than warehousing materials. Some medical libraries have embedded library staff, services, and seating throughout learning areas on campus. Others have situated curricular activities related to simulation, visualization, and problem-based learning into the footprint occupied by library services. For example, Louis Stokes Health Sciences Library at Howard University, designed by Hillier Group in association with Amos Bailey + Lee,

incorporated a 5-seat telemedicine consultation room into its design (http://www.founders.howard.edu/HSL new/Program.htm).

The library can be thought of as a third place. Conceptually, a first place is one's home and a second place is one's workplace. Library space can serve as a third place for affiliated personnel without private workspace for study, collaboration, and consultation. Creative work related to imagining new spaces gives librarians the impetus to question how and where library operations and services are conducted.

This chapter will offer insights into the creative and logistical processes necessary to plan, implement, and evaluate a successful library renovation or construction project. Examples will include libraries from a variety of medical and nonmedical settings including academic medical centers, hospitals, health organizations, and universities. Suggested approaches are appropriate for anyone planning a library project now, next year, or in the distant future. These ideas and principles apply to any type of library renovation or construction project in a variety of settings.

Roles and Responsibilities

The health care librarian should be the central figure throughout the planning process, from start to finish. Because librarians are responsible for the effective use of the space given to the library, they must become experts in planning the space. This expertise can be developed and maintained by reading, attending workshops on space planning, talking to librarians who have recently planned new space, and visiting other libraries. Weise and Tooey (1995) provide an excellent overview of the planning process. A compilation of library renovation/construction case studies includes practical examples from academic medical centers, hospitals, and other health care settings (Connor, 2005). It is commonplace for librarians planning a renovation or construction project to visit other libraries to gather ideas. Michaels (2003) has developed a useful checklist for documenting visits to libraries. When visiting other facilities, the librarian should ask what did not work and what would have been done differently. In addition to becoming an expert on library space, the librarian should assume a leadership role in the planning process. This role includes initiating the study of space requirements, planning a solution to space problems, writing the building program or hiring someone else to do this, acquiring administrative approval for plans, and working with the building team to translate plans into a functional library. To succeed, the librarian must be attuned to political dynamics and continually analyze the situation to determine effective ways to initiate action or remove blocks to progress.

Importance of Institutional Master Plans and Strategic Plans

Many institutions have master plans that describe library space. Elements of master plan discussions should include anticipated bed size, enrollments, curricular changes, new programs, and other growth areas that can affect library operations, services, and facilities. If a library renovation or construction project is not mentioned in this plan, it is unlikely that the project will be funded.

To be successful, librarians need to assess their institution's needs. Those who develop new services that are highly valued by their institution and have strong supporters among key user groups stand the best chance of obtaining additional or new space. Present and potential services need to be carefully assessed before beginning renovations or planning a new facility. The first step in the space-planning process is the development of a three-to-five-year strategic plan for the library. Input from a broad cross section of the organizational community, including administration, should be an essential part of the library's strategic-planning process.

In particular, strategic planning should explore critical issues, such as the library's existing relationships with other departments, especially media services, patient library, information technology, and continuing education. Will the library be assuming new responsibility for any of these activities? Should the library include additional space for consumer information and resources, an electronic classroom, conference rooms, a collection of computer software, or a learning resource center?

The planning process should consider all clientele, especially library services for patients, their families, and unaffiliated users, such as members of the community or other professionals. Without a strategic plan that has been accepted by the administration and received broad support from the organization, it is difficult to develop a workable, long-term space plan for the library. Strategic plans need to be updated periodically so that when the library space plan is implemented, it is based on the most current needs assessment. Although time-consuming, strategic planning is necessary for making informed decisions regarding space; it can also increase the librarian's credibility and influence within the organization. See more on planning in general in Chapter 3.

Identifying and Involving Constituent Groups

The importance of input from various constituencies (administrators, clinicians, faculty, researchers, students, employees, librarians and library staff) cannot be overstated. Project planners for McMaster University's renovation of Thode Library in Hamilton, Ontario, Canada, hosted consultations geared toward undergraduate students, graduate students, faculty, university staff, and held additional "open call" sessions (Thode Library, 2010b, 2010c). The purpose of these conversations was to gain input and support. At the University of Massachusetts Medical School, the library's Remodel Planning Team worked with architects to hold focus group discussions related to "what people liked about the current library and what improvements needed to be made" (Lucia and Piorun, 2005: 125).

The administrative officer to whom the librarian reports can be the most effective advocate for the development of a good library. Therefore, the librarian should involve the administrator in assessing space needs and involving constituent groups. Through this process, the administrator can gain a clear understanding of how the library functions and how it contributes to the quality of patient care. If committed to the essential role of the library, the administrator will participate actively in the preparation of the space proposal, often to the library's advantage. When the completed proposal is referred to the committee or board responsible for decisions on space, the administrator can be a knowledgeable advocate for the space proposal. Depending on the circumstances, money to finance the project may be sought before or after final approval.

Forming Project Teams

One individual alone rarely does planning for new or renovated space in a department. Sometimes space planners or architects work with departments to determine space requirements. Many institutions organize planning teams for a particular project. The library committee, which usually represents various user groups, is often very effective in this role because the members are familiar with the library. Another approach is to appoint a special committee of interested, committed, and influential users. Frequently one or two nonusers are also appointed to the committee to provide insight into why people do not use the library. The purpose of the planning team or committee is to explore and press user needs and desires, react to all aspects of planning, and apply pressure to bring about an effective outcome. In some larger library settings, different teams are formed to handle specific aspects of the project (Lucia and Piorun, 2005; Thode Library, 2010a).

Developing Assumptions

Foote points out that "many building types, libraries among them, are shackled by outdated imagery at the same time that they remain the centers of intellectual purpose" (Foote, 1995: 351). Just as many librarians imagine a larger "shoebox" in which to situate services, resources, and personnel, some architects view libraries as opportunities to build iconic space replete with soaring staircases, atria, and skylights without consideration of how space can be used to transform teaching and learning.

Other good starting points for librarians who are inexperienced with envisioning future space and developing assumptions would be to read Scott Bennett's thoughtful articles about learning, libraries, and higher education (Bennett, 2003; Bennett, 2007; Bennett, 2009).

Assessing Existing Space

The space-planning process may be initiated by the librarian or necessitated by changes within the organization. Renovation or the construction of new space is expensive and space is usually scarce. Before a request for new space is made, the librarian should evaluate the existing space to determine its limitations, identify specific, existing space needs, and forecast future needs.

Although many of the space needs formulae were developed for public libraries, these tools can be adapted for other types of libraries. For example, Maine State Library's Public Library Standard 2007 includes a worksheet for calculating space needed for collections, readers, staff, meetings, special uses, and nonassignable areas (Maine State Library, 2007). Dahlgren's worksheet focuses on similar calculations for present and future library materials, staff, and users (Dahlgren, 2009).

Data should be gathered on the use of existing space, user populations, and standard or typical library space needs. For example, Vaska, Chan, and Powelson (2009) administered a user survey to determine whether a health sciences library renovation project was warranted. Analyzing use of the existing space includes the size of the total space in square feet, the collection size and its annual growth rate, a list of all computers and other equipment with their space requirements, seating capacity,

and staff size. The librarian should also determine both present and potential user populations according to job category, such as staff physician, resident, nurse, pharmacist, etc.

Measuring the size of the collections and forecasting projected growth can be daunting. Since collections have traditionally required the largest area in libraries, careful analysis of collection size is essential. The number of volumes of books and journals can be used to determine the current size of the collection. The librarian should consider the costs and advantages of ownership versus access. Factors to consider include:

1. the high cost of space and storage costs;
2. the trend toward shifting budget funds from print collections to electronic resources;
3. the replacement of print reference tools and journals with their electronic counterparts; and
4. same-day document delivery options that make it unnecessary to retain infrequently used journals.

The librarian should assess the needs of users and evaluate current and retrospective collections. This information can be used to determine whether it is more cost-beneficial to own or provide access to an item. Kane recommends that a library maintain a core collection of high-demand materials "based on the standard '20 percent' rule, which is that 20 percent of the collection will satisfy 80 percent of the information needs of patrons" (Kane, 1997: 65). For materials that are moderate to low use, Kane recommends that libraries "purchase access to the information rather than the information itself" (Kane, 1997: 65). Bastille and Mankin recommend continuous use studies to "make reasonable decisions on the optimum allocation of space to fill the highest percentage of demand with available funds" (Bastille and Mankin, 1980: 358). In addition to raw use data, they looked at density of use, that is, the number of uses divided by the number of linear feet required to shelve the journal, and concluded that "density of use ranking seems to produce a higher quality collection by providing a larger yield of titles to satisfy a maximum of uses in the least space and at the least cost" (Bastille and Mankin, 1980: 365). Schneider, Mankin, and Bastille (1995) update this work and describe how usage data are collected.

Collection use studies should be started early in the planning process. Later on, if space trade-offs need to be made, even preliminary use data can be helpful. Regardless, the data will be useful for space and collection planning. After studying usage, the librarian should consider the following:

1. Withdrawing infrequently used items

2. If cost efficient, increasing the use of interlibrary loan and document delivery services

3. Implementing cooperative collection sharing arrangements with other libraries

4. Expanding use of electronic full-text databases

However, before such policy measures are implemented, these approaches should be discussed with the library committee and administration. If adopted, the number of items withdrawn and decisions regarding future purchases should be documented. Estimates of collection size can be revised to incorporate these decisions; space saved should be documented.

Design Trends

Recent library designs have emphasized clusters, webs, and nodes that allow for the distribution of learning throughout campus. For example, architectural firm DEGW (http://www.degw.com) has pioneered higher education space that is location independent (Dugdale, Torino, and Felix, 2009; Dugdale, 2009; Welch Medical Library, 2010). These multiple ambiences allow "library" space and librarian expertise to be dispersed throughout campus. This dispersal or embedding helps establish and maintain horizontal and vertical relationships of services, collections, and personnel (Council on Library and Information Resources, 2005). Location of library personnel in work areas occupied by others also provides immediacy and a texture of contact unlike interactions experienced in standard library facilities.

Basic Design Principles

Librarians involved in renovation/construction projects can familiarize themselves with

> basic principles related to composition (arranging or grouping of objects into a unified whole), proportion (dimensions or quantity of objects relative to each other or the whole), balance, scale (size of an object relative to other objects), style, perspective (point of view, particularly related to the illusion of depth), form (shape or structure of an object), light, and color. (Connor, 2008: 371)

With practice, "the eye can be trained to detect the characteristics of well-designed spaces that are proportional and balanced, resulting in aesthetically pleasing facilities" (Connor, 2008: 371).

Selecting a color scheme is important in the design of a new library. People are affected by color, but their reactions are diverse. The use of primary colors, for example, attracts some people and repels others. Conversely, subdued tones may be oppressive to some people and soothing to others. Therefore, it is important to create an environment comfortable for most. Choosing colors for the most effective impact requires an expert such as an architect, interior designer, or furniture salesperson. The librarian can exert influence on the outcome by expressing preferences, discussing the psychological effect desired, or reacting to the expert's selections. If no expert assistance is available, the librarian should coordinate the color scheme.

Color design by committee does not work well, since people may have conflicting tastes. Staff and other members of the planning team can participate in the selection by reacting to the effect of the overall scheme, thus supporting or helping to amend the choices. When selecting colors, it is best to start with the color of the largest area first—the walls. The choice of an off-white color for the walls is the most popular solution to the problem of various color tastes. The next area, the carpet, should have color variations. Tweed patterns provide such a variation and will hide dirt or lint. The ceiling should be white or a light shade so that light can be reflected effectively. Bright splashes of color can be used on small walls or on stack ends as long as the colors are kept uniform throughout the library. A neutral, warm, off-white color should be selected for areas of concentrated study. In areas of high activity, such as the information desk, the librarian can use stronger colors. Consider outlining specific areas with different colors, such as the journal collection in one color, the books in another. This makes it easier to give directions or for patrons to navigate through the space with minimal assistance. Some libraries use glass as transitional space, as one moves from one part of the library to the other. For example, a glass paneled lobby beckons people to visit other visible parts of the space.

Color selection for fabrics, paints, carpets, and wood finishes should all be matched under the light and on the surface where they are to be used. Matte finishes, which reduce glare, should be used for walls and surfaces of workstations. For a more extensive discussion on color, librarians should read works published by Cohen, Cohen, and Cohen (2006) and Cohen and Cohen (1979). Carol R. Brown's (2002) book on library interior design and Tish Murphy's (2007) guide to planning library furnishings are other excellent sources of inspiration and guidance.

Innovative Features in Library Space

Individuals anticipating an upcoming renovation or construction project can benefit from recent trends in library facility design that have emphasized collaborative activities over warehousing of materials. Brown recommends design of spaces that foster studio-based learning (Brown, 2006). As electronic collections obviate the need to use most of a facility to display and store library materials, opportunities abound to focus on users by understanding their needs and planning accordingly.

User-Oriented Spaces

The location and design of the library entranceway cannot be underestimated. The entranceway provides the "First Impression" to the library. This first impression sets the stage for inviting people to enter and linger. Cohen et al. (2006: 24) suggest that a well-functioning library design features "small, circular zones of related activities." By paying close attention to the adjacencies within a building, planners can design a facility that is logically planned and draws users through the footprint, contributing to effective traffic flow. Clear sight lines also draw people through the space and allow them to find key areas without much assistance. ADA (Americans with Disabilities Act) aspects of signage are discussed in another section of this chapter.

Historic Buildings

Library space situated in historic buildings can pose renovation and design challenges. Fleet Library at the Rhode Island School of Design (RISD) in Providence, Rhode Island, is a dramatic example of creating progressive mixed-used space within an historic bank building (Rhode Island School of Design, 2010; Johnson, 2007; Pearson, 2007; Terry, 2007). Architects Nader Tehrani and Monica Ponce de Leon (http://www.officeda.com) designed nine floors of living and learning space above the library's two-and-a-half floors. The architects had not designed a library before and as a result, they held no preconceived notions of how a library should look, but library director Carol Terry was totally involved in the project every step of the way to ensure that the space could function as a library (Terry, personal communication, December 3, 2009). Of particular note are the Stair Pavilion and Circulation Island within a 114-ft x 180-ft. Grand Hall. Both areas are "packed with program" (Terry, personal communication, December 3, 2009), meaning that each space is filled to the brim with services, resources, and people. The Stair Pavilion evokes the Spanish Steps, a gathering place in Rome, but functions

as a freestanding structure within the grand hall, and has been described as follows:

> A new multi-level study/gathering platform breaks up the hall and adds a balcony tier to the first floor. The study island on top has flexible seating to accommodate group or individual study. Housed underneath the stair pavilion are individual work carrels on each side, as well as two classrooms, a group study area, and video viewing room below. The balcony level and stairs leading to it provide space for informal gathering and study, an easy vantage point for people watching, open platforms for sketching, as well as stadium seating for public events and readings. (Rhode Island School of Design Unveils New Fleet Library, 2006)

The Circulation Island includes staff offices, course reserve materials, pre-shelving areas on the back end, and computers that rim the perimeter edges of the structure. This unique architectural feature has been described as follows:

> At the other end of the ground floor a circulation island visually balances the stair pavilion and is the centralized resource for library information, check out, reserve books, and staff guidance. Both of these major structures have been conceived to respect the historic hall and preserve the integrity of the original building features while offering the key resources needed in a contemporary student library. ("Rhode Island School of Design Unveils New Fleet Library," 2006)

Various collections (current/bound periodicals, books, videos/DVDs/CDs, reference books, oversized materials, theses) are located on the first floor. Along the long side of the first floor are Reference and Readers' Services offices, instructional classroom, video viewing rooms, conference room, and library director's office. The second floor of Fleet Library is used for archives, special collections, slide collection, picture collections, and technical services (staff offices, staff work areas, staff conference room, classroom).

The Library Services Department of the Naval Medical Center Portsmouth (NMCP) in Portsmouth, Virginia, is an example of a medical library situated in a historic building (Pellegrino and Eblen, 2005). At NMCP, the challenge included renovating space within a structure built in 1830, but the final result preserved architectural details that include "chisel-dressed Virginia freestone, with a portico of ten Doric columns fronted by twenty steps" (Pellegrino and Eblen, 2005: 91).

Learning Commons

Sometimes referred to an Information Commons, the Learning Commons concept represents and fosters the creation and synthesis of new knowledge by creating accessible and comfortable space for computing and collaborating. Halbert describes the Information Commons developed at Emory University in Atlanta, Georgia as a high technology area that has "empowered and challenged the staff...in many ways" (Halbert, 1999: 91). In its Collaborative Learning Area, Murphy Library at the University of Wisconsin LaCrosse includes low-profile workstations that can be used individually or by groups (Smith, 2004). In an effort to reduce the barrier-like effect of a typical reference desk, Holberg at Covenant College in Lookout Mountain, Georgia, "created a reference table—six feet long with two padded, rocking chairs...placed side-by-side, with a flat screen monitor on the desktop" (Holberg, 2006: 43).

The University of Colorado Health Sciences Center Library in Aurora, Colorado, was designed by DEGW (http://www.degw.com) and represents a progressive view of the library as a hub (Dugdale et al., 2009; Dugdale, 2009). The library's Learning Commons occupies 11,700 net square feet and features collaborative work areas, teaching labs, a visualization lab, café, drug information center, and a consultation bar originally intended to be staffed by mobile librarians (University of Colorado Denver, 2010). Other areas of the 113,000 square foot library focus on collections, readers, and staff with group study rooms, reading rooms, exhibition space, decks, terraces, and work areas.

Mazurek Medical Education Commons at Wayne State University occupies a three-story building that situates a variety of teaching and learning space such as classrooms, computer laboratories, group study rooms, reading areas, clinical skills center, and simulation laboratories; administrative offices; and Shiffman Medical Library for the School of Medicine (Wayne State University, School of Medicine, 2006).

Learning Commons @ Thode (Thode Library of Science and Engineering at McMaster University in Hamilton, Ontario, Canada) is an example of creating "enhanced spaces for research and IT assistance" (Thode Library, 2010b, 2010c). Features include small group study rooms, breakout rooms, classrooms, and collaboration spaces. Equipment includes interactive whiteboards, plasma displays, and video conferencing. Thode's study areas are called Learning Zones, intended "to promote the Library as a space for research, reflection, discovery, and learning" (Thode Library, 2010b, 2010c). Different zones focus on groups, conversation, cell phone use, quiet study, and silent learning. Thode established a "set of expectations, benefits, and cautions" for each zone (Thode Library, 2010b, 2010c).

Meeting Space

If possible, one or more conference rooms should be included in the library building program. Conference rooms in the library can be used by the library staff for teaching and meetings, such as the library committee or journal club. A room 16 feet by 16 feet can comfortably seat 16 at tables arranged in a hollow square; it can be easily reconfigured for use as a group study room. In the future, such a design decision will provide space for the library to expand.

Seating

The librarian will want to provide a variety of seating facilities to accommodate an assortment of library activities, such as quick consultation, relaxed reading, group study and concentrated study. Although a variety of seating should be provided, any writing surfaces should have a light color matte finish to reflect the light. Chairs must fit under tables and carrels. Often it is better to pay more for a chair that guarantees durability. Sturdiness, fit, and comfort are more important than look or design. Lounge chairs add to the comfort and attractiveness of the library. They are appropriate as long as their size is proportional to the space available. Sturdy coffee tables provide a place for newspapers or journal issues and are a practical accompaniment to lounge chairs. Sofas are not recommended; people do not like to sit close to each other while reading. The librarian and other staff members should sit in the chair before approving its selection. See also the section devoted to ergonomic furnishings.

Shelving (Regular, High Density, Robotic, Offsite)

Standard steel shelving provides versatility, especially when supplementary components are added, such as slanted journal display shelves, slotted shelves with dividers for audiovisual software or journal issues, and coat racks that fit the standard brackets. Sliding reference shelves allow users to quickly consult materials right in the stacks; these can be located in a standard location, for example, the middle shelf at the end of every other tier of shelving and painted a different color for easy identification.

Freestanding, braced, double-faced stacks are preferred. They provide a uniform, clean, and simple shelf arrangement for users and make an effective sound barrier for study tables and carrels. Individual, adjustable shelves offer maximum flexibility; this is especially important in health care libraries because many medical textbooks and journals are higher than the 12-inch space between standard shelves. It is best to avoid built-in shelving or alcoves of counter-height shelving, although some libraries use half-height shelves to encourage consultation of heavy volumes and to keep open vistas throughout the library space.

Discussions about types of shelving are necessary during the early planning stages as the regular shelving requires a floor that can withstand a live load of 150 to 175 pounds per square foot while high-density stack units exert 300 pounds per square foot. A building must be able to support dead load and live load. Dead load refers to the weight of the elements in the structure, such as steel, wood and concrete. The live load refers to the elements that can be moved around in the building, such as furnishings and people. At a minimum, library floors must be able to support 150 pounds of live load per square foot. Because most hospital floors are built to support a live load of about 70 pounds per square foot, this requirement often presents a problem for hospitals and may severely restrict suitable locations for the library. The ability of the floor to bear the weight of stacks can be determined only by a structural engineer. The formulas presented for space assume 3-foot aisles between stacks that require a live load capacity of 150 pounds. Compact and multitiered shelving require 300 pounds, as do microforms.

Enforcing the weight-bearing capacity of the floor is very costly, but it provides a more flexible use of the space. The cost of requiring 300 pounds throughout "is only 10% of the structural cost of the project. This translates to roughly 2% of the overall cost of construction" (Foote, 1995: 353). Amrhein and Resetar (2004) explain the use of robotic shelving at Valparaiso University in Indiana. A comprehensive document about remote shelving is available from the Association of Research Libraries (2006).

Service Points

In many library settings, the information desk is situated near the library entrance for both convenience and control of library materials. The most comfortable desk for both users and staff has a counter at standing height (38 inches) on the user's side and a desk-height surface (28 inches high) on the staff side. The desk can be bought commercially or designed by the architect to fit a particular location. Under the counter, locking cabinets with adjustable shelving can be used to store supplies; locking file drawers are useful to store records and petty cash. Electrical and data communications wiring need to be taken into consideration for the functions that will take place at any service point.

In larger medical libraries, the trend has been to reduce the number of service points from several (circulation, reference, computer troubleshooting) in efforts to provide more effective assistance (Murphy et al., 2008; Bradigan and Rodman, 2008; Moore, McGraw, and Shaw-Kokot, 2001). A planned renovation or construction project is a perfect opportunity to reconsider the number and/or placement of service points.

Work Areas and Offices

During a renovation/construction project, staff work areas are sometimes overlooked or deemphasized. It is fallacious to assume that the same amount of space, or something slightly larger, will be sufficient. That said, it is shortsighted to design a work area for specific employees rather than specific positions or work duties. Staff work areas and offices should have good lighting and be comfortable, well organized, and well ventilated to support effective, productive performance.

The librarian should give the staff work area a high priority when determining what is adequate. Adequate space should be designated for receiving and processing materials, for holding cartons of books or bound journals on the floor, for book trucks, and an exit door to the corridor. If more space is needed than institutional standards permit, the librarian should develop a detailed plan of activities, such as technical processing, and the space and equipment required. Space for staff should equal 25 percent of the space allocated for collections and users (Leighton and Weber, 1999).

In libraries with only one or two staff members, an ideal location for the work area is behind the information desk. The work area should be a separate room. The librarian should consider the pros and cons of installing a glass wall or a door with a glass panel in this room. A door with a glass panel protects the library staff working in this room from interruptions by users; it also discourages staff from working in the office rather than at the information desk. A glass wall or half wall allows staff to work in the office and still monitor the information desk; it also makes the staff member highly visible to library users. If the glass panel is equipped with Venetian blinds or curtains, the library staff has the option of good visibility or privacy, as the situation requires.

The staff workroom should be designed for efficient operation and employee comfort. Thought should be given to the tasks to be performed at each work area and the equipment, space, and storage required. Frequently used items, such as telephones or manuals, should be within easy reach. Library staff should be involved in analyzing tasks to be performed and their space requirements.

The librarian should consider the ways to adjust the space in the future when requirements, staffing, or equipment may change. The work area should be furnished with standard office furniture. Most library tasks require substantial amounts of desk or table space. The best way to accomplish this is modular furniture; for maximum flexibility choose all pieces of the same width. Workstations that are U-shaped are a functional arrangement for staff offices. To provide adequate workspace, desk surfaces should be at least 30 inches deep. Ergonomic guidelines recommend adjustable height (from 23 to 28 inches) for work surfaces with computer monitors; if this is not possible, the work surface should be at 26 inches; a 28-inch work surface can be used with a keyboard tray (Cohen and Cohen, 1979).

The librarian should plan for generous work surfaces, storage areas, and shelving space behind the scenes. Steel shelving sections and a 30-inch deep work surface for processing materials are necessary items. Near the workroom exit to the main corridor, an area should be established for receiving mail, books, and supplies. Floor space should also be available for holding and receiving cartons. Storage cabinets should be no deeper than 24 inches over work counters of the same depth. Non-glare task lighting should be placed under all cabinets. Other important items that should be included in the workroom are a locking drawer for handbags and personal items for each staff member; file cabinets; space for book trucks; a small sink; counter space for a coffeepot and microwave; a coat closet; large wastebaskets, and a recycle bin. If there is a separate librarian's office, it should have a computer workstation, at least two chairs for visitors, and generous shelving. To be prepared for future changes, extra space should be planned for at least one additional staff member, and additional computer workstations.

Library Projects of Note

This section will describe some contemporary projects from various library settings. As mentioned, there are several excellent sources of information about recent projects, and persons anticipating a building project in the near or distant future can review such resources to get updated ideas and contacts. If an institution benchmarks itself against its peers or aspirant peers, it would be useful to keep track of projects planned or underway at these locations, for purposes of meaningful comparison. It would make little sense for a small library located in a small not-for-profit hospital to be compared to a library renovated or built for a university-based academic medical center, but excellent ideas can be derived from libraries in different settings.

Health Sciences Libraries

A good source of information related to renovation/construction projects in academic medical libraries is the Association of Academic Health Sciences Libraries' *Library Space Trends* blog (http://aahslspacetrends.blogspot.com). In 2003, the National Library of Medicine hosted a symposium titled, "The Library as Place," that focused on the need for collaborative space, noise control for a variety of different activities, functional public space, and highly visible and available staff (National Library of Medicine, 2005).

Each year, the Buildings Projects editor of *Journal of the Medical Library Association* compiles information about recent medical library projects. In 2010, a survey of medical libraries yielded information about 78 new construction or renovation projects conducted from 1999 to 2009 (Ludwig, 2010).

The library construction project at A. T. Still University of the Health Sciences in Kirksville, Missouri, resulted in the incorporation of clinical simulation, distance education, and group breakout activities within library space (A. T. Still Memorial Library, 2006; Ludwig, 2010).

MANAGEMENT IN ACTION 9.1

A. T. Still University of the Health Sciences

Location: Osteopathic Medical School

Description of Problem/Project: Emphasizing the need to integrate information-seeking behavior with clinical training—leading to a lifelong pattern of information management at the point of care.

Impact On: Direct Student Education and access to information services at the simulated bedside leading to information-seeking behavior as a part of routine medical practice.

People Involved: B. Douglas Blansit, Library Director.

Strategies for Success: Two strategies were pursued. First, tables for osteopathic manipulative procedures were placed within the library. With the new library building these are moveable tables in proximity to the group study rooms allowing student groups to deal with noise and privacy issues. Second, the students have sessions where they diagnose and treat a patient simulator, placed near the library so that student groups have convenient access to the physical library materials. The scenario was similar to seeing a patient and reporting on the patient to the attending.

(Continued)

MANAGEMENT IN ACTION 9.1 *(Continued)*

Library staff attended these sessions to emphasize the ease in using electronic clinical reference tools to provide a higher level of health care. Integrating Information-Seeking behavior with clinical practice leads to an increased usage of information tools. It is hoped that this habit will continue throughout the physicians' lives.

Barriers Encountered: The provision of OMM (osteopathic manipulative medicine) tables within the library was openly supported by staff and students. Problems were rare, dealing mainly with noise issues and the sacrifice of materials space for two tables (each about the size of a twin bed). Of course, the tables are intentionally placed in an area that receives more traffic and noise. This was successful only because the library had been planned to provide areas ranging from open conversation to ultra-quiet isolation for focused study. Placing a librarian within the clinical simulations was difficult due to the balance of time devoted to clinical didactics as opposed to instruction in the use of the various resources. There was also some friction between the clinician's database of choice and those offered by the library.

Take-Home Points:
- Plan for various usage patterns.
- Take the opportunity to show the relevance of the library to clinical practice, continuing education, and lifelong learning.
- Integrate information-seeking behavior within a clinical scenario as it models the ideal practice of medicine.
- Provide a location with a clinical practice table with the ready availability of both online and physical resources that allows the students to actively critique their knowledge and performance.

Contact Information: B. Douglas Blansit, Library Director, A. T. Still Memorial Library, A. T. Still University of the Health Sciences, Kirksville, Missouri. E-mail: bblansit@atsu.edu.

At Commonwealth Medical College Medical Library in Scranton, Pennsylvania, construction of a new library facility is underway to support a new medical school (Commonwealth Medical College, 2010; Ludwig, 2010). The plan will result in group study rooms, an information commons, informatics instruction areas, and a conference room.

Simmy and Henry Ginsburg Health Sciences Library at Temple University in Philadelphia, Pennsylvania, occupies a tenth of the total space available in a new medical education building (Temple University, 2009;

Ludwig, 2010). The emphasis is on individual study, group study, and instructional space. Features include

> over 175 public workstations; seating for nearly 1,000 throughout the library; two classrooms to meet the library's instructional needs, one of which can be converted into a conference room; over 30 group study rooms; wireless access throughout the entire library space; flat-screen panels with directory information, hours, and other essential information for navigating the Ginsburg Library; ten collaborative learning rooms that include flat screen panels for displaying and reviewing electronic information. (Temple University, 2009)

Hospital Libraries

The renovation of Mount Sinai School of Medicine's Levy Library resulted in an integrated service desk that situates circulation staff, reference librarians, and computer help desk staff in one convenient location (Mount Sinai School of Medicine, 2010). Although this project did not add additional seating to the space, integrating services into one place made the services more accessible and visible, computer workstations were increased, and teleconferencing capabilities were incorporated into space dedicated to faculty collaboration (Ludwig, 2010).

Riverview Hospital Library in British Columbia, Canada, is an example of revitalizing existing space; the renovation focused on improving visibility and capitalizing on underutilized patio space (Ballantyne and Bassett, 2008).

At Kalispell Regional Medical Center's Medical Library in Kalispell, Montana, plans are underway to move the library from the basement and situate the new, larger facility adjacent to key clinical areas such as the emergency room, pharmacy, and operating rooms (Ludwig, 2010; Kalispell Regional Medical Center, 2010).

Booker Health Sciences Library at Jersey Shore University Medical Center in Monmouth County, New Jersey, is an example of new construction that merged a medical library collection with a school of nursing library and added a new consumer health component (Boss, 2005). Challenges included securing outside funding for the $1.5 million project and finding a suitable location (Boss, 2005).

In 2000, plans to merge two city hospitals—Elizabeth General Medical Center and St. Elizabeth Hospital, in Elizabeth, New Jersey—resulted in "one [library] collection with half the space and half the manpower, while satisfying escalating demands for service" (Jacobsen, 2005: 61). This merger project's "delays brought both benefits and frustrations" to library staff and patrons alike (Jacobsen, 2005: 68).

Saint Francis Health Sciences Library in Tulsa, Oklahoma, underwent a remodeling project that resulted in improved traffic flow, an updated color scheme, an office for the medical librarian, and an open computing area within a 1,500-square-foot area that already accommodated a Drug Information Center and "more than 100 current print journals [and] 1,200 books" (Stewart, 2005:73).

Other Types of Libraries

Libraries in settings other than hospitals or academic medical centers can afford glimpses into creative solutions to common design dilemmas and features not always associated with libraries. The Centers for Disease Control (CDC) Library features a collaboratory, visualization forum, digital research lab, and suites for knowledge management staff. Designed by DEGW, these areas emphasize visible evidence of collaboration and project work (Dugdale et al., 2009; Dugdale, 2009).

Fayetteville Public Library in Fayetteville, Arkansas, is an example of a library building that focused on sustainable design (Fayetteville Public Library, 2010). Designed by Meyer, Scherer & Rockcastle (MS&R), this building's unique features include rainwater recycling and waterless urinals. Rated LEED Silver, FPL's flooring includes carpet, cork, ceramic tile, concrete, terrazzo and linoleum. LEED is Leadership in Energy and Environmental Design, an industry rating system used to categorize green and sustainable buildings (Stoss, 2010).

Project planners for Princeton Public Library in Princeton, New Jersey, listened closely to what the community and librarians had to say when envisioning a new library (Burger and Rizzo, 2005). After describing the new building as "the community's living room," focus group sessions were held to yield ideas. The resulting design "[varies] little from floor to floor, which allowed the creation of recognizable zones on each level" (Burger and Rizzo, 2005: 43).

> Burger and Rizzo (2005: 43) go on to say:
> Color brings visual focus to areas linked to a core library function, such as the circulation or information desks, whereas reading nooks and other "passive" spaces are bathed in neutral tones…Librarians sought quiet places to work, but they most wanted visible centers to interact with patrons—both at traditional service desks and at "quick hit" spots throughout each collection area.

The Skillman Library of Lafayette College (Lafayette College, 2010) in Easton, Pennsylvania, was designed by Schwartz Silver Architects and Ann Beha Architects. The Reading Room is a showplace that features a unique piece of furniture that can be used for informal reference consultations. Skillman Library also includes an Instruction Room and Reference Studio.

The library/information commons building project at the Massachusetts Maritime Academy is a direct offshoot of New England Association of Schools and Colleges (NEASC) concerns about the adequacy of library space (Massachusetts Maritime Academy Library, 2010). To that end, the resulting building project will include a 11,525 square-foot library and 16,720 square-foot Information Commons. The commons will feature a Mission Bridge Simulator for marine transportation students, tiered 50-seat classroom, café, conference room, and meeting rooms.

Practical Considerations

Throughout the life cycle of a project, a number of issues need to be considered and taken into consideration. These issues include accessibility, acoustics, information technology infrastructure, ergonomics, flooring, furnishings, "green" design, electrical and plumbing, heating/air conditioning, insurance, landscaping, layouts and traffic flow, lighting, mechanical systems, moving of materials, and non-assignable space. Several excellent publications focus on incorporating green principles into library design (McBane-Mulford and Himmel, 2010; Miller, 2010).

Accessibility

In addition to consulting the requirements for libraries set forth by The Americans with Disabilities Act (ADA) of 1990 (United States Access Board, 2004), project planners should refer to city, state, and county accessibility guidelines. These guidelines are intended to eliminate discrimination and to provide easy navigation from handicapped parking spaces through the entry doors, up and down the book stack aisles, at the service desks, in the restrooms, and at least one table, counter, and carrel that follow the ADA requirements for clearance and reach. Other accommodations for persons with visual and/or other physical disabilities or limitations include lever-type door handles, lever faucets, automatic sliding doors, and other accoutrements. Project planners can consult with occupational therapy staff to design a facility that is welcoming and easy to maneuver for all.

Acoustics

Sometimes librarians have little or no input into important considerations such as acoustics. Depending on the involvement in such specifications, it is worthwhile to familiarize oneself with the value of acoustic ceilings, high noise reduction coefficient, and the installation of sound batts in walls that surround mechanical rooms, conference rooms, offices, and restrooms. Such concerns can be communicated to the library consultant hired to write the program statement and/or mentioned during discussions with project planners. Additional information about the issues of acoustics in libraries is available from several sources (Brown, 2002; Cavanaugh, Tocci, and Wilkes, 2009).

Information Technology Infrastructure

Library renovation and construction projects continue to plan computing areas and labs despite the ubiquity of handheld devices and laptops. In many hospital settings, clinical staff is restricted by use-specific workstations, meaning that use of specific computers might be limited by function such as checking laboratory results. Such limitations have implications for libraries providing sufficient numbers of workstations to be used by clinical staff and others.

The desire for ubiquitous wireless communications sometimes deludes project planners into believing that the proposed plan does not need as many electrical outlets as specified. Regardless of whether workstations and devices connect to the network through hardwired or wireless connections, electrical outlets are still needed at regularly spaced intervals to handle the electrical equipment used on a day-to-day basis and to handle the recharging of various handheld devices carried by staff and patrons. If possible, wiring for telecommunications and electrical supply should be installed through the ceiling; this will allow almost unlimited expansion. Some building project managers hire information technology consultants early in the project planning phases.

Flooring

For sound absorption, carpet may be the best material for most libraries. Carpet can be cleaned inexpensively, and it is easy to maintain. Carpet should be placed in every area of the library. Although more expensive, carpet tiles are the best choice for two reasons. First, they are easier to maintain; dirty or worn tiles can be easily replaced. Second, flat wiring can be installed under carpet tiles; this is an excellent way to retrofit an area with cable or to add flexibility for the future.

If carpet tiles cannot be used, nylon or another synthetic with a low cut or loop pile is preferable. Anti-static carpeting should be used in all areas with computers. Carpet should be glued to the floor without padding; this allows book trucks to roll more easily. If new space is planned, it is easier and less expensive to lay the carpet first and then place the stacks over it. If new carpet is to be placed in the existing space, it is easier to use carpet tile or to cut the carpet to fit around the stacks than to remove the books and the stacks to lay the carpet. Cohen and Cohen (1979) present an extensive discussion on carpeting.

Furnishings and Ergonomics

Ergonomics, or human engineering, is the design and placement of furniture, equipment, and physical working conditions to meet the requirements of users. Well-designed space with comfortable furniture of the appropriate types and sizes increases efficiency and satisfaction. A renovated or new library provides an opportunity to update furniture and redesign workstations to reduce fatigue and repetitive use injuries, such as carpal tunnel syndrome. The growing literature on ergonomics and library design indicates its importance, even in the electronic library. Thibodeau and Melamut (1995) discuss common ergonomic problems, work environment, specific design issues, and workstation design. Wilkinson and Krug (1993) provide a checklist for assessing computer workstations. Morris and Dyer (1998), in their comprehensive book about library automation, address ergonomic workplace design in depth. For the latest research and standards, the Internet is an excellent source; several library ergonomics websites provide links to ergonomic guidelines for workstation design, library furnishings, and equipment. In addition to the literature, staff from the occupational therapy department may be able to assist with ergonomic issues.

Ergonomic design includes the selection of ergonomic furnishing, such as chairs and desks; design of workstations; lighting; the placement of computer screens in relation to windows; color and finishes of furniture and walls; and the way all of these components work together. Mason (1984) reported that ergonomic furniture can increase productivity in libraries by 10 to 25 percent. The following is a brief discussion of the ergonomic factors that should be considered in the selection of chairs and design of workstations. Chairs are a critical component and a good first step in ergonomic design. The Task Force on Ergonomics Guidelines of the University of Texas Libraries (1995) recommends that chairs selected for library offices include the following ergonomic features:

Legs: 5 legs for stability and casters for easy movement.

Height: pneumatically adjustable while seated, a range of 15 to 21 inches off the floor. Thighs should be horizontal, feet flat on the floor. Seat height should allow a 90-degree angle at elbows for typing.

Seat: width of 17 to 20 inches; deep enough to permit the back to contact the lumbar backrest; swivel easily. The front edge should be padded and rounded.

Backrest: should be 12 to 19 inches wide; offer firm support, especially in the lumbar region; easily adjustable both in angle and height.

Armrests: optional, should permit arms to move comfortably to perform required tasks.

The height of chairs should be adjusted so that feet can be placed firmly on the floor. For short individuals, a footrest, which can be adjusted for height and angle, should be used to support weight from the lower leg and reduce pressure on the thighs. Reasonably priced ergonomic chairs for offices, workstations, study space, and casual seating areas are available. Often, furniture companies will provide several chairs for library patrons and staff to test. This is an excellent way for these constituent groups to be involved in the process of furnishing the library. All chairs should be field tested before purchase, especially by people of different sizes and builds. Workstations are another critical component of ergonomic design. Morris and Dyer (1998) suggest considering the following factors:

- Adequate clearance for thighs. Desks with drawers directly below the working surface often do not provide adequate clearance.
- Desktops or work surfaces free of sharp edges and large enough to accommodate all the items needed to perform given tasks, including a computer workstation.
- Work surface at the correct height. For writing and general office work, the desktop should be about 6 inches above the user's elbow; for typing, the home row of the keyboard should be level with the user's elbow.
- Adequate storage for the tasks performed at the workstation and for the staff members who use it.

- Appropriate variety of storage space (hanging files, shallow drawers, deep drawers) to store supplies needed for the tasks performed at the workstation.
- Space for heavy manuals, if necessary, that can be reached without twisting, bending, or stretching.
- Space for feet. Trailing wires should be taped to workstation or floor.

Librarians must become knowledgeable consumers about ergonomic factors in library design. They should consider ergonomic factors whenever they redesign space and purchase furnishings. Improved workstation design increases productivity and library staff satisfaction.

Lighting

Natural daylight is an important psychological element in libraries, but crucial decisions need to be made about low-glare artificial light early in the planning of renovation and construction projects. Lighting consultants are valuable project partners when planning a library construction or renovation project, and their recommendations should be included in the program statement as the choice of lighting fixture is governed by ceiling height and architectural details such as soffits. It is also recommended that as few types of lighting as possible be used when planning a building renovation or construction project, for ease of light replacements and maintenance.

Incandescent lights give off a good color but are inefficient. Fluorescent light fixtures are efficient but require a ballast in each lighting unit. High intensity discharge (HID) lights do not provide a good color, are unsuitable for indoor use, and delay in turning back on after being turned off. Off white acoustic ceiling tiles can reflect 90 percent of the uplights directed at it.

The tendency for architects to design atrium features or skylights in libraries is both regrettable and legendary (Schlipf and Moorman, 1998, 2000, 2006). Some of the most beautiful libraries in the world (De Laubier, 2003) feature a combination of abundant natural and artificial light. Clerestory windows (tall units used in areas with double-story ceiling heights) are more effective at bringing natural light into library space than an atrium or skylight, which is likely to leak over time and is difficult to keep clean.

It is a good idea to familiarize oneself with terms used and lighting levels recommended by the Illumination Engineering Society (DiLaura et al., 2010). In the past, libraries were lighted above the level of 100 foot candies. The term "foot candle" describes the amount of light produced by one plumber's candle at a distance of one foot. Today, it is used as a measure of the level of lighting available. The present level for overall lighting is about 30 foot candles. Table and desktop lighting requires a higher level of illumination, from 50 to 100 foot candles depending on the detail of the work and the duration. Librarians should avoid over illumination; at carrels and in the reference and journal display areas readers should be comfortable reading, writing, or using computers

Recommended lighting levels for those planning libraries include stacks (30 vertical foot candles at 30 inches above finished floor); reading rooms (30 to 50 horizontal foot candles); service desks (50 horizontal foot candles); staff work areas (50 to 70 horizontal foot candles); conference rooms (30 to 50 horizontal foot candles and 5 vertical foot candles at face height); hallways (5 to 10 horizontal foot candles); and restrooms (10 to 20 horizontal foot candles and 5 to 10 vertical foot candles). More information about lighting in libraries is available in several library design books (Brown, 2002; Pierce, 1980).

Insurance

It is advisable to obtain comprehensive insurance coverage for replacement and rebuilding costs for the library building and its contents. The librarian may wish to prepare an estimate of replacement costs in the advent of a disaster, and update as needed.

Mechanical Systems

The importance of effective mechanical systems cannot be overemphasized in the daily functioning of a library facility. Some forethought, vigilance, and self-study can alleviate problems during the project, and later during the life cycle of the building.

Electrical and Plumbing

A detailed equipment list will assist the librarian in determining any unusable locations for electrical outlets and plumbing fixtures. This list needs to be completed early in the planning process. When the architect or planner develops the floor plan, the location of all electrical outlets, telephone jacks, network connections, and plumbing fixtures should be clearly marked. Ideally, electrical receptacles will be spaced six feet apart along all walls. Additional outlets can be situated in floors, again allowing six-foot intervals throughout all public and work areas. Outlets close to tables or carrels should be quadruplex.

Bazillion states that "ideally, no point . . . should be further than three feet from a potential connection (electrical, telecommunications, cable). Technology changes

too quickly for one-time installations intended to meet only current needs" (Bazillion and Braun, 2001: 81). Managing cables is another challenge for effective library design. Loose cables on or under workstations, carrels, or desks can be pulled out or tripped over. This can damage the connection pins or pull the equipment off the surface. Some modular furniture units have panels that hide conduits or cables at either the base or desktop; others offer cabling inside desk legs or through screens or dividers. Equipment bars that handle a variety of electrical and telecommunications features provide flexibility for equipment in confined areas. Morris and Dyer (1998) provide an excellent discussion of cable management. Some furniture vendors employ engineers who will assist librarians with wire management for carrels and other library furniture. Regardless of the method chosen, wire management should be planned carefully for both the present and any future expansions or changes. Planning for the future is crucial. It is easier to have funds allocated at the time of the initial project. A well-thought-out plan will help. Changes after the initial installation are much more expensive, and architects are often unaware of the magnitude of electrical, cable, and telecommunications requirements of an electronic library.

Heating, Ventilation, and Air Conditioning (HVAC)

Adequate heating and cooling systems are not the major responsibility of the librarian. However, some knowledge of these areas is essential. A librarian must work with the engineer and the architect to make sure that library requirements are satisfied by the systems they design.

Moving of Collections, Equipment, and People

Additions, renovations, and new construction alike involve the eventual movement of office files, supplies, collections, equipment, furniture, and personnel. Some renovation projects require storage of valuable items until the renovation phase is completed (Kurth and Grim, 1966). In any case, a decision needs to be made about whether inventory and moving processes will be conducted by library staff or professional movers (Kurth and Grim, 1966; Wisconsin Bureau for Library Development, 1990b). The challenges of moving medical library collections in hospital settings are addressed by Roth (1985) and Bridges (2009). Jacobsen reported the frustrations of dealing with "commercial movers [who] were not prepared to move a library collection by chronological, alphabetical, or classification order and needed constant supervision" (Jacobsen, 2005: 70).

Nonassignable Space

Nonassignable space occupies about 20 to 30 percent of a building's square footage. Gross square footage is comprised of nonassignable and assignable space, and is the basis upon which the project budget is calculated. For the most part, nonassignable space is comprised of entrance foyers, housekeeping closets, mechanical rooms, restrooms, storage areas, and the like. Housekeeping activities require dedicated storage spaces that include running water.

ADA—Americans with Disabilities Act

Some of the weakest elements of a project can be the interior signs, if not included in the original interior design. An audit of the existing library will show a plethora of signs. A signage consultant can be employed to improve overall wayfinding. Some libraries have used flooring and color schemes to direct patrons toward service areas, but flexible and easily changed signage is necessary throughout the facility. The Americans with Disabilities Act (ADA) provides some recommendations about specific signs inside and outside the library (United States Access Board, 2002).

Step-by-Step Planning Processes

Predesign Planning

Although less planning is required for smaller projects, the steps in the planning process are the same whether the project is the reorganization, and perhaps revitalization or renovation, of one room or a new multiroom or multilevel library. Labree (2000) offered a 16-step approach to planning a renovation project, as shown in Figure 9.1.

Several methods can be employed to develop a design concept. Survey questions, focus groups, scenario writing, and interviews (both formal and informal) can be employed to determine positive and negative features of the existing library, and to ascertain wants, needs, and preferences for future space. For example, library staff can be tasked with writing or revising a mission, values, and vision statement to be used to guide future planning. The surveys and/or focus group sessions can be used to ask library staff and various constituencies to describe the following:

Figure 9.1. 16-Step Approach to Planning a Library Project

1. Developing a strategic plan
2. Evaluating existing space
3. Evaluating collection size
4. Considering alternatives to new space
5. Planning and design for the electronic library
6. Estimating general space requirements
7. Estimating space requirements by area function
8. Developing support for renovated or new library space
9. Writing the library building program statement
10. Making a detailed space estimate
11. Comparing estimates and making trade-offs
12. Choosing between renovation and new space
13. Designing library space
14. Monitoring construction
15. Planning for signage
16. Moving the library

Source: Adapted from Labree, 2000.

- Favorite library settings in terms of location and size
- Design, lighting, furnishings, and functions
- What persons entering the new library would see
- Different functions and services available to specific constituencies (faculty, clinician, researcher, student, staff, etc.)
- Habits and patterns of usage by specific constituencies (faculty, clinician, researcher, student, staff, etc.)
- Features or designated spaces lacking in the present library
- Possible shared or joint use of space
- Possible adjacencies within a building or campus

As mentioned, focus groups are one way to receive suggestions from a broad cross section of the organization. If possible, the librarian should arrange to have someone from outside the library to facilitate these sessions; the person responsible for planning in the organization may be an ideal facilitator. Often, the facilitator becomes a strong advocate for the library. During the focus groups, participants should be encouraged to brainstorm and share all ideas, suggestions, and criticisms even if they seem impractical. The most useful plans are developed when the planning process and library staff members are receptive to all suggestions. Thinking should be bold and creative.

Another useful aspect of predesign planning is reading broadly about teaching, learning, and library space that is conducive to studying (Appleton, 2009; Antell and Engel, 2006), and/or perceived as congenial (Houlihan, 2005) or social (Bryant, Matthews, and Walton, 2009). Other resources provide an excellent background for understanding and justifying the centrality of effective library space in the business of teaching, learning, and research (Council on Library and Information Resources, 2005; "Designing the Space," 2003; Foote, 2004; Shill and Tonner, 2004; Thomas, 2000).

At Clemson University in South Carolina, university faculty and staff collaborated with students to identify and imagine existing space that could be repurposed and renovated to yield spectacular areas for learning (Weaver, 2009). An old swimming pool was transformed into a classroom called the "sandbox." Three insights from Clemson's collaboration include these:

- Keeping an open mind on how to redesign unused spaces—including theaters and swimming pools—can help a campus obtain additional classroom space.

- Collaborating across campus can help generate funding and implementation of experimental classroom designs like the Clemson sandbox.

- Building flexibility into a classroom design allows incorporation of new technologies as they come along. (Weaver, 2009)

Remodeling or New Construction

The decision to remodel existing space or to construct a new library facility depends on a number of factors including the institutional master plan, projected funding, and age/condition of the present facility. In some situations, if the cost of a renovation project exceeds a certain percentage of projected new construction costs, the project will not be approved for funding.

An architect, space planner, or draftsman provides assistance in planning by preparing schematic drawings, floor plans, construction documents, and specifications. Boss (1987) recommends that an architect should be retained for any project over $10,000 that involves partitioning, electrical work, air conditioning, or other major systems. The architect, institutional engineer, or planner will check state and local code, as well as the Americans with Disabilities Act (United States Access Board, 2004) requirements, and confer with mechanical, electrical,

and structural engineers. This person may assist with the selection of furniture, color schemes, carpeting, wood finishes, and stacks.

Sometimes a health care organization will employ an interior designer or ask the advice of a designer on the staff of a large furniture supply firm. This specialist can prepare a layout for library areas, select furniture, decor, colors, carpeting, and wood finishes. Commercial shelving companies can be a useful source for advice on placement of shelving. The range of services provided by these professionals and the overlapping of abilities make it essential that librarians have some knowledge of every aspect of design. With such knowledge, librarians can make more informed decisions on design, furniture, and aesthetics.

Construction work can be done by the organization's maintenance department or by a hired contractor. If a contractor is hired, he or she may use subcontractors for special jobs, such as electrical or ventilation work. Usually a contractor agrees to do all the work indicated on the final plans for a fixed price. Any changes or additions to those plans are charged at a substantial, additional fee. Therefore, it is extremely important for the librarian to plan all the details carefully so that all necessary work is covered in the original agreement.

Site Selection

The process of selecting a site for a new library building involves a number of issues that may be too complicated for one person to make. In an ideal situation, this decision is made jointly by the architect, library consultant, and project manager (librarian). An ideal site is four times the size of the library envelope, allowing for parking, setbacks, and landscaping.

Developing Planning Documents

Types of planning documents include formal requests for proposal, program statements, and building maintenance plans.

Requests for Proposals

While reviewing submitted requests for proposal (RFPs), the librarian should take note of similar projects completed by the proposal submitter. Some RFP documents include letters of reference for specific projects, or contact information for past projects.

Library Building Program Statements

Will the library be a stand-alone building or part and parcel of an existing building or a planned facility?

Normally, a stand-alone building figures prominently on campus, and its relative importance is signaled by key adjacencies. If a library does not occupy its own free-standing building, it can be connected within shared space. It is helpful to position library renovation/construction projects as part of campus or organization-wide planning rather than departmental planning.

While it makes perfect sense for a library director and/or project manager to write the building program statement, outside expertise should be sought for this important process as the statement shapes many future decisions and the final product prepared by an external expert may be better accepted than a statement that reflects just internal views. It is customary to hire a library consultant familiar with writing such statements, based on discussions and interviews with library faculty/staff and various campus and community constituencies.

In a nutshell, a program statement addresses "the purpose, functions, and operations of a particular library in terms of its space, environmental requirements, and characteristics" (Wisconsin Bureau for Library Development, 1990a: 65). This statement serves many practical purposes: to communicate with potential architects; describe, and justify the proposed project to constituents and funding partners; identify workplace issues that can be addressed in a new design; and provide an outline against which a project plan can be evaluated and tracked.

The person selected or hired to write this statement should be familiar with state standards for similar renovation/construction projects. The process of addressing state criteria for construction and renovation is useful for preparing the information needed to write a building program statement. For example, Minnesota's *Guidelines and Criteria for Library Construction and Renovation Projects* (Minnesota Library Planning Task Force, 2001) requires detailed information about context and need, mission, customers, interlibrary collaboration, facility need and offsite alternatives, project overview (estimated square footage and costs), project program, budget, and factors related to modular design, expansion, wiring distribution, materials handling, lighting standards, and furniture design.

Other publications that provide useful guidelines for preparing necessary planning documents include those of the state of Connecticut (Connecticut State Library, 2002) and Society for College and University Planning (2002). For the most part, if a design element or architectural feature is not mentioned in the program statement, it will not be included in either the design or the construction. That said, the resulting design needs to be flexible enough to accommodate changes that occur over time.

Building Maintenance Plans

Renovated and newly constructed spaces alike require a comprehensive building maintenance plan to address routine cleaning, bulb replacement, air filter replacement, and other associated costs. The project's general contractor can provide detailed instructions for maintaining all materials and equipment and this information can be stored with drawings associated with the project, Also, it is useful to request additional stock of extra materials such as wall coverings, ceiling tiles, flooring tiles, carpeting, paint, air filters, light bulbs, and such.

Estimating Space Needs

There are three different ways to estimate space requirements: (1) by number of users; (2) by areas and their functions; and (3) by a detailed space plan. Each approach is useful at various stages in the planning process. First, the librarian or consultant usually calculates general space requirements based on number of library users. The librarian should have a realistic space estimate, based on programmatic needs and projected collection growth, to cite early in the process of selling the library's space needs. For example, although a 50 percent increase in present space may seem reasonable at first, projections may show that such space would only alleviate the space problem temporarily. Therefore, the librarian must not only calculate realistic figures at the start of the planning process, but also demonstrate the advantages, including costs, of arranging for flexible space that can be used effectively for a period of ten years. The librarian can make a general estimate of the total amount of space needed for all library activities by calculating the number of seats needed to accommodate users during peak periods. This number is based on 10 to 25 percent of the number of potential users. The percentage of potential users may be divided into primary users (those who use seats regularly) and secondary users (those who use the library infrequently). For many health care libraries, seating 10 percent of primary users and 1 percent of secondary users provides adequate seating (*Suggested Minimum Guidelines for Connecticut Health Science Libraries*, 1970; Hitt, 1988). For hospitals and other organizations with extensive teaching commitments, seating 15 to 25 percent of heavy users, such as students; 10 percent of moderate users, such as residents; and 1 percent of light users, such as social workers or dietitians, may be more realistic. After the number of seats has been determined, the total is multiplied by 100 to 120 square feet (Hitt, 1988). This estimate usually provides an adequate amount of space for all the furniture, equipment, and materials needed for the entire facility. See Figure 9.2 for more specifics. Figure 9.2 is rendered as a spreadsheet on the **accompanying CD-ROM**. Also included on the CD-ROM is a spreadsheet for counting primary users.

Working with Consultants, Architects, Engineers, and Contractors

It is advisable to hire a library building consultant prior to developing a program statement, issuing requests for proposals, or engaging an architectural firm. When finances are secured, specialists are appointed to implement the approved plans. The Medical Library Association's "Standards for Hospital Libraries 2002" suggest that

a hospital library consultant serve "as advisor to the hospital administration, medical staff, library staff, library committee, or any combination thereof in defining and designing hospital library services and facilities to meet the informational, educational, research, and patient care–related needs of the entire hospital community…" (Gluck et al., 2002). The consultant should have extensive experience and knowledge in planning libraries so that he or she can help analyze needs, prepare the written plan for use of library space, and recommend whether to remodel the existing area or provide new space. He or she should have experience with the information technologies the library intends to include in its building program.

The consultant's services are particularly useful in writing, reviewing, and/or critiquing the building program. This expert opinion may influence the revision of

Figure 9.2. Estimating Space Requirements

Type	Guideline	Example	Space Required
Books	10 vols./sq. ft. (shelving with aisles) 25 vols./sq. ft. (compact shelving)	1,000 books	100 sq. ft. (normal 84–90-inch-high units with aisles) 40 sq. ft. (compact shelving)
Journals	divide number of current titles by 1.5 multiply backfile titles by .5 per title and multiply by number of years retained	150 current titles 10 yrs. backfiles	100 sq. ft. 750 sq. ft.
Computer workstations	50 sq. ft. per workstation	computer area with 4 workstations	200 sq. ft.
Seats	30 sq. ft. per seat	10 seats	300 sq. ft.
Staff	125–150 sq. ft. per staff member (this figure can be used for staff assigned at service points, private and shared work space)	3 FTE library staff	375–450 sq. ft.
Meeting room space	10 sq. ft. per seat plus 100 sq. ft. for podium area	15-seat space with podium area	150 sq. ft. 100 sq. ft.
Instructional space	50 sq. ft./workstation 80 sq. ft. for instructor	10 work-stations with space for instructor	500 sq. ft. 80 sq. ft.
Subtotal for this example			2595–2730 sq. ft.
Non-assignable space	1/5 to 1/3 of total space		~560–900 sq. ft.
Total space for this example			~3200–3600 sq. ft.

Source: Adapted from Connor, 2008: 380.

the program or add support to the planning team's recommendation. In many instances, an appropriate library consultant can be located through the National Network of Libraries of Medicine (NN/LM) Regional Medical Library (RML) system, the Medical Library Association (MLA), reviews of new health sciences library projects published annually in *Journal of the Medical Library Association*, Library Administration and Management Association (LAMA) consultant, word of mouth, or recommendations through the state library.

While it is essential to involve many people in project planning and to keep many others apprised of the project's progress, the library director and/or project manager need to keep close tabs on the project, and make sure that in most cases, just one person communicates decisions and changes with the project team.

The librarian is responsible for working with the architect to develop the architectural drawings for the project. After discussing the library's building program with the architect, each set of architectural drawings should be reviewed and carefully checked to ensure that all the essential elements of the library's building program have been included. While the librarian and library consultant have the primary responsibility for reviewing the drawings, it may be useful to include the institutional planner or engineer, library staff, special planning team, and the library committee. If tradeoffs or space reductions need to be made, their inclusion is especially important. Once the plans have been signed off, these documents can be exhibited in the library for all to see. The librarian should keep copies of the final construction, HVAC plans, and wiring (cables, telecommunications, and electrical) plans for future reference. These will be invaluable when additions or changes are required during the life of the project. As soon as the architectural drawings are completed, work should begin on the interior design. If possible, the librarian should see all swatches and finish chips for furnishings. Interior designers develop concept boards that include sample fabrics, finishes, and color schemes.

Keeping track of the project's progress includes attending regular meetings with architectural, construction, and project personnel, and taking detailed minutes of decisions and change orders made. It is essential to take notes related to each meeting, and keep all project documents in one easily accessible location. Once construction begins, daily site walk-through visits are necessary to observe progress, provide input, and identify and address problems as they occur. Librarians who anticipate a renovation or construction project in the future can familiarize themselves with the jargon used by architects, engineers, and construction personnel, as some of the commonly used terms are unfamiliar to laypeople (American Institute of Architects, 2010; Schmidt and Wilson, 2010).

Managing Renovation and Construction Projects

Many libraries appoint one individual to serve as the project manager. As mentioned, a single voice that represents the opinions and recommendations of many will streamline the decision-making processes. This individual can track project progress and communicate project milestones to various constituencies.

Tracking Project Progress

Several successful library renovation/construction projects created project sites that helped communicate and document the progress of the project from start to finish. San Francisco State University's Library Building Project has a website (http://www.library.sfsu.edu/about/building/index.php) that provides useful project information about service locations, presentations, photographs, and updates. At McMaster University, Thode Library maintained a renovation blog that tracked progress throughout the duration of the project (Thode Library, 2010b, 2010c).

Medical library examples of project sites include

- Herman Robbins Medical Library at New York University Medical Center (http://library.med.nyu.edu/HJD/renovation/ Home.html)
- Health Sciences Library at the University of North Carolina, Chapel Hill (http://www.hsl.unc.edu/AboutLib/building/renovation.cfm)

Staying on Track

Even though change orders (requests to deviate from original construction decisions) can be costly, the timeline for a typical renovation/construction project is so lengthy that invariably, changes need to be made to the original plans. Change orders are examples of decisions that need to be coordinated by just the library director and/or project manager, as the final budget and completion date depend on the number and nature of changes. Three excellent sources of information for keeping a renovation or construction project on track include McCarthy (2007), Hagloch (1994), and Woodward (2000).

Conclusion

This chapter was intended to stimulate thinking and planning processes necessary to initiate and complete a successful project. Thoughtfully planned and aesthetically pleasing space is essential to providing good library services. Both library users and staff need comfortable, well-designed spaces and work areas. Ever-evolving technology and user needs may mandate that libraries need to be remodeled or redesigned more frequently. Over time, expectations and demand for library functions and services evolve. It behooves the project planner to monitor the successes and failures of the project. Open or modular space with a generous telecommunications and power grid will accommodate future adaptations and modifications. In many organizations, library use increases significantly when space is renovated or a new library is built.

Each library facility project is unique in terms of how it is imagined, planned, implemented, and evaluated. Through careful planning, forward thinking, and effective communication, and the use of flexible design elements, signature space can function well and be adapted to changing needs for many decades to come.

Individuals planning renovated or new library space deserve a finished result that features collaborative learning space (Adamson and Bunnett, 2002) that invites people in, encourages them to linger, learn, and interact in ways never possible or imagined before. A beautiful library is a physical manifestation of an institution's commitment to scholarship. It also serves as a neutral space, capable of unifying other parts of the organization and forging new and fruitful partnerships.

References

A. T. Still Memorial Library. 2006. "A. T. Still Memorial Library Virtual Tour." Kirksville, MO: A. T. Still University. Accessed November 5, 2010. http://www.atsu.edu/library/virtual_tour/libtour4.html.

Adamson, Martha C., and Brian P. Bunnett. 2002. "Planning Library Spaces to Encourage Collaboration." *Journal of the Medical Library Association* 90, no. 4 (October): 437–441.

American Institute of Architects. 2007. *You and Your Architect: A Guide for a Successful Partnership*. Washington, DC: American Institute of Architects. Accessed November 5, 2010. http://howdesignworks.aia.org/pdf/You_and_Your_Architect.pdf.

Amrhein, Rick, and Donna Resetar. 2004. "Maximizing with Library Storage High-Tech Robotic Shelving." *Computers in Libraries* 24, no. 10 (November/December): 6–8, 51–56.

Antell, Karen, and Debra Engel. 2006. "Conduciveness to Scholarship: The Essence of Academic Library as Place." *College & Research Libraries* 67, no. 6 (November): 536–560.

Appleton, Rachel. 2009. "The Library Is for Studying: Student Preferences for Study Space." *Journal of Academic Librarianship* 35, no. 4 (July): 341–346.

Association of Research Libraries. 2006. *Remote Shelving Services*. SPEC Kit 295. Washington, DC: Association of Research Libraries.

Ballantyne, Brooke, and Dawn Bassett. 2008. "Revitalization and Renewal: Renovations in Special Libraries May not be as Challenging as You Think." *Wired West* 11, no. 2. (Winter). Accessed June 25, 2010. http://units.sla.org/chapter/cwcn/wwest/v11n2/article_renovations.shtml.

Bastille, Jacqueline D., and Carole J. Mankin. 1980. "A Simple Objective Method for Determining a Dynamic Journal Collection." *Bulletin of the Medical Library Association* 68, no. 4 (October): 357–366.

Bazillion, Richard J., and Connie Braun. 2001. *Academic Libraries as High-tech Gateways: A Guide to Design & Space Decisions*. Chicago: American Library Association.

Bennett, Scott. 2003. *Libraries Designed for Learning*. Washington, DC: Council on Library and Information Resources.

Bennett, Scott. 2007. "First Questions for Designing Higher Education Learning Spaces." *Journal of Academic Librarianship* 33, no. 1 (January): 14–26.

Bennett, Scott. 2009. "Libraries and Learning: A History of Paradigm Change." *Portal: Libraries and the Academy* 9, no. 2 (April): 181–197.

Boss, Catherine M. 2005. "Booker Health Sciences Library." In *Planning, Renovating, Expanding, and Constructing Library Facilities in Hospitals, Academic Medical Centers, and Health Organizations*, edited by Elizabeth Connor, 47–59. Binghamton, NY: Haworth Information Press.

Boss, Richard W. 1987. *Information Technologies and Space Planning for Libraries and Information Centers*. Boston, MA: G. K. Hall.

Bradigan, Pamela S., and Ruey L. Rodman. 2008. "Single Service Point: It's All in the Design." *Medical Reference Services Quarterly* 27, no. 4 (Winter): 367–378.

Bridges, Jane. 2009. "Moving a Hospital Library." *Medical Reference Services Quarterly* 28, no. 1 (Spring): 77–87.

Brown, Carol R. 2002. *Interior Design for Libraries: Drawing on Function & Appeal*. Chicago: American Library Association, 2002.

Brown, John Seely. 2006. "New Learning Environments for the 21st Century: Exploring the Edge." *Change* 38 (September/October): 18–24. Accessed July 23, 2010. http://net.educause.edu/ir/library/pdf/ffp0605.pdf.

Bryant, Joanna, Graham Matthews, and Graham Walton. 2009. "Academic Libraries and Social and Learning Space: A Case Study of Loughborough University Library, UK." *Journal of Librarianship and Information Science* 41, no. 1 (March): 7–18.

Burger, Leslie, and Joseph C. Rizzo. 2005. "Princeton PL's Interior Mix." *Library Journal* 130 (part Library by Design, Fall): 43.

Carleton College, Gould Library. 2008. "Athenaeum." Northfield, MN: Carleton College. Accessed June 25, 2010. http://apps.carleton.edu/campus/library/about/ athenaeum/.

Cavanaugh, William J., Gregory C. Tocci, and Joseph A. Wilkes. 2009. *Architectural Acoustics: Principles and Practice.* 2nd ed. Hoboken, NJ: John Wiley and Sons.

Cohen, Aaron, and Elaine Cohen. 1979. *Designing and Space Planning for Libraries: A Behavioral Guide.* New York: R. R. Bowker.

Cohen, Alexander, Aaron Cohen, and Elaine Cohen. 2006. "The Visual Scan and the Design for Future-Oriented Libraries." *Public Library Quarterly* 24, no. 1 (April): 23–32.

Commonwealth Medical College. 2010. "Medical Library." Scranton, PA: The Commonwealth Medical College. Accessed November 5. http://www.thecommonwealth medical.com/oth/Page.asp?PageID=OTH000031.

Connecticut State Library. 2002. *Library Space Planning Guide.* Hartford, CT: Connecticut State Library.

Connor, Elizabeth. 2005. *Planning, Renovating, Expanding, and Constructing Library Facilities in Hospitals, Academic Medical Centers, and Health Organizations.* Binghamton, NY: Haworth Information Press.

Connor, Elizabeth. 2008. "Library Space Planning." In *Introduction to Health Sciences Librarianship*, edited by M. Sandra Wood, 369–396. New York: Haworth Press, Routledge.

Council on Library and Information Resources. 2005. *Library as Place: Rethinking Roles, Rethinking Space.* CLIR Publication No. 129. Washington, DC: Council on Library and Information Resources. Accessed July 10, 2010. http://www.clir.org/pubs/reports/pub129/contents.html.

Dahlgren, Anders C. 2009. *Public Library Space Needs: A Planning Outline.* Wisconsin Department of Public Instruction. Accesed June 25, 2010. http://dpi.wi.gov/pld/plspace.html.

De Laubier, Guillaume. 2003. *The Most Beautiful Libraries in the World.* New York: Harry N. Abrams.

Demas, Sam, and Jeffrey A. Scherer. 2002. "Esprit de Place: Maintaining and Designing Library Buildings to Provide Transcendent Spaces." *American Libraries* 33, no. 4 (April): 65–68.

"Designing the Space: A Conversation with William J. Mitchell." 2003. *Syllabus* 17, no. 2: 10, 13, 41. Accessed June 25, 2010. http://campustechnology.com/articles/2003/08/ designing-the-space-a-conversation-with-william-j-mitchell .aspx.

DiLaura, David, Kevin Houser, Richard Mistrick, and Gary Steffy. 2010. *IES Lighting Handbook.* 10th ed. New York: Illuminating Engineering Society of North America.

Dugdale, Shirley. 2009. "Space Strategies for the New Learning Landscape." *EDUCAUSE Review* 44, no. 2 (March/April). Accessed July 10, 2010. http://www.educause.edu/ EDUCAUSE+Review/EDUCAUSEReviewMagazine Volume44/SpaceStrategiesfortheNewLearni/163820.

Dugdale, Shirley, Roger Torino, and Elliot Felix. 2009. "A Case Study in Master Planning the Learning Landscape: Hub Concepts for the University at Buffalo." *EDUCAUSE Quarterly* 32, no. 1. Accessed July 10, 2010. http://www.educause.edu/ EDUCAUSE+Quarterly/EDUCAUSEQuarterlyMagazine Volume32/ACaseStudyinMasterPlanningtheL/163848.

Fayetteville Public Library. 2010. "Library History." Accessed June 25. http://www.faylib.org/information/history.asp.

Foote, Steven M. 1995. "An Architect's Perspective on Contemporary Academic Library Design." *Bulletin of the Medical Library Association* 83, no. 3 (July): 351–356.

Foote, Steven M. 2004. "Changes in Library Design: An Architect's Perspective." *Portal: Libraries and the Academy* 4, no. 1 (January): 41–59.

Gluck, Jeannine Cyr, Robin Ackley Hassig, Leeni Balogh, Margaret Bandy, Jacqueline Donaldson Doyle, Michael R. Kronenfeld, Katherine Lois Lindner, Kathleen Murray, JoAn Petersen, and Debra C. Rand. 2002. "Standards for Hospital Libraries 2002." *Journal of the Medical Library Association* 90, no. 4 (October): 465–472.

Hagloch, Susan B. 1994. *Library Building Projects: Tips for Survival.* Englewood, CO: Libraries Unlimited.

Halbert, Martin. 1999. "Lessons From the Information Commons Frontier." *Journal of Academic Librarianship* 25, no. 2 (March): 90–91.

Hitt, Samuel. 1988. "Administration: Space Planning for Health Sciences Libraries. In *Handbook of Medical Library Practice*, 4th ed., vol. 3, edited by Louise Darling, David Bishop, and Lois Ann Colaianni, 387–467. Chicago: Medical Library Association.

Holberg, John E. 2006. "Relational Reference: A Challenge to the Reference Fortress." In *An Introduction to Reference Services in Academic Libraries*, edited by Elizabeth Connor, 39–46. Binghamton, NY: Haworth Information Press.

Houlihan, Ron. 2005. "The Academic Library as Congenial Space: More on the Saint Mary's Experience." *New Library World* 106, no. 1-2 (January): 7–15.

Jacobsen, Elisabeth. 2005. "A Tale of Two Libraries: Overview of a Merger." In *Planning, Renovating, Expanding, and Constructing Library Facilities in Hospitals, Academic Medical Centers, and Health Organizations*, edited by Elizabeth Connor, 61–72. Binghamton, NY: Haworth Information Press.

Johnson, Matthew H. 2007. "Reconsidering Value Engineering: The Rhode Island School of Design Library Project." *Civil Engineering* 77, no. 2 (February): 36–45, 84–85.

Kalispell Regional Medical Center. 2010. "Medical Library." Accessed November 5. https://www.nwhc.org/krmc/content/index.cfm?cm_id=269.

Kane, Laura T. 1997. "Access Vs. Ownership: Do We Have to Make a Choice?" *College & Research Libraries* 58, no. 1 (January): 58–66.

Kurth, William H., and Ray W. Grim. 1966. *Moving a Library.* New York: Scarecrow Press.

Labree, Rosanne. 2000. "Space Planning." In *Medical Library Association Guide to Managing Health Care Libraries*, edited by Ruth Holst and Sharon A. Phillips, 135–175. New York: Neal-Schuman.

Lafayette College. 2010. "About the Lafayette Libraries." Accessed June 25. http://library.lafayette.edu/description oflibraries.

Leighton, Philip D., and David C. Weber. 1999. *Planning Academic and Research Library Buildings.* 3rd ed. Chicago: American Library Association.

Leslie, Don. 1999. "Industry Experts Gather to Map Future of Libraries." *The Electronic Library* 17, no. 3 (June): 149–153.

Lucia, Deanna, and Mary E. Piorun. 2005. "Managing a Library Renovation Project: A Team Approach." In *Planning, Renovating, Expanding, and Constructing Library Facilities in Hospitals, Academic Medical Centers, and Health Organizations*, edited by Elizabeth Connor, 117–132. Binghamton, NY: Haworth Information Press.

Ludwig, Logan. 2010. "Health Sciences Libraries Building Survey, 1999–2009." *Journal of the Medical Library Association* 98, no. 2 (April): 105–134.

Maine State Library. 2007. "MLA Public Library Standards 2007—Space Needs Worksheet." Accessed November 5, 2010. http://www.maine.gov/msl/libs/standards/appendixF.htm.

Mash, Samuel D. 2008. *Technology, Forecasting, and Ambiguity: A Study of University Decision Making During the Construction of Twenty-first Century Academic Libraries.* Thesis (PhD). Columbia, SC: University of South Carolina.

Mason, Robert M. 1984. "Mason on Micros. Ergonomics: The Human and the Machine." *Library Journal* 109, no. 3 (February 15): 331–332.

Massachusetts Maritime Academy Library. 2010. "MMA Library/Information Commons Construction Project." Accessed June 25. http://library.maritime.edu/internal/construction.html.

McBane-Mulford, Sam, and Ned A. Himmel. 2010. *How Green is My Library?* Santa Barbara, CA: Libraries Unlimited.

McCarthy, Richard C. 2007. *Managing Your Library Construction Project: A Step-by-Step Guide.* Chicago: American Library Association.

Michaels, Andrea Arthur. 2003. "Before Sizing Your Building, Reinvent It: Think New Services, Connections, and Equipment." In *Planning the Modern Public Library*, edited by Gerard B. McCabe and James Robert Kennedy, 17–30. Englewood, CO: Libraries Unlimited.

Miller, Kathryn. 2010. *Public Libraries Going Green.* Chicago: American Library Association.

Minnesota Library Planning Task Force. 2001. *Guidelines and Criteria for Library Construction and Renovation Projects.* Accessed July 20, 2010. http://www.ohe.state.mn.us/pdf/library/sunsetprojects.pdf.

Moore, Mary E., Kathleen A. McGraw, and Julia Shaw-Kokot. 2001. "Preparing Staff to Work at a Single Service Desk." *Medical Reference Services Quarterly* 20, no. 1 (Spring): 79–86.

Morris, Anne, and Hilary Dyer. 1998. *Human Aspects of Library Automation.* 2nd ed. Aldershot, Hampshire: Gower, pp. 190–193.

Mount Sinai School of Medicine. 2010. "Levy Library Renovation." New York: Mount Sinai Medical Center. Accessed November 5. http://library.mssm.edu/reference/news/renovation08.shtml.

Murphy, Beverly, Richard A. Peterson, Hattie Vines, Megan von Isenburg, Elizabeth Berney, James Robert, Marcos Rodriguez, and Patricia Thibodeau. 2008. "Revolution at the Library Service Desk." *Medical Reference Services Quarterly* 27, no. 4 (Winter): 379–393.

Murphy, Tish. 2007. *Library Furnishings: A Planning Guide.* Jefferson, NC: McFarland & Co.

National Library of Medicine. 2005. "Libraries in the Digital Age." *National Library of Medicine News* (Spring). Accessed June 25, 2010. http://www.nlm.nih.gov/pubs/nlmnews/spring05/60sp_newsline.pdf.

Pearson, Clifford A. 2007. "Office dA Inserts a New Sensibility Within a Historic Shell to Create the Fleet Library at RISD." *Architectural Record* 195, no. 6 (June): 200–203.

Pellegrino, Jane A., and Lisa R. Eblen. 2005. "Blending the New With the Old: Designing a New Library in a Historic Naval Hospital." In *Planning, Renovating, Expanding, and Constructing Library Facilities in Hospitals, Academic Medical Centers, and Health Organizations*, edited by Elizabeth Connor, 87–101. Binghamton, NY: Haworth Information Press.

Pierce, William S. 1980. *Furnishing the Library Interior.* New York: Marcel Dekker.

Rhode Island School of Design. 2010. "Fleet Library at RISD." Accessed November 5. http://www.risd.com/cfm/pdf/fleet libraryrisd.pdf.

"Rhode Island School of Design Unveils New Fleet Library." 2006. *Dexigner Newsletter* (October 8). Accessed June 25, 2010. http://www.dexigner.com/design_news/7838.html.

Roth, Britain. 1985. "Moving a Medical Center Library." *Special Libraries* 76, no.1 (Winter): 31–34.

Schlipf, Fred, and John Moorman. 1998. "Seven Deadly Sins of Library Architecture." Presented by Fred Schlipf and John Moorman at the Public Library Association Conference. Accessed June 25, 2010. http://urbanafreelibrary.org/about/affiliations/presentations/sevensins/sevensins.pdf.

Schlipf, Fred, and John Moorman. 2000. "(Un)desiderata: 27 Snappy Rules for Good and Evil in Library Architecture." Presented by Fred Schlipf and John Moorman at the Public Library Association Conference. Accessed June 25, 2010. http://urbanafreelibrary.org/about/affiliations/presentations/undesiderata/.

Schlipf, Fred, and John Moorman. 2006. "The Curse of Carnegie: Can Modern Public Libraries Find True Happiness in Historic Buildings?" Twenty-One Useful Aphorisms by Fred Schlipf and John Moorman prepared for the Public Library Association Conference. Accessed June 25, 2010. http://www.urbanafreelibrary.org/about/affiliations/presentations/carnegie/.

Schmidt, Janine, and Hamilton Wilson. 2010. "The Architect/Librarian Team: Ensuring Excellence in Library Design." University of Queensland, Australia. Accessed November 5. http://www.library.uq.edu.au/papers/paper archives/the_architect_librarian_team.pdf.

Schneider, Elizabeth, Carole J. Mankin, and Jacqueline D. Bastille. 1995. "Practical Library Research: A Tool for Effective Library Management." *Bulletin of the Medical Library Association* 83, no. 1 (January): 22–26.

Shill, Harold B., and Shawn Tonner. 2004. "Does the Building Still Matter? Usage Patterns in New, Expanded, and Renovated Libraries, 1995-2002." *College & Research Libraries* 65, no. 2 (March): 123–150.

Smith, Stefan A. 2004. "Designing Collaborative Learning Experiences for Library Computer Classrooms." *College & Undergraduate Libraries* 11, no. 2 (December): 65 83.

Society for College and University Planning. 2002. "The SANE Space Model: Its Implications for Higher Education Planning." Knowledge From SCUP. Accessed September 20, 2010. http://www1.scup.org/downloads/annualconf/37/proceedings/S37-C39.htm.

Stewart, Veronica Dawn. 2005. "Renovating a Small Hospital Library." In *Planning, Renovating, Expanding, and Constructing Library Facilities in Hospitals, Academic Medical Centers, and Health Organizations*, edited by Elizabeth Connor, 73–86. Binghamton, NY: The Haworth Information Press.

Stoss, Frederick. 2010. "Libraries Taking the LEED: Green Libraries Leading in Energy and Environmental Design." *Online* (Weston, CT) 34, no. 2 (March/April): 20–27.

Suggested Minimum Guidelines for Connecticut Health Science Libraries. 1970. New Haven, CT: Connecticut Regional Medical Program.

Temple University. 2009. "Grand Opening of the Simmy and Harry Ginsburg Health Sciences Library." Accessed June 25, 2010. http://blog.library.temple.edu/liblog/archives/2009/06/grand-opening-o.html.

Terry, Carol. 2007. "From Grand Banking Hall to the Art and Design School Library of the 21st Century." *Art Libraries Journal* 32, no. 4: 11–16.

Thibodeau, Patricia L., and Steven J. Melamut. 1995. "Ergonomics in the Electronic Library." *Bulletin of the Medical Library Association* 83, no. 3 (July): 322–329.

Thode Library. 2010a. "Project Teams." Thode Library of Science & Engineering, McMaster University, Hamilton, Ontario, CA. Accessed June 25. http://thodereno.blog.lib.mcmaster.ca/project-teams/.

Thode Library. 2010b. "Thode Renovation: Everything You Want to Know about the Reno." Thode Library of Science & Engineering, McMaster University, Hamilton, Ontario, CA. Accessed June 25. http://thodereno.blog.lib.mcmaster.ca/.

Thode Library. 2010c. "Update on Renovations at the Thode Library of Science & Engineering." Thode Library of Science & Engineering, McMaster University, Hamilton, Ontario, CA. Accessed June 25. http://library.mcmaster.ca/thode/renovation/update.htm.

Thomas, Mary Augusta. 2000. "Redefining Library Space: Managing the Co-Existence of Books, Computers, and Readers." *Journal of Academic Librarianship* 26, no. 6 (November): 408–415.

United States Access Board. 2002. "ADA Accessibility Guidelines for Buildings and Facilities (ADAAG): 4.30 Signage." Accessed June 25, 2010. http://www.access-board.gov/adaag/html/adaag .htm#4.30.

United States Access Board. 2004. "Guide to the Updated ADA Standards." Accessed June 25, 2010. http://www.access board .gov/ada-aba/guide.htm.

University of Colorado Denver. 2010. "Health Sciences Library." Denver, CO: University of Colorado Denver. Accessed November 5. http://hslibrary.ucdenver.edu/.

University of Texas Libraries. 1995. Task Force on Ergonomics Guidelines. Ergonomic Guidelines: Workstation Health Information for General Libraries Staff. Austin, TX: University of Texas Libraries. Accessed September 20, 2010. http://www.lib.utexas.edu/ergonomics/.

Vaska, Marcus, Rachel Chan, and Susan Powelson. 2009. "Results of a User Survey to Determine Needs for a Health Sciences Library Renovation." *New Review of Academic Librarianship* 15, no. 2 (November): 219–234.

Wayne State University, School of Medicine. 2006. "Our Future" [video]. Accessed November 5, 2010. http://www.med.wayne.edu/medical_education/special_events/Movies/ourfuture.asx.

Weaver, Barbara. 2009. "Collaborating With Users to Design Learning Spaces: Playing Nicely in the Sandbox." *EDUCAUSE Quarterly* 32, no. 1. Accessed June 25, 2010. http://www .educause.edu/EDUCAUSE+Quarterly/EDUCAUSE Quarterly MagazineVolum/CollaboratingwithUserstoDesign/163855.

Weise, Frieda O., and M. J. Tooey. 1995. "The Building-Planning Process: Tips from the UMAB Experience." *Bulletin of the Medical Library Association* 83, no. 3 (July): 315–321.

Welch Medical Library. 2010. "Welch Library Architectural Study." Welch Medical Library, Johns Hopkins University School of Medicine, Baltimore, MD. Accessed June 25. http://www.welch.jhu.edu/architecturalstudy/index.html.

Wilkinson, Frances C., and Ruth Krug. 1993. "Computer Workstation Design and Assessment." *Technical Services Quarterly* 10, no. 4: 43–52.

Wisconsin Bureau for Library Development. 1990a. "Chapter 4. The Library Building Program Statement." In *Wisconsin Library Building Project Handbook*, edited by Raymond M. Holt, Anders Dahlgren, and the Wisconsin Bureau for Library Development. Madison, WI: Wisconsin Department of Public Instruction. Accessed November 5, 2010. http://dpi.state.wi.us/pubsales/lbrary_3.html.

Wisconsin Bureau for Library Development. 1990b. "Chapter 12. Construction." In *Wisconsin Library Building Project Handbook*, edited by Raymond M. Holt, Anders Dahlgren, and the Wisconsin Bureau for Library Development. Madison, WI: Wisconsin Department of Public Instruction. Accessed November 5, 2010. http://dpi.state.wi.us/pubsales/lbrary_3.html.

Woodward, Jeannette A. 2000. *Countdown to a New Library: Managing the Building Project*. Chicago: American Library Association.

III

Services

On-Site and Web-Based Information Services

Educational Services

Information Practice

Knowledge Services

Health Information for Patients and Consumers

Associated Services

Solo Librarians

10

On-Site and Web-Based Information Services

Susan Lessick

Information and document delivery/interlibrary loan services in health care libraries have undergone considerable change over the past ten years. New service models and service desk configurations have evolved, such as tiered reference and consolidated service points.

Library services have also moved beyond the walls to reach customers in their physical and virtual spaces. Virtual reference and social networking sites have taken a larger role in reaching and serving customers. Libraries have continued to refine their web presence to give customers more immediate and self-sufficient access in ways that are personally relevant and participatory. Context-embedded information services have emerged and are beginning to make a difference in health care and research processes.

In the first section of this chapter, the foundations for success in providing both information services and document delivery services are discussed, including service policies and procedures, customer service, and guidelines for maintaining clientele privacy. In the second section, information services, a variety of new service models are explored. The section describes current practices, performance measures, and staff development practices needed to manage increasingly complex knowledge based information and technologies. The third section of the chapter covers document delivery and how customers' expectations for speed and accessibility to digital information at any time from anywhere has transformed these services and the way scholarly content is shared among libraries. While all aspects of interlibrary loan and document delivery are discussed, the section focuses on new emerging information technologies that are changing delivery methods and sources used for document delivery, as well as the role of document delivery itself.

Foundations for Success

Service Policies and Procedures

Many libraries have policies in place that delineate service philosophy and goals and spell out customers served, type and level of services provided to all potential user groups, and library fees, if applicable. Policies should establish standards of service, define excellent customer service, and provide guidelines for protecting users' privacy. While policies and procedures are time-consuming to write and maintain, there are many good reasons to develop a written policy and procedure manual for information services.

- The process of writing policy statements helps to clarify service goals and objectives.
- Policies establish service priorities, levels, and limits for various user groups.
- Once service policies are determined, they ensure more consistent actions and decisions, hence more consistent service to customers.
- During periods of staffing shortages due to absences, hiring freezes, etc., policies and detailed

procedures can help the department function more smoothly.

- Policies support the library staff, who have to explain and enforce service priorities and practices.
- Policies are useful in training new staff members, volunteers, and student workers, and as an ongoing reference manual for experienced staff.
- A policy and procedure manual is a convenient place to gather information on forms, special procedures, handling patron complaints, and key contacts for referrals, guidance, and emergencies.

Library policies should complement the goals, objectives, and priorities of the parent institution. To the extent possible, policies, which reflect the "rules" of the library, should be stated in a positive manner and stress services and privileges that are available to customers and staff, rather than focusing on restrictions. Policies should be sufficiently flexible to allow for decision making and professional judgment within established guidelines. Procedures, on the other hand, represent the implementation of policies and serve as usable, step-by-step work instructions for library processes. Effective procedures increase staff productivity, ensure consistency, and eliminate confusion. Written procedures should have a standard format so they are easy-to-follow and have clear, simple, concise wording. Unlike policies, it is expected that procedures continually evolve as new tools and processes emerge, so staff should be expected to challenge outdated procedures and/or call them to the attention of library management. As services and procedures are added or changed, policies and procedures should be revised with the involvement of affected staff members.

An up-to-date print copy of the policy and procedure manual should be kept in a location that is easy to access by staff. This copy often consists of a loose-leaf notebook with a detailed table of contents and section tabs that allow for quick consultation. Copies of all forms used in a procedure with a sample completed form should be included. It is essential to have an on-site print copy that is always available in the event of emergencies should computer systems go down. A copy of the manual should also be posted on an internal webpage or shared drive, so staff can access policy and procedure information from a variety of locations. An online manual can also be developed and maintained by using database or wiki technology. A policy and procedure manual wiki can be an especially useful application since it provides a collaborative online space in which multiple staff members can create and edit a shared manual. User policy statements should be widely communicated and posted on the library website or a FAQ page with pertinent links.

Clemmons and Schwartz (1994) provide background reading on developing information services policies, and Brumley (2006) has authored a compilation of reference service policies and forms from approximately 200 academic and public libraries. It may also be helpful to do a Google search or request policies and procedures from other health care libraries of similar size, characteristics, and programs.

Categories of Library Customers

One of the most important functions of an information service policy is to identify the categories of customers who are eligible for services. Customer categories vary with the type of library, e.g., small hospital libraries, large teaching hospital libraries, academic health sciences libraries, etc. They also differ in terms of the missions and goals of the parent organization. For example, if an institution has strong relationships with affiliated programs, the library may be expected to provide the maximum level of service to affiliated health professionals. In many cases decisions about which clientele to serve is a resource issue, so libraries need to have policies that ensure the needs of primary clientele are paramount and that secondary and possibly tertiary users are not diverting services away from the library's most important customers. Many libraries out of necessity make a distinction among customer categories and assign different levels of services to each category, i.e., primary, secondary, and tertiary clientele.

The *Standards for Hospital Libraries 2007* (Hospital Libraries Section Standards Committee, 2008), available on the **accompanying CD-ROM**, identify core user groups served by hospital libraries. Primary users that are accorded the highest priority of service in a hospital library include:

- clinical staff, including medical, nursing, and allied health staff;
- administrative and managerial staff;
- residents and third- and fourth-year medical students, if the hospital has a strong affiliation with a medical school;
- research staff, if the hospital has an active research program;
- patients and their families;
- staff located in off-site locations; and
- other groups as appropriate, i.e., affiliated programs or clinics.

Hospital libraries may designate temporary and retired employees as secondary users, as well as Loansome Doc users if the hospital library is a Loansome Doc provider. Hospital libraries usually do not have tertiary users.

Primary clientele in academic medical libraries are usually faculty, staff, and students, often including visiting faculty and graduate students, retirees, and adjunct and volunteer clinical faculty. University faculty in non-medical academic divisions, affiliates, alumni, and spouses and dependents of faculty are frequently considered secondary users. Unaffiliated health professionals may also be designated as secondary users, especially if an academic medical library is a resource library in the National Network of Library of Medicine (NN/LM) with contractual responsibilities to provide services to unaffiliated health professionals who lack access to health information. Individual community members and companies are usually considered tertiary users and charged fees for services.

Levels of Service

The library's information services policy should define the kinds of services provided with a brief explanation of each service. Policy statements should also specify the services that are available to each category of user. Because most libraries have to prioritize the limited resources they have, many health sciences libraries have been compelled to examine their goals and clientele to best manage the demands for services by different user groups. In order to maintain a proper balance of services, the library may offer maximum assistance to primary users and provide differing levels of services to secondary users. Libraries may also find it necessary to assess fees for services to nonprimary users on a cost-recovery basis or to create revenue to support the library's budget. Factors to consider when determining the level of service for each user category are:

- mission of the parent institution,
- number of library staff,
- use patterns of services and resources,
- applicability of services,
- number of potential users,
- impacts of service on primary users, and
- cost of providing services.

A useful way to display policy information about services available to various user groups is in a chart (Figure 10.1). The chart consists of a list of services by customer categories and notes special conditions and fees. Libraries may need to use other solutions to display services by customer category if they provide different levels of service to numerous groups of secondary and tertiary users. Service policies and lists of affiliated groups should be readily available to both staff and clientele with an internal version maintained in the policy and procedure manual and a public version posted on the library's website. The figure is also available on the **accompanying CD-ROM**.

Customer Service

In libraries as in other services, providing a positive customer "experience" has taken on a new focus and an increased urgency. In writing about customer service in academic libraries, Woodward (2009: 178) says:

> One of the many reasons why it is helpful to use the term customers . . . is to remind us of this new emphasis on running higher education as a business enterprise. . . . Customers . . . demand high quality facilities,

resources, and services. They want a library that is focused on their needs, and they have no intention of going out of their way to meet the library's needs or expectations.

What is the essential component of high quality customer service? In his blog Steven Bell (2010) says, "We should invest time and effort in understanding the community, and then designing a unique experience that delivers on and exceeds their library expectations."

There are several steps in first understanding our community and then in designing a unique experience. Dudden in Chapter 6 provides a number of tools the librarian can use to ascertain customer needs.

Who are our customers? McKnight and Booth (2010) suggest that identifying and understanding the various segments of our user community comes first. It is likely that members of these groups have different information needs and expectations of library services. Residents in training may have different needs than staff nurses writing

Figure 10.1. Information Services Available by Customer Categories

Services	Hospital staff, residents and students	Retired Employees and Alumni	Local Health Professionals (and Loansome Doc)	Community and Business
Borrowing Privileges	Free borrowing card	May purchase card for $50/year	Free borrowing card	No
Books	2 weeks/one renewal	1 weeks/no renewals	1 week/no renewals	No
Journals and Audiovisuals	3 days	No	No	No
Copying/Printing	$5 per article	$5 per article	$10 per article	$10 per article
Physical access to library resources	Yes	Yes	Yes	Yes
Walk-in Reference	Yes	Yes	Yes	Yes
Electronic Reference	Yes	Yes	Yes	Yes
Mediated searches	Yes	Yes + $10	Yes + $10	Yes + $25
Electronic resources (with passwords)	Yes	No	No	No
Off-campus Access	Yes	Remote access not allowed	Remote access not allowed	Remote access not allowed
Workshops and Tours	Yes	Yes	Yes*	$30 per class or tour*
Interlibrary Loan/ Document Delivery	Yes	$16 per article	$16 per article	Yes + $30 per article

*Tours must be scheduled in advance.

policies. These expectations may change over time as the library is able to meet user needs more quickly and in a more focused way. The Customer Value Discovery research methodology essentially "seeks to contextualize the library service for the customer and seeks the customers' perceptions of service excellence" (McKnight and Booth, 2010: 28). It is a way to find out what customers think is important rather than giving them a list of "pre-specified priorities." This type of research may be too time-consuming for many health care libraries, but part of the value in learning about it may be to help the library staff take a different approach to developing a customer service culture in their library. Whatever approach the librarian takes, the key is not to assume that we already know what is most important to our customers.

Woodward (2009: 152) says, "I am convinced that the survival of the twenty-first-century academic library depends on people, library people...Central to almost every library survival strategy is the library staff...their expertise and their interaction with customers." Several chapters in this book encourage health care librarians to leave the physical library and work more closely with their customers. Enyeart and Weaver describe their efforts in relationship marketing, in which they conducted a series of one-on-one interviews with different segments of the hospital population. The authors state that "These productive interviews...laid the foundation for a new customer service relationship orientation" (Enyeart and Weaver, 2005: 92).

Chamberlain (2008: 6) suggests that "To transform customer service...one must believe in the power of one encounter with one person—in our libraries, that means each and every encounter with customers and staff out on the floor, in our workrooms, and in our board rooms." To this list the health care librarian can add the hospital unit, the committee meeting, and the classroom.

There are many resources that discuss the fundamentals of excellent customer service. Some of them use principles from retail services and hotels such as Nordstrom and Ritz Carlton. Mark P. Bernstein (2008) has provided an excellent summary of these ideas and others. He also provides the essential philosophy underlying them as noted in the sidebar.

> Without the service mission and the people who provide that service, the library is nothing more than a warehouse. As service organizations, libraries must adapt, evolve, and change as users learn to use new tools and ways to communicate and receive information. Service is what will allow libraries to not only survive, but thrive. (Bernstein, 2008: 21)

In addition, the library's parent organization may have defined certain basic service expectations that all employees must follow. Figure 10.2 is an example of one health care system's service behavior philosophy that provides general principles that are relevant to the library as well. If an organization does not have such a statement, the library can develop and post one as a promise to customers regarding how they will be treated.

Developing and sustaining a culture of customer service is one of the challenges health care librarians must embrace. Todaro and Smith (2006) have developed a comprehensive training manual that can provide a variety of approaches for different situations and learning styles. Most important is the health care library manager's commitment to providing a consistent and reliable customer experience.

Privacy

As Woodward (2007: ix) so eloquently states, "Few professionals are as concerned about the privacy of their customers as librarians." Woodward specifically is addressing privacy concerns in the digital age, but even paper-based systems require attention to privacy. In addition to safeguarding records produced by the library and library systems, librarians must also think about the

Figure 10.2. Service Behaviors

Communicate Effectively	Act Respectfully	Promote Teamwork
We listen carefully to what our customers have to say.	We acknowledge our customers and welcome them to the library.	We want to get to know you and build a positive working relationship with you.
We ask questions to be sure we understand your request.	We introduce ourselves and let you know our role in providing service to you.	We follow through on commitments we make to you.
We respond to your request in a timely manner.	We honor your need for and right to privacy and confidentiality in all our interactions.	We treat you as a professional and recognize your expertise.

Source: Adapted from Exempla Healthcare Service Behaviors, 2003. Used with permission.

problems created by public access computers. For health care libraries, the latter issue also pertains to the use of library computers by health care professionals to access patient information. In health care libraries where the computer filters and other controls are maintained by the IT department, the librarian should consult with IT to be sure privacy issues are also considered.

Chapter 6 mentions privacy as it relates to information gathering for evaluation and assessment. Nicholson and Smith (2007) suggest that some elements of HIPAA regarding the de-identification of patient health information may be useful to librarians who want to use patron records for research. Both the Medical Library Association (MLA) and the American Library Association (ALA) have strong statements on privacy and confidentiality in their respective ethics codes (see sidebar).

- The health sciences librarian respects the privacy of clients and protects the confidentiality of the client relationship. (Medical Library Association, 2010a)
- We protect each library user's right to privacy and confidentiality with respect to information sought or received and resources consulted, borrowed, acquired, or transmitted. (American Library Association, 2008a)

Public libraries and libraries accessible by the public are governed by state privacy laws (Neuhaus, 2003). It is beyond the scope of this chapter to delve into the specifics of state laws or the USA Patriot Act that address the retention of and access to library records. What follows are some tips that health care librarians can use in developing privacy policies and procedures, as recommended by ALA:

- Limit the degree to which personally identifiable information is collected, monitored, disclosed, and distributed.
- Avoid creating unnecessary records.
- Limit access to personally identifiable information to staff performing authorized functions.
- Dispose of library usage records containing personally identifiable information unless they are needed for the efficient and lawful operation of the library.
- Ensure that those records that must be retained are secure.
- Avoid library practices and procedures that place personally identifiable information on public view.
- Conduct an annual privacy audit to ensure that information processing procedures meet privacy requirements by examining how information about library users and employees is collected, stored, shared, used, and destroyed. (American Library Association, 2006).

In addition to stating that the library respects each user's privacy, the policies and procedures should attempt to spell out specific steps that that the library takes to ensure it as much as possible. Some authors suggest using a checklist that helps identify how the library handles activities and records with respect to privacy (Adams, 2009; Magi, 2007). Such a checklist can be used as a periodic audit and also for training staff and volunteers. Figure 10.3 lists some possible items but each library should develop its own checklist based on the kinds of services as well as the technologies that are in use. The checklist is also available on the **accompanying CD-ROM**.

The library collects patron data in various places and in various systems: interlibrary loan records, circulation systems, search request forms. Web browsers on public access computers also collect information about patron activities. It may be hard to know all the places where identifiable patron information may be located. Coombs used the ALA Privacy Toolkit (ALA, 2007) for a list of places to look for privacy data as she was developing her own library's practices. Whatever approach is used, it is helpful to remember what Coombs (2005: 20) has shared:

Figure 10.3. Library Privacy Checklist

Item	Met	Date
The library has a privacy policy.		
The privacy policy is audited annually.		
Staff are trained and tested annually on the privacy policy.		
The privacy policy is posted in a public area.		
Patron names are removed from interlibrary loan records at the end of the month.		
E-mail reference requests are deleted upon completion.		
Patron names are removed from search logs quarterly.		
Patron names are removed from circulation cards.		
Warnings about protecting privacy are posted in the public computer area.		
Browsing histories are purged daily from public computers.		

Source: Adapted from Adams, 2009: 55.

I learned five key points while working on this project:

1. A privacy policy is more than a written document.

2. Data can be stored in places you didn't think of.

3. How you purge user data can affect your library's ability to function.

4. You don't always control the systems where your user data is being stored.

5. Privacy policies and procedures are dynamic, living things.

Information Services

More than merely a collection of books, modern health care libraries are increasingly being redefined as service organizations and places to go to get access to information. In a digital world, this means that libraries are now providing both physical and digital spaces to facilitate information access. The Medical Library Association (MLA) "Standards for Hospital Libraries 2007" (Hospital Libraries Section Standards Committee, 2008), which further define The Joint Commission knowledge-based information (KBI) standards (Joint Commission, 2007), reaffirm the hospital library's centrality in providing ready access to knowledge-based information. Providing information services, guides, and tools is essential to the library's greater role in information access.

In an increasingly digital world, library customers need expert and personalized assistance to navigate and use an expanding array of online resources to meet their particular information needs for clinical decision making, institutional success, life-long learning, patient safety, and research excellence. The National Library of Medicine (NLM) long range plan, *Charting a Course for the 21st Century* (2006), available on the **accompanying CD-ROM**, suggests that medical libraries will continue to be vital in the future as providers of products and services tailored to the information needs of individuals. Dillon (2007: 39) argues that the "the future of libraries is likely to be where it has always been, in providing a particular community with value-added information services that they cannot get elsewhere." This view is echoed by Starr (2010), who speculates that libraries need to refocus their efforts on developing value-added services and tools that enhance the use of information to differentiate and fortify the library's future role in the evolving information environment. The ubiquity of the Internet and the super-abundance of available information have made value-added information services all the more crucial.

Information Services Defined

In this fast-paced, dynamic environment, information services can be defined as any assistance given by library staff to customers seeking and using information. The definition and goals for information services, frequently referred to as reference services, have been developed by the American Library Association's (ALA) Reference and User Services Association (RUSA). They state:

> The goal of information services is to provide the information sought by the user. Information service should anticipate as well as meet user needs. It should encourage user awareness of the potential of information resources to fulfill individual information needs...The library should develop information, reference, and directional services consistent with the goals of the institution or community it serves. (Reference and User Services Association, 2000)

Information services in the digital environment include a wide array of mediated and unmediated services that are provided both on-site and electronically using Internet technology to communicate with remote customers. Libraries continue to provide traditional services, such as answering information inquiries and teaching customers one-on-one about sources in the library, usually at a library service desk, and creating print access and subject guides that offer assistance in using particular resources and searching for sources on specific topics. Newer types of service solutions are emerging in combination with traditional library services. These include providing "virtual reference" services using a wide variety of information and social networking technologies; building and refining websites, developing aids and tools that can be used independently, in-house, or remotely, to anticipate and satisfy user information needs; and offering specialized, mediated services that are embedded into user work flows. For purposes of this chapter, end-user instruction in the context of information services refers to individualized library instruction that is provided either at the desk or via individual research consultation. The various aspects of educational services are covered in-depth in Chapter 11.

Evolution of Services

Since the first edition of the *Medical Library Association Guide to Managing Health Care Libraries* was published in 2000 (Holst and Phillips, 2000), the focus of information services has shifted dramatically. Libraries in general are seeing a slowing of traffic to the physical library and service desks, while seeing huge increases in the use of the library's online resources. Although libraries continue to offer traditional information services, new technologies have enabled service models that provide ways of accessing information and communicating with customers previously unavailable. Libraries are also responding to changes in the health information environment and new health care, education, and research initiatives as discussed in Chapter 2.

Libraries are addressing evolving customer demands by providing a wide range of virtual resources and services. Reference work is increasingly based on electronic means of communication. Customers ask questions 24/7 through virtual reference and expect an immediate response. Customers access electronic resources through web interfaces, guides, and tools that librarians have authored and organized. New social networking tools are being applied daily in libraries as librarians reach out to customers and meet them in their digital spaces.

In the current digital environment, the nature of medical reference work has also deepened and expanded to include more complex mediated user assistance. Tenopir and Ennis (2001) examined the changing nature of reference questions in research libraries and noted that reference questions, while declining in numbers, have become more complex and technical than in years past and take more time on the average to answer. The authors attribute these changes to patrons answering basic questions on their own and relying on librarians to help with harder, more obscure searches. At the same time, librarians need to explore and teach a vastly expanded array of resources which adds to the complexity of the reference process. To address the need for more customer assistance and personal attention, many libraries now have added a research consultation model and provide appointment-based research consultations and one-on-one instruction on use of library resources. Face-to-face reference assistance, consultation, and instruction have also expanded to locations outside the library within clinical settings and departmental workspaces.

Mediated services have taken many creative forms in medicine's knowledge-intensive environment and enriched traditional reference services. Evidence-based medicine (EBM), which emphasizes the value of information and importance of finding quality evidence in the scientific literature as the basis of clinical decision making, has elevated and broadened the librarian's historical role as mediated searcher and instructor with evidence-based searching, quality filtering, and synthesis functions. In addition to the emphasis on EBM, the publicity surrounding the untimely death of a participant in the clinical study at Johns Hopkins University (Savulescu

and Spriggs, 2002), which exposed the need for the inclusion of "expert searchers" in the development of research protocols, has had a strategic impact on the profession. This incident spurred a resurgence of interest in mediated, expert searching, further underscoring the essential role that librarians play in research design and clarifying the responsibilities and skills of the expert searcher, and the expert search process itself (Medical Library Association, 2010b). In a similar vein, the concept of an information specialist working within a domain or "in-context," first introduced by Davidoff and Florance (2000) and further explored by the MLA Task Force on the Information Specialist in Context (ISIC) (Medical Library Association, 2006), has provided opportunities for librarians with searching and domain expertise to more fully participate in the clinical decision making, research, and educational processes.

On-Site Services

On-site services continue to be highly valued by library customers in both hospital and academic library settings. In spite of increasing online access to both information resources and services and decreasing library visits by patrons, libraries still function as important service centers in their institutions for accessing, managing, and distributing print and electronic information (Weise, 2004). With regard to information services, customers continue to obtain the majority of access and information assistance during on-site visits to the library. De Groote, Hitchcock, and McGowan (2007) found that while the distribution of medical reference questions had changed over the 18-year period they studied, traditional questions asked at an on-site desk remained at the core of information service. Today's customers visit the library to get personalized assistance, expertise, and training for searching, using, evaluating, and obtaining knowledge-based resources. Increasingly customers also want a convenient place to access public workstations and get assistance in utilizing multiple technologies to access knowledge-based resources such as desktop, laptop, wireless, and PDA support. Other key "place-centered" activities include browsing and checking out materials from the print collection, picking up and returning print resources on loan from other institutions, and finding quiet spaces for individual study and collaborative work.

On-Site Desk Services

While very little literature exists on the latest trends about the use of the reference or information desks in hospital libraries, it is assumed that most offer some type of desk assistance during the open hours of the library and that key library functions such as information, reference, and circulation are generally combined into one service point. While a single service point has been standard practice and a staffing necessity in hospital and small libraries for years, academic libraries have only more recently been moving away from multiple service points to a single consolidated service point, sometimes called the information or learning commons (Bradigan and Rodman, 2008; Allegri and Bedard, 2006; Naismith, 2004). Many libraries now see advantages to providing "one-stop" assistance to decrease user confusion about where to go for help, provide a consistent level of quality customer service, and optimize constrained staffing resources. The consolidated service desk serves as a focal point for all types of library services. See the sidebar for services offered at the service desk.

Libraries now staff the service desk differently than in the past. Most libraries use a variety of staff to cover service desk functions. In the hospital library with limited staff support, it is common practice for all staff to be cross-trained for essential functions to ensure a consistent level of service and backup to cope with unexpected absences and emergencies. In academic libraries it has become accepted practice to use librarians and paraprofessionals with broadened responsibilities at the desk, along with other specialists if the desk has merged functions (Scherrer, 2004). This "tiered" staffing model is based upon meeting baseline user needs at the desk, i.e., directional and routine questions, with the option of making *immediate* referrals to on-call or backup librarians or other specialists to answer complicated or in-depth reference questions.

While this staffing model can be efficient and effective, it does require significant advanced planning to implement, ongoing training to learn skills necessary for basic reference and the online circulation system, and the development of in-depth service desk documentation to ensure that the diverse staff is comfortable and capable of meeting a wide variety of user needs and providing good customer service at the desk (Murphy et al., 2008). Ross, Nilsen, and Radford (2009) caution that a tiered approach rests on the assumption that straightforward and complex questions can be easily recognized based on the initial question and oftentimes this may not be the case. Because the real query is frequently discovered *after* the reference interview has been conducted, libraries with tiered service models should have well-defined and documented referral procedures to librarians that will prevent frontline staff from providing insufficient service to the user. The most important advantage of a tiered

Services Offered at a Consolidated Desk

- Information and reference queries
  - Received:
    - In-person
    - Telephone
    - Virtual Reference
      - E-mail
      - Chat reference
  - Simple directional, policy, or procedural questions
  - Brief reference assistance (ready reference)
  - Mediated searches
  - One-on-one instruction
  - Referrals
    - Expert consultations
    - Other services or libraries
- Technical support
  - Browsing and accessing electronic resources
  - Public access computers & printers
  - PDAs
  - Laptops
  - Wireless connection
- Circulating print materials from collection
  - Checking out/returning of library materials
  - Collecting fines
  - Registering borrowers
  - Checking status of library requests
- Helping with ILL/DDS requests
- Guest Registration for library use by non-affiliated people

staffing approach at the desk is that it allows librarians to be more involved in teaching classes and other online and outreach activities that redefine and extend existing services into clinical and research workflows.

There is no one service desk or staffing model that will fit every library. Libraries must review the many options and examples of desk service structures available in the literature and try out new arrangements that address local challenges, library and institutional goals, and user expectations (Flanagan and Horowitz, 2000; Moore, McGraw, and Shaw-Kokot, 2001; Naismith, 2004; Allegri and Bedard, 2006; Bradigan and Rodman, 2008; and Murphy et al., 2008).

The Reference Interview

Customers approach a librarian at the service desk or in their work environment or contact a librarian online to request information and expect to get answers and assistance. However, librarians often discover that the real question was not the first one asked, or the customer's question was not defined in sufficient depth and breadth. To ensure the librarian understands what the customer really needs, to avoid mistakes, and to save everyone's time, the librarian asks additional clarifying questions to determine the actual content of the request and then provides the information that will help the customer reach that goal. When conducted effectively, the reference interview elicits sufficient information for the librarian to conduct a successful search strategy that identifies and evaluates specific sources that meet the customer's need. This is the reference interview in a nutshell.

While the phrase "reference interview" implies a short face-to-face interchange between the librarian and the customer, it is often a complex process to get a more complete picture of what a customer wants to know. "The user's initial question often needs to be clarified, narrowed down, made more detailed, and contextualized" (Ross, Nilsen, and Radford, 2009: 3). In addition, the reference interview includes all related functions such as greeting and establishing rapport with the customer; providing information, advice, or instruction; getting feedback; and following up to assess customers' satisfaction on the information provided, and ending the interaction (Ross, Nilsen, and Radford, 2009). The reference interview has been written about extensively in the library literature. While each reference interview varies in length, complexity, topic, and sources provided, authors have discussed common structural features or stages of the reference interview (Lankes et al., 2004; Ross, Nilsen, and Radford, 2009; and Cassell and Hiremath, 2009). Usually the stages of the reference interview are:

- greeting/establishing rapport;
- negotiating the question;
- developing the search strategy;
- finding the information;
- presenting the information to the customer; and
- follow-up/closure.

The initial introductory communication between the librarian and customer is very important. Because many customers are hesitant to ask for help, being friendly and approachable is the first step in giving good customer service. It has also been suggested that librarians may want to review the layout of the library's reference/information desk, itself, from the user's perspective, since signage and layout can be barriers for library customers seeking help (Ross, Nilsen, and Radford, 2009). Kazlauskas (1976) identified behaviors that make librarians less approachable, including lack of immediate acknowledgment, reading, tapping one's finger, among other behaviors.

Radford (1998) identified factors that make librarians more approachable. These include such things as using eye contact, verbal reinforcement, availability, proximity, familiarity, etc. The RUSA (Reference and User Services Association, 2004a) "Guidelines for Behavioral Performance of Reference and Information Service Providers" underscore the importance of being friendly and approachable to make the customer feel more comfortable asking for the help they need. While many librarians believe that answering the customer's question correctly is the most important aspect of the reference interaction, studies show that customers are more likely to return to a librarian that is courteous even if they did not get the information they needed (Cassell and Hiremath, 2009). As Cassell and Hiremath (2009: 15) state in *Reference and Information Services in the 21st Century*, "conduct is as important as content."

The next stage is to question the library customer about his or her query, which Lankes (2004: 101) describes as "the heart of the reference interview." Librarians should never accept the initial question on face value. They need to ask good questions without using library jargon, avoid rushing to provide a quick answer, and then rephrase the question back to the user to make sure the real request is understood before proceeding to find any information. Many approaches have been suggested for negotiating the question and they have been summarized (Cassell and Hiremath, 2009). Jankowski (2008) discusses the goals, stages, and challenges of the reference interview for health-related comprehensive literature searches. Usually a mix of open-ended and closed questions works the best to enable the librarian to do a successful search. Open-ended questions are useful at the beginning of the interview because they encourage customers to express what they need in their own words, for example "What would you like to know about that topic?" or "What aspect of that topic are you most interested in?" Once the librarian understands the request, closed questions are helpful in narrowing the search to establish parameters for search, such as languages, publication type, and years covered. An example of a closed question is "Do you want recent articles on that topic?" Ross, Nilsen, and Radford (2009: 94) also suggest using "neutral questions" or "sense-making questions" to guide the interview because they have more structure than open questions. This sense-making question model tries to find out three things, specifically:

- the context of the question,
- the user's real question, and
- how the information will be used.

Examples of the sense-making questions are:

- "What prompts you to ask this question?"
- "What would you like to know about [the topic]?"
- "How do you plan to use the information?" (Ross, Nilsen, and Radford, 2009: 98, 101)

After asking some open or sense-making questions, the librarian should rephrase or summarize the question for the customer to be sure that he or she really understands what is needed. The librarian needs to remain objective and should not make judgments about the subject or question. The librarian should also include the customer in the search process to the extent possible. For example, the librarian can turn the monitor to the customer while searching databases to verify if he or she is proceeding in the right direction and to guide the requester through the process.

The next stage is finding the information. This involves constructing a search strategy, identifying the most appropriate database, website, or print source, such as an almanac or data book, and finding the right answer or information. Some requests may result in referrals to other librarians, services, or libraries. As the search is developed, the librarian should explain the process and any search results always working within the customer's time frame. The librarian should continuously check in with the customer to determine whether the information retrieved meets the request and if necessary refine the search. The conclusion of the search is the follow up and confirming with the customer that the question has been answered. In addition, the librarian should invite the customer back to ask for additional help.

There are many resources that discuss the fundamentals of the reference interview. Cassell and Hiremath (2009) provide a summary of relevant issues, approaches, and studies. Ross, Nilsen, and Radford (2009) have developed a comprehensive training manual that provides excellent information, tips, exercises, examples, and references on conducting the reference interview. The virtual reference interview is discussed later in the chapter.

Virtual Reference Services

While information/reference desk services continue to play an important role in aiding customers, desk services are now only one of many reference delivery methods. The challenge for today's library is to distribute services outward and provide assistance through multiple channels. Increasingly health care libraries and library consortia are extending reference service over the Internet to provide reference assistance, thus reaching outward to

patrons who might not otherwise come to the library (Dee, 2003a,b, 2005; Cleveland and Philbrick, 2007). Virtual reference enables customers to get direct assistance from librarians wherever and whenever they need it.

The literature refers to virtual reference by a variety of terms, including digital reference, e-reference, chat reference, instant messaging reference, live reference, and Ask a Librarian reference. Most health care libraries use the phrase "Ask a Librarian" to label their virtual reference services (Stone et al., 2003; Cleveland and Philbrick, 2007). There are also many definitions of this concept. For purposes of this chapter, the term virtual reference services and the definition of virtual reference services developed by Reference and User Services Association (RUSA) of ALA will be used. The definition offered by RUSA states that "virtual reference is reference service initiated electronically, often in real-time, where patrons employ computers or other Internet technology to communicate with reference staff, without being physically present" (Reference and User Services Association, 2004b). Various technologies are used in virtual reference, including e-mail and webform, chat, co-browsing, and text messaging.

There are two general categories of virtual reference: asynchronous and synchronous. Asynchronous reference, such as e-mail and web form questions, involves the patron submitting a question with the librarian responding with answers and information at a later time. Synchronous reference, such as chat, instant messaging (IM), and text messaging, involves the patron and librarian communicating in real time. Academic libraries primarily use web forms, e-mail, chat, and IM to deliver virtual reference services (Cleveland and Philbrick, 2007).

Several studies have examined the types of questions received through virtual reference service (Powell and Bradigan, 2001; Jerant and Firestein, 2003; Markgren, Ascher, and Crow, 2004). DeGroote (2005) compared the types of questions asked at the reference desk with questions asked via e-mail and chat. She found that in-person questions primarily consisted of journal holdings, book holdings, and technical and access issues, whereas chat questions focused on finding articles on a particular topic, and e-mail questions focused on journal holdings, media items, and finding articles on a particular topic.

Health sciences libraries have addressed the issue of staffing differently to distribute the additional workload created by chat reference services. Dee's study of digital chat reference in academic libraries indicated that most academic libraries provided chat service from librarians' offices with librarians monitoring the chat service in regularly scheduled shifts. Some libraries integrate chat service into reference desk work provided there was sufficient staff to cover both the desk and online questions, while others share staffing with paraprofessionals or consortial colleagues (Dee, 2005).

Some libraries provide virtual reference services collaboratively with other libraries. These collaborations can be between campus library units, through a consortium, regional, or across time zones to spread the expense and extending hours of operation (Parker and Johnson, 2003; McClellan, 2003).

Virtual reference is frequently underused simply because customers are not aware of it. It is important that libraries highlight and make the service visible on all pages on their website, as well as market the service to create awareness of the service. Cleveland and Philbrick's review article (2007) of virtual reference services is an excellent source on marketing virtual reference services and discusses various issues, such as naming the service, locations of links to the service, and using multiple formats to promote the service. Libraries can publicize virtual reference services in a variety of ways, including links to the service on all library webpages, newsletters, institutionwide e-mail announcements, on bookmarks, and demonstrations in orientations and instructional sessions (McGraw, Heiland, and Harris, 2003).

E-mail, Chat, IM, and Text Messaging

E-mail reference has been offered by libraries since the mid-1980s and is the most common form of virtual reference service in hospital and academic health sciences libraries. A key element of e-mail reference is a well-designed form that is prominently placed on the library website to prompt the user for details about their information need. Capturing detailed information on a form is essential since it is difficult to ask remote customers follow-up questions. Sample e-mail reference forms can be found on many health sciences library websites. Although it is hard to conduct a reference interview on e-mail, e-mail reference has the advantage of giving the librarian time to do research and provide a more thorough answer. E-mail responses should include an invitation to the customer to return for more information or to use the service again.

Chat reference services are increasingly being implemented in academic health sciences libraries due to the popularity of chat applications in the home computing market. Chat reference can be provided by using simple instant-messaging (IM) software that is either free or reasonably priced. See the sidebar for examples of widely available commercial IM networks.

Examples of IM networks
- AOL Instant Messenger (http://www.aim.com/)
- MSN Messenger (http://explore.live.com/windows-live-messenger)
- Yahoo! Messenger (http://messenger.yahoo.com/)
- Google Talk (http://www.google.com/talk/)

IM aggregator programs
- Meebo (http://www.meebo.com/)
- Trillian (http://www.trillian.im/)
- Pidgin (http://www.pidgin.im/)

IM aggregators are particularly useful in managing chat reference because they can combine multiple IM services into a single application and offer additional features, such as file transfer, encryption of IM communications, and transaction logs (Jayaraman, 2009). They are also easy to use and require little support from IT staff. In addition, Meebo provides a MeeboMe widget that can be embedded on a library home page or hospital intranet. For these reasons, Rios (2008) recommended the use of IM tools for virtual reference in hospital libraries. Jayaraman (2009) discussed the benefits to the librarian and the end user of IM reference in an academic medical library. Kipnis and Kaplan's case study (2008) examined question types and usage patterns and found that most customers were well satisfied with the IM service and would use it again in the future. Ruppel and Fagan (2002) found that customers valued IM reference service for its convenience, anonymity, and quick help.

Because IM chat messages are sent and responded to quickly, they often lack context and clarity. Since interactions are also quite short, customers may not provide contact information to follow up. Furthermore, it is difficult to know when a question is finished in the chat environment. In the fast-paced environment of IM reference it is recommended that librarians should respond to IM chat queries in a succinct manner with small amounts of information and requests for clarification (Ross, Nilsen, and Radford, 2009). They should also try to get a user's e-mail address to do follow-up or encourage customers to come to the library for further assistance.

Chat reference is also commonly provided using vendor-provided packages called web contact or call center software. Examples include OCLC's Question Point (http://www.questionpoint.org/), VRLplus (http://www.altarama.com/page/VRLplus.aspx), Tutor.com (http://www.tutor.com/), and LivePerson (http://www.liveperson.com/). These interactive programs, which are patterned after commercial software, can be rather expensive, which has prompted some academic libraries to create consortia to offset the costs (Cleveland and Philbrick, 2007). Most programs manage incoming calls, maintain statistics, and provide transcripts. They may also include cobrowsing and application sharing, which allow the librarian to push pages onto the user's screen and point out particular items of interest while having a chat conversation with the user. User perceptions of chat reference are not well documented in the medical library literature. However, one case study has found that feedback from customers of the chat service were generally positive about the service (Jerant and Firestein, 2003). Dee (2003a,b) provides a comprehensive overview of chat reference management issues for librarians investigating chat reference service.

SMS (Short Message Service), also known as text messaging appears to be effective and viable, and an upward trend in libraries (Kroski, 2009). SMS allows customers to send short text messages on their cell phones via SMS from any location. SMS communication is limited by a message length of 160 characters. Several vendors offer fee-based SMS services that allow libraries to efficiently manage SMS reference. Examples of products include Altarama (http://www.altarama.com.au/refxsms .htm), which delivers text messages to a library email address for monitoring and handling, and Mosio's Text a Librarian (http://www.textalibrarian.com/), which offers libraries a web-based gateway that librarians can log into to monitor and handle text messages. Text a Librarian also offers special services for medical libraries and library cooperatives.

The Virtual Reference Interview

Reference interviewing in the virtual environment, specifically in the chat medium, has many similarities to face-to-face reference. Because there is an opportunity to communicate back and forth and provide guidance, the virtual reference interview has the same structural features as the face-to-face interview. However, a virtual reference interview lacks the advantage of having nonverbal cues, such as the customer's tone of voice, facial expressions, and body language, that provide constant feedback to the librarian in understanding the customer's information needs. On the positive side, Cassell and Hiremath (2009) point out that despite this disadvantage, virtual reference can be a powerful opportunity to reach more types of individuals because some customers cannot leave their work or clinical areas or they prefer to communicate using a keyboard rather than verbal communication.

When serving customers who ask a question through a chat service, the librarian should set a friendly tone for the encounter by greeting the user in a friendly, upbeat manner, such as "Hello. How can I help you?" or "You have a very interesting question for me." The librarian should also try to use the customer's name if known. Sometimes in the chat medium canned messages are used to welcome the customer and ask for their affiliation. If this is the case, the librarian should add a personal greeting and respond with "hello" or some other greeting to set up a more personal online working relationship. Ross, Nilsen, and Radford (2009) offer many suggestions for increasing approachability, including having the link and service hours for Ask a Librarian prominently displayed on all library webpages.

The central role of question negotiation in the reference interview does not change in the virtual environment (Lankes et al., 2004). Because the librarian and user are physically separate and chat messages are sent and responded to quickly, they often lack context and clarity. In this environment it is the responsibility of the librarian to ask clarifying questions to ensure that both parties understand each other and to save time. The librarian should ask the same types of open-ended or sense-making questions as in the face-to-face interview to give the user an opportunity to type out his or her request. Responses and clarification questions should be succinct and conveyed with small amounts of information using shortcuts, abbreviations, and emoticons while chatting online with customers (Ross, Nilsen, and Radford, 2009). Librarians also need to rephrase the question to get confirmation before searching. It is important to explain what steps are being taken and frequently ask for feedback since the customer cannot see what the librarian is doing. When information is found, the librarian should provide a URL or co-browse with the customer if this feature is available.

Online interactions are often followed up with a telephone call, e-mail message, or in-person interaction, if the question requires a complex search or in-depth training. Follow-up e-mails should be supportive and invite customers to use the library again virtually or in person. Because librarians often provide patrons with URLs with additional information, it is very important to keep library webpages up-to-date with current policies and procedures so staff and patrons can find needed information quickly. There are many resources that discuss the reference interview in the digital environment. Cassell and Hiremath (2009) summarize relevant issues, approaches, and studies on virtual reference. Lankes et al. (2009) provide information on current practices, theories, studies, and trends on virtual reference. Ross, Nilsen, and Radford (2009) have a chapter devoted to the reference encounter in virtual environments. It is an excellent resource for text-based strategies and tips, common chat abbreviations, and comparisons between e-mail, chat, and face-to-face interviews, with many exercises, examples, and references on conducting virtual reference interviews.

Use of Social Networking and Media Sites in Reference

Since their introduction in the late 1990s, social networking sites have attracted millions of people, many of whom have integrated these sites into their daily practices. As of this writing, three of the top ten most visited websites in the world are social networking sites (Facebook, YouTube, and Twitter, in that order) (Alexa Internet Inc., 2010). These new social networking sites have shown great promise for use by libraries and libraries have moved quickly to investigate and use them for end-user services and internally for library staff. Given the reach of these sites and the emphasis on providing timely reference at the user's point of need, the use of social networking sites is increasingly prevalent in health sciences libraries to deliver and market services, especially reference services. By tapping into specialized online communities that users are already using or will be in the future, librarians can reach customers who might never have considered using library services and collections before.

The definition and terminology used for social networking sites (SNS) vary widely and continue to evolve due to rapidly shifting online cultures and the different perspectives of authors. Definitions range from using social networking as an umbrella term to cover a broad range of sites that have implemented SNS features (Connor, 2007; Rethlefsen, 2007), to a narrower more nuanced typology of web applications that primarily focus on making and accumulating "friendship" connections (Cassell and Hiremath, 2009; Steiner and Madden, 2008). In this chapter, social networking sites are defined somewhat narrowly as websites that are structured to facilitate online user interaction and the open sharing of data. Sites such as Facebook (http://www.facebook.com/) and Twitter (http://twitter.com/) are prime examples of social networking sites. Other types of social networking sites that have great relevance to health care libraries are sites that are designed to share specific types of media. These sites contain mostly user-generated media content and are referred to as social media sites. Examples of these social media sites are YouTube (http://www.youtube.com) and Flickr (http://www.flickr.com).

Within each of these online communities, users interact and share ideas with other individuals with similar interests by creating user profiles, sharing media and

websites, and directly communicating with one another within the SNS. From the user perspective, they are easy to use since they are already familiar with the capabilities, limitations, and conventions of these sites. They are also convenient and provide ubiquitous access for users—information can be shared and viewed as many times as needed, from anywhere, at anytime. These sites also work with other SNS platforms and cell phones.

While each of these social networking sites have similarities, each have unique features and differences that should be taken into account in order for librarians to effectively use them to increase library awareness, offer services and resources, and meet customers' information needs within these online environments. Facebook is immensely popular with college students, provides gated networks based on regions, schools, and interest groups, and a "wall" for scrolled messages and threaded discussion lists. Facebook also encourages developers to create embedded applications in Facebook. Twitter is part "microblog" and part SNS. It was designed to exchange pithy, real-time messages, called "tweets," that are limited to a maximum of 140 characters each. Twitter can integrate with other webpages to access Twitter updates. YouTube, purchased by Google in 2006, is a video-sharing social media site. Users of YouTube can upload, share, tag, post comments on, and rate videos. YouTube also allows videos hosted on its site to be embedded in other webpages, Facebook, and Twitter. Flickr, purchased by Yahoo in 2005, is a photo management and sharing social media site that offers two versions: a basic account that is free and a fee-based premium account that provides unlimited, high-resolution storage. Flickr users can upload and tag photos, indicate whether photos are public or private, specify copyright permissions, browse others' photos, and add comments and annotations to photos.

Self-organizing groups of users within Facebook, such as affinity groups with library, education, health, or research interests, afford targeted marketing opportunities for libraries. Homegrown applications for Facebook have been created by libraries to help answer reference questions and search local online catalogs. Other functional applications, developed by organizations and vendors, have direct bearing in health care settings, such as PubMed, WorldCat, LibGuides, and medical journal applications, such as JSTOR. The study by Hendrix and others (2009) on the extent and nature of institutional Facebook use in academic health sciences libraries provides an informative review of existing research-oriented studies on libraries and Facebook, usage benchmark data, and insights into the current uses of Facebook in academic libraries. The study showed that most health sciences academic libraries did not maintain Facebook pages, and that libraries with Facebook pages reported they used it to provide a presence in the social network, to market the library, and push out announcement to library customers, to post photos, and to provide reference (Hendrix et al., 2009).

Various articles in the library literature have pointed out the potential and actual uses of Twitter by library institutions. Libraries have shared brief news announcements about events, changes in library hours, workshops, new title lists, among other uses (Cassell and Hiremath, 2009; Rodzvilla, 2010). In the same way that clickers facilitate active learning, Twitter can be used by attendees of classes or conference sessions to ask questions and share thoughts in real time with others at the event and with those who are unable to attend. This application was used at the Medical Informatics Section's Top Technology Trends session at MLA 2010 Annual Meeting. Stuart (2010) reported that currently over 400 libraries have a library presence on Twitter and that most libraries primarily broadcast news and information about the library and highlight library resources. Fewer than 30 percent of the libraries in Twitter post daily updates, and even less are interactively engaged in conversation with customers. Milstein (2009) has provided helpful suggestions, or "twittequette," for libraries to effectively communicate and build relationships with library customers in Twitter.

Libraries are using YouTube to post videos for promotion, outreach, instruction, and archiving. Examples of videos that have been created by libraries and posted in YouTube include library orientation videos, tutorials, video repositories, and entertaining library videos. Del Castillo's course wiki (2008) provides an excellent introduction to YouTube for libraries and includes many examples, references, and resources for libraries investigating video development and YouTube applications.

Flickr has numerous uses for health sciences libraries. The reader has only to browse the Libraries and Librarians group in Flickr, which has over 3,000 members and a pool of over 35,000 photos, to discover ways in which libraries are using this tool. Mention should also be made of the successful Library of Congress's pilot project to place over 5,000 historical photos on Flickr to increase the public's awareness and spark creative engagement of the library's collections (Remarkable Outreach, 2009). Excellent suggestions have been offered as to how libraries could use Flickr to enhance services (Smith, 2010; Ekart, 2010; Anderson, 2007; Rethlefsen, 2007; and CollegeDegrees.com, 2008). Some of these suggestions include publicizing library events, recognizing library staff and patrons, presenting collections of historical

photos, promoting images of workshops, and creating a digital collection repository to mention only a few. Libraries have also embedded Flickr "slideshows" in library webpages and blogs to present virtual library displays and tours. Furthermore, libraries are using Flickr to store screenshots and images for later re-use in publications (Rethlefsen, 2007). Reference librarians should also remember that the vast collections of images in Flickr (and videos in YouTube) can provide digital inspiration and be used by patrons for presentations, provided there are no copyright restrictions.

The use of social networking sites by health sciences libraries is still evolving. Currently libraries are using these sites primarily for library marketing, reference, and instruction. Some libraries have not yet "taken the leap," but are exploring the pros and cons of offering and promoting services in these increasingly mainstream online environments. Unfortunately, many hospital libraries are not able to use social networking technologies, especially Facebook and YouTube, because of security and bandwidth issues.

For reference librarians, social networking sites provide yet another "space" in which to offer reference assistance; a space that affords unprecedented access to library customers. See the sidebar for ideas on possible reference uses of social networking sites.

Reference Uses of Social Networking Sites

- Privately answer questions from individual customers
- Provide a public forum for asking and answering questions
- Create an Ask A Librarian application for questions
- Use chat feature within SNS to answer questions
- Join group discussions to anticipate questions and provide assistance

Librarians can choose to message customers directly to answer private questions or provide a public forum for customers to ask reference questions and see responses, potentially generating discussion and further questions. Librarians can also use the communication tools provided by the social networking services, such as an Ask A Librarian application or chat tool within a site, to provide chat reference services, allowing customers to seek reference help without leaving the page.

Library outreach is another important benefit of joining users in "their space," enabling librarians to stay connected to what customers want and need. Mathews (2008: 91) argued that social networking calls for a "preemptive approach" that seeks out customers, rather than waiting for customers to visit the reference desk or library website. Social networking allows the librarian to become more approachable, better able to anticipate patron needs, and better equipped to inform customers of appropriate search strategies and resources much earlier than before. The idea of exposing reference services at the point of need (user work flows) carries over to other health care information service models that will be discussed later in the chapter.

While there is an abundance of literature about social networking in libraries, most articles still provide an overview of the sites and discuss potential library uses of them in general. With few exceptions, research-based articles that evaluate the use and benefits of social networking sites to health sciences libraries are lacking. As library use of these sites become more prevalent, more high-quality research is needed to demonstrate the value of these services in comparison to other methods of reference delivery. That being said, it is essential for libraries to continue to innovate and experiment with new emerging reference service formats and strategies. By finding new creative ways to branch out, virtually and physically, libraries can blend in more with the communities they serve, gain a richer understanding of how libraries services are perceived and used, and forge a new identity and relevance.

Development of Websites

Information services in the digital environment include a wide range of web-based activities, such as building webpages, web-based subject guides, portals, and incorporating Web 2.0 customization tools that can be used independently or collaboratively, in-house or remotely, to anticipate and satisfy user information needs. Rapid advances in digital technology have led to the astonishing growth of library web-based information and services over the past 15 years. Today's library web presence serves as the virtual front door of the library, a gateway to high quality electronic resources in full-text and multimedia formats, and as a mission-critical service point that offers fast and easy online assistance, guidance, and instruction in navigating often difficult to use resources and systems found in the health sciences environment.

Health sciences libraries began developing websites almost immediately after Mosaic, the world's first web browser, was released in 1993 (Brower, 2004). Brower (2004) observed that by the mid-1990s most academic health sciences libraries had developed their own websites. While little can be found in the literature of early efforts of hospital libraries, it can be assumed that once

hospitals obtained Internet connectivity (sometimes at the urging of the hospital librarian), hospital librarians were quick to begin to explore and develop individual library sites (Fuller and Hinegardner, 2001). Early websites consisted of simple, individual webpages with static lists, directories and guides. Archived revisions of individual library websites over time are available from the Internet Archive WayBack Machine (Internet Archive, 2010).

Since the early days in the mid-1990s health sciences library websites have gone through multiple revisions and grown tremendously in size and sophistication. Most current library websites are dynamically driven with user-centered interfaces that provide patrons access to online catalogs, subscribed resources, and other electronic content. Some also create virtual environments that enable patrons to personalize the selection and presentations of resources through portals, while others include federated search tools, electronic reference services (e.g., Ask A Librarian), enriched content (e.g., annotated resource lists, book covers, etc.), and Web 2.0 tools to engage in two-way communication and collaborations with library customers.

Design, organization, structure, content, and maintenance issues for library websites are vital because the library website is now the primary vehicle used to distribute library information, services, and collections to customers. While design elements are quite subjective, it is important for library websites to conform to institutional standards to the extent possible, and be easy to navigate with consistent elements throughout the pages and a logical organizational structure that makes sense to relevant user groups. Many excellent guides are available on website design and are listed in the Further Reading section at the end of the chapter. Several articles provide excellent discussions of design considerations and suggestions of best practices for library websites (Tennant, 1999; Zhou, 2003; Brower, 2004; and Detlor and Lewis, 2006). Librarians can read the website design literature, visit other library websites, and incorporate usability testing into design plans. If the library staff does not possess sufficient graphic design expertise, it may be necessary to seek help either from professionals in the parent institution or outside design firms.

The basic structure and organization of the website should be cohesive and contain a useful set of information services and resources that reflects the user's perspective. Zhou (2003) observed that most library websites are generally hierarchical or audience oriented. The hierarchical websites reflect the library's physical hierarchical structure, mainly organized by library units or functions, e.g. reference, access service, cataloging, interlibrary loan, reserve service, etc. The audience website is organized by user types, such as faculty, students, clinicians, nurses, patients, researchers, donors, etc. Health sciences library websites are also organized by specific disciplines or subjects. Often library websites use a combination of hierarchical, audience, and discipline structures for their home pages. A fourth type of library website is the portal, although this type of site is less frequently used by libraries. The portal website, which is a unified gateway that can be customized by individual users to automatically filter information from the web, can be a built-in function in a library website or it can be incorporated into another institutional portal. Library portals are discussed more fully later in the chapter.

Subject Guides

Most health sciences websites steer users to discipline-based virtual collections, often called subject guides or research guides, of locally provided resources and other external links. These subject-oriented pages include subscription databases, reference aids, online research and literacy tutorials, virtual reference assistance, and links to select free Internet resources outside the institution. Subject guides are tailored to assist users with their information needs at the point of care, in their research, or in the classroom. Subject guides or collections are also useful in reference queries because librarians answering questions may or may not be familiar with the subject area of the questions. Subject guides are also helpful in education and training.

Linking to free external resources should be used judiciously. Finding and organizing links to external sites consumes a great deal of time and they must be regularly checked and evaluated for continuity and quality control (Ryan, 2003). Therefore it is best to link only to well-established sites. As noted in Chapter 7, external link selection criteria should also be consistent with the library's collection development policy. Each external link should be evaluated for currency, authority, organization, and accessibility.

Dahl (2001) recommends that links to subject guides should be easy to locate on the library home page. Libraries should also consider putting subject guide records in the local online catalog to give them more exposure because some evidence suggests that this may increase their use (Jackson and Pellack, 2004; Simpson et al., 2005). The use of subject guides can be demonstrated at library instructional sessions when patrons are most likely to use them.

There are a number of maintenance issues with subject guides. Subject guides need to be checked and updated frequently. Free link checkers are available that will test access and detect bad connections or redirected pages, which may indicate a change in authoring agency. At some institutions, an automated link checker is run every month to check all of the sites listed in the guides. Even with a link checker, the links should always be reviewed manually to determine if the URL or content of the page has changed. Examples of free link checkers are WWW Consortium Link Checker (http://www.w3.org/QA/Tools/), which allows one to enter a URL to check for dead links, DoctorHTML (http://www.fixing yourweb site.com/drhtml.html), and Web Design Group's HTML Validator (http://www.htmlhelp.com/tools/validator). Guides should always include page revision dates.

Over the past few years, librarians have been exploring alternative ways to quickly create and update subject guides and to make them more accessible and engaging. These newer methods, such content management tools, database driven solutions, and Web 2.0 tools are cost-effective options and improve the process of updating content.

A new fee-based content management tool called LibGuides (http://www.springshare.com/libguides) has become increasingly popular in health care libraries because it allows librarians to quickly create subject guides, course guides, or information portals on a wide variety of clinical and biomedical research topics in a customizable fashion using Web 2.0 applications. While the top banner and color scheme of the home page can be customized with local library branding, LibGuides has the same structure with a home page and tab navigation system for secondary pages within the guide. Librarians can also create a profile box that contains standard contact information and a photograph. Other options include embedded widgets for instant messaging, podcasts, RSS feeds, links to the library catalog, and interactive polls. LibGuides can also be linked to other Web 2.0 applications such as Facebook, Twitter, and Delicious. LibGuides keeps detailed usage statistics and includes a handy Post to LibGuides toolbar feature for librarians to use to populate links in the guides when browsing the Web. Management in Action 10.1 describes how a hospital library manager saw a product such as LibGuides as a possible solution to improving user access to resources when other technologies weren't available.

Corrado and Frederick (2008) review popular open source, database-driven solutions that have been used by libraries to streamline maintenance tasks related to subject guides and they discuss the functionality, strengths, and weaknesses of each option. The authors recommend social bookmarking and wiki applications for smaller

MANAGEMENT IN ACTION 10.1

Overcoming Technological Limitations to Improve User Access to Resources

Location: Library Services in a Three-Hospital System.

Description of Problem/Project: The hospital system IT department controls user access to all patient and financial information through an enterprise portal that authenticates the users. Since there is no web-based intranet, all of the electronic resources provided by the libraries have to be accessed through this same portal so that patrons can use them offsite. Patrons download a Citrix client to their home or office computers to access the proxy server. The portal has a limited number of publishing forms so there is little flexibility in how resources can be presented. Single resources such as commercial databases, article link resolvers, and the online catalog are represented with icons that are programmed by IT to invoke the Citrix client to provide offsite access. Subject lists such as journals licensed by only one library or subject guides to resources can not use the Citrix client. The librarians were looking for a better way to present some of their resources for ease of access by library customers. The e-books are included in the online catalog and they recently added e-books to their link resolver, but neither of these approaches has been totally satisfactory in providing users with a convenient way to know about them and access them. In addition, the librarians wanted to provide subject guides to support the work of the various teams they work with in the hospital such as patient safety, ethics committee, and nursing research council.

Impact On: Library customers, library staff.

People Involved: Library staff, IT department, product vendor, colleagues in other libraries.

Strategies for Success: One of the library managers learned about a product called LibGuides that could be licensed to create subject-specific webpages. They looked at the pages of other libraries including hospital libraries that use LibGuides. They thought this would be a way to provide access using Web 2.0 technology that they currently couldn't use. They could showcase their e-books and other web resources on an attractive platform. The resources could include embedded URLs so their patrons could go directly to the resource. The link to LibGuides could be on the portal page for users to access offsite but could also be something internal users could bookmark on their desktop browsers without going through the portal that often timed them out. The library manager contacted colleagues for feedback on ease of use and customer satisfaction and based on that information decided to approach the IT department to be sure there were no barriers to using the product. Initial contact was made with an IT director that the library manager had worked with on other projects. This IT director made the connection with the appropriate individual in charge of network security.

Barriers Encountered: The IT department had concerns that had to be addressed. First, that no Patient Health Information could somehow be compromised, and second, that there was nothing such as ActiveX controls that needed to be downloaded. These concerns were answered satisfactorily so the library manager could proceed with implementation of LibGuides.

Take-Home Points: Hospital librarians often have restrictions in using newer Web 2.0 technologies because of security issues. It is important to keep looking for solutions that provide better and easier access to resources for our customers. Having a good working relationship with the IT department is essential. When planning implementation of a new technology, library managers should review current processes to ascertain any changes that need to be made. Customer input and feedback must be solicited to ensure success.

Further Reading: Gonzalez, Alisa C., and Theresa Westbrock. 2010. "Reaching Out with LibGuides: Establishing a Working Set of Best Practices." *Journal of Library Administration* 50, no. 5/6 (July/September): 638–656.

libraries with limited budgets and staff. Social bookmarking and wiki tools are especially well-suited to hospital libraries because they can be used successfully as a subject guide platform and they do not require systems staff to be updated.

Social bookmarking sites are used for bookmarking websites, articles, images, and other web-based materials. Bookmarks are portable and are able to be accessed from any computer instead of being limited to browser-based bookmarks on the user's desktop. Librarians can easily organize the bookmarks into categories and they can be

searched by others looking to explore new websites and content. Librarians can also add descriptions and multiple tags to categorize each bookmark saved, which provides multiple access points for other users browsing tags to discover new resources. Delicious (http://www.delicious.com/), acquired by Yahoo in 2005, is one of the most popular social bookmarking sites. Kroski (2008) provides excellent information on social bookmarking tools, best practices, and examples of how libraries are using social bookmarking. Herzog (2007) offers a useful resource guide for creating subject guides utilizing Delicious.

Landau (2010), a solo hospital librarian with severe time constraints, discusses the creative use of Delicious to create a library home page and subject guide for nurses as a way to expand services beyond the hospital intranet and firewall. See sidebar for possible uses of social bookmarking in libraries.

Social Bookmarking Uses in Libraries

- Organize personal research by subject area.
- Track up-to-the-minute links on particular topics.
- Collaborate with like-minded colleagues to share web resources with comments on topics of mutual interest.
- Browse other user's tags of favorite bookmarks to discover new resources.
- Create library websites, i.e., PMC Library Webpage (http://www.delicious.com/pmclibrary).
- Create subject guides for patrons (http://www.swissarmylibrarian.net/2007/07/28/library-subject-guides-using-delicious).
- Create and share reading lists for library classes (set up class tag for easy searching).
- Provide lists of recommended resource links on library webpages.
- Display link rolls of bookmarks on sidebar of library webpage.
- Syndicate RSS feeds of library bookmarks to blogs, Facebook, Twitter, etc.
- Display tag clouds and link rolls on library webpages so users can browse tagged subject collections.

Wikis are customizable websites that allow multiple users to add, remove, and edit information on a site without the need to know any computer programming language. The ability to easily personalize and add content makes wikis ideal for team collaboration, i.e., working on collaborative websites or group projects. Examples of popular wiki programs are PBWorks (http://pbworks.com/), Webpaint (http://www.wetpaintcentral.com/), a free hosted service, and Wiki Plus, a social computing add-on for SharePoint (http://www.kwizcom.com/ProductPage.asp?ProductID=524). When selecting a wiki, librarians should consult WikiMatrix (http://www.wikimatrix.org), which provides information and comparisons of different wikis available. Excellent resources are available that provide overviews, examples of subject guides, and other ideas for using wikis in libraries (Damani and Fulton, 2010; Lombardo, Mower, and McFarland, 2008; Dennis, 2007; Sodt and Summey, 2009; Kroski, 2008; and Holmes and Dubinsky, 2009). See the sidebar for possible uses of wikis in libraries.

Wiki Uses in Libraries

Internal Uses

- Develop and update policies and procedures.
- Develop a strategic plan.
- Plan and manage projects.
- Write grant application with a team.
- Write articles and presentations with multiple authors.
- Store and update training resources and documents.
- Store and update IT department documentation.

External Uses

- Create, update, and share subject guides, i.e., Medical Matters Wiki (http://usabiomedmatters.wikidot.com/).
- Store, update, and share frequently asked reference questions.
- Store, update, and share instruction resources, i.e., handouts, tutorials, etc.
- Deliver literature search results to clinical teams.
- Create knowledge bases, i.e., HLWIKI, a wiki for health librarians (http://hlwiki.slais.ubc.ca); and Library Success, a best practices wiki for field of library and information science(http://www.libsuccess.org).

Web Portals

Current trends in web development in libraries involve the concepts of personalization, customization, and portal development. Modeled after commercial services, such as My Yahoo and Amazon.com, some libraries have built web portals in response to users' need to take control over their information environment, i.e., MyLibrary and MyNCBI services. Shedlock et al. (2010) observed that libraries began adopting portals as digital libraries grew in size and complexity. Because most library websites contain more content than users want to know or manage, libraries began creating tools to help users highlight high-quality online information sources and streamline access to frequently used websites and library resources, thereby reducing information overload that can distract and confuse users.

The terms "customization," "personalization," and library portals can be confusing, because these concepts have evolved over time and authors sometimes view them differently depending on their perspective. Nielsen (1998) distinguishes between customization and personalization. Customization occurs when the user explicitly makes selections among options, such as having the ability to select online resources to include on a MyLibrary webpage, while "personalization" is driven by the computer as a way to automatically individualize pages based on a profile of some type, i.e., online library catalogs that retain users' searches or save lists. Various definitions have been put forward for web portals. Two helpful definitions view a library portal as "a doorway that can be customized by individual users to automatically filter information from the Web" (Zhou, 2003: 120) and as "a customized learning and transactional Web environment, designed purposefully to enable an individual end-user to 'personalize' the content and look of the website for his/her own individual preference" (Lakos, 2004: 9). Shedlock et al. (2010: 98) equated customization with web portals and pointed out that this practice will play an increasingly important role in higher education. This is underscored by the *Horizon Report* that identified the personal web, which allows users to "reorganize, configure, and manage online content rather than just viewing it," as a key emerging technology that will have a large impact on teaching, learning, or creative inquiry on college and university campuses within the next five years (Johnson, Levine, and Smith, 2009: 19).

Boss (2008) has suggested common features for library portals. He maintains that a portal is not a mere gateway to select online resources, but that a portal combines a number of elements: (1) an easy-to-navigate user interface that can be personalized using user-profile information to deliver personalized content, (2) federated searching or the ability to search across multiple databases and sources with a single search, (3) a patron authentication component that authorizes and certifies that users qualify to use the library portal and electronic resources through a single authorization, and (4) link resolvers that allow users to navigate from search results or citations to full-text, or a catalog search for materials about the same topic, or to an interlibrary loan request. See the sidebar for common features of library portals.

Common Features of Library Portals

- User interface that stores profiles
- Federated searching
- Patron authentication
- Link resolvers to resources, catalog, reference, and document delivery services
- Management information and usage statistics

Four basic approaches exist for creating library portals: building a portal, joining a campus or institutional portal, partnering with other libraries for portal development, or hiring a portal vendor. Another particularly interesting development for libraries concerns "vortals," which Zhou (2003: 127) defines for libraries as "a portal that organizes information in a hierarchical subject structure." Little

(2001) suggests that building subject guides as vortals may be a first step in supporting the university-wide enterprise portal and the channel distribution system.

Besides developing stand-alone library portals, some libraries are investigating the promising and cost-effective alternative of providing library information to their patrons through one or more "channels" on their parent institution's portal. Channels are modules of a portal that can appear as a small block of screen space or as a folder tab with either dynamic or static content. They have the capability of delivering prepopulated information resources and services based on user profiles within a course management system, such as Blackboard or WebCT, or a campus or organization portal (McDonald, 2004). In times of tight budgets and given the high cost of portal development, academic health sciences libraries can take advantage of services and expertise of campus technology staff and the fact that campus portals may be more likely to be used by faculty and students than stand-alone library portals (Stoffel and Cunningham, 2005). Likewise in the hospital library environment, libraries can explore opportunities to participate in larger institutional portal efforts (Bandy and Fosmire, 2004).

The technology used to create portals is inherently complex and libraries will need access to technical support and expertise either among the staff or in collaboration with other IT departments to develop an in-house portal, manage commercial portal applications, or develop and integrate library channels into other portals. Shedlock et al. (2010) provides an informative case study that outlines and assesses benefits and issues of implementing a locally developed library portal tool in an academic health sciences library. Boss (2002) provides an overview of major third-party library portal vendors and lists of open-source portal software that are available. Most vendors of integrated library systems also offer a portal feature. Librarians can consult with the website of their library's integrated library system vendor to learn more about portal services. Excellent resources on library portals are available in the library literature and on the web (Boss, 2002; Zhou, 2003; Library of Congress, 2004; Lakos, 2004 [special section on portals]; Michalak, 2005; and Shedlock et al, 2010). More portal information can also be found on the EDUCAUSE website by browsing the term "portal" (http://www.educause.edu/Resources/Browse/Portals/17599).

Managing Off-Site Customers

In today's mobile society with ubiquitous computing and fast Internet access from homes and workplaces, providing affiliated users with remote access to the library's electronic resources and services is a necessity. Libraries subscribe to many electronic resources and journals, which have license agreements that almost always limit use to on-site users or to affiliated users. Generally, authentication is handled by vendors through IP authentication, also called IP validation or IP filtering, although some vendors provide username/password authentication, e.g., PDA software licenses. In the case of IP authentication, librarians comply with license agreements by registering qualified IP addresses with the vendors who, in turn, allow access from any computers with a valid address within the registered IP range. For situations where vendors provide password authentication, it is the responsibility of librarians to distribute them to patrons and keep track of the passwords for multiple different resources. Because managing passwords can be time-consuming and confusing, it is standard practice for librarians to insist on IP authentication when negotiating licenses.

Given this highly restrictive environment, the question for libraries is how best to provide remote access to legitimate affiliated users who want and need to access library resources from a wide variety of off-site locations. Customers expect easy 24/7 access and vendors require access by valid users only. Librarians must balance these needs and create mutually beneficial solutions for both vendors and users (Lawrence, 2009).

Academic health sciences librarians have the advantage of being able to work with their campus IT departments to determine the best way to authenticate affiliated users and provide them with off-campus access using highly sophisticated, reliable, and secure methods. Hospital librarians have a bigger challenge because they struggle with limited IT support, firewall issues, and hospital IT staff who are very concerned with breaches of network security that may compromise the hospital network and patient confidentially. Lawrence (2009) observed that most connection problems that are reported relate to computer or workplace firewalls. Mitchell and Ennis (2010) suggest that hospital librarians obtain an understanding of the technology behind firewalls in order to work with their hospital's IT department to develop network firewall policies, obtain agreed-upon exceptions in the hospital's firewall, and implement good remote access solutions for library customers.

To provide assistance to remote customers outside regular working hours, it is important that libraries provide well-documented instructions, guidelines, and FAQs on the library webpages. Webpages should include contact names, e-mail addresses, and phone numbers of staff who can provide assistance, should self-help guides

be insufficient. Chat reference can also be option for remote users to start the help process.

TYPES OF REMOTE ACCESS TO ELECTRONIC RESOURCES AND SERVICES

There are a variety of current and evolving methods for providing access to electronic resources to off-site customers. These are outlined below along with the advantages and disadvantages of each.

1. **Dial-in access**: Some institutions still provide dial-in modem access through dial-in server(s) for users that do not use commercial Internet Service Providers (ISPs). Because users are increasingly getting high-speed Internet access using DSL and cable modem technologies via commercial ISPs, the use of dial-in access has dropped off significantly in recent years.

2. **Proxy server**: A popular way of providing off-site access is by a proxy server that is usually managed by the organization's IT department. A proxy server requires users to log in or authenticate with a username and password assigned by the organization or campus. When the user logs in, the program operates as a go-between between users and the vendor's database. Since the server software runs on a validated network, the database vendor sees the requests as coming from an IP address on the campus network and allows access. Some proxy servers require users to configure their own browsers, which needs to be turned on and off. This requires the library to provide directions for multiple browsers and for turning the configuration on and off after use.

   Another type of proxy server is a "URL rewriting" proxy server. An example of this type of server is EZproxy (http://www.oclc.org/us/en/ezproxy/default.htm), which was purchased by OCLC in 2008. Once the user has logged in, the proxy server rewrites each URL requested and routes it though the server's IP address. Besides vendor databases, the library's online catalog as well as other course management systems can be proxied (Lawrence, 2009). Any browser can work with this type of server, which is very convenient for the user and librarian. Similar to other proxy servers, a URL rewriting server works with a list of URLs of library resources that the library subscribes to. This list must be kept up-to-date with frequent configuration changes as electronic resources are added and removed. Like other remote access methods, some browser, operating system, and specific database combinations can be problematic. Firewalls also present difficulties so a special configured network connection should be used that is outside the campus firewall (Lawrence, 2009).

3. **Virtual private network**: Many universities, large organizations, and companies create their own virtual private network (VPN) over the Internet to transport encrypted data in a way that gives only authorized users remote access to on-site networks and resources. VPNs work at a network infrastructure layer below that of a web proxy server, but they accomplish the same result in a highly secure manner. Similar to a proxy server, users must have their own ISP, log in to the network, and then they are authenticated into the vendor's resource by IP address.

4. **Athens access management**: The Athens Management System, also referred to as Athens, is a purchased service that enables off-site customers to get access to library resources. Kraft provides a very useful review of Athens in *JMLA* (Kraft, 2008). Athens is available from Eduserv Technologies and since its introduction at the Medical Library Association Annual Meeting in 2006, hospital libraries have begun using Athens as a method for remote access. Athens offers users a single sign-on using a simple access portal called MyAthens and does not require the installation of any software or hardware.

Once a library subscribes to Athens, it is given an Athens ID number that the librarian then gives to each online database and journal provider. Many online publishers are "Athens-enabled;" a full list can be found at http://www.athensams.net/dsp/. Even though a large number of vendors participate, not all vendors are Athens-enabled so librarians will need to contact each subscribed vendor and request that they activate Athens authentication for off-site access. Librarians also need to set up and maintain a patron and resource database in Athens. Librarians can populate the patron database in several ways through a local authentication database, a bulk upload, manually, or patron self-registration. All users in the database are given their own unique username and password, which is used to log into all of the library's online resources. Once library customers are added to the database, they are able to view their account and access online library resources using the library's own webpages or via the MyAthens portal at the vendor website. The single sign-on enables users to conduct research without the need to constantly log in to each resource. Maintenance of the resource and patron database and contacting vendors about MyAthens activation require some time and effort on the part of the librarian. Even though there are some maintenance tasks for the librarian, Athens is ideal for hospital libraries with limited budgets and technical support, and with firewall issues, because they can offer affiliated users remote access to online resources by giving them their own personal log in and password that works for all the library's online products.

5. **Shibboleth**: Shibboleth is an emerging technology that refers to an open source, standards-based access management solution based on Security Assertion Markup Language (SAML). Shibboleth's basic premise is that it provides or prohibits access to electronic content on the basis of individual users' attributes, as opposed to IP authentication or username/password credentials that are now widely used by libraries and vendors. The Shibboleth initiative started in February 2000 as a project of Internet2 and a leading group of campus middleware architects (Thompson, 2006). Shibboleth is now in release 2.2.0 and has been implemented by many websites spanning academia, research, government and industry.

The user uses a single sign-on to gain access to all resources to which they are entitled. Since the access management infrastructure is web-based, there is no connection to the physical location of the user. On the vendor side, there is no more need for IP address management, which currently requires a great deal of administrative support (Thompson, 2006). Another key advantage with Shibboleth is its distributed infrastructure that allows users to maintain their privacy with vendors, because all personal identity information is maintained at the user's institution. For up-to-date information on Shibboleth, including FAQs, technical specifications, and lists of Shibboleth-enabled vendors, readers can visit the Shibboleth website at http://shibboleth.internet2.edu/shib-intro.html.

Mediated Search Services

Many libraries provide assistance to their health care institutions through mediated online searches and personalized consulting as a way of meeting the information and educational needs of the individual user. Both of these user-centered services are highly relevant in today's library because they add value to the information search, retrieval, and evaluation process through the assistance, guidance, and instruction of a highly trained and experienced expert searcher. Homan (2010: 55) notes that health science librarians as expert intermediaries and knowledge coaches have continuing relevance in the evolving digital ecology and "promote both individual and institutional success in the context of patient care excellence, patient safety, research competitiveness, and conservation of that scarce and precious resource of time for decision making." Mediated searching is defined as database searching that is done by someone other than the person who uses the search results (Jankowski, 2008). When a librarian performs an online search for an end-user, the librarian is often referred to as expert intermediary or expert searcher. Other terms that are used interchangeably for mediated searching are database searching, literature searching, online searching, and expert searching. Mediated searching is often contrasted to end-user searching, which is characterized as database searching performed by the individual (end user) who directly uses the results and information that are retrieved in the search.

Mediated search services have been offered by health care libraries for many years. This is especially true of the hospital library environment where many clinical cases require the close review and evaluation of available evidence by an expert searcher. The origins of mediated searching reach back to the 1960s when the first databases were developed and searching was done almost exclusively by librarians. As database interfaces became more user-friendly in the late 1980s and Internet usage became more commonplace in the 1990s, end-user searching became the norm. In recent years, there has been a renewed interest in mediated searching by expert librarians. Prompted by an increased emphasis on evidence-based practice and quality literature searching by highly trained experts, the Medical Library Association has forcefully promoted the unique value and critical role of librarians as expert searchers in health care and biomedical research through publications, presentations, and continuing-education courses (Medical Library Association, 2010b). As a result, mediated searching, or expert searching, is actively practiced and promoted by librarians in both hospital and academic libraries.

The expert search interview differs somewhat from other reference interviews in that there is an emphasis on the iterative and collaborative nature which is necessary

for comprehensive literature searches. Jankowski (2008) sees the interview as "a continuous cycle" that begins during the preliminary discussion before the search is run (pre-search phase), with checkpoints throughout the search process at which times the expert searcher checks back with the user to renegotiate the search (search phase). The process concludes (postsearch phase) with documentation, including a cover letter, search strategy and results, and a postsearch evaluation of the results and process, which may begin the cycle again to explore another avenue or start a new question.

With the widespread adoption of evidence-based medicine, clinicians often structure their search requests as well-built clinical questions using the PICO mnemonic (Patient/Population, Intervention, Comparative Intervention, Outcome Desired). Three techniques for building search strategies are in common use: the building block method, successive fractions method, and the pearl-growing technique. These techniques are used separately or in combination, depending on the personal preference of the expert searcher, the topic in question, and database search features available. In her excellent training guide, Jankowski (2008) recommends that both natural language (keywords) and subject descriptors (MeSH terms) be used in combination for the most successful comprehensive searches. Searching on any given topic almost always requires the searching of multiple databases due to the complementary nature of databases and the increasingly interdisciplinary nature of research. Multiple databases should be searched sequentially if possible rather than through a federated search engine due to the lack of common access points and vocabularies across databases.

Many libraries furnish structured search request forms for customers to complete and submit at the desk or via a web-based form. These requests will require a follow-up discussion to further define the user's information needs. Some libraries charge patrons a fee for mediated searches because of budgetary constraints. Search fees vary based on local conditions. Some are set up to allow free mediated searches under a certain number of citations, while others are based on time spent processing the search, direct vendor charges, and the method of delivery of the results.

Expert Consultation Services

To address the need for more in-depth and customized user assistance, most libraries now have added a research consultation model and provide appointment-based research consultations and one-on-one instruction on use of library resources. Expert consults are an ideal solution for customers with lengthy and complex research or educational needs that require more time on the part of the librarian than answering a typical reference query. Scheduling procedures for research consults differ for each library. Some libraries ask customers to contact the reference desk or appropriate liaison librarian, while others provide a web-based consultation appointment request form.

Expert searching and consultation play a critical role in conducting a rigorous examination of the published evidence prior to clinical and administrative decision making, in research studies, and in the training of health care providers. Attebury, Sprague, and Young (2009) summarize additional benefits of research consults that have been reported in the literature. Among the benefits they mention is the fact that one-on-one sessions deal with the actual immediate needs of customers rather than needs perceived by librarians because face-to-face sessions provide instant feedback for both the librarian and user. The consultation model also allows the librarian to prepare ahead of time, adjust the session for different learning styles, and allow focused time with the user free of interruptions. In addition, highly personalized librarian-mediated services promote good public relations and a positive public image of the librarian as expert searcher and knowledge coach.

Expert consultation requires the same knowledge base and skill set required for expert searching, clinical medical librarians, and embedded information specialists. Librarians consult in many areas that include:

- evidence-based search methodology and literature evaluation;
- systematic reviews;
- current awareness searches and e-mail alerts;
- database evaluation and selection;
- expert search instructional design and training;
- bibliographic management technology; and
- publishing, journal selection practices for indexing in databases, NIH deposits, and copyright.

Expert consultations can take place in the library, clinical and research settings, departmental offices or meeting rooms, laboratories, or classrooms. Librarians serve as expert consultants on a wide variety of clinical and biomedical research teams providing clinical and research decision support. They also use their knowledge and expertise in database searching to create and share "hedges," defined as "a list of terms that are either synonymous, related, or of variant spelling" (Alpi and Delgado, 2007: 14). Hedges are used as one of the building blocks of a search strategy.

Outreach Service Model

Many librarians contribute their skills, talents, and resources in proactive and creative ways to enhance the activities and goals of their user communities at locations outside the physical library. Tao et al. (2009) described a department-specific outreach project in an academic medical center library that delivered onsite reference service with regular hours to public health faculty, students, and staff located at a remote campus location. The authors noted a marked increase in the numbers of reference inquiries and liaison contacts by this population, and in the use of in-library services and resources as compared to previous years, as well as other benefits, as directly attributable to the onsite service. Handler, Lackey, and Vaughan (2009) described department-specific outreach programs that offered a combination of onsite and online reference office hours in three different schools and observed that they produced positive secondary benefits, such as increased good will for the library, stronger teaching and research partnerships, and enhanced librarian-faculty relationships. Freiburger and Kramer (2009) believed the implementation of decentralized models of embedded liaisons in three academic programs were successful, based on the inclusion of liaisons in numerous grants, significant increases in teaching activities, and enhanced user perceptions of the role of librarians. Polger (2010) describes delivering all hospital library services to clinical units in the hospital and reported that the outreach program significantly increased the number of library instruction sessions, as well as the usage of other services, and had a positive impact on the clinicians' professional lives.

Hospital librarians also provide outreach support within their institutions by actively participating on committees and teams that focus on improving patient care. Some librarians serve in a consultant status on committees and teams while other librarians serve as permanent members. Librarians are proactively involved with patient safety teams and institutional review boards to provide information and promote the role of evidenced-based decisions (Zipperer and Sykes, 2004; Frumento and Keating, 2007). Bandy, Condon, and Graves (2008) described various examples of hospital librarian participation in clinical microsystems or multidisciplinary teams in a hospital to improve patient care. They noted numerous benefits of participation for both the community of practice participants and the librarian.

Clinical Medical Librarian (CML) Service Model

Librarians also extend library and information services into the clinical health care environment by serving as clinical team members and clinical medical librarians. Clinical medical librarian (CML) services have been implemented in a variety of clinical settings since the 1970s. Librarians accompany physicians on patient rounds (Burdick, 2004; Brandes, 2007), participate in teaching conferences and journal clubs (Wagner and Byrd, 2004; Bandy, Condon, and Graves, 2008), and attend morning report (Atlas et al., 2003; Schwing and Coldsmith, 2005; Banks et al., 2007), where they provide expert searching assistance, critical appraisal of results, and training in collaboration with clinicians and other health professionals. The added value and benefits of these clinical collaborations are manifold and have been well described in the literature. Wagner and Byrd's (2004) systematic review of studies of CML programs is particularly helpful in showing the general characteristics of these programs in various clinical settings over a 30-year period. Cumulatively, the studies show that health care professionals found the information provided by the librarians to be useful and of high quality and CML services contributed to improved patient care. Other key benefits of librarian-generated searches and assistance at the point of clinical need have been described in recent literature. Librarian support within clinical teams has changed patient protocols (Brandes, 2007), enhanced the educational experience of students and residents (Atlas et al., 2003; Schwing and Coldsmith, 2005), and led to a positive impact on length of stay and hospital charges (Banks et al., 2007). See Chapter 12 for more discussion of this service.

Informationist in Context Model

The informationist in context service model, also called the information specialist in context (ISIC) model, has grown out of long standing library outreach practices, such as the work of hospital librarians serving as full members of clinical teams, academic library liaisons working outside the library, and the clinical medical librarian model. The informationist model was first proposed by Davidoff and Florance (2000), who described this emerging professional as a clinical knowledge worker who is trained in both information and clinical sciences and able to find, appraise, synthesize, and present medical information for clinical health care teams. Following Davidoff and Florance's editorial, both the National Library of Medicine and MLA provided strong support in the further development and implementation of the concept. NLM sponsored a special conference at NLM (Shipman et al., 2002) and offered a grant program for informationist training fellowships for several years. MLA also played an active leadership role in spurring strong interest in the model by hosting an open forum at an annual meeting and appointing a Task Force that commissioned a report to define roles and training needs and to advance the implementation of the informationist model (Giuse, Sathe, and Jerome, 2006).

Since the original editorial, there has been a sustained interest in the model as reflected in programs springing up in clinical, biomedical research, and public health settings, and in the numerous case reports and opinion papers about informationists that have appeared in the literature. Rankin, Grefsheim, and Canto (2008) synthesized the literature related to the informationist between the years 2000–2006, pointing out that the informationist concept is currently in the early adopter stage, and proposed four defining program attributes based on the literature: formal training in both information sciences and a subject domain; deep understanding of work culture; in-context work as team member and/or expert consultant; and skills in critical appraisal/literature synthesis and/or bioscience data analysis. While the definition of informationist in context is somewhat in flux, there is a general consensus that both subject domain and information science knowledge are defining attributes of the model. This characteristic differentiates this model from the other outreach models described above, i.e., clinical medical librarians. While there is still little evidence of the effectiveness of existing informationist programs, Rankin, Grefsheim and Canto (2008) highlighted many positive outcomes of the studies, some of which include adding staff and resources as a result of the expanded role, user satisfaction with the programs, personal growth of librarian participants, and increased usage of other library services. See Chapter 12 for more discussion of this service model.

Current Awareness Services

Current awareness services (CAS) provide library customers with a different information experience than searching does. CAS or information awareness is different from explicit information seeking or literature searching in that it provides awareness of relevant content and references proactively. The goal of CAS is not necessarily to delve deeply into a particular topic, but rather to have an overall picture of what information might be available on a topic. Awareness tools aim to make customers aware of potentially useful information sources in a timely manner. The past and present CAS tools are only a fore-shadowing of future developments combining many Internet and database technologies such as described by Powell, Collins, and Martinez (2009).

Before the advent of e-journals, scientists and physicians would come to the library to scan print journals for new information as well as reading their personal subscriptions. Many also subscribed to *Current Contents* from ISI and even purchased postcards that they would send to authors to request reprints. In addition, information services departments would provide current awareness services to complement this activity. Previously called Selective Dissemination of Information (SDI), in the 1970s there were manual and automated services involving NLM's SDILINE and the print monthly *Index Medicus* (Wood and Seeds, 1974; Yunis, 1973). Many libraries had services that copied and circulated print tables of contents or even routed the entire journal. For many years the capability of creating stored searches on very specific subjects that could be executed on a periodic basis have been provided by database vendors such as Ovid, Dialog, and PubMed. PubMed's My NCBI and Ovid's AutoAlert system are perhaps the most used in health care libraries. These can be received via e-mail and now by RSS feed. Librarians can help users set up efficient searches, teach these technologies, and provide help screens on their websites.

Customers can be encouraged to set up individual e-mail alerts from individual journals. Electronic Table of Contents (eTOC) is easy to do and is done at each publisher's site. Concerning these various methods, Johnson, Osmond, and Holz (2009: 52) list the disadvantages:

- Print material routed to multiple people moves slowly.
- Distributing photocopies of tables of contents is labor intensive.
- Browsing print material requires extra time and active participation, even if they were available in the digital age.
- Saved searches used as auto-alerts require the customer to be expert in this area and make continual search amendments.
- E-mail alerts flood inboxes already overflowing with unread items.

The technology RSS (really simple syndication) is more complicated than eTOC but can be convenient. Several articles describe how libraries have used RSS feeds (Badman and Hartman, 2008; Cooke, 2006; Farkas, 2008; Fletcher, 2009; Landau 2010; Rothman, 2007). RSS was originally used for reading multiple blogs and news sites all at once. Instead of going out to blogs or news sites of interest one at a time using bookmarks or a favorites list, an RSS feed allows the user to access one place and look at many sites at a time. Journal publishers started using RSS in the early 2000s and now most journals provide eTOC RSS feeds with abstracts provided. For those that don't, another option is a PubMed RSS feed. David Rothman's *Favorite RSS Resources and Tools* is listed in the sidebar. Health care librarians will find the book *Internet Cool Tools for Physicians* by Rethlefsen, Rothman, and Mojon (2009) very helpful as well.

One very innovative project in this area comes from the Ebling Library for the Health Sciences, University of Wisconsin–Madison. (http://ebling.library.wisc.edu/rss/index.cfm). As described by Johnson, Osmond, and Holz (2008), the library used an outline processor markup language (OPML) to collect and bundle journal feeds. Access to the tables of contents is not limited to affiliated users of the Ebling Library although access to the full text will depend on the end-user's own affiliation.

In between total use of RSS feeds and the simpler email eTOCs is a British site called ticTOCs Journal Tables of Contents Service. This service makes it easy for library users to keep up-to-date with newly published scholarly material by enabling them to find, display, store, combine, and reuse thousands of journal tables of contents from multiple publishers (http://www.tictocs.ac.uk/).

Explanation of RSS Technology

There is an excellent video on the basics at Common Craft (http://www.commoncraft.com/rss_plain_english). Another site is David Rothman's *Favorite RSS Resources and Tools* (http://davidrothman.net/2008/01/14/favorite-rss-resources-and-tools/). The first step is to subscribe to a feed reader. Evaluate the various readers as they do act differently. Some, such as Google Reader, are on the Web and some operate as an add-on to your browser. An overview of this selection process can be found at http://rss-tutorial.com/rss-select-an-rss-reader.htm. If this takes too much time just choose one of the most popular, Google Reader. Then find your favorite blogs, news feeds, and journals and click on the orange or blue RSS symbol. Confirm adding the feed to the reader. Organize the feeds into folders. Go to the RSS Reader periodically and review all new eTOCs, blogs, and news. Welcome to 21st century current awareness!

Tracking Use of Information Services

Techniques of evaluation and assessment of services are covered in Chapter 6 but there are unique problems with what to count and how to count information services. Logan (2009: 225) states, "Does a hash mark really reflect the reference transaction? And does a statistic adequately represent the quality or value of reference?" Each type of information service reviewed in this chapter could be the target of an assessment. Suggested measurement categories include number of transactions, accuracy of answers, quality of the service encounter, and patron satisfaction. Each of these categories would reflect the purpose of the evaluation. Logan (2009) in his comprehensive article gives a broad overview of the trends in these areas. Høivik (2003) covers the issues involved in reporting statistics for reference.

Reports in the literature reflect many methods that are being tried to develop criteria for evaluation. Most now use a database system where many criteria can be captured for various dimensions for various uses. Good examples of a multidimensional database use can be found in Smith (2006) and in Garrison (2010). Many libraries today have database systems available to them such as MySQL, Access, or FileMaker Pro. Often these systems can be made available on the web for the staff to fill out a data entry form.

The first question is: What is a transaction? Every reference transaction would be a record in the database. A record would be started by either recording the question or by checking off a more basic question such as a directional question. The Association of Research Libraries (ARL) recently provided this definition for their 2009 annual questionnaire:

> A reference transaction is an information contact that involves the knowledge, use, recommendations, interpretation, or instruction in the use of one or more information sources by a member of the library staff.

The term includes information and referral service. Information sources include (a) printed and nonprinted material; (b) machine-readable databases (including computer-assisted instruction); (c) the library's own catalogs and other holdings records; (d) other libraries and institutions through communication or referral; and (e) persons both inside and outside the library. When a staff member uses information gained from previous use of information sources to answer a question, the transaction is reported as a reference transaction even if the source is not consulted again. (Association of Research Libraries, 2009)

If the library reports to ARL, the total count of records for the year could be the figure reported.

The subsequent question regarding staffing is: how long did it take to answer the question and at what staffing level? This could require a categorization such as represented in Figure 10.4. The categories were developed by Warner (2001) and recently adapted by Meserve et al. (2009). Gerlich and Berard (2007, 2010) have developed a similar scale called the READ Scale (Reference Effort Assessment Data). Their point is that "counting traffic numbers at the traditional reference desk is no longer sufficient as a measurement that reflects the effort, skill, and knowledge associated with this work" (Gerlich and Berard, 2010: 117). As total reference questions continue to drop, this kind of categorization can show that the complexity rises and the time it takes to answer the questions continues to grow (Garrison, 2010).

Other dimensions of the customer interaction could be:

- How did the question originate and how much time did it take? Was the question received in-person at the desk, by telephone, by email, or from an online

Figure 10.4. Categories of Reference Service

Level I: Nonresource-based	Questions that do not require a resource to answer and might be answered by a sign or help sheet (e.g., geographic or policy questions). Usually answered at the service desk.
Level II: Skill-based	Questions that require a demonstration to answer (i.e., "how-to" questions that might be answered by a well-developed set of directions). Most often the library staff must move to a location and demonstrate a skill. The same question should always get the same answer.
Level III: Strategy-based	Questions that require the formulation of a strategy to locate an answer and require selection of resources. May require individualized subject approaches.
Level IV: Consultation	Usually longer encounters outside of regular desk duty. May be for the selection of curriculum materials. The librarian will often have to research recommendations or prepare reports for consultation work.

Source: Adapted from Warner, 2001: 53.

digital reference services? Was the librarian in the field on an outreach project? How is this activity recorded? (Del Bosque and Chapman, 2007)

- Why is this question being asked and by whom? These questions could help steer planning efforts to see who is using the service or how the clientele is growing in complexity (Garrison, 2010).

- What resources were used? This would add a dimension to the online use statistics being gathered and help in decisions to purchase expensive databases.

- Evaluation of staff performance: As mentioned above, are they answering the questions correctly? A field to record the answer or copy in the whole online search strategy would help supervisors review responses in a more efficient manner.

- Use for marketing and promotion: Is this activity improving information literacy? Can there be a field where you can build a library "story" of success or a change in someone's life, a story that could be used in promotion? We tend to forget the stories but they could be recorded here right after they happened.

- What about librarian initiated interactions or contacts? When a librarian sees a piece of information a customer would like and e-mails it to him or her, this could be recorded.

- Integration with web statistics of virtual reference. This concept is covered in Welch, 2007.

The value of such a system is that it can collect statistics in one place for many uses. Each question should have a purpose. To encourage the staff to participate in the data collection, the manager should show them the results of their effort and they should see this information used in reports. Some libraries are using commercial web-based products such as Desk Tracker (http://www.desktracker.com/) or RefTracker (http://www.altarama.com/page/RefTracker.aspx) for this purpose.

The quality of the service encounter and patron satisfaction cannot be answered by such a database. Quality evaluations have their own problems (Logan, 2009; Smith, 2006). Chapter 6 covers general information on measuring quality. Chapter 12 discusses looking at outcomes of information services. Logan (2009: 231) states: "Individual programs should develop their own list of qualities associated with good reference service." His suggested list of qualities of a reference service is noted in the sidebar. Logan concludes that while there is no ideal measurement tool, "every reference department

must nonetheless examine its service" so that it can "define and articulate its level of commitment to meeting people's information needs" (Logan, 2009: 231).

Qualities of a Reference Service

Behavioral characteristics:
- Attitude
- Ability to communicate
- Approachability

Basic knowledge of resources and collections

Subject knowledge

Reference skills:
- Ability to discern appropriate level of help
- When to refer
- Use of resources
- Time limitations
- Interviewing technique
- Relevance
- Accuracy
- Perspective
- Bias

Training and Maintaining Skills

The educational policy statement of MLA, available on the **accompanying CD-ROM**, has a direct bearing on information services. The policy states that "lifelong learning must be a cornerstone of every individual's professional development plan to achieve success in the health sciences environment and that individuals must assume greater personal responsibility for defining their ongoing learning goals" (Medical Library Association, 2007). As such, health care librarians need to proactively seek lifelong education and professional development opportunities throughout their careers to develop and enhance their knowledge and skills of information services, including the health sciences environment, information technology, and research methodology, specifically critical appraisal and filtering of research literature. Employers of health care librarians should also place a high priority on staff development and make it an explicit budget objective with earmarked funds devoted to regular training activities because ongoing training is an essential ingredient of a library's success. Continuous learning keeps staff up-to-date, stimulates innovation, and leads to continuous improvement of information services.

Four basic staff competencies are required to ensure that the library offers high quality information services.

Various self-study training programs and resources are available for each competency. See also the **CD-ROM**.

1. **Conducting an effective reference interview**
   - The Ross, Nilsen, and Radford workbook (2009) that focuses on learning and practicing traditional reference interviewing skills one skill at a time.
   - RUSA offers an 8-module online course on the reference interview (http://www.ala.org/ala/mgrps/divs/rusa/development/referenceinterview/).
   - Ohio Library Council's Ohio Reference Excellence (ORE) on the web provides an online self-study program that includes modules on the reference interview (http://www.olc.org/ore/).
   - Reference interviewing resources and training for support staff is available at LibrarySupportStaff.com (http://librarysupportstaff.com/librefpg.html#interview).

2. **Finding and using core reference materials**
   - Huber, Boorkman, and Blackwell's (2008) unique and comprehensive work describes key health sciences reference sources that are consulted for specific and immediate information.
   - Cassell and Hiremath (2009) discuss the nature of answering reference questions, developing answering skills, and identifying common pitfalls. This process involves categorizing the answer as well as determining what type of answer is needed. The work also has descriptions of major health resources used in reference work.
   - Definitions of a reference question from the data definitions of the 2007 MLA Benchmarking Survey (http://mlanet.org/resources/benchmark07/definitions.html).
   - Definitions of reference transactions (ALA, ARL, and NCES) (http://www.ala.org/ala/mgr ps/divs/rusa/resources/guidelines/definitionsref erence.cfm).
   - RUSA's "Guidelines for Behavioral Performance of Reference and Information Service Providers" (http://www.ala.org/ala/mgrps/divs/rusa/resources/guidelines/guidelinesbehavioral.cfm).
   - RUSA's "Guidelines for Medical, Legal, and Business Responses" (http://www.ala.org/ala/mgrps/divs/rusa/resources/guidelines/guidelinesmedical.cfm).

3. **Mediated searching**
   - Librarians should read Jankowski's training guide (2008) that provides information, practice exercises, and resources on expert searching.
   - *Bates InfoTip Newsletter* (http://www.batesinfo.com/index.html) provides information and tips on information retrieval for expert searchers.
   - MLA's Public Services Section manages a moderated listserv on expert searching (http://pss.mlanet.org/mailman/listinfo/expertsearching_pss.mlanet.org).
   - "Expert Searchers" column in the *MLA News* (http://mlanet.org/members/mla_news/) that appears quarterly features information and tips on expert searching.
   - NLM Training Manuals used in classes offered by NTCC are available online (http://www.nlm.nih.gov/pubs/web_based.html).
   - The NLM Technical Bulletin covers specific NLM database features, indexing issues, and search strategies (http://www.nlm.nih.gov/pubs/techbull/).

4. **Virtual reference**
   - The Ross, Nilsen, and Radford workbook (2009) has an excellent chapter on reference encounters in virtual environments with tips, exercises, and examples.
   - Ward (2003) article that describes the use of chat transcripts for training, including checklists.
   - "Anytime, Anywhere Answers: Building Skills for Virtual Reference" is a curriculum that was created for a Washington state Virtual Reference Project (http://vrstrain.spl.org/).
   - Ohio Library Council's Ohio Reference Excellence (ORE) on the web provides an online self-study program on Library 2.0 and virtual reference (http://www.olc.org/ore/purpose.htm).
   - Vendors of various virtual reference products provide tutorials, instructional materials, and training sessions.
     - QuestionPoint 24/7 Reference (http://questionpoint.org/education/)
     - VRLplus (http://www.altarama.com/page/Resources.aspx)
     - Tutor.com (http://www.tutor.com/libraries/products/virtual-reference)

The library work environment should support opportunities for both independent and group learning.

If an experienced librarian is available, librarians usually obtain on-the-job training from a senior staff person who serves as a role model and coach. Time should be set aside in staff meetings for informative and practical problem-solving sessions or for special monthly reference training sessions to demonstrate new resources, share difficult reference questions, and for the peer review of searches. Special in-service sessions can be arranged to practice interview and virtual reference techniques. Solo librarians can partner with librarians at nearby institutions to organize peer coaching sessions, workshops, and vendor demonstrations or create reference support groups. In addition, area librarians can work together or with a chapter group to invite outside experts to provide staff training in reference skills. Librarians also need "off-desk" time to upgrade their skills, and to continue their education through reading, distance education programs, and attending off-site classes.

Health care librarians should take advantage of self-development opportunities, such as scanning the contents of major library and health sciences journals, participating in professional listservs, browsing blogs and wikis, such as The Krafty Librarian (http://kraftyl ibrarian.com/), and using RSS feeds to increase their awareness of current trends and issues. Lists of various MLA Web 2.0 communication tools are available on MLANET at http://mlanet.org/resources/web20_resources .html. The "Weblogs—Medical Librarian" page lists numerous medical librarianship blogs (http://liswiki .org/wiki/Weblogs_-_Medical_Librarianship). Database vendors are another important continuing education source and they are increasingly offering web or video-based training. Individual health sciences librarians also need to take responsibility for their own continuing education through memberships in professional associations, such as MLA or chapter groups, and by attending face-to-face and online training sessions that these associations provide.

The Medical Library Association (MLA) strongly supports lifelong learning by offering numerous educational courses geared to health sciences librarians in conjunction with their annual and regional meetings. MLA courses are organized in tracks according to the professional competency areas as described in MLA's *Competencies for Lifelong Learning and Professional Success* (Medical Library Association, 2007).

MLA also offers a wide range of health sciences library-related online learning that covers reference fundamentals, emerging technologies, and environmental trends. MLA's eLearning opportunities include webcasts for individuals or groups, web-based courses, web-based degree programs in partnership with universities, and self-paced tutorials. Examples such as MLA's CE e-Learning courses are the Online Bootcamp for New Health Sciences Librarians, which provides a core curriculum for beginning librarians, and MLA online tutorials on evidence-based practice for health sciences librarians. Librarians can also participate in other types of independent education opportunities, such as MLA's independent reading program, a self-directed learning program that allows librarians to design their own courses of study, or discussion groups with other professionals on a topic of mutual interest. Descriptions of courses offered at MLA annual meetings appear in the MLA annual meeting registration information and on MLANET, MLA's website (http:// mlanet.org/). Course information on MLA's e-Learning programs is available from MLANET (http://mlanet .org/education/web/). These web-based courses and self-directed learning programs are ideal for librarians who find it difficult to attend courses outside the local area or for the solo librarian.

The National Network of Libraries of Medicine (NN/LM) is another major continuing education resource for hospital and academic health sciences librarians. NN/LM workshops, along with those offered by the regional medical libraries, are usually low cost or free. The National Training Center and Clearinghouse (NTCC) trains health information professionals, health professionals, and members of the general public on searching techniques of PubMed and various other NLM databases. Class descriptions, schedules by regions and locations, and registration information are available at NTCC website (http://nnlm.gov/ntcc/). NTCC also offers many online classes, webcast, and online tutorials on NLM databases that are available at http://www.nlm .nih.gov/bsd/dist_edu.html.

Other associations such as the various units of American Library Association (ALA) also offer numerous online education courses that have relevance for information services. RUSA (Reference and User Services Association) offers online courses on the reference interview and customer service via Moodle, a free web application that educators use to create online learning sites. ACRL (Association of College and Research Libraries) offers online courses on academic librarianship, and LITA (Library and Information Technology Association) offers online courses on information technology. More information on these workshops is available on the Online Learning page of the ALA website (http://www.ala.org/ala/onlinelearning/ index.cfm).

Document Delivery Services

Technology has expanded document access and delivery options beyond traditional library-to-library transactions. In today's library, a variety of nontraditional means are available to library customers to ensure them maximum accessibility. Methods include unmediated requests, direct-to-user delivery, purchase-on-demand options, and increasing full-text availability.

Document Delivery and Interlibrary Loan Services Defined

In this emerging environment, the concepts and definitions of interlibrary loan and document delivery continue to evolve. The definition found in the National Interlibrary Loan Code for the United States will be used in this chapter (American Library Association, 2008b). Interlibrary loan service (ILL) refers to the process of requesting and supplying physical materials (originals or copies) library to library. Document delivery, on the other hand, focuses on alternative delivery options and represents the transfer of full-text documents directly to library customers or external libraries and organizations. The terms "requesting library" and "supplying library" are used in the chapter whenever possible in preference to "borrowing library" and "lending library" to include the exchange of copies as well as loans.

Impact of New Information Technologies

The marked growth of online searching, discovery tools, and availability of full-text online journals has had a huge impact on interlibrary loan operations, although the long-term implications for ILL still remain unclear. Lacroix and Collins (2007) provide a highly informative discussion of major large-scale and individual library studies that have explored this impact. In terms of ILL traffic, the studies indicate that changes in ILL demand are not uniform across libraries. Some studies indicate ILL has actually increased, others indicate decreases, while still others say ILL traffic has stayed more or less the same. Lacroix and Collins's large-scale study of DOCLINE requests in health sciences libraries showed that they have remained relatively flat since the late 1990s (Lacroix and Collins, 2007), although more recent DOCLINE data shows a further decline in ILL activity since that study (Collins, 2010).

Trend data also suggest that there may be a shift away from the most recent material, which possibly can be attributed to the widespread licensing of recently published full-text articles online, the online indexing of older materials, and the ongoing need to obtain landmark articles (Lacroix and Collins, 2007; Beaubien, 2007). In addition, publisher restrictions on ILL and time-embargoes on current e-journals may be limiting interlibrary loan access to articles published electronically ahead of print issues (Lacroix and Collins, 2007).

Given this evolving information landscape, there is every reason to believe that ILL will continue to play a key, albeit different, role in health sciences libraries in the years to come. ILL and document delivery services will continue to simplify processes and improve delivery options and turnaround times for customers. Hard-pressed libraries facing space constraints and budget reductions will need to rely on ILL to ensure access to older issues, the latest issues available electronically but not in print, articles from out-of-scope titles, and for little-used materials.

National Network of Libraries of Medicine

Since 1965 health sciences libraries in the United States have participated in a national network of regional medical libraries, known as the National Network of Libraries of Medicine (NN/LM) (http://nnlm.gov/). The cornerstone of the program is to provide all health professionals with equal access to biomedical information and to improve the public's access to health information. The network is coordinated by the National Library of Medicine (NLM) and consists of more than 4,000 primary access libraries, over 150 resource libraries, eight regional medical libraries, and NLM (U.S. National Library of Medicine, 2009b).

This hierarchical network allows small primary access libraries, primarily located in hospitals, to obtain materials from larger medical libraries in their geographical region and refer requests they are unable to fill to a regional library or to NLM. Participation in the NN/LM also requires involvement in a number of related activities, such as contributing to union lists or databanks of serial holdings and maintaining ILL performance standards. In addition to coordinating interlibrary loan services, NN/LM provides training and consultation services to network librarians and outreach services to underserved health professionals and user populations.

Library Consortia

Library consortial arrangements in health sciences libraries are longstanding and can often offer a wide range of services and benefits to small and large libraries alike. Consortial groups can be local, regional, or interstate. Some are multitype library cooperatives, such as the Medical Libraries Consortium of Hawaii. Others are homogeneous consortia that have member libraries with the same or similar collections and services, such as a small group of hospital libraries clustered in one regional area. Still others can be limited to libraries in one specialty, such as the Northern California Consortium of Psychology Libraries (NCCPL). Consortia can be formally organized by bylaws and agreements with paid professional staff and centralized services, or more informal and largely run by volunteers.

Health sciences library consortia came into existence primarily as a vehicle to facilitate resource sharing among hospital libraries. Holst and Bensing (2000) provide an informative discussion and further reading on consortium formation and cooperative efforts among hospital and other health-related libraries to foster interlibrary loan cooperation. These traditional consortial activities usually include filling loan requests from other members at no charge, maintaining holdings in union lists, aligning DOCLINE routing cells according to consortia membership via the Library Group feature in DOCLINE, submitting statistics, and adhering to various network rules. Sometimes consortia may even have their own courier or delivery services to ensure prompt and efficient sharing of print resources.

While facilitating resource sharing has remained a key purpose for many consortia, it is now the norm for consortial members to employ electronic document receiving and sending capabilities in order to cut interlibrary loan turnaround times and reduce paper and mailing costs (Hill, 2009). Consortia are partnering together to leverage their purchasing power to negotiate significant price advantages for electronic journals and databases. In general, library consortia that provide fast turnaround times on ILL requests, expedited document delivery options, and expanded access to electronic titles at an affordable cost have numerous advantages for the individual library. More information and listings of local library consortia, cooperatives, and networks can be found by contacting the regional office of the NN/LM or the local chapter of the Medical Library Association (http://mlanet.org/chapters/chapters.html).

Basic Operations of ILL

Interlibrary loan and document delivery involve work procedures that may vary from library to library. Holst and others have explained in detail all the daily functions

that are associated with the workflow of traditional interlibrary loan processing (Arnold and Fishel, 1996; Boucher, 1996; and Holst and Bensing, 2000). The increasing use of electronic systems to request, manage, and deliver documents has fundamentally changed the ILL landscape and become a key to providing faster and more convenient ILL service. Also, many publishers now provide electronic access to journals instead of, or in addition to, print formats. This transition brings into play new licensing issues that affect day-to-day ILL activities. Copyright issues, especially with regard to emerging technologies, also continue to play an important part in ILL work. It is essential in this evolving digital environment of ILL to have clearly written, up-to-date procedures to provide guidance and enable staff members at all levels to perform their tasks efficiently and consistently. Training of personnel is also of paramount importance with the advent of networking and new ILL systems to assure quality and increase efficiency.

Requesting Tasks

The daily functions associated with requesting are listed in Figure 10.5 and are also available on the **accompanying CD-ROM**. The methods patrons use to submit interlibrary loans depend on the policies and technologies employed by the individual library. In the last few years, an increasing number of libraries have offered patrons the option of submitting their interlibrary loan requests online while continuing to provide traditional or manual avenues for submission, such as postal mail, fax, e-mail, or phone. Larger health sciences libraries have been early adopters of electronic requesting systems that enable patrons to initiate interlibrary loan requests from a web-created form or while searching online catalogs or locally mounted databases. Embedded interlibrary loan links in catalogs and databases through new linking technology automatically map specific citations to an interlibrary loan request. This has the advantage of enabling patrons to request materials via ILL without having to leave a particular database. If a library uses an ILL Management System (IMS) with a request module, this initial electronic request record can also be updated and tracked throughout the ILL processing cycle. Some IMS systems with password-protected webpages even allow patrons to check the real-time status of their own orders online. Further discussion of ILL Management Systems can be found in the ILL Management System section of this chapter.

All types of interlibrary loan requests are located by searching bibliographic records for potential suppliers. Usually requests for articles are searched and sent through DOCLINE because it offers powerful tools for

Figure 10.5. Document Requesting Daily Functions

List of Daily Requesting Functions

- Collect new requests (from electronic, fax, email, and paper forms)
- Review requests for patron eligibility, legibility, completeness of bibliographic information, and local availability, noting any special instructions or deadlines
- Determine copyright compliance
- Locate potential suppliers (DOCLINE, OCLC, online catalogs, and commercial sources)
- Input article requests into DOCLINE system (or use alternate means for "returnable" items)
- File requests and update electronic records
- Receive and process filled requests (match/pull records from paper files, update record in DOCLINE, and/or update record in IMS)
- Notify patrons and deliver materials (physical or electronic delivery to patrons)
- Follow up on pending requests as needed
- Prepare physical, "returnable" items for shipping back to supplier
- Resolve any problems
- Perform record keeping activities, including updating records (physical and electronic), inputting statistics, and generating reports (may be done less often than daily)

Source: Adapted from Arnold and Fishel, 1996: 111.

locating biomedical serials and for automatically requesting those materials from other health sciences libraries. Monographs, nonprint materials, and out-of-scope materials are located by searching the online catalogs of other libraries, consortial union catalogs, LocatorPlus (http://locatorplus.gov), the National Library of Medicine's online catalog, or WorldCat (http://www.worldcat.org), OCLC's immense online union catalog representing books, journals, dissertations, audio-visual materials, and manuscripts in libraries worldwide.

Because today's library is a hybrid of physical and automated processes and print and electronic resources, received or filled requests are processed in multiple ways. This usually involves matching and pulling records from paper files or updating electronic records in an IMS database, updating electronic transaction records in DOCLINE (discussed later in this chapter), and notifying patrons, usually by e-mail, that their materials are ready for pickup or online viewing. More and more supplying libraries deliver requested articles to other libraries in a digital format. Electronic document delivery options will depend on the technology used, document delivery services offered, and patron preferences.

Supplying Tasks

The daily functions required in supplying materials from a library's own collection to other libraries are listed in Figure 10.6 and on the **accompanying CD-ROM**. Generally new requests from other libraries are received on

DOCLINE, although this may vary depending on the type of request and system used. Many health sciences libraries now use scanners to digitize articles, book chapters, and medical images, and specialized software to send electronic copies to other libraries via the Internet. This process normally involves the supplying library scanning documents into the computer using ARIEL software and then sending them over the Internet to the requesting library. Scanned documents can also be converted to PDF and e-mailed to the requesting library. This method is used by smaller libraries that can't use ARIEL. These digitized documents can then be printed out for the patron, emailed to the patron as an attachment, or transferred to a secure web server for patron pickup provided the patron has a password or personal identification number (PIN) to view or print them. Some ILL systems can also automatically send an email notification to the patron indicating that the material is ready for pickup.

Record Keeping and Statistics

Accurate and detailed record keeping is an essential and sometimes underrated part of a successful ILL program. Records provide documentation for decision making, assessment, and demonstrating a library's value and impact on customers. They also provide financial data for payments to supplying institutions and for billing patrons and other libraries as necessary. They are needed

---

Figure 10.6. Document Supplying Daily Functions

List of Daily Supplying Functions
- Collect new requests (from DOCLINE, ARIEL, Odyssey, fax, mail, or other sources)
- Review requests for local availability, accuracy, completeness, and special handling and delivery requirements
- Search catalog for call numbers and locations and sort for efficient retrieval of materials
- Retrieve physical items (pull physical items from stacks; photocopy or scan items)
- Check out physical items to be loaned and prepare them and accompanying forms for mailing or other delivery method
- Retrieve electronic items (review ILL licensing terms for requested item and handle accordingly; download original file or photocopy, scan, and transmit per requesting library preference)
- Update systems with request status; notify requesting library and refer requests as needed
- Prepare invoices or other billing method as appropriate
- Receive and check in returned material; follow up on pending loans as needed
- Resolve any problems
- Perform record keeping activities, including updating records (physical and electronic), inputting statistics, and generating reports (may be done less often than daily)

Source: Adapted from Arnold and Fishel, 1996: 114.

---

for reporting ILL activities to outside agencies. In general most libraries track the following:

- Date material was requested, received, and returned or supplied to other libraries
- Number of items borrowed from specific institutions
- Number and category of patrons requesting materials
- Number of items supplied to specific institutions
- Format of materials
- Copyright compliance information
- Number of requests that could not be filled and for what reasons
- Costs of items
- Turnaround times

It is important to update ILL records as they move through the ILL process from submission to completion. This is essential to review changing conditions, react accordingly, and reply to patrons inquiries. Libraries can also choose to maintain electronic records of ILL requests using current software technologies. If a library uses an IMS system that contains up-to-the-minute accurate data, staff can provide patrons with status checks quickly and efficiently. Some libraries even have the capability of providing online status checks with password-protected webpages that allow patrons to check their own orders.

Interlibrary loan records are organized in anticipation of patron and operational needs. Usually borrowing records for pending requests are filed by patron name so that staff can quickly determine the status of requested items and follow up on problems for patrons. Supplying records are commonly filed by date or institution to track the status of outstanding loans and due dates, renewals, and overdue items. Financial records are arranged by patron if they were charged for the service or by the lending institution to provide accurate records of paid and outstanding accounts. Summaries of interlibrary loan activities can be compiled and analyzed to track ILL patterns and collection development needs. They are also reported to outside agencies, such as local consortia. DOCLINE provides detailed reports of a library's interlibrary requesting and supplying activities that can be generated on quarterly and annual basis.

The decision as to what records are retained is often dictated by the policies of the parent institution and the need to report these activities to outside agencies. Retrospective tracking of requests is facilitated by filing requests alphabetically by journal title and within a title by year of publication to ensure that the CONTU (Commission on New Technological Uses of Copyrighted Works) guidelines on photocopying for interlibrary loan activities described below are followed by the requesting library. Records for filled article requests should be kept for three years. Financial data for payments to lending institutions and for billing patrons and other libraries is usually maintained according to the guidelines of the parent institution.

Many interlibrary loan units in health sciences libraries have made great strides moving to "paperless" processes. Knox (2010) observes that "although ILL processes can still consume a large amount of paper, ILL is no longer a paper-driven service." It is essential for all libraries, no matter the size, to automate as much of the ILL tracking process as possible to improve efficiency and facilitate the sharing of data. Knox (2010) suggests best "paperless" practices and affordable technologies to support ILL services in small and one-person libraries. For medium and larger libraries with bigger budgets, numerous technology solutions are available that can assist in simplifying and enhancing ILL operations, such as commercially available document delivery systems and comprehensive ILL management systems. Further discussion of ILL technology systems is found below under ILL Management Systems.

Document Delivery Technologies

DOCLINE

DOCLINE is NLM's automated ILL request and routing system that serves nearly all of the medical libraries in the United States, Canada, and Mexico at no cost (U.S. National Library of Medicine, 2009a). The DOCLINE ILL routing algorithm is unique in its ability to hierarchically and "intelligently" route requests based on detailed library holdings and library preferences to potential supplying libraries that hold the needed items. Health sciences libraries, libraries in institutions with a health sciences mission, and NLM-affiliated libraries are eligible to apply for access to DOCLINE. Libraries can apply for membership and a system account by contacting the regional office of the NN/LM at their regional medical library. The NN/LM has provided a list of DOCLINE Best Practices available at http://nnlm.gov/rsdd/docline/bestpractices.html.

DOCLINE consists of three main components: Institutions; SERHOLD (Serial Holdings); and Request modules. Libraries maintain their own institutional records in DOCLINE. Information in each institutional record includes the institutional name and address, interlibrary loan policies, and routing information. Each institutional record is assigned a LIBID (Library Identifier) that is used throughout the system to identify individual libraries.

Data stored in the SERHOLD module of DOCLINE provides serial information used by DOCLINE's automatic routing feature. SERHOLD currently includes over 1.6 million holdings statements from 3,018 health sciences libraries in the United States, Canada, and Mexico (U.S. National Library of Medicine, 2009c). Libraries may add, edit, or delete holdings records at any time.

Libraries create interlibrary loans, receive requests, and update transaction records using the Request module in DOCLINE. The Request system provides several ordering options and then sends the request automatically to a library that owns the requested material, based on SERHOLD data and a stored routing table of the potential lenders created by the requesting library. Libraries regularly receive reports of ILL activity that can be used for assessment, planning, and collection development purposes.

Beginning in 2006, DOCLINE introduced the Library Group routing feature. Membership in various Library Groups, such as library consortia, can range from 11 libraries to more than 1,000 libraries. During routing, DOCLINE randomly selects up to a maximum of 20 libraries per Library Group to which requests will route. DOCLINE can also designate requests by service level (rush and urgent patient care) and delivery methods, such as e-mail (PDF), ARIEL, mail, fax, web (PDF), etc. With the release of DOCLINE Version 4.5 in August 2010, the system added Odyssey as an electronic document delivery option. Further information about Odyssey is found in the section on ILL Management Systems.

DOCLINE also provides a free resource-sharing option for DOCLINE libraries via the FreeShare Library Group (http://nnlm.gov/rsdd/freeshare/). FreeShare is an interstate DOCLINE Library Group whose members agree to fill DOCLINE requests free of charge on a reciprocal basis. Any DOCLINE library can participate in FreeShare except "Borrowing Only" DOCLINE libraries. Over 1,300 DOCLINE libraries participate in the FreeShare Library Group.

Loansome Doc

NLM's Loansome Doc service provides document delivery for articles found in the NLM's databases by tapping into the DOCLINE network of health sciences libraries. Individual users of PubMed and NLM Gateway, including international users, have the ability to order documents directly from the list of citations retrieved from these databases. Before ordering documents in these databases, users must first register with a participating medical library or libraries that use DOCLINE for service. For current instructions on how to use Loansome Doc from PubMed and the NLM Gateway, NLM provides an up-to-date Fact Sheet with detailed instructions and contact information for all new users (http://www.nlm.nih.gov/

pubs/factsheets/loansome_doc.html). Although Loansome Doc requests have been decreasing since 2002 (Collins, 2010), the system is still actively used by the general public and has had a positive impact on end-users because of its convenience (Paden, Batson, and Wallace, 2001).

OCLC Interlibrary Loan System

The OCLC interlibrary loan system is an often used method of request transmission in health care libraries. The OCLC ILL system, called WorldCat Resource Sharing (http://www.oclc.org/resourcesharing/overview/default. htm), allows the user to create, send, and track interlibrary loan requests. This system is the most used electronic interlibrary loan system in the United States. The system is tightly integrated with OCLC's online union catalog, WorldCat.org, with over one billion holdings that cross all disciplines, languages, and cultures, and FirstSearch, a large abstract and index database that covers a wide range of topics. Interlibrary loan staff uses a variety of OCLC services. WorldCat.org and FirstSearch provide bibliographic verification and location of an enormous variety of library materials. The WorldCat Registry and the Policies Directory are two other OCLC programs of help to interlibrary loan. The OCLC ILL Fee Management (IFM) system described below is designed to decrease the workload burden of financial transactions between institutions. A statistical management tool is also available through WorldCat Collection Analysis. WorldCat Resource Sharing is offered on an annual subscription fee basis depending on size of institution and level of ILL activity.

ARIEL

ARIEL software is now used routinely by libraries to provide library-to-library electronic document delivery. Since it was introduced in 1991 by Research Libraries Group (RLG), it has grown in popularly and currently serves as a de facto standard for document transmission software for libraries. ARIEL allows libraries to scan articles and images in high image resolution and send them over the Internet via ftp or email address to other institutions that also utilize the ARIEL software. ARIEL uses multipage TIFF (Tag Image File Format) to scan and deliver materials to and from libraries. These received TIFF files are then quality checked, printed, and processed manually by ILL staff, or they can be converted to PDF (Portable Document Format) for patron desktop delivery.

Installation of ARIEL software requires a great deal of systems support and expertise to set up and maintain. This is especially true for hospital libraries that need special adaptations to use ARIEL from behind a hospital firewall. ARIEL's reliance on an open port server, which poses security concerns and special installation problems, has slowed ARIEL's adoption by hospital libraries that generally lack sufficient staffing and technology support (McKnight, 2002). In addition to this technical impediment, full vendor support is no longer offered for ARIEL, leaving software issues that arise to be solved by local systems staff (Elliott and Longacre, 2010). Because of these obstacles, it is important for libraries to work closely with their institution's systems staff to successfully implement, configure, and upgrade ARIEL software. Small and rural hospital libraries faced with significant barriers should investigate other types of Internet document delivery solutions that have been described in the literature to take advantage of the benefits of electronic document delivery (McKnight, 2002; Schnell, 2007).

ARIEL is compatible with most commercially available hardware and requires a computer workstation, a scanner, a high-resolution laser printer, and a compatible Internet connection. Current equipment recommendations are available at the Information Center (http://www4.info trieve.com/ariel/ricari.html). ARIEL can be used in conjunction with other transmission software, such as Prospero (http://bones.med.ohio-state.edu/prospero/), which provides conversion from TIFF to PDF and transfers files to an authenticated web server.

ARIEL operates with most IMS systems, such as the Clio System and ILLiad, which facilitate desktop document delivery, posting documents on a Web server, and sending email alerts to the patrons. Many commercial document delivery services also offer ARIEL delivery as an option. The ARIEL delivery method is also available in DOCLINE. Since 2003 the ARIEL software product has been available from Infotrieve (http://www.infotrieve .com/ariel).

ILL Management Systems

Interlibrary loan Management Systems (IMS) are an increasingly important component of the document delivery process. These systems can automate routine procedures associated with requesting and supplying documents and track requests electronically. An IMS consists of a back-end database, which can manipulate ILL records "offline" and import and export records and data to other systems. They can generate a wide variety of reports and facilitate electronic document delivery.

ILL management systems vary in cost and complexity and can run as stand-alone systems or as part of larger integrated packages. Lower volume libraries with straightforward work flows will benefit from implementing IMS systems, such as QuickDOC and ClioBasic. These basic IMS systems are reasonably priced, expedite processing, and significantly reduce the time required to process requests. Both QuickDOC and ClioBasic interoperate with DOCLINE and Loansome Doc, and prepare EFTS files, statistical reports, and copyright compliance and billing documents. ClioBasic also interfaces with OCLC. Both systems can be installed on a single computer workstation or on multiple networked workstations. Originally developed in 1987 by Jay Daly, since 2010 the QuickDOC software product is supported by New England Survey Systems (http://newsurv.com). Clio Software (http://www.cliosoftware.com) offers two packages, ClioBasic and the Clio System. The Clio System provides basic management functions, as well as a patron web interface piece and desktop delivery of articles via ARIEL and Odyssey.

High-volume libraries with more complex workflows and multiple sites will benefit from using more robust and customizable systems, such as OCLC ILLiad (http://www.atlas-sys.com/products/illiad) and Relais (http://www.relais-intl.com). These comprehensive systems are server-based and have many customization and reporting features. They can be hosted either by the implementing library or the off-site vendor for an additional cost. Installing and maintaining an IMS server on-site requires significant systems staff support, as well as web services support for customizing and programming patron and staff interfaces. While Relais is tightly integrated with DOCLINE, Loansome Doc, and OCLC, ILLiad lacks a direct connection with DOCLINE and Loansome Doc, causing some processing inefficiencies (Norton and Stover, 2003). Since 2003 ILLiad has offered a "free" stand-alone Odyssey module for Internet document transmission between other ILLiad libraries, similar to the ARIEL protocol described above. Odyssey (with the Trusted Sender setting enabled) has the advantage of unmediated delivery of articles, which has been shown to reduce staff time and turnaround time (Connell and Janke, 2006).

Additional Methods for Locating Full-Text Documents

Link Resolvers for Document Delivery

One of the most innovative online services to evolve in the past several years is "link resolver" or "link server" software. This popular new technology works with an OpenURL standard that is designed to support linking from an information source, such as a bibliographic citation or bibliographic record, to a target resource, such as a full-text journal article. Not only do link resolvers give library users the ability to directly link to the full-text article, they can also link to an online catalog to locate articles in print if the electronic version is not available, or to a self-populating interlibrary loan form. This saves users time, allows users to focus their efforts more on research and writing, and can dramatically increase the efficiency and accuracy of interlibrary loan operations.

Many journal publishers and aggregators (e-journal and e-book vendor sites), bibliographic databases, interlibrary loan services, OPACs, and web search engines are now OpenURL-enabled, including EBSCOhost, Elsevier, OVID, PubMed, and Google Scholar to name only a few. A list of OpenURL compliant resources is available from the ExLibris SFX website (http://www.exlibrisgroup.com/category/SFXResources).

A growing number of companies also offer standalone link resolver services. Some of the more widely used commercial services include Ex Libris SFX (http://www.exlibrisgroup.com/category/SFXOverview), Serials Solutions 360 Link (http://www.serialssolutions.com/360-link/), and EBSCO LinkSource (http://www2.ebsco.com/en-us/ProductsServices/linksource/Pages/index.aspx). SFX and LinkSource are available as a remotely or locally hosted product. 360 Link is only offered as a remotely hosted solution and does not work for any non-journal citations.

Open Access

With the advent of the Open Access (OA) movement, a growing number of scholarly, peer-reviewed articles are now freely available on the Internet. Open access articles include both published articles that are available free of charge on the publisher's website and articles that the authors themselves have self-archived and made freely available over the Internet. Chapter 7 provides information and resources related to Open Access.

Commercial Document Suppliers

Many libraries use commercial document suppliers to augment their library-to-library document delivery services. Commercial document services can expand service options and provide a greater capability in meeting user expectations. Using a document supplier is a viable option when a guaranteed, expedited request is of critical importance. They can be an alternative when a library is about to or has exceeded the limit of five articles per copyright guidelines or if multiple articles from the same volume are needed because service fees include a royalty payment to publishers. They can also be used for out-of-scope materials. Commercial suppliers can provide a convenient solution for nonaffiliated users if they are willing to pay a fee.

Because studies have shown that there is a wide variation in the performance of commercial suppliers, librarians should carefully select a document supplier based on local needs and if they meet certain performance criteria. Jackson discusses four criteria for selecting an effective document delivery supplier: fast turnaround time, expedited delivery options, known fees and payment options, and different methods to submit requests (Jackson, 2004). Shipman's Document Delivery Suppliers webpage (http://library.med.utah.edu/docsupp) provides an up-to-date listing of commercial document suppliers, as well as detailed service and contact information for each supplier.

In some situations libraries may also want to consider the option of taking direct online purchases of articles and books to content providers and booksellers to fill requests. Buchanan (2009) suggests using this alternative when the cost of purchase is less than the copyright fee.

International Sources of Document Delivery

International interlibrary loan is growing due to the use of the Internet and other electronic sources, such as WorldCat. As library patrons become aware of an immense universe of content that was previously hidden, libraries should develop international document delivery procedures for searching, requesting, supplying, paying for, and returning internationally held items. International ILL practices should be guided by the standards in the National Interlibrary Loan Code for the United States (American Library Association, 2008b) and the International Federation of Library Associations and Institutions' (IFLA) guidelines (http://www.ifla.org/files/docdel/documents/international-lending-en.pdf) (International Federation of Library Associations, 2009). Both cover the responsibilities of requesting and supplying libraries.

When requesting international items be sure to allow sufficient time for transmittal of the request and the receipt of the material. Copyright laws can also be different in other countries, so libraries need to strictly adhere to U.S. copyright law, the CONTU Guidelines, and the Berne Convention (1988) regarding international copyright. More information on international resources and document delivery is available from NLM (http://www.nlm.nih.gov/services/getting_fulltext_articles.html) and on the IFLA website (http://www.ifla.org/en/about-the-docdel-section).

Developing Document Delivery Policies

All health sciences libraries need to develop written ILL/document delivery policies and procedures because they provide guidelines and a framework for consistent and effective ILL/document delivery services and operations. Policies should be compatible with the mission and values of its parent organization and clearly designate the scope and goals of service.

Because of differing requirements and responsibilities of the requesting and supplying functions, it is useful to develop separate policy statements for each function. A suggested outline for a document delivery/ILL policy appears in Figure 10.7 and is available on the **accompanying CD-ROM.**

Figure 10.7. Document Delivery Policy and Procedure Manual, Suggested Outline

1 **Goals of interlibrary loan and document delivery services**
2 **Policies and procedures for requesting materials from other libraries**
   2.1 Eligible library customers
   2.2 Acceptable methods for submitting requests
   2.3 Types of materials that may be requested
   2.4 Copyright compliance
   2.5 Sources for obtaining materials
   2.6 Procedures for requesting materials
   2.7 Average turnaround time
   2.8 Charges and financial responsibilities
   2.9 Confidentiality of records
   2.10 Record keeping
3 **Policies and procedures for lending materials to other libraries**
   3.1 Eligible libraries
   3.2 Types of materials that may be lent
   3.3 Licensing restrictions
   3.4 Loan duration and restrictions
   3.5 Procedures for supplying materials
   3.6 Packing requirements
   3.7 Average processing time
   3.8 Charges
   3.9 Billing procedures
   3.10 Record keeping
   3.11 List hours, mailing address, phone number, fax number, e-mail address, and ARIEL address

Source: Adapted from Holst and Bensing, 2000: 305.

Requesting Policies

Requesting policies should itemize who is eligible to use ILL/document delivery. Eligibility criteria should be spelled out not only for clinical staff, but for all applicable groups, such as staff in off-site locations, students in affiliated programs, patients and their families, and other applicable groups. Libraries that participate in the Loansome Doc program will also need to include policies for unaffiliated users. Eligibility decisions should be based on organizational goals and the availability of library staff and economic resources to carry out these services.

Supplying Policies

Most libraries are expected to participate in reciprocal ILL/document delivery services. In general, libraries, no matter the size, benefit from having as nonrestrictive lending policies as possible, although smaller libraries with very limited staff may have some restrictions. Lending policies should specify eligible libraries and the types and formats of materials that circulate through interlibrary loan. They should indicate loan periods, routine and expedited charges, renewal protocols, and methods for delivery and return of ILL/document delivery materials.

Supplying policies should specify charges for routine and expedited requests and provide guidelines for collecting fees. Supplying policies should also cover the use of telefacsimile (fax) and electronic methods of document delivery, and the handling practices of requests by each service level. Supplying libraries usually process requests via DOCLINE as part of the normal workload unless otherwise designated as "rush" or "urgent patient care."

Policies of Other Libraries, Networks, and the NN/LM

It is important for all libraries to have a basic understanding of the document delivery policies of other regularly used, supplying libraries and to be able to locate the policies of other libraries. Lending policies can be obtained by collecting individual policy statements from other frequently used libraries or by consulting online ILL policy directories, such as Institutional Records in DOCLINE, the OCLC Policies Directory, or the Interlibrary Loan Policies Directory (Morris, 2002).

Other pertinent lending policies to collect include those of any consortia and regional networks to which the library belongs. Because most health sciences libraries participate in the NN/LM, the policies of both the Resource and Regional Medical Libraries and the NLM

should also be readily available. NN/LM regional ILL/document delivery policies are generally available through the websites of various Regional Medical Libraries.

Medical librarians should also consult the National Interlibrary Loan Code for the United States (American Library Association, 2008c) and accompanying explanatory supplement (American Library Association, 2008b) that fully describe borrowing and lending responsibilities that apply to all document delivery requests between libraries with no specific agreements. International guidelines for document delivery are also available from IFLA, which include helpful guidelines and forms for international email and fax requests (International Federation of Library Associations, 2009).

Service Continuity in Disasters

Health sciences libraries provide important public services that would be compromised during catastrophic failures due to a weather event, a public health threat, or a power outage. Core services like interlibrary loan that support direct patient care are critical for their institutions and communities throughout a disaster and during postdisaster recovery (McHone-Chase, 2010). With careful forethought and preparation, libraries should develop a service continuity plan to ensure that core services are always available in disasters and these support institutional and other regional network efforts. Chapter 3 provides useful information on disaster planning including information on the National Emergency Preparedness & Response Toolkit (http://nnlm.gov/ep/).

Copyright and Licensing in the Digital Environment

Copyright law has a direct bearing on ILL/document delivery services and establishes different requirements for requesting and supplying libraries. Librarians can refer to several helpful resources in making determinations about copyright compliance and for suggested practices for health sciences libraries. The Medical Library Association provides up-to-date information (http://mlanet .org /government/index.html#copyright). The MLA web publication, *The Copyright Law and the Health Sciences Librarian* is included on the **accompanying CD-ROM**. The Copyright Act of 1976 is best understood and applied in conjunction with other guidelines prepared by the National Commission on New Technological Uses of Copyright Works (CONTU) (Copyright Law of the United States, 1976; National Commission, 1978). Under the law and guidelines, the copyright responsibilities of the requesting library exceed those of the lending library because the law makes the requesting library responsible for certain aspects of copyright compliance.

Borrowing requirements for copies of materials (non-returnable requests) include:

- copyright warning notification,
- limits on systematic reproduction,
- copyright representation for requests, and
- record maintenance for interlibrary borrowing requests.

The requesting library is required to display a copyright warning notice with prescribed wording where requests for copies are accepted. This copyright warning notice must also be included on all order forms, including electronic request forms. See Figure 10.8 for wording of notice.

As more libraries convert their journal subscriptions and textbooks to electronic access, they must increasingly manage the use of these resources under the terms agreed to in a license. Librarians should read these contracts carefully to determine how interlibrary loans are handled, as libraries are required to abide by these terms, rather than copyright requirements. ILL terms in a license are likely to be more restrictive than the rights accorded under copyright law. Interlibrary loan compliance to licensing terms can be difficult, especially when licensing clauses related to interlibrary loan are varied and, in some cases, open to interpretation. Types of restrictions

that frequently appear in licenses include: sending requests with original digital files; filling requests for individuals; filling requests for non-profit libraries; and filling requests from foreign countries.

Librarians should make every effort to negotiate favorable licenses for electronic resources that preserve all interlibrary loan rights under the Copyright Act and remove any overly restrictive clauses. Maintaining spreadsheets or databases of licensing terms is helpful to track licensing terms for interlibrary loan. Some libraries input this information in a MARC field in the local online catalog. These tools aid in complying with licensing terms of specific journal titles that the library subscribes to. Librarians can consult open access directories of publisher copyright policies, such as the Liblicense site (http://www.library.yale.edu/~llicense/publishers.shtml) and SHERPA/RoMEO (http://www.sherpa.ac.uk/romeo/), for information on ILL terms set by different publishers and aggregators (Yale University Library, 2007; SHERPA, 2006–2008).

Fees and Financial Management of Document Delivery

Health care libraries often charge for ILL/document delivery services in order to recoup some of the associated costs necessary to obtain items through interlibrary loan or to generate funds for additional staffing and equipment. Whether and how much a library decides to charge for ILL/document delivery services depends on many factors, including the service philosophy of the library, the prevailing practices of other libraries, and the availability of resources. Document delivery fees fall into two categories: borrowing and lending charges. The financial aspects of the library's document delivery service, including payment requirements and options such as departmental recharge accounts and billing procedures, should be a part of a policy and procedure manual. Having these financial details in writing and easily accessible to patrons helps clarify responsibilities and reduce confusion and misunderstandings about the assessment of fees.

User Fees for ILL Requests

Requesting fees are those fees that are assessed to the customer for obtaining items though ILL/document delivery from other libraries. Each library must determine if it will implement a cost-recovery program for interlibrary loans or provide free interlibrary loans to other libraries that request materials. Holst and Bensing provide specific questions to consider when deciding

---

Figure 10.8. Copyright Warning Notice

NOTICE: WARNING CONCERNING COPYRIGHT RESTRICTIONS

The copyright law of the United States (Title 17, United States Code) governs the making of photocopies or other reproductions of copyrighted material.

Under certain conditions specified in the law, libraries and archives are authorized to furnish a photocopy or other reproduction. One of these specified conditions is that the photocopy or reproduction is not to be "used for any purpose other than private study, scholarship, or research." If a user makes a request for, or later uses, a photocopy or reproduction for purposes in excess of "fair use," that user may be liable for copyright infringement.

This institution reserves the right to refuse to accept a copying order if, in its judgment, fulfillment of the order would involve violation of copyright law.

Source: U.S. Code of Federal Regulations, 1995.

whether to charge library customers for document delivery services (Holst and Bensing, 2000: 304). Some libraries are able to subsidize all requesting costs through the library's operating budget, but most libraries must pass along some or all of these costs to their library users. Usually a library passes on only the direct costs for which they are billed by another library. Indirect costs, or costs that would be incurred whether or not a library participated in document delivery, are generally not passed on to the user. Most libraries do not charge the user for items that are obtained for free. Many libraries also provide the option of charging departments rather individual requesters.

Fees Levied on Other Libraries for Supplying ILL Requests

Of equal concern to health science libraries are charges that are levied on external institutions for supplying a loan request. Many libraries bill only those libraries that charge for their document delivery services and provide free services to those that reciprocate with free loans. Others charge special fees for rush requests and may charge borrowers for overdue fees and shipping charges for materials loaned in their original format. ILL/document delivery charges will vary from library to library depending on the service philosophy of the library, library specific costs, fee systems of Resource and Regional Medical Libraries and the National Library of Medicine, among other factors. Since 2002, the maximum amount charged by Resource and Regional Medical Libraries for journal and monographic requests is $11, although not all libraries charge the maximum fee. Beginning in December 2003, NLM charges $9 for each filled domestic request, regardless of method of delivery, i.e., e-mail (PDF), ARIEL, or mail.

Financial Management of Document Delivery

The development of an operating budget for ILL/document delivery depends on the overall budgeting structure of the library or parent institution and the amount of revenue that is generated by the service itself. Smaller net-borrowing libraries or libraries that have reciprocal borrowing agreements with other institutions can use simple expense summaries to keep track of costs. Larger libraries that are net-lenders and generate substantial amounts of revenue use more elaborate fund accounting systems to offset expenditures with revenue to determine final net income. It is useful to understand the economics of document delivery because having cost data allows for preparing and forecasting budgets, more accurate lending fees to be established, comparing and selecting

potential lenders, and collection development decisions. Various methods and tools have been described in the literature to determine accurately actual document delivery costs that can be applied to health care libraries (Dickson and Boucher, 1989; Lessick, 1996). Libraries that charge either library patrons or other libraries need to keep careful account of transactions and should use a front-end ILL management system or a spreadsheet program to help manage transactions and billing operations.

Fee Management Systems

Health sciences libraries of various types and sizes can benefit from using ILL fee management systems. These systems eliminate the need to create invoices and write checks for reimbursement for interlibrary loan and document delivery between participants, which is a tedious but necessary part of interlibrary loan.

Since the early 2000s most health sciences libraries have participated in the Electronic Fund Transfer System (EFTS) (https://efts.uchc.edu/EftsPublic/faq.aspx), which eliminates the need for DOCLINE libraries to bill and receive payments from other libraries. EFTS administered by the University of Connecticut Health Center is a net reimbursement system that is fully integrated into DOCLINE. Participants establish an account by completing an online application and submitting a Memorandum of Agreement along with deposit funds to the University of Connecticut Health Center. Lenders upload billing data for DOCLINE and other non-DOCLINE transactions. Their accounts are credited and requestors' accounts are debited. Lenders pay a 5 percent fee of the amount collected. Detailed reports are available online. The EFTS can also handle varying charges per type of request and affiliation. Management in Action 10.2 describes successful adoption of EFTS in a hospital library.

Another widely accepted ILL fee management system that is used by larger health sciences libraries is the OCLC Interlibrary Loan Fee Management (IFM) system (http://www.oclc.org/support/questions/resource sharing/ifm/) that works in conjunction with the OCLC interlibrary loan subsystem (WorldCat Resource Sharing). IFM tracks the debit and credit activities of member libraries through a monthly report that provides a detailed breakdown of transactions. A requesting library specifies a maximum cost that it is willing to pay within a request. The IFM also supports reciprocal agreements. Libraries are charged an IFM administrative fee for completed borrowing transactions.

International interlibrary transactions are often handled by using vouchers sponsored by IFLA, rather than money. The reuseable plastic vouchers represent a

MANAGEMENT IN ACTION 10.2

Adoption of EFTS by a Hospital Library

Location: Metropolitan Teaching Hospital

Description of Problem/Project: In order to support a large teaching program and an active physician medical group, the hospital library borrowed several thousand articles each year. The number of individual invoices that needed to be paid became increasingly burdensome for the library manager. The library manager also thought that it was expensive for the hospital accounting department to write all those individual checks and that lending partners might not be getting prompt payment. The library manager had heard about EFTS and decided to investigate it as a solution to the problem.

Impact On: Improvement in efficiency and reduction in the cost of paying ILL invoices.

People Involved: Library manager, accounts payable department, financial services division, chief financial officer.

Strategies for Success: Some individuals in the financial services division were hesitant to set up a deposit account with a third party that would be handling payment. The library manager explained the process and showed how many libraries were already using the system. The library manager also investigated the cost to the institution of writing one check, which at that time was $25 per check. After being told that approval would need to come from the highest level, the library manger e-mailed the chief financial officer (CFO) directly and explained the cost benefit to the institution and the detailed reports that would be available for tracking payments. With this information the CFO readily approved the hospital library joining EFTS.

Barriers Encountered: The main barrier was the concerns by some in financial services of having a third party handle the financial transactions.

Take-Home Points: In adopting a new system that changes a current process, the library manager must learn as much as possible about the issues involved. In this case the manager needed to know as much as possible about EFTS and also about the concerns of the financial services department. It is easy to look at things only from the library's point of view. To get buy-in from other shareholders the library manager needs to thoroughly investigate the matter and respond to concerns clearly and objectively.

Further Reading: Lewis, Jacqueline. 2007. "The DOCLINE Electronic Funds Transfer System (EFTS)." *Journal of Interlibrary Loan, Document Delivery & Information Supply* 17, no 3: 75–83.

standard payment for one transaction. Each supplying library determines the quantity of vouchers needed for the loan and keeps them to be reused for borrowing transactions from other libraries at a later date. Net lender libraries can redeem the vouchers through IFLA. Supplying libraries are encouraged to accept a standard "payment" of one voucher for supplying a loan or a photocopy of up to 15 pages. More information about the IFLA Voucher Scheme is available on the IFLA website (http://www.ifla.org/en/voucher-scheme).

Conclusion

For the foreseeable future there will be on-site customers and one desk that serves a variety of functions. Customers will be able to reach librarians for expert assistance by a dynamic and rich mixture of methods and modes meeting users at their point of need—at the reference desk, in offices by appointment, from bench-to-bedside, via digital technology, and in the Web 2.0 universe. Librarians will have increased flexibility and skills to provide context-embedded information services such as embedded liaison, CML, and informationist services. They will continue to test, measure, and refine embedded information service regimes to better support health care processes and outcomes. In addition, librarians will continue to develop web-based information services, including the library's website, subject guides, portals, and Web 2.0 tools to distribute and promote services and resources to present and potential users.

Document delivery services will continue to use technology to streamline processes, expand delivery options, and reduce turnaround times for users. For the foreseeable future document delivery will be the primary vehicle for obtaining knowledge-based information in nondigital formats and for accessing embargoed and less-used content.

The future of health sciences libraries will be to provide value-added services to health practitioners, researchers, educators, students, patients, and the public that they can not get elsewhere. Dillon (2007: 40) identifies three value-added services that can "carve out an effective and sustaining pathway to the future...access to information that is not easily available over the Internet, and to information in context that makes a difference, as well as a place where information seekers gather." Hospital and academic health sciences libraries have had a long tradition of innovation and leadership in many professional areas, among them resource sharing, expert searching, quality filtering, and critical appraisal of the literature.

The success of context-embedded information services to elicit and meet information needs at the point of care to potentially shape patient outcomes has implications for practice outside of health sciences libraries and may potentially propel a broader "reference renaissance" (Harmon and Westbrook, 2010:85). Health care libraries are especially well-positioned to leverage these strengths to compete and succeed in the maelstrom of change and to create better health for individuals and communities.

References

Adams, Helen R. 2009. "Privacy Checklist: Evaluating the Library Media Program." *School Library Media Activities Monthly* 25, no. 7 (March): 55.

Alexa Internet Inc. 2010. "Global Top Sites." Alexa the Web Information Company. Accessed August 21. http://www.alexa.com/topsites.

Allegri, Francesca, and Martha Bedard. 2006. "Lessons Learned from Single Service Point Implementations." *Medical Reference Services Quarterly* 25, no. 2 (June): 31–47.

Alpi, Kristine, and Diana Delgado. 2007. "Search Hedges: Cutting Across the Trees of MeSH." *MLA News* no. 399 (September): 14.

American Library Association. 2006. "Resolution on the Retention of Library Usage Records" (June 28, 2006). Accessed September 11, 2010. http://www.ala.org/ala/about ala/offices oif/statementspols/ifresolutions/libraryusage records.cfm.

American Library Association. 2007. "Privacy." (May 29, 2007). Accessed September 11, 2010. http://www.ala.org/ala/aboutala/offices/oif/iftoolkits/toolkitsprivacy/privacy.cfm.

American Library Association. 2008a."Code of Ethics of the American Library Association." (January 22, 2008). Accessed September 11, 2010. http://www.ala.org/ala/aboutala/offices/oif/ifgroups/cope/Code%20of%20Ethics%202008.pdf.

American Library Association. 2008b. "Interlibrary Loan Code for the United States: Explanatory Supplement." Chicago: American Library Association. Accessed October 17, 2010. http://www.ala.org/ala/mgrps/divs/rusa/resources/guide lines/interlibraryloancode.cfm.

American Library Association. 2008c."National Interlibrary Loan Code for the United States." Chicago: American Library Association. Accessed October 17, 2010. http://www.ala.org/ala/mgrps/divs/rusa/resources/guidelines/inter library.cfm.

Anderson, P. F. 2007. "31 Flavors: Things to Do with Flickr in Libraries." OCLC (September 14, 2007). Accessed August 23, 2010. http://www.webjunction.org/technology/web-tools/articles/content/450126.

Arnold, Gretchen N., and Martha R. Fishel. 1996. "Interlibrary Loan and Document Delivery." In *Information Access and Delivery in Health Sciences Libraries*, edited by Carolyn E.

Lipscomb, 101–143. Current Practice in Health Sciences Librarianship. Chicago: Medical Library Association.

Association of Research Libraries. 2009. *ARL Statistics Questionnaire, 2008–09: Instructions for Completing the Questionnaire.* Accessed September 12, 2010. http://www.arl.org/bm~doc/09instruct.pdf.

Atlas, Michel C., Elizabeth M. Smigielski, Judith L. Wulff, and Mary T. Coleman. 2003. "Case Studies from Morning Report: Librarians' Role in Helping Residents Find Evidence-Based Clinical Information." *Medical Reference Services Quarterly* 22, no. 3 (Fall): 1–14.

Attebury, Ramirose, Nancy Sprague, and Nancy J. Young. 2009. "A Decade of Personalized Research Assistance." *Reference Services Review* 37, no. 2: 207–220.

Badman, Derik A., and Lianne Hartman. 2008. "Developing Current Awareness Services: Virtual Reading Rooms and Online Routing." *College & Research Libraries News* 69, no. 11 (December): 670–672.

Bandy, Margaret, Joyce Condon, and Ellen Graves. 2008. "Participating in Communities of Practice." *Medical Reference Services Quarterly* 27, no. 4 (Winter): 441–449.

Bandy, Margaret, and Brenda Fosmire. 2004. "The Hospital Library and the Enterprise Portal." *Medical Reference Services Quarterly* 23, no. 1 (Spring): 63–72.

Banks, Daniel E., Runhua Shi, Donna F. Timm, Kerri Ann Christopher, David Charles Duggar, Marianne Comegys, and Jerry McLarty. 2007. "Decreased Hospital Length of Stay Associated with Presentation of Cases at Morning Report with Librarian Support." *Journal of the Medical Library Association* 95, no. 4 (October): 381–387.

Beaubien, Anne K. 2007. "ARL White Paper on Interlibrary Loan." Chicago: Association of Research Library (June 2007). Accessed November 29, 2010. http://www.arl.org/bm~doc/ARL_white_paper_ILL_june07.pdf.

Bell, Steven. 2010. "The Future of the Library Is not the Apple Store" (September 3). Accessed September 12, 2010. http://dbl.lishost.org/blog/2010/09/03/the-future-of-the-library-is-not-the-apple-store/.

Berne Convention Implementation Act of 1988. 1988. Circular 92. Washington, DC: U. S. Government Printing Office. Accessed November 29, 2010. http://www.cni.org/docs/infopols/US.Berne.Convention.html.

Bernstein, Mark P. 2008. "Am I Obsolete? How Customer Service Principles Ensure the Library's Relevance." *AALL Spectrum* 13, no. 2 (November): 20–22.

Boss, Richard W. 2002. "How to Plan and Implement a Library Portal." *Library Technology Reports* 38, no. 6 (November/December): 1–54.

Boss, Richard. 2008. "Library Web Portals." *Tech Notes* [series]. Chicago: American Library Association, Public Library Association (May 28, 2008). Accessed September 22, 2010. http://www.lita.org/ala/mgrps/divs/pla/plapublications/pla technotes/ALA_print_layout_1_510659_510659.cfm.

Boucher, Virginia. 1996. *Interlibrary Loan Practices Handbook.* 2nd ed. Chicago: American Library Association.

Bradigan, Pamela S., and Ruey L. Rodman. 2008. "Single Service Point: It's All in the Design." *Medical Reference Quarterly* 27, no.4 (Winter): 367–378.

Brandes, Susan. 2007. "Experience and Outcomes of Medical Librarian Rounding." *Medical Reference Services Quarterly* 26, no. 4 (Winter): 85–92.

Brower, Stewart. 2004. "Academic Health Sciences Library Website Navigation: An Analysis of Forty-one Websites and Their Navigation Tools." *Journal of the Medical Library Association* 92, no. 4 (October): 412–420.

Brumley, Rebecca. 2006. *The Reference Librarian's Policies, Forms, Guidelines, and Procedures Handbook with CD-ROM*. New York: Neal-Schuman.

Buchanan, Sherry. 2009. "Interlibrary Loan Is the New Reference: Reducing Barriers, Providing Access and Refining Services." *Interlending & Document Supply* 37, no. 4: 168–170.

Burdick, Amrita. 2004. "Informationist? Internal Medicine Rounds with a Clinical Medical Librarian." *Journal of Hospital Librarianship* 4, no. 1: 17–27.

Cassell, Kay Ann, and Uma Hiremath. 2009. *Reference and Information Services in the 21st Century*. New York: Neal-Schuman.

Chamberlain, Jane. 2008. "What Does It Take? Transforming Customer Service Today." *Illinois Library Association Reporter* 26, no. 1 (February): 4–7.

Clemmons, Nancy W., and Diane G. Schwartz. 1994. "Management of Reference Services." In *Reference and Information Services in Health Sciences Libraries*, edited by M. Sandra Wood, 179–243. Metuchen, NJ: Medical Library Association; Scarecrow Press.

Cleveland, Ana D., and Jodi L. Philbrick. 2007. "Virtual Reference Services for the Academic Health Sciences Librarian 2.0." In *Medical Librarian 2.0; Use of Web 2.0 Technologies in Reference Services*, edited by M. Sandra Wood, 25–49. New York: Haworth Press. (Also published as *Medical Reference Services Quarterly* 26, Supp. 1, 2007: 25–49).

CollegeDegrees.com. 2008. "How to: Make Flickr Work for Your Library—50+ Resources." (September 24). Accessed August 23, 2010. http://www.collegedegrees.com/blog/2008/06/24/how-to-make-flickr-work-for-your-library-50-resources/.

Collins, Maria E. 2010. "MLA 2010 Docline Update." PowerPoint slides presented at the Annual Meeting of the Medical Library Association, Washington, DC, May 24, 2010. Accessed July 17. http://www.nlm.nih.gov/docline/presentations/MLA_2010_DOCLINE_Update.ppt.

Connell, Ruth S., and Karen L. Janke. 2006. "Turnaround Time Between ILLiad's Odyssey and Ariel Delivery Methods." *Journal of Interlibrary Loan, Document Delivery & Electronic Reserve* 16, no. 3: 41–56.

Connor, Elizabeth. 2007. "Library 2.0: An Overview." In *Medical Librarian 2.0; Use of Web 2.0 Technologies in Reference Services*, edited by M. Sandra Wood, 5–23. New York: Haworth Press. (Also published as *Medical Reference Services Quarterly* 26, Supp. 1, 2007: 5–23).

Cooke, Carol A. 2006. "Current Awareness in the New Millennium: RSS." *Medical Reference Services Quarterly* 25, no. 1 (Spring): 59–69.

Coombs, Karen A. 2005. "Protecting User Privacy in the Age of Digital Libraries." *Computers in Libraries* 25, no. 6 (06): 16–20.

Copyright Law of the United States. Title 17, §§101, 106-108. 1976. Accessed August 1, 2010. http://copyright.gov/title17/.

Corrado, Edward M., and Kathryn A. Frederick. 2008. "Free and Open Source Options for Creating Database-Driven Subject Guides." *Code4Lib Journal* 2 (2008-03-24). Accessed September 28, 2010. http://journal.code4lib.org/articles/47.

Dahl, Candice. 2001. "Electronic Pathfinders in Academic Libraries: An Analysis of Their Content and Form." *College & Research Libraries* 62, no. 3 (May): 227–237.

Damani, Shamsha, and Stephanie Fulton. 2010. "Collaborating and Delivering Literature Search Results to Clinical Teams Using Web 2.0 Tools." *Medical Reference Services Quarterly* 29, no. 3 (July-September): 207–217.

Davidoff, Frank, and Valerie Florance. 2000. "The Informationist: A New Health Profession?" *Annals of Internal Medicine* 132, no. 12 (June 20): 996–998.

De Groote, Sandra L. 2005. "Questions Asked at the Virtual and Physical Health Sciences Reference Desk: How Do They Compare and What Do They Tell Us." *Medical Reference Services Quarterly* 24, no. 2 (Summer): 11–23.

De Groote, Sandra L., Kristin Hitchcock, and Richard McGowan. 2007. "Trends in Reference Usage Statistics in an Academic Health Sciences Library." *Journal of the Medical Library Association* 95, no. 1 (January): 23–30.

Dee, Cheryl R. 2003a. "Chat Reference Service in Medical Libraries: Part 1—An Introduction." *Medical Reference Services Quarterly*, 22, no. 2 (Summer): 1–13.

Dee, Cheryl R. 2003b. "Chat Reference Service in Medical Libraries: Part 2—Trends in Medical School Libraries." *Medical Reference Services Quarterly*, 22, no. 2 (Summer), 15–28.

Dee, Cheryl R. 2005. "Digital Reference Service." *Medical Reference Services Quarterly* 24, no. 1 (Spring): 19–27.

Del Bosque, Darcy, and Kimberly Chapman. 2007. "Your Place or Mine? Face-to-Face Reference Services Across Campus." *New Library World* 108, no. 5/6: 247–262.

Del Castillo, Melissa. "Academic Libraries and YouTube." Tallahassee, FL: Florida State University (December 7, 2008). Accessed August 23, 2010. http://lis5313.ci.fsu.edu/wiki/index.php/Academic_Libraries_and_YouTube.

Dennis, Sharon. 2007. "Getting Started with Wikis." *Latitudes* (October 24). Accessed September 14, 2010. http://nnlm.gov/psr/newsletter/?p=173.

Detlor, Brian, and Vivian Lewis. 2006. "Academic Library Web Sites: Current Practice and Future Directions." *Journal of Academic Librarianship* 32, no. 3 (May): 251–258.

Dickson, Stephen P., and Virginia Boucher. 1989. "A Methodology for Determining Costs of Interlibrary Lending." In *Research Access through New Technology*, edited by Mary E. Jackson, 137–159. New York: AMS Press.

Dillon, Dennis. 2007. "Google, Libraries, and Knowledge Management." *Journal of Library Administration* 46, no. 1:27–40.

Ekart, Donna F. 2010. "Flickr Four by Four." *Computers in Libraries* 30, no.7 (September): 46–47.

Elliott, Sarah, and Rosa Longacre. 2010. "Software and Scanner: A Comparison of Procedures in University of California, San Diego's Interlibrary Loan and Course Reserves Units." *Journal of Interlibrary Loan, Document Delivery & Electronic Reserve* 20, no. 1: 43–51.

Enyeart, Amanda L., and Debbie Weaver. 2005. "Relationship Marketing in a Hospital Library." *Medical Reference Services Quarterly* 24, no. 4 (Winter): 89–97.

Farkas, Meredith. 2008. "Reading Rooms Online. " *American Libraries* 39, no. 6 (June/July): 48.

Flanagan, Pat, and Lisa R. Horowitz. 2000. "Exploring New Service Models: Can Consolidating Public Service Points Improve Response to Customer Needs?" *Journal of Academic Librarianship* 26, no. 5 (September): 329–338.

Fletcher, Adelaide Myers. 2009. "Free-range RSS Feeds and Farm-raised Journals: What to Expect When Using RSS as a TOC Service." *Medical Reference Services Quarterly* 28, no. 2 (April/June): 172–179.

Freiburger, Gary, and Sandra Kramer. 2009. "Embedded Librarians: One Library's Model for Decentralized Service." *Journal of the Medical Library Association* 97, no. 2 (April): 139–142.

Frumento, Katherine, and Judith Keating. 2007. "The Role of the Hospital Librarian on an Institutional Review Board." *Journal of Hospital Librarianship* 7, no. 4 (September): 113–120.

Fuller, Diane M., and Patricia G. Hinegardner.2001. "Ensuring Quality Website Redesign: The University of Maryland's Experience." *Bulletin of the Medical Library Association* 89, no. 4 (October): 339–345.

Garrison, Judith S. 2010. "Making Reference Service Count: Collecting and Using Reference Service Statistics to Make a Difference." *The Reference Librarian* 51, no. 3: 202–211.

Gerlich, Bella Karr, and G. Lynn Berard. 2007. "Introducing the READ Scale: Qualitative Statistics for Academic Reference Services." *Georgia Library Quarterly* 43, no. 4 (Winter): 7–13.

Gerlich, Bella Karr, and G. Lynn Berard. 2010. "Testing the Viability of the READ Scale (Reference Effort Assessment Data): Qualitative Statistics for Academic Reference Services." *College & Research Libraries* 71, no. 2 (March): 116–137.

Giuse, Nunzia B., Nila Sathe, Rebecca Jerome. 2006. "Task Force on the Informationist Specialist in Context (ISIC) Final Report: Envisioning the Informationist Specialist in Context (ISIC): A Multi-Center Study to Articulate Roles and Training Models." Chicago: Medical Library Association. Accessed August 28, 2010. http://mlanet.org/research/informationist/.

Handler, Lara, Mellanye Lackey, and K.T.L. Vaughan. 2009. "'Hidden Treasures': Librarian Office Hours for Three Health Sciences Schools." *Medical Reference Services Quarterly* 28, no. 4 (October-December): 336–350.

Harmon, Glynn, and Lynn Westbrook. 2010. "Unconscious Cognition in the Genesis of Reference Queries." In *Reference Renaissance*, edited by Marie L. Radford and R. David Lankes, 81–98. New York: Neal-Schuman.

Hendrix, Dean, Deborah Chiarella, Linda Hasman, Sharon Murphy, and Michelle L. Zafron. 2009. "Use of Facebook in Academic Health Sciences Libraries." *Journal of the Medical Library Association* 97, no. 1 (January): 44–47.

Herzog, Brian. 2007. "Library Subject Guides using del.icio.us." Chelmsford, MA: *Swiss Army Librarian* (July 28). Accessed October 1, 2010. http://www.swissarmylibrarian .net/2007/07/28/library-subject-guides-using-delicious.

Hill, Thomas W., and Karen L. Roth. 2009. "Electronic Document Delivery; A Six-Year Study to Benchmark the Shift to Electronic Interlibrary Loan in Two Hospital Libraries." *Journal of the Medical Library Association* 97, no. 1 (January): 54–57.

Høivik, Tord. 2003. "Why Do You Ask? Reference Statistics for Library Planning." *Performance Measurement and Metrics* 4, no. 1: 28–37.

Holmes, Kristi L., and Ellen K. Dubinsky. 2009. "Integration of Web 2.0 Technologies in the Translational Research Environment." *Medical Reference Services Quarterly* 28, no. 4 (October-December): 309–335.

Holst, Ruth, and Karen M. Bensing. 2000. "Document Delivery." In *The Medical Library Association Guide to Managing Health Care Libraries*, edited by Ruth Holst, 295–310. New York: Neal-Schuman.

Holst, Ruth, and Sharon A. Phillips, eds. 2000. *The Medical Library Association Guide to Managing Health Care Libraries.* New York: Neal-Schuman.

Homan Michael J. 2010. "Eyes on the Prize: Reflections on the Impact of the Evolving Digital Ecology on the Librarian as Expert Intermediary and Knowledge Coach, 1969–2009." *Journal of the Medical Library Association* 98, no. 1 (January): 49–56.

Hospital Libraries Section Standards Committee, Margaret Bandy, Jacqueline Donaldson Doyle, Anne Fladger, Katherine Stemmer Frumento, Linné Girouard, Sheila Hayes, and Diane Rourke. 2008. "Standards for Hospital Libraries 2007." *Journal of the Medical Library Association* 96, no. 2 (April): 162–169.

Huber, Jeffrey T., Jo Anne Boorkman, and Jean Blackwell. 2008. *Introduction to Reference Sources in the Health Sciences.* New York: Neal Schuman.

International Federation of Library Associations. 2009. "International Lending and Document Delivery: Principles and Guidelines for Procedure." The Hague, Netherlands: IFLA (February 2009). Accessed July 18, 2010. http://www.ifla .org/files/docdel/documents/international-lending-en.pdf.

Internet Archive. 2010. *Wayback Machine.* San Francisco, CA: Internet Archive. Accessed September 25. http://www .archive.org.

Jackson, Mary. 2004. "Selecting the "Best" Document Delivery Supplier." *Interlending & Document Supply* 32, no. 4: 242–243.

Jackson, Rebecca, and Lorraine J. Pellack. 2004. "Internet Subject Guides in Academic Libraries: An Analysis of Contents, Practices, and Opinions." *Reference & User Services Quarterly* 43, no. 4 (Summer): 319–327.

Jankowski, Terry Ann. 2008. *Medical Library Association Essential Guide to Becoming an Expert Searcher: Proven Techniques, Strategies, and Tips for Finding Health Information.* New York: Neal-Schuman.

Jayaraman, Shobana. 2009. "Selecting an IM Aggregator for a Virtual Reference Service at UT Southwestern Medical Center Library." *Journal of Hospital Librarianship* 9, no. 4: 433–438.

Jerant, Lisa Lott, and Kenneth Firestein. 2003. "Not Virtual, but a Real, Live, Online, Interactive Reference Service." *Medical Reference Services Quarterly* 22, no. 2 (Summer): 57–68.

Johnson, Larry, Alan Levine, and Rachel Smith. 2009. *The 2009 Horizon Report.* Austin: The New Media Consortium. Accessed October 16, 2010. http://www.nmc.org/pdf/2009-Horizon-Report.pdf.

Johnson, Stephen M., Andrew Osmond, and Rebecca J. Holz. 2009. "Developing a Current Awareness Service Using Really Simple Syndication (RSS)." *Journal of the Medical Library Association* 97, no. 1 (January): 52–54.

Joint Commission. 2007. *CAMH: Comprehensive Accreditation Manual for Hospitals: The Official Handbook.* Oakbrook Terrace, IL: The Commission.

Kazlauskas, Edward. 1976. "An Exploratory Study: A Kinesic Analysis of Academic Library Public Service Points." *Journal of Academic Librarianship* 2, no. 3: 130–134.

Kipnis, Daniel, and Gary E. Kaplan. 2008. "Analysis and Lessons Learned Instituting an Instant Messaging Reference Service at an Academic Health Sciences Library." *Medical Reference Services Quarterly* 27, no. 1 (Spring): 33–51.

Knox, Emily. 2010. *Document Delivery and Interlibrary Loan on a Shoestring.* New York: Neal-Schuman.

Kraft, Michelle. 2008. "Athens Management System." *Journal of the Medical Library Association* 96, no. 2 (April): 176–177.

Kroski, Ellyssa. 2008. *Web 2.0 for Librarians and Information Professionals.* New York: Neal-Schuman.

Kroski, Ellyssa. 2009. "Text Message Reference: Is It Effective?" *Library Journal* (October 15, 2009). Accessed August 17, 2010. http://www.libraryjournal.com/article/CA6701869 .html.

Lacroix, Eve-Marie, and Maria E. Collins. 2007. "Interlibrary Loan in U.S. and Canadian Health Sciences Libraries 2005: Update on Journal Article Use." *Journal of the Medical Library Association* 95, no. 2 (April): 189–190.

Lakos, Amos A., ed. 2004. "Portals in Libraries (Special Section)." *Bulletin of the American Society for Information Science and Technology* 31, no. 1 (October/November): 7–25.

Landau, Rebecca. 2010. "Solo Librarian and Outreach to Hospital Staff Using Web 2.0 Technologies." *Medical Reference Services Quarterly* 29, no. 1 (January–March): 75–84.

Lankes, R. David, Joseph Janes, Linda C. Smith, and Christina M. Finneran, eds. 2004. *The Virtual Reference Experience: Integrating Theory into Practice.* New York: Neal-Schuman.

Lawrence, Peg. 2009. "Access When and Where They Want It: Using EZproxy to Serve Our Remote Users." *Computers in Libraries* 29, no. 11 (January): 6-7, 41–43.

Lessick, Susan. 1996. "Administration and Organization of Services." In *Information Access and Delivery in Health Sciences Libraries* edited by Carolyn E. Lipscomb, 1–58. Current Practice in Health Sciences Librarianship. Chicago: Medical Library Association.

Library of Congress. 2004. "Library & Information Technology Publications & Articles." Library of Congress, Portals Applications Issues Group (August 24, 2004). Accessed August 17, 2010. http://www.loc.gov/catdir/lcpaig/articles .html.

Little, John R. 2001. "A Librarian's Perspective on Portals." *EDUCAUSE Quarterly* 24, no. 2: 52–54.

Logan, Firouzeh F. 2009. "A Brief History of Reference Assessment: No Easy Solutions." *The Reference Librarian* 50, no. 3 (July/September): 225–233.

Lombardo, Nancy T., Allyson Mower, and Mary M. McFarland. 2008. "Putting Wikis to Work in Libraries." *Medical Reference Services Quarterly* 27, no. 2 (Summer): 129–144.

Magi, Trina J. 2007. "Protecting Library Patrons' Confidentiality: Checklist of Best Practices." *Illinois Library Association Reporter* 25, no. 6 (December): 14–16.

Markgren, Susanne, Marie T. Ascher, and Suzanne J. Crow. 2004. "Asked and Answered—Online: How Two Medical Libraries Are Using OCLC's QuestionPoint to Answer Reference Question." *Medical Reference Services Quarterly* 23, no. 1 (Spring): 13–28.

Mathews, Brian S. 2008. "Preemptive Reference: Coming Out from Behind the Desk." In *The Desk and Beyond: Next Generation Reference Services*, edited by Sarah K. Steiner and M. Leslie Madden, 91–98. Chicago: American Library Association.

McClellan, Cynthia S. 2003. "Live Reference in an Academic Health Sciences Library: The Q and A NJ Experience at the University of Medicine and Dentistry of New Jersey Health Sciences Library at Stratford." *Internet Reference Services Quarterly* 8, no. 1/2: 117–126.

McDonald, Robert H. 2004. "Portals in Libraries: An Environmental Landscape." *Bulletin of the American Society for Information Science and Technology* 31, no. 1 (October/November 2004): 10–11.

McGraw, Kathleen A., Jennifer Heiland, and Julianna C. Harris. 2003. "Promotion and Evaluation of a Virtual Live Reference Service." *Medical Reference Services Quarterly* 22, no. 2 (Summer): 41–56.

McHone-Chase, Sarah M. 2010. "The Role of Interlibrary Loan in Disaster Preparedness and Recovery." *Journal of Interlibrary Loan, Document Delivery & Electronic Reserve* 20, no. 1: 53–60.

McKnight, Michelynn. 2002. "ARIEL and Hospital Libraries." *Journal of Hospital Librarianship* 1, no. 4 (March): 1–16.

McKnight, Susan, and Andrew Booth. 2010. "Identifying Customer Expectations Is Key to Evidence-Based Service

Delivery." *Evidence Based Library and Information Practice* 5, no. 1: 26–31.

Medical Library Association. 2006. "Informationist/Information Specialist in Context." Chicago: Medical Library Association. Accessed July 25, 2010. http://mlanet.org/research/informationist/.

Medical Library Association. 2007. *Competencies for Lifelong Learning and Professional Success: The Educational Policy Statement of the Medical Library Association* (February). Chicago: Medical Library Association. Accessed October 12, 2010. http://mlanet.org/education/policy/.

Medical Library Association. 2010a. "Code of Ethics for Health Sciences Librarianship." Chicago: Medical Library Association. Accessed September 11. http://mlanet.org/about/ethics.html.

Medical Library Association. 2010b. "Expert Searching." Chicago: Medical Library Association. Accessed July 25. http://mlanet.org/resources/expert_search/.

Medical Library Association. 2010c. "Joint Commission Accreditation Resources." Chicago: Medical Library Association. Accessed July 22. http://mlanet.org/resources/#jcaho.

Meserve, Harry C., Sandra E. Belanger, Joan Bowlby, and Lisa Rosenblum. 2009. "Developing a Model for Reference Research Statistics: Applying the Warner Model of Reference Question Classification to Streamline Research Services." *Reference & User Services Quarterly* 48, no. 3 (Spring): 247–258.

Michalak, Sarah C, ed. 2005. *Portals and Libraries*. New York: Haworth Press.

Milstein, Sarah. 2009. "Twitter for Libraries (and Librarians)." *Online* 33, no. 2 (March/April): 34–35.

Mitchell, Nicole, and Lisa A. Ennis. 2010. "Scaling the (Fire) Wall." *Journal of Hospital Librarianship* 10, no. 2: 190–196.

Moore, Margaret E., Kathleen A. McGraw, and Julia Shaw-Kokot. 2001. "Preparing Staff to Work at a Single Service Desk." *Medical Reference Services Quarterly* 20, no. 1 (Spring): 79–86.

Morris, Leslie R. 2002. *Interlibrary Loan Policies Directory*. 7th ed. New York: Neal-Schuman.

Murphy, Beverly, Richard A. Peterson, Hattie Vines, Megan von Isenburg, Elizabeth Berney, Robert James, Marcos Rodriguez, and Patrica Thibodeau. 2008. "Revolution at the Library Service Desk." *Medical Reference Services Quarterly* 27, no. 4 (Winter): 379–393.

Naismith, Rachael. 2004. "Combining Circulation and Reference Functions at One Desk." *Journal of Access Services* 2, no. 3: 15–20.

National Commission on New Technological Uses of Copyright Works. 1978. "CONTU Guidelines on Photocopyright under Interlibrary Loan Arrangements." Washington, DC: Library of Congress. Accessed August 1, 2010. http://www.cni.org/docs/infopols/CONTU.html.

Neuhaus, Paul. 2003. "Privacy and Confidentiality in Digital Reference." *Reference & User Services Quarterly* 43, no. 1 (Fall): 26–36.

Nicholson, Scott, and Catherine Arnott Smith. 2007. "Using Lessons from Health Care to Protect the Privacy of Library Users: Guidelines for the De-identification of Library Data Based on HIPAA." *Journal of the American Society for Information Science and Technology* 58, no. 8 (June): 1198–206.

Nielsen, Jakob. 1998. "Personalization Is Over-Rated." *Alertbox* (October 4). Accessed September 21, 2010. http://www.useit.com/alertbox/981004.html.

Norton, Melanie J., and Michelle A. Stover. 2003. "Review of OCLC ILLiad." *Bulletin of the Medical Library Association* 91, no. 3 (July): 379–380.

Paden, Shelley L., Andrea L. Batson, and Richard L. Wallace. 2001. "Web-based Loansome Doc, Librarians, and End Users: Results from a Survey of the Southeast Region." *Bulletin of the Medical Library Association* 89, no. 3 (July): 263–271.

Parker, Sandi K., and E. Diane Johnson. 2003. "The Region 4 Collaborative Virtual Reference Project." *Medical Reference Services Quarterly* 22, no. 2 (Summer): 29–39.

Polger, Mark Aaron. 2010. "Information Takeout and Delivery: A Case Study Exploring Different Library Service Delivery Models." *Journal of Hospital Librarianship* 10, no. 1 (January): 3–22.

Powell, Carol A., and Pamela S. Bradigan. 2001. "E-Mail Reference Services: Characteristics and Effects on Overall Reference Services at an Academic Health Sciences Library." *Reference & User Services Quarterly* 41, no. 2 (Winter): 170–178.

Powell, James E., Linn Marks Collins, and Mark L. B. Martinez. 2009. "The Fierce Urgency of Now: A Proactive, Pervasive Content Awareness Tool." " *D-Lib Magazine* 15, no. 5/6. Accessed September 15, 2010. http://www.dlib.org/dlib/may09/powell/05powell.html.

Radford, Marie L. 1998. "Approach or Avoidance? The Role of Nonverbal Communication in the Academic Library User's Decision to Initiate a Reference Encounter." *Library Trends* 46, no. 4 (Spring): 699–717.

Rankin, Jocelyn A., Suzanne F. Grefsheim, and Candace C. Canto. 2008. "The Emerging Informationist Specialty: A Systematic Review of the Literature." *Journal of the Medical Library Association* 96, no. 3 (July): 194–206.

Reference and User Services Association, American Library Association. 2000. "Guidelines for Information Services." Chicago: American Library Association. Accessed October 22, 2010. http://www.ala.org/ala/mgrps/divs/rusa/resources/guidelines/guidelinesinformation.cfm.

Reference and User Services Association, American Library Association. 2004a. "Guidelines for Behavioral Performance of Reference and Information Service Professionals." Accessed October 6, 2010. http://www.ala.org/ala/mgrps/divs/rusa/resources/guidelines/guidelinesbehavioral.cfm.

Reference and User Services Association, American Library Association. 2004b. "Guidelines for Implementing and Maintaining Virtual Reference Services." Chicago: American Library Association. Accessed August 11, 2010. http://www.ala.org/ala/mgrps/divs/rusa/resources/guidelines/virtrefguidelines.cfm.

"Remarkable Outreach: Flickr Project Draws 10 Million Views." 2009. *Library of Congress Information Bulletin* 68, no. 1/2 (January/February): 22–24.

Rethlefsen, Melissa. 2007. "Social Networking." In *Medical Librarian 2.0; Use of Web 2.0 Technologies in Reference Services*, edited by M. Sandra Wood, 117–141. New York: Haworth Press. (Also published as *Medical Reference Services Quarterly* 26, Supp. 1, 2007: 117–141).

Rethlefsen, Melissa L., David L. Rothman, and Daniel S. Mojon. 2009. *Internet Cool Tools for Physicians.* Berlin: Springer.

Rios, Gabriel. 2008. "Creating a 'Virtual Expert' Presence in the Hospital Library." *Journal of Hospital Librarianship* 8, no. 4: 457–463.

Rodzvilla, John. 2010. "New Title Tweets: Using Twitter and Microsoft Excel to Broadcast New Title Lists." *Computers in Libraries* 30, no. 5 (June): 26–30.

Ross, Catherine Sheldrick, Kirsti Nilsen, and Marie L. Radford. 2009. *Conducting the Reference Interview: A How-To-Do-It Manual for Librarians.* 2nd ed. New York: Neal Schuman.

Rothman, David L. 2007. "Getting Started with RSS Feeds." *Journal of Hospital Librarianship* 7, no. 3: 75–83.

Rupple, Margie, and Jody Condit Fagan. 2002. "Instant Messaging Reference: Users' Evaluation of Library Chat." *Reference Service Review* 30, no. 3: 183–197.

Ryan, Susan M. 2003. "Library Web Site Administration: A Strategic Planning Model for the Smaller Academic Library." *Journal of Academic Librarianship* 29, no. 4 (July): 207–218.

Savulescu, Julian, and Merle Spriggs. 2002. "The Hexamethonium Asthma Study and the Death of a Normal Volunteer in Research." *Journal of Medical Ethics* 28, no. 1 (February): 3–4.

Scherrer, Carol. 2004. "Reference Librarians' Perceptions of the Issues They Face as Academic Health Information Professionals." *Journal of the Medical Library Association* 92, no.2 (April): 226–232.

Schnell, Eric. 2007. "Document Delivery Using docMD." *Journal of Interlibrary Loan, Document Delivery, & Electronic Reserve* 17, no. 3: 99–107.

Schwing, Laurie J., and Elizabeth E. Coldsmith. 2005. "Librarians as Hidden Gems in a Clinical Team." *Medical Reference Services Quarterly* 24, no. 1 (Spring): 29–39.

Shedlock, James, Michelle Frisque, Steve Hunt, Linda Walton, Jonathan Handler, and Michael Gillam. 2010. "Case Study: The Health SmartLibrary Experiences in Web Personalization and Customization at the Galter Health Sciences Library, Northwestern University." *Journal of the Medical Library Association* 98, no. 2 (April): 98–104.

SHERPA. 2006–2008. "SHERPA/RoMEO: Publisher Copyright Policies & Self-Archiving." Nottingham, UK: University of Nottingham (2006–2008). Accessed July 18, 2010. http://www.sherpa.ac.uk/romeo/.

Shipman, Jean P., Diana J. Cunningham, Ruth Holst, and Linda A. Watson. 2002. "The Informationist Conference: Report." *Journal of the Medical Library Association* 90, no. 4 (October): 458–464.

Simpson, Betsy, Priscilla Williams, Shelley Arlen, and Peter Bushnell. 2005. "Accessing Locally Created Subject Guides via the Library's Catalog." *Collection Management* 30, no. 4: 31–42.

Smith, Michael M. 2006. "A Tool for All Places: A Web-based Reference Statistics System." *Reference Services Review* 34, no. 2: 298–315.

Smith, Virginia M. 2010. "Internet Reviews: Flickr for Your Library." *Kentucky Libraries* 74, no. 2 (Spring): 26–27.

Sodt, Jill M., and Terri Pedersen Summey. 2009. "Beyond the Library's Walls: Using Library 2.0 Tools to Reach Out to All Users." *Journal of Library Administration* 49, no. 1: 97–109.

Starr, Susan. 2010. "The Customer versus the Container." *Journal of the Medical Library Association* 98, no. 22 (April): 95–96.

Steiner, Sarah K., and M. Leslie Madden. 2008. *The Desk and Beyond: Next Generation Reference Services.* Chicago: American Library Association.

Stoffel, Bruce, and Jim Cunningham. 2005. "Library Participation in Campus Web Portals: An Initial Study." *Reference Services Review* 33, no. 2: 144–160.

Stone, Martha E., Carole Foxman, Maura Sostack, Lori Francar, Patrice Hall, and Linda Garr Markwell. 2003. "Ask a Librarian." *Medical Reference Services Quarterly* 22, no. 2 (Summer): 93–105.

Stuart, David. 2010. "What Are Libraries Doing on Twitter?" *Online* 34, no. 1 (January/February): 45–47.

Tao, Donghua, Patrick G. McCarthy, Mary M. Krieger, and Annie B. Webb. 2009. "The Mobile Reference Service: A Case Study of an Onsite Reference Service Program at the School of Public Health." *Journal of the Medical Librarian Association* 97, no. 1 (January): 34–40.

Tennant, Roy. 1999. "Digital Libraries: User Interface Design: Some Guiding Principles." *Library Journal* 124, no. 17 (October 15): 28–29.

Tenopir, Carol, and Lisa A. Ennis. 2001. "Reference Services in the New Millennium." *Online* 25, no. 4 (July/August): 40–45.

Thompson, Tracy L. 2006. "From authentication to access management: The potential of shibboleth." *AALL Spectrum* 10, no.4 (February): insert10-11.

Todaro, Julie Beth, and Mark L. Smith. 2006. *Training Library Staff and Volunteers to Provide Extraordinary Customer Service.* London: Facet.

U. S. National Library of Medicine. 2006. *Charting a Course for the 21st Century: NLM's Long Range Plan 2006–2016.* Bethesda, MD: NLM Board of Regents: U.S. Department of Health and Human Services, Public Health Service, National Institutes of Health, National Library of Medicine. Accessed October 17, 2010. http://www.nlm.nih.gov/pubs/plan/lrp06/NLM_LRP2006_WEB.pdf.

U.S. National Library of Medicine. 2009a. "DOCLINE Fact Sheet." Bethesda, MD: National Library of Medicine, August 25. Accessed October 17, 2010. http://www.nlm.nih.gov/pubs/factsheets/docline.html.

U.S. National Library of Medicine. 2009b. "National Network of Libraries of Medicine Fact Sheet." Bethesda, MD:

National Library of Medicine, July 27. Accessed October 17, 2010. http://www.nlm.nih.gov/pubs/factsheets/nnlm.html.

U.S. National Library of Medicine. 2009c. "SERHOLD Fact Sheet." Bethesda, MD: National Library of Medicine, June 24. Accessed October 17, 2010. http://www.nlm.nih.gov/pubs/factsheets/serhold.html.

Wagner, Kay Cimpl, and Gary D. Byrd. 2004. "Evaluating the Effectiveness of Clinical Medical Librarian Programs: A Systematic Review of the Literature." *Journal of the Medical Library Association* 92, no. 1 (January): 14–33.

Ward, David. 2003. "Using Virtual Reference Transcripts for Staff Training." *Reference Services Review* 31, no. 1: 46–56.

Warner, Debra G. 2001. "A New Classification for Reference Statistics." *Reference & User Services Quarterly* 41, no. 1 (Fall): 51–55.

"Warnings of Copyright for Use by Certain Libraries and Archives." 1995. *U.S. Code of Federal Regulations*, v.37, sec.201.14(b) (1995).

Weise, Frieda. 2004. "Being There: The Library as Place." *Journal of the Medical Library Association* 92, no. 1 (January): 6–13.

Welch, Jeanie M. 2007. "Click and Be Counted: A New Standard for Reference Statistics." *The Reference Librarian* 47, no. 1: 95–104.

Wood, M. Sandra., and Robert S. Seeds. 1974. "Development of SDI Services from a Manual Current Awareness Service to SDILINE." *Bulletin of the Medical Library Association* 62, no. 4 (October): 374–384.

Woodward, Jeannette A. 2007. *What Every Librarian Should Know about Electronic Privacy*. Westport, CT: Libraries Unlimited.

Woodward, Jeannette A. 2009. *Creating the Customer-Driven Academic Library*. Chicago: American Library Association.

Yale University Library. 2007. "Licensing Digital Information: Licenses Provided by Publishers." (October 13, 2007). Accessed October 17, 2010. http://www.library.yale.edu/~llicense/publishers.shtml.

Yunis, Susan S. 1973. "The Implementation, Evaluation, and Refinement of a Manual SDI Service." *Bulletin of the Medical Library Association* 61, no. 1 (January): 4–14.

Zhou, Joe. 2003. "A History of Web Portals and Their Developments in Libraries." *Information Technology in Libraries* 22, no. 3 (September): 119–128.

Zipperer, Lorri, and Jan Sykes. 2004. "The Role of Librarians in Patient Safety: Gaps and Strengths in the Current Culture." *Journal of the Medical Library Association* 92, no. 4 (October): 498–500.

Further Reading

Information Services

Aamot, Gordon, and Steve Hiller. 2004. "Library Services in Non-Library Spaces." *Association Research Libraries SPEC Kit 285.* Washington DC: Association Research Libraries (November).

Robertson, Justin, Judy Burnham, and Ellen Sayed. 2008. "The Medical Matters Wiki." *Medical Reference Services Quarterly* 27, no. 1 (Spring): 21–32.

Stephens, Michael. 2006. "Steal This Idea: Flickr for Librarians." *Tame the Web: Libraries and Technology* (September 18). Accessed August 23, 2010. http://tametheweb.com/2006/09/steal_this_idea_flickr_for_lib.html.

Interlibrary Loan and Document Delivery

Arcari, Ralph, Jackie Lewis, and Edward Donald. 2004. "The Electronic Fund Transfer System." *Journal of the Medical Library Association* 92, no. 4 (October): 493–495.

Baich, Tina, Tim Jiping Zou, Heather Weltin, and Zheng Ye Yang. 2009. "Lending and Borrowing Across Borders." *Reference & User Services Quarterly* 49, no. 1 (Fall): 54–63.

Crowe, William J. 2009. "The Revolution Continues: Resource Sharing and OCLC in the New Century." *Journal of Library Administration* 49, no. 7: 669–673.

Croft, Janet B. 2005. "Interlibrary Loan and Licensing." *Journal of Library Administration* 42, no. 3: 41–53.

Deardorff, Thomas, and Heidi Nance. 2009. "WorldCat Local Implementation: The Impact on Interlibrary Loan." *Interlending & Document Supply* 37, no. 4: 177–180.

Dell, Esther Y. 2007. "Access to Medical Literature: Interlibrary Borrowing and Lending in an Electronic Age." *Journal of Interlibrary Loan, Document Delivery & Electronic Reserve* 17, nos. 1/2: 37–43.

Dudden, Rosalind F., Sue Coldren, Joyce E. Condon, Sara Katsh, Catherine M. Reiter, and Pamela L. Roth. 2000. "Interlibrary Loan in Primary Access Libraries: Challenging the Traditional View." *Bulletin of the Medical Library Association* 88, no. 4 (October): 303–311.

Hill, Thomas W. 2005. "Document Delivery for the Hospital Library, 2005." *Journal of Hospital Librarianship* 6, no. 2: 85–94.

Hill, Thomas W. 2006. "Document Delivery for the Hospital Library, 2006 Part 2." *Journal of Hospital Librarianship* 6, no. 3: 97–109.

Hilyer, Lee A. 2006. "Chapter 2. Governing Policies for Interlibrary Loan." *Journal of Interlibrary Loan, Document Delivery & Electronic Reserve* 16, no. 1: 11–15.

Hilyer, Lee A. 2006. "Chapter 3. Borrowing." *Journal of Interlibrary Loan, Document Delivery & Electronic Reserve* 16, no. 1: 17–39.

Hilyer, Lee A. 2006. "Chapter 4. Lending." *Journal of Interlibrary Loan, Document Delivery & Electronic Reserve* 16, nos. 1/2: 41–51.

Hilyer, Lee A. 2006. "Chapter 5. Copyright in the Interlibrary Loan Department." *Journal of Interlibrary Loan, Document Delivery & Electronic Reserve* 16, nos. 1/2: 53–64.

Hilyer, Lee A. 2006. "Part II: Resources." *Journal of Interlibrary Loan, Document Delivery & Electronic Reserve* 16, no. 1: 81–106.

Jayaraman, Shobana, and Karen Harker. 2009. "Evaluating the Quality of a Link Resolver." *Journal of Electronic Resources in Medical Libraries* 6, no. 2: 152–162.

Morrison, Heather G. 2006. "The Dramatic Growth of Open Access." *Journal of Interlibrary Loan, Document Delivery & Electronic Reserve* 16, no. 3: 95–107.

Norton, Melanie J., Daniel T. Wilson, and Susan S. Yowell. 2009. "Partnering to Promote Service Continuity in the Event of an Emergency: A Successful Collaboration Between Two Interlibrary Loan Departments." *Journal of the Medical Library Association* 97, no. 2 (April): 131–134.

Zopfi-Jordan, David. 2008. "Purchasing or Borrowing: Making Interlibrary Loan Decisions That Enhance Patron Satisfaction." *Journal of Interlibrary Loan, Document Delivery & Electronic Reserve* 18, no. 3: 387–394.

Library Websites

Davidsen, Susanna, and Everyl Yankee. 2003. *Web Site Design with the Patron in Mind: A Step-By-Step Guide for Librarians.* Chicago: American Library Association.

Lynch, Patrick J., and Sarah Horton. 2009. *Web Style Guide: Basic Design Principles for Creating Web Sites.* 3rd ed. New Haven, CT: Yale University Press.

Morville, Peter, and Louis Rosefeld. 2006. *Information Architecture for the World Wide Web.* 3rd ed. Sebastopol, CA: O'Reilly Media.

Nielsen, Jakob. 2007. *Jakob Nielsen's Alertbox: Top Ten Mistakes in Web Design.* Accessed September 26, 2010. http://www.useit.com/alertbox/9605.html.

Simpson, Betsy, Priscilla Williams, Shelley Arlen, and Peter Bushnell. 2005. "Accessing Locally Created Subject Guides via the Library's Catalog." *Collection Management* 30, no. 4: 31–42.

Song, Yuwu. 2003. *Building Better Web Sites: A How-To-Do-It Manual for Librarians.* New York: Neal-Schuman.

Veldof Jerilyn R., and Shane Nackerud. 2001. "Do You Have the Right Stuff? Seven Areas of Expertise for Successful Web Site Design in Libraries." *Internet Reference Services Quarterly* 6, no. 1: 13–38.

Wilson, A. Paula 2004. *Library Web Sites: Creating Online Collections and Services.* Chicago: American Library Association.

11

Educational Services

Lisa K. Traditi

The author wishes to acknowledge the outstanding work of Jacqueline Doyle and Kay Wellik, co-authors of this chapter in the first edition of the MLA Guide to Health Sciences Library, whose work provided the foundation for and remains integrated into the current chapter.

Although health care library customers are highly trained in their respective fields, they may require additional knowledge and skills to make effective use of the library. In this context, the librarian takes on the role of instructor to help health professionals gain needed skills in information retrieval and information management. Because the need to provide education and training to library users is growing, the coverage of educational services has been expanded from the previous edition of this book into its own chapter.

This educational activity on the part of library staff has historically been called bibliographic instruction, library instruction, or instructional services. A phrase formerly used in academic libraries was "information management education." In recent years academic libraries have adopted the concept of Information Literacy (IL), which is discussed in a subsequent section. This chapter uses the term "educational services," to include the broad range of activities focused on the teaching of information-related topics and skills. The terms "training," "instruction," and "education" are used synonymously.

Educational services, like information services, are designed and delivered based on the librarian's knowledge of the organization's information-related educational needs. They vary, therefore, depending on the mission of the organization and the type of customers served. These services can range from a "welcome aboard" tour for new physicians and nurses to database and Internet training for cardiology fellows to using a smartphone to access web-based information tools at the point of care. The breadth and depth of educational services depends on the results of the needs assessment described earlier in Chapter 6 combined with the availability of educational resources elsewhere in the organization.

Based on the needs assessment and the librarian's existing knowledge of the organization, learning objectives for each educational activity should be defined and potential instructors identified. The librarian must define the role of the library staff in the delivery of educational offerings. For example, the library may actually provide the training or act as a facilitating department for training provided by an interdisciplinary team of information-savvy health professionals. Instructors may be library staff members, health care professionals with special skills, or computer experts from any area of the organization.

Environmental Trends

A number of trends have influenced the need for and delivery of educational services in health care settings. Included among those trends are direct access to databases, information literacy, lifelong learning and evidence-based practice, and the growth of medical informatics.

Direct Access to Databases

Beginning in the mid-1980s, the National Library of Medicine (NLM) introduced a series of products and subsequent enhancements to improve online access to the MEDLARS files, particularly MEDLINE. Grateful Med, Loansome Doc and, later, Internet Grateful Med and PubMed, changed the way health professionals accessed the NLM databases. In addition, commercial vendors of electronic databases began to market their enhanced versions of these databases directly to the public. This access, coupled with higher levels of computer competencies and improved access to computer technology within health care organizations, has enabled more health professionals to perform their own searches. Health care librarians have adapted their libraries' education services to meet the needs and expectations of these computer-savvy health professionals.

Information Literacy

Information Literacy (IL) is a concept primarily adopted and executed by academic libraries. Brower (2008) has provided a number of insights on the meaning of information literacy and how the concept can be used in program development. IL relates well to the idea of lifelong learning discussed below since IL programs cover a broad array of competencies. Brower (2010: 218) notes that the Information Literacy Standards of ACRL "have been widely adopted, particularly in academic undergraduate and graduate school libraries.". The ACRL standards are summarized on their website:

> An information literate individual is able to:
> - Determine the extent of information needed
> - Access the needed information effectively and efficiently
> - Evaluate information and its sources critically
> - Incorporate selected information into one's knowledge base
> - Use information effectively to accomplish a specific purpose
> - Understand the economic, legal, and social issues surrounding the use of information, and access and use information ethically and legally (Association of College and Research Libraries, 2010)

While development of a full-blown IL program may be beyond the resources available to managers of smaller health care libraries, it is helpful to understand the concept and adapt some of the instructional ideas to their setting. The rest of the chapter will provide some details on how selective programming can accomplish these aims. Brower also edits an electronic journal *Communications in Information Literacy* (http://www.comminfolit.org/index.php/cil/index) that provides information and links to additional resources.

Lifelong Learning and Evidence-Based Practice

Schools of medicine, nursing, and allied health have increasingly integrated the concepts of lifelong learning and evidence-based practice into their programs (Schulte, 2008). For example, the landmark GPEP Report (Association of American Medical Colleges, 1984) recommended that medical students be taught information management skills that would enhance their ability to improve their medical skills and increase their knowledge throughout their professional lives. The Medical School Objectives Project Report II *Contemporary Issues in*

Medicine: Medical Informatics and Population Health (Association of American Medical Colleges,1998) was another significant and influential report that health care librarians have used to frame instructional programs that can be integrated in curriculum. Health care librarians serving residency programs look to the General Competencies of the Accreditation Council for Graduate Medical Education (ACGME), which requires that residents must be able to "locate, appraise, and assimilate evidence from scientific studies related to their patients' health problems and use information technology to optimize learning" (Accreditation Council for Graduate Medical Education, 2007).

Evidence-based medicine "stresses the examination of evidence from clinical research" (Evidence-Based Medicine Working Group, 1992: 2420). Consequently, physicians and other health professionals are developing new skills that include efficient literature searching and the critical appraisal of biomedical literature. Health professionals exposed to these concepts during training will have different expectations for library services, and health care librarians must be prepared to develop services to support these expectations (Scherrer, Dorsch, and Weller, 2006).

Health care librarians in all environments should be involved in these activities. As noted in a recent Vital Pathways Task Force report, "As the clinical practice environment becomes increasingly technology driven... health care professionals will require information management and informatics knowledge and skills to function effectively. In addition... professional development activities will also increasingly require knowledge and skill in using many different technological resources... Facilitating the advancement of these skills among health care provider trainees—whether at the undergraduate, graduate, or postgraduate level—will remain an essential role and responsibility of the health sciences librarian" (Schwartz et al., 2009: 283).

Growth of Medical Informatics

Information technologies are ever changing. Definitions are changing as well, but Shortliffe's 1990 description of medical informatics endures: "a field of study concerned with the broad range of issues in the management and use of biomedical information, including medical computing and the study of the nature of medical information itself" (Shortliffe and Perreault, 1990: 658). Computers are being used in an increasingly wider range of medical applications, from bedside patient care and patient education to health records management and online physician order entry. Health care organizations are integrating Internet and intranet technologies into the information system infrastructure to enhance electronic sharing of information resources. Librarians need to keep abreast of new developments in this field so that they can apply whatever tools and methods will improve the library's information systems and assist in integrating library systems into the organization's information systems overall (Albert, 2007; Haynes, 2007; Ellero, 2009).

Clinical translational science is the latest effort of the national informatics community, with multi-million dollar grants awarded by the National Institute of Health (NIH) to more than 70 health sciences universities across the United States. These grants, called Clinical and Translational Science Awards (CTSA), fund projects that often include informatics education efforts in which the library can play a useful role (Kon, 2008).

What Is Clinical Translational Science?

To improve human health, scientific discoveries must be translated into practical applications. Such discoveries typically begin at the "bench" with basic research—in which scientists study disease at a molecular or cellular level—then progress to the clinical level, or the patient's "bedside." Scientists are increasingly aware that this bench-to-bedside approach to translational research is really a two-way street.

Basic scientists provide clinicians with new tools for use in patients and for assessment of their impact, and clinical researchers make novel observations about the nature and progression of disease that often stimulate basic investigations.

Translational research has proven to be a powerful process that drives the clinical research engine. However, a stronger research infrastructure could strengthen and accelerate this critical part of the clinical research enterprise. The NIH Roadmap attempts to catalyze translational research in various ways (NIH Common Fund, 2009).

Types of Educational Services

The librarian might choose to work collaboratively with other information or health care professionals. For example, employees in the information systems department could have expertise in a particular piece of computer software and could instruct students in the use of that software. Physicians with critical appraisal or web skills may be interested in teaching new physicians, house staff, or other health care professionals. Nurses with knowledge of research methods may want to teach other nurses how to search the nursing literature for information relevant to nursing quality improvement. The librarian may be invited to teach information seeking skills within a curriculum on evidence based practice or a research course. Working collaboratively with health, education, research, and computer professionals to develop and provide effective educational experiences expands the librarian's perceived and actual value to the organization. It also spreads the burden of the curriculum development and teaching over a greater number of individuals, making it easier to offer a greater range and variety of offerings.

Educational programs offered under the library's auspices are varied and may include:

- general user orientation,
- focused library instruction,
- individual consultation,
- curriculum-integrated programming,
- database and literature searching education,
- topic-specific searching instruction,
- bibliographic management tools instruction, and
- handheld and smartphone tools.

See Figure 11.1 for educational services ideas for different types of health sciences libraries.

General User Orientation

Some librarians offer a general orientation for all new employees or, more specifically, for new physicians or new nurses. This event is frequently the first time a new employee or health care professional sees the library, and as such, it is a good opportunity to educate potential new customers about the purpose and functions of the library. The orientation might include a library tour, information about resources, or a demonstration of the library's electronic access systems. If it is difficult to get new employees or medical staff to actually come to the library, the librarian might consider developing a handout, a poster display, or a web-based video library orientation program. The latter could be mounted on the organization's Intranet for access from workstations throughout the facility. A web-based orientation could also be viewed within a classroom or included in general orientation.

Focused Library Instruction

Librarians will find that not all health professionals or administrators conduct their own library research. They may delegate that task—sometimes to a nurse, a secretary, a student or intern, a physician assistant, or a volunteer. Providing training to these individuals will enhance their effectiveness as library users. Examples

Figure 11.1. Educational Services Ideas

	Non-teaching community hospital library	Teaching community hospital library	Tertiary care research hospital library	Corporate health sciences library	Community college library	University library: under-graduate	Academic health sciences university library with University Hospital
One-on-One Consultations	●	●	●	●	●	●	●
Small Group Consultations	●	●	●	●	●	●	●
Grand Rounds	●	●	●				●
Departmental Continuing Education Meetings	●	●	●	●	●	●	●
Ethics Committee	●	●	●	●			●
Nursing Research Group	●	●	●				●
Nursing Magnet Committee	●	●	●				●

(Continued)

Figure 11.1. Educational Services Ideas (Continued)

	Non-teaching community hospital library	Teaching community hospital library	Tertiary care research hospital library	Corporate health sciences library	Community college library	University library: under-graduate	Academic health sciences university library with University Hospital
Quality Improvement Group	●	●	●	●			●
Staff Development	●	●	●	●	●	●	●
Health Care Provider Development	●	●	●				●
Faculty development		●	●	●	●	●	●
Continuing Education Department	●	●	●	●	●	●	●
Departments with Practicum Students		●	●	●			●
Allied Health Professionals (PT, OT, Dieticians, Social Work, etc.)	●	●	●				●
Research Teams		●	●	●		●	●
Orientations (New Staff, Faculty, Employees, Students)	●	●	●	●	●	●	●
Residency and Fellowship Programs		●	●				●
Morning Report		●	●				●
Clinical Rounds		●	●				●
Evidence-Based Practice Trainings		●	●				●
"One-off" classes within the Curriculum					●	●	●
"How to Do Research" Sessions					●	●	●
"Searching for the Evidence" Sessions					●	●	●
Research Courses					●	●	●
Full-Term Courses within the Curriculum					●	●	●
Evidence-Based Practice Course					●	●	●
Fundamentals of Research					●	●	●
Public Health					●	●	●
Health Literacy					●	●	●

of instruction might include using the library's online catalog of books and other materials, basic end-user database searching, introduction to the contents of the reference collection, or completion of interlibrary loan request forms.

Training sessions should be scheduled as needed, perhaps once per quarter. Offerings can be publicized in organization wide e-mails, online or print newsletters, or with posters in key locations.

Individual Consultation

Adults learn best in a focused, personalized setting and at the time they experience a learning gap. Librarians can provide one-on-one instruction and consultation to meet those needs. Individual consultations can be considered the ultimate reference interview, where the librarian not only answers specific questions but also provides skills the customer can use to answer future questions.

Curriculum-Integrated Programming

Another highly effective teaching program is one tied into the curricula of academic health sciences centers. Librarians often work with faculty of their university schools and colleges of medicine, nursing, dentistry, pharmacy, public health, physician assistant, and physical therapy, as well as graduate schools in basic and advanced sciences. Teaching students how to find, evaluate, and manage information fits well in research courses, as well as those focused on evidence-based practice. Topic specific courses are also good spots for such instruction— offering courses on finding women's health topics or infectious diseases.

Also, university and teaching hospital residency and fellowship programs offer rich opportunities for teaching information literacy skills. Learning how to ask and answer background and foreground questions in a clinical setting, when time is of the essence, is the key to clinical success. Librarians can teach residents how to use clinical point of care information resources, how to find online calculators for risk assessment or number needed to treat, and how to use resources from a smartphone or PDA. Another technique is to attend the residency morning report sessions and then do a literature search and send out information on the important questions of the day. Alternatively, the librarian can demonstrate searching for those answers live during the morning report session, offering real-time learning opportunities for the participants.

Database and Literature Searching Education

The growth and ease of use of the World Wide Web and the increasing number of health professionals who prefer to conduct their own online searches goes hand in hand. Personal computer use and database search training are now a common part of both undergraduate and graduate education for health professionals. Librarians working in teaching hospitals will want to be actively involved in training house staff, nurses, and other health professionals to search databases or to teach the idiosyncrasies of the database systems in place. New physicians, nurses, and other health professionals bring with them the expectation of end-user search capabilities and remote access to library information resources.

End-user searching education frequently serves as the core of a medical informatics program. Education about literature searching should provide library users with a basic introduction to methods for accessing medical and related literature, as well as an awareness of the variety of formats in which it can be found, including licensed online databases, free web-based resources, and print materials. Most health care libraries offer at least one end-user system, if not several, and build their literature-searching curriculum around these products.

Regular, ongoing training should be offered to the users of the resources selected. Studies have compared end-user search results with those of experienced professional searchers (McKibbon and Walker-Dilks, 1995). Inexperienced searchers frequently miss many relevant citations and search inefficiently, underscoring that literature-searching education is a vital component of library education services. Training end users to do their own database searching often results in the trainees' gaining a greater appreciation for the librarian's skills and expertise. Using a simple pre-test to assess the trainees' prior knowledge of searching will make it possible to direct the training session to a level appropriate to the individual or group being trained. See Figure 11.2 for an example of a pre- and post-test (Fox, 2008). The pre- and post-test is also on the **accompanying CD-ROM**.

Printed guides or online handouts should be available for any resources offered so that health professionals can learn at home or in their office. Examples of learning materials might include a list of available databases with descriptive scope notes; formulation of a sample search strategy; and instructions on how to display, print, and download results. The basic elements of searcher training for new or inexperienced searchers might include:

MANAGEMENT IN ACTION 11.1

Everyday Educational Packages

Location: Metropolitan Teaching Hospital

Description of Problem/Project: When faced with clinical questions not answered by their attending, residents either used the local health sciences university library or other resources, but not the hospital library. The library manager wanted to connect the residents to the hospital library and its staff in a vital and consistent way by providing follow-up information in a timely and meaningful manner. After meeting with the residency director, she decided to attend morning report.

Currently, every Monday through Friday, the residents meet in a conference room, where one resident is assigned to present an interesting case. One of the librarians attends the session, listens to the case presentation and discussion, then returns to the library and looks up articles, book sections, and websites to help the residents learn more about what was discussed. She then copies the case report written by the chief resident, includes the items found, and distributes this in an e-mail.

Impact: In July 2010, almost 150 people were on their distribution list: 99 percent are physicians, but a few are from other areas in the hospital, such as risk management.

People Involved: The three staff librarians alternate on which days they attend morning report. Important note: All three librarians total 2.5 FTEs and the library has no other library staff.

Strategies for Success:
1. Ask how to be involved. The library manager took the initiative to approach the residency director and offered to be involved.
2. Deliver. A librarian shows up at morning report, regularly.
3. Add value. The librarian tracks the cases, researches the answers, and delivers information to the residents.
4. Be timely. The "learning package" goes out every day via e-mail.
5. Build on success. The librarian added the case report to the "learning package" so that those who did not attend that session have some context for the information provided. Also, the residents are archiving the completed "learning packages" on their internal website.
6. Keep improving the product. The library manager would like to add a registration link to the library's website, so that anyone on the hospital staff can sign up to receive the packages. Also, she is working with the residents to make the archive accessible to affiliated community physicians.

Barriers Encountered: Besides making the time to attend the meeting and research the questions, the greatest initial barrier was that, since this service had never been provided before, the physicians had no idea why a librarian would attend morning report. At that time, the e-mail was only going to the chief residents and the presenter; the other attendees never saw any benefit. As time went on, the librarian was given an e-mail distribution list of the residents and regular attending physicians so that everyone present could benefit from the library information. However, those who missed the presentation were still not getting the full benefit of the materials. Last year, the library manager asked for and received permission to include the case presentation itself, since that is more useful for the people who were unable to attend. Corporate compliance told her what parts of the case presentation had to be removed because of HIPAA, then gave their blessing to include the rest of the information.

Take-Home Points: Proving your worth is often no different than simply showing up and following up. The word of mouth on the email "learning packages" is huge and has spread to residency programs at the local university hospital residency program.

Further Reading: Enyeart, Amanda and Debbie Weaver. "Relationship Marketing in a Hospital Library." *Medical Reference Services Quarterly* 24, no. 4 (Winter): 89–97

- introduction to the common databases, including MEDLINE/PubMed, CINAHL, and Embase, or specialty-specific files such as PsycINFO or Micromedex;
- differentiation of bibliographic and full-text databases and how that difference affects searching strategy;
- an overview of searching commands, especially for subjects, keywords, and authors;
- introduction to the Boolean operators AND, OR, and NOT;
- explanation of how to use the controlled vocabulary effectively;

Figure 11.2. Example of a Pre- and Post-test

Used to measure changes in participants' knowledge. Medical Informatics Elective for the Primary Care Internal Medicine Residency, 1997–2008

Medical Informatics Elective

Pre- and Post-test

1. Select the best choice for success when looking for electronic, full-text articles in professional journals through Denison Library's databases.
    a. ☐ UpToDate
    b. ☐ INFOTRAC
    c. ☐ IMPULSE Catalog
    d. ☐ Web of Science
    e. ☐ All of the above

2. When [bracketed] titles appear in Ovid or PubMed MEDLINE search returns, it is clear that the language of the article is English.
    ☐ True   ☐ False

3. Do all the articles indexed in the MEDLINE database include abstracts?
    a. ☐ No. Abstracts are available in the MEDLINE database only if the original journal article includes an abstract in its publication.
    b. ☐ Yes. The MEDLINE indexers create abstracts for all the journal articles indexed in the MEDLINE database.

4. When searching the PubMed MEDLINE database, which statement is true?
    a. ☐ PubMed automatically does an "explosion" of terms.
    b. ☐ PubMed does not automatically do an "explosion" of terms.

5. The MEDLINEplus website includes general (non-medical) publications - providing a view of what your patients may be reading.
    ☐ True   ☐ False

6. It is frequently useful to see where a particular reference has been cited in other professional journals. Which of these databases gives you this opportunity?
    a. ☐ Ovid MEDLINE
    b. ☐ INFOTRAC
    c. ☐ PubMed MEDLINE
    d. ☐ Web of Science
    e. ☐ None of the above
    f. ☐ All of the above

7. The Micromedex database allows one to search for items owned by Denison Memorial Library, including the full-text journals to which the library subscribes.
    ☐ True   ☐ False

8. Which of the following items is good to review when assessing the potential relevance of a reference returned from an Internet search?
    a. ☐ The glove size of the author
    b. ☐ The number of words in the title
    c. ☐ The last revision date
    d. ☐ The score of the last Broncos-Chiefs game
    e. ☐ None of the above

(Continued)

Figure 11.2. Example of a Pre- and Post-test (*Continued*)

9. The Ovid MEDLINE system defaults to controlled vocabulary searching.

   ☐ True   ☐ False

10. Using the Boolean operators OR and AND in the same search statement is not an effective way to search.

    ☐ True   ☐ False

11. Which of the following is the most effective way to search for specific age groups in Ovid MEDLINE or in PubMed MEDLINE?

    a. ☐ Use the limit feature for the specific age group(s)
    b. ☐ Use the terms "geriatrics," "pediatrics," etc.
    c. ☐ Neither. There is no effective way to search for age groups.
    d. ☐ Both a. and b.

12. If a web search yields no results, you can assume the information you seek simply has not yet made it to the web.

    ☐ True   ☐ False

13 Electronic Medical Records are easily transferred from one hospital to another.

    ☐ True   ☐ False

15. Everything one needs to know to practice evidence-based medicine can be memorized, if one only works hard enough.

    ☐ True   ☐ False

Source: Fox, Lynne M. Health Sciences Library/University of Colorado Anschutz Medical Campus, 2008. Used with permission.

- how to save search strategies as auto-alerts or permanent searches;
- directions for printing, and for selecting what is to be printed;
- overview and comparison of the variety of access methods available, including any provided as part of the library's digital collections and those offered free of charge through such providers as NLM (PubMed, GenBank, etc.);
- directions for downloading references to the user's personal citation library for future word processing; and
- overview of database access options available to the user; including those accessible from a remote location.

Topic-Specific Searching Instruction

A natural offshoot of database and literature searching sessions are educational sessions on searching for specific topics—drug information or physical therapy/rehabilitation literature, for instance. Rather than teach users to search only in one database, helping them discover topic specific information across a variety of databases, print materials, and free internet resources can show the richness of the library's resources, as well as of the librarian's

knowledge. Providing online or printed topic-specific tip sheets or pathway tools is another teaching tool that can offer learning in a just-in-time way or when library staff are not available. Commercial tools, such as LibGuides (Springshare, 2010), are another popular way to provide guided instruction on specific topics.

Evidence-Based Health Care and Critical Appraisal Methods Training

Definition of Evidence-Based Medicine

Evidence-based medicine is the conscientious, explicit, and judicious use of current best evidence in making decisions about the care of individual patients. The practice of evidence-based medicine means integrating individual clinical expertise with the best available external clinical evidence from systematic research. The practice of evidence-based medicine means integrating individual clinical expertise with the best available external clinical evidence from systematic research. (Sackett et al. 1996: 71)

The rise of Evidence-Based Health Care (EBHC) has created numerous opportunities for librarians. Librarians can translate general literature searching classes into instruction on EBHC by teaching health care students and professionals how to ask answerable questions (Richardson et al., 1995), locate and use the best database resources to answer those questions, and critically appraise what is discovered.

The goal of critical appraisal skills training is to enable the health professional to assess the value of a published study or group of studies before applying the results to patient care. Many medical, nursing, and other health professional graduate schools include these methods in the curriculum, usually during the clinical experience years. For faculty and staff, critical appraisal training may be offered as a joint venture with the medical or nursing education departments or as part of a journal club. Librarians can play a role in all aspects of EBHC and critical appraisal from teaching courses to helping find and make available online and print tools to assist in the learning process (Lynn, 2010).

Critical appraisal tools are available online, both free and for a subscription. Free resources include examples and guides found online, such as those at the University of Toronto's Center for Evidence-Based Practice (http://www.cebm.utoronto.ca/practise/ca/). More specific and detailed appraisal techniques for guidelines and systematic reviews are now available through the GRADE Working Group (http://www.gradeworkinggroup.org/) and AGREE Collaboration (http://www.agreecollaboration.org/). A series of articles on EBM Teaching Tips is published in the *Journal of General Internal Medicine*, making its first appearance in 2007 (Lee et al., 2009; McGinn et al., 2008; Prasad et al., 2008; Kennedy et al., 2008; Richardson et al., 2008). Previous papers in this series were published in the *Canadian Medical Association Journal* (*CMAJ*) (*CMAJ* Evidence-Based Medicine Series, 2010). Another popular and useful tool is the "Users' Guides to the Medical Literature," originally a series of articles published in *JAMA* beginning in 1993 (Oxman, Sackett, and Guyatt, 1993). This series of articles describes how skillful use of the medical literature enables health professionals to practice evidence-based medicine. The Users' Guide is now available as a free, pre-publication text resource through the Centre of Health Education at the University of Alberta (http://www.cche.net/users guides/main.asp), as an available-for-purchase print text with an accompanying DVD (Guyatt, 2002), and as an online subscription-based tool through the AMA (http://pubs.ama-assn.org/misc/usersguides.dtl).

Critical appraisal skills training is also closely linked to traditional literature search techniques. For example, selecting the proper database or databases to be searched is an appraisal skill. Using MeSH or other vocabularies to construct an effective search strategy and using the "publication type" feature to locate research studies are also common appraisal techniques. Teaching critical appraisal skill is an important part of information literacy training (Brown and Nelson, 2003). See Chapter 12 for more on EBHC.

Personal Computer and Software Training

Computer and software training can be the domain of the Information Systems or the Human Resources departments. However, if public access computers are available in the library then basic computer training should be considered within the library education curriculum. A systematic personal computer training service will enhance the ability of health professionals and other personnel to use the library's resources more effectively, as well as save staff time providing assistance and troubleshooting on an ad hoc basis (Chmiei, 1997). The content of a basic computer training course or series of courses might include:

- an introduction to Windows or whatever operating systems are in use within the organization;
- a tutorial on how to use the e-mail system;
- word-processing techniques or desktop publishing software;
- spreadsheet development and conversion of spreadsheet data to graphic display;
- PowerPoint or other professional presentation;
- statistical software packages;
- bibliographic management software and online resource instruction;
- use of scanners and other peripheral equipment; and
- basic computer maintenance and trouble-shooting.

Internet Training

There are many ways to access the Internet, from dedicated high-speed data lines to wireless data connections. Connectivity of information systems within and among health care institutions and other educational institutions provides an exciting opportunity for the librarian to become an institutional information-management leader. Indeed, a major advantage of library involvement in this electronic connectivity is that it gives library professionals an opportunity to demonstrate the vital role they play in ensuring effective use of the Internet. A librarian who takes the lead in this endeavor will not only be providing a valuable teaching component for the institution, but will also be enhancing awareness of the value of the Internet as a source of knowledge-based information (Shaw Morrison and Krishnamurthy, 2008).

Librarians can target specific user groups using Internet technologies (Landau, 2010), assist in design procedures for library websites (Wisniewski, 2009), and provide guidelines for the evaluation of websites (Crespo, 2004). In addition, the library staff may want to take on responsibility for requesting, issuing, and maintaining passwords for the entire institution. Connection to the Internet will provide health professionals with access to electronic mail, health-related discussion groups, and the vast resources of the web. Instruction in using the Internet might include these elements:

- Brief history of the Internet and the web
- Demonstration of various web browsers and plug-ins
- Setting and using bookmarks/favorites
- Selection and use of search engines and search engine tips and tricks
- Explanation of how searching on the web differs from the familiar literature searching techniques (Brettle, Hulme, and Ormandy, 2007)
- Evaluation of websites, particularly medical and health-related sites, for authority, attribution, disclosure, currency (Gagliardi and Jadad, 2002)
- Copyright and intellectual property issues in the digital environment
- Instruction on Web 2.0, 3.0 and beyond (for details, see Chapters 10 and 15)
- Tips on setting up iGoogle pages and other specialty web services

Handheld and Smartphone Tools

The development and growth of personal digital assistant (PDA) devices and now smartphone devices has allowed increasingly ubiquitous access to the Internet and database tools. BlackBerry and iPhone devices are common sights in all health care settings. Many licensed online resources offer a PDA version, including NLM's PubMed, and all are searchable from a smartphone with wireless web access. Many now offer mobile versions of their search engines. Librarians can not only create and maintain a list of useful resources for PDAs and smartphones, but also offer classes and individual consultation on using these resources and devices.

Principles of Adult Learning

Current adult education theory has its roots in the 1920s with the work of Eduard C. Lindeman and others, who believed adults learned through situations and life experience. Malcolm Knowles, who considered Lindeman one of his mentors, expanded on this theory in his writings (Knowles, 1970; Knowles, 1998). Knowles used the term "andragogy" to distinguish adult teaching and learning from pre-adult teaching and learning called "pedagogy." As summarized by Smith, Knowles held five fundamental assumptions about adult learners:

- The adult learner is self-directed,
- has life experience that is a learning resource,
- learns as the need arises,
- wants to apply the new knowledge immediately, and
- is self-motivated. (Smith, 2002)

Riggs (2010: 388) points out that it is important to understand the difference between pedagogy and andragogy. "Pedagogy is content focused and involves one person leading the educational session. This person is considered "the expert."... Andragogy is focused on learner-driven education, incorporating motivational principles, placing value on life and learning experiences, and highlighting processes." At times the pedagogical approach may need to be used, especially when there are time constraints and a great deal of content to be shared, but librarians who consider adult learning concepts when developing educational sessions will engage learners more effectively and provide a superior teaching and learning experience. These theories allow the librarian, and, in fact, any instructor, to facilitate the learning experience rather than be put into the role of expert or "the sage on the stage." Many resources are available to help librarians understand effective ways to teach adult learners (Stern and Kaur, 2010). Riggs (2010) has listed eight useful strategies, summarized here:

- Ask the students to contribute their ideas.
- Consider different learning styles.
- Design an informal atmosphere more conducive to sharing.
- Investigate the learner's goals.
- Respect that the learners are self-directed.
- Encourage learners to contribute their experience but don't let individuals dominate.
- Provide practical application whenever possible.
- Try to build on the knowledge base of the learner.

Developing and Delivering Educational Services

Educational services should be offered in a variety of modes. The mode selected for use is based on the needs that have been assessed, the target audience, and educational objectives, and might include:

- formal lectures,
- demonstrations,
- hands-on experience,
- distance learning, e.g., teleconferencing, video-conferencing via the web (see Chapter 15 for more technological details),
- group exercises,
- web-based self-paced instructional video or tutorial, and
- one-to-one training.

As noted previously, it is important for the librarian and teaching staff to know the target audience's preferred learning styles. For example, busy, practicing physicians might prefer individualized and personalized one-to-one training, while other professionals such as nurses might be inclined to want to learn together in small, informal groups. Medical students and other health professionals who work in locations remote from the library may need instruction delivered by either the Internet or video conferencing systems. Some populations may prefer the convenience of viewing a pre-recorded demonstration or web-based tutorials on their own time, called asynchronous education.

Librarians are encouraged to work with the hospital education department or university human resources training division during the planning phase of an education program. Education professionals will be able to provide assistance with setting educational objectives, defining target audiences, and determining the best methods of instruction for each type of content or audience. Many universities have online technology experts who can assist librarians with learning web-based and online tutorial software products that can be used to deliver educational content.

The library's computer lab can be viewed as one way to deliver information-management education in either one-to-one or group settings. The lab could also offer computer-based training (CBT) programs in support of the organization's clinical teaching or in-service education programs. The appropriate mode or modes for each educational offering, suitable training and promotional materials, and evaluation methods should be developed systematically during the initial planning process.

If the needs of the library's user population warrant it, a multiuser computer lab may be desirable to expand service to more health professionals. University settings often have computer labs in the health sciences library or available elsewhere on the campus. Some libraries have invested in mobile computer lab equipment, using laptops and a data projector on a computer cart to take the computer lab to the learners (Le Ber et al., 2004).

Computer and Information Literacy are frequently goals of nursing and medical education programs in both undergraduate and graduate education settings. In addition, library users may be interested in taking advantage of the library's computer resources to improve their information management skills. Health professionals are often pursuing advanced degrees and may want to use library equipment to prepare papers or dissertations.

A computer lab can provide timely and cost-effective access to a broad range of resources and services in a networked and seamless manner. Also, hands-on training meets the needs of adult learners for self-directed and "just-in-time" learning. Specific objectives of a computer education service might include one or more of the following:

- To introduce health professionals to new information technologies and electronic resources
- To enhance health professionals' research capabilities
- To incorporate information management concepts into clinical and research processes
- To assist in learning the institution's electronic medical records system
- To provide opportunities to improve writing skills (Chmiei, 1997)

Institutional commitment is required to ensure dedicated space and equipment for even a small computer lab in a hospital setting. Librarians with limited space can consider partnering with Human Resources, Education, and/or Information Systems to create a shared computer lab training room. Computer labs may already be available as hospitals increasingly adopt Electronic Medical Records systems and integrated order entry and billing systems. Gaining the support of experts in the Information Systems department is crucial and will provide the library staff with assistance in selecting equipment and workstations, maintaining the hardware, and updating the software.

Educational Resources and Tools

A wealth of resources and tools are available for the librarian who wants to develop education programming. The problem is finding the time to develop courses, especially in smaller libraries with few staff. Luckily, help is at hand. Libraries and library service organizations have already created classes and handouts that they will happily share with those libraries just starting or looking to enhance their educational services.

Educational Resources

Following are a few resources where librarians can find assistance in developing educational programs.

- **NN/LM Training Center**: The National Network of Libraries of Medicine creates and makes freely available a number of training tools and handouts at http://nnlm.gov/training/.

- **NN/LM National Training Center and Clearinghouse (NTCC)**: The NN/LM provides trainers through the Regional Medical Libraries and through the NTCC. Information is available at http://nnlm.gov/ntcc/.

- **Medical Library Association (MLA) CORE Toolbox**: Members of the Medical Library Association have access to the MLA CORE Toolbox, available from http://www.mlanet.org, where librarians can post examples of lesson plans, tutorials, handouts, and webpage links to a wide variety of educational services and tools. All are created and maintained by members, so remember to ask for permission from the author before copying.

- **ACRL PRIMO**: The Association of College and Research Libraries PRIMO (http://www.ala.org/ala/mgrps/divs/acrl/about/sections/is/projpubs/primo/index.cfm) project promotes and shares peer-reviewed instructional materials created by librarians to teach people about discovering, accessing, and evaluating information in networked environments.

- **Vendor material**: Most databases to which the library will subscribe offer online tutorials or will send trainers to work with library staff or end-users. Ask the vendor representative about free training available from their company.

Technologies for Teaching

Computer and web technology grows so fast that several new tools will be available before this chapter is published. The librarian should have a strategy for keeping up with new educational technologies and tools—keeping in mind that sometimes the tried and true live web demonstration may be all that's required. The concept of the learning commons is introduced in Chapter 9 as a space planning issue and in Chapter 15 in relation to students having a place to access the hardware and software necessary to produce projects in a variety of formats for different learning requirements. Other technologies are covered in Chapter 15 under the heading supporting multimedia creation and collections.

- **PowerPoint**: Using Microsoft PowerPoint or another slide presentation software can be an excellent teaching tool for presentations where a live Internet connection is not available or if the connection may be unreliable. Screenshots of the database or resource being taught may be more visible on a slide than on a live web screen.

- **Web tutorials**: A variety of software programs, such as Adobe Captivate or Jing, are available to capture a demonstration and edit a voice recording over the presentation. It can then be posted to a webpage for asynchronous learning.

- **Course Management Systems—fee-based and free**: Many institutions license course management programs such as Blackboard. Moodle and Ning are web-based free course management programs, often used by nonprofit and professional society organizations. For educational services where more than one session is required, these tools may be worth exploring.

Evaluating the Quality of Library Educational Services

It is important for the library manager to continuously measure the quality and impact of library sources and services. A quality improvement process should measure the library's success in filling identified needs and suggest methods for improving the quality of the services and resources provided. This is especially important for educational services. Many librarians collect data to measure the effectiveness of library educational services. They also measure user satisfaction with the educational services offered. Whatever measures are selected, they should align with the organization-wide quality improvement process (see also Chapter 6).

A paper or web-based form can be used to gather feedback from learners in each session. Feedback can be used to verify that the educational offerings are on target or to improve and change them. In some organizations, the quality review or management department may request a monthly statistic called a quality indicator that demonstrates how well the library is meeting established quality goals. Here are some examples of quality indicators:

- All requests for classes or individual consultations are to be responded to within 24 hours of receiving the request (excluding weekends).

- 90 percent of participants in the MEDLINE searching course were satisfied that they had improved their searching skills.

- 95 percent of the questions raised during medical rounds were satisfactorily answered by the librarian in clinical morning report rounds.

Statistics should be kept on how many classes and of what type, how many learners along with their status and affiliation (faculty/staff/students and school or department), and the number of teaching hours. These statistics can show the quantitative effect of the education programs. Statistics are useful for reporting to internal organizations and external ones, such as the Association of Academic Health Sciences Libraries.

The librarian should consult with the administration to determine what reports are needed. Statistics may be used in monthly reports or, creatively, to publicize what the library can do for the organization. Making statistical reports meaningful will ensure that they actually are read. If the library belongs to a consortium, data recommended by the group for comparative analysis should also be collected.

To assess the user's perspective on the quality of educational services in the library, the librarian might find the following questions helpful:

- Did the educational information provided help in patient care or research?

- Was the educational information provided appropriate for the need?

- Was it provided in a timely manner?

- Was it in a format adequate to the learners needs?

- Did this educational session meet your expectations? Achieve its objectives?

- Will the knowledge/skill you gained in this session change the way you do your job?

- Will the searching techniques you learned affect the way you manage your patients?

Quality management programs focus on the customer, attempting to bring customer expectations and library performance closer together. For this reason, it is important to analyze how education services are conducted, to identify ways to improve the service, and to assess the impact that the library's educational services have on patient care. The quality improvement process is a continuous one, using feedback to make improvements as needed.

Conclusion

Educational services are a vital part of the library function. Librarians cannot expect end users to intuitively understand the value and breadth of the resources the library provides. Offering training, orientation, and personalized consultation gives visible proof of the value-added services the professional librarians can provide to their customers and organizations. The goal of the health care library is to provide information services and resources to support the mission of the organization. With thorough and thoughtful planning, the librarian can demonstrate the value of the library to the organization by providing effective educational services that connect library users with knowledge-based resources and enhance the effectiveness of that connection.

References

Accreditation Council for Graduate Medical Education. 2007. *Common Program Requirements: General Competencies.* Accessed October 12, 2010. http://www.acgme.org/outcome/comp/GeneralCompetenciesStandards21307.pdf.

Albert, Karen M. 2007. "Integrating Knowledge-based Resources into the Electronic Health Record: History, Current Status, and Role of Librarians." *Medical Reference Services Quarterly* 26, no. 3 (Fall): 1–19.

Association of American Medical Colleges. 1984. "Physicians for the Twenty-First Century: Report of the Project Panel of General Professional Education of the Physician (GPEP) and College Preparation for Medicine." *Journal of Medical Education* 59, no. 11 pt. 2 (November): 1–208.

Association of American Medical Colleges. 1998. *MSOP: Medical School Objectives Project.* Accessed October 12, 2010. http://www.aamc.org/initiatives/msop/.

Association of College and Research Libraries. 2010. "Information Literacy Competency Standards for Higher Education." Accessed November 5. http://www.ala.org/ala/mgrps/divs/acrl/standards/informationliteracycompetency.cfm.

Brettle, Alison, Claire Hulme, and Paula Ormandy. 2007. "Effectiveness of Information Skills Training and Mediated Searching: Qualitative Results from the EMPIRIC Project." *Health Information and Libraries Journal* 24, no. 1 (March): 24–33.

Brower, Stewart M. 2008. "Information Literacy Education in Health Sciences Libraries." In *Introduction to Health Sciences Librarianship*, edited by M. Sandra Wood, 217–240. New York: Routledge.

Brown, Janis. F., and Janet L. Nelson. 2003. "Integration of Information Literacy into a Revised Medical School Curriculum." *Medical Reference Services Quarterly* 22, no.3 (Fall): 63–74.

Chmiei, Kathryn. 1997. "Education and Training: The Challenges of Computer Training in a Small Hospital." *Medical Reference Services Quarterly* 16, no. 4 (Winter): 83–87.

"CMAJ Evidence-Based Medicine Series." 2010. Canadian Medical Association. Accessed October 12. http://www.cmaj.ca/cgi/collection/evidence_based_medicine_series.

Crespo, Javier. 2004. "Training the Health Information Seeker: Quality Issues in Health Information Web Sites." *Library Trends* 53, no. 2 (Fall): 360–374.

Ellero, Nadine. 2009. "Crossing Over: Health Sciences Librarians Contributing and Collaborating on Electronic Medical Record (EMR) Implementation." *Journal of Hospital Librarianship* 9, no. 1 (January): 89–107.

The Evidence-Based Medicine Working Group. 1992. "Evidence-Based Medicine. A New Approach to Teaching the Practice of Medicine." *JAMA; Journal of the American Medical Association* 268, no. 17 (November 4): 2420–2425.

Fox, Lynne M. 2008. "Example of a Pre- and Post-Test Used to Measure Changes in Participants' Knowledge." Unpublished manuscript. Health Sciences Library/University of Colorado Anschutz Medical Campus.

Gagliardi, Anna, and Alejandro R. Jadad. 2002. "Examination of Instruments Used to Rate Quality of Health Information on the Internet: Chronicle of a Voyage with an Unclear Destination." *BMJ (Clinical Research ed.)* 324, no. 7337 (March 9): 569–573.

Guyatt, Gordon, Drummond Rennie, Evidence-Based Medicine Working Group, and American Medical Association. 2002. *Users' Guides to the Medical Literature: A Manual for Evidence-Based Clinical Practice*. Chicago: AMA Press.

Haynes, Craig. 2007. "Linking to Knowledge-Based Systems from the Electronic Health Record." *Journal of Hospital Librarianship* 7, no. 4 (September): 121–129.

Kennedy, Cassie C., Roman Jaeschke, Sheri Keitz, Thomas Newman, Victor Montori, Peter C. Wyer, and Gordon Guyatt. 2008. "Tips for Teachers of Evidence-Based Medicine: Adjusting for Prognostic Imbalances (Confounding Variables) in Studies on Therapy or Harm." *Journal of General Internal Medicine* 23, no. 3 (March): 337–343.

Knowles, Malcolm S. 1970. *The Modern Practice of Adult Education*. New York: Association Press.

Knowles, Malcolm S. 1998. *The Adult Learner*. 5th ed. Houston: Gulf Publishing Company.

Kon, Alexander A. 2008. "The Clinical and Translational Science Award (CTSA) Consortium and the Translational Research Model." *American Journal of Bioethics* 8, no. 3 (March): 58–60.

Landau, Rebecca. 2010. "Solo Librarian and Outreach to Hospital Staff using Web 2.0 Technologies." *Medical Reference Services Quarterly* 29, no. 1 (January–March): 75–84

Le Ber, Jeanne Marie, Nancy T. Lombardo, Alice Weber, and John Bramble. 2004. "Portable Classroom Leads to Partnership." *Medical Reference Services Quarterly* 23, no. 2 (Summer): 41–48.

Lee, Anna, Gavin M. Joynt, Anthony M. H. Ho, Sheri Keitz, Thomas McGinn, and Peter C. Wyer. 2009. "Tips For Teachers of Evidence-Based Medicine: Making Sense of Decision Analysis Using a Decision Tree." *Journal of General Internal Medicine* 24, no. 5 (May): 642–648.

Lynn, Valerie A. 2010. "Foundations of Database Searching: Integrating Evidence-Based Medicine into the Medical Curriculum." *Medical Reference Services Quarterly* 29, no. 2 (April-June): 121–131.

McGinn, Thomas, Ramiro Jervis, Juan Wisnivesky, Sheri Keitz, and Peter C. Wyer. 2008. "Tips for Teachers of Evidence-Based Medicine: Clinical Prediction Rules (CPRs) and Estimating Pretest Probability." *Journal of General Internal Medicine* 23, no. 8 (August): 1261–1268.

McKibbon, K. Ann, and Cynthia J. Walker-Dilks. 1995. "The Quality and Impact of MEDLINE Searches Performed By End Users." *Health Libraries Review* 12, no. 3 (September): 191–200.

NIH Common Fund. 2009. "Re-engineering the Clinical Research Enterprise." Accessed October 12, 2010. http://commonfund.nih.gov/clinicalresearch/overview-translational.asp

Oxman, Andy D., David L. Sackett, Gordon H. Guyatt, Evidence-Based Medicine Working Group. 1993. "Users' Guides to the Medical Literature. I. How to Get Started." *JAMA: Journal of the American Medical Association* 270, no. 17 (November 3): 2093–2095.

Prasad, Kameshwar, Roman Jaeschke, Peter Wyer, Shari Keitz, and Gordon Guyatt. 2008. "Tips for Teachers of Evidence-Based Medicine: Understanding Odds Ratios and Their Relationship to Risk Ratios." *Journal of General Internal Medicine* 23, no. 5 (May): 635–640.

Richardson, W. Scott, Mark C. Wilson, Sheri A. Keitz, and Peter C. Wyer. EBM Teaching Scripts Working Group. 2008. "Tips for Teachers of Evidence-Based Medicine: Making Sense of Diagnostic Test Results Using Likelihood Ratios." *Journal of General Internal Medicine* 23, no. 1 (January): 87–92.

Richardson, W Scott, Mark C. Wilson, Jim Nishikawa, and Robert S. Hayward. 1995. "The Well-Built Clinical Question:

A Key to Evidence-Based Decisions." *ACP Journal Club* 123, no. 3 (November-December): A12–A13.

Riggs, Connie J. 2010. "Taming the Pedagogy Dragon." *Journal of Continuing Education in Nursing* 41, no. 9 (September): 388–389.

Sackett, David L., William M. C. Rosenberg, J. A. Muir Gray, R. Brian Haynes, and W. Scott Richardson. 1996. "Evidence-Based Medicine: What It Is and What It Isn't." *BMJ (Clinical Research ed.)* 12, no. 7023 (January 13): 71-72.

Scherrer, Carol S., Josephine L. Dorsch, and Anne C. Weller. 2006. "An Evaluation of a Collaborative Model for Preparing Evidence-Based Medicine Teachers." *Journal of the Medical Library Association* 94, no. 2 (April): 159–165.

Schulte, Stephanie J. 2008. "Integrating Information Literacy into an Online Undergraduate Nursing Informatics Course: The Librarian's Role in the Design and Teaching of the Course." *Medical Reference Services Quarterly* 27, no. 2 (April-June): 158–172.

Schwartz, Diane G., Paul M. Blobaum, Jean P. Shipman, Linda Garr Markwell, and Joanne Gard Marshall. 2009. "The Health Sciences Librarian in Medical Education: A Vital Pathways Project Task Force." *Journal of the Medical Library Association* 97, no. 4 (October): 280–284.

Shaw Morrison, Ruby, and Mangala Krishnamurthy. 2008. "Customized Library Tutorial for Online BSN Students: Library and Nursing Partnership." *Nurse Educator* 33, no. 1 (January-February): 18–21.

Shortliffe, Edward H., and Leslie E. Perreault. 1990. *Medical Informatics: Computer Applications in Health Care.* Reading, MA: Addison-Wesley.

Smith, Mark. K. 2002. "Malcolm Knowles, Informal Adult Education, Self-Direction and Anadragogy." The Encyclopedia of Informal Education. Accessed October 12, 2010. http://www.infed.org/thinkers/et-knowl.htm.

Springshare. 2010. "LibGuides: Web 2.0 Sharing System for Libraries." Accessed October 12. http://springshare.com/libguides/.

Stern, Caroline, and Trishanjit Kaur. 2010. "Developing Theory-Based, Practical Information Literacy Training for

Adults." *International Information & Library Review* 42, no. 2 (June): 69–74

Wisniewski, Jeff. 2009. "The Pitfalls of Redesign and How to Avoid Them." *Online* (Weston, CT) 33, no. 4 (July/August): 54–57.

Further Reading

Appelt, Kristina M., and Kimberly Pendell. 2010. "Assess and Invest: Faculty Feedback on Library Tutorials." *College & Research Libraries* 71, no. 3 (May): 245–253.

Brower, Stewart M. 2010. "Medical Education and Information Literacy in the Era of Open Access." *Medical Reference Services Quarterly* 29, no. 1 (January-March): 85–91.

Cheren, Mark. 2002. "A Concise Review of Adult Learning Theory." *Journal of Continuing Education in the Health Professions* 22, no. 3 (Summer): 199–201.

Fox, Susannah. 2009. *The Social Life of Health Information: Americans' Pursuit of Health Takes Place Within a Widening Network of Both Online and Offline Sources.* Pew Internet & American Life. Accessed October 12, 2010. http://www.pewinternet.org/Reports/2009/8-The-Social-Life-of-Health-Information/01-Summary-of-Findings.aspx?r=1.

Looney, Ryan P., and Ellen C. Ramsey. 2006. "Multimedia Bootcamp: Encouraging Faculty To Integrate Technology In Teaching." *Medical Reference Services Quarterly* 25, no. 3 (Fall): 87–92.

Mani, Nandita S. 2008. "Library-on-the-Go: Utilizing Technology to Provide Educational Programming." *Journal of the Medical Library Association* 96, no. 3 (July): 230–232.

Merriam, Sharan B., ed. 2001. *A New Update on Adult Learning Theory. New Directions for Adult and Continuing Education Series. Number 89.* San Francisco: Jossey-Bass.

Shurtz, Suzanne. 2009. "Thinking Outside the Classroom: Providing Student-Centered Informatics Instruction to First- and Second-Year Medical Students." *Medical Reference Services Quarterly* 28, no. 3 (July-September): 275–281.

12

Information Practice

Michele Klein-Fedyshin

A national epidemic of unasked or unanswered questions may be occurring in physicians' offices and in hospitals. U.S. government statistics calculate that there are 95,616 patients in the hospital during any single day (DeFrances and Podgornik, 2006). With an average of five questions per patient encounter in academic hospital settings, and at most only 55 percent of these being pursued, that leaves 215,136 questions a day going unanswered (Klein-Fedyshin, 2010). Looking at it from the family physician's side, "the typical physician has about 10 questions per day of which about one half go answered; that is more than 2 million unanswered questions per week by family physicians alone" (Ebell, 2010: 407). How many of the 98,000 patient deaths a year calculated by the Institute of Medicine (IOM) are attributable to unasked or unanswered questions? The level of knowledge brought to patient care matters. Patient care suffers because of inadequate or nonexistent searching (Ramsay, 2001; *Harbeson v. Parke-Davis*, 1985).

Conversely, care is changed by the addition of information. The use of bibliographic information on an individual case basis is reported less, but is evident in the literature as shown by the article, "A Rare Complication of Pneumonectomy: Diagnosis Made by a Literature Search" (Crosbie et al., 2005). When applied, information influences clinical decision-making and often changes care (King, 1987; Marshall, 1992). Patients who are discussed at evidence-oriented forums like Tumor Board are more likely to receive recommended care (Abraham et al., 2006; Petty and Vetto, 2002). Patients whose providers have a timely literature search performed are released faster and incur lower charges (Klein et al., 1994). A systematic review on the value of information supplied by library services for patient care suggested that they do have an impact on health outcomes and may lead to time savings for health care professionals (Weightman et al., 2005). Time savings for health care professionals translate into more time available for other patient care pursuits and increased provider productivity.

Medicine is an information-intensive discipline. The quantification of information need described previously attests to a more "hands on" role for the information provider; not just as a procurer but as a participant. Given the increased complexity of health care, it is likely that the library manager in the health care setting will recognize the need for more advanced information services. This chapter suggests the transformation of librarianship into Information Practice (IP). It introduces the concept, definition, and historical evolution toward Information Practice. The value-added components are explained as the goals and roles of Information Practice are discussed. Outcomes for Information Practice, its management and future conclude the chapter.

> Information Practice is not fully formed.

Evidence-based library and information practice (EBLIP) is part of the concept of Information Practice, not its equivalent. The two are not synonymous. EBLIP provides the research base for all kinds of librarianship, including information practice. EBLIP provides a basis for the standards for IP and its high quality, evidentiary basis. EBLIP is discussed in more detail in Chapter 6.

This chapter positions the profession for the future and builds on the rich history and the current practice of providing clinical information within the health care realm to practitioners, patients, staff, and students. The advances in electronic information access have impressed upon professionals and those they treat that decision making is a shared process best based on scientific evidence and individual values. For such collaborative health care, information is needed at moments when physicians have the least time to find it and patients are least prepared to understand it. IP seeks to best serve them all. IP builds on the current practice of information provision on the hospital units, within clinics, associations, and research institutions. It envisions the ongoing development of information technology and new directions for information scientists. This is indeed a challenge for the library manager, but it is one that promises both a greater contribution to improved health care and a greater professional fulfillment for the health care librarian.

The management of the day-to-day provision of an in-library and web-based reference service is covered in Chapter 10. Here, it is postulated that the development of Information Practice will require new skills for the reference librarian and will take the Information Practitioner out of the library.

Information Practice for the Twenty-First Century

Information Practice for the twenty-first century contains new roles for the health care librarian. An elaboration of the model alternately known as the knowledge hierarchy or wisdom tool elucidates the changes. The model is composed of Data-Information-Knowledge-Wisdom. Figure 12.1 illustrates these components. Using the interpretation of a prostate-specific antigen (PSA) test as an example, data is the most elemental level, and it consists of basic numerical information such as a PSA level found in a specific patient to be 6.0, post-prostatectomy. Information has meaning, such that a prostate-specific antigen (PSA) level of 8 is high and less than 4 is normal. This can be found in a book. Knowledge requires interpretation such as an understanding that after a prostatectomy, the PSA level should eventually drop. Knowledge requires comprehension and insight into information. Wisdom is the level of the knowledge where the person knows that if the PSA continues to rise consistently over the next two years, the patient needs to go back for more testing. Wisdom requires manipulation of information and knowledge.

Traditionally, librarians use information and incorporate knowledge, but not data. This feature is added in information practice. The absence of data in the reference interview illustrates the issue. The typical search form used in the reference interview lacks entries or questions on a patient's lab values/data or physical findings of

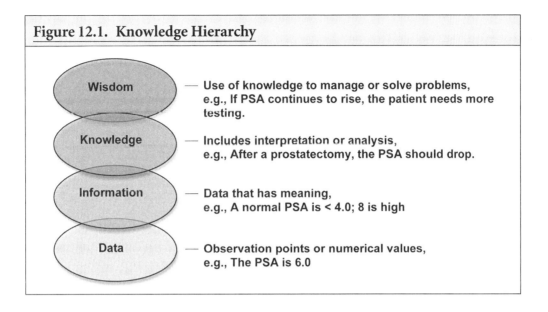

Figure 12.1. Knowledge Hierarchy

Wisdom — Use of knowledge to manage or solve problems, e.g., If PSA continues to rise, the patient needs more testing.

Knowledge — Includes interpretation or analysis, e.g., After a prostatectomy, the PSA should drop.

Information — Data that has meaning, e.g., A normal PSA is < 4.0; 8 is high

Data — Observation points or numerical values, e.g., The PSA is 6.0

significance. Critical values are those that have life-threatening significance. They may even have provoked the question from the physician. Yet librarians may not ask about the lab values. Other places where Information Practitioners (IPR) may need to request data are:

- looking for or calculating effect sizes when quality filtering articles;
- creating Electronic Health Record order sets;
- searching in genomics and molecular biology; and
- providing assistance with evidence tables.

Situations involving decision support for direct patient care for individuals are becoming more complex. When an IPR is asked for a search on abdominal pain, the clarifying follow-up questions are patient centric: does the patient have constipation? Is the patient on narcotics or postoperative? The search would take a different path if one knew the patient is on chemotherapy for leukemia and has right lower quadrant pain. In this new paradigm, the standard reference interview questions like "how far back should I search" are extended to questions relating to the care at hand: what is the patient's prior medical history, physical findings, and medication history. Formally incorporating blood counts, basic electrolyte values, physical findings, formulas for incidence and prevalence, sensitivity and specificity, and other standard health care parameters allows the librarian to respond to information queries at a greater depth of knowledge. IPRs integrate data with information retrieval to participate in decision making.

In addition, with data, the IPR can apply *information analysis* to institutional goals, be they patient care, research

or education. The IPR may work individually or as part of a team. Part of the process is inherently information search and retrieval, but IP goes further to contribute to decision making. Information Practitioners don't just retrieve information, they manipulate it too. In a hospital, Information Practice is searching for and synthesizing data-laden information to solve patient questions.

Information Practice is not just using information technology to support patient care, which is what clinical staff does when they retrieve labs or input vital signs. Information Practice is using information and *data* to advance patient care. When database search forms or the reference interview asks about important laboratory or physical findings, relevant data sets, or a quantitative value for the information need, then Information Practice is employed. This adds a new dimension to the process of information retrieval and requires additional skills for the librarian.

Definition

As an evolving concept, Information Practice has not been formally defined before, although articles in the library literature have begun discussing implications for practice of their results (Klein-Fedyshin et al., 2005; McKnight, 2006). Recent articles using an Information Practice perspective look at where clinical librarianship is being practiced (Harrison and Beraquet, 2010). It is the culmination of ongoing developments within library science and an extension of recent trends. Information Practice conforms to the shift toward the practical applications of information to patient care via evidence-based science and health care guidelines. It views the use of information in the context of a professional practice that requires education and training due to the impact information has on the outcome of care. Information Practice recognizes the professional aspects of information retrieval and elevates the standards required for an organization to claim the availability of quality information resources. Information Practice is defined as the survey and application of information in a comprehensive, yet focused manner for a practical, specific use to affect a positive outcome in a particular situation.

Information Practice involves the analysis, interpretation, synthesis and application of information to a particular situation. Retrieval is just the beginning.

Environment for Information Practice

The environment for Information Practice includes hospitals, health care institutions, academic health sciences centers, research institutions, public health organizations and initiatives, consumer health organizations, associations, and pharmaceutical research companies. Assisting at the point of care is only one locale. Clinical conferences, IT departments incorporating best practices into protocols, merging clinical vocabularies in the EHR, or health-related associations charged with issuing evidence-based guidelines are all venues suitable for Information Practice.

Small institutions are as much candidates for an Information Practice as large ones. The consulting service of an Information Practitioner brings to rural or remote staff the latest knowledge and scientific evidence for the treatment under debate. In urban areas, health departments considering epidemic disease and health promotion techniques offer the community as a venue for Information Practice. The focus of this chapter will be on health care facilities.

Outreach to the Organization

Information Practice is a form of outreach within the home organization. Why is this important? Electronic libraries are simultaneously everywhere and nowhere. Like the electronic mediums, the Information Practitioner must be willing to go where the customer needs information, be it their office, the hospital unit, the research lab, the lunch room, or a committee meeting. The IPR's presence in these environments reminds staff that they have a library and the services its personnel offer. Staff should feel that "help is on the way" when they call the IPR and know that there is back-up support

for their information needs. It isn't just "Ask a Librarian"; it's "Ask your Librarian."

There is a spectrum of Information Practice ranging from embedded librarians to dual degree specialists. These IPRs actively bridge domain activities, connecting Information Practice to the practice of medicine and allied health. Law librarians form an example from our sister discipline. According to the American Association of Law Libraries, approximately 30 percent of law librarians also have a JD (http://www.aallnet.org/committee/rllc/resources/education.asp). Medical librarians benefit from courses in the sciences or having an undergraduate degree related to allied health. As the profession transitions to recognizing advanced informationist skills, IPRs will use data, information, knowledge, and wisdom to develop their information-integration roles and responsibilities. In this scenario, librarians will start using additional training and standards of practice as the basis for their professionalism.

Naming the New Professional

Naming the new professional offers several challenges. Some might see it as an outgrowth or extrapolation of the role of a clinical librarian. Should that name be retained? With the advance toward evidence-driven medicine, is an Evidence-Based Practitioner more encompassing of the duties? Does the term Informationist, as advanced in 2000 by Davidoff and Florance (2000), best define the new professional? If the Informationist is the professional, then what they do is Information Practice.

Thus, it may be most apt to call the professional an Information Practitioner. The name structure parallels that of Nurse Practitioner, Family Practitioner, Infection Control Practitioner, or Evidence-Based Practitioner. At a fundamental level, an Information Practitioner is an information scientist. It is a general title and yet conveys that the individual is performing at a professional level of practice. Once the scope of practice is set, the title will be useful for job descriptions and organizational charts.

There are certain parallels with the Information Specialist in Context (ISIC) concept. The MLA Task Force on the ISIC commissioned a study of this subspecialty, which culminated in the report *Envisioning the Information Specialist in Context (ISIC): A Multi-Center Study to Articulate Roles and Training Models* (Giuse, Sathe, and Jerome, 2006). It helped "elucidate the knowledge and training requirements for information specialists who work as peers in the patient care and research settings" (Florance, Giuse, and Ketchell, 2002: 49). The Information Specialist in Context (ISIC) report to MLA considered the importance of the clinical knowledge base of this new profession. Health care/research professionals ranked it 4.2 out of 5 in importance. After eliminating general business skills (communication, professionalism, ability to translate complex knowledge), the task force found that comprehensive subject knowledge ranked second to only critical appraisal and synthesis of evidence/information in importance. In the study, librarians rated knowledge of specialized database and information seeking higher. By 2002, ISIC programs found a need for domain specific knowledge. The Clinical Informatics Consult Service at Vanderbilt University Medical Center noted, "It is essential that rounding librarians acquire a solid personal understanding of clinical medicine" and recommends "applicable courses" (Florance, Giuse, and Ketchell, 2002: 53). An article from the United Kingdom found that core duties of a Clinical Librarian, who meets the criteria as working in context, includes information evaluation, ward rounds, case conferences, and clinical guidelines development (Sargeant and Harrison, 2004).

The Information Practitioner takes the field one step further by incorporating data into the knowledge set required for the position. As an example, an IPR would know normal lab and vital sign values. Statistical concepts like effect size, number needed to treat, and significance would be part of the data knowledge set (Mays and Melnyk, 2009). An article from the United Kingdom noted the lack of a "nationally accepted practice" for Clinical Librarians (Sargeant and Harrison, 2004). There is the need to establish one for specialized Information Practitioners in the United States as well.

Developmental Milestones and History of Information Practice

When looking at a timeline of development of the concepts underlying the Information Practice there is a progression that isn't immediately evident. The timeline documents the building trend toward using information practically, specifically, and regularly in the health care environment. How both the science and use are developing is more clearly seen in the scenarios and milestones detailing its discovery and application. The timeline goes beyond any one profession into a professionally cross-cultural labyrinth including physicians, nurses, geneticists, information scientists, medical librarians, pharmacists, dieticians, educators, and authors. Highlights illustrating the growth of the librarian as an Information Practitioner are on the **accompanying CD-ROM.**

Notably, the first medical library in the United States was a hospital library in Philadelphia opened in 1762 (Thompson, 1956). In the early 1800s, libraries became more firmly rooted in European institutions (Weimer-skirch, 1965). Mental institutions used books for treatment and de escalation of emotional agitation. In 1836, the Library of the Surgeon General's Office, the precursor of the National Library of Medicine, was founded. (Blake, 1986). In the mid-1800s, American mental institutions began offering patient libraries. Begun in 1880, the Index Catalog of the Library of the Surgeon General was the first index of medical literature (Blake, 1986). By 1919, a hospital librarian was discussing the therapeutic benefits of her hospital library (Green and Schwab, 1919).

Literature Attached to Charts (LATCH) was an early product of the clinical medical librarianship (CML) concept. LATCH began at the Washington Hospital Center in 1967 where it was developed by its former medical librarian, Jane M. Fulcher, using a Medical Library Resource Grant from NLM (Sowell, 1978). This was followed in 1971 with the first Clinical Medical Librarian (CML) project established at University of Missouri Kansas City by Gertrude Lamb (Cimpl, 1985). Clinical Medical Librarians attended clinical meetings and left the library to engage their customers at their clinical sites on rounds. LATCH persisted in some institutions as a way to offer CML services without committing a librarian for long periods outside of the library.

Attending morning report on a patient care unit meant a more limited time commitment out of the library than full CML services. For small facilities, it was easier to return information to a requesting user via numerous methods, such as paper output or the pneumatic tube system. Now the role is more generally called clinical librarian. With every citation kept or discarded during the selection process of a search, clinical librarians are making clinical decisions. Automated ordering of LATCH as well as patient education literature enabled staff to submit library requests in the same work flow as lab or other orders (Klein, 1989). Currently numerous library resources are integrated with the Electronic Health Record or accessible from hospital unit computers to be constantly present at the point of care. Digitized articles can be e-mailed to requestors as attachments. The timeline on the **accompanying CD-ROM** notes the growth of services moving beyond library walls.

The march of librarians beyond the physical library continued in both hospital and academic health science libraries. Liaison librarians provide outreach to academic departments often in a university-affiliated health science institution. Embedded librarians are by definition housed in the sponsoring department and not the library. Freiburger and Kramer (2009: 140) call them "liaison librarians in context." Beyond assisting individual customers at on-site departments and units, librarians received formal appointments to councils and committees as their ability to facilitate information use was increasingly recognized. Patient safety, quality improvement, journal clubs, research and evidence based practice (EBP) councils are typical of the larger group venues served by librarians. From their efforts, librarians have begun receiving formal acknowledgement or co-authorship. The Family Practice Inquiries Network (FPIN) weaves a librarian into retrieval and use of information. They are cited as co-authors on the eventual publications (Ward, Meadows, and Nashelsky, 2005). Another incorporation of librarians' skill is in systematic reviews, and they may be cited as co-authors there as well (Forsythe et al., 2008). Sometimes the credit is as simple as, "A trained medical reference librarian assisted with the literature search" (Goddard and deShazo, 2009: 1358).

From the early recognition of bibliotherapy to today's co-authored systematic reviews, librarian's skills and their information products have become increasingly integrated into the ranks of health professionals. The health care team now includes an Information Practitioner, a practitioner with a long history and many names.

Goals for Information Practice

Information Practice goals are proactive and reflect involvement in the operations of the institution. They include general overview goals as well as more specific elements to define the practice. These goals could be used as a starting point for a manager wanting to start an Information Practice or revise how a traditional reference service is operated or perceived. They might also form the basis for a hospital policy on Information Practice.

Goal 1. To improve health and health care on both the individual and population level: This would be accomplished by increasing the effectiveness of information through analysis and synthesis. The value-added components of analysis and synthesis enhance the utility of the Information Practitioner who becomes an active contributor to the solution.

Goal 2. To implement timely interventions for positive outcomes: This goal focuses on doing and not just informing. The information product delivered is time bound. The output seeks to validate, change if needed, and ameliorate outcomes for the patient, institution, and community. It may revise surgical plans or medications. The intervention might be a policy or protocol change. The IPR contributes to the decision or implementation process.

Goal 3. To define a Level of Practice within an institution that doesn't focus only on the person (librarian) or place (library), but the products of Information Practice: The product might be a synthesized report written by an individual or a team-based product such as a systematic review. It draws on the special skill set of a masters-prepared Information Practitioner to incorporate data into information search and retrieval, evaluate it, and merge it with existing knowledge to make a cogent analysis (wisdom).

Goal 4. To establish standards of Information Practice that the organization can use to credential/rate its level of "knowledge readiness" within the institution to support evidence-based decision making: Determining knowledge readiness would be based on a formula derived from need and based on recommended or established capability for information provision. It is similar to the ranking of a trauma center, e.g., Level 1 Trauma Center designation, (American College of Surgeons, 2006) or "most-wired" status (Solovy, 2010: 17). One refers to how comprehensive the trauma care is while most wired status is a marker for the implementation of health information technology. Both reflect the resources suggested for quality patient care. Knowledge readiness would factor in the knowledge resources for optimal patient care. Information products that might factor into ratings for a knowledge center are outlined in Figure 12.2. The resulting score might eventually connect to the development of new information handling standards. Fewer information resources mean less access and use of materials (Schell, 2009) and would rate at a lower level of knowledge readiness.

As will be seen later, these goals begin to lay a foundation for specific Standards of Information Practice as well as scope of services. They differ from existing Medical Library Association Standards for Hospital Libraries (Hospital Libraries Section Standards Committee, 2008), in that they incorporate other organizations' standards for informational retrieval such as PRISMA (Liberati et al., 2009), evidence-based practice in the ANCC Magnet Recognition Program (Allen et al., 2009), or comprehensive literature review as conducted for Cochrane reviews (Cochrane Collaboration, 2010). By adopting

Figure 12.2. Potential Factors in Knowledge Readiness		
Factor	Points	Evidence-base
Search design assistance available from qualified IPR available 40 hours a week —available 20 hours a week	2 1	PRISMA Standards
Searches performed by a qualified IPR available 40 hours a week —available 20 hours a week	2 1	PRISMA Standards
Turn-Around Time (TAT) for delivery of off-site documents is within 24 hours TAT within two days	2 1	(Hill and Roth, 2009)
Number of databases licensed: 4 or more: 1–3	2 1	(Lemeshow et al., 2005)
Knowledge-based resources are available 24/7	2	Joint Commission IM.03.01.01

and incorporating these other organizations' standards, IPRs accentuate the value placed on their services and expertise.

Roles for Information Practitioner

The specific roles for an Information Practitioner are described in this section. These roles fit within the definitions and goals described previously. It should be mentioned that a single person would not do all these things. Universities may have all of the programs whereas a smaller health care library might be participating in only one or two of these initiatives. Even a solo librarian as described in Chapter 16 might participate in Magnet programs. Increasing involvement in the electronic health record, clinical decision-support, and evidence-based informatics described as follows expands the focus of IPR tasks to information utilization more than information retrieval.

Supporting Evidence-Based Medical Practice

In 1996, David Sackett defined evidence-based medicine (EBM) as, "the conscientious and judicious use of current best evidence in making decisions about the care of individual patients. The practice of evidence-based medicine means integrating individual clinical expertise with the best available external clinical evidence through systematic research" (Sackett et al., 1996: 71). Current thinking sees EBM as knitting together the evidence with clinical experience along with the patient's values. The patient's preferences are recognized as an important addition to the scientific perspective.

The EBM Process

Sackett et al. (2000) defined five steps in the EBM process. These are elaborated upon here to include the incorporation of the Information Practitioner. Where the role of the librarian may cease after the evidence is found, the IPR role is woven throughout the evidence-driven

---

MANAGEMENT IN ACTION 12.1

Integration of an Information Practitioner on a Nursing Evidence-Based Practice Committee

Location: Metropolitan Teaching Hospital

Description of Problem/Project: The institution has decided to apply for Magnet status from the ANCC. They recognize that Magnet status connotes that the organization ensures quality nursing care through the use of evidence-based practice (EBP). To promulgate bedside care that is evidence based, nurses need to be able to find, assess, and apply research as evidence for patient care. An EBP Committee can assist nurses in finding research, learning how to evaluate it, and then assisting with policy changes to adopt the retrieved best practices. What is the best technique to inculcate evidence into the EBP council and teach nurses the necessary literature retrieval and analysis skills?

Impact On: The use of evidence for patient care in the hospital and the demonstration of that as part of a successful Magnet application.

(Continued)

MANAGEMENT IN ACTION 12.1 *(Continued)*

People Involved: Chief Nursing Officer, unit nurses managers, advanced practice nurses, interested staff nurses, a PhD nurse with an interest in research either as an advisor to the group or committee member, and the Information Practitioner.

Strategies for Success: An offer was made to the proposed chair of the new committee to assist with teaching information retrieval and critical appraisal of the identified materials. This resulted in an invitation to be a founding member of the committee, which was accepted. By the third meeting, a request to teach at a meeting of the newly formed committee was extended to the IPR. Further teaching requests came as topics evolved from literature searching to critical appraisal to knowledge synthesis.

Barriers Encountered: Nurses joined and left the committee for several meetings until it stabilized with an interested group of participants. Classes taught at the inception of the group needed to be repeated. Some nurses found time a barrier and an endorsement from the CNO helped convince them to devote their lunch hour to it.

Take-Home Points: If the administration doesn't think of including the IPR in such relevant committees, an offer to participate by the IPR may still be welcome.

Further Readings:

Rader, Tamara, and Anita J. Gagnon. 2000. "Expediting the Transfer of Evidence into Practice: Building Clinical Partnerships." *Bulletin of the Medical Library Association* 88, no. 3 (July): 247–250.

Wise, Nancy J. 2009. "Maintaining Magnet Status: Establishing an Evidence-Based Practice Committee." *AORN Journal* 90, no. 2 (August): 205–213.

process. No handoff occurs after step 2, but continual involvement persists with the project. Figure 12.3 shows the steps of IPR Involvement in EBM.

STEP 1. IDENTIFY THE PRACTICE/POLICY/PATIENT PROBLEM

The problem may revolve around a single patient's unusual presentation, a larger population-based issue of how all patients with a particular problem do best, or a protocol needing clarification. A single patient presentation example could be: When is the best time to restart anticoagulation in a patient who requires it for a mechanical heart valve after a GI bleed? An example at a more macro level would be: In adult patients who smoke, what is the effect of Wellbutrin on smoking cessation compared with nicotine replacement? Framing the question is a critical step and the first phase of identifying the problem is forming it into an answerable clinical question. This usually takes on a PICO format (Population, Intervention, Comparison, Outcome). The requestor frames the question in preparation for step 2. The IPR can assist in the framing of these questions.

STEP 2. SEARCH FOR THE EVIDENCE

Librarian involvement has traditionally begun and ended with this phase. A comprehensive literature review searching multiple databases is needed. Finding extant guidelines in repositories (e.g., guidelines.gov) and checking out associations for their consensus/recommendations are all part of the search process. This phase needs to be thorough to the level of requestor need, be it searching multiple sources to retrieving thousands of

Figure 12.3. Information Practitioner Involvement in EBM

Information Practitioner Involvement in EBM	
Sackett's Five Steps	**IP Roles in EBM/EBP**
1. Convert the need for information into an answerable question (often in PICO form).	1. Identify interventions and comparisons.
2. Find the best evidence.	2. Find best evidence and relate it to extant organizational knowledge (policies and procedures).
3. Critically appraise its validity, impact, and applicability.	3. Organize the evidence into a cumulative review with grades. Calculate effect sizes and appraise the closeness of the studies to the situation at hand.
4. Integrate this with expertise and the patient's values and circumstances.	4. Assist with planning, application, or writing of outcome.
5. Evaluate the effectiveness.	5. Assist with evaluation.

citations for a systematic review. A definite need for searching more than one database is known (Lemeshow et al., 2005). At this point, in the past, librarians tended to hand off their work and their involvement ceased. With this new concept of Information Practice, added in are steps researching the EHR or organizational practice manuals plus checking recently completed, unpublished trials for relevant outcomes. Integration of the IPR continues in the next phases.

Step 3. Perform Cumulative Review of the Retrieved Studies

This is a systematic evaluation of the results of the studies and the strength of this evidence. Evaluating the strength of the evidence in a systematic manner requires tools. One such tool is an Evidence Table that enables compilation and comparison of each study's results. Once an article is selected for inclusion, it is critically appraised using a template form. Having a template helps with transferring data from each article to the review table. A template is included on the **accompanying CD-ROM**. A generic table would include such categories as the study's citation, its design, interventions applied, relevant results, and a grade of the study's strength. Data for the evidence comes from the studies' methods and results.

Statisticians are usually involved to check calculations of effect sizes or manipulate the data. One example of a grading mechanism for individual articles and then a total grade comes from the Centre for Evidence-Based Medicine in Oxford, United Kingdom (http://www.cebm.net/index.aspx?o=1025). Their "Levels of Evidence" document rates the individual articles from 1a-5. Based on this, an overall grade can be given for the derived recommendation from A–D. The cumulated review compares the studies' findings in relation to the population and outcome of interest.

An example of a completed Evidence Table can be found in Figure 12.4 (Exempla Saint Joseph Hospital Nursing Research Council, 2009). Other examples of evidence tables can be found online at the NHCBI (http://www.nhlbi.nih.gov/guidelines/obesity/ob_evtbl.htm) or AHRQ (http://www.ncbi.nlm.nih.gov/bookshelf/br.fcgi?book=cer8&part=A42219).

The AHRQ has a different scale that is useful to sum the individual articles evidence grades and give an overall score for the strength of the combined results (http://www.ahrq.gov/clinic/3rduspstf/ratings.htm). Either one might be used; some associations prefer to redefine their own. The GRADE Working Group (Atkins et al., 2004) and the Strength of Recommendation Taxonomy (Lin and Slawson, 2009) are just two examples. The interest

and enthusiasm for grading evidence and the strength of subsequent recommendations testifies to the importance placed in using the right literature, for the right patient, at the right time.

The IPR role is ongoing and could include completing sections of the integrated review on study design, inclusion/exclusion criteria, variables, interventions, and grading the articles. Another IPR role might be calculating effect sizes and scoring strength of the evidence. With their grasp of the question and the knowledge of the subject's evidential data, they could offer alternatives and help craft the comparisons. The resulting data may be used for an order set in Computerized Physician Order Entry software, patient care, or development of new guideline.

Step 4. Create a Decision/Form a Policy/Protocol and Implement It

The information provided may lead to a decision in a particular patient's case at the individual level. The data from the review may be used to create new guidelines or revise existing ones. Generally with the input of a clinical expert or a team consensus approach, new policies or protocols may be written and implemented from the review. The IPR role is active here as well. They may help plan how to apply or implement the determination derived from the cumulated review. Taken one step further, they may write part of the new guideline or the methodological basis for the decision. Handling the clinical record, calculating effect sizes, and assuming accountability for the options presented are part of the IPR role.

Step 5. Have the Team/Committee Evaluate the Decision, Processes, Outcome

The IPR role would continue by creating templates for the evaluation, outcome comparisons, and data sets. Being intimately involved with the whole process, the IPR could organize evaluation of the decision or process outcome. Factors with the *comparison* element of PICO would be positioned against their *outcomes*. New data or articles would come from the IPR's alerts or RSS feeds. Information would be assimilated, evaluated, and synthesized for the team.

Utilizing Informatics Technology

Another technique for IPRs to support EBM is adding technology components to evidence procurement and distribution. As an example, an early application brought "evidence carts," which contained multiple resources including textbooks, databases, and critical appraisals to

Figure 12.4. Completed Evidence Table

Question: In Patients with Intermittent IV Infusions, Is Capping or Looping IV Tubing Equally Safe?

Article/ Resource	Type of Evidence/ Methodology	Article Focus	Results	Conclusions/ Recommendations
CDC 2002[1]	Evidence-based guideline	Prevention of Intravascular Catheter-Related Infections	Use maximum sterile techniques. Use local guidelines (institutional). "Cap…when not in use."	Use maximum sterile techniques. Use local guidelines (institutional). "Cap when not in use."
INS 2006 #48[2]	Evidence-based guideline	Administration Set Change	Cap IV tubing.	Cap IV tubing (sterile cap, new each time).
INS 2006 #29[3]	Evidence-based guideline	Add-on Devices and Junction Securement	Stopcock covered with sterile cap when not in use.	Cap IV tubing (sterile cap, new each time).
Gorski 2008[4]	Evidence-based guideline	Summary of INS standard #48	Refer to manufacturer guidelines. Sterile cap decreases contamination and infection. Aseptic technique and disinfection of injection ports and connections.	Cap IV tubing (sterile cap, new each time). Aseptic technique and disinfection of injection ports and connections.
Casey 2007[5]	Meta-analysis	Disinfect with chlorhexidine versus alcohol. Compared different needleless systems	Clean (disinfect) both before and after port use. Consider barrier cap.	Clean (disinfect) both before and after port use. Consider barrier cap.
ISMP 2007[6]	Expert opinion	IV tubing not being capped. Port not being cleaned	Patient exposure to contaminants due to failure to clean access port with alcohol swabs or cap IV tubing with a sterile cap. Regular compliance rounds to document extent of problem and improvement. HAND HYGEINE Do not recommend looping of IV tubing (INS standards). Only appropriate staff to manage IV tubing.	Clean access port or cap IV tubing with a sterile cap. Do not recommend looping of IV tubing (INS standards). Document requirement for capping and/or disinfection procedures in policies/procedures. Address/emphasize technique in initial professional orientation/ competencies.

(Continued)

Figure 12.4. Completed Evidence Table (Continued)

Question: In Patients with Intermittent IV Infusions, Is Capping or Looping IV Tubing Equally Safe?

Article/ Resource	Type of Evidence/ Methodology	Article Focus	Results	Conclusions/ Recommendations
Stoker 2008[7]	Observational study	Survey of healthcare workers practice of managing IVs and use of aseptic technique	Place a sterile cap every time disconnect IV tubing. Follow INS recommendation to not loop IV tubing. Use alcohol swabs for disinfection and allow alcohol to evaporate. Recommend best practice for capping administration sets is to use a single-use sterile cap.	Recommend best practice for capping administration sets is to use a single-use sterile cap. Emphasize correct technique among staff.

References

1. O'Grady, N. P., Mary Alexander, E. Patchen Dellinger, Julie L. Gerberding, Stephen O. Heard, Dennis G. Maki, Henry Masur, et al. 2002. "Guidelines for the Prevention of Intravascular Catheter-Related Infections. Centers for Disease Control and Prevention." *MMWR. Recommendations and Reports: Morbidity and Mortality Weekly Report. Recommendations and Reports/Centers for Disease Control* 51, no. RR-10 (August 9): 1–29.

2. Infusion Nurses Society. 2006. "Infusion Nursing Standards of Practice. 48. Administration Set Change." *Journal of Infusion Nursing: The Official Publication of the Infusion Nurses Society* 29, no. 1 Supp. (January/February): S48–S51.

3. Infusion Nurses Society. 2006. "Infusion Nursing Standards of Practice. 29. Add-On Devices and Junction Securement." *Journal of Infusion Nursing: The Official Publication of the Infusion Nurses Society* 29, no. 1 Supp. (January/February): S32.

4. Gorski, Lisa A. 2008. "Standard 48: Administration Set Change." *Journal of Infusion Nursing: The Official Publication of the Infusion Nurses Society* 31, no. 5 (September/October): 267–268.

5. Casey, Anna L., and Tom S. J. Elliott. 2007. "Infection Risks Associated with Needleless Intravenous Access Devices." *Nursing Standard (Royal College of Nursing [Great Britain]: 1987)* 22, no. 11 (November 21): 38–44.

6. "Failure to Cap IC Tubing and Disinfect IV Ports Place Patients at Risk for Infections." 2007. *ISMP Newsletter* (July 26). Accessed September 28, 2010. http://www.ismp.org/newsletters/acutecare/articles/20070726.asp.

7. Stoker, Ron. 2008. "One Less Problem; Safe Practices When Administering IV Therapy. 2008. *Managing Infection Control* (June): 14–18.

Source: Exempla Saint Joseph Hospital Nursing Research Council. 2009. "Capping or Looping IV Tubing Evidence Table." Used with permission.

rounds with house staff (Sackett and Straus, 1998). New Web 2.0 products, such as the *Morning Report* blog at the University of Pittsburgh Health Sciences Library System (http://www.hsls.pitt.edu/morningreport/), list a topic or question with links to articles that respond to the query. Comments to a blog post and links to PubMed may also be available. "Tags" applied to the blog posts can give subject access points to the questions poised and answered for later reference. Medical Subject Headings (MeSH) terms offer an authoritative basis for these tags. The blog joins the information armamentarium with accessibility from multiple access points, browsability and clinical applicability. Updating would be needed to keep it current. A variety of blogs exist that demonstrate library staff involvement with house staff rounds. For question tracking, using PubMed's My NCBI's Collections, RefWorks, or EndNote for the citations facilitates the reuse and revision of answered questions.

Other technologies can link the institution's Electronic Health Record (EHR) for either order entry of requests, links to evidence, or appending a synthesis to a patient record. Automated order entry of library requests from the patient care unit isn't new, but as the technology has advanced so has the ability to more fully integrate library resources. Many systems now link to some form of evidence, and other functions allow linking to library resources from the EHR. Prior to purchase, librarians contribute expert evaluation of information products and their content. Other involvement reformulates library resources for clinical use, such as the University of Pittsburgh's Clinical Focus (http://www.hsls.pitt.edu/guides/clinical/) from the Health Sciences Library System. Use of library resources through the EHR extends the reach of knowledge to the unit. Weaving evidence into the EHR positions the IPR for the future since the government has mandated the use of EHRs as discussed in Chapter 2.

Clinical Librarian and Informationist Roles

Within the United States, the IPR may be titled clinical librarian (CL), embedded librarian, or informationist. An informationist, like the ISIC term, is broader in concept than CL. A systematic review of the informationist specialty found 15 model programs in public health, research, and health policy as well as clinical settings (Rankin, Grefsheim and Canto, 2008). The practice roles the authors delineated included knowledge translator, evidence educator, critical appraiser, and synthesizer of the literature. They found the practice setting as located outside the library, although the qualifications included graduate preparation in either a subject discipline and/or information sciences.

One of the most developed informationist programs in the United States is Vanderbilt University Medical Center (UVMC)'s Clinical Informatics Consult Service (CICS) (Giuse et al., 2005). In an example of advanced Information Practice, the expert evidence syntheses of the CICS staff are integrated into VUMC's electronic record. This allows their staff input into the patient's file, fostering a closer functional relationship between clinicians and IPRs. They accept requests from a variety of units including intensive care and emergency medicine (http://www.mc.vanderbilt.edu/biolib/services/cics.html).

Funding for CLs and informationists may come from the parent institution, the library budget in particular, or a clinical department's allocation. Enabling the IPR to bill for services, much like a consultant would, expands the revenue base of the sponsoring library.

The IPR role extends beyond the good article selection, which is a main skill of the informationist (Rosenbloom et al., 2005). In addition to selecting information, the IPR merges data with the articles selected to become a more active participant in the decision-making process. Access to the medical record helps inform the IPR and integrates them onto the patient care team. In advanced Information Practice, the IPR could access current clinical information, prior medical history, and participate on rounds. The IPR could incorporate the extant body of recorded knowledge with patient findings. Information Practice goes beyond retrieval to include analysis and synthesis of evidence along with the patients' lab records, drugs, and physical findings. Participating in ward rounds and interacting with the patient to answer questions raised during the information consultation helps the IPR present more accurate information back to the team and increases the productivity of the team as a whole.

Although clinical librarians did not originate in the United Kingdom, there is a developing movement there. Perhaps due to the origination of the Cochrane Collaboration in Oxford, United Kingdom, a leader in evidence-based health care and systematic review, the initiative to promote the CL is active and ongoing. The National Health Service of the United Kingdom (http://www.library.nhs.uk/) issued a report reviewing Health Library Services in England. It sees the clinical librarian as supporting clinical decision making and recommends in this report that the current complement of CLs be increased to 800 from about 50 at present. It envisions this as part of a major transformation of the delivery service model to one where librarians work directly with clinicians. It also advocates a knowledge transformation that moves librarians to venues where information is needed and used (Hill, 2008). This authoritative report values the work of clinical librarians, and thereby strongly supports the need for Information Practitioners.

An important note from both the U.S. and U.K. movements toward Information Practice is the application of the terminology of a *professional practice* to these roles. These roles are solidifying into a recognizable set of skills and abilities that form a level of professionalism. Recommendation 5 from the U.K. report suggested their "National Library for Health should act as a clearing house for examples of good practice in NHS health library services and facilitate their widespread adoption" (Hill, 2008: 30). Rankin's review specifically defined the informationist's environment as *practice roles* and settings (Rankin, Grefsheim and Canto, 2008).

Supporting Guideline Development, Meta-Analysis, and Systematic Reviews

Supporting the literature review for the guideline development, systematic reviews, or meta-analysis is an advanced skill which some librarians currently offer (Harris, 2005). Librarians may include multiple activities such as expert searching, citation management, data collection, or writing the search methodology section of the review. Expert searching employs an underlying knowledge of database structure, Boolean logic, and command line searching techniques. Librarians and IPRs understand what goes on behind the scenes when users click the Search button. Expert searching is a movement within the practice of librarianship that promotes high quality, complete searching (Medical Library Association 2005). The Medical Library Association Policy Statement on the Role of Expert Searching in Health Sciences Libraries is included on the **accompanying CD-ROM**.

The Canadian Agency for Drugs and Technology in Health (CADTH) compiled an evidence-based checklist to promote the methodological quality needed in a comprehensive search (http://www.cadth.ca/index.php/en/publication/781). Their Peer Review of Electronic Search Strategies (PRESS) Checklist includes the elements of a quality search (Sampson et al., 2009). These efforts acknowledge that a comprehensive search is needed to provide a valid evidence base. Establishing these parameters helps ensure a high quality search and elevates the expectations for what a search should be. For large projects, the IPR might set up a shared My NCBI account at NLM for the team. Using citation management software such as RefWorks or EndNote to store, organize, and manipulate the retrieved citations may follow. IPR roles include harvesting terms, documenting the search strategies used, and perhaps writing the search methodology section of the final product.

The AGREE Instrument is useful if one is conducting an evaluation of guidelines. The AGREE Collaboration is an international organization established to improve guideline development by using a common tool for their assessment. The AGREE collaboration is coordinated by the Health Care Evaluation unit at St George's Hospital Medical School in London. The instrument they developed is a clear, easy-to-use tool to help evaluate guidelines (http://www.agreecollaboration.org/instrument). This tool is more oriented to the quality of clinical guidelines rather than their validity. For those working with committees writing clinical guidelines, a helpful manual

published online by the American Heart Association is available for work on their guidelines (American College of Cardiology and American Heart Association, 2010).

In circumstances where a thorough search of all relevant sources is needed, it helps to follow a stepwise approach. Figure 12.5 illustrates the steps involved in conducting a comprehensive literature search in flow chart form. The flow chart details IPR's involvement in the guideline construction. Of additional note, there are numerous activities that are labeled the responsibility of the "research analyst" in the AHA flow chart that fall within the scope of Information Practice. Detailed search records are useful for search methodologies, risk management, malpractice, magnet status applications, and annual reports. For systematic reviews and these other activities, keeping a spreadsheet of the primary and subsequent search histories may be needed.

A Systematic Review is, "A review of a clearly formulated question that uses systematic and explicit methods to identify, select, and critically appraise relevant research and to collect and analyse data from the studies that are included in the review. Statistical methods (meta-analysis) may or may not be used to analyse and summarise the results of the included studies" (Green and Higgins, 2005). The Cochrane Collaboration disseminates many such reports and creates manuals for their creation. Systematic reviews differ from the solely mathematical approach taken to integrating research results in meta-analysis. These assimilate data to draw conclusions.

PRISMA stands for Preferred Reporting Items for Systematic Reviews and Meta-Analyses. They are standards developed by an international group of clinicians, authors, editors, a methodologist, and consumers as a quality tool for reporting systematic and meta-analysis. A 27-item checklist covers the whole process from structured abstract, methods, results, discussion, and funding in some detail (Liberati et al., 2009). Like the PRESS checklist, these items are among the tasks an IPR might assume for a systematic review or meta-analysis. Writing the search methodology section accompanying the report is critical to the integrity of the review and it should be reproducible. The overall aim of the PRISMA is to promote a high quality information product. PRISMA prescribes the elements to include, which are adapted and depicted in Figure 12.6.

Of note, PRISMA standards stipulate the reporting of who formulated and executed the search. This reflects the importance of the qualifications of the searcher and the increasing recognition that the quality of the search itself determines the evidence considered and eventual conclusions drawn from it. Whether an individual life is at stake

Figure 12.5. Process for Conducting a Comprehensive Literature Search

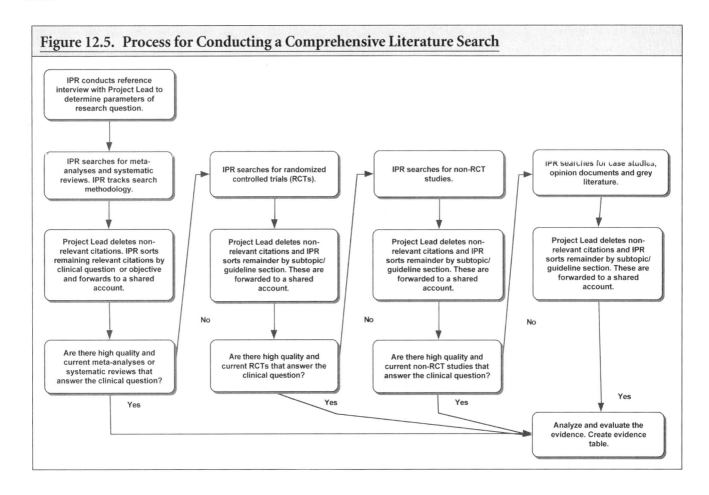

Figure 12.6. Components of a Search Methodology

PRISMA:

Writing the Methods Section

- Details About the Search Process
  - Information Sources Used
    - For every database, include database, platform, or provider
    - Start and end date for search of each database
  - Who developed and conducted the searches
  - Any supplementary approaches
    - Hand-searching
    - Trials registries
    - Cited reference searching
    - Individuals or organizations contacted
- Search Terms
  - Present the full search strategy for at least one database, including limits used, such that the search could be repeated
  - Have an archive of all search strategies

Source: Adapted from PRISMA, Liberati et al., 2009: W72-73. Used with permission of Mary Lou Klem.

or that of a group using a guideline, the retrieval of high quality, relevant citations with a thorough review to avoid important omissions is central to the outcome. These stipulations form a quality check for the search itself.

Some cumulated reviews involve merging multiple studies results to look for statistical outcomes for a meta-analysis. The results of selected studies on a topic are combined to create a larger sample size to potentially detect different or stronger effects. For instance, the effectiveness of a therapy that had been in doubt may be clear if the samples are pooled to increase the power via combining study results to derive consensus. Sometimes tools which are used for systematic reviews are also employed for meta-analysis such as the PRISMA guidelines. Search formulation, conduction, and study retrieval may be part of the meta-analysis support offered by an IPR.

The searches behind queries or reviews are acquiring increasing importance. In addition to the searches behind a systematic review or meta-analysis, the search strategies underlying PubMed's Clinical Queries can be viewed. These were developed by R. B. Haynes et al. (2005) to be either broad and sensitive or narrow and specific. PubMed lists a dozen articles devoted to the development of these "optimal search strategies" (http://www.nlm.nih.gov/pubs/techbull/jf04/cq_info. html). Even single study reports are beginning to describe the search methodology. The true strategic thinking, the art and science involved with a good search strategy, is now appreciated.

Supporting Nursing Practice, Research, and Magnet Status

Nursing has embraced and incorporated the notion of applying evidence to patient care and practice policies. Some of these initial efforts began by forming Research Councils that eventually evolved into Evidence-Based Practice (EBP) Committees. Their efforts are buoyed and encouraged by hospitals seeking to attain Magnet Status. The American Nurses Credentialing Center (ANCC), a subsidiary of the American Nurses Association, certifies health care institutions who meet five components derived from their original 14 Forces of Magnetism. This coveted recognition acknowledges attributes of the work environment and aids nurse recruitment and retention. The goals of the Magnet Recognition Program involve promoting quality in professional practice, identifying excellence in the delivery of nursing services, and promulgating "best practices" in nursing. IPRs have a particular role to play in researching the evidence for the best practices and supporting policy development built around them. By attending to nursing research and

evidence-based practice, Magnet hospitals build patient safety into care.

IPRs fill many roles in assisting institutions on their "Magnet journey." They primarily teach or bring evidence retrieval skills to Research/EBP committees. They may assist in the collection and organization of evidence associated with each force or standard. They search for articles appropriate to policy or practice questions. Some host portions of the site visit or centralize the documents needed. The importance of librarian participation can be seen in a survey of Magnet coordinators where 82 percent reported librarian involvement often as the only non-nurse (Sherwill-Navarro and Allen, 2008). Specific duties entailed EBP support for guideline development, citation management, teaching, and searches. Additional Information Practice roles can include the following:

- Assuring the organization is informed and knowledgeable of Magnet standards and process
- Participating in gap analysis relative to forces and standards of nursing excellence
- Identifying and supporting nursing research opportunities

The importance of librarians to the Magnet process is seen by the results that 94 percent of Magnet-certified hospitals have a nursing or medical library within the medical center complex, and 96 percent of responders reported the library added value to the institution and its employees (Sherwill-Navarro and Allen, 2008).

Nursing education has also embraced evidence-based practice. Nursing schools offer graduate research classes oriented around EBP and nursing informatics courses as part of the educational fundamentals imparted to the graduating nurse. Basic search skills training is part of the curriculum along with research fundamentals, often coordinated with the library as described in Chapter 11. Some students are required to complete evidence tables, write an EBP protocol, and evaluate the evidence base of practices for grade and strength.

Supporting Patient Safety and Patient-Centered Practice

The National Quality Forum (NQF) has identified serious adverse health care events (National Quality Forum, 2006). National quality incentives have followed and Medicare has selected conditions that have evidence-based guidelines for reimbursement changes. The rising costs for health care will impel the government and insurers to find measures that increase efficiency and decrease unnecessary care. They will use the evidence base as it develops to reimburse only what is proven to work. For example, Medicare will no longer pay for the extra care required for catheter-related infections, as well as numerous other events considered preventable. Thus, they pay only for expected care costs. Both Medicare and commercial insurers are driving the initiative by reducing payments for non-participation in its "Pay for Performance (P4P)" initiative.

An example of a role for the IPR is suggested by Medicare's elimination of the payment for protracted stays due to urinary tract infections from an indwelling catheter. An IPR might work with an interdisciplinary committee made up of floor nurses, unit directors, the Infection Control Practitioner, and a urology resident to develop a protocol for when to remove a urinary catheter. The resulting protocol would be part of the hospital's Policy and Procedure Manual and used on the units. Being seen as a needed part of the committee's structure to formulate hospital policy is an important step for the IPR. These efforts conform to The Joint Commission's listing of National Patient Safety Goals. These goals change annually and are focal points for The Joint Commission accreditation inspections. The regulatory compliance office helps the hospital conform to a host of additional regulators. The Leapfrog Group, CCHIT certifications, American College of Surgeons, ACGME, and other accreditations form regulatory compliance issues that may also be a focus of IPR activities. Chapter 2 has information about these initiatives and agencies.

By incorporating evidence into unit policies, institutional protocols and immediate, individual patient-care, errors may be avoided. Contentious practice, tradition-based policies and undocumented procedures may give way to fact-based, referenced actions as patient safety takes hold. An evidence-based specialty like Information Practice could find and recommend the safest approaches. This would minimize errors by searching for and applying evidence to support patient care activities. "Why do we do it this way" and "Is it time to operate on this patient" will be questions asked *and answered.*

Complying with regulators and using evidence-based health care is core to the foundation of ensuring safe and effective health care outcomes. *Knowledge-based information not only supports the process, it drives the process by furnishing the evidence undergirding it.* As the AHRQ asserts, "Questions are the answer" (http://www.ahrq.gov/questionsaretheanswer/). It goes beyond the five rights of drug administration (right drug, to the right patient, with the right dosage, at the right time, by the right route) to patient safety in surgery, hospital infection control, and evidence-based implementation throughout patient care activities. (Taylor et al., 2008).

This suggests the five rights of Information Practice developed as follows:

- Right source (search engine, database, platform, guideline, book, article for questions at hand. Not just what is easy and cheap (Google)
- Right search strategy (blend of recall, relevance, and precision)
- Right evidence (high grade, good strength)
- Right for the particular patient (allergies, insurance, values)
- Right answer (to decrease errors in medicine)

Supporting Research Projects

In an effort to maximize the government's health care dollars, the Institute of Medicine established 100 priorities of Comparative (treatment) Effectiveness Research (CER) (Iglehart, 2009). Recommendations for funding priorities also grew from the Federal Coordinating Council for Comparative Effectiveness Research (Federal Coordinating Council). These recommendations are being fueled by the American Recovery and Reinvestment Act. This research may eventually tie into Pay for Performance. Subsequently, what works is what will be reimbursed. Yet, evidence is a fluid commodity and institutions need IPRs to monitor the changing evidence about what constitutes best practice. Given that literature reviews are included as possible study methods for CER, and dissemination methods to ensure "translation of CER results into best practices" would be needed, there will be a role for the IPR to play (Iglehart, 2009: 327).

Many institutions, especially those with research centers, have Clinical Research Coordinators (CRC). They enroll patients in trials, ensure informed consent, and coordinate with the Institutional Review Board (IRB). In addition to acting as a liaison between the study's sponsor and the investigators, they interact with patients on their protocols to check for medication and injection compliance. IPRs may assist coordinators by staying current with new research, creating current awareness searches, and locating relevant articles being published. They can critically appraise articles coming out that question or support the ongoing research.

Supporting Health Information Technology Certification

The Department of Health and Human Services has developed certification criteria for Electronic Health Records to help foster their development and propagation.

Hospitals and physician practices will be required by providers to make "meaningful use" of a certified EHR to decrease errors and increase safety (http://healthit.hhs .gov/portal/server.pt?open=512&objID=2996&mode=2). Organizations will need personnel to help design and implement order sets and screens. Given their informatics experience, IPRs can work with programmers to define systems according to certification needs.

One of the biggest problems of the EHR is updating multiple files impacted by changes in practice. Tracking what works for patients at various levels of risk will result in practical knowledge clinicians can use, and keeping it current will be critical to guide practice choices. Verifying that clinical decision support guidelines are current will be an ongoing project of IPRs assigned to the EHR.

Impact and Outcome of Information Practice Services

The body of literature to support the value and impact of libraries and their staffs in various roles exists already (Holst et al., 2009). Well-referenced reviews and articles document the solid outcomes when knowledge-based services are applied to institutional needs.

Patient Outcomes

Beginning with the King study (1987), followed by Marshall's study (1992), Klein et al's research (1994), and Banks et al.'s more recent evaluation of morning report (2007), a strong body of literature supports the impact of librarian-supplied information (Weightman et al., 2005). The body of evidence exists and grows to document the shift of librarianship to Information Practice. Now it needs to be codified so that the provision and application of information are weighed into the quality of care and the institutional resources. Institutional capabilities in information handling could be rated and certified for health care library information handling expertise. By rating the ability of institutions to supply knowledge resources, patients and providers could anticipate the level of knowledge that could be brought to their care.

Cost Impact: Effect on Institutional Bottom Lines

Numerous studies have found that libraries save hospital staff time (King, 1987; Marshall, 1992; Klein et al., 1999),

decrease length of stay (Klein et al., 1994; Banks et al., 2007), and are cost effective (Scura and Davidoff, 1981). Time savings translate into increased physician and nurse productivity. If the right evidence is retrieved the first time around, its quality merits best practices, and outside articles are retrieved quickly, then policies or decisions can be made and implemented sooner. That is the essence of why information retrieved earlier in the patient's stay results in lowers cost and charges. Shorter committee duration and fewer meetings due to having the right information retrieved first allows physicians and nurses to focus on hands-on patient care. Fewer hours are spent in committee to develop policies and protocols, and those that are become more productive.

Educational and Certification Outcomes of Hospital Staff

Besides the information provision role, librarians train health professionals and students in the retrieval and use of literature. They negotiate database licenses, implement the software and teach it. This results in a higher percentage of degreed and certified nurses as can be seen in Magnet hospitals that have a greater information penetration (Allen et al., 2009). As suggested by Magnet hospitals, in hospitals with libraries there is a higher level of nursing staff knowledge. Greater information availability in the institution translates into greater information use for staff education as well as patient care. With many nurses seeking certification and needing continuing education, the need for the hospital to provide information resources to support staff grows.

Product Outcomes

Information Practitioners produce tangible information products that can be seen, read, and referred to. Examples include answers provided in the form of a knowledge synthesis, a meta-analysis, an evidence table, the methodology section of a systematic review, etc. Librarians hand off their efforts and often lose acknowledgment in the process. Having a physical product and record of its transmission to the requestor documents the originator of the product and promotes recognition by both the customer and administration. Statistical documentation, as well as innovations, newsletters, and accolades, is important for library managers to maintain and use in annual library reports, performance reviews, and budget justifications.

The evidence-driven health care movement is an acknowledgment of the value of information for improved outcomes. Comparative effectiveness research will institute the role at a national level and add to the formal recognition that information heals.

Management of an Information Practice Service in the Health Care Library

Three library services increasingly being deployed are training, search protocol projects, and clinical library services (Thibodeau and Funk, 2009). The evidence-based care movement and the expansion of knowledge links to the EHR may underlie this growth. Managers can position their library to respond positively to project openings and step into such roles. The particular environment of the institution will dictate how best to offer specialized services. A full range of services may be considered depending on institutional needs and the size and talents of the staff, but they can also include systematic reviews, assisting with evidence for order sets, and documented search methodologies. A robust response from customers may lead to increased staffing. While "back justifying" staff creates temporary hardships as responsibilities mount, it may be the only way to add positions. IPR roles and functions open the door for graduated staffing increases. The library manager initiates the IPR's involvement with evidence-based care and institutional projects.

Policy and Practice Documentation

Health care facilities have both institutional and departmental policy/procedure manuals. Having a policy in the institution's manual for using knowledge would extend the library's reach and demonstrate the importance of using evidence. Some evidence-driven institutions may implement top-down a requirement for its staff to document polices, protocols, and decisions with references to the literature. The library manager may be asked to write such a policy for inclusion. The goal of the policy is to improve care in real-time, real-world settings by using the best knowledge to identify best practice in individual or population care questions. This integrates the knowledge content with the patient's context. A sample policy for using knowledge-based evidence for high quality patient care is included on the **accompanying CD-ROM**.

Being able to document search methodologies is an inherent value-added part of IP. Search terms, search strategies with retrieval figures, along with the database name and platform all assist with the replicability of the methodology. By printing or saving the search strategy and postings, the IPR can document the search process.

Another part of the "how to" is to tie critical lab or imaging findings into the EHR as triggers for a search request form to be completed by staff. Critical values and unusual patient courses should require an information consultation and not just a consult with a rheumatologist. Case example: A patient post carotid endarterectomy has a creatinine level that hits critical unexpectedly. This triggered a search that found a crystal cholesterol embolism and promoted the initial trial of therapeutics.

Procedural and Technical Aspects

Procedural and technical aspects involved in managing the service may include having staff available on pager to meet any turnaround time goals that are set by the clinicians. There are a variety of ways to offer timely service.

EHR-based automated search ordering is one means to offer services to customers. Some institutions embed links in the patient record to guidelines used for the care of an individual patient (Giuse et al., 2005). This documents what level of knowledge is brought to the patient's care. It is important to note that anything in a patient record is actionable for legal review. "Ask A Librarian" links are another means, yet they require users to leave either their e-mail system or the EHR to find the library's website. Simple e-mails via the clinical/medical center e-mail to the clinical librarians are easy and efficient, although responses are limited to library operational hours. Linking library resources to the EHR so "end users" can find information themselves is another option.

Customer preference is an important factor in how the output is delivered. The methods include hard copy or electronic articles or links, and the format may involve a synthesis, question-and-answer approach, specific forms, or a spreadsheet of harvested search terms with the strategy used.

Be prepared to respond to urgent patient care questions that the clinical staff has not been able to answer. The library may be the information source of both first and last resort. An example may be a call from the unit if no policy exists in the hospital manual on extravasation of a particular drug. The customers want to know if there is any information in the literature. The question is for patient care and is an emergency situation. The librarian may be the "First Responder" for such questions. Poison Control Centers and Drug Information Centers may also call the library when they are stymied.

Packaging, branding, and marketing the information product is important regardless if the output is in paper or electronic form. This follows a business model with a tangible product. Brand e-mails, websites, covers for articles, and "Ask A Librarian" responses should include a recognizable logo and follow a standardized format. Be willing to package projects according to the institution's conception. If the new thrust is Patient-Centered Care services, then enfolding family library concepts into this theme enables expansion.

Barriers to Information Practice

Among the barriers to IP acceptance is the lack of a peer-to-peer relationship in Information Consultation. The psychological component of "asking for help" is compounded by this lack of a peer-level interaction between clinicians and library staff. When physicians consult with one another or even another perceived clinician (nurse), it is seen as one clinician to another. In what may be a comment of an under-observed consideration of information needs, Smith (1996: 1066) finds that the need for information is often more than a question about medical knowledge. "Doctors are looking for guidance, psychological support, affirmation, commiseration, sympathy, judgment and feedback."

If this is truly the case, technical solutions are not the full answer, and training users to search still will not address the psychological component of the information need. One opportunity to overcome this obstacle may be the "Resident Project." Teaching programs require trainees to do evidence-based projects; the environment fosters need for information and rewards information-seeking behavior. Thus it should become reputation boosting to use information and not be seen as relinquishing role responsibilities. Librarians' orientation to service aids this perspective, although librarians also need to be acknowledged as vital to the process.

Being part of a team and actively participating means literally sitting at the table at morning report. It engenders collegiality. Having an ongoing relationship with the requestor or department integrates library activities with department needs. Opportunities to socialize, join institutional gatherings, or attend relevant grand rounds should be seized. This breaks down barriers and enhances staff willingness to contact the IPRs because they are seen more as peers.

Other barriers perceived in implementing IPR-type roles involve the increasing technological abilities of customers themselves and synthesized point-of care tools (Sathe, Jerome, and Giuse, 2007). The information specialist needs to be able to evaluate that information and comprehend its application for the specific situation

to provide value-added services, making the contact worthwhile to the customer.

Future of Information Practice

Solidifying Standards of Information Practice

Scopes and Standards of/for Information Practice will need to be developed. They would function like a Standards of Care for IP. Standards are being set for information retrieval and analysis for patient care by the organizations and agencies discussed below. Information Practitioners could review these and adopt or revise them as appropriate for Standards of Practice. Standards are already devised, endorsed, or accepted by such major organizations as those behind PRISMA. Scientists and physicians are recognizing and accepting them.

Scopes of practice are developing already by virtue of increasing specialization and Hospital Library Standards of Practice incorporated into state laws for hospital licensing (Davis, 2009). To enable further evolution, librarians need to codify a scope of practice and embrace the standards relevant to the profession developing around library work. Below is an example of existing standards that might be included:

- **PRISMA standards** (Liberati et al., 2009): Standards are being set for information retrieval by PRISMA as noted. They pertain to both the search strategy for the retrieval of abstracts/articles and formulated review of them. They can be accepted and adopted as part of the IP Scope of Practice.
- **PRESS checklist** (Sampson et al., 2009): The PRESS checklist implies an audit of search and attests to the vital importance of search strategies to retrieving an accurate, adequate literature base.
- **Cochrane Handbook and website**: While created by an evidence-based collaboration, parts of the handbook may become used as an accepted foundation for organizational endeavors to incorporate evidence-based concepts. In particular, their description of a search strategy needing to include both unpublished and non-English materials relates to information professionals (Cochrane Collaboration, 2010).
- **Quality of evidence grades for articles used in evidence-based care applications, policies, protocols, or procedures**: Using an agreed-upon set of

grading ranks, e.g., AHRQ, ACP, or others, articles can be graded for their strength. IPR's familiarity with the literature and research design should position them to grade articles that are used by staff to substantiate policies or protocols.

The above standards are outside of such regulatory agencies as JCAHO and CMS. These organizations are promulgating information-related standards that are endorsed and accepted by the scientific communities they serve. They can contribute to the Scopes and Standards for Information Practice.

Future Standards

In addition to the standards already established and discussed, other information-related standards might be developed that incorporate research about information quality. Some potential concepts to use when building an evidence base are:

- **Number needed to retrieve (NNR)** (Booth, 2006): How many citations need to be retrieved to give due consideration to a topic? In systematic reviews, it is all relevant articles that meet inclusion criteria and may include hundreds of articles. If the topic involves a rare diagnosis, it may be a dozen or so. Booth's interesting article may demonstrate a method to determine not just when to stop searching, but the cost effectiveness of continuing.

- **Span of search/Number needed to access (NNA)**: Information retrieval should come from more than two scientific databases or guidelines to reach target sensitivities of about 90 percent of relevant publications for a topic (Lemeshow et al., 2005). Better results come with increasing the number of databases/sites searched. Using just one database for a search could result in the loss of more than half of the available literature on a subject (Lawrence, 2008). In addition, the database platform matters. One study found that the EBSCO AMED platform missed more than 70 percent of possible relevant articles (Younger and Boddy, 2009). The number of searches needed for a comprehensive review is an important parameter.

- **Recall and precision statistics for a search output**: This reflects quality of the search engine, indexing, as well as the searcher. If the search is for a systematic review or meta-analysis, the Lead Reviewer will remove nonrelevant citations from the librarian's retrieval. It may be helpful to track the statistics on

this to use for evidence-based information practice at some point.

- **Search turnaround time if the request is for patient care**: Like critical lab values, if it is a critical patient care situation, start the search within 1–10 minutes. As the evidence base for IP grows, this number could be more fully documented with outcomes.

- **Use of databases that are current within two months**: Google Scholar has year-old PubMed data (Falagas et al., 2008). Also, Google Scholar posts results in the order of times visited by users, which is essentially a popularity contest that favors older literature (Falagas et al., 2008). Especially in medicine, there can be implications if current data is missed. Conversely, the earliest citations are also important as older articles may contain valuable, formative data.

- **Turnaround time for outside information**: Document delivery is achievable within 24–36 hours (Hill and Roth, 2009). This may become a standard for institutions.

- **A need for more meta-information about reference itself**: This is seen in the lack of quantitative valuing of patient care questions, prediction rules for answering them, or measures pertaining to information need or use. Future research would be needed to derive standards or a tool to use as a basis for comparison for queries themselves.

With this extant body of knowledge, the profession can move forward. Authoritative bodies, such as the IOM, Academies of Science, Medical Boards who bear vetting responsibility for the educational level of their residents, and medical executive groups have the base from which to note and acknowledge the foundations on which scientific advancement, cost-efficient care, and error reduction rest. Flowing from the acknowledgment that quality information retrieval makes a difference will be that quality-seeking, safety-oriented organizations will seek a level of information retrieval compatible with emerging standards once those levels are spelled out.

Funding Models

Beyond departmental or institutional budgets, other funding models may be gleaned from existing ones. Within specific circumstances nurses, dieticians, and pharmacists can become certified diabetic outpatient educators (CDOE's) and obtain provider numbers to bill third party payers for counseling services (Lieder, 2001).

The stages involved in securing insurance compensation presume data to justify the impact and positive benefits (Michael, 2000). Medical Nutrition Therapy (MNT) is covered under Medicare in hospital outpatient departments, independent practices, or most other settings except inpatient or skilled nursing facilities. MNT are currently disease-specific services for those with diabetes (including gestational diabetes) and kidney diseases. When librarians are the teachers, should it be any different?

Pharmacists form another model. Pharmacists are increasingly involved in "cognitive services" for patients and may bill for them in some circumstances. Pharmacists are concerned with medication questions, but only IPRs extend their evidence focus to diseases, complications, and diagnostic issues. Nurse practitioners can bill for certain services a physician would perform. If a physician would access, select, and retrieve information but then hand this responsibility off to an IPR, it would seem knowledge consultation could be a billable, cognitive service.

Selling the library's services might become a literal statement and not just marketing. Working on a systematic review? Bill back the benefiting department for your services. Kurup and Hershey's article on the perioperative librarian calls for "new outcome measures to define success" that may be translated into new evidence-driven standards for information output/products (Kurup and Hersey, 2007: 585). The economic considerations they call for could be built in at an institutional level. Smaller institutions may consider hiring a consultant IPR if they are offered a project too large for a one-person library but important to the organization. A collaboration could result that would extend the reach of the home facility. The concerns of organizations are revenue and productivity. Even non-profits need to have a positive bottom line. Many articles on library services note that they save hospital staff time. This could be translated into a Utility Analysis that focuses on how librarians and the facility's services increase the productivity of the staff. Want to save staff time? Route the requests to a trained IPR. Other calculators for a library's worth have been established by the Midcontinental Region of the NN/LM and several may be found at http://nnlm.gov/mcr/evaluation/calculator.html.

Conclusion

The Information Practitioner is not to be confused with an enhanced information retrieval or delivery mechanism. It is an evolution beyond those concepts. Imagine the value-added delivery of patient-sensitive, applicable information tailored to the question at hand and validated with evidence-based, full-text information from the literature, web, international community, guidelines, and latest research results. Not just librarianship with a high-touch component, this profession involves incorporating roles not previously part of the profession. It affords the collegiality and confirmation sought in the hallway consultation, the fact-based data of scientific foundations, the evidence-base of literature retrieval, and the hands-on, physically there, patient relevant information professional totally missing on most patient care teams.

The haphazard nature of amateur information retrieval (such as using Google for a systematic review), is not the same as the iterative, organized process followed by IP professionals. Evidence-based health care decision making leads to evidence-based health care delivery and may improve care while lowering costs.

Someday evidence-based practice will be as basic to health care as the physical exam. Calls for an interdisciplinary, innovative point-of-care professional to create an infrastructure to anchor patient care activities into evidence come from multiple sources (Porter-O'Grady and Malloch, 2008). Ciliska (2006: 39) describes this person as someone who "could recognize clinical problems, having the time, skills and resources to access the research literature and translate the findings in a way front-line staff can understand." It is a work in progress. There is a need for someone to look at the data in articles and guidelines coupled with the patient's values and make a preliminary evaluation. At that point, IPRs can move from "this looks relevant to this type of patient" to "this looks relevant to this patient." With 215,136 questions a day to two million per week still going unanswered, one might conclude that evidence-driven health care delivered with an Information Practitioner is an idea whose time has come.

References

Abraham, Neena S., J. Travis Gossey, Jessica A. Davila, Sarah Al-Oudat, and Jennifer K. Kramer. 2006. "Receipt of Recommended Therapy by Patients with Advanced Colorectal Cancer." *The American Journal of Gastroenterology* 101, no. 6 (June): 1320–1328.

Allen, Margaret (Peg), Melody M. Allison, Margaret M. Bandy, Joy C. Kennedy, and Pamela Sherwill-Navarro. 2009. "The Magnet Journey: Opportunities for Librarians to Partner with Nurses." *Journal of the Medical Library Association* 97, no. 4 (October): 302–307.

American College of Cardiology and American Heart Association. 2010. "Manual for ACC/AHA guideline writing committees." Dallas: American Heart Association. Accessed July 9. http://circ.ahajournals.org/manual/manual_IIstep2.shtml.

American College of Surgeons. 2006. *Resources for Optimal Care of the Injured Patient 2006*. Chicago: American College of Surgeons.

Atkins, David, Dana Best, Peter A. Briss, Martin Eccles, Yngve Falck-Ytter, Signe Flottorp, Gordon H. Guyatt, et al. 2004. "Grading Quality of Evidence and Strength of Recommendations." *BMJ (Clinical Research Ed.)* 328, no. 7454 (June 19): 1490.

Banks, Daniel E., Runhua Shi, Donna F. Timm, Kerri Ann Christopher, David Charles Duggar, Marianne Comegys, and Jerry McLarty. 2007. "Decreased Hospital Length of Stay Associated with Presentation of Cases at Morning Report with Librarian Support." *Journal of the Medical Library Association* 95, no. 4 (October): 381–387.

Blake, John B. 1986. "From Surgeon General's Bookshelf to National Library of Medicine: A Brief History." *Bulletin of the Medical Library Association* 74, no. 4 (October): 318–324.

Booth, Andrew. 2006. "The Number Needed to Retrieve: A Practically Useful Measure of Information Retrieval?" *Health Information & Libraries Journal* 23, no. 3 (September): 229–232.

Ciliska, Donna. 2006. "Evidence-Based Nursing: How Far Have We Come? What's Next?" *Evidence Based Nursing* 9, no. 2 (April): 38–40.

Cimpl, Kay. 1985. "Clinical Medical Librarianship: A Review of the Literature." *Bulletin of the Medical Library Association* 73, no. 1 (January): 21–28.

Cochrane Collaboration. 2010. "Structure of a Cochrane Review." The Cochrane Collaboration. Accessed November 5. http://www.cochrane.org/cochrane-reviews/review-structure.

Crosbie, P. A. J., A. N. Cooper, S. Ray, and R. O'Driscoll. 2005. "A Rare Complication of Pneumonectomy: Diagnosis Made by a Literature Search." *Respiratory Medicine* 99, no. 9 (September): 1198–1200.

Davidoff, Frank, and Valerie Florance. 2000. "The Informationist: A New Health Profession?" *Annals of Internal Medicine* 132, no. 12 (June 20): 996–998.

Davis, Barbara B. 2009. "Small State, Great Aspirations: Strengthening Health Sciences Libraries in Rhode Island." *National Network* 34, no. 2 (11): 4.

DeFrances, Carol J., and Michelle N. Podgornik. 2006. "2004 National Hospital Discharge Survey." Advance Data from Vital and Health Statistics; no 371. Table 1. Hyattsville, MD: National Center for Health Statistics.

Ebell, Mark. 2010. "In Reply." *American Family Physician* 81, no. 4 (February 15): 407.

Exempla Saint Joseph Hospital Nursing Research Council. 2009. "Capping or Looping IV Tubing Evidence Table." Unpublished manuscript.

Falagas, Matthew E., Eleni I. Pitsouni, George A. Malietzis, and Georgios Pappas. 2008. "Comparison of PubMed, Scopus, Web of Science, and Google Scholar: Strengths and Weaknesses." *The FASEB Journal: Official Publication of the Federation of American Societies for Experimental Biology* 22, no. 2 (February): 338–342.

Florance, Valerie, Nunzia Bettinsoli Giuse, and Debra S. Ketchell. 2002. "Information in Context: Integrating Information Specialists into Practice Settings." *Journal of the Medical Library Association* 90, no. 1 (January): 49–58.

Forsythe, Raquel M., Charles B. Wessel, Timothy R. Billiar, Derek C. Angus, and Matthew R. Rosengart. 2008. "Parenteral Calcium for Intensive Care Unit Patients." *Cochrane Database of Systematic Reviews (Online)* (4), no. 4 (October 8): CD006163.

Freiburger, Gary, and Sandra Kramer. 2009. "Embedded Librarians: One Library's Model for Decentralized Service." *Journal of the Medical Library Association* 97, no. 2 (April): 139–142.

Giuse, Nunzia B., Taneya Y. Koonce, Rebecca N. Jerome, Molynda Cahall, Nila A. Sathe, and Annette Williams. 2005. "Evolution of a Mature Clinical Informationist Model." *Journal of the American Medical Informatics Association: JAMIA* 12, no. 3 (May-June): 249–255.

Giuse, Nunzia B., Nila A. Sathe, and Rebecca N. Jerome. 2006. *Envisioning the information specialist in context: A multicenter study to articulate roles and training models*. Chicago: Medical Library Association. Accessed July 15, 2010. http://www.mlanet.org/members/pdf/isic_final_report_feb06.pdf.

Goddard, Jerome, and Richard deShazo. 2009. "Bed Bugs (Cimex Lectularius) and Clinical Consequences of their Bites." *JAMA: The Journal of the American Medical Association* 301, no. 13 (April 1): 1358–1366.

Green, Elizabeth, and Sidney I. Schwab. 1919. "The Therapeutic Use of a Hospital Library." *Hospital Social Service Quarterly* 1: 147.

Green, Sally, and Julian Higgins, eds. 2005. "Glossary." *Cochrane Handbook for Systematic Reviews of Interventions 4.2.5*. Last updated May. Accessed July 24, 2010. http://www.cochrane.org/resources/handbook/.

"*Harbeson v. Parke-Davis*. Supreme Court of Washington, January 6, 1983 (98 Wash.2d 460, 656 P.2d 483). Malpractice." 1985. *Medicine and Law* 4, no. 2: 189–194.

Harris, Martha R. 2005. "The Librarian's Roles in the Systematic Review Process: A Case Study." *Journal of the Medical Library Association* 93, no. 1 (January): 81–87.

Harrison, Janet, and Vera Beraquet. 2010. "Clinical Librarians, a New Tribe in the UK: Roles and Responsibilities." *Health Information & Libraries Journal* 27, no. 2 (June): 123–132.

Haynes, R. Brian, K. Ann McKibbon, Nancy L. Wilczynski, Stephen D. Walter, Stephen R. Werre, and Hedges Team. 2005. "Optimal Search Strategies for Retrieving Scientifically Strong Studies of Treatment from Medline: Analytical Survey." *BMJ (Clinical Research ed.)* 330, no. 7501 (May 21): 1179–1182.

Hill, Peter. 2008. *Report of a National Review of NHS Health Library Standards in England: From Knowledge to Health in the 21st Century.* United Kingdom: National Health Service (March 2008). Accessed July 15th, 2010. http://www.library .nhs.uk/nlhdocs/national_library_review_final_report_ 4feb_081.pdf.

Hill, Thomas W., and Karen L. Roth. 2009. "Electronic Document Delivery: A Six-Year Study to Benchmark the Shift to Electronic Interlibrary Loan in Two Hospital Libraries." *Journal of the Medical Library Association* 97, no. 1 (January): 54–57.

Holst, Ruth, Carla J. Funk, Heidi Sue Adams, Margaret Bandy, Catherine Mary Boss, Beth Hill, Claire B. Joseph, and Rosalind K. Lett. 2009. "Vital Pathways for Hospital Librarians: Present and Future Roles." *Journal of the Medical Library Association* 97, no. 4 (October): 285–292.

Hospital Libraries Section Standards Committee, Margaret Bandy, Jacqueline Donaldson Doyle, Anne Fladger, Katherine Stemmer Frumento, Linné Girouard, Sheila Hayes, and Diane Rourke. 2008. "Standards for Hospital Libraries 2007." *Journal of the Medical Library Association* 96, no. 2 (April): 162–169.

Iglehart, John K. 2009. "Prioritizing Comparative-Effectiveness Research—IOM Recommendations." *New England Journal of Medicine* 361, no. 4 (July 23): 325–328.

King, David N. 1987. "The Contribution of Hospital Library Information Services to Clinical Care: A Study in Eight Hospitals." *Bulletin of the Medical Library Association* 75, no. 4 (October): 291–301.

Klein, Michele S. 1989. "Adapting IAIMS to a Hospital Library Level." *Bulletin of the Medical Library Association* 77, no. 4 (October): 357–365.

Klein, Michele S., Cathy H. Eames, Pippa M. Simpson, Cheryl A. Szof, Richard A. Humes, and Ralph E. Kauffman. 1999. "Information at the Point of Care: Effect on Patient Care and Resource Consumption." *Journal of Healthcare Information Management: JHIM* 13, no. 1 (Spring): 67–81.

Klein, Michele S., Faith VanToll Ross, Deborah L. Adams, and Carole M. Gilbert. 1994. "Effect of Online Literature Searching on Length of Stay and Patient Care Costs." *Academic Medicine: Journal of the Association of American Medical Colleges* 69, no. 6 (June): 489–495.

Klein-Fedyshin, Michele. 2010. "It Was the Worst of Times; It Was the Best of Times: Positive Trends Influencing Hospital Libraries." *Journal of the Medical Library Association* 98, no. 3 (July): 196–199.

Klein-Fedyshin, Michele, Michelle L. Burda, Barbara A. Epstein, and Barbara Lawrence. 2005. "Collaborating to Enhance Patient Education and Recovery." *Journal of the Medical Library Association* 93, no. 4 (October): 440–445.

Kurup, Viji, and Denise Hersey. 2007. "The Perioperative Librarian: Luxury or Necessity?" *Current Opinion in Anaesthesiology* 20, no. 6 (December): 585–589.

Lawrence, David W. 2008. "What Is Lost when Searching Only One Literature Database for Articles Relevant to Injury Prevention and Safety Promotion?" *Injury Prevention: Journal of the International Society for Child and Adolescent Injury Prevention* 14, no. 6 (December): 401–404.

Lemeshow, Adina R., Robin E. Blum, Jesse A. Berlin, Michael A. Stoto, and Graham A. Colditz. 2005. "Searching One or Two Databases Was Insufficient for Meta-Analysis of Observational Studies." *Journal of Clinical Epidemiology* 58, no. 9 (September): 867–873.

Liberati, Alessandro, Douglas G. Altman, Jennifer Tetzlaff, Cynthia Mulrow, Peter C. Gotzsche, John P. A. Ioannidis, Mike Clarke, P. J. Devereaux, Jos Kleijnen, and David Moher. 2009. "The PRISMA Statement for Reporting Systematic Reviews and Meta-Analyses of Studies that Evaluate Health Care Interventions: Explanation and Elaboration." *Annals of Internal Medicine* 151, no. 4 (August 18): W65–94.

Lieder, Tzipora R. 2001. "Rhode Island Insurers Pick Up Tab for Diabetes Self-Management Education." *American Journal of Health-System Pharmacy: AJHP: Official Journal of the American Society of Health-System Pharmacists* 58, no. 9 (May 1): 751–752, 754, 756.

Lin, Kenneth W., and David C. Slawson. 2009. "Identifying and Using Good Practice Guidelines." *American Family Physician* 80, no. 1 (July 1): 67–70.

Marshall, Joanne G. 1992. "The Impact of the Hospital Library on Clinical Decision Making: The Rochester Study." *Bulletin of the Medical Library Association* 80, no. 2 (April): 169–178.

Mays, Mary Z., and Bernadette Mazurek Melnyk. 2009. "A Call for the Reporting of Effect Sizes in Research Reports to Enhance Critical Appraisal and Evidence-Based Practice." *Worldviews on Evidence Based Nursing* 6, no. 3: 125–129.

McKnight, Michelynn. 2006. "The Information Seeking of On-Duty Critical Care Nurses: Evidence from Participant Observation and In-Context Interviews." *Journal of the Medical Library Association* 94, no. 2 (April): 145–151.

Medical Library Association. 2005. "Role of Expert Searching in Health Sciences Libraries." *Journal of the Medical Library Association* 93, no. 1 (January): 42–44.

Michael, Pam. 2000. "The Three Cs of MNT: Coverage, Codes, and Compensation." *Journal of the American Dietetic Association* 100, no. 10 (October): 1140–1141.

National Quality Forum. 2006. "Serious Reportable Events in Healthcare—2006 Update: A Consensus Report." Washington, DC: National Quality Forum. Accessed December 9, 2010. http://www.qualityforum.org/Publications/2007/03/ Serious_Reportable_Events_in_Healthcare%E2%80%9320 06_Update.aspx.

Petty, John K., and John T. Vetto. 2002. "Beyond Doughnuts: Tumor Board Recommendations Influence Patient Care." *Journal of Cancer Education: The Official Journal of the American Association for Cancer Education* 17, no. 2 (Summer): 97–100.

Porter-O'Grady, Tim, and Kathy Malloch. 2008. "Beyond Myth and Magic: The Future of Evidence-Based Leadership." *Nursing Administration Quarterly* 32, no. 3 (July–September): 176–187.

Ramsay, Sarah. 2001. "Johns Hopkins Takes Responsibility for Volunteer's Death." *Lancet* 358, no. 9277 (July 21): 213.

Rankin, Jocelyn A., Suzanne F. Grefsheim, and Candace C. Canto. 2008. "The Emerging Informationist Specialty: A Systematic Review of the Literature." *Journal of the Medical Library Association* 96, no. 3 (July): 194–206.

Rosenbloom, S. Trent, Nunzia Bettinsoli Giuse, Rebecca N. Jerome, and Jennifer U. Blackford. 2005. "Providing Evidence-Based Answers to Complex Clinical Questions: Evaluating the Consistency of Article Selection." *Academic Medicine: Journal of the Association of American Medical Colleges* 80, no. 1 (January): 109–114.

Sackett, David L., William M. C. Rosenberg, J. A. Muir Gray, R. Brian Haynes, and W. Scott Richardson. 1996. "Evidence Based Medicine: What It Is and What It Isn't." *BMJ (Clinical Research Ed.)* 312, no. 7023 (January 13): 71–72.

Sackett, David L., and Sharon E. Straus. 1998. "Finding and Applying Evidence During Clinical Rounds: The 'Evidence Cart.'" *JAMA: The Journal of the American Medical Association* 280, no. 15 (October 21): 1336–1338.

Sackett, David L., Sharon E. Straus, W. Scott Richardson, William Rosenberg, and R. Brian Haynes. 2000. *Evidence-Based Medicine: How to Practice and Teach EBM.* 2nd ed. Edinburgh; New York: Churchill Livingstone.

Sampson, Margaret, Jessie McGowan, Elise Cogo, Jeremy Grimshaw, David Moher, and Carol Lefebvre. 2009. "An Evidence-Based Practice Guideline for the Peer Review of Electronic Search Strategies." *Journal of Clinical Epidemiology* 62, no. 9 (September): 944–952.

Sargeant, Sally J. E., and Janet Harrison. 2004. "Clinical Librarianship in the UK: Temporary Trend or Permanent Profession? Part I: A Review of the Role of the Clinical Librarian." *Health Information & Libraries Journal* 21, no. 3 (September): 173–181.

Sathe, Nila A., Rebecca Jerome, and Nunzia Bettinsoli Giuse. 2007. "Librarian-Perceived Barriers to the Implementation of the Informationist/Information Specialist in Context Role." *Journal of the Medical Library Association* 95, no. 3 (July): 270–274.

Schell, Mary Beth. 2009. "The Impact of Loss of Access to a Point-of-Care Resource: A Case Study of the North Carolina AHEC Digital Library." *Journal of Hospital Librarianship* 9, no. 1 (2009): 8–14.

Scura, Georgia, and Frank Davidoff. 1981. "Case-Related Use of the Medical Literature. Clinical Librarian Services for Improving Patient Care." *JAMA: The Journal of the American Medical Association* 245, no. 1 (January 2): 50–52.

Sherwill-Navarro, Pamela, and Margaret (Peg) Allen. 2008. *Final Report: NAHRS/MLA Magnet Coordinator Survey, July 2007.* Chicago: Medical Library Association (April 28, 2008). Accessed September 26, 2010. http://nahrs.mlanet .org/activity/mapping/research/magnet_surveyreport_ final20080429.pdf.

Smith, Richard. 1996. "What Clinical Information Do Doctors Need?" *BMJ (Clinical Research Ed.)* 313, no. 7064 (October 26): 1062–1068.

Solovy, Alden. 2010. "Health Care's Most Wired Gets Redesigned." *Hospitals & Health Networks / AHA* 84, no. 1 (January): 17.

Sowell, Steven L. 1978. "LATCH at the Washington Hospital Center, 1967–1975." *Bulletin of the Medical Library Association* 66, no. 2 (April): 218–222.

Taylor, Carol, Carol Lillis, Priscilla LeMone, and Pamela Lynn. 2008. *Fundamentals of Nursing: The Art and Science of Nursing Care.* Philadelphia: Lippincott Williams and Wilkins.

Thibodeau, Patricia L., and Carla J. Funk. 2009. "Trends in Hospital Librarianship and Hospital Library Services: 1989 to 2006." *Journal of the Medical Library Association* 97, no. 4 (October): 273–279.

Thompson, Kathryn S. 1956. "America's Oldest Medical Library: The Pennsylvania Hospital." *Bulletin of the Medical Library Association* 44, no. 4 (October): 428–430.

Ward, Deborah, Susan E. Meadows, and Joan E. Nashelsky. 2005. "The Role of Expert Searching in the Family Physicians' Inquiries Network (FPIN)." *Journal of the Medical Library Association* 93, no. 1 (January): 88–96.

Weightman, Alison L., Jane Williamson, and Library & Knowledge Development Network (LKDN) Quality and Statistics Group. 2005. "The Value and Impact of Information Provided through Library Services for Patient Care: A Systematic Review." *Health Information & Libraries Journal.* 22, no. 1 (March): 4–25.

Weimerskirch, Philip J. 1965. "Benjamin Rush and John Minson Galt, II. Pioneers of Bibliotherapy in America." *Bulletin of the Medical Library Association* 53, no. 4 (October): 510–526.

Younger, Paula, and Kate Boddy. 2009. "When Is a Search Not a Search? A Comparison of Searching the AMED Complementary Health Database via EBSCOhost, OVID and DIALOG." *Health Information & Libraries Journal* 26, no. 2 (June): 126–135.

Further Reading

Albert, Karen M. 2007. "Integrating Knowledge-Based Resources into the Electronic Health Record: History, Current Status, and Role of Librarians." *Medical Reference Services Quarterly* 26, no. 3 (Fall): 1–19.

Ellero, Nadine P. 2009. "Crossing Over: Health Sciences Librarians Contributing and Collaborating On Electronic Medical Record Implementation." *Journal of Hospital Librarianship* 9: 89–107.

Fuller, Sherrilynne S., Debra S. Ketchell, Peter Tarczy-Hornoch, David Masuda. 1999. "Integrating Knowledge Resources at the Point of Care: Opportunities for Librarians." *Bulletin of the Medical Library Association* 87, no. 4 (October): 393–403.

"Value of Libraries Project." New York: NN/LM Middle Atlantic Region (July 1, 2010). Accessed July 24, 2010. http://nnlm.gov/mar/about/value.html.

13

Knowledge Services

Lorri Zipperer

Properly understood knowledge is paradoxically both a thing and a flow. (Snowden, 2002: 102)

Knowledge is information combined with experience, context, interpretation and reflection. (Davenport, De Long, and Beers, 1998: 43)

What exactly *is* knowledge? Definitions of knowledge and information have been discussed among librarians, administrators, cognitive scientists, and educators for years (Skinner, 2008). Knowledge is difficult to define, which makes it all the more difficult to manage (Sheffield, 2008). Despite the debate and the term's use as both a role clarifier and a marketing slogan, knowledge as a concept is still thought by many to be best defined within the context of the actual environment within which it is enabled. The context for knowledge that guides this chapter is a human-centered one. A focus on the tacit, social side of knowledge is applied.

This approach is not meant to undermine the importance of and respect for the established and recognized impact librarians have on making information (i.e. articles, books, guidelines, and databases) accessible (Garcia and Wells, 2009). However, this author believes that the human-centered approach presented here will stimulate a conversation around knowledge services as a way of enabling individuals, teams, and organizations to share "what they know" through personal interaction, dialogue, and feedback. This approach will support an extension of the skill set of health care librarians into an area that will help determine and contribute to the design and development of knowledge-sharing initiatives. This role is seen as one that can affect the delivery of high quality, safe care in the acute care environment. Through human engagement, knowledge can be shared in effective and systemized ways to facilitate collaboration, communication, and learning. This focus on the librarian as manager/strategist/leader/champion in knowledge services seeks to enable innovation in shaping a new role: developing projects and programs, defining metrics, and designing improvement mechanisms to help make explicit the tacit knowledge existing in health care organizations.

This chapter begins with terminology to guide the exploration of the role of librarians in knowledge management (KM). It next provides perspective on KM in industries outside of health care librarianship to bring context to the points made. The author advocates a human, not technology-focused, approach to knowledge management as an innovation for librarians who seek an opportunity for expansion of their role in the acute care environment. This chapter will emphasize knowledge services as a way of building opportunities for "knowers" to interact in an effective way that can result in tangible improvements and learning, rather than focusing on the technology that can make that exchange possible.

Several foundational concepts to inform and expand the reader's understanding of this role in health care organizations are provided to help them embrace this opportunity. Quality, patient safety, and clinical applications are employed to illustrate the viability of this perspective. A discussion follows that highlights the armamentarium of skills librarians can leverage to proactively apply expertise to knowledge-sharing work. To make the discussion applicable in the field, the text includes strategies to employ these abilities that are coupled with a selected set of tools to support the work. The chapter closes with a compilation of activities that can enable the librarian to find direction to start or contribute to human-centered tacit knowledge-sharing efforts.

Context and Terminology for This Chapter

Language used to discuss the management and use of knowledge varies among peers and across professions. Some examples of terms used are knowledge creation, sharing, organization, transfer, translation, reuse, identification, application, and normalization. For this chapter, the phrase "knowledge management" is used as a general term for these concepts. The author recognizes that this is too generic for the multifaceted and nuanced series of processes and products that affect knowledge delivery and sharing. Its use here is to serve as a backbone for the discussion. The author and editors envision that a response to this chapter and discourse stemming from it could result in consensus among health care librarians as to general and specific terms related to this work.

There is a standard hierarchy first noted by Russell Ackoff (1987) that illustrates the development and application of data and how it matures into wisdom. Knowledge plays a central role in this trajectory.

- Data: Data include facts and numbers, discrete "nuggets."
- Information: Data that is processed and repurposed and printed for distinct use.

- Knowledge: What an individual knows. It is broader, deeper, and richer than information or data (Davenport and Prusak, 1998). It is dynamic in nature and embedded in the actions of experts. It is multifaceted and context-specific. Its value emerges over time and is influenced by the knower (Sheffield, 2008).
- Understanding: the process of taking knowledge and creating new knowledge from it. Understanding builds on the information and know-how one currently holds (Bellinger, Castro, and Mills, 2004).
- Wisdom: "Wisdom is essentially systemic" (Bellinger, Castro, and Mills, 2004). It provides understanding through bringing a certain consciousness to what is known in a moralistic, philosophical way based on experience, sensitivity, and maturity.

Several terms provide a foundation for the discussion in this chapter:

- Explicit knowledge is knowledge that is easily expressed, captured, stored, and reused. It can be transmitted as data and is found in databases, books, manuals, and messages (Nonaka, 1991). Hansen suggests treatment of this type of knowledge requires a "codification strategy" (Hansen, Nohria, and Tierney, 1999: 107). Knowledge in explicit form is most likely the "mental model" many librarians harbor and apply to their work when considering knowledge management (Schwarzwalder, 1999).
- Tacit knowledge is the knowledge that is carried around in our heads. Polanyi describes it as "indwelling" (Dixon, 2000: 27). Tacit knowledge serves as a rich source of expertise and is most apt to leave an organization with employees (Anderson and Willson, 2009). It is internal to human understanding of the application of experience that is formed through work, beliefs, and understanding. Hansen and colleagues labeled this approach as a "personalization strategy" (Hansen, Nohria, and Tierney, 1999: 107).
- Knowledge management: Despite the fact that there is no fully agreed upon definition for KM, the list below provides a few contextual examples:
  - **Clinical practice**: The term often is connected with health care information technology concepts—computerized practitioner order entry, electronic health or medical records, evidence-based medicine, and decision support.
  - **Quality improvement**: "The accumulated intellectual resources of the organization.... Knowledge assets are the "know-how" that an organization

has available to use, to invest and to grow" (Baldrige National Quality Program, 2009: 62).

- **Organized medicine**: Knowledge management creates processes to systematically acquire, disseminate, and apply what is known. Knowledge management will help an organization be clear about the knowledge it takes in, how that knowledge is used within the organization and what knowledge is useful for their clients (Donaldson and Gray, 1998).

- **Knowledge-based information**: In 1994, The Joint Commission (TJC)—then called the Joint Commission on Accreditation of Healthcare Organizations, or JCAHO—began to use the phrase knowledge-based information in its documentation (Joint Commission on Accreditation of Healthcare Organizations, 1994). TJC's definition of Knowledge-Based Information aims to create a segment of the information base that is of higher applicability and quality. This term resonates with health care practitioners, administrators, and medical librarians alike: "A collection of stored facts, models, and information. This includes medication-related information such as drug interactions, drug therapy, side effects, toxicology, dosage, indications for use, and routes of administration. Knowledge-based information is found in the clinical, scientific, and management literature" (Joint Commission, 2010, GL-15-16).

- **Evidence**: Another term that requires clarification is "evidence." In academic circles, evidence refers to the scientifically sound, fully researched, and validated information and data collected during the pursuit of the understanding and validation of a hypothesis. In others, evidence can refer to what someone's experience has been. Certainly this view of evidence plays a role in what individual practitioners, patients, and families can bring to the table to enable organizational learning and improvement through the sharing of stories and experience, a tactic explored by the World Bank and others as an effective learning tool (Denning, 2004; Conway, 2008). How evidence relates to knowledge in an organization should be considered when designing KM programs and tactics.

- **Evidence-based medicine (EBM)**: "The conscientious, explicit, and judicious use of current best evidence in making decisions about the care of individual patients" (Sackett et al., 1996: 71). Refer to Chapter 12 regarding the viability of EBM as a

strategy to address urgent problems; it is recognized here that use of good information that can be applied in real time is an important strategy to support effective health care (Healy, 2006).

Lessons from Outside of Health Care Librarianship

Efforts from the corporate arena provide interesting models for health care. Knowledge management, as a process and emphasis for work, became prevalent in the 1990s (Davenport and Glaser, 2002). As the business and consultant arena has been a primary home for KM work, specific strategies and frameworks are too numerous to mention and are beyond the scope of this chapter. The references and further reading sections list some core texts.

Librarians in the corporate sector have had the opportunity to engage in a more person-centric role in knowledge sharing. Health care librarians should tap into the experience of their colleagues in the corporate world to understand how knowledge sharing could inform KM efforts in the acute care setting.

The Special Libraries Association (SLA) has taken the lead in advocating for librarians and information professionals as leaders in knowledge management work. This dedication to nurturing professional experience in this area is evidenced by the many conference sessions held and articles written. Online courses are produced and attended by members of this broad-based professional organization. SLA provides access to a variety of resources that demonstrates this commitment, including information on an online KM certificate program (http://www.sla.org/content/learn/certificates/kmcert/index.cfm). In 2006, an SLA division dedicated to knowledge management was formed. The division website hosts a members-only discussion list, wiki, speaker's bureau, and job board relevant to KM practitioners (http://wiki.sla.org/ display/SLAKM/).

American Society for Information Science and Technology (ASIS&T) has a Special Interest Group on Knowledge Management (SIG-KM). Formed in 1999, it endeavors to address a wide range of issues that support the successful implementation of strategies to enable organizations to share knowledge effectively. The SIG-KM annually hosts a meeting in conjunction with the annual ASIS&T conference focusing specifically on these issues and publishes materials related to the sessions in a variety of formats (http://www.asis.org/SIG/sigkm/). Other information management organizations such as the American Medical

Informatics Association (AMIA) and the Health Information Management Systems Society (HIMSS) have shown interest in KM with some use of the phrase in their conference content and journal coverage. At initial glance, these health care professional groups seem to focus on technology rather than social and cultural factors in knowledge management. They tend to discuss knowledge in a data-centric context. Nonetheless, it is important that knowledge management is included in the scope of these professional organizations to enable health care librarians to situate KM as part of the scope of work in their environment. Given the intersection demonstrated by these select groups, librarians are well positioned to craft a role for themselves in the knowledge management spectrum within health care organizations.

Several organizations have statements that advocate for the health care librarian's role in KM, but through a traditional prism. In 2003 the Association of Academic Health Science Libraries (AAHSL) distributed a statement supporting a role for health sciences librarians in explicit knowledge management initiatives (Association of Academic Health Science Libraries, 2003). This vision encompassed some elements of a person-to-person context for this work (Littleton, 2009; Association of Academic Health Science Libraries, 2003). The current Medical Library Association Academy of Health Information Professionals (AHIP) Essential Areas of Knowledge (EAK) do not emphasize skills that support a knowledge-sharing role with a focus on tacit and human-centered strategies (Medical Library Association, 2006). This lack of an existing concrete endorsement of a social, systems-focused, person-to-person interaction-oriented approach to developing the expertise of librarians in knowledge sharing for organizational learning presents an opportunity for the profession to shape a broader role for themselves in this work. It illustrates the innovation this chapter could articulate for the profession. Again, the library-oriented statements describe a skill base that is relevant to knowledge management, but primarily within the established framework of managing information and explicit resources. They lack a focus on how people interact to share what they know and transfer that back to the organization to enable it to learn from the managed experience. The future is in "connecting people and helping them find one another, rather than in capturing resources" (Prusak, 2009: 11).

Other evidence that the human context of knowledge management may be a growth area for medical librarians materialized during the analysis of a comparative study of the role of librarians in patient safety work. Examples used in a 2006 survey to illustrate KM roles in hospitals included:

- creating expertise directories,
- managing communities of practice, and
- collecting and sharing best practices.

Providing examples of KM roles was important in eliciting more accurate feedback. While only 26.10 percent of the survey respondents (n 318) in 2006 reported being involved in KM activities, almost half (48.43 percent) of respondents said they did not participate in KM activities once they were clearly defined. This is a 20.38 percent decline from the 2003 survey, where the knowledge management roles were not defined in any way (Zipperer and Sykes, 2004, 2009).

This opportunity has just begun to be leveraged by the health care librarian community. The Medical Library Association (MLA) is taking a leadership role with the publication of this chapter at this time. In addition, recent efforts and writings have emerged to help support the early adopters of these concepts in the health care environment (Hamasu, 2009; Robb and Zipperer, 2009). Such activities may create momentum for those in the field to embrace these ideas.

> The future is in "connecting people and helping them find one another, rather than in capturing resources." (Prusak, 2009: 11)

Knowledge Management in Health Care

As a general concept, knowledge management has achieved some traction in the acute care environment (Sheffield, 2008). Corporate applications of knowledge transfer tactics may have gained more visibility in health care organizations because of the increased call for upper management accountability to drive and implement quality improvement successes (Rangachari, 2008). Some health care studies suggest that knowledge services should focus on how to enable organizations to *respond* to knowledge, rather than to acquire or disseminate knowledge (Gowen, Henagan, and McFadden, 2009). This study supports the need for librarians to shift their focus from explicit knowledge activities to the development of tacit knowledge roles.

Orientation Contexts

The concepts of complexity, systems thinking, and organizational learning are invaluable to the library manager's

The IOM also noted in 2004 that hospitals need to "use knowledge management practices to establish the organization as a 'learning organization'" (Institute of Medicine, 2004: 3–4).

understanding of how to best implement knowledge services in the health care organization. These approaches were all considered in the Insitute of Medicine (IOM) seminal reports on quality and safety as being fundamental to driving and sustaining improvement (Kohn, Corrigan, and Donaldson, 2000; Institute of Medicine, 2001). They support knowledge sharing to enable learning, given that knowledge is multifaceted and context specific. The synergies are worth leveraging to drive improvement. The IOM also noted in 2004 that hospitals need to "use knowledge management practices to establish the organization as a 'learning organization'" (Institute of Medicine, 2004: 3–4).

These practices aid in creating a mindfulness of how organizations actively function (complexity) and take into account a strategy for preparing them to enable effective and sustainable change (systems thinking). This approach then enables continued feedback of experience into the organization to ensure that the knowledge

gained is available to be applied through effective sharing (learning organization).

Complexity

Health care organizations are complex entities. "Complex systems typically have fuzzy boundaries. Membership can change, and agents can simultaneously be members of several systems. This can complicate problem solving and lead to unexpected actions in response to change" (Plsek and Greenhalgh, 2001: 625). Complex systems are inherently different than linear systems (Rangachari, 2009).

Recognizing that systemic complexity is inherent in health care is an important step in initiating knowledge management activities (Sheffield, 2008). Librarians should demonstrate an understanding of these unique characteristics and their effect on knowledge sharing while they implement services and design knowledge responsibilities for themselves and colleagues. The leap from a complicated to a complex mind-set could provide librarians with an effective role that could enhance and expand their impact on a health care organization. Figure 13.1 demonstrates the differences in a simple, complicated and complex environment eloquently.

Figure 13.1. Simple, Complicated, and Complex Activities

SIMPLE	COMPLICATED	COMPLEX
Following a Recipe	*Sending a Rocket*	*Raising a Child*
The recipe is essential	Rigid protocols or formulas are necessary	Protocols have a limited application
Recipes are tested to assure easy replication of success	Sending one rocket increases assurance of future success: key elements are identical	Raising one child provides experience but no assurance of future success
No particular expertise is required (cooking skills can improve the success rate)	High levels of expertise in a variety of fields are necessary for success	Expertise can contribute but is neither necessary nor sufficient to assure success
Recipes produce standardized, predictable results every time	Rockets are similar as there is a high degree of outcome predictability	Every child is a unique individual with unpredictable "outcomes"

Source: Adapted from Westley, Patton, and Zimmerman, 2006, and McCandless, 2008. Used with permission of Zimmerman and McCandless.

The characteristics of complexity along with those of systems thinking, discussed below, may be in conflict with traditional more rule-based, linear management strategies (Sewell, 2004; Ollhoff and Walcheski, 2006). Librarians are traditionally associated with a linear management style, which is useful for an adherence to structured constructs and standardization. Adopting a complexity mind-set would present the work of libraries and how it intersects with other efforts in an organization in a new light.

Systems Thinking/Systems Approach

Systems thinking is a process that enables one to better perceive the whole (e.g., the corporation), the elements of which continually affect each other over time and (ideally) operate toward a common purpose. It supports openness to learning from failure, being sensitive to the impact of one's actions across the system, and respecting time and feedback as elements of driving improvement and understanding the environment. It is an engineering analysis concept that was popularized for general business application by Peter Senge (1990) in his book *The Fifth Discipline*.

Systems thinking and its associated techniques have been posited as mechanisms not only to drive and sustain improvement in the safety and quality of health care, but also to illuminate librarians' role in their environment (Leape, 1994; Zipperer and Tompson, 2006). The connection between systems thinking and the learning organization draws this work into the discussion of knowledge management (Littleton, 2009).

Viewing an organization's knowledge-sharing weaknesses from a systems-thinking perspective will illustrate the need for a multitiered, nonsiloed approach to solutions. To nurture the behavior required from both individuals and institutions, and share knowledge and lessons learned, the systems thinker will employ a variety of tools including training, shadowing, and after-action reviews (Milton, 2010). Systems-thinking mechanisms should be applied to help uncover organizational forces that work against sharing. They help inform the deployment of solutions that consider the longer term and systemic effects of change. They can help design a process to ensure that feedback from the system is embodied in the work of the organization. This feedback serves as a knowledge conduit that requires planning to be effective and sustainable. The Evidence-Based Medicine training knowledge exchange strategy described in Management in Action 13.1 brought the librarian into the world of the quality office to share knowledge about searching, and also infused the quality officer into the function of the

library to share what she does and what quality is about at the hospital. So each group learned from each leader as knowledge-sharing opportunities were designed into the initiative.

> This feedback serves as a knowledge conduit that requires planning to be effective and sustainable.

Organizational Learning

Organizational learning requires the involvement of individuals at various levels in an institution. Leadership needs not only to provide vision to ensure resources, but to embody the philosophy and infuse learning into daily work through policies and human resources functions. Line managers or informal "network" leaders—both of which groups could include librarians—"weave the organization together" (Carroll and Edmondson, 2002: 54). The broad view requires these leaders to energize learning and facilitate feedback. It bespeaks a commitment to a systems understanding of the work they do and the organization they function in, and their responsibility to effect improvement across disciplines and among their peers.

> Organizational learning is a process of increasing knowledge and innovative work routines through the interplay of action and reflection that is more extensive than individually focused training and repetition. (Carroll and Edmondson, 2002: 55)

Organizational Culture

The above concepts all focus on the key element of culture. The importance of an organizational culture on the ability to build and sustain knowledge management initiatives cannot be understated. If such a culture is not already established, it is difficult to build one (Davenport, De Long, and Beers, 1998). However, it has also been noted that effective knowledge sharing can in fact help put in place the culture of learning (Dixon, 2000). Also, it has been documented that culture is unit-specific in health care organizations (Sexton et al., 2007). Either way, it should be noted that the learning organization supports values, behaviors, and activities that can enable successful knowledge sharing by exhibiting and supporting the following attributes:

- Employees feel safe to share ideas.
- Credit for ideas is recognized.
- There is a willingness to learn from failure.
- Value is placed on learning on and off the job.

MANAGEMENT IN ACTION 13.1

Structured Librarian and Quality Department Knowledge Sharing

Location: Hospital System

Description of Project: The goal of this project was to get two departments within Via Christi Hospitals more acquainted with each other's functions and roles and facilitate tacit knowledge sharing within the larger institution. The two departments are the Center for Clinical Effectiveness (CCE) and the Libraries.

Impact On: Knowledge sharing would improve the departments' understanding of each other and, therefore, enable both to collaborate more effectively and efficiently.

People Involved: The librarians and CCE staff.

Strategies for Success: A pre-survey was done in the CCE to determine informational needs. This was used to develop two in-services presented by the librarian for the CCE staff. The librarian demonstrated the online services available and stressed the benefits of involving a librarian in CCE projects. A CCE department member reciprocated with an in-depth presentation to the librarians on her department's functions and their potential informational needs.

Barriers Encountered: Scheduling the meetings was a challenge due to infrequency of the CCE department meetings (monthly) and that the agenda is typically full. The original plan was to complete a post survey to measure improvement. However, of the original 15 CCE department members, three do not search for information, three are no longer here, and there are three new members in the department.

Take-Home Points: There was unexpected benefit of referrals to the Libraries as a result of CCE department interactions with other departments and their new knowledge about the Libraries' services. For example, the IV team contacted the Libraries for assistance and requested a literature review for their project. Although a post-survey no longer seems feasible, comments have supported the perceived usefulness of the in-services. In addition, there are plans to continue the librarians' presence at the monthly staff meetings but with much shorter sound bytes. Keeping a "face" on the Libraries should prove useful to both departments.

Contact Information: Camillia A. Gentry, MLS, Medical Librarian (cam.gentry@viachristi.org); Marsha Healy, MPH, RD, LD, Clinical Practice Improvement Coordinator (marsha.healy@via-christi.org). Via Christi Hospitals, Wichita, Inc, Wichita, KS

Further Reading:

Darling, Margaret. 2006. "Librarians' Roles in the Patient Safety Movement." *Access* 12, no. 3 (Spring): 61–62.

Weightman, Allison, and Jane Williamson. 2005. "The Value and Impact of Information Provided through Library Services for Patient Care: A Systematic Review." *Health Information and Libraries Journal* 22, no. 1 (March): 4–25.

Williams, Linda, and Lorri Zipperer. 2003. "Improving Access to Information: Librarians and Nurses Team up for Patient Safety." *Nursing Economics* 21, no. 4 (July-August): 199–201.

Domains of Application: Two Examples

Both quality and safety improvement initiatives and knowledge management work emphasize the notions presented above. The quest for clinical reliability and efficiency gives visibility to the involvement of librarians in driving improvement. The following examples could provide useful leverage points for KM efforts.

Quality/Safety Applications

Connecting KM to quality and patient safety will demonstrate a synergy that could promote the importance of knowledge-sharing programs. This alignment strategy could raise the profile of knowledge management in the eyes of top administration. Making this specific connection could enable a role for librarians and provide opportunities to leverage information manage-

ment and knowledge sharing/brokering expertise in health care (Gowen, Henagan, and McFadden, 2009). Several visible programs may provide librarians with this opportunity:

- **Baldrige KM**: The Malcolm Baldrige National Quality Award is a prestigious honor for an organization to receive. Established by Congress in 1987, and opened to health care organizations in 1999, the annual award recognizes performance excellence in health care, manufacturing, service, small business, education and nonprofit organizations. It is typically presented by the president of the United States. The Baldrige program highlights exceptional performance practices and shares what has been learned with other organizations to enable excellence in American business. At this writing 11 health care organizations have won the award (http://www.baldrige.nist.gov/Contacts_Profiles.htm). Knowledge management is one element in the Baldrige criteria set. This solidly places KM as an important element in achieving excellence for hospitals and health systems. Using these criteria and connecting KM projects to this process could help ensure that upper management supports the concepts.

- **Institute for Healthcare Improvement Collaboratives**: The Boston-based Institute for Healthcare Improvement (IHI) is a leader in patient safety and quality improvement. It utilizes a variety of collaborative and leadership development efforts to support the learning and the spread of initiatives. Its use of learning networks (e.g., the 100K and 5 Million Lives Campaigns) has helped infuse evidence-based practice into the field (http://www.ihi.org). Knowledge management skills served as a cornerstone of the successful spread of these successes. Stating their importance in the rapid collection, review, and distilling of insight from members of their collaborative, the knowledge manager's facilitative role was recognized as crucial to the success of any large scale improvement programs (McCannon and Perla, 2009).

- **Joint Commission Knowledge-Based Information (KBI)**: The Joint Commission's (TJC) foray into understanding and tracking knowledge sharing has a strong focus on explicit representations of knowledge. Note here that there is no indication of the role of culture and person-to-person interaction in the success of knowledge sharing. The Joint Commission commitment supporting a safety culture is documented (The Joint Commission, 2009). Unfortunately, the role of knowledge management as a contributor to a safe culture or librarians' potential role as contributors to that work through the application of their skills is not mentioned, but librarians could leverage their skills in applying KM to their organizations safety culture.

These examples demonstrate opportunities to highlight the importance of the role of knowledge management processes in effective provision of care. They present medical librarians with an opportunity to advocate for involvement in their institutions' quality improvement efforts through partnership, knowledge service design, content development, social network strategy, and health information technology implementation.

Clinical Applications

In this environment opportunities exist for librarians to infuse their knowledge into the process of clinical work.

- **Evidence-based medicine training and transfer of expertise**: The role of librarians in improving access to evidence-based information or KBI in the clinical setting is established (Banks et al., 2007; Dunn, 2009). Chapter 12 covers this aspect of librarianship. A discussion of activities and strengths librarians have to affect the translation of evidence to affect clinical care could also apply to other areas of the business. Helping teams utilize a wide variety of "evidence," from how care is delivered to how the organization learns from its experience, places this training competency as a skill that presents librarians with a knowledge-sharing innovation opportunity. Approached from this perspective, EBM training and awareness efforts can position librarians to serve as boundary spanners and knowledge brokers. The librarian can learn from the practitioner about medical decision making, application of the evidence on the front lines, and the realities of using tools and published studies in the daily work of clinical medicine. Librarians in turn share what they know by working directly with clinical colleagues on the process of identifying high quality relevant and actionable evidence in a way that impacts patient care. Through these interactions, librarians can help dismantle silos and facilitate learning and effective sharing throughout a health care organization (Bandy, Condon, and Graves, 2008).

- **Information Specialist in Context (ISIC)**: The role of librarians in rounding has also been studied (Banks et al., 2007; Brandes, 2007; Bandy, Condon, and Graves, 2008). The implementation of these programs is covered in Chapter 12. As a knowledge management strategy, embedded work roles enable librarians to understand how knowledge is shared and used on the front lines. The participation of librarians in rounds should be seen not only as reference work—as advocated for by the Medical Library Association in the "Vital Pathways for Hospital Librarians" effort—but as a proactive strategy to enhance knowledge sharing within the unit and the organization. (Medical Library Association, 2009). Librarians can help build awareness of how knowledge is shared among the clinical team and of what barriers exist. Observation of clinical simulations could provide the librarian with an excellent opportunity to understand knowledge sharing during clinical events in an environment situated to learning.

- **Integration of knowledge services with the organizational information systems**: As stated earlier, the health care arena has a distinct framework from which to disseminate data. Chapters 2, 7, and 12 in this text discuss these points in more detail. While these technologies assist in the standardization of the information system that is useful, in and of itself it is an ineffective knowledge management strategy (Sheffield, 2008). It is important for librarians to see this as an opportunity to apply what they know to health information technology projects. This could form a foundation from which to expand their skill and influence. Librarians can provide insights and apply both explicit strategies and their own "know how" to collaborate for the effective use of the following tools:
  - Electronic health record / electronic medical record
  - Personal health record
  - Computerized provider order entry
  - Medical error reporting mechanisms
  - E-library requests/automated order entry
  - Clinical decision-making, decision-support systems, teaching, and research (Albert, 2007; Zipperer, 2009)
- **Terminology development and application**: Librarians are trained to be aware of taxonomies and their effective application to location and use of materials. Similar skills can be used to develop tools to help knowledge workers find other knowledgeable individuals. For example, the creation of mechanisms to support organic Web 2.0 tagging processes can provide the redundancy required to ensure/insure their reliability through structured categorization, while still reflecting the natural way users think (McDermott, 2000).

Successful Knowledge Service: Skills, Strategies, and Steps

The following section highlights professional abilities librarians can apply to knowledge-sharing efforts, strategies for application of those skills, and recommended strategies to launch KM efforts. These ideas will help the library manager develop a viable knowledge service.

Skills for Effective KM

Nancy Dixon in *Common Knowledge* highlights the following skills she brings to organizations as a KM consultant (Dixon, 2000). These are skills that librarians possess and that they can deploy:

- **Interviewing**—builds the needed rapport and asks the right questions to draw out in-depth knowledge from executives to front-line workers
- **Analysis**—has a special ability to find patterns in what is happening within an organization
- **Knowledge transfer**—creates innovative methods for knowledge to be transferred from one part of the system to another

Relationship building and networking are mainstays of librarianship that have been applied to learning from colleagues, addressing resource gaps, coordinating consortial and organizational subscription commitments, and making community outreach efforts. These skills can also be applied to knowledge-sharing project management.

A 2007 workshop of hospital librarians on forming knowledge-sharing roles identified five areas of expertise that could be applied to knowledge-sharing efforts:

- Communication
- Knowledge (of their domain and their organization)
- Gap recognition and reduction
- Culture identification
- Change agent role (Robb and Zipperer, 2009)

Strategies Supported by Librarians' Skills

Proactive efforts seek to alter the communication process to enable effective knowledge sharing (Rangachari, 2008).

A number of strategies have been identified that exploit the skills that librarians possess.

- **Knowledge maps/expertise location systems**: (Snowden, 2002; Zipperer, Gluck, and Andersen, 2002). This concept is now clearly seen in a variety of tools that facilitate discussion across organizations and peer groups (see section on social networks). From a tacit sharing perspective, the strategy must be accompanied by a leadership commitment to give employees the time and support needed to respond to queries and participate wholly. Otherwise, there is a risk of gaps in access and barriers that might result in hoarding of information for power or inordinate influence, which could inadvertently result in failure. (Kiechel, 2010).

- **Meetings**: Despite the often bemoaned inefficiency of meetings, they do offer a substantial opportunity for the dissemination of both explicit and tacit knowledge (Gowen, Henagan and McFadden, 2009). It is essential that they be run efficiently and effectively with strong facilitation and clear goals. Asking for evaluation by participants at the end of a session facilitates learning from the experience in rapid time. This tactic also demonstrates a willingness to have a transparent, open rapid learning mechanism built into the process.

- **Collaborative projects/work**: Cross-functional team participation outside the library can support a librarian's heightened awareness of how knowledge is shared (Wheaton, 2009). The dissemination of innovations from team to team, as noted by Dixon, is a useful outcome. The likelihood that the idea will be reinvented as teams apply the concepts in their own context helps the innovation to be concrete, or to "spread" (Berwick, 2003). The sharing of knowledge that needs a translator or boundary spanner from one group to another has been noted as an effective knowledge transfer strategy by the Institute for Healthcare Improvement and others (Dixon, 2000; McCannon and Perla, 2009). Librarians should also seek this as an opportunity to collaborate with patients by serving as knowledge coaches (Association of Academic Health Science Libraries, 2003). Applying patient experience and knowledge to the work of librarianship in the health care organizational setting should be recognized as a valuable innovation for the future of health care. Observing patients' interaction with a variety of silos as they progress through the system provides a unique opportunity for librarians to see systems interactions they may not directly encounter.

- **Embedded librarianship**: A heightened sense of how the work really gets done can be achieved by working at the front lines (Moore, 2006). Being embedded is different from the collaborative projects noted above in that it transfers a keen awareness of knowledge flow and application in daily work through such avenues as participation in rounds (safety, clinical and administrative) (Garcia and Wells, 2009; Greco et al., 2009; Robison, Ryan, and Cooper, 2009; Banks et al., 2007). The basic construct of embedded librarianship is a key element of the nature of information provision work:

50 percent of respondents to a national study designate that customer groups are serviced in this way (Shumaker, Talley, and Miervaldis, 2009). Being embedded also can facilitate the librarian's exposure to "water cooler" methods of sharing that can identify experts, process and information failures, and in turn support safety culture through open and trustful communications between peers and colleagues (Waring and Bishop, 2010: 325).

- **Story dissemination**: Stories have been recognized as a key knowledge-sharing strategy (Denning, 2004). Stories have a place in informing patient safety and quality improvement activities, both within and outside an organization (Conway, 2008). Using stories to build on data and evidence will enhance learning about incidents and increase the urgency to drive improvements. Librarians can apply their skills to systemize the feedback experience and implement tools so teams can use stories broadly. Proactive efforts seek to alter the communication process to enable effective knowledge sharing (Rangachari, 2008). The telling of stories also lends itself well to audio and digital video capture and social networking applications (McGrath, 2008). Librarians can use these tools along with information and social networking technologies to develop effective story collections and sharing mechanisms. This concept is discussed further in the section below, noting both key opportunities and barriers to their adoption and use in the health care environment.

- **Organizational knowledge retention**: The loss of institutional knowledge through employee retirement and job change is recognized as a key driver for knowledge management efforts. In health care, for example, it should be a strategic imperative to develop processes that minimize the loss of nursing insights due to the aging of the nursing workforce and the diminishment of team and unit expertise as they leave (Bleich et al., 2009). Librarians can build on their relationships with staff to envision methods to capture that knowledge and transfer it to their direct reports. It is also important that KM programs are designed to ensure these ideas feed back into the collective intellectual construct of the organization.

- **Reading groups, journal clubs, and other organized opportunities for expert exchange**: Discourse opportunities should include established tools for review and discussion of the literature.

This work can be positioned as a tacit knowledge sharing initiative to expand the librarian's role beyond the identification and distribution piece of the program typically associated with it (Bandy, Condon, and Graves, 2008; Jaffe, 2006). The librarian can select items and facilitate dialogue and learning among the participants instead of relying on a didactic presentation of the facts of the publication. Building in a feedback mechanism is an important element in knowledge-sharing/learning organization development (Tompson and Zipperer, in press). The feedback into the organization can serve as an opportunity for continued learning. In addition, this can serve as an opportunity for librarians to learn by actively participating rather than serving only to identify and acquire session resources.

Tools for Knowledge Sharing

To transfer tacit knowledge from individuals into a repository, organizations usually use some sort of community-based electronic discussion. (Davenport, De Long, and Beers, 1998: 45)

Our profession has long since surpassed the notion that a good set of index cards could serve as a knowledge management tool (Davenport and Prusak, 1998). A "build it and they will come" mentality is a major myth to be debunked when building technologies to support knowledge sharing (Dixon, 2000). Traditionally recognized technologies—databases, for example—are established tools for librarians. This section will instead focus on enabling interaction through the use of social networking technologies in the field today, providing the infrastructure needed to enable this work (Davenport, De Long, and Beers, 1998). Social networking offers growth opportunities for librarians in knowledge-sharing activities. The following brief discussion of these tools is not technical in nature, but rather positions social networking in a person-centered context.

The Web 2.0, social networked knowledge-sharing environment of today is like the Wild West. Experimentation is possible due to the freedom of easy-to-use technologies with low technical development thresholds. Despite its potential, social networking has its skeptics. The time it takes to use the tools effectively has elicited both negative and positive reactions. It is reasonable to discuss social networking as a process of sharing what is known, building community, bringing together teams from disparate organizations, and harnessing the "wisdom

of crowds" to address problems (Sarasohn-Kahn, 2008: 5). A 2009 survey of health care information technology professionals found that 90 percent believed it was acceptable for health care organizations to use social technologies as a means to communicate with the broader public (Health Information Management Systems Society, 2009).

Web-based social networking technologies support tacit knowledge sharing (Bandy, Condon, and Graves, 2008; Garcia and Wells, 2009). The librarian manager must remember that the technologies are only tools. A knowledge-sharing culture must first be explored and enabled to facilitate knowledge management (Davenport and Prusak, 1998). Once that is in place, these tools can be as effective as popular belief would have them to be.

From the knowledge-sharing perspective, library managers launching initiatives based on these tools should require an emphasis on participation rather than on their use for passive content review or posting information nuggets. This activity will enable a depth of insight and degree of mindfulness for librarians as they develop and support the tools. An interest in multidisciplinary dialogue can expand sharing and assist in translation of what is known throughout a network outside their peer group. In health care, this multidisciplinary collaborative approach could enable silo degeneration, boundary spanning, and other opportunities that not only facilitate knowledge flow, but also strategically impact information service design and deployment. Several tools can be used in this fashion: e-mail lists, communities of practice, blogs, wikis, Facebook, Twitter, SharePoint, Second Life, and YouTube. Suggestions of how to use a few of them follow.

E-mail Discussion Groups

E-mail discussion groups are established tools that facilitate information sharing. Librarians have been using this primary technology for years, both within their organizations and for external networking, information delivery, and resource acquisition. As this technology enters the social networking arena, librarians' skills in increasing the effectiveness of e-mail lists could be applied to knowledge work. Management and moderation of the other networking tools discussed below provide logical extensions of this skill set.

Communities of Practice

Communities of practice (CoPs) are thought to enable learning among peers, both novices and experts, in a social context (Li et al., 2009a). They have existed in the corporate arena for 20 years with limited uptake in health care (Li et al., 2009b). Typically associated with the work of Wenger, the concept has morphed over time and is still interpreted in a variety of ways (Wenger, 1998; Li et al., 2009a). A study of 57 non-health care CoPs uncovered both success and failure points in their administration (Probst and Borzillo, 2008). The results were somewhat tactical in nature, but the authors highlight the need for an organization to be willing to allow for the free exchange of ideas in an environment that is risk-free. This engenders the notion of culture supporting the conversation and enabling the community to flourish (Probst and Borzillo 2008). Librarians can contribute to embodying that culture through the use of technology and by participation on care teams (Bandy, Condon, and Graves, 2008). These communities can be enabled via a variety of free social networking platforms (Facebook, Ning, blogs and wikis). An initiative using technology to support a community of practice as a knowledge-sharing strategy is described in Management in Action 13.2. While working within existing technology constraints the goal was to enable the teams to work together more effectively. The richness of the tacit knowledge-sharing opportunities enabled by out-of-the-box thinking positioned the librarian as a leader, and strategist, and opened doors to other types of knowledge exchange opportunities.

YouTube

The types of short audio files and video distributed via an open video channel such as YouTube can be used to translate what the "knower knows" into a tangible, portable format. Once captured this way, it can be made accessible from a variety of devices, thereby facilitating knowledge-sharing spread, and broad feedback through associated social networking mechanisms.

MANAGEMENT IN ACTION 13.2

Librarians Support Communities of Practice

Location: Metropolitan Teaching Hospital

Description of Problem/Project: A number of multidisciplinary clinical microsystems were being developed and the library manager was invited to join the ICU Microsystem Lead Team. Additional library staff members joined two other Microsystem Lead Teams. After participating in the team for several months, it became apparent to the librarians that there was no plan for how to share and capture knowledge within and among the groups.

Impact On: Knowledge sharing would improve the groups' ability to create charters, aims, surveys, and other tools. It would avoid each group having to "recreate the wheel" and enable them to draw from the experience of the group so they could focus on the specific needs of their patient population. As new microsystems were developed they would benefit from lessons learned overtime.

People Involved: Microsystem leadership (physician, nurse, and administrator), facilitator, and librarian.

Strategies for Success: (*action taken*) A prototype content management website was developed using open source software. The site had work areas for each microsystem but allowed for sharing across groups as well. Components of the site included document management, a forum, links to resources, news feeds, and a wiki.

Barriers Encountered: Although there was enthusiasm on the part of the leadership, the IT infrastructure would not support an open source application.

Take-Home Points: The goal of a tool that would support robust knowledge sharing was not realized. However, the librarian refocused the goal on an available tool on the hospital portal, called a microsite. A microsite was developed to support the work of the ICU microsystem, and as it became successful it was expanded to support the work of other groups in the ICU, including the Nurse Practice Council. The success positioned the library manager as an expert in helping teams and councils improve their awareness of the importance of explicit and tacit knowledge sharing. The librarian consulted on the development of microsites for the Education Council, Nursing Research Council, Shared Decision-Making Council, PICC-IV Team, and the Ethics Committee.

Contact Information: Margaret M. Bandy, Medical Librarian, Exempla Saint Joseph Hospital, Denver, Colorado. E-mail: bandym@exempla.org

Further Reading:

Dixon, Nancy M. 2000. *Common Knowledge: How Companies Thrive by Sharing What They Know* (online book excerpt). Boston: Harvard Business School Press. Accessed July 24, 2010. http://www.acm.org/ubiquity/book/n_dixon_1.html.

Wenger, Etienne. 1996. "How to Optimize Organizational Learning." *Healthcare Forum Journal* (July/August): 22–23.

This type of tool can enable fairly immediate capture and reuse of important knowledge and insight. For example, interviewing experts, team members, and senior employees prior to their departure may allow for their knowledge to be captured for a variety of uses (McGrath, 2008).

This tactic may allow knowledge to be translated into a form that becomes part of the corporate memory more rapidly than the laborious process of a peer-reviewed article or award lecture, case report or commentary. As with any initiative, the goals of the project can affect the final product. This technology is perfect for sharing stories, noted earlier as a key element in knowledge-sharing programs. In addition to capturing the primary content, the emotion and commitment inherent in the story is transmitted visually and by tone of voice. Not only are interviews useful for knowledge sharing, but they may in turn provide marketing dividends should an interviewee prove to be exceptionally witty, photogenic, or articulate.

Other Online Considerations

There are a number of challenges in using these tools:

- Firewall and security issues in the health care environment may limit the use of these technologies. Nonetheless, librarians should seek avenues to use similar tools that have been approved for use in their environments.

- Bandwidth concerns can also result in reservations to the adoption of social networking tools. Health care organizations that struggle with this directly, or that are based in communities with bandwidth issues, may seek to address the problem by just disallowing their collective use.

- Site development and design play a role in the success of online communication functions, but they are a means to an end. The technology should be seen only as a tool. Organizations and librarians should understand that the engagement needed to drive experts and visitors to use the tool to share what they know, mine the community for what they don't know, and seek and share solutions, is a key strategic effort.

Getting Started: What Is a Manager to Do?

The context provided above provides grounding on tacit versus explicit knowledge roles for librarians. Library managers should find direction here to expand their knowledge-sharing impact within the acute care arena. Given that there are many ways to define this work and

inculcate it, depending on the organizational culture, the following suggestions may establish the librarian as a key partner in determining effective KM strategies and tactics.

1. *Determine need*:
   - Audit a multidisciplinary set of clients, colleagues and nonusers.
   - Conduct group interviews and/or focus groups.

2. *Build a cadre of champions*:
   - Engage leadership (Davenport, De Long, and Beers, 1998).
   - Educate: Develop and seek opportunities to explore knowledge-sharing concepts with others. Take part in and facilitate dialogues to enable shared meaning around what "knowledge" and "knowledge management" mean at your organization. Trumpet the findings and use them to frame the strategy and related initiatives.
   - Network with HR, leadership, health information technology (HIT), clinicians: Building an effective and sustainable KM effort means working with the right people. Develop explicit and measurable job requirements that articulate the role of knowledge sharing to will draw the right person to the job, or empower the right work to be done within an existing position. Be prepared to make individuals and their managers accountable for their participation, and be accountable for letting them do the work.

3. *Pull together a multidisciplinary team*: Enable a group to work together that is small, engaged, and comfortable learning together. Include participants who are innovative and entrepreneurial. Consider involving a volunteer committee of retirees with extensive organizational knowledge and process orientation. Ensure that the patient perspective is represented not only by a professional who works with patients, but if possible with actual patients and/or family members.

4. *Build a strategy that aligns with the hospital's mission and goals, not necessarily the library's goals*: Library managers know how to do this (see Chapter 3). With a strategy that incorporates the goals of other operational units, knowledge management terminology and impact can be seen as a core value and an element of success and effective patient care. The importance will resonate with those who are contributing to the work and will support the sharing of knowledge more effectively

(Davenport, De Long, and Beers, 1998). Aligning the work with the mission of the organization, rather than that of the library is key (Wheaton, 2009). Obviously, it goes without saying that the library's mission should also be aligned with the organization's mission, but recognizing the larger mission scope is important.

5. *Determine opportunities for improvement*:
   - Assess audit results.
   - Attend sessions to see systemic "knowledge gaps."
   - Apply systems thinking tools to explore solutions and assess impact at an organizational level over time (Zipperer and Tompson, 2006).

6. *Build a tool and process for sharing that works for everyone and commit to using it*: This should be enabled by a multichannel strategy (online, phone, Internet, face to face) with appropriate robust use by leaders and management to demonstrate and support the behavior (Davenport, De Long, and Beers, 1998).

7. *Be flexible and create a flexible process and program structure* (Davenport, De Long, and Beers, 1998).

8. *Demonstrate knowledge sharing behaviors both as a team participant and a manager*:
   - Respond to e-mails/queries with knowledge, not only with citations.
   - Connect people to individuals, not just to materials.
   - Share what you know in a way that enables exchange and dialogue.

9. *Be realistic*:
   - Define what you mean—the multidisciplinary team will assist in ensuring that the language for the program is meaningful to all disciplines. Knowledge management and information work in general has its own jargon. The definitions used to describe the work need to mean something to everyone involved in implementing the program so language may need to be amended to resonate appropriately.
   - Start small—recognize the culture is local (Sexton et al., 2007).
   - Test effectiveness—it is important to know if the changes that will be suggested to improve knowledge sharing actually work. Rapid cycle change methods can be used to create a sense of urgency around the proposed improvements

and the need to move from point A to point B without elongated study times and substantive resource use. A Plan-Do-Study-Act method is just one example of this strategy (Robb and Zipperer, 2009; Wheaton, 2009).

10. *Use metrics that demonstrate impact*: Gowen and colleagues provide some interesting tactics for measurement (Gowen, Henagan, and McFadden, 2009). Baldrige also provides a question that may provide some ideas to gather data to measure knowledge-sharing impact in its review criteria:
    "How do you manage organizational knowledge to accomplish:
    - The collection and transfer of workforce knowledge
    - The transfer of relevant knowledge to and from patients and stakeholders, suppliers, partners and collaborators
    - The rapid identification, sharing, and implementation of best practices, and
    - The assembly and transfer of relevant knowledge for use in the strategic planning process." (Baldrige National Quality Program, 2009:17)

11. *Facilitate the learning for both the organization and the team*: Do not assume training will provide knowledge sharing in a real way. Training is important, but not as rich a sharing opportunity as collaboration on multidisciplinary teams, working with outside experts, embedded work (as a clinical librarian or otherwise), and dialogue participation (Sewell, 2004).
    - Be sure to enable people not only to collect knowledge, but to report it back to others.
    - Reward the activity, although do not assume incentives will sustain it.

12. *Define knowledge management as being about a shift in culture and engagement, which is enabled by technology, but is not ABOUT technology* (Strong, Davenport, and Prusak, 2008): The notion is to facilitate an environment within which the knowledge is shared (Collison and Parcell, 2005).

Technology projects—which may be easier to launch due to their tangibility, seeming immediacy, and "hipness"—lend themselves to knowledge sharing if designed with this in mind. As described in Management in Action 13.3, the librarians developed a blog for residents to support their work in preparing for morning report. This tool was more focused on information sharing and process improvement, but it opened the door for the

MANAGEMENT IN ACTION 13.3

Residents' Blog for Morning Report

Location: Primary Children's Medical Center and University of Utah Department of Pediatrics

Description of Problem/Project: Morning report is a time before rounding in which a resident presents a case he or she feels will bring a learning point to the other residents. Morning report starts with the presentation of a patient and questions are asked to obtain the patient history. The next stage is how the patient presented at the time of examination and what tests and labs should be ordered with values given if the tests or labs were actually performed. A differential diagnosis is discussed and then the actual diagnosis is presented along with a learning point about the diagnosis. This knowledge was shared but never archived so there was no access to past morning report presentations or the knowledge that was gained from treating a particular patient. The librarians and research coordinator created a blog for University of Utah pediatric residents that practiced at Intermountain's Primary Children's Medical Center to share what was learned through presentations at morning report (http://www.pcmcmorningreport.blogspot.com). PowerPoint presentations by the residents were embedded in the blog and the librarian and research coordinator included further citations and resources for residents to learn more about the topics posted to the blog. On days when there was not morning report the librarian would sometimes post tips on how to search or interpret medical information in journals or other information resources.

Impact On: The residents would have access to learning points they may have missed by not attending morning report. Also, because this is a public access blog the broader population of hospital attending physicians, community pediatricians, and family medicine doctors could benefit as well.

People Involved: The medical librarian at Primary Children's Medical Center partnered with a research coordinator in the University of Utah Department of Pediatrics along with the chief pediatric residents.

Strategies for Success: Working with the associate medical director and the director of the pediatric residents along with the support of the chief pediatric residents, the librarian and research coordinator were able to participate three times a week when morning report occurred. The kick-off of the blog was presented at a noon conference lunch to the broader resident and attending population. Residents have told attending and clinic physicians about the blog and this has increased readership. Also, the pediatric residents felt that the blog was a great resource and willingly shared their information to be posted to the blog. A public access blog site that was free was used to facilitate the knowledge exchange. This allowed visitors to view the blog while at the hospital but also outside of the hospital's online network.

Barriers Encountered: Full-text resources could not be posted to the blog because of copyright. Sometimes morning report was missed by the blog administrators and getting the morning report topic was sometimes difficult as the residents did not always respond to the request for the topic.

Take-Home Points: A successful project requires administrative support. Be open to suggestions, as this was not the initial knowledge management project idea. If an electronic format for the work is chosen, it is better to have it accessible inside the organization as well as outside on the Internet. Use what the organization IT staff will allow through a firewall. A web application is better to use than software that needs to download to a computer. If a blog is the chosen tool, post to it regularly or it will become unread. If a public blog is created, keep in mind to not post anything that would reveal patient identification. Be creative; it increases learning and knowledge sharing.

Contact Information: Emily Eresuma, MLS, Senior Medical Librarian, Primary Children's Medical Library, Salt Lake City, Utah. E-mail: emily.eresuma@imail.org

Further Reading:

Anderson, Jane A., and Pamela Willson. 2009. "Knowledge Management: Organizing Nursing Care Knowledge." *Critical Care Nursing Quarterly* 32, no. 1 (January-March): 1–9.

Bhargava, Rohit. "How Hospitals Are Quietly Leading the Way with Social Media." *Fresh Influence*. Ogilvy Public Relations Worldwide (September 25, 2009). Accessed October 2, 2010. http://blog.ogilvypr.com/2009/09/how-hospitals-are-quietly-leading-the-way-with-social-media/.

Billings, Diane M. 2009. "Wikis and Blogs: Consider the Possibilities for Continuing Nursing Education." *Journal of Continuing Education in Nursing* 40 no. 12 (December): 534–535.

Srikantaiah, T. Kanti, and Michael E.D. Koenig, eds. 2000. *Knowledge Management for the Information Professional*. Medford, NJ; Information Today.

librarians to get more involved and share their knowledge about all kinds of information tactics, raised their visibility as part of the team, and helped the librarian understand the issues around morning report, so that tactic knowledge was gathered through the participation enabled by the availability of the technology.

Barriers and Opportunities for Improvement

Do you have the time, to "halve" the time? (Collison and Parcell, 2005: 66)

Core work in knowledge management is similar to culture change efforts and can be stymied by the same types of problems. The following list of barriers is presented to prepare the library manager to circumvent oft-stated arguments against knowledge-sharing efforts:

- **Time**: Similar to other change efforts, the time it takes to put them in place can be a legitimate issue, but if a long-term vision is attached to the work, the ultimate time savings may help justify the effort.

- **Hierarchy**: The hierarchy of medicine can be a tremendous obstacle to improvement and culture change efforts in a health care organization. Knowledge management initiatives are also vulnerable to this problem.

- **Technology**:
  - Design and internal access are poor (McKnight, 2006).
  - Taxonomies do not reflect how users think (McDermott, 2000).
  - Links are not always easy to use. A process for using URLs that are short and robust should be designed. Using open URL programs like TinyURL (http://tinyurl.com/) or digital object identifiers (DOI) (http://www.doi.org/) may create links to explicit resources that stand the test of time.
  - External networking sites are blocked by firewalls.
  - Reading-to-learn is not embedded in the culture and is seen as suspect (McKnight, 2006).

- **Cross-discipline communication**: Clear purpose and language are very important to success (Davenport, De Young, and Beers, 1998). Anecdotal results from the authors' survey development project with hospitals to assess learning organization characteristics, behaviors, and the intersection of information,

evidence, and knowledge access indicated that a lack of clarity across silos can undermine even small efforts (Zipperer unpublished data, 2004). In addition, the perception by staff of the librarian's traditional role in the organization could also stymie innovation.

- **Not folding the process into "daily work" to demonstrate its enhancement of daily work**: If contributing to or accessing knowledge tools is seen as just one more task to add to a busy day, the complexity of getting work done is a barrier to contribution. A study interviewing medical librarians about their use of established information-sharing tools found that catalogers used them because they could easily see the benefits of the knowledge capture system as a memory bank (for catalog record development) that reduced duplication and saved time (Ralph and Tijerino, 2009).

- **ROI difficult to calculate (especially with tacit knowledge)**: There is a recognized lack of empirical research on the impact of KM in health care organizations (Zack, McKeen, and Singh, 2009). However, metrics and questions posited by Baldrige may provide an industry-recognized example with which to initiate the measurement process (Baldrige National Quality Program, 2009). Measure for management, not only for the use of the library. The numbers should speak to the champions to drive acceptance of the program.

Conclusion

Hospitals have been challenged to adopt a mind-set and activities that support organizational learning. Influential organizations across the health care spectrum have begun to discuss knowledge management as a quality improvement and best practice dissemination process. Knowledge management can serve as an important element supporting that strategy (Institute of Medicine, 2004). Successful error reduction efforts rely on sharing experience and better practice in a constructive way that enables learning from failure.

Librarians have the skills to participate in these functions, but have not collectively been designated as a specific player in this work. The application of the skills that librarians routinely apply to information- and evidence-sharing efforts could enhance the nascent efforts to establish knowledge management and organizational learning initiatives in health care organizations (Zipperer and Sykes, 2009). Knowledge management serves as an opportunity for librarians to have an impact on quality, leadership transformation, and clinical care by presenting their skills in this context.

References

Ackoff, Russell L. 1989. "From Data to Wisdom." *Journal of Applied Systems Analysis* 16: 3–9.

Albert, Karen M. 2007. "Integrating Knowledge-Based Resources into the Electronic Health Record: History, Current Status, and Role of Librarians." *Medical Reference Services Quarterly* 26, no 3 (Fall): 1–19.

Anderson, Jane A., and Pamela Willson. 2009. "Knowledge Management: Organizing Nursing Care Knowledge." *Critical Care Nursing Quarterly* 32, no. 1 (January-March): 1–9.

Association of Academic Health Sciences Libraries. AAHSL Charting the Future Task Force. 2003. "Building on Success: Charting the Future of Knowledge Management within the Academic Health Center." Accessed October 4, 2010. http://www.aahsl.org/mc/page.do?sitePageId=84882. Viewable document at: http://kuscholarworks.ku.edu/dspace/bitstream/1808/217/1/Charting_the_Future_viewable.pdf.

Baldrige National Quality Program. 2009. "Health Care Criteria for Performance Excellence 2009-2010." Gaithersburg, MD: NIST. 2009.

Bandy, Margaret M., Joyce Condon, and Ellen Graves. 2008. "Participating in Communities of Practice." *Medical Reference Services Quarterly* 27, no. 4 (Winter): 441–449.

Banks, Daniel E., Runhua Shi, Donna F. Timm, Kerri Ann Christopher, David Charles Duggar, Marianne Comegys, and Jerry McLarty. 2007. "Decreased Hospital Length of Stay Associated with Presentation of Cases at Morning Report with Librarian Support." *Journal of the Medical Library Association* 95, no. 4 (October): 381–387.

Bellinger, Gene, Durval Castro, and Anthony Mills. 2004. "Data, Information, Knowledge, and Wisdom." Accessed October 4, 2010. http://www.systems-thinking.org/dikw/dikw.htm.

Berwick, Donald M. 2003. "Disseminating Innovations in Health Care." *JAMA: The Journal of the American Medical Association* 289, no 15 (April 16):1969–1975.

Bleich, Michael R., Brenda L. Cleary, Kathleen Davis, Barbara J. Hatcher, Peggy O. Hewlett, and Karen S. Hill. 2009. "Mitigating Knowledge Loss: A Strategic Imperative for Nurse Leaders." *Journal of Nursing Administration* 39, no. 4 (April): 160–164.

Brandes, Susan. 2007. "Experience and Outcomes of Medical Librarian Rounding." *Medical Reference Services Quarterly* 26, no. 4 (Winter): 85–92.

Carroll, J. S., and Amy C. Edmondson. 2002. "Leading Organisational Learning in Health Care." *Quality and Safety in Health Care* 11, no. 1 (March): 51–56.

Collison Chris, and Geoff Parcell. 2005. *Learning to Fly—Practical Knowledge Management from Leading and Learning Organizations.* 2nd ed. West Sussex, UK: Capstone.

Conway, James B. 2008. "Could It Happen Here? Learning from Other Organizations' Safety Errors." *Healthcare Executive* 23, no. 6 (November/December): 64–67.

Davenport, Thomas H., and John Glaser. 2002. "Just-in-Time Delivery Comes to Knowledge Management." *Harvard Business Review* 80, no. 7 (July): 107–111, 126.

Davenport, Thomas, H., David W. De Long, and Michael C. Beers. 1998. "Successful Knowledge Management Projects." *Sloan Management Review* 39, no. 2 (Winter): 43–57.

Davenport, Thomas H., and Laurence Prusak. 1998. *Working Knowledge: How Organizations Manage What They Know.* Boston: Harvard Business School Press.

Denning, Steve. 2004. "Telling Tales." *Harvard Business Review* 82, no. 5 (May): 122–129.

Dixon, Nancy M. 2000. *Common Knowledge: How Companies Thrive by Sharing What They Know.* Boston: Harvard Business School Press.

Donaldson, Liam J., and J. A. Muir Gray. 1998. "Clinical Governance: A Quality Duty for Health Organizations." *Quality in Health Care* 7, (Supp):S37–S44.

Dunn, Kathel. 2009. *Value of Libraries Bibliography* (September 9). Accessed October 4, 2010. http://nnlm.gov/mar/about/pdf/valuearticles090909.pdf.

Garcia, Jenny L., and Karen K. Wells. 2009. "Knowledge-Based Information to Improve the Quality of Patient Care." *Journal for Healthcare Quality* 31, no. 1: 30–35.

Gowen, Charles R., III, Stephanie C. Henagan, and Kathleen L. McFadden. 2009. "Knowledge Management as a Mediator for the Efficacy of Transformational Leadership and Quality Management Initiatives in U.S. Health Care." *Health Care Management Review* 34, no. 3 (April-June): 129–140.

Greco Elisa, Marina Englesakis, Amy Faulkner, Boguslawa Trojan, Lorne E Rotstein, and David R. Urbach. 2009. "Clinical Librarian Attendance at General Surgery Quality of Care Rounds (Mortality and Morbidity Conference)." *Surgical Innovation* 16, no. 3: 266–269.

Hamasu, Claire. 2009. "Knowledge Sharing in Hospitals: The Workshop." *Plains to Peaks Post* 8, no. 1 (July): 6–7.

Hansen, Morten T., Nitin Nohria, and Thomas Tierney. 1999. "What's Your Strategy for Managing Knowledge?" *Harvard Business Review* 77, no. 2 (March/April): 106–115.

Health Information Management Systems Society. 2009. *Social Technology Tools in Health Care. Vantage Point.* Accessed October 4, 2010. http://www.himss.org/content/files/vantage point/pdf/VantagePoint_200912.pdf.

Healy, Bernadine. 2006. "Who Says What's Best?" *U.S. News & World Report* 141, no. 9 (September 11): 75. Accessed October 2, 2010. http://health.usnews.com/usnews/health/articles/060903/11healy.htm.

Institute of Medicine. 2004. Committee on the Work Environment for Nurses and Patient Safety, Board on Health Care Services, A. Page, ed. *Keeping Patients Safe: Transforming the*

Work Environment of Nurses. Washington, DC: National Academies Press.

Institute of Medicine. Committee on Quality of Health Care in America, 2001. *Crossing the Quality Chasm: A New Health System for the 21st Century.* Washington, DC: National Academies Press.

Jaffe, Judy. 2006. "Meet the Special Library: The Wacker Knowledge Center." *SLA Boston Bulletin* 71, no. 3 (Fall).

Joint Commission. 2009. "Leadership Committed to Safety." *Sentinel Event Alert* 43 (August 27): 1–3. Accessed January 22, 2011. http://www.jointcommission.org/assets/1/18/SEA_43.PDF.

Jaffe, Judy. 2006. "Meet the Special Library: The Wacker Knowledge Center." *SLA Boston Bulletin* 71, no. 3 (Fall).

Joint Commission. 2010. "Glossary." In *2010 Hospital Accreditation Standards* (pp. GL-15–GL-16). Oakbrook Terrace, IL: Joint Commission.

Joint Commission on Accreditation of Healthcare Organizations. 1994. "Standard IM.9." In *Comprehensive Accreditation Manual for Hospitals 1994-1995.* Oakbrook Terrace, IL: The Commission.

Kiechel, Walter. 2010. "One More Time, Don't Hoard Information." *The Conversation: Harvard Business Review Blog* (March 4). Accessed October 4, 2010. http://blogs.hbr.org/cs/2010/03/one_more_time_dont_hoard_information.html.

Kohn, Linda T., Janet M. Corrigan, and Molla S. Donaldson, eds. 2000. *To Err Is Human: Building a Safer Health System.* Washington, DC: Committee on Quality of Health Care in America, Institute of Medicine. National Academies Press.

Leape, Lucian L. 1994. "Error in Medicine." *JAMA: The Journal of the American Medical Association* 272, no. 23: 1851–1857.

Li, Linda C., Jeremy M. Grimshaw, Camilla Nielsen, Maria Judd, Peter C. Coyte, and Ian D. Graham. 2009a. "Evolution of Wenger's Concept of Community of Practice." *Implementation Science* 4: 11.

Li, Linda C, Jeremy M. Grimshaw, Camilla Nielsen, Maria Judd, Peter C. Coyte, and Ian D. Graham. 2009b. "Use of Communities of Practice in Business and Health Care Sectors: a Systematic Review." *Implementation Science* 4: 27.

Littleton, Dawn. 2009. "Supporting Academic Health Centers with Knowledge Management: Learning from the Web." *Medical Reference Services* Quarterly 28, no. 2 (April): 164–171.

McCandless, Keith. 2008. *Safely Taking Risks: Complexity and Patient Safety.* Social Invention Group. Accessed October 2, 2010. http://socialinvention.net/Documents/McCandless%20-%20Safely%20Taking%20Risks.pdf.

McCannon, C. Joseph, and Rocco J. Perla. 2009. "Learning Networks for Sustainable, Large-scale Improvement." *Joint Commission Journal of Quality and Patient Safety* 35, no. 5 (May): 286–291.

McDermott, Richard M. 2000. "Knowing in Community: 10 Critical Success Factors in Building Communities of Practice." *IHRIM Journal* 4, no.1 (March): 19.

McGrath, Sean. 2008. "Leverage Web Technologies to Capture and Manage Knowledge Assets." *IT World* (January 7, 2008). Accessed October 4, 2010. http://www.itworld.com/knowledge-management-nlsebiz-080107.

McKnight, Michelynn. 2006. "The Information Seeking of On-Duty Critical Care Nurses: Evidence from Participant Observation and In-Context Interviews." *Journal of the Medical Library Association* 94, no. 2 (April): 145–151.

Medical Library Association. 2006. "The Academy of Health Information Professionals Essential Areas of Knowledge." Chicago: MLA. Accessed October 4, 2010. http://www.mlanet.org/academy/knowledge.

Medical Library Association. 2009. *Vital Pathways for Hospital Librarians: Addressing the Hospital's Information and Training Needs.* Chicago: Medical Library Association. Accessed October 4, 2010. http://www.mlanet.org/resources/vital/vitalpathways_execsumm.pdf.

Milton, Nick. 2010. *The Lessons Learned Handbook: Practical Approaches to Learning from Experience.* Oxford, UK. Chandos Publishing.

Moore, Michael F. 2006. "Embedded in Systems Engineering: How One Organization Makes It Work." *Information Outlook* 10, no. 5 (May): 23–25.

Nonaka, Ikujiro. 1991. "The Knowledge Creating Company." *Harvard Business Review* 69, no. 6 (November–December): 96–104.

Ollhoff, J., and M. Walcheski. 2006. "Making the Jump to Systems Thinking." *The Systems Thinker* 17, no. 5 (June/July): 9–11.

Plsek, Paul E., and Trish Greenhalgh. 2001. "The Challenge of Complexity in Health Care." *British Medical Journal* 323, no. 7313 (September 15): 625–628.

Probst, Gilbert, and Stefano Borzillo. 2008. "Why Communities of Practice Succeed and Why They Fail." *European Management Journal* 26, no. 5: 335–347.

Prusak, Lawrence. 2009. "You Can Never Have Too Much Knowledge." *Information Outlook* 13, no. 8 (December): 10–13.

Ralph, Lynette, and Cathy Tijerino. 2009. "Knowledge Management and Library Culture." *College and Undergraduate Libraries* 16, no. 4: 329–337.

Rangachari, Pavani. 2008. "Knowledge Sharing Networks Related to Hospital Quality Measurement and Reporting." *Health Care Management Review* 33, no. 3 (July–September): 253–263.

Rangachari, Pavani. 2009. "Knowledge-Sharing Networks in Professional Complex Systems." *Journal of Knowledge Management* 13, no. 3: 132–145.

Robb, Beth G., and Lorri Zipperer. 2009. "Knowledge Management in Hospitals: Drawing from Experience to Define the Librarian's Role." *Journal of Hospital Librarianship* 9, no. 3: 307–317.

Robison, Rex R., Mary E. Ryan, and I. Diane Cooper. 2009. "Inquiring Informationists: A Qualitative Exploration of Our Role." *Evidence-Based Library and Information Practice* 4, no. 1: 4–16.

Sackett, David L., William M. C. Rosenberg, J. A. Muir Gray, R. Brian Haynes, and W. Scott Richardson. 1996. "Evidence-Based Medicine: What It Is and What It Isn't." *BMJ* 312, no. 7023 (January 13): 71–72.

Sarasohn-Kahn, Jane. 2008. *The Wisdom of Patients: Health Care Meets Online Social Media.* Oakland: California HealthCare Foundation (April 2008). Accessed October 4, 2010. http://www.chcf.org/publications/2008/04/the-wisdom -of-patients-health-care-meets-online-social-media.

Schwarzwalder, Robert. 1999. "Librarians as Knowledge Management Agents." *Econtent* 22, no. 4 (August/September): 63–65.

Senge, Peter M. 1990. *The Fifth Discipline.* New York: Random House.

Sewell, Jacquie. 2004. "Building a Learning Organization @ Your Library." *MLA Forum* 3, no 1, (February 24). Accessed October 4, 2010. http://www.mlaforum.org/volumeIII/ issue1/Article3learningOrg.html.

Sexton, J. Byran, Lori A. Paine, James Manfuso, Christine G. Holzmueller, Elizabeth A. Martinez, Dana Moore, David G. Hunt, and Peter J. Pronovost. 2007. "Check-up for Safety Culture in 'My Patient Care Area.'" *Joint Commission Journal on Quality and Patient Safety* 33, no. 1: 699–703.

Sheffield, James. 2008. "Inquiry in Health Knowledge Management." *Journal of Knowledge Management* 12, no. 4: 160–172.

Shumaker, David, Mary Talley, and Wendy Miervaldis. 2009. *Models of Embedded Librarianship. Final Report.* Prepared under the Special Libraries Association Research Grant 2007 (June 30, 2009). Accessed October 4, 2010. http://www.sla.org/pdfs/EmbeddedLibrarianshipFinalRpt Rev.pdf.

Skinner, Ben. 2008. "Web Alert: Resources to Support the Development of a Knowledge Management Strategy." *Quality in Primary Care* 16, no 4: 295–299.

Snowden, David. 2002. "Complex Acts of Knowing: Paradox and Descriptive Self-Awareness." *Journal of Knowledge Management* 6, no. 2: 100–111.

Strong, Bruce, Thomas H. Davenport, and Laurence Prusak. 2008. "Organizational Governance of Knowledge and Learning." *Knowledge and Process Management* 15, no. 2: 150–157.

Tompson, Sara, and Lorri Zipperer. In press. "Systems Thinking for Success" In *Best Practices for Corporate Libraries*, edited by Marjorie J. Porter and Sigrid Kelsey. Santa Barbara: ABC-CLIO.

Waring, Justin J., and Simon Bishop. 2010. "'Water Cooler' Learning: Knowledge Sharing at the Clinical 'Backstage' and its Contribution to Patient Safety." *Journal of Health Organization Management* 24, no 4: 325–342.

Wenger, Etienne. 1998. *Communities of Practice. Learning, Meaning, and Identity.* Cambridge, UK: Cambridge University Press.

Westley, Frances, Michael Quinn Patton, and Brenda Zimmerman. 2006. *Getting to Maybe.* Toronto: Random House Canada.

Wheaton, Ken. 2009. "Making the Transformation to Sharing Knowledge." *Information Outlook* 13, no. 6 (September): 20–24.

Zack, Michael, James McKeen, and Satyendra Singh. 2009. "Knowledge Management and Organizational Performance: An Exploratory Analysis." *Journal of Knowledge Management* 13, no. 6: 392–409.

Zipperer, Lorri. 2009. "Knowledge Workers, Librarians and Safety: Opportunities for Partnership." In *Handbook of Research on Information Technology Management and Clinical Data Administration in Health Care*, edited by A. Dwivedi, 495–506. London, UK: IGI Global.

Zipperer, Lorri, Jeannine Gluck, and Susan Anderson. 2002. "Knowledge Maps for Patient Safety." *Journal of Hospital Librarianship* 2, no. 4: 17–35.

Zipperer, Lorri, and Jan Sykes. 2004. "The Role of Librarians in Patient Safety: Gaps and Strengths in the Current Culture." *Journal of the Medical Library Association* 92, no. 4: 498–500.

Zipperer, Lorri, and Jan Sykes. 2009 "Engaging as Partners in Patient Safety: The Experience of Librarians." *Patient Safety and Quality in Healthcare* 6, no. 2 (March/April): 28-30, 32-33.

Zipperer, Lorri, and Sara Tompson. 2006. "Systems Thinking: A New Avenue for Involvement and Growth." *Information Outlook* 10, no. 12 (December): 16–20.

Further Reading

Currie, Graeme, Justin Waring, and Rachael Finn. 2008. "The Limits of Knowledge Management for UK Public Services Modernization: The Case of Patient Safety and Service Quality." *Public Administration* 86, no. 2: 363–385.

Garvin, David. 1993. "Building a Learning Organization." *Harvard Business Review* 71, no. 4: 78–92.

Garvin, David A., Amy C. Edmondson, and Francesca Gino. 2008. "Is Yours a Learning Organization?" *Harvard Business Review* 86, no. 3: 109–116.

Guptill, Janet. 2005. "Knowledge Management in Health Care." *Journal of Health Care Finance* 31, no. 3 (Spring): 10–14.

Keeling, Carole, and Sian Lambert. 2000. "Knowledge Management in the NHS: Positioning the Health Care Librarian at the Knowledge Intersection." *Health Libraries Review* 17, no. 3: 136–143.

Nonaka, Ikujiro, and Hirotaka Takeuchi. 1995. *The Knowledge-Creating Company: How Japanese Companies Create the Dynamics of Innovation.* New York: Oxford University Press.

O'Dell, Carla. 1998. *If Only We Knew What We Know: The Transfer of Internal Knowledge and Best Practice.* New York: Free Press.

Plsek, Paul E., and Tim Wilson. 2001. "Complexity, Leadership, and Management in Health Care Organisations." *BMJ* 323, no. 7315 (September 29): 746–749.

14

Health Information for Patients and Consumers

Michele Spatz

Patients and health care consumers need and want access to sound health information, and who better to provide it than health sciences librarians, the twenty-first century's knowledge navigation experts. This chapter takes a comprehensive look at providing patient and consumer health information, from its importance in the health of our nation and contributions toward quality patient care, to the nuts and bolts of service provision. Practical aspects such as legal and ethical issues as well as establishing services, developing collections across a spectrum of available information media, promotion and outreach, and finally, measuring effectiveness are all discussed. The chapter author would like to gratefully acknowledge the work of the previous edition's chapter author, Margaret Bandy.

Much has changed in the 11 years since the first edition of this book was published, when providing consumer health information was considered novel. Today, regulatory and market pressures compel the health care system to reform its delivery model while the health care industry itself strives toward patient-centered care. These two forces are creating an expectation that patients and consumers need to take more responsibility and control of their health in order to make health care sustainable. Patient and consumer health information services are vital to the emerging model of patient-centered or patient-driven health care.

Importance of Patient/Consumer Health Information in Health Care Settings

National Health Initiatives

In recent years, people involved in all sectors of health care have called for more patient-focused care. There are organizations, such as Planetree, whose mission is to advance the practice of patient-centered care in a variety of health care settings such as hospitals, long-term care facilities, and inpatient mental health settings. The Joint Commission tells patients that they should become active participants in their heath care decisions. Its National Patient Safety Goals "encourage patients' active involvement in their own care as a patient safety strategy" (Joint Commission, 2009). Hospitalized patients are asked to "Speak Up" and say something when things don't seem right (Joint Commission, 2010).

At the same time that organizations are trying to engage patients in their care, lengths of stay have shortened. For example, 30 years ago, a heart attack patient was hospitalized five to six weeks and was surrounded by skilled health care professionals. Today, heart patients typically go home within seven days, are quickly on their own and given instruction lists, medications, follow-up appointments, and very little skilled support. This may be all well and good if patients understand how to manage their care at home. However, national data show approximately 43 percent of U.S. adults have basic or below basic health literacy skills, meaning they have difficulty using text to accomplish everyday tasks (Joint Commission, 2007).

Lack of health literacy is a national health problem, costing the United States approximately $106–$238 billion annually in one analysis (Vernon et al., 2007). The human cost in terms of quality of life and lives lost is even more compelling. A 2004 Institute of Medicine report found that adults with low health literacy skills don't understand their chronic illness or how to change their behaviors for proper self-care, and did not know how to use appropriate preventive health services. As a result, they used the health care system more—especially emergency room services. They consistently reported poorer states of health (Nielsen-Bohlman, Panzer, and Kindig, 2004).

Librarians' Role on the Patient Care Team

Health care librarians find themselves in a perfect storm of skyrocketing health care costs, an emphasis on patient safety, and the problems of health literacy coupled with an industry move toward patient-centered care. Librarians who work with patients and their family members are important members of the patient care team. Because they are health information knowledge navigators, librarians connect patients with health information in appropriate formats and, with print information, appropriate reading levels. They may make patient information visits or rounds, talking with patients and helping them identify diagnosis-specific information needs (Spatz, 2009).

Librarians can identify and provide patients with resources to help them understand their diagnosis and treatment options as well as to have meaningful conversations with their health care providers. They connect patients to helpful community resources such as support groups and diagnosis-specific self-management classes. In the interest of patient safety, health sciences librarians may lead or participate in the hospital's health literacy efforts by teaching staff how to identify nonreaders and to write low literacy documents for patient use. They can be important members of the hospital's patient education committee, suggesting new and effective patient teaching tools and methods. These and other activities have been described in the MLA/CAPHIS policy statement updated in 2010 titled "The Librarian's Role in the Provision of Consumer Health Information and Patient Education" (Medical Library Association, 1996). The statement is available on the **accompanying CD-ROM**.

The **accompanying CD-ROM** also contains the Consumer Health Information Survey Summary Report. "The intent of this survey was to assess hospital administrators' and health care providers' awareness and understanding of consumer health information resources and services, and its value in support of patient care" (Medical Library Association, 2008: 1). This information may be useful to librarians beginning to plan consumer health information and health literacy services. Other health literacy information and tools are available at http://www.mlanet .org/resources/healthlit/hil_project.html.

Patient Libraries as a Community Benefit

Providing and reporting community benefit is required for hospitals to be tax-exempt charitable organizations under section 501(c)(3) of the U.S. Internal Revenue Code. This report highlights the significant contributions the hospital makes to the overall health and well-being of the community (Chastain-Warheit and Henry, 2010). The Catholic Health Association publishes a yearly guide to help hospitals prepare their annual community benefit report and lists "consumer health libraries" as a reportable community benefit (Catholic Health Association of the United States, 2008: 281). Patient or consumer health libraries provide a safe and trusted place for individuals to learn about diseases and conditions to support personal decision making regarding their health and well-being. Added community benefit may be derived from hosting patient support group meetings, community health education presentations or classes, or through any number of community outreach programs. No federal guidelines currently exist for determining the financial value of consumer health libraries for tax-exempt reporting purposes, so it's best to work with someone in your hospital's finance department or the preparer of the hospital's community benefit tax filing in arriving at a figure. As suggested in Chapter 4, *Measuring Your Library's Value: How to Do Cost-Benefit Analysis for Your Public Library* provides help in determining any library's benefit (Elliott et al., 2007).

Providing Services to Patients and Consumers

Assessing Service Needs

A number of steps are essential when planning a patient or consumer health library. A needs assessment provides an important first step by identifying and evaluating the demand for patient health resources and information services. It helps ascertain how and where materials and services might best be offered to patients. Needs assessments support project justification and help secure hospital administrative support and funding. Chapter 6 of this book provides a vivid, real-world illustration of the importance of a library's needs assessment in growing its services.

The needs assessment requires data. Consider forming a small committee (i.e., nurse educator, health sciences librarian, physician, members of the general public, hospital administrator or board member) to help identify, collect, and evaluate data. Such a broad-based committee will ensure that the needs assessment is approached from different perspectives and helps facilitate a balanced assessment.

Data Gathering

To gather relevant data, a written, online, or telephone survey may be conducted. If resources permit, this task may be outsourced to a third party. Another viable way of assessing needs is to host a series of focus groups, asking pertinent questions such as, "Are your health information needs being met? If so, where? If not, why not? In regard to locating or finding health information, what is missing? Is health information available in language that is easy to understand and in formats that are conducive to learning? Are culturally relevant materials available across a variety of diagnoses and conditions?" Questions should focus on perceived or real access to information, and the quality and timeliness of information. Patients and community members' voices are vital in the needs assessment process and focus groups are a proven way to hear and record their concerns (Frampton et al., 2008).

Consider the following potential library user groups when conducting a needs assessment:

- Public library users and public librarians
- Former hospital patients or their family members
- Area health care providers: i.e., physical therapists and mental health care providers
- People in waiting areas in the hospital, physician clinics, or other health care providers' offices
- Members of the community-at-large, such as parent groups at schools, church members, local business people, senior centers, day care centers, self-help or local support groups

A thorough needs assessment will include an examination of the health care library's current requests for patient and consumer health information. Items to analyze may include the following:

- **Reference requests** to determine what percent of requests is patient or consumer health related.
- **Document delivery** borrowing records to determine the number of lay health resources requested.
- **Circulation statistics** to determine what percent of items circulating is patient or consumer health related.

Explore the status of the current patient or consumer health collection in the library by examining the following:

- **The existing collection** to determine what percent is patient or consumer health related. Assess the collection's reading level, currency, and the depth and breadth of health subjects covered.
- **The library's existing space** to determine space and any shelving requirements needed to add or expand patient or consumer health resources. Determine whether the existing space permits patient or consumer health information delivery.
- **Other public and hospital library services in the area** to determine the scope of their patient and consumer health information resources and services.
- **The hospital's website usage** related to health information.

A thorough needs assessment will also include an analysis of current diseases the organization treats as well as the health status of the larger community. To identify these, take a look at the following:

- **Existing programs or services** developed to respond to the health needs of its patients. Determine what type of education, if any, is offered to patients with specific diagnoses. Are the patients' health information needs being met through curricula and resources? What kind of health information materials might patients feel are needed to support them in their learning and self-care?
- **The hospital's top 10 or 20 Diagnosis Related Groups (DRGs)** to determine what health resources best support hospital inpatients and family members' need for diagnosis-related information. The top inpatient DRG's are likely indicators of health concerns within the community at large. Benchmark this by requesting the local public health department's top 10 causes of morbidity and mortality.
- **Community resources**, such as health agencies and health-related support groups, to determine what materials and information are currently available locally and how accessible it is to patients and the lay public.

- **Healthy People 2020's local implementation plan**, to determine which national health concerns are being addressed as community priorities.

Finally, looking at local community demographics and its socioeconomic aspects will help formulate an understanding of who might use consumer health information services and what specific needs they might have. For example, you will want knowledge of the following:

- Overall population size and its age distribution
- Median educational level
- Median income
- Economic base of the community
- Climate
- Primary language and important secondary languages
- Important cultural characteristics

Oftentimes, the U.S. Census Bureau, state labor market agencies, county economic development offices and the local chamber of commerce are sources of this important information.

Evaluating the Data

Evaluate the information gathered in your needs assessment to determine whether patient or consumer health information resources and services are indeed warranted. Where does a need exist? Is it a narrow niche, such as women's health concerns; cancer patients and their families; people with musculoskeletal problems? Or a very great need, such as the community at large or the entire patient population of a hospital or health system?

Perhaps your target audience is predefined, such as a directive from the hospital's administration or board to start a women's health collection or patient library. Whether your target audience is mandated or arrived at through painstaking data collection and analysis, it is important in all aspects of decision making. Defining your target audience determines the kind of facility you develop, where you locate it, the scope and content of your resources, and what services are offered.

Mission and Goals

Once need has been assessed and a target audience identified, the next task is to develop a mission statement that describes the intention and purpose of the patient or consumer health library. A mission statement is the philosophy or ideal to which the patient or consumer health library and its services aspire. It serves as a valuable point of reference in the planning, development, and ultimate management of the consumer health library. A compelling mission will help garner support for your project. Ultimately, like a compass, it provides guidance and direction in difficult junctures, because it always leads one back to the heart of the project. The sidebar provides a sample mission statement.

> *The Anytown Hospital Patient Library creates and supports innovative programs and services designed to provide patients and their families with access to a wide variety of health and medical information in order to help them become active participants in their health and medical care.*

In moving the mission forward, goals are required. Goals outline the steps that support and lead to the successful completion of the library's mission. They are statements of purpose and are both meaningful and measurable. Because goals are essential to accomplish the library's mission, they too are an important tool in planning, developing and managing a patient or consumer health library or service. The sidebar presents sample goal statements.

> Here are two sample goals that support the mission statement:
>
> *The Anytown Hospital Patient Library will provide open access to a broad spectrum of current health and medical information to the public, patients and family, by providing a current collection of books, journals, magazines, newsletters, pamphlets, fact sheets, multimedia materials, and electronic sources of health and medical information.*
>
> *The Anytown Hospital Patient Library, seeking to empower individuals to make informed health-care decisions and encouraging individuals to take greater responsibility for their own health, will provide to hospital inpatients a packet of health and medical information on a topic of their choice.*

Services

In the first edition of this book, Bandy (2000: 329) writes, "Because health care libraries vary in size, staff, services, support, location, and many other factors, there is no perfect model for providing patient and consumer information services that will fit every situation." She advocates a continuum approach, starting with limited services and then expanding as demand for services and the level of funding grows. A decade later it's still true: to get started, the larger vision of a patient library with robust services may need to start small. A graduated plan of growth, from a modest beginning but adding equipment and services as success and more financial

support are achieved, is the surest route to long-term sustainability.

When considering services, there are myriad possibilities. What is most critical given the results of the needs assessment study? The services provided will be based upon the identified needs of the target audience and the amount of committed funding. It's important to keep the mission statement in mind when considering what services to offer, as the latter should support the former. As shown in Figure 14.1, there are a number of potential services to consider.

Funding

Most of the expenses associated with providing a patient library are operational or on-going costs, making sustained funding a priority. The type of library, the number of staff, and the extent of the services planned will drive the start-up costs. Once the library is established, the larger the volume of service (or the more people served), the greater the return on the fixed costs. In other words, it pays to be successful! In starting out, it's important to have solid host institution commitment in writing with an agreed upon time frame. For example, if your administration or board decides to implement a patient library or information service, ask for a minimum three-year commitment. Like any new business, a new patient library needs enough time to become established and grow its service.

There are many creative funding ideas worth exploring to help make a patient library feasible. Here are a few suggestions:

- Build partnerships that share costs. Secure partnerships with interagency contracts clearly outlining all financial commitments for a specified time.

- Work with your institution's foundation as a funding and fundraising source.

- Establish an endowment fund with financial contributions from grateful patients and family members to provide a sustained funding stream, once start-up costs are achieved.

- Offer opportunities for people to leave bequests, or to donate major equipment or furnishings to the library.

- Have an annual fund-raising drive of local businesses and civic groups to raise money for specific equipment or to support special subject areas of the collection. For example, the local Lions Club may sponsor the eye care collection.

Figure 14.1. Possible Services Chart

E-Services	Print	Multimedia	Reference/Circulation	Outreach
Patient databases	Book collection	Audio CDs	On-site reference assistance	Health screenings
Internet Access	Medical textbooks	DVDs	Telephone reference assistance	Health education talks/demonstrations
E-books	Magazines	Podcasts	Chat or virtual reference assistance	Lectures on health and medical topics
E-magazines	Newsletters	Webcasts	Information by mail	Host support group meetings
Patient/Family Website Portal	Pamphlets	Low literacy resources	Patient information rounds	Health Fairs
Low literacy resources	Low literacy resources	Foreign language or multicultural resources	Circulating collection of materials	Teaching: web-based resources; utilizing databases...
Foreign language or multicultural resources	Foreign language or multicultural resources		Develop and distribute fact sheets on health and medical topics	Health promotion & advocacy

Staffing

Staffing will of course depend upon the breadth and depth of services provided as well as the number of hours the library is open each week. *The library's staff is its most valuable asset.* The greatest assembly of materials and virtual resources won't get a patient or family member far if the staff is unapproachable or unknowledgeable. Great care must be taken in determining who the staff members will be. A professional librarian plays a key role in managing the consumer health library or service. A health sciences librarian has the professional expertise to identify and provide appropriate services and materials as well as organize and manage diverse types of collections. Furthermore, a professional librarian has highly-developed information research skills and the communication skills necessary to discover a library user's real health information concern. A critical skill that librarians possess is the ability to evaluate health information for its credibility, reliability, bias, currency, and relevancy to a user's information request, which is increasingly valuable in a society of "information overload." Librarians have the expertise to locate and provide resources that meet the user's reading level, are culturally relevant and in a language the user can understand.

Support staff may consist of clerical support or technicians trained in library work. Strengths to consider include proficiency with computers coupled with strong interpersonal communication and empathy skills.

Volunteer Staff

Many consumer health libraries use volunteers to *help* staff the facility. Volunteers are a wonderful support staff—they can orient new users, perform many clerical functions, and staff the circulation desk. Library volunteers must work under the direction of a professional librarian. While volunteers demonstrate that the patient resources are easily accessible, it is not advisable to schedule volunteers to staff the library alone. Volunteers have a different focus and orientation from paid staff. Many volunteers are retired and thus have other hobbies or interests, which they may favor over their volunteer work. Hence, they are unreliable as a consistent workforce. There are legal and ethical issues involved in providing health information, which demand a qualified staff member, rather than a volunteer with limited expertise. Finally, as patients become more adept at finding health or medical information, the questions they bring to the library are more difficult and complex. Volunteers do not have the skill and proficiency to answer the complexity of reference questions posed by patients today because they've had no formal training.

When using volunteers as helpers in the patient library, here are some ideas to consider:

1. Request a weekly commitment of four hours/week, to make having a volunteer worthwhile. Just as if they are paid staff, volunteers will require training and supervision.

2. Set up a probationary period, similar to that for a paid employee, allowing time to determine whether the volunteer is a good fit in the patient library.

3. Inquire about the potential volunteer's comfort level with the ALA's Library Bill of Rights (American Library Association, 1996) and censorship issues. It's important that volunteers not impede the free flow of information nor be judgmental of patients' requests.

4. Inquire about any work background relating to the health sciences—such as former biologists, EMT workers and such. Familiarity with medical terminology is a big plus.

5. Make sure the individual can distinguish between locating information and giving medical advice, which is forbidden in the library volunteer as well as the librarian's role.

6. Have volunteers sign a volunteer agreement outlining their responsibilities and commitment.

Include volunteers in staff meetings and training sessions and honor them often and in creative ways with small rewards. Because they are active members of the community, volunteers' hard work and dedication contribute to the success of the patient library both on and off the job.

Budgeting

A budget is a plan that outlines the patient library's financial and operational goals. A budget may be thought of as an action plan: planning a budget helps the librarian allocate resources, evaluate the library's financial performance, and formulate plans for the future. While planning a budget can occur at any time, for many patient libraries, planning a budget is an annual task, where the past year's budget is reviewed and compared to actual expenditures, and budget projections are made for the next one to three years.

The basic method of planning a patient library budget involves listing and analyzing the library's fixed and variable costs on a monthly basis and then deciding on an allocation of dollars to maintain or expand the library's operational costs. A budget supports the library's goals, which are rooted and spring forth from its mission.

In building a budget, it's important to have a thorough understanding of the day-to-day, monthly, and annual expenses of the library's operational expenses. Keep careful records of all expenses and thoroughly review these at annual budget time. Walk through the library, if necessary, to record all the supplies, items, and service contracts required for the library's operation at its current level of service. Use budgeting software to help streamline this process. Many hospitals use proprietary budgeting or financial software, which are invaluable tools for tracking expenses and making budget projections.

Budgets are largely forecasts. Forecasting is the process of analyzing current and historical data to determine future trends. In planning a future budget, forecasting begins with data collection. As mentioned previously, budgeting software may help to adequately categorize and then track budget expenditures for each expenditure category throughout the year. When it's time to budget, real data exist to base budget forecasts for each category for the coming year. In a typical year, consider adding approximately 3–5 percent to each budget category. Market trends influence pricing of many things, such as health insurance, and natural resources, such as oil. These trends will affect everything from heating costs to mileage reimbursement to delivery charges.

Remember, a budget is a goal or action plan and as such, there is typically some flexibility in its management. Careful review of monthly budget expenditures provides the information needed to make adjustments throughout the current budget cycle.

Typical items to consider when constructing a patient library budget are as follows:

- Salaries and benefits
- Office supplies: pens, pencils, paper, post-it notes, etc.
- Library supplies: book labels, barcode labels, etc.
- Photocopy supplies: toner, paper
- Computer supplies: paper, toner, software upgrades, ink cartridges
- Fax supplies: paper, toner
- Book budget
- Subscriptions: magazines, newspapers, newsletters, E-resources, databases
- Postage and ground delivery service
- Document delivery fees/ Copyright Clearance Center
- Printing costs for letterhead, envelopes, bookmarks, publicity, etc.
- Professional memberships, dues
- Staff education, training and travel
- Equipment maintenance/repair cost

Figure 14.2 illustrates some of the typical costs of patient library materials. Additional information on library budgeting may be found in Chapter 4 of this book.

Figure 14.2. Typical Costs of Patient Library Materials

Material	Cost
Books	$18
DVDs	$100-$150
Audio CDs	$25
Magazine Subscriptions	$30

Establishing and Writing Policies and Procedures

Written policies and procedures are essential for the effective and smooth operation of the patient library. Together, they describe both the method and the rationale for how the library functions.

A policy states a guiding principle and is analogous to the North Star. Policies keep library staff on track with the library's mission and values by serving as a guideline to action and decision-making when presented with a given set of circumstances. A policy ensures uniformity and fairness of response to individual or group demands that lie within the framework of the library's mission and values.

Procedures are developed to support policy. A procedure outlines a template of the steps to follow to accomplish a task. Procedures set a uniform and consistent manner to achieve a desired result.

Policies and procedures often go hand in hand. A policy will state an overarching principle while a procedure describes how that policy is put into practice or the steps that are taken to reach the library policy's fulfillment. A formal voice is used when writing policies and procedures to give them heft and weight. Clarity in writing policies and procedures is essential so that library users understand their meaning. Consider inviting someone who is not familiar with the library to review its policy and procedure statements for clarity. Figure 14.3 provides a guideline of suggested policies and procedures for a patient library.

Legal and Ethical Issues

Librarians working in patient and consumer health libraries have long practiced under the ethical guidelines of their professional organization—the Medical Library Association. These recently revised and adopted ethics uphold an individual's right to access health information, a respect for privacy and confidentiality, the provision of

quality information and service without discrimination (Medical Library Association, 2010). The MLA Ethics Statement may be found on the **accompanying CD-ROM**. For librarians undertaking a new venture in the delivery of patient or consumer health information, these ethics remain and hold true today. By providing health information service to all who seek it, in a confidential and nonjudgmental manner with the best resources possible, the librarian will fulfill the patient's expectations.

Many librarians live in fear of the legal issues of providing health information to patients and consumers. While there are some considerations to be aware of, to date there have been no lawsuits brought by patients or consumers against health sciences librarians. In *Answering Consumer Health Questions*, Spatz (2008: 54) states, "It is outside the scope of practice for...librarians to interpret, advise, recommend, or give their personal opinion about the content of the information shared with a patron." It is most important to remember to give information, not opinion or advice. By adhering to their scope of practice and practicing within their professional ethics, librarians will provide much-needed support to patients and consumers seeking health information without crossing legal or ethical lines.

In addition to following legal and ethical principles, a common safeguard used by many librarians is a disclaimer statement. Spatz (2008: 58) writes, "A disclaimer is a legal declaration renouncing one's right or claim of responsibility or connection to the actual content of materials in the collection." Disclaimers may apply to

Figure 14.3. Suggested Policies and Procedures

Circulation	Collection Development
Confidentiality	Copyright Compliance
Document Delivery	Electronic Database Use
Exhibits & Displays	Fees & Charges
Gifts to the Library	Hours of Operation
Intellectual Freedom & Censorship	Interlibrary & Interagency Cooperation
Internet Access by the Public	Opening & Closing
Patron Complaints	Privacy
Public Relations	Reference (all forms)
Scheduling Use of Library by Outside Groups	Staffing

any resource, from print to electronic databases to multimedia. Many librarians not only post them in the library, but also stamp one on materials shared with patients. Figure 14.4 lists some common disclaimers in use today. You may want your legal department or administration to review and approve any disclaimer you use. Sample disclaimers are also available on the **accompanying CD-ROM.**

Collection Development

There are many studies illustrating the complexity of communication between physicians and patients in the clinical setting. Given that important and highly personal information is exchanged and may not be completely understood, patients may need to follow up their doctor visit with a visit to the library. Careful collection development ensures that the library has appropriate materials to meet patients' information needs.

The information gathered in the exhaustive needs assessment will prove valuable in planning the library's collection. It will clarify the subject areas to concentrate on to meet the particular information needs of the hospital's patient community. For example, look at the top 10 Diagnosis-Related Groups for the hospital by asking someone in the hospital's Health Information Management (formerly Medical Records) department to compile the data, and then plan to build strong collections in those particular areas. Pay special attention to information needs identified across the community. For example, if the public library reports they have many patrons requesting information on heart disease, while coronary artery disease is listed by physician offices as being a common diagnosis, and the hospital's #4 DRG is coronary artery disease, by all means strive to have an outstanding collection of materials on heart health and coronary artery disease in particular.

Collection Development Policy

As discussed in Chapter 7, a collection development policy is a statement of the principles, policies, and guidelines for the selection of all print and nonprint materials in the library. A comprehensive collection development policy will support the mission and goals of the library and provide parameters as to what is considered appropriate material and why. The document will provide the framework from which to build the collection and will also provide support, in terms of rationale, should items in the collection be challenged.

Figure 14. 4. Sample Disclaimers

Sample 1

The materials provided in the Anytown Hospital Patient Library are intended for informational and educational purposes only. Use of library materials or resources is not a substitute for the examination, diagnosis, and medical treatment provided by a licensed and qualified health professional.

Sample 2

The materials and resources of the Anytown Hospital Patient Library are provided for information only and should not be construed as medical advice, instruction, or endorsement.

Sample 3

Information from the Anytown Hospital Patient Library is not intended to substitute or replace the professional medical advice you receive from your physician. Materials and resources provided are for informational purposes only, and is not designed to diagnose or treat a health problem or disease. Please consult your physician with any questions or concerns you may have regarding your health or medical condition.

A sound collection development policy will include the following elements:

- **Definition of purpose**—state the purpose of the collection development policy. For example, "the purpose of the collection development policy is to provide resources to meet the health and medical information needs of the patients, family members, and general public of Anytown, USA."

- **Scope of the collection**—State the types of materials collected, the subject areas covered, the breadth and depth of coverage, and issues regarding currency.

- **Selection responsibilities**—State who is responsible for selecting materials and how suggestions for purchase are handled.

- **General selection guidelines**—List any general principles that are applied when selecting items for the collection. For example, "in general, materials will be purchased to circulate from the collection." Or, "when need or demand warrants it, two copies will be purchased for the collection."

- **Criteria for selection of materials**—List the criteria you consider when purchasing an item. These may include: subject content, currency, qualifications of author, foreign language, cost, etc.

- **Collection development tools**—Name any items that aid you in the identification of new materials, i.e., book reviews, core library lists, publisher or distributor lists, websites, etc.

- **Donations to the collection**—Describe how (and if) donations of materials are accepted. State the conditions of acceptance. Explain what happens to materials that are accepted and later deemed inappropriate.

- **Collection review**—State how often the collection is reviewed and weeded. What are the conditions for removal of items from the collection?

- **Controversial materials**—Explain how objections to material in the collection are submitted and resolved.

Selection Criteria

With a vast array of health materials available to choose from, selection criteria serve as measures to help determine the potential value of a work. An outline of selection criteria is in the sidebar.

Selection Criteria

1. The author's or publisher's qualifications
2. The content of the work
3. Accuracy
4. Currency
5. Scope of coverage and organization of material
6. Readability and tone
7. Language
8. Ease of use
9. Consumer orientation
10. User demand
11. Collection scope
12. Cost

Budget limitations combined with great demand for health materials makes careful selection a necessity. Here is a list of typical selection criteria:

1. **The author's or publisher's qualifications:** Look at the author's or publisher's credentials or background. For authors, determine whether they have a degree and if their degree is *relevant* to their subject. Are they a health professional or a professional writer? Do they have personal experience with the subject matter? What is their institutional or association affiliation?

The essential question is: *Does the author have the necessary education, experience, and training to be writing authoritatively on this subject?* For example, be wary of a book such as, *Dr. May's Complete Book of Heart Surgery Techniques*, where Dr. May is a podiatrist. With publishers, determine if it is it a reputable publishing house, part of a university or medical center, or a mom-and-pop operation. If it is a mom-and-pop operation, determine their credentials and expertise.

2. **The content of the work:** Look for objective content—a balanced approach. Watch for potential bias on the part of the author or publisher. For example, ethical bias exists for some subjects, like physician-assisted suicide. Such subjects may be explored through a given ethical point of view, and this is fine as long as the ethical bias is clearly indicated and opposing views are also presented or represented in the collection. Bias may come in the form of selling a particular product or certain approach to therapy, or may come in other forms. In selecting materials, be aware of ethnic or gender biases as well.

3. **Accuracy:** The information should be based on sound medical research that is documented or referenced. Be wary of unproven claims. Usually these are easy to spot through their advertising material, which will announce, "Things the FDA doesn't want you to know about cancer treatments!" or "The miracle cure the AMA is hiding!"

4. **Currency:** What is the copyright date or currency of the work? It should reflect current knowledge or an aggregate of medical thinking on the subject. Currency is paramount in the diagnosis and treatment aspects of diseases and illnesses. Strive to purchase and maintain materials published within the current three years for most medical diagnoses and conditions. There is more latitude for general health materials, such as resources on coping, stress, caregiving, death and dying.

5. **Scope of coverage and organization of material:** For print materials, the table of contents outlines the scope of coverage and should give a clear sense of what is discussed in the book. The coverage should match the author's claims. Ask "the three bears" question regarding the intended coverage: is it too much? Not enough? Just right? Look at the content organization and determine if it makes sense. Does it flow in a natural sequence; for example, causes of problem, diagnosis, treatment, lifestyle considerations, etc.

6. **Readability and tone**: Check for readability. Is the quality of writing clear and to the point? Does it flow? Another important aspect to consider is the tone of the material. It should be matter-of-fact and nonthreatening. It should neither minimize the problem nor blow it out of proportion. Nor should it be overly emotional, so that important factual information gets lost or buried in the feelings. Steer clear of material that is condescending or preachy.

   Ideally, you want the tone to be straightforward and respectful. Look at the introductory remarks for *sensitivity to the problem* discussed. For example, a resource on lung cancer that begins, "8 out of 10 people with lung cancer die within 3 years of their diagnosis" is not a very sensitive approach. Look for resources with a more empathetic approach.

7. **Language**: Make sure the language is appropriate to the intended audience. The language should not be filled with jargon or impossible or undefined acronyms. Look for good illustrations, tables, charts and drawings to help people visualize complex problems or procedures. Review language for its literacy level and strive for a range of materials from third grade to highly technical. For a list of resources to help you evaluate reading level, visit the Harvard School of Public Health: Health Literacy Studies (2010) website at: http://www.hsph.harvard.edu/healthliteracy/practice/innovative-actions/index.html.

8. **Ease of use**: Can specific information be readily found? Adequate indexing is important here. Helpful indexing includes the use of "see" references. If possible, avoid books that use inverted medical terms in the index; for example cardiomyopathy, *alcoholic* instead of the more straightforward *alcoholic cardiomyopathy*. Look for the inclusion of a glossary, with simple definitions for lay users.

9. **Consumer orientation**: Resources with a patient's or consumer's interest at heart will include discussions on decision making and provide leads to further information through bibliographies, documentation of research, and contact information for relevant agencies, organizations, support groups, treatment centers, etc.

10. **User demand**: Is there a potential or known demand for a specific item? User requests should be honored, if at all possible; it's just good customer service. Popular health authors may be in demand, for example, Andrew Weil, Mehmet Oz, and Michael Roizen. Subject demand or collection gaps may be determined by careful analysis of reference requests.

11. **Collection scope**: Does the item fit within the scope of your collection development policy? Does it support or complement other materials the library already owns in a subject area or does it fill a known gap in the collection, making it a valuable addition?

12. **Cost**: By using the above criteria, does the value of the material justify its cost?

Health care library managers can use the definitions and examples listed above or adapt the selection criteria to their own situations. Defined selection criteria may prove important in winning approval for the library program as illustrated in the Management in Action scenario in the sidebar.

MANAGEMENT IN ACTION 14.1

Winning Medical Staff Approval for a Patient/Consumer Library

Location: Community Hospital

Description of Problem/Project: The Patient Educator and Medical Librarian have been working on a proposal to establish a Patient/Consumer Library. Members of the medical staff have expressed concern about the quality and validity of the materials to be provided in the library.

Impact On: Winning approval of the medical staff will be critical to the success of the patient/consumer library. Support from the administration also hinges on the acceptance of the project by physicians.

People Involved: Patient Educator, Medical Librarian, Patient Education Committee, representatives of the medical staff, selected allied health professionals.

Strategies for Success: The librarian and the patient educator developed a tool for evaluating the materials that would be added to the collection. The selection criteria included the author's or publisher's credentials or background, accuracy of content, currency of the material, literacy level, and other criteria. A scoring system was devised to determine the lowest acceptable score for materials acquisition. A multidisciplinary advisory panel of health professionals was asked to score the new acquisitions using the evaluation tool prior to the materials being added to the collection.

Barriers Encountered: Applying the evaluation tool was time-consuming and created delays in processing the new materials. Some health professionals took too long to evaluate the materials.

(Continued)

Therapeutic Categories in Consumer Health Information

Patient or consumer health librarians should be aware of five primary categories of health-related remedies. These were developed by John H. Renner, MD, and the staff of the Consumer Health Information Research Institute, Kansas City, Missouri, and published in *Consumer Health Information: Managing Hospital-Based Centers* (Kernaghan and Giloth, 1991). Knowledge of these categories will provide insight and understanding when purchasing resources as well as in reference work with patients and consumers. The sidebar outlines the categories of health-related remedies.

Primary Categories of Health-Related Remedies

- Folklore   ▪ Unproven   ▪ Proven
- Quackery   ▪ Investigational

The five categories are:

1. **Folklore:** These are remedies handed down from generation to generation and based on local wisdom or custom. Typically, these remedies are not harmful and may primarily be comfort measures. Folklore treatments are generally spread by word of mouth or sometimes written record. A good example of a folklore remedy is the *use of chicken soup to treat a cold.*

2. **Quackery:** These remedies are often for sale, and may have a hefty price tag associated with them. The therapeutic claims are bold, as is the heavy promotional campaign for these items.

    Even so, there has been little or no scientific research to support the safety or efficacy of the remedy. There may be potential harm in applying these remedies to an individual's treatment plan, especially if there is a recommendation to forego current conventional treatment. Often the claims are heavy on words like "cure," "miracle," and "wonder drug." Example: *The use of mangosteen juice for urinary tract infections.*

3. **Unproven:** Similar to quackery, although not as bold in its claims, unproven remedies *suggest* there is sound scientific support for this particular approach. In actuality, there are no scientific studies or evidence to lend credence to the remedy, which makes this category, in some ways, just a softer sell of quackery. It may, in fact, be harmful to an individual to use an unproven remedy. Example: *Le Gac Therapy (antibiotics plus hot tubs) for multiple sclerosis.*

4. **Investigational:** This remedy has some scientific merit or basis in scientific fact, such that it is currently undergoing investigation or research within the scientific community. The fact that use of an investigational remedy is being suggested before the research is complete indicates that early or initial research results look promising. Yet use of these remedies has the potential to be harmful, because they are not yet fully understood. Example: *The National Cancer Institute is conducting Phase III clinical trials adding cetuximab (Erbitux) to high-intensity radiotherapy for locoregionally advanced head and neck cancer. Preliminary results show improved overall survival and extension of the duration of local control, without exacerbating adverse effects such as mucositis in patients receiving cetuximab.*

5. **Proven:** The remedies in this category are based on sound, repeated scientific investigations with demonstrated results. While side effects are possible, the safety and efficacy of this remedy for its intended use has been demonstrated. Example: *Insulin for diabetes.*

Identifying Consumer Health Materials

Core lists for patient and consumer health materials are available, but care must be taken as most are not updated regularly; since currency of information is paramount, a core list may be used as a starting point rather than an absolute. Use the core list as a benchmark with which to research the newest edition of an item or as a guide to the types of titles in a typical consumer health library.

Two sources of core lists are the Consumer and Patient Health Information Section of the Medical Library Association (http://caphis.mlanet.org) and Healthnet: Connecticut Consumer Health Information Network's "Recommended Books for a Consumer Health Library" (http://library.uchc.edu/departm/hnet/pdf/corelist.pdf).

Book reviews and new book lists are other good ways of learning about potential resources. A few publications that offer notable reviews or new book lists are: *The New York Times*, *Booklist*, *Journal of the American Medical Association*, *New England Journal of Medicine* and *Library Journal*. Each issue of *Library Journal* contains reviews of health books and medical reference books as well as DVD/videotape and audio CD reviews. A regular "Collection Development" feature offers an in-depth, annotated guide to selected resources with consumer health topics highlighted about once or twice per year. *Yoga Journal* and *Natural Health* magazines consistently offer reviews of complementary medicine books.

Doody's Review Service (http://www.doody.com/DRS/) provides another option for material identification and selection. This subscription service offers an extensive database of health sciences book and software reviews. Updated weekly, the service contains more than 20,000 reviews and includes consumer health titles.

Many publishers and book vendors supply consumer health materials, such as Baker and Taylor Books (http://www.btol.com), Majors Books (http://www.majors books.com), Rittenhouse Books (http://www.rittenhouse.com), and Matthews Books (http://www.matthewsbooks.com). In addition to their websites, publishers and vendors may offer a "new book" e-mail alert in addition to print catalogs. Health care organizations, associations, and agencies are often sources of books, pamphlets, and other educational materials.

Don't overlook a trip to a local bookstore where you can browse the health, nutrition, psychology, self-help, women's health, and parenting sections. As you browse, bear in mind that bestsellers do not necessarily equate to best sources of sound health information, so using sound selection techniques is in order. A trip to the electronic bookstore may also help identify resources. Many electronic bookstores are searchable by subject and also provide book reviews as well as reader reviews or ratings. Examples include Amazon Books (http://www.amazon.com), Powell's Books (http://www.powells.com), and Barnes and Noble (http://www.barnesandnoble.com).

Finally, visit other patient or consumer health libraries in the area to benchmark their collections. Ask which resources are well used and recommended, bearing in mind the uniqueness of the patients and consumers served by the library.

Organizing the Collection

Cataloging and organizing the collection is essential so patients and consumers can easily find the materials they are seeking. A variety of approaches are discussed in the following section.

Classification Schemes

A classification scheme is an essential component of any well-organized collection of materials. Although many classification schemes are available, most will need to be adapted to the particular nuances of patient and consumer health collections. Here are some potential classification schemes you may want to consider:

- **The Planetree Classification Scheme**: Developed specifically for consumer health libraries, this scheme was originally published in 1991 and is currently undergoing a complete revision with publication expected in 2010. The first edition was developed by two medical librarians with expertise in providing consumer health information, two physicians, and a registered nurse. The system assimilates materials and follows a sequence that makes browsing *related* subjects easy. For example, a book on yoga and the disabled would be found with books on physical disability rather than yoga. This allows patients browsing the physical disability section to find all relevant materials they might not have originally considered. If you are interested in purchasing this classification scheme, contact the national Planetree office, http://www.planetree.org, for its cost and availability.

- **Library of Congress (LC) and Dewey Decimal Systems**: The Library of Congress and Dewey Decimal systems have long, established histories in library sciences. Unfortunately, neither system offers the subject specificity that consumer collections warrant.

- **National Library of Medicine (NLM) Classification System**: The National Library of Medicine (NLM) was born as the first surgeon general's library and by design was meant to serve the nation's health care professionals. Historically, its classification scheme was never intended to support cataloging of patient or consumer health collections. While the NLM's mission has expanded in modern times to include the provision of patient and consumer information, the classification scheme remains unchanged. The terminology of the system is very technical and the schematic organization scatters subjects that may be more beneficial to the patient or the consumer if they are kept together. For example, dermatology books are classified between obstetrics and pediatrics. Ideally for patient or consumer ease, pediatric materials (child care) would follow obstetric materials (pregnancy and childbirth).

The LC, Dewey, and NLM classification schemes were developed before the explosion of consumer health information, and this is evident in their subject content and coverage. While these classification schemes can be used in the consumer health setting, it's likely these systems would need to be adapted by the patient or consumer health librarian for use in the patient library. For example, you may have to translate the technical term to a lay term, or reverse inverted subject headings when developing a catalog or online resources database. Even the Planetree system must be adapted to new or evolving consumer health terminology. Using a commercial supplier of catalog records may be a factor in determining which cataloging and classification scheme is selected.

Shelf Labels

Aside from classification schemes, a simple way to guide users to specific areas of the collection is to apply shelf labels. Shelf labels are small signs attached to the bookshelves that highlight significant areas of the collection, such as "cancer," "children's health," "nutrition," and "depression."

Cataloging Software

The selection of cataloging software will depend upon the size of the collection, its expected growth, and whether or not the library is required to participate in a specified proprietary cataloging and circulation system. For the smaller collection, here are a few possibilities:

- **Library Thing** (http://www.librarything.com) is a web-based cataloging community, where you may enter 200 books for free and more for a nominal fee.
- **Cybertools for Libraries** (http://www.cybertoolsforlibraries.com) offers an affordable web-based Integrated Library System for special libraries such as a patient or consumer health library.
- **InMagic** (http://www.inmagic.com) was founded by a librarian in 1982 and today offers separate web-based ILS and catalog products.

- **ResourceMate** (http://www.resourcemate.com) provides affordable web-based cataloging, searching, and circulating software.
- **Primasoft PC Software: Small Library Organizer Pro, v1.8** (http://www.primasoft.com/pro_software/library_software_pro.htm) provides in-house cataloging, searching, and circulation for library collections.

Media

When organizing media, consider how they might best be brought to the user's awareness. Some librarians intershelve media with the print collection, so everything on one subject is brought together, regardless of its format. Others prefer a separate shelving arrangement.

Pamphlets

Pamphlets can be a management nightmare in terms of restocking and currency. Maintaining a pamphlet collection can be very time-consuming. Ruti Volk, a librarian at the University of Michigan's Comprehensive Cancer Center in Ann Arbor, Michigan, developed *Brochure Boss*, "an automated solution for ordering and managing brochure collections." Visit the *Brochure Boss* website at http://www.cancer.med.umich.edu/support/brochure_boss.shtml.

Magazines

Special shelving can be made or purchased through library supply catalogs that will display and store current magazine collections very nicely. The library's collection development policy should address how many back issues are kept for print titles. For consumer health titles, just the current year is recommended since most patient and consumer health libraries will provide electronic access to magazine content.

Decisions regarding the organization of library resources will, of course, depend upon the size and scope of the collections and the available space for this purpose. Well-thought-out organization is crucial because it determines the ease with which patients and consumers find the information they are seeking. Seeing the collection from their point of view will help guide these important decisions.

Electronic Patient and Consumer Health Resources

In addition to the Internet, many vendors provide web-based proprietary electronic patient and consumer health information products. Any product must be purchased within the parameters of the library's collection development policy. When purchasing electronic resources, there are a few considerations to keep in mind. Chief among them are the product's affordability and how well the content meets the health information needs of patients and consumers. As with all consumer health materials, a reading level between sixth and eighth grade is a priority as many studies have determined that even highly literate individuals prefer health information in an easy-to-understand format. Many vendors claim to meet this threshold, but upon close review often fall far short. Patient-friendly products will provide helpful visuals and include pictures as well as multimedia options to either support or supply an alternative to text. Ease of use by patients and consumers is another key consideration. The product should be intuitive and easy to navigate.

It's wise to preview any electronic product prior to purchase. Put the product through its paces by using it in the reference setting. Ask library users for feedback and be sure to do an independent analysis of the reading level of the material.

Providing Electronic Health Information

Planning for use of the Internet and electronic resources helps prevent most problems and is an essential component of managing a patient or consumer health library. Careful planning and development of a written policy will help you establish a service that meets library users' needs and minimizes potential problems.

Consider how many terminals and printers to provide and whether the stations will be dedicated to Internet use or double as e-resource workstations for subscription products. Bear in mind that many users will need training or quick, jump-start lessons on e-resources.

In placing computer stations, always consider user privacy. Are the workstations in a private area for patients or loved ones to search or are they located in areas where their results are on display for all to see? There are advantages and disadvantages to either location. In a private area, the confidentiality of the user's information need is protected, but monitoring use is difficult and intrusive. In a more "public" area, individual privacy is compromised, but monitoring is relatively easy.

Heavy computer usage may necessitate a per-page printing charge to help users think carefully before printing information. A per-page print charge cuts down on unneeded printing and paper waste, and may also help offset the cost of the paper. This may be necessary for printer stations in libraries with heavy usage or for libraries on really tight budgets. Some libraries compromise and offer a limited number of pages free, after which there is a per-page charge. Another approach is to ask users to "think green" before printing to lessen the environmental impact.

Where usage is heavy and the number of search stations is limited, some libraries have initiated a sign-up system, where users schedule or reserve half-hour to one hour time slots to use search stations. For confidentiality reasons you may not want to keep a printed list or you might shred the list at the end of each workday. Search time may also be limited through an honor system or through library software products, such as PC Management by Envisionware (http://www.envisionware.com/pc_reservation) or Cybrarian (http://www.cybrarian.com/). These software products automatically log users off after a preset time period has expired.

Another important consideration is to determine who will train the novice computer user or Internet searcher. For one-person libraries the answer is self-evident; for larger libraries, staff are typically cross-trained to provide this type of assistance.

Issues of censorship, via electronic filtering software, or the use of your search stations by minors should be deliberated. In hospitals, filtering software is common and this may be a decision the librarian does not get to make. In some circumstances, the filtering software is so strict it precludes successful Internet searches on specific health topics. With Information Systems support, consider offering Internet stations that are not behind the hospital firewall and hence subject to the strict filtering software.

Youth have grown up in a wired world, so think long and hard about restricting access to the library's Internet stations and e-resources based upon age. If you are going to restrict access, then this must be included in the library's policy on use of electronic systems or in a broader policy on unaccompanied minors.

E-resources Use Policy

A policy on use of electronic systems serves first to prevent, and second, to provide a protocol for effectively resolving problems stemming from use or misuse of the library's public computer search stations. The policy should cover:

- the intended use or purpose of the electronic system;
- user response to hardware or software failure;
- a statement concerning copyright compliance;

- a definition of inappropriate use of the hardware, software, or electronic system;

- procedures an individual must follow in order to use the library's e-resources;

- a statement on the library's use of electronic filtering software; and

- a statement on who may or may not use your electronic system.

Figure 14.5 presents a sample policy on library electronic resources, while Figure 14.6 provides a list of selected electronic resources suitable for a consumer health library.

Figure 14.5. Sample Policy on Use of the Library's Electronic Resources

I. Purpose

The purpose of this policy is to define the appropriate use of the library's electronic resources at the Anytown Hospital Patient Library (AHPL).

II. Policy

The use of AHPL owned, contracted, or operated information systems and technology, computer hardware and software are intended for personal health or medical information purposes only. All other use is prohibited.

While using AHPL owned, contracted, or operated information systems and technology including, but not limited to, hardware, software programs, templates, and files, it is the user's responsibility to report any hardware or software failure or damage to the AHPL staff.

Users shall not perform maintenance or repair on any AHPL owned, contracted, or operated computer or electronic communications equipment.

AHPL, in compliance with federal law, prohibits duplication or downloading of copyrighted software or materials.

All software and hardware are to be used in the location in which it has been installed and is not to be moved by anyone other than employees of AHPL.

The use of profane, abusive, discriminatory, harassing, or defamatory language or images is prohibited on AHPL owned, contracted, or operated information systems or electronic communication equipment.

Files, data, and messages stored in AHPL computers and electronic communications equipment may be subject to the subpoena powers of a court and/or other court-related activities.

The use of AHPL computers and electronic communications equipment for the advertisement or solicitation of goods, services, donations, politics, or any other matter relating to personal interest or gain is strictly forbidden.

The policy on use of electronic resources is also on the **accompanying CD-ROM**.

Quality Health Information on the Internet for Patients and Consumers

According to a 2009 *Pew Internet and American Life* study called "The Social Life of Health Information," 61 percent of adults look online for health information. Of those, 66 percent look online for information about a specific disease or medical problem, while 55 percent look online for information about a medical treatment or procedure (Fox and Jones, 2009). Much is written in the professional literature about whether patients know how to find health information they can trust online. As health information specialists, it's incumbent upon librarians to teach patients how to find information that is not only trustworthy, but meaningful, and in language and a cultural context that they understand.

What constitutes quality health information on the Internet? These basic criteria apply:

- **Accurate**: The information should be up-to-date and referenced.

- **Clear**: The information should be simply stated.

- **Relevant**: The information should be written with the patient in mind. Look for information that is important (need-to-know vs. nice-to-know) and addresses the patients' concerns about their diagnosis or condition.

When guiding patients toward quality health information on the Internet, use the following principles:

- **Sponsorship of the website**: Websites should clearly indicate who is responsible for the information. Websites that are sponsored by established institutions, medical organizations, or associations with professional credibility are more likely to have reliable and trustworthy health information. Outside sponsors and partnerships should also be indicated, whether financial, professional, commercial, or personal. It should be clear if any outside sponsor provides content for the website. A contact link for questions and comments about the website should be provided. Teach patients to check the "About Us" section of a website to establish sponsorship. Also teach them the difference between the meanings of URL extensions: .com, .edu, .net, .org, .gov.

- **Purpose**: What is the stated purpose of the website? Is it intended to educate or is it trying to sell a product?

Figure 14.6. Selected Electronic Patient and Consumer Health Products

Clinical Reference Systems McKesson Corporation 800-237-8401 http://www.patienteducation.com	Clinical Reference System Health Advisor series offers nine different topic modules, providing full-text information in both English and Spanish. Materials in each module are reviewed annually. There are sample materials on their website. Products include: ■ **Adult Health Advisor** Over 700 medical and surgical topics, in English and Spanish. Information included has been favorably reviewed by the American Academy of Family Physicians Foundation. ■ **Pediatric Advisor** Over 900 topics in English and Spanish for parents on newborn care, childhood illnesses, and behavioral problems and adolescent health. ■ **Senior Health Advisor** Covers extensive range of senior health topics with a focus on the medical, psychological, and social issues of older adults. Also includes caregiver topics. ■ **Women's Health Advisor** Approximately 600 women's health topics, including conditions and procedures from ob/gyn to primary care issues. Other Health Advisor product modules include: ■ Behavioral Health Advisor ■ Sports Medicine Advisor ■ Cardiology Advisor ■ Medication Advisor ■ Eye Advisor
The Health and Wellness Resource Center Thomson/Gale 800-877-4253 http://www.gale.cengage.com/Health/HealthRC/about.htm	The Health and Wellness Resource Center features: ■ Health and medical journals and pamphlets (nearly 70 percent in full-text) ■ Health articles from 2,200 general-interest publications ■ A broad collection of full-text Gale reference titles ■ Links to key health websites ■ Streaming video library
EBSCO Information Services P.O. Box 1943 Birmingham, AL USA 35201-1943 205-991-6600 205-995-1518 (Fax) http://www.ebscohost.com/healthLibrary/	EBSCO Information Services offers: **Health Library** This product is designed to serve as a web portal to hospital-based patient and consumer health information. It offers: ■ Evidenced-based patient and consumer health information ■ Low reading level material ■ Numerous illustrations, images, and multimedia content to support understanding ■ Available in both English and Spanish
Krames Krames-Corporate HQ Krames-West Coast 780 Township Line Rd 1100 Grundy Lane Yardley, PA 19067 San Bruno, CA 94066 800-333-3032 info@krames.com http://www.krames.com/	Krames offers several electronic patient education products: ■ wiredMD Patient education videos (400+ videos in 9 languages) ■ Over 1,500 patient education pamphlets (English & Spanish) ■ Krames online - a patient and consumer health website portal (articles, streaming videos, and interactive tools) ■ Go-To Guides for self-management of chronic diseases (web-based, interactive tools on the leading causes of chronic illness)

- **Patient orientation**: Does the website provide specific information about a particular medical diagnosis or condition, including treatment options, lifestyle issues, coping, and prevention? If the website provides links to other sites for more information, how reliable are those links? Does the site offer other resources, such as an online support group, or other social media for patients to connect to one another?

- **Authorship**: Who writes the information? Is it based on fact and well supported by evidence? Does the author have the qualifications to write on a specific disease or medical problem? Where references are given, patients should be able to link easily to them.

- **Currency**: The date of original publication should be easily identified along with the latest revision and review dates. Teach patients about the importance of locating up-to-date medical or health information.

- **Privacy issues**: Websites that ask for personal information should state exactly how it will be used. Teach consumers to read privacy policies in order to understand how personal information may be used.

Many librarians provide direct links to patient-friendly websites from the hospital library's webpage. This is a valuable aid, as patients don't have to second-guess the quality of information on the website. Using a topical or subject display of recommended health website links helps patients hone in on a specific area of information, saving them time by offering a targeted approach to their information search.

Promoting Patient and Consumer Health Information Services

In the hospital setting, a crisis often precipitates a visit to the patient library. Typically, the need for patient and consumer health information is the result of a recent diagnosis or some type of stressful health event. Because these needs are episodic, actively and continually promoting the patient and consumer health information services must be a priority. The goal is to have the library come to mind when someone needs personal health or medical information.

General Promotion Ideas

The library's biggest advertisement is its satisfied users. Pleased users will tell their loved ones, friends, and neighbors about the library's staff and services. Similarly, disappointed users will do the same. Professional service coupled with a warm and welcoming environment will help library visitors feel comfortable with staff.

There are many ways to promote the library's services. If the hospital or library has a public relations department, seek their help and support. The cost of promotion can vary greatly, depending upon, for example, whether a paid advertisement is placed or a public service announcement is used. Consider the following ways to promote the patient or consumer health library:

- Run regular newspaper or radio ads. Submit public service announcements (PSAs) to local radio stations.

- Participate in communitywide events, such as a health fair.

- Offer health screening clinics on a regular basis to attract new patrons.

- Provide space for on-going health-related support group meetings as a way to promote the library's collection and services. Make sure the library has a policy in place covering what groups may use the library, how room reservations should be made, and acceptable activity and noise levels. Be sure to include an "out" clause in the policy, in case a group is not a good fit.

- Offer a recurring health lecture or health education series to entice new users to the library. Some health libraries offer a year-round series, while others offer it on an annual or semi-annual basis.

- Distribute a newsletter (print or electronic) to keep users in touch with what's new at the library. Mailing lists can be generated from the library's circulation database, if users register for library cards. Be sure to request the library user's permission to receive mailings from the library.

- Develop a website to offer 24/7 services.

- Use Web 2.0 services such as a library blog, wiki, Facebook page, or Twitter feed. Because hospitals have very strict security settings and firewalls, it may be necessary to have a separate server (outside the hospital's firewall) in order to offer Web 2.0 services.

- Join local library resource-sharing networks. Library users will be able to identify the patient or consumer health library's materials from their home or any desktop PC.

- Visit local support groups and health care organizations to talk about the library's services and resources. Keep the presentation specific to their information needs.

■ Place the library's bookmarks, flyers, or brochures in key locations such as physician waiting rooms, chamber of commerce offices, health agency offices, hospital waiting areas, coffeehouse bulletin boards, etc.

■ Set up a display showcasing materials on a specific disease or health condition. You can include the corresponding book jacket covers or favorite websites. For inspiration, visit the National Health Information Center's Health Observances Calendar at http://www.healthfinder.gov/nho/nho.asp.

■ Distribute press releases or publicize significant milestones. Examples of milestones are the 1000th visitor, the library's first anniversary, fifth anniversary, and so on, or the 1000th library card issued.

■ Write a monthly column on a health-related topic for publication in the hospital or library newsletter or the local newspaper. Include a short list of resources available in the library's collection for readers to "check out" if they want to know more, and include recommended websites for readers to visit. Consider e-publications as well.

■ Provide orientation tours to interested groups from public officials to business owners to church groups as a way of attracting new users.

Remember to promote the library's success and its value to Administration. Along with reporting use, share thoughts from a Comments Book, written thank-you notes, and so forth. It's very important to tell the library's *story*. Use examples of gratitude to show how the library and its services have had an impact on patients, family members, and members of the community. Sharing these stories helps Administration appreciate the significant contribution the patient or consumer health library service makes to supporting individuals' need for accurate, timely, and trusted health information.

Outreach and "In-Reach"

Today, it's not enough to provide patient and consumer health service within the four walls of the library. Librarians are designing and participating in outreach activities within their communities or reaching out to audiences within their institution, a form of outreach dubbed "in-reach." Outreach is as its name implies: reaching out to others. It means forming partnerships within the larger community or within the institutional community to

further common health goals. Outreach (or in-reach) provides an opportunity for librarians to broaden the reach of their services by making others aware of the richness and depth of resources and information skills librarians have to offer. Outreach connects people who need health information to a source of support and available services. Good outreach brings out the best in all partners and, through shared resources and expertise, expands service delivery beyond the capabilities of any single agency, department, or individual. By definition, outreach requires librarians to *"get outside"* their library.

In-reach may include such services as performing patient information rounds in the hospital and then delivering tailor-made packets of information on a particular diagnosis or condition. These information packets can be paper or paperless—by pushing full-text information electronically or sending specific links to webpages that respond to a patient's information request. Planetree Health Resource Center in The Dalles, Oregon, has provided this service for years. Such a service may be offered to all patients at small facilities or to patients on a specific unit or medical service, such as oncology or the cardiac care unit in larger hospitals.

It's important to work with the unit's nursing administration when developing such a service. Explain that the service is designed to supplement the nurse's role as patient educator, not supplant it. If met with resistance, offer to trial the service for three months and then evaluate it for patient utilization and satisfaction.

Outreach may involve working with other community groups, for example senior centers or schools, to further the library's mission of providing meaningful health information. One approach to a senior center involves bringing a wireless laptop and providing on-site reference work. Connect to a wireless printer so that the seniors can take the information home with them for later reference. Visiting high school health classes as a guest lecturer to lead classes on critically evaluating health websites helps teach young health care consumers how to identify and locate health information they can trust. These are just a few possibilities. Where outreach and in-reach are concerned, the possibilities are limited only by one's imagination!

Measuring Effectiveness

As mentioned previously, it's not enough to count basic library statistics, such as number of user visits, telephone calls, website hits, etc. as a measure of success. Certainly, these numbers matter. But in order to keep in touch with and be responsive to library users, it's important to find out what they are thinking about the service or services the library provides. The essential question is: what is a service's *value* to library users? While Chapter 6, "Evaluation and Improvement Management," discusses this in depth, we'll discuss utilizing a customer survey as a measurement tool here.

Any measuring should be done against the library's mission statement, goals and objectives. Measurement is a tool used to determine future direction by evaluating current performance and apparent value. In planning a measurement survey, consider these questions:

- What is to be measure and why? Is there a problem to be solved? Budgetary concerns? Considering a service expansion?

- Is a survey the best tool to measure? Will the survey provide the necessary information for decision making?

- Which audience will be surveyed? Patients? Hospital staff? Administrators?

Always include library staff in planning any type of customer service survey. Allow staff the opportunity to help design, critique, and administer the survey. Staff participation is essential in interpreting survey results and using the results to improve service. When conducting a survey, do the following:

- Plan a timeline for development, implementation, and analysis of the survey results. Typically a survey takes about three months to plan, execute, and analyze.

- Decide how the survey will be administered: paper, electronic, in-person interviews, or focus groups. Each has its pluses and minuses regarding response rate, ability to reach target audience (for example, not everyone reads e-mail), and time to administer the survey.

- Sample the survey to make sure survey takers understand the questions without additional explanation. A small group of three to five people can give realistic feedback.

- Administer and then send follow-up reminders to bolster return rates.

- If possible, use incentives as motivation for completion. (i.e., offer to put names into a drawing for a gift card to a local bookstore, restaurant, the hospital gift shop, etc.).

- Assess the results carefully so they provide a plan of action.

- Communicate the results with staff and stakeholders.

Surveys do not necessarily need to be long, complex affairs. One quick survey that you might use is a "bull's-eye" survey. The survey form is a simple target with a bull's-eye. You may pose any question, such as "How close to the bull's-eye were you in getting your information needs met today? Place an 'X' on your spot." The results of this survey may be used to determine whether a more in-depth survey is needed.

Free online tools exist with which to perform a survey. Typically these sites allow the user to design a short survey (for example, 10 questions with a maximum of 100 responses) using a survey template and then collect responses online free of charge. This is an especially helpful tool for librarians in smaller institutions. For a graduated annual fee, larger surveys can be conducted and more powerful functionality is available. Two such online survey sites are SurveyMonkey (http://www.surveymonkey.com) and Zoomerang (http://www.zoomerang.com).

Acquiring Consumer Health Expertise

According to Zionts et al., "librarians are the front-line workers in consumer health literacy" (2010: 350). The study also found that, nevertheless, public librarians in particular are not specifically prepared to respond to consumers' demands for meaningful health and medical information. The same may be true for medical and academic librarians who have spent the majority of their career assisting health care professionals with their information needs. Given the task of responding to patient and consumer health questions, they may find they are unexpectedly unprepared. The Medical Library Association offers many consumer health continuing education programs both in-person and via web-based classroom technology. These courses offer a solid foundation in consumer health resources and reference work, together with topical education for keeping skills current. Participation in these specialized continuing education courses may lead to MLA's certificate of Consumer Health Specialization. For more information about this program, visit http://www.mlanet.org/education/chc/.

Furthermore, the Consumer and Patient Health Information Section (CAPHIS) of the Medical Library Association (http://caphis.mlanet.org/) provides ongoing networking support to individuals with a special focus on consumer and patient health information service and offers invaluable peer support through its active Listserv and website.

The National Network of Libraries of Medicine (NN/LM) through its Regional Medical Library Network offers support to librarians engaged in consumer health information delivery. Each of the regional NN/LM offices has a consumer health outreach librarian on staff. In addition, NN/LM offers free education on consumer health topics; participation is open to any librarian. There are also helpful consumer health resources and tools on its website. Visit the NN/LM website and find your Regional Medical Library at: http://nnlm.gov/.

Conclusion

In a rapidly changing world of health information and health information technology, librarians provide order and meaning to vast resources. Patients and consumers benefit from the skills and expertise librarians bring to health information in the hospital setting (Weightman and Williamson, 2005). With careful planning and a clear mission to further individuals' ability to become true partners in their health care, the patient or consumer health library will be a vital part of any organization.

References

American Library Association. 1996. "Library Bill of Rights." Chicago: American Library Association. Accessed May 4, 2010. http://www.ala.org/ala/issuesadvocacy/intfreedom/librarybill/lbor.pdf.

Bandy, Margaret. 2000. "Health Information for Patients and Consumers." In *The Medical Library Association Guide to Managing Health Care Libraries*, edited by Ruth Holst and Sharon A. Phillips, 329–350. New York: Neal-Schuman.

Catholic Health Association. 2008. *A Guide for Planning and Reporting Community Benefit (2008 Edition)*. St. Louis, MO: Catholic Health Association of the United States.

Chastain-Warheit, Christine, and Barbara Henry. 2010. "How Hospital Librarians Can Demonstrate Internal Revenue Service-Mandated 'Community Benefit' for Their Non-profit Organizations." *MLA News* 50, no. 8: 1, 7.

Elliott, Donald S., Glen E. Holt, Sterling W. Hayden, and Leslie Edmonds Holt. 2007. *Measuring Your Library's Value: How to Do Cost-Benefit Analysis for Your Public Library*. Chicago: American Library Association.

Fox, Susannah, and Sydney Jones. 2009. "The Social Life of Health Information." Washington, DC: Pew Internet and American Life Project (June 2009). Accessed September 23, 2010. http://www.pewinternet.org/Reports/2009/8-The-Social-Life-of-Health-Information/2-Certain-medical-treatment-or-procedure.aspx?view=all.

Frampton, Susan, Sara Guastello, Carrie Brady, Maria Hale, Sheryl Horowitz, Susan Bennett Smith, and Susan Stone. 2008. "Myth #12: Our Patients Aren't Complaining, so We Must Be Meeting All Their Needs." In *Patient-Centered Care Improvement Guide*. Derby, CT: Planetree and Picker Institute. Accessed September 23, 2010. http://www.planetree.org/publications.

Harvard School of Public Health: Health Literacy Studies Web Site. 2010. Accessed September 18, 2010. http://www.hsph.harvard.edu/healthliteracy/practice/innovative-actions/index.html.

Joint Commission. 2007. "'What Did the Doctor Say?' Improving Health Literacy to Protect Patient Safety." Chicago: The Joint Commission, 2007. Accessed January 22, 2011. http://www.jointcommission.org/assets/1/18/improving_health_literacy.pdf.

Joint Commission. 2009. "Facts about the National Patient Safety Goals." Chicago: Joint Commission. Accessed January 22, 2011. http://www.jointcommission.org/assets/1/18/National_Patient_Safety_Goals_12_09.pdf.

Joint Commission. 2010. "Facts about Speak-Up Initiatives." Chicago: Joint Commission. Accessed January 22, 2011. http://www.jointcommission.org/speakup.aspx.

Kernaghan, Salvinija G., and Barbara E. Giloth. 1991. *Consumer Health Information: Managing Hospital-Based Centers*. Chicago: American Hospital Association.

Medical Library Association. 2008. "MLA Health Information Literacy Research Project. Consumer Health Information Survey Summary Report." Accessed September 19, 2010. http://www.mlanet.org/pdf/resources/hil_chi_survey_summary_bmla_211b.pdf.

Medical Library Association. 2010. "Code of Ethics for Health Sciences Librarianship." Chicago: Medical Library Association. Accessed May 4. http://www.mlanet.org/about/ethics.html.

Medical Library Association, Consumer and Patient Health Information Section (CAPHIS). 1996. "The Librarian's Role in the Provision of Consumer Health Information and Patient Education. Policy Statement by the Medical Library Association and the Consumer and Patient Health Information Section (CAPHIS/MLA)." *Bulletin of the Medical Library Association* 84, no. 2 (April): 238–239. Updated 2010. Accessed October 1. http://mlaguide.info/rev3cd/chap14/LIbrarian%27s_Role_in_Consumer_Health.pdf.

Nielsen-Bohlman, Lynn, Allison M. Panzer, and David A. Kindig. 2004. "Extent and Associations of Limited Health Literacy." *Health Literacy: A Prescription to End Confusion*, 59–107. Washington DC: The National Academies Press.

Spatz, Michele A. 2008. *Answering Consumer Health Questions: The Medical Library Association Guide for Reference Librarians*. New York: Neal-Schuman.

Spatz, Michele A. 2009. "Personalized Health Information." *American Journal of Nursing* 109, no. 4 (April): 70–72.

Vernon, John A., Antonio Trujillo, Sara Rosenbaum, and Barbara DeBuono. 2007. "Low Health Literacy: Implications for National Health Policy." Boston, MA: Partnership for

Clear Health Communication at the National Patient Safety Foundation, October. Accessed November 29, 2010. http://npsf.org/askme3/pdfs/Case_Report_10_07.pdf.

Weightman, Allison, and Jane Williamson. 2005. "The Value and Impact of Information Provided through Library Services for Patient Care: A Systematic Review." *Health Information and Libraries Journal* 22, no.1 (March): 4–25.

Zionts, Nancy D., Jan Apter, Julianna Kuchta, and Pamela K. Greenhouse. 2010. "Promoting Consumer Health Literacy: Creation of a Health Information Librarian Fellowship." *Reference and User Services Quarterly* 49, no. 4: 350–359.

Further Reading

Allen, Christine W., and Bruce H. Allen. 2007. "Outreach Marketing in a Community Health Library: Creating and Delivering Value through Target Marketing." *Journal of Hospital Librarianship* 7, no. 2: 17–29.

Brawn, Tammy S. 2005. "Consumer Health Libraries: What Do Patrons Really Want?" *Journal of the Medical Library Association* 93, no. 4: 495–496.

Eastwood, Elizabeth J., and Bernadine Goldman. 2007. "Help Your Health! Establishing a Consumer Health Program in a Small Public Library." *Journal of Hospital Librarianship* 7, no. 2: 57–66.

Kane, Laura Townsend and others. 2008. *Answers to the Health Questions People Ask in Libraries.* New York: Neal-Schuman.

Kennedy, Joy. 2006. "The Healing Library Environment." *Journal of Hospital Librarianship* 6, no. 3: 67–74.

Mays, Tammy L. 2005. "Consumer Health Issues, Trends, and Research, Part I: Strategic Strides toward a Better Future." *Library Trends* 53, no. 2 (Fall): 265–388.

Mays, Tammy L. 2005. "Consumer Health Issues, Trends, and Research, Part 2: Applicable Research in the 21st Century." *Library Trends* 53, no. 3 (Winter): 395–511.

Thomas, Deborah A. 2005. "The Consumer Health Reference Interview." *Journal of Hospital Librarianship* 5, no. 2: 45–56.

15

Associated Services

Hope Leman, Donna Beales, Daniel Sokolow, Alison Aldrich, and Marlene Englander

In health sciences libraries, there is a core set of services to meet the information needs of the library's primary users and support the mission-critical goals of the institution. These services and programs are described in the previous chapters. Many libraries also provide services that could be considered outside this core or what we are calling associated services. Many librarians will spend much of their time on these services and duties and others may never find themselves dealing with the matters discussed here. Some of these services are assigned to a librarian in budget-tightening times, sometimes to the detriment of library services. At other times, the librarian may choose to offer these services as value-added services that may be seen to ensure the survival of the library. Others may see some of these services as truly part of the core of a library.

The services discussed in depth in this chapter were chosen because they are areas that many libraries, hospital or academic, are managing. In the previous edition, audiovisual management was its own chapter and archives were touched on briefly. Here the editors are giving the readers more in-depth coverage of these value-added services.

The authors sought input in October 2009 from the readers of electronic discussions lists in the medical library profession on what constitutes associated services. In the responses, some librarians listed a priority service of theirs that in other libraries might be considered a core service. Excluding the services discussed in depth in this chapter, we were able to identify 30 services that we considered to be more uncommon or associated, as listed here:

1. Providing business information, human resource information, and insurance information services

2. Facilitating the health care institution's marketing program

3. Facilitating the health care institution's Internet presence

4. Managing the hospital website

5. Curating intranets, Sharepoint sites, and staff wikis

6. Providing information support for air ambulance FAA Guidelines adherence

7. Providing information support for grant seekers

8. Providing information support for the institution's employee/volunteer orientation program

9. Serving as institution tour guide

10. Considering implementing a program in support of GPS tracking devices, teaching map reading and plotting grids, checking out GPS handheld devices, and curating topographic and raised relief maps in the medical library

11. Providing computer application and/or computer training

12. Housing on-demand patient education system hardware and staff continuing education DVDs

13. Housing patient education kiosks and dealing with vendors of such

14. Working with nurse educators on implementing new programs

15. Serving as software/database evaluator for other departments

16. Providing support to journal clubs

17. Circulating recorders for students to use for classes

18. Circulating flash drives

19. Providing discounted book-buying services to all employees

20. Managing various nonlibrary IT services of the institution

21. Managing hospital policy and procedure database: editing, setting standards, organizing, database management, indexing, etc.

22. Maintaining a consumer health web database

23. Providing a notary service

24. Photographing staff for and maintaining photo gallery of institutional staff

25. Helping staff and members of the public with résumé creation and revision

26. Leading résumé workshops and grants workshops

27. Providing counseling on accessing government assistance programs

28. Providing Wii and other gaming equipment and services

29. Maintaining lending libraries of materials for recreational reading

30. Advising staff on professional publishing matters such as editing and proofreading papers

Could any of these be considered core services? Some librarians may think so and others may not. A few of them are covered in the section Other Associated Services. Chapter 3 has an additional list of services in Figure 3.1. Interestingly, the two lists hardly match at all with Figure 3.1 adding 17 different associated services to the list of possibilities. When it comes to associated services, library managers can be found doing many creative programs that add value to their library service.

Essentials of Continuing Medical Education Delivery

What Is Continuing Medical Education?

Medicine is a rapidly shifting discipline. Accepted practice changes constantly as new studies are published and novel technologies evolve. Physicians must keep up with the current state of medical knowledge so that they can provide the finest care for their patients based on the best available evidence. Continuing Medical Education (CME) is the ongoing, formalized process of career-long learning for physicians and certain other medical specialties. Health care facilities, academic institutions, and specialty societies and organizations can be accredited to provide CME, which keeps medical professionals abreast of current information about diagnosis, treatment, prevention, and etiology of disease states and conditions. CME also elucidates such topics as medical ethics, avoidance of malpractice, physician-patient communication, risk mitigation, and even behavioral coaching.

CME formats vary. Most often, CME is presented in traditional lecture-style fashion. However, many other styles of learning are also employed. Hands-on sessions using simulated "patients" and case presentations in which a particular patient's medical problem is presented and participants are asked to determine the care of the patient are acceptable. Even mock malpractice trials can qualify for CME credit. In addition, CME can occur in print materials, DVDs, streaming videos, interactive online tutorials, and self-directed (also called "point of care") learning.

Purpose of CME

In the United States, all physicians and osteopaths are licensed to practice medicine. Frequently, licensure requirements stipulate that doctors attend a minimum of 100 hours of accredited continuing medical education during a two-year period. Some allied health specialties also allow their members to attend CME programs, which count toward certification or licensure.

The purpose of these requirements is to address "practice gaps." Practice gaps are areas where an individual or group's knowledge, professional competence, or actual performance may be deficient. Often, astute medical professionals can self-identify their practice gaps. However,

sometimes gaps are identified through data analysis by a health care facility or as a result of poor patient outcomes. CME is vital because it attempts to address practice gaps. No patient wants to be treated by a doctor who isn't employing the best medical knowledge available, who lacks competence, or whose actual practice has been shown by objective measures to be below standard. Ultimately, the best care of the individual patient is at stake.

CME can be used as a measure of "quality improvement" (QI). QI is the process of examining aggregated data to determine how overall patient care can be improved or enhanced. For example, if a surgical specialty society creates a guideline or determines through hard evidence that a certain drug should be administered to all surgical patients within one hour of surgery, the records of many patients can be examined to determine if the drug is indeed being administered appropriately. If not, education may be warranted to attempt to rectify the identified gap in actual practice, which in this example is failure to administer the drug.

Over the last few years, a paradigm shift has occurred in CME, garnering both praise and controversy in professional CME circles. The shift is toward requiring "outcomes measurement." Outcomes measurement is the process of assessing the success or failure of a CME program as it relates to an identified practice gap. In order to conduct outcomes measurement, CME providers must now identify a gap in knowledge, performance, or competence, describe how an educational program will address the gap, conduct the educational intervention, and then use one of several processes to determine if the program had any impact on closing the gap.

The strongest measures of educational outcomes are data driven. To build upon the above example, if a medical facility identified through data analysis that its surgical patients weren't being given a necessary drug and made an educational intervention, it would be easy for the facility to choose a timeline to revisit the data to see if the numbers show an improvement after the educational event.

There's a problem with this approach, however. Although numbers may improve, there's no way to prove that education was the reason. The best that can be said is that the educational activity correlated with the desired change. Correlation, however, is not causation.

Furthermore, it's possible that numbers may actually worsen after a CME program. Reasons may be difficult to interpret. Human variables come into play, including expert differences of opinion about guidelines, corporate culture factors, and personal biases about how medicine should be practiced. For these reasons, data-driven outcomes measurement is controversial. Post-tests are another form of outcomes measurement. Ideally, gaps in knowledge can be identified through the use of a pre-test, completing the circle of gap identification, educational intervention, and measurable outcome in the form of a post-test.

Problems with post-testing abound. They don't measure the knowledge base an individual brings to the table prior to an educational program, and they measure short-term knowledge, not retention over time. Too, knowledge doesn't always translate to actual practice. An individual may score 100 percent on a post-test and yet fail to apply what is known to patient care. Barriers that have nothing to do with a physician's understanding may exist, such as financial constraints that prevent implementation, or lack of access to current technology. Moreover, if the physician disagrees with the information presented in an educational program, he or she may actively choose not to follow it in practice, regardless of his or her level of comprehension. Finally, physicians may balk at a post-test approach. Physicians are accustomed to obtaining CME credit based on simple program attendance; therefore, they may avoid CME programs in which measurable performance is a part.

"Softer" outcomes measurement tools include use of an audience response system (ARS), program evaluations, and attendee surveys. These are subjective methods of measurement. An audience response system uses small remote handsets to poll attendees for their answers to specific questions. The handsets transmit individuals' answers to a computer, which then immediately displays collective results. An ARS can be used to track individuals' responses to a post-test. This type of use is most commonly found in academic settings. In nonacademic institutions, ARS technology is often employed to poll for collective opinions and group knowledge so aspects can be explored and discussed in real-time.

No matter what form outcomes measurement takes, the purpose of CME is to advance the quality of medical care through education and to demonstrate quantifiable improvements. Practice gap analysis and outcomes measurement are vital and have positive implications for the future of CME. They may serve to justify the expense of maintaining a viable CME program by showing administrators that education not only adds value, it can cut substandard practice costs, and, most important, save lives.

Accreditation, Regulations, and Guidelines

The American Medical Association (AMA) originated CME in the form of the AMA Physician's Recognition Award, which sets forth what medical doctors must accomplish to maintain their licenses. The Accreditation Council for Continuing Medical Education (ACCME) oversees the educational component of AMA licensure requirements. In the United States the lion's share of CME programs are accredited by the ACCME. The American Academy of Family Practice also offers accredited CME coursework for its members, and the processes of accreditation as well as the requirements for individuals' participation differ somewhat from those of the ACCME. As well as maintaining a close relationship with the AMA, ACCME partners with seven member organizations, including the American Hospital Association and the American Board of Medical Specialties. This and other information about the ACCME referenced herein can be found on the organization's website, http://www.accme.org.

ACCME-accredited CME consists of two "designations," or levels. "Category 1" credit is that which is offered by accredited CME providers, who track participation and maintain attendance records. "Category 2" credit is CME that individuals do entirely on their own by reading journals or engaging in other learning activities while keeping track of their own participation. Many doctors shun Category 2 participation, which they consider bothersome to maintain.

The following section focuses on ACCME accreditation requirements for CME providers offering Category 1 credit. The ACCME sets forth the "rules" of how CME providers must operate their overall programs if they wish to be accredited. These requirements are known as the "ACCME Essential Areas and Elements" (ACCME, 2006a).

The Elements themselves are relatively straightforward, although their implementation can be difficult. They require providers to:

- draft a mission statement,
- have an overall educational plan,
- clearly communicate the purpose of activities to learners, and
- ensure that CME educational content is free of bias.

Providers must ensure that those who are in control of educational content, such as CME committee members, planners, and employees, have no commercial conflicts of interest. Providers must also:

- evaluate effectiveness of educational programs,
- provide adequate funding to ensure quality, and
- operate the CME program utilizing acceptable corporate polices pertaining to personnel management, legal obligations, and financial accountability.

Of these requirements, the second most important role of CME providers after the provision of quality education is to ascertain that corporate interests are kept separate from education (Mazmanian, 2009; Goold and Campbell, 2008). The importance of this role cannot be overstated. That the practice of medicine should be free of the influence of industry should go without saying. However, because medical practice is so intertwined with the use of pharmaceutical products and medical technologies, conflicts of interest can occur (Brody, 2009).

The ACCME Elements have distinct requirements to ensure that a sound firewall exists between industry and CME. These requirements are called the *ACCME Standards for Commercial Support* (ACCME, 2006b). The Standards were put in place as an indirect result of suits brought against CME providers who invited physician speakers with corporate interests to present accredited educational programs. These speakers promoted off-label use of pharmaceutical products, a practice prohibited under federal law. "Off label" refers to use that is not approved by the Food and Drug Administration. Often, little if any evidence exists to support off-label prescribing. Physicians, however, are free to prescribe drugs for unapproved uses despite a paucity of factual support. Therefore, it benefits industry to try to sway doctors to embrace off-label prescribing; companies sell more products as a result (Mello, Studdert, and Brennan, 2009).

In one particularly disturbing example, "off-label" use of a drug for adolescents with bipolar disorder was touted at a CME program. As a result, a physician attendee prescribed Neurontin, an epilepsy drug marketed by Parke-Davis (since acquired by Pfizer), for 16-year-old bipolar patient Dustin Yankus. Neurontin has no proven efficacy in the treatment of bipolar disorder. Yankus committed suicide. A successful suit resulted against Pfizer's Warner Lambert division, which pled guilty and paid $430 million (U.S. Department of Justice, 2004). More recently, in 2009 the pharmaceutical giant Pfizer made the largest payout in American history when the Department of Justice found the company guilty of a felony violation for promoting off-label use of its drug Bextra. According to a *New York Times* story, Pfizer paid $2.3 billion dollars in fines (Harris, Gardiner, 2009). Yet as Smith (2006) reports, the payout represented less than 5 percent of Pfizer's more than $50 billion dollar 2006 annual sales figures as reported by *CNN Money*. In 2009 alone, 14 companies were cited by the FDA for misleading advertising (Edwards, 2009).

Considering that corporations plan for worst-case scenarios, even such staggering fines may prove to be ineffective in deterring companies from engaging in questionable activities. Over a five-year period, the money Pfizer will pay out will be less than 1 percent of its yearly earnings, which is an easily absorbable cost. In any corporation, such a small percentage may be perceived as simply the cost of doing business. Moreover, companies often build such costs into their product pricing structure. Thus, such losses are often offset before they even occur.

The pharmaceutical industry recognized the potential for backlash against its questionable practices. The Pharmaceutical Research and Manufacturers of America, a trade group for the industry, developed a code of conduct called the "Code of Interactions with Healthcare Professionals," known informally as the "PhRMA Code." The efficacy of this code has yet to be determined (PhRMA, 2010). To date, it appears to have had little effect on the actual practices of companies.

The ACCME Standards require providers to solicit information from every CME presenter about the presenter's financial interests and relationships, to determine if the speaker will be discussing any off-label use of a medication, as well as to "vet," i.e., pre-screen, content that will be presented during a lecture in order to verify that it is free of bias (ACCME, 2006b). For example, obvious promotion such as the inclusion of corporate logos or product trade names is prohibited, and vetting ensures that none is present. Vetting also ensures that the information to be presented is supported by scientific literature. Selective use of literature is a subtle form of bias that can be difficult to detect.

The Standards require CME providers to publicly disclose presenters' commercial ties and any declared intent to discuss off-label use during the course of a program. Presumably, this arms audience members with information to identify bias in lecture content. However, studies show that medical professionals' prescribing practices are influenced by even such innocuous activities as provision of small items like branded mugs or pens (Schneider et al., 2006; Weber and Bissell, 2006). A presentation by a lauded expert with vested interests is likely to have similar effects, despite disclosures. The dynamics of this relationship, including ethics, bias, and the influence of drug companies, have been studied and reported in the literature (Chimonas, Brennan, and Rothman, 2007; Cornish and Leist, 2006; Ellison et al., 2009; Greene and Podolsky, 2009; Harris, Gwyn, 2009; Price, Havens, and Bellman, 2009; Theodorou et al., 2009).

Procedures for creating industry firewalls are seriously flawed. In most CME programs, execution of the Standards is built around use of the honor system, assuming that presenters will fully self-disclose their financial interests and relationships. However, unscrupulous professionals are an unfortunate reality in every discipline. Alarmingly, even in cases where a CME provider is able to identify overt promotion on the part of a presenter, as of this writing, the ACCME has no formal mechanism in place for providers to report violations. Thus, unscrupulous presenters may slip from provider to provider unhindered as the onus is on each CME provider, not the ACCME, to maintain the integrity of its individual CME program.

Recently, the ACCME, pressured by a 2007 Senate Finance Committee report detailing abuses, moved to announce that it will post information about a small number of investigations it conducted related to reported violations of the Standards. It's too soon to tell if this will be effective in preventing further problems (Tanne, 2009; Hosansky, 2009).

In summary, although other AMA accredited CME institutions exist, CME is governed primarily in the U.S. by the ACCME, which has specific accreditation requirements. The two basic issues addressed by these requirements are to ensure that CME programs are of high quality, and that they remain free of commercial bias. Meeting these requirements is challenging, especially in difficult economic times, when quality may suffer as a result of funding cuts. In terms of adequate commercial firewalls, industry continues to attempt to blur the line between product promotion and education, often with considerable financial resources behind their efforts and often with subtle efficacy (Campbell and Rosenthal, 2009).

State Medical Societies and State Regulations

To aid in managing the process of national accreditation standards, the ACCME accredits state medical societies and organizations. These state organizations in turn accredit CME programs in hospitals, medical practices, academic institutions, and other health care facilities within each state. Interpretation of ACCME requirements varies slightly from state to state. State medical societies have some autonomy to make additional requirements and to differ somewhat from the ACCME, although recent trends indicate that this is changing to a more uniform approach.

The uniformity drift has particular import for medical librarians. Some states, such as Massachusetts, did away with requirements mandating the inclusion of medical libraries as part of CME accreditation requirements. In contrast, Connecticut has distinctly strong hospital library requirements. Jeannine Cyr Gluck, MLS, AHIP, serves as a member of the Connecticut State Medical

Society CME Committee. Gluck states that she contacted the ACCME, "... to determine whether additional standards over and above those of the ACCME were still allowable" (Personal communication, November 25, 2009). No impediment was identified. Connecticut retains its standards for libraries in CME-accredited hospitals and remains a national leader in this regard (Gluck, 2004; Gluck and Hassig, 2001).

Library requirements have often been used to justify budgets and even as leverage for continued operation. Without them, the increasing trend to close the doors of medical libraries can only be expected to grow. Unless librarians lobby at a national level to convince major health care organizations to add medical libraries to their lists of requirements, or at very least to necessitate the presence of a qualified librarian, medical libraries will continue to struggle to survive in a bottom-line driven health care climate.

Library issues aside, other variations in state requirements exist. One of them is the inclusion of what is called "risk management" CME. Risk management is the process of mitigating potential hazards before they arise. Examples of risk management CME include avoidance of malpractice, patient-physician communication, and any entity that poses a threat to patients because of identified gaps. H1N1 influenza is a good example of a disease that presented an obvious gap because it had never been encountered before. Thus, there was a pressing need for CME education. Some states require physicians to attend a set number of risk management CME programs and have guidelines about the kinds of programs that can carry the designation "risk management;" others have no risk requirements at all.

Some states are moving toward strictly controlling the interaction between industry and medical providers. Massachusetts was one of the first states to enact such legislation, Chapter 111N of the Massachusetts General Laws, which specifically delineates what commercial enterprises may and may not engage in related to continuing medical education. It also makes provisions for mandating presenter transparency. In Massachusetts, the ACCME Standards for Commercial Support (SM) and the "PhRMA Code of Interactions with Healthcare Professionals" are now written into law (General Laws of Massachusetts, 2010).

Roles the Librarian Can Play in Delivery of CME

Regardless of whether a medical librarian has job responsibility for the operation of a CME department or serves

MANAGEMENT IN ACTION 15.1

Handling Difficult Customers as a CME Coordinator

Location: Community Hospital

Description of Problem: As a CME Coordinator, one role is to vet the audiovisual slides of CME presenters before passing them along to the Director of Medical Education (DME). The institution has a philosophy that every person using services is a customer, including all co-workers. Dr. Jones is a well-known speaker from a nonprofit tertiary center in the area. She's coming to present in two months. First, she gets angry when told that it's required that her slides get vetted before her presentation. She appears to have never heard of the requirement before although she speaks often. Dr. Jones refuses to comply until only four days before the scheduled program, and then submits a presentation with 14 trade names included that refer to one drug. The drug does have a generic name. It is communicated politely to Dr. Jones that all 14 instances must be eliminated. She resubmits her slides, but now there are six references in different places in the presentation. There is a follow-up communication. She gets angry and is sure there is a "mistake" in the vetting. She resubmits her slides a third and a fourth time and each time trade names are referenced. Dr. Jones' tone becomes increasingly belligerent, and she threatens to cancel her talk two days before the program.

Impact On: Compliance with issue of conflict of interest; scheduling of CME programs.

People Involved: Librarian/CME Coordinator, Physician Speaker, Director of Medical Education, Speakers Bureau Coordinator

Strategies for Success: The librarian/CME coordinator has kept the Director of Medical Education in the loop with every communication and also sought the advice of the Corporate Compliance Officer. The speaker had previously disclosed several commercial involvements. The referenced trade name was a monoclonal antibody, and the speaker was involved in its development, a fact uncovered by the librarian's research. Since the incident happened in Massachusetts, it was agreed that the next communication to the speaker would be copied to the manager of the tertiary center's speakers program, Mr. Smith. A carefully worded e-mail contained not only the actual ACCME Standard about trade name exclusion, but also a reference to Massachusetts General Law 111N, to the effect that "Dr. Jones, Mr. Smith can best apprise you about how this law may apply to you." Following this interaction, the speaker did comply and went on to give a reasonably unbiased presentation.

Barriers Encountered: Annoyance on the part of a speaker in relation to complying with the rules; perhaps Dr. Jones did not know the rules, i.e., needed to be informed.

Take-Home Points: The librarian/CME coordinator knew the rules, communicated the problem to the supervisor and sought advice from experts such as the compliance officer. The supervisory staff supported the people doing the work.

solely as a medical librarian but works in a CME-accredited institution, librarians have a specialized skill set that dovetails nicely with the demands of CME. These skills can enrich and enhance operation of a CME program and provide a rewarding experience for the library professional. However, prudence is warranted; before any master's-level library professional considers or accepts a position that formally combines CME duties with those of the medical library, a few inquiries should be made.

Due to its stringent requirements, CME entails a considerable amount of clerical work. Therefore, librarians considering solo positions in health care institutions should ask key questions, such as the following, when interviewing for dual Library/CME jobs:

- What clerical support will be provided?
- What percentage of my time will I be spending on CME?

- What specific duties are entailed in the area of CME?
- What library skills have been brought to bear on your CME program in the past?

Behavioral interviewing techniques such as, "Can you give me an example of a time when the librarian's duties and responsibilities conflicted with those of the CME department?" may highlight potential pitfalls faced by predecessors. Ultimately if the interviewers can't provide good answers to these questions, then caveat emptor. A common complaint of "CME librarians" is that they feel underemployed and that, as voiced by one colleague, "I didn't spend all that time in graduate school to do this," i.e., CME.

But there are ways librarians can bring valuable expertise to the CME table. Literature searching is a good example. Specific kinds of searches apply to CME programs:

- **Bibliographies**: The most obvious search, and the one library professionals most frequently perform, is done to put together bibliographies that pertain to individual CME programs.

- **Locating quality speakers**: One way of ensuring quality is to select speakers based on a review of their publications. Librarians have access to many tools that enable them not only to locate publications by author, but also to use advanced search techniques to narrow these publications to those that are evidence-based, current, and well-cited by others—or not.

- **Retraction alerts**: Searching expertise can be used to ascertain if an author has ever been involved in writing an article that has later been retracted. For example, Scott Reuben, MD, was a prominent Boston-area anesthesiologist who published extensively in his field and spoke at numerous CME programs. Reuben allegedly fabricated data to support "multimodal therapy" or the use of multiple drugs simultaneously for pain control in postsurgical patients. Reuben's employer, Baystate Medical Center in Springfield, Massachusetts, discovered that Reuben may have completely falsified data to support his multimodal therapy conclusions, which had been widely accepted in the field. Baystate in turn called for the retraction of 21 of his published articles according to Winstein and Armstrong (2009). Librarians can alert CME department personnel about such instances, as forewarned is forearmed.

- **Current trends**: By combing medical newsfeeds and keeping abreast of what's being published in the popular press on medical topics, librarians can help CME departments anticipate the kinds of questions physicians are likely to encounter from their media savvy patients, and ensure they're informed enough to provide good care based on up-to-date information.

- **Content vetting**: Librarians can be included in the first round of vetting in two ways. First, they can research drugs mentioned in slides to ascertain that no trade names, which are forbidden by the ACCME Standards, are included. Second, many presentations contain published references. Librarians can locate the referenced abstracts or retrieve full-text articles for evaluation by CME personnel, and add expertise in determining if the references are considered evidence based.

- **Research validity checking**: Librarians with a background in research can evaluate references for validity based on study population size, study design, and statistical validity. Even those without a research background can perform a more basic "compare and contrast" function, comparing studies used to justify the speaker's position against evidence-based studies on the same topic where available, or by exploring current guidelines.

- **Financial disclosure**: Perhaps the most intriguing, and difficult, use of a librarian's search skills may be in the arena of financial disclosure. Since most CME providers rely on the use of speaker self-disclosure of commercial interests, a little research may reveal situations where a speaker has failed to make full disclosure or even misrepresented information. The Internet can sometimes yield indirect associations between presenters and companies, or provide evidence that a speaker has a vested interest in a product. Such associations are not always immediately evident; it often takes a bit of sleuthing to bring them to light. Not all speakers indulge in such bias because they're out to make a buck; some are legitimately committed to their research and believe in their work. However, bias is still bias, and librarians can bring balance to CME education through their search skills.

CME Delivery via Various Media

Another potential CME role for the skilled librarian is the media specialist role. "Media specialist" is a subset of library education primarily geared for colleagues who wish to teach in accredited academic settings. The specialty usually demands coursework in pedagogy, curriculum development, learning theory, and audio-visual applications for educational settings. All media specialist disciplines can be applied to CME programs.

For example, audiovisual and web technology expertise can directly enhance CME offerings. Time constraints may prevent medical professionals from attending live CME activities. Too, the hospitalist movement may impact CME attendance. Fewer internists and family practitioners need to be on site at hospitals; thus, they turn their attention to seeing more patients in place of making trips out to attend educational programs.

Librarians can employ their skills in web development to create interactive learning tools. One such example is point-of-care learning, also known as point-of-need, or self-directed learning. Educational theorists posit that people learn best when they have an immediate need to know about a topic because finding an answer either provides benefit to them or helps them avoid a negative consequence. Point-of-care CME is about the "teachable moment." Perceived need prompts doctors to seek out literature to help them best treat their patients. Most are surprised that they can actually receive Category 1 credit for their efforts when the process is managed and tracked by an accredited CME provider. Librarians can facilitate the process by designing easy-to-use webpages and forms that meet all Category 1 requirements (Muallem, 2007).

Streaming video can be used for CME delivery. Some librarians with undergraduate media backgrounds use screencasting or videotape, then edit and produce accredited CME programs. Others evaluate and purchase products to serve the purpose. Either way, librarians' professional skills are employed to enhance the CME experience. Librarians' expertise in copyright is important to any fixed medium creation.

Librarians' ability to keep abreast of current technologies, including trialing new software applications and exploring and adopting new audiovisual hardware, such as audience response technologies, can increase their value to the organizations they serve. Other audiovisual applications useful in managing CME may include proficiency in the use of touch screen technologies. Modern AV systems often incorporate use of computers, digital overhead projectors, webcasting equipment, satellite technologies, and more. All areas of audiovisual know-how can make a librarian an integral, highly visible member of a CME team.

A foundation in pedagogy and curriculum development is essential for CME programs; however, no specific requirements exist for Directors of Continuing Medical Education to complete any educational coursework. Although no minimum standards or educational credentials are required to head a continuing medical education program, most directors in universities and large hospitals are MDs or PhDs. Many organizations, especially community hospitals, may not have a CME Director but function with a CME committee chaired by a physician with support from a CME Coordinator to handle the paperwork. A CME certification movement is in the works, but it remains optional.

CME Section Summary

In summary, a great deal of specialized knowledge is necessary to successfully function in the CME arena. CME rules and regulations and potential operational pitfalls demand attention to detail, vigilance, integrity, and courage to do the right thing. The more broadly a librarian can apply her skill sets within CME education,

the more valuable she will be to her employer. More job diversity may mean more job satisfaction and possibly more job security, although there are no guarantees.

Library professionals must take care to avoid entrapping themselves in CME-related jobs that underutilize their valuable professional talents, marginalize their contributions, or usurp the time they need to operate a medical library efficiently. Yet, despite its problems, CME can be a rewarding experience in one other important way and you realize your efforts do make a difference. In the searing instance where the rubber ultimately hits the road, you'll know that all your efforts really matter, when:

- Mr. McFarland comes through the door of Dr. Casey's office unable to breathe and Dr. Casey is able to successfully open McFarland's airway because she went to that hands-on Grand Rounds about in-office intubation;

- hospital data reveals that more orthopedic patients are receiving antibiotics within an hour of surgery as outlined in national guidelines, and fewer patients are developing infections, probably as a result of more education; and

- Dr. Yi personally thanks you because he learned something during a CME program that will help him communicate more efficiently with his patients.

Managing Archives

Of all the managed services, archival services are closest to the core functions of the medical library, and yet the differences are great enough to leave the most experienced librarian confused and uncertain how to proceed. While many health care organizations have full or part-time archivists on staff, more do not and the archival function can often fall under the purview of the medical library and its staff.

What happens when the librarian, and specifically the medical librarian, is asked to handle the archives of the organization? The purpose of this section is to help medical librarians answer that question.

Additional readings and resources can be found on the **accompanying CD-ROM**. The *SAA Archival Fundamentals Series* is recommended. This seven-volume series provides a basic introduction to many aspects of archival management, from selection to preservation and everything in between. Other books and brochures may be found by searching at the SAA Bookstore (http://www.archivists.org/catalog/index.asp). Readers are also referred to this section author's article "You want me to do what? Medical librarians and the management of archival collections" (Sokolow, 2004). Also of interest is the new book by Laura A. Millar, *Archives: Principles and Practices* (Millar, 2010).

It should be noted that many archival responsibilities could be addressed with the help of an archival consultant. While many institutions cannot afford to hire a full-time archivist, an archival consultant can be brought in to assist in the planning and development of an archival program. The professional input of a trained archivist will ensure that the mission and plan for the archives is appropriate for the institution, and provide perspective on issues of costs, management, and continuing development of the archival program.

Defining an Archive and Archival Responsibilities

The first step in managing an archive is to understand what an archive actually is. Some librarians have been introduced to the basic concepts of archival management in graduate school, but many others will be learning of it for the first time. In essence, an archive is a collection of unique materials, of permanent value, specific to an organization or an individual. The key here for librarians is the uniqueness of the materials. The texts and electronic materials of the modern medical library are often reproduced exactly from one institution to another. For an archive, items that exist in one hospital archive will have little relation to the materials in another.

This difference can be a hurdle for some librarians—standardized rules of cataloging and arrangement have little or no application to an archive. There are certainly commonly used arrangement practices in the archival world—provenance (the trail materials have taken to get from record creator, through various owners, to the archive) and original order are critical to properly maintain a collection. But the passage of time, the complicated travels of departmental files, and the maddening changes of administrations and organizations create difficulties not seen in the more orderly world of book cataloging. The archivist (and every librarian handed this responsibility becomes an archivist, like it or not) is responsible not only for maintaining order, but in many cases creating it.

One critical note here—an archival document is archival irrespective of the medium in which it is created. Paper records, photographs, video, born-digital records, e-mails—all of these can be archival records requiring permanent retention. The information may sit on a piece of paper, a portable flash drive, $1/2$" videotape, or a 5.25" floppy disk, but in all cases the record has permanence.

Preservation of the different media raises very complicated issues, but in all cases the records should be kept if possible.

A second area of definition is the purpose of the archive; why is the archive there or why is it being created? Often there is an anniversary or other significant event that leads the organization to begin collecting and preserving its historical materials. In other cases there are legal or business needs behind the drive to preserve the past. As a last example, there are times when a long-serving or retiring executive or physician sees the archive as an opportunity to preserve his legacy with the institution. Any of these valid reasons for beginning an archive require some further definition before the archive opens for business. Is the archive going to be available for internal or external use, or both? Will the archive continue its efforts once the initial impulse (i.e., the anniversary) is past? Is there sufficient support for the archive to continue as an ongoing concern? The answers to these questions will help define what the archive is to accomplish and what the archivist needs to concentrate on.

The last area of definition that the librarian needs to address is collection scope. What does the organization want to collect? Like the library's nonarchival collection, the librarian will be responsible for choosing what materials have permanent value to the organization. Some of these choices will be easy: board minutes, for example, have both historical and legal value, and should automatically be kept. Other materials, like billing records, will probably never find their way to an archive, and if they do they can be discarded in accordance with state and federal record-keeping statutes.

The complications arise when materials arrive that have no clear resolution. If a doctor donates his notebook documenting his experiments, what should the newly minted archivist do? Perhaps the doctor will one day win the Nobel Prize for his work. Archivists need to determine what kind of archive they are creating and managing—a home for institutional records only, or do they intend to collect faculty/staff papers, related donations, etc. Resources, funding, and management support will play a significant role in determining how the archive will be defined.

Appraisal: Determining the Value of Archival Records

A particular difficulty for librarians facing the archive is the need to create archival collections from nothing. In some cases the new archivist is directed to a room full of old materials and told, "Here you are. Make some sense out of this." In many other cases, librarians find themselves part of a committee to create an archive, often in connection with an upcoming anniversary (and those committees never plan these things far enough in advance). Unlike a library, where one can prepare a list of items to be purchased, archival materials have to be found from the masses of records produced by modern hospitals. Ferreting out the hidden gems of the institution's past is a forensic task, suited to those with high levels of patience and a strong stomach to deal with the poor conditions where records are often found. There is a great deal of negotiation involved as well, as records owners are not always happy to lose control over their materials.

The phrase "you wouldn't want that" is one often heard in the course of archival collection development. The creators or custodians of the records in question have leapt to the conclusion that they know the long-term value of the records better than the archivist. The author's usual response is to politely point out that he must be the best judge of what has permanent value.

This does raise the question of how the medical librarian turned archivist can best select materials for the archives. There are, unfortunately, no hard-and-fast rules. A hospital with a specialty in cancer research will have to concentrate on that area, while another will need to focus on its renowned cardiology department. One cannot save it all, and that is the first rule an archivist should go by; resources are limited, space is limited; thus, we need to save as best we can. Selecting records for permanent archival retention is a form of triage—each group of materials measured against the available resources and competing collections. The basic goal of collection appraisal and development is to provide as complete a picture as possible of the institution's activities. It may make more sense to collect fewer things from a number of different departments than a large group from a single department.

Here are some basic guidelines the beginning archivist can work by. They are by no means comprehensive or universal, but they should enable the librarian to begin the process. There are several measurements of relative archival value, including legal evidence, historical evidence, and evidentiary value. Each of these items fits into one of these areas, or may fall into more than one.

- **Board minutes**: These records are essential, and are in most cases permanent by statute. Minutes from the governing body provide insight into the creation of the institution, as well as illuminating decisions made by the Board. Again, as these are required by law to be kept, they should automatically be saved.
- **Medical Board minutes**: Like the organization's Board, the Medical Board's minutes are also often

required by law to be kept. In addition, they can help the institution and researchers understand actions taken by the medical board.

- **Other legally required materials**: In consultation with the hospital's legal department or outside counsel, the archivist should determine what records must be saved by law.
- **Public relations**: Many of the items that come from a hospital's Public/Community Relations department prove valuable to the institution and researchers. The PR department may provide the best overview of the varied activities of the hospital, as they often work with every clinical and nonclinical department to produce material. Newsletters, press releases, brochures, and advertisements can all be used both for the information they contain and as evidence of the work the hospital has done in the past.
- **Department files**: Depending on resources, a hospital archive should attempt to obtain some materials from as many departments as possible, both clinical and nonclinical. Again, the relative importance of the department to the hospital can be used as a guide.
- **Audiovisual materials**: These are often the most used and most valuable parts of an archival collection. Video material can be reused in new video presentations, as an example, employee orientation; still images can be used in brochures, advertisements, etc.
- **Individuals' papers**: This is a matter of choice for the archives. The author's repository does not collect personal papers, only institutional materials. Some archives do collect materials from individuals connected to the organization. This is usually a matter of resources and focus, and the institution must decide what it wants to pursue. As a matter of organization, an individual's materials are usually considered his own collection, independent of the institutional collections.
- **Medical records**: The question of medical records has gotten more complicated because of Health Insurance Portability and Accountability Act (HIPAA) regulations.

There is tremendous value to the records for historians, but the privacy rules of HIPAA make administering the records more difficult than it has been in the past. Additional HIPAA information about its relationship to archives is available at Society of American Archivists

There is a developing area of literature on the subject of HIPAA and historical collections. As the regulations surrounding HIPAA continue to evolve, numerous archivists in the Health Sciences have been writing about the trends and issues surrounding its impact on historical collections. The most up-to-date collection of articles and commentary on the subject can be found on the website of the Science, Technology and Health Care Roundtable of the Society of American Archivists. (http://www.library.vcu.edu/tml/speccoll/hipaa.html). There are a number of important articles and links on the site, including congressional testimony by several health care archivists and articles.

(SAA)'s Science, Technology, and Health Care Round Table (http://www.archivists.org/saagroups/sthc/index .html). With effort, the records can be made available to researchers through a number of methods: all Personal Health Information (PHI) can be removed, consent forms obtained from all individuals, or a waiver for use of the records may be possible through the facility's Institutional Review Board (IRB). The first would likely remove most of the useful information from the records; the second is both difficult and would likely need to be repeated for each new investigation; the third, while complicating reference, is the one option likely to preserve the value in the medical records. The increasing concern of health care facilities about these records means they may never find their way to the archive. Even so, the archivist should be aware of the historical importance of the materials, and may wish to participate in any discussions about the disposition of these records with the relevant medical records personnel, the facility's compliance officer, and the IRB (Lawrence, 2007).

Stephen Novak, Head of Archives & Special Collections, Augustus C. Long Health Sciences Library, Columbia University Medical Center, pointed out in a personal communication that there is a difference between medical records of different eras. As he wrote, "…research access to records of those presumed deceased is considerably easier than access to records of those we can reasonably assume are alive. Patient records predating 1920 are relatively rare in this country and if a hospital still has any of these, every effort should be made to save all or part of them" (Personal communication, 2003).

It should be noted that finding these materials and actually transferring them to the archive are two different matters. Finding them is often by luck, but the usual first step is tracking down long-serving employees or medical staff who may remember where they are or who had them last. Getting the materials transferred requires tact, negotiation, and (with any luck) support from the powerful, who will insist that these materials be moved to a proper home.

Organizing and Preserving Archival Materials

Once the materials have been collected, the next step is to arrange, describe, and re-house the materials. Where possible, archivists prefer to base their organization on two principles—provenance and original order. Provenance means keeping records from different departments and records creators intellectually separate from one another, and tracking as best you can the path the records have taken from the creator to the archives. The value of this approach is that users can understand the creator's intentions and uses of the materials as they were created. Original order, as it implies, means maintaining the order in which the records creator arranged the materials.

As one might expect, many records arrive in the archives in a poorly organized mass rather than in a controlled, well-planned transfer. Provenance and original order are often impossible to determine in these cases, and instead the archivist must create an arrangement from nothing. In these cases, one needs to anticipate users' needs, and create an arrangement that makes sense to almost anyone. Bear in mind that others will follow the archivist, and it is useful to develop a system that can be grasped quickly by another person. Separating administrative departments from clinical, for example, is one way to organize materials, and likely reflects the provenance of the materials. It is somewhat a matter of taste, but good judgment will lead to a workable system.

As the sample organization found on the **accompanying CD-ROM** indicates, the author has chosen to arrange the materials from the different components of the North Shore-LIJ Health System ("the System") separately rather than following like subjects. Thus, the materials from the System's Glen Cove facility are filed independently of the material from Long Island Jewish Medical Center. Despite certain parallels (for example, both have a Department of Medicine and an Auxiliary), the materials really have no connection to one another. In addition, the archival concept of provenance—keeping records from different record creators distinct from each other—should lead the archivist to distinguish between two historically separate institutions.

Archivists are often confronted by the complications of large conglomerates like the hospital systems. Now that there is one overarching corporate body, the thinking goes, is there a strong reason to combine the various parts into a single collection? Since the departments of pediatrics at the various hospitals are merging, should their archival collections merge as well? In situations where administrative rearrangements are frequent, organizational schemes for archival collections can get very complicated. There is no simple answer, but in the author's situation he has decided to maintain parallel collections even where mergers have taken place. The addition of a "Hospital System" collection to the individual hospital collections creates a place for materials from newly merged entities, while maintaining the hospital collections allows hospital-specific information to reside in its natural location.

As a concrete example, the creation of a hospital system-wide Community Relations Department has effectively limited the continuing development of the hospital-based community relations material. All press releases come from a central location; thus, even hospital-specific releases are filed with the hospital system community relations material. While newsletters for particular hospitals are still filed with their respective institutions, most of the rest of the community relations material now belongs to the Hospital System collection.

Whatever the arrangement, a clear descriptive guide to the collections will resolve any issues of how materials are organized. Organization is a matter of intellectual control rather than physical control, and making one's intentions clear in a finding aid or electronic catalog will make life simpler when the archivist is unavailable. Training staff in the whys and wherefores of the archive will enable them to perform basic reference, and a clearly designed guide will enable them to find the materials even in the archivist's absence. Database systems are ideal for archival catalogs, as related but physically separate materials can be linked easily. If, for example, a patron is interested in the development of pediatrics in an area, a database catalog will allow a search through multiple collections containing the right materials. There are archival database programs available for purchase, but this author feels that any decent database, properly constructed, should serve as a good catalog.

There are predetermined means of cataloging archival material: the MARC format has a set of rules for Archives & Manuscripts Control, and there is a more recent effort underway in the archival community to standardize the language and description of archival materials known as EAD, Encoded Archival Description. Using the SGML and XML markup languages, the format is designed to enable institutions to share information about their collections using standardized language,

share their finding aids over the web, as well as link directly to digitized documents.

The idea of sharing the institution's information with the general public, or at least others in the archival community, is an open question for each archives. The value of these different approaches should be measured against the amount of time necessary to master them versus the value of adhering to these standards.

Regardless of the scheme or software used, basics like folder title, box number, location, and collection name are a necessity. In addition, certain critical information about the materials in a collection should be preserved regardless of the scheme used:

- **Names**: Since much of the reference work for archival collections surrounds individuals, a names field is essential.

- **Dates**: General or specific, it is helpful to researchers to be able to find the period they are interested in quickly.

- **Organization**: The author divides this information into two categories, in two separate fields—internal and external. This generic term covers divisions within hospitals, departments, external companies, etc.

- **Notes**: A generic, catch-all field that allows for any additional information that is not easily categorized.

Whatever arrangement is decided on, most archives will need a certain level of customization to fit their own needs.

Basic preservation work should begin as the collections arrive at the archive and any budget for an archive must include funds for archival containers and folders purchased from reputable archival supply houses. A short list of archival suppliers can be found on the **accompanying CD-ROM** in the Additional Readings and Resources document. As the materials are organized, they should be rehoused in nonreactive, acid-free containers. Often the materials will arrive in an odd lot of records containers, U-haul cartons, and grocery-store boxes. Paper materials should be removed from whatever folders they arrive in and be placed in acid-free folders, the folders placed in acid-free archival boxes or record cartons. Board minutes can usually be removed from three-ring or other binders and placed in folders. The rings wear at the paper, and unless there is some evidentiary value to the binder itself, the binders can be discarded.

Like all library materials, boxes should be on shelves and raised above floor level to protect against flooding.

If environmentally sound space can be provided, that is ideal. That is usually not the case, so the medical archivist should work diligently to at the least avoid placement below ground level in spaces with water pipes running through. The space should not be subject to prolonged sun exposure to minimize light damage to materials, and should be secured against unsupervised entry.

Administering Archival Collections

The final goal of the archivist is to make the collections available for use. An unused archive serves no purpose; keeping the materials on the shelf unopened is a pointless exercise. By and large, the archivist does not drive the use of materials; he or she responds to the needs of others. This is not to say that the archivist cannot suggest projects that take advantage of the collections, but most medical librarians taking on this role will already have enough to do.

If an anniversary or similar event drives the formation of the archives, the first use is determined in advance. The organization and description of the materials will enable event planners to see what is available to use for the event, and the archivist can pull the materials as needed. If the collections are significant and the public is made aware of them, outside researchers will contact the archives seeking to use the materials. This does raise an access issue, as some of the materials will be confidential. Archives are usually restricted access by definition, as comparatively few researchers need the primary source materials available there. The archivist should consult with legal counsel about restricting access to sensitive or proprietary materials, as well as vetting materials for HIPAA-protected information.

Other uses that may develop are in-house exercises like newsletters, advertisements, intranet or Internet sites, and other similar public relations activity. Auxiliaries or the medical board may want to review old board minutes or by-laws as part of a process of making changes to those documents. Departments may wish to decorate their spaces with images of former staff members or departmental activity. The legal department may need to see old board minutes so as to understand the institution's obligations or responsibilities in a legal case. In all of these instances the medical archivist will be dealing with in-house clientele, and the relationship should be similar to the one he has in his role as medical librarian. One difference is that archival materials ideally should not circulate, as they have a habit of disappearing forever.

Members of the general public may present more of a challenge. Many archives decide to remain closed to outside users, and the medical archivist may choose that route. If the archive is open to the public, one simply needs to be aware that outsiders arrive with their own needs and desires, which may conflict with the mission of the institution. The archivist may be put in the position of balancing those competing needs when providing access. Bear in mind, though, that section VI of the professional code of ethics for archivists, developed by the Society of American Archivists, stipulates that once records are open to the public, the archivist is obligated to provide equal access to the records (Society of American Archivists, 2005).

Other Concerns

There are numbers of additional issues in archival management that librarians should be aware of. They are well beyond the scope of this limited discussion, but there are several that readers should consider when planning and implementing an archives program.

Records Management

In many organizations there is a direct connection between a Records Management (RM) program and the archive. Briefly, RM is defined by the Association of Records Managers and Administrators (ARMA) as the systematic control of records throughout their life cycle: in short, keeping track of documents from creation through final disposition. If an organization has a records manager, it is vital that the archivist work closely with the manager to ensure that permanent documentation is not lost. The records manager can ensure that permanently valuable materials are transferred to the archive and not mistakenly discarded or destroyed. The archivist can still serve as final decision maker on the permanence of records, but a strong records management program can provide the vital feeder system that delivers critical materials to the archives.

Legal Issues

As stated earlier, one of the key reasons for maintaining an archive is to ensure compliance with relevant federal, state, and local records law. The archivist is not required to be a legal expert on document retention, but it is essential to have a basic familiarity with legal issues surrounding archival materials. This is a complex area, but the following are some basics each archivist should learn something about:

- **Records retention**: What are the statutes and regulations regarding the permanence of materials?

- **HIPAA**: Is the organization a covered entity under HIPAA? Do the materials contain any Protected Health Information (PHI)? Note that photographs, particularly full faces, are considered PHI, and many hospital photographic collections include patient photos.

- **Discovery**: The archives may contain discoverable information in the case of litigation; is the legal department aware of the materials contained in the archives?

- **Copyright**: Archives are covered under the fair use section of U.S. copyright law (see sections 107 & 108 of the U.S. Copyright Code), but archivists need to understand their obligations under these sections. Likewise, noninstitutional records (e.g., faculty papers) may have copyright ramifications when the papers are donated.

- **Donation/gift issues**: When noninstitutional records are donated or gifted to the archives, legal documentation needs to be drawn up to ensure the donation is spelled out clearly, and that all obligations, funding, and tax issues are spelled out correctly to protect both donor and institution.

Again this is a very complex area of archival effort. The national and local archival organizations listed on the **accompanying CD-ROM** in the Additional Readings and Resources document can provide valuable reference tools.

On-Site versus Off-Site Storage

One question that often comes up is the idea of storing archival records off-site. Space is usually at a premium, and many archives cannot afford to develop the proper secured, environmentally controlled storage areas that would be best for these records. Some archives do indeed ship their archival records to off-site storage, but there are concerns that archivists should be aware of.

For one, many off-site storage facilities do not store records under ideal environmental conditions. They may offer it as an additional service, but users will pay more for that controlled space. Second, and probably more important, archivists need to understand all the costs involved in off-site storage. The basic monthly or annual cost for storage is often minimal; $1 per linear foot or less is not unusual. The retrieval fees, however, are considerably higher, especially if the boxes are required quickly. It's vital that the archivist does a proper cost analysis of both storage and retrieval/return costs before looking to store materials off-site.

Electronic Records

The subject of born-digital records is a hot topic in archival literature these days, and probably the most difficult for archivists to manage. As more of an organization's business is done electronically, the management of permanent records has gotten progressively more complex. In addition to understanding the basics of archival value, the archivist needs to understand the varieties of digital formats, storage media, backup and disaster planning, and a host of other IT-related concerns. It's not even enough to be able to save the files; can the archivist also maintain the software programs that read those files? A Microsoft Word document is hard enough to manage; what about WordStar or other discontinued software packages?

It is highly unlikely that the average smaller organization, or the average librarian for that matter, will have the ability to implement a full e-records archival management program. It is important, however, to lay the groundwork by approaching the IT department to seek its help. With enough effort and some IT buy-in, the archivist may be able to minimally identify crucial e-records for long-term preservation. It will probably have to be restricted to the most significant institutional records, but it is a start on a highly complex issue.

Archives Section Summary

The mission of the medical librarian turned archivist is to preserve, protect, and promote to the best of his or her ability the historical record of the institution. This requires skills close enough to their everyday work to be familiar and yet far enough away to leave the newly minted archivist feeling lost. The key items for the new archivist to remember are these:

- The materials in each facility will be unique to that institution.

- There needs to be institutional support for the program in order to be successful.

- The involvement of an archival consultant can greatly assist the planning process, and help the program avoid major mistakes.

- A well-thought-out organizational scheme, planned in advance, will simplify the task.

- The organizational scheme needs to be clear and easy for a successor to understand and maintain.

- Databases or finding aids should provide enough information to allow the collections to be used quickly and easily.

- Basic preservation work through rehousing of materials is absolutely essential to preserve the materials for posterity.

A basic understanding of the differences between a librarian and an archivist, some background learning or coursework, and a lot of determination will enable the librarian to become an archivist almost painlessly.

Supporting Multimedia Creation and Collections

The life cycle of information involves three interrelated phases: creation, management, and use. An information resource is *created* when ideas are written down, recorded, or captured in some way. It is *managed* when it is organized, described, and classified with subject terms and other metadata. Information is *used* by practitioners, students, and researchers to inform decision making and/or to advance scholarship by feeding into the creation of new information resources. The circular nature of these phases is illustrated in Figure 15.1.

Traditionally, librarians have functioned in the *management* and *use* phases of the information life cycle, organizing physical collections and facilitating or controlling access to them. These will continue to be important functions. However, as collections become increasingly digital and search interfaces more end-user friendly, the idea of the librarian as the ultimate gatekeeper to information is rapidly eroding. Fortunately, our skills as information professionals help us adapt to new roles if we remain open to nontraditional possibilities.

Many emerging roles for librarians have increased emphasis on the *creation* phase of the information life cycle. This section describes ways for librarians to support information resource creation within academic, research, and health care organizations.

Audio, Video, and Presentations

In an effort to better prepare students for real-world work experiences, health sciences curriculum developers are incorporating more group work and problem-based learning (Neville, 2009; Koh et al., 2008). Written papers are no longer the only products from assignments. Students (and the health professionals they become) work in nontext formats such as digital audio and video. They produce presentations and websites involving complex graphics and data visualizations. For more information about trends in health sciences education and the library's involvement, see Chapter 11.

The concept of the learning commons (sometimes called an information commons, or knowledge commons) was introduced in Chapter 9 as a factor to consider when planning library spaces. The learning commons is a place for library users to gather and process information, then to synthesize that information into new resources they create (Steiner and Holley, 2009). Put more concretely, it is a place to access the hardware and software necessary to produce projects in a variety of formats. The learning commons is also a place for users to connect with knowledgeable staff, often a mix of library and IT staff, who can provide some level of technical instruction and troubleshoot hardware and software issues. Two web examples are the Oregon State University Libraries with their *Library a la carte* (http://alacarte.library.oregonstate.edu/) and the University of Iowa Libraries with their *Information commons* (http://www.lib.uiowa.edu/hardin/infocommons.html).

Faculty, students, and other stakeholders should be involved in the early stages of planning, because the best mix of hardware and software varies widely according to the institution's specific needs. Following is a list of hardware and software, beyond the standard office suite, that might be included in a modern learning commons.

Figure 15.1. The Life Cycle of Information

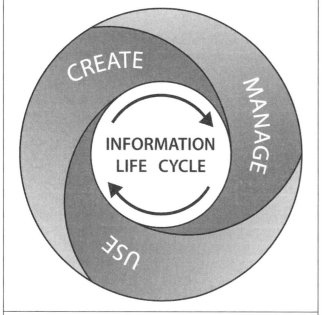

Source: Adapted from University of Kansas, http://www.provost.ku.edu/infomanagement/info.shtml.

- For loan: Laptops, DVD players, digital projectors, digital video cameras, tripods, audio recorders, microphones, mobile devices, and e-book readers
- Video and audio production software
- Studio space for audio and video recording
- Computer stations with large monitors to facilitate group work
- Interactive whiteboards such as SMART boards for presentation practice
- Color printers
- High-quality scanners
- Image manipulation software
- Statistical and graphing applications
- Virtual reality and simulation software
- Web development software

In many ways, the learning commons concept is an extension of more traditional library audiovisual services. In the first edition of this book, the chapter "Managing Audiovisual Services" includes step-by-step guidance about selecting, processing, maintaining, and circulating AV equipment; providing projectionist services; and designating space in the library to be an AV viewing area. Some of the equipment described (slide projectors, VCR/TV monitors, audiocassette players) is nearing obsolescence, but the chapter remains an excellent reference for those who are new to selecting and maintaining media equipment (Phillips and Weitkemper, 2000).

This idealized vision of the learning commons may seem out of reach for most medical libraries, which are smaller, have more specialized clientele, and face significant budget challenges due to the high cost of medical journals and monographs. The degree to which library staff can support a learning commons depends on the number of available staff, their skills and interests, and competing priorities. Physical space limitations are also a big concern, as making room for more computer equipment often involves significant weeding of the circulating collection. Given these challenges, however, medical library managers should think about how to scale back the commons idea to develop services that are practical, sustainable, and customized to the needs of their organization (Boyd, 2008).

Supporting Distance Education

Distance education technologies such as virtual learning environments and web conferences are frequently used to deliver instruction to health sciences students. These same technologies provide a convenient and cost-effective way for health care providers to access continuing education opportunities. Distance education also presents new technological and pedagogical challenges to instructors. Medical library staff might support distance education by providing facilities, decision support, and training for instructors looking to optimize their use of new technology.

Blackboard (http://www.blackboard.com), Moodle (http://moodle.org), and Second Life (http://secondlife.com) are examples of virtual learning environments. These products allow instructors to build customized course portals by choosing from a menu of module options. A course portal typically includes links to readings, schedules, assignments, and syllabi, a discussion board, and (if the course is for credit) a place for students to upload assignments. Other features, such as live chat, videos, and interactive quizzes, may be incorporated as well. Some virtual learning environment software, such as Blackboard, is proprietary. Open source software is an option for organizations with limited funds but adequate IT and server support. Moodle and Sakai (http://sakaiproject.org) are two open source virtual learning environments with active developer communities. Second Life is a graphics-intensive virtual world in which participants create avatars and navigate through different environments, interacting with other avatars as well as virtual objects. A number of educational institutions, health care organizations, and even the Centers for Disease Control and Prevention have experimented with using Second Life as a way to engage learners (Beard et al., 2009).

Web conferences allow students and instructors to interact in real time, but from different geographic locations. As the technology has improved, web conferencing is increasingly accepted as a viable alternative to in-person meetings. It saves on travel costs and reduces the burden of schedule conflicts. Librarians may be asked for (or could offer to provide) input on web conferencing software solutions that would be the best fit for the organization. Most software providers allow free trial periods, allowing potential customers to host test meetings in order to evaluate usability and test various features. Factors to consider in evaluating web conferencing software include:

- System requirements, operating system and browser compatibility
- Price and billing structure
- The maximum number of attendees per meeting
- The method of audio. Is it VoIP (voice over internet protocol) or telephone-based?

- Overall picture and sound quality
- Site security and privacy options
- Requirements for meeting attendees. Will they need to install software and/or plug-ins in advance?
- File sharing options. Is it possible to upload presentation files and other documents? Is upload speed a problem?
- Availability and usability of desired extra features, which might include text chat, webcam support, the ability to record and play back meetings, polling, and collaboration tools
- Quality of user support services and help files

Libraries with learning commons, classroom, or conference room space can also support the organization by allowing those spaces to be reserved for group participation in web meetings and video broadcasts. When lectures and other events are held on site, the library might provide video recording and/or streaming media services to make these events accessible to more people. Streaming media is so named because it is delivered to the users in a continuous stream over the Internet, rather than being downloaded. Streaming media requires a specialized web server and some knowledge of video file compression formats. A chapter in the book *Medical Librarian 2.0* provides guidance on how to establish streaming media services, along with a case study about digital video production at the University of Utah's Eccles Health Sciences Library (Lombardo, Dennis, and Cowan, 2007).

Library database instruction lends itself to screencasting: the recording of actions performed on a computer screen, sometimes with audio narration, for purposes of demonstrating a computer-based task. Screencasts also serve other purposes within health care organizations. For example, they could be used to help train clinical staff in the use of a new electronic health record system. Adobe Captivate (http://www.adobe.com/products/captivate/), TechSmith Camtasia (http://www.techsmith.com/camtasia.asp), and similar software can be used to record and edit professional-looking screencasts. A number of free and inexpensive web-based screencasting tools are also available and are perfectly sufficient for recording quick demonstrations. Many of these tools are integrated with popular online social networks for easy sharing. Screencasts produced in formats such as .swf (Flash), .mov (Quicktime), and .wmv (Windows Media Player) can be easily incorporated on course pages and websites. Other production settings generate screencasts optimized for mobile devices.

For examples of high-quality screencast productions, watch the series of video tutorials from Yale University's Cushing/Whitney Library (http://cwml-tutorials.blogspot.com/).

Library managers should, at the very least, be aware of the distance education technologies in place at the parent institution. Instruction librarians should seek out opportunities to integrate links to library resources and tutorials when appropriate. In some cases, the library may be in charge of maintaining distance learning platforms, such as web conferencing software subscriptions and course management tools, for the entire organization. Full and optimal support for distance learning technology by a library would involve part-time commitments from acquisitions staff, systems staff, and instruction librarians.

Social Media

Social media websites like blogs, wikis, and social networking are in wide use at academic institutions but are often blocked by IT at hospital libraries due to security concerns or the perception that employees would waste time if allowed to access these tools. In recent years, though, social media has become an integral part of how we interact as professionals and with our constituents. Restrictions are loosening, especially as hospitals see the value in using social media for public relations. Hospital web manager Ed Bennett has assembled a list of more than 800 hospitals currently using Facebook, Twitter, and YouTube (Bennett, 2010).

Librarians can take a proactive role in shaping social media policy in organizations that are new to the idea by staying current on effective uses of the technology as well as privacy and ethical issues that accompany its use. The Medical Library Association, the Special Libraries Association, and the National Network of Libraries of Medicine frequently offer continuing education courses and webinars about emerging technology topics. Many of these social media courses are taught online using the same social media tools being discussed. Rethlefsen, Piorun, and Prince (2009) reported on one such successful course in which more than 600 MLA members participated in 2008.

Managing Traditional Audiovisual Collections

The first edition of this book describes a number of pre–digital audiovisual program formats, such as 35mm slides, videocassettes, and overhead transparencies, which have been important elements of library collections in the recent past (Phillips and Weitkemper, 2000). With the hardware needed to view these media formats nearing obsolescence, most health science libraries now make it a policy to only collect audiovisual materials in digital formats. If materials in older formats are still in high demand and similar materials are not available in a newer format, the library will likely need to maintain the equipment, such as 35mm slide projectors, necessary to use the media. Equipment like this is rarely produced anymore so is difficult to replace. Another option is to use a service to have the material migrated to a digital format. This can be expensive and there are copyright considerations involved.

In most libraries, managing physical audiovisual program collections requires sufficiently less staff time today than it did a decade ago. Today, it is common for medical textbooks to come with supplementary material on compact disc. DVD and high definition Blu-ray discs have replaced videotape. These new formats are generally a lot more durable than tapes and films, requiring very little physical maintenance beyond cleaning discs periodically and replacing cracked and broken cases. They can also be used on library computers, eliminating the need for the library to maintain televisions and audio players on site.

Presentation programs such as PowerPoint and Keynote have replaced 35mm slides and transparencies. High quality images, streaming audio and video content can now be licensed online, eliminating the need for individual libraries to manage any physical media at all, although licensing does present its own unique challenges. While not considered "technology" necessarily, anatomical models are an exception to the rule of ever-changing formats. Physical models of the skeleton and organ systems are still collected by medical libraries and, despite computer-based options, remain popular with students and health care providers.

Supporting Multimedia Creation and Collections Summary

Providing support for multimedia creation challenges librarians to expand their own proficiencies with hardware and software beyond the standard office and library applications. Likewise, maintaining a useful and used audiovisual collection requires staying tuned in to library users' preferred viewing formats, and to the particular ways in which consuming media is part of their workflow. As time and resources permit, taking on these challenges can be a good way to position the library as an even more indispensable unit within the larger educational setting or hospital.

Supporting Scholarly Publications

Scholarly publications include research articles, book chapters, reviews, and case studies, usually for peer-reviewed journals or textbooks. The scholarly publishing landscape is in a period of significant change right now due to a proliferation of electronic journal options and the growing open access movement. Chapter 7 introduces some of the implications of electronic journals and open access from a collection development perspective. This section introduces some practical ways for librarians to guide health sciences researchers through the publication process.

Citation Managers

Libraries commonly provide print style guides and manuals for the appropriate formatting of manuscripts. Research libraries might also consider purchasing a site license for bibliographic citation management software such as EndNote, RefWorks, or a similar product. Citation management software integrates with most commercial databases to import and save bibliographic information, which can then be formatted and reformatted according to any number of citation style formats. This software also integrates with word processing software to greatly simplify the process of creating parenthetical citations, footnotes, and reference lists. The University of Wisconsin-Madison Libraries maintain a detailed chart comparing popular citation management programs in terms of cost, technical specifications, database and record structure, and import, export and other features (http://www.library.wisc.edu/citation-managers/comparison.html). It is possible to search the MEDLINE database from directly within many citation manager interfaces. This method, however, is not recommended for in-depth searching (Gomis, Gall, and Brahmi, 2008).

Submitting Manuscripts for Publication

Another way librarians can facilitate information resource creation is to support researchers in the process of submitting article manuscripts for publication. Potential authors are concerned with finding the widest and most appropriate readership for their articles, then moving through the submission, peer-review, resubmission and publication processes as efficiently as possible.

Potential authors should be made aware of the benefits and drawbacks of choosing to publish in open access journals and institutional repositories. These benefits include greater exposure for the work, often a faster time to publication, and eliminating the need for the library to have to "buy back" by subscribing to the journal.

Journal reputation is an important factor to consider when seeking the widest possible audience for a scholarly article. The most well-known metric for journal reputation is the impact factor, which is calculated annually by Thomson Reuters (previously from the Institute for Scientific Information) and published in *Journal Citation Reports*. The impact factor is "a measure of the frequency with which the 'average article' in a journal has been cited in a particular year or period" (Thomson Reuters, 2010).

Researchers should take care to avoid overreliance on the impact factor as a measure of journal quality and professional success. Likewise, librarians should use caution when considering the impact factor, or any general journal quality metric, in collection development decisions. The impact factor has been criticized for being too easily influenced by the types of articles journals choose to publish, and for not accounting for citation pattern differences in different fields (Althouse et al., 2009; Thomson Reuters, 2010). Two alternative reputation metrics are the Eigenfactor (Bergstrom, 2007), which uses an algorithm for ranking journals based on the idea of Google's algorithm for ranking webpages and the H-index, which evaluates the impact of journal articles individually as well as the reputations of authors (Hirsch, 2005).

Once a potential author has come to a decision about where to submit a manuscript, he or she must determine the appropriate next steps. Publishers have different procedures and requirements for article submission, and it can be a challenge to keep track of the details. The University of Toledo's Mulford Library maintains a database of links to Instructions for Authors pages for more than 6,000 health science journals (http://mulford.utoledo .edu/instr/) that can be linked from the library webpage. The database is searchable by journal title or keyword.

Copyright and Authors' Rights

Authors and librarians share a mutual interest in making published articles as accessible as possible within the bounds of the law. Information creators such as published authors could benefit from knowing more about their intellectual property rights. Librarians, being already acquainted with copyright from an information use perspective (in the context of interlibrary loan, for example), can be natural partners in helping potential authors make sense of copyright issues associated with information creation.

Partly in response to unsustainable journal price increases, the Association of Research Libraries developed the Scholarly Publishing & Academic Resources Coalition (SPARC) in 1997 to mobilize libraries to advocate for open access scholarly communication models. One of SPARC's many successful projects has been its Authors' Rights initiative. In signing contracts with journal publishers, authors often unnecessarily sign away certain rights, such as the rights to reproduce, share, and repurpose the article for noncommercial purposes. SPARC's Author Rights Addendum (http:// www.arl.org/sparc/author/index.shtml) is a useful template document authors can attach to publication contracts to ensure that these rights are maintained.

The NIH Public Access Policy

The NIH Public Access Policy, passed into law in 2008, imposes new requirements on authors who publish articles based on research that was funded by the National Institutes of Health (National Institutes of Health, 2010). These requirements include depositing the work, via the NIH Manuscript Submission (NIHMS) system, into the PubMed Central repository within twelve months of publication. Authors of articles based on NIH research must cite specific identifiers on all future grant applications. The consequences of noncompliance are significant. Those who fail to comply may find themselves delayed or ineligible to receive future funding from NIH. Librarians supporting NIH-funded authors should maintain an awareness of this policy in order to provide guidance to those who are confused about navigating the unfamiliar procedures and requirements. A PowerPoint presentation developed by MLA's Ad Hoc Committee for Advocating Scholarly Communication provides a useful overview for librarians and is included on the **accompanying CD-ROM**. MLA's website on the subject (http://www.mlanet .org/resources/publish/sc_nih_policy.html) has background information and links to various libraries that have programs to support this law.

Institutional Repositories

An institutional repository is an online archive of intellectual works produced at a university or other academic or research institution. Items deposited in an institutional repository typically include text documents such as article manuscripts, dissertations, and theses, but may also include teaching materials, presentation slides, videos, laboratory notes, and even datasets. As of this writing, the Directory of Open Access Resources lists 252 institutions in the United States with Institutional Repositories (University of Nottingham, 2010).

As discussed in Chapter 7, repositories offer a way for institutions to take back some control over access and preservation of their intellectual property. Information professionals have a critical role in the successful implementation and development of repositories. However, embarking on such a project requires a substantial investment of money and staff time.

Responsibility for repository development commonly falls to one librarian with a position related to digital libraries and scholarly communication initiatives. Possible job titles include Institutional Repository Librarian, Scholarly Communication Librarian, Metadata Librarian, and Digital Services Librarian. This librarian should have digital preservation experience and a working knowledge of open source and proprietary digital library platforms. He or she should also be familiar with traditional and open access publishing practices, author's rights, copyright, and associated issues. Political savvy is another important attribute for institutional repository developers. Faculty and administrators may need to be convinced of the benefits of contributing their work to a repository.

In addition to the How-To-Do-It Manual cited in Chapter 7 (Reese and Banerjee 2008), SPARC maintains a list of helpful resources for learning about and implementing institutional repositories (http://www.arl.org/sparc/repositories/index.shtml). Among these resources is a report from the Association of Research Libraries Digital Repository Issues Task Force (Association of Research Libraries, 2009). This report assesses the current state of affairs with regard to library involvement in digital repositories and suggests strategies for future success. It includes case studies about several specific repositories representing a range of service delivery options.

Most institutional repositories, like most academic institutions, are multidisciplinary and incorporate content from the arts and humanities as well as the sciences. Because of this, there are relatively few examples in the literature about institutional repositories falling under the auspices of the health sciences library. At Thomas Jefferson University, a health sciences campus, librarians have maintained the Jefferson Digital Commons repository since 2005. Koopman and Kipnis (2009) describe this project, which has evolved over time into an original publishing platform. Piorun and Palmer (2008) of Lamar Souter Library at the University of Massachusetts Medical Center provide a detailed analysis of the costs and processes involved in digitizing more than 300 dissertations for a new institutional repository.

MANAGEMENT IN ACTION 15.2

New Services to Meet Evolving Customer Needs

Description of Problem/Project: The Arnold Library at Fred Hutchinson Cancer Research Center (FHCRC) in Seattle, Washington, has implemented a number of services to guide faculty through complex new publication and grant requirements resulting from the NIH Public Access Policy. These services include training for faculty and support staff, direct NIHMS deposits, and NIHMS usage coaching, follow-up with publishers regarding proper submission of manuscripts to PubMed Central, and the hosting and promotion of an Institutional Repository.

Impact On: Improved institutional and faculty compliance with the NIH Public Access Policy; greater exposure for faculty works; significant time and money savings for FHCRC faculty and staff

People Involved: Library Director, Scholarly Communications Librarian

Strategies for Success: Develop a brand identity and follow up with an intense promotion of the new services through awareness-raising presentations, individual face-to-face communication, e-mail, newsletters, posters, flow charts, and frequent training sessions. Coordination of service design and practice with General Counsel's office and the Office of Sponsored Research.

Barriers Encountered: Working through the complexities of copyright, the new rules and regulations, and keeping up with evolving NIHMS protocols.

Take-Home Points: The staff at Arnold Library worked quickly to create new services that are directly related to an urgent need for their constituents.

Resource: Fred Hutchinson Cancer Research Center, Arnold Library. Open Access Service. Accessed October 1, 2010. http://www.fhcrc.org/science/shared_resources/library/services/authors/index.html.

Supporting Scholarly Publications Summary

Librarians have long been called upon to assist authors with manuscript preparation and obtaining or retaining copyright permissions. New citation management tools such as the ones mentioned in this section provide new opportunities for librarians to respond to these standard needs. On the other hand, the open access movement, the NIH Public Access Policy, and the institutional repositories concept are all emerging ideas and will continue to increase in relevance for library users. The MLA webpage "Scholarly Communications Issues" (http://www.mlanet.org/resources/publish/) is a great starting place to learn about these issues and well as keep up with trends. Librarians would be well-advised to stay ahead of the curve.

Tracking Institutional Publications

Librarians are experienced in searching the literature, and also have a working knowledge of publisher standards. Therefore, it is appropriate for librarians to play an active role in collecting information about their institution's scholarly publishing and assisting, as needed, in managing this function. Whether the parent institution is large or small, or if only a few people publish each year, librarians can still track this information and publicize the results in innovative ways. Besides the section author's article (Englander, 2003), there are several other reports in the literature about various programs (Fitzpatrick, 2007; Goe, Herrera, and Mower, 1998; Mischke et al., 2004; O'Brien, Davis, and Leman, 2008).

Designing Your Product: Who, What, Where, How

When perusing websites of other institutions, or those of physicians, one will often find a link to publications. These links can be to an internally developed database or to an external database, such as PubMed. Sometimes the link goes to a word-processed file or PDF, or perhaps a CV compiled by the clinician or someone compiling it on his behalf. To avoid inconsistencies in style and format, even within one organization, it is advantageous to have this managed from a central location, and the library is an obvious partner. If all the institution's data are collected in one place, subsequent publicity and dissemination of this information would be standardized and uniform.

In conjunction with the institution's administration, or Library Committee, the first step would be to determine whose publications to collect and what types of publications will be included. After these questions are answered, the librarian can then strategize on how to identify these materials, how to manage them, and how to help produce a final product.

The anticipated quantity of publications may help determine how to manage the information. If there are only a few publications a year, information could be maintained in a word-processed document, or on a wiki or blog, as long as steps are taken to ensure that all data

are keyed similarly. If there are many publications, a database program may be better. A reference management program will help ensure standardization for formats and outputs. If maintaining physical copies of all publications is part of the process, the volume will help determine the proper storage venue. It may be a file cabinet, a PDF collection stored on a computer, or it may be links to external databases or electronic journals. AutoAlerts can be created in a variety of databases to help regularly identify publications in a timely manner. In addition, employees can submit information directly, and publisher sites and book vendors can also be valuable resources.

Identifying the Proper Publications

Once the process begins, it will become clear where there may be challenges in gathering appropriate information. Perhaps there are people with common names and isolating the appropriate publications doesn't seem possible. Scoville, Johnson, and McConnell (2003) describe strategies for capturing publications by the correct author. Or, perhaps there is a new journal in which employees are publishing, but access to the journal to verify the information is not possible. Solutions to these issues will vary. Contacting the clinician directly may be a good start; contacting the journal publisher to help verify a reference is also an option.

Final Product

After the information is gathered and the format is standardized, it is time to share and publicize the results. The institution's needs along with the volume of data will determine the scope of the publicity. It can be as formal as a web-based database or a printed book, to something as informal as names on a bulletin board or in a newsletter. Some institutions may also be interested in associating these publications with impact factors, or other indices, and using publications information in outcomes and productivity reports.

Tracking Publications Summary

Involving the library in gathering, managing, and disseminating the institution's scholarly publication activity is appropriate. Librarians can ensure quality and consistency in documentation. Their knowledge of publishing practices, indexing, and database searching strategies can be useful when specific questions arise and to identify appropriate resources. Whether the process is handled

Checklist for Tracking Institutional Publications

The following list provides some questions to consider as you develop your product; the questions were adapted from Englander (2003: 85). Since each institution is unique, there will be a lot of variation in the response to these questions. Englander also provides additional questions, including detailed examples from the Cleveland Clinic's experience (Englander, 2003).

- What data will be collected? Articles, books, book chapters, book reviews, product reviews, letters to the editor, editorials, electronic publications, Internet-only publications, meeting abstracts, oral presentations, poster sessions, blogs, newspaper columns, websites, patents? What about other nontraditional sources of scholarly publication?
- Whose data will be collected? Physicians, nurses, all employees? If the institution is part of a multisite network, will publications from other sites be of interest?
- How will the data be stored and organized? Which commercial products will be evaluated?
- How will the data be used? What output and search strategies will be necessary? If the database management program doesn't support every desired function, how can the software be modified or adapted to meet specific needs?
- How will appropriate publications be identified? Which databases/other sources should be checked? How often? How can literature searches be constructed for optimum retrieval? What direct input will employees have?
- Are all journals equal? Does it matter if a journal isn't peer-reviewed? What about journals that aren't indexed? What about newsletters? Will items that cannot be verified at all be included? What about online only, Open Access, ahead of print, in press, and submitted publications?
- How will discrepancies in indexing standards/data entry between vendors be handled? In absence of an original, what will be the authoritative source? Will information from a monographic serial be considered a book chapter or a journal article?
- Will keywords or subject headings be assigned to citations? If so, how will the vocabulary be standardized?
- Will additional information be included with the citations, and, if so, what? Summaries, abstracts, Digital Object Identifiers (DOIs), other vendor accession numbers? Data that tie the citation to the library's collection?
- Will links to electronic access or full-text be included? Depending on licensing issues, this can be a valuable asset.
- Will print copies of each publication be maintained? This may be influenced by staff time, financial resources available, size of the database, and space.
- Will information be accessible to others, and how will this be accomplished?
- If plans include posting information on a public website, will the library be able to supply print copies, if asked? If so, how will this be accomplished and how will copyright be handled?
- What will the final product be? How will it be promoted and advertised?
- Is publishing required for promotion or tenure? Will publications information be included in annual reports or other marketing materials? If so, can your product be the institution's resource for this information?
- Will authors be honored/acknowledged? If so, how?

manually, or whether automated programs are used, involving the library in the process will be worthwhile.

In addition, knowledge of an institution's publishing patterns and trends can assist with the library's acquisitions and serials management functions. Knowing the number of institution-authored publications in various journals can help determine whether specific titles should be added to the library's collection, how long to maintain a subscription, or whether to subscribe to a title electronically.

Although most physicians have an idea of what they have published, they often don't have copies of these articles or document the publications accurately. Physicians, secretaries, and administrators will be relieved to know that there is a centralized source for this information and that data are standardized and current. Regardless of the final product and its related uses, the institution and all authors will be proud of these publishing accomplishments.

Library Staff Publications of a Marketing Nature

Marketing and promoting library service is covered in Chapter 3 with descriptions of various traditional media such as newsletters, brochures, and annual reports that can be used to bring library services to the attention of it's customers. Some of these traditional outlets, such as a newsletter, can be transformed into a blog. Some library services can be used by the web public and need a different kind of promotion. These types of services can be promoted using Web 2.0 technologies.

Increasingly, librarians are taking advantage of the opportunities that Web 2.0, such as blogs and wikis and social media such as Facebook, Twitter, or YouTube, offer to raise the visibility of their libraries. Librarians can also establish their own personal brands, which can act as the public face of their libraries among their peers, patrons, and the general public. The upside of this trend is that it leverages the skills librarians already possess such as writing ability, excitement about one's field, and a plethora of library services to showcase. The downside is that what goes out onto the web generally stays on the web and one can sometimes be somewhat overly and imprudently candid in one's comment in social media venues.

Maintaining an active web presence is also labor intensive and time-consuming. It sometimes takes a hard sell to one's managers, both in the library and to administrators generally. The list below outlines various types of venues where the library staff can publish information about their unique services or if they have a new twist on a traditional service.

- **Articles in scholarly journals**: One can publish articles about web services the library has developed so as to showcase them to the library community. Scholarly articles also give community web services some substance and weight that can appeal to grantors.

- **Articles in non-peer-reviewed, information science-related periodicals**: Writing here about services the library has developed can showcase them to the wider library community and the producer can connect with those who are engaged in similar projects.

- **Articles in professional association newsletters**: Here one can connect with peers both within and outside of one's region and discuss issues of interest to all.

- **Blog postings on professional association blogs**: Besides networking within the library profession, in this medium one can ask for assistance or input

MANAGEMENT IN ACTION 15.3

Promoting the Use of a Web Service via Networking among Professional Organizations and Periodical Publication

Location: Hospital Library

Description of Problem: Need for greater awareness among the general public, and library colleagues in particular, of a web service developed by library staff. The hit rates for the service need to go up and remain high to continue.

Impact On: The library staff and the hit rate of the web service.

People Involved: Librarian and librarian's supervisor

Strategies for Success: The librarian joins sections of the Medical Library Association (e.g., the Nursing and Allied Health Resources; Technical Services) to learn about similar services and to note opportunities to publish in section newsletters or to post items in their electronic discussion lists about her service. Librarian also joins other professional organizations such as the Special Libraries Association (SLA), the American Society for Information Science & Technology (ASIST), and various committees of the Association of College and Research Libraries (ACRL) to do much the same thing among their divisions and special interest groups. She learns via the discussion lists of these groups not only about opportunities to publish items in their newsletters about her service but about calls for papers for scholarly journals and calls for presentations at conferences that offer additional opportunities to promote her service. Librarian also notes calls for papers on blogs such as A Library Writer's Blog (http://librarywriting.blogspot.com/) and lines up publishing opportunities via emails to editors of publications such as *Online* and *Computers in Libraries*.

Barriers Encountered: Membership in multiple professional organizations can reach into the low four-figures and travel to conferences is often not funded by librarian's institution. In addition, it can be hard to quantify time spent on professional networking and manager must be flexible and allow librarian to work at home when the latter is working on an article with a fast approaching deadline.

Take-Home Points: Promoting a web service is a never-ending process and requires money for professional organization membership, for travel to conferences at which librarian presents papers or posters, and time for writing and correspondence with editors about articles. Managers should confer with librarian periodically so as to agree on when such activities are valuable to the promotion of the web service and when too much of this activity causes problems with the smooth functioning of the library.

about services under development. The comment feature can be used to collect ideas.

- **Blog postings and comments on nonlibrary blogs and websites**: This is an excellent way to reach out to those outside the library profession such as those in scholarly publishing, informatics, the e-patient, participatory medicine, and open science movements. An example of the open science movement blog would be Significant Science (http://significantscience.com).

- **Podcasts of interviews of others conducted by library staff**: Interviews of clinical or administrative staff at one's own institution or of community leaders in health care could be featured on the library's website or blog.

- **Podcasts of interviews with library staff about library science matters generally**: These also could be featured on the library's website or blog.

- **Profiles of library staff in outside publications**: These could be in-print publications, blogs, or websites of other libraries or institutions. These are an excellent way to raise the web profile of one's library and institution and to increase traffic to the services mentioned in the interview. In talking to the media, there may be a corporate policy to go through the public affairs or public relations department first.

- **Video presentations or screencasts**: Web video clips or screencasts (see above) can showcase a library's services and illustrate their features and use. These can be used by other librarians who need to explain the same material to their users. Such uses by other libraries can increase the library's web presence.

Bookstores and Other Retail Services of Libraries

Libraries sometimes conduct retail operations to raise funds. Some public libraries have started bookstores run by volunteers (Barr, 2004). In health care, these operations can be as informal as simple book ordering services for staff or book corners in hospital gift shops, wellness centers, or pharmacies. They can also be formal, such as bookstores clearly identified as such, either within the library itself in a separate room or in a setting elsewhere in the larger institution. They might have a small stock of new books but rely mostly on ordering upon request. In academic settings, there is usually a campus bookstore so having a bookstore in the library is less likely.

The positive side of maintaining such operations is that librarians can sometimes raise the visibility of their libraries and increase foot traffic simply by leveraging their know-how in stocking the latest in medical, nursing, or consumer health titles. The negative side is that keeping up on such matters and devoting the time it takes to make a success of it in retail. On the informal side, most libraries sell their withdrawn books, either on a shelf continuously or at an annual sale. Some libraries are now using a bookseller to sell their withdrawn books on the Internet. If working for a not-for-profit, always clear such activities with accounting and/or materials management.

Operations such as coffee shops or cafés run by the library would require food-handling licenses and capital outlay, so many libraries contract with outside restaurants or chains to operate the service. The interactions with the public, regular patrons, and staff from other departments compensate for occasional difficulties. Cafés or coffee shops inside libraries help create a sense of place and create friendly and inviting spaces. If designing a new or renovating library space as discussed in Chapter 9, this idea should be considered. The idea of providing great service, giving people a reason to spend time in the library, and simply offering enjoyment is too great an opportunity to disregard (Harris, 2007). Ray Oldenburg (1991), an urban sociologist, in his book *A Great Good Place*, hypothesized that time is primarily spent in isolated first (home) and second (work) places. In contrast, third places offer a neutral public space for a community to connect and establish bonds. Third places host the regular, voluntary, informal, and happily anticipated gatherings of individuals beyond the realms of home and work. This theory could be expanded to include the workplace in general with one's office being the first place and perhaps meetings being the second place. So the library could see itself as in competition with the staff lounge or the cafeteria for the third place. Many hospital libraries are situated near the medical staff lounge. The librarian could take advantage of that in some way, perhaps treating it as if it were the library's coffee shop and allowing coffee to be brought into the library space.

Although beverages are not crucial in developing a third place, the enjoyment of conversation over a cup of coffee certainly adds to the experience. Due to their ability to attract a large and diverse range of users and the prominent position they hold in many communities, public libraries are creating a sense of community. Their cafés appear to be an integral part of their development as a new third place. (Harris, 2007: 145)

Gorbe (2005) studied the issue of library coffee shops in her master's thesis, incorporating the ideas of Oldenburg. Looking into the debate in the library community concerning whether libraries should invest in library coffee shops, she found most writings were based on personal opinions, unsubstantiated by experience. She surveyed library managers and found an overwhelming theme was apparent and every manager reported a coffee shop to be a positive addition to a library, whether they had started it or it had existed when they were hired.

Institutional Satellite Facilities

Many librarians these days find themselves responsible for managing multiple and disparate sites in the form of institutional satellite facilities. Examples include small libraries in health career training centers for professions such as radiology technicians, pharmacy technicians, surgical technologists, certified nursing assistants, etc.; wellness center libraries such as those catering to heart and diabetes patients or those seeking complementary and alternative treatments; cancer center libraries; and those libraries for nursing education programs. The most common satellite facility is a consumer health service somewhere near the center of patient activity. The principles of this service are covered in Chapter 14.

Each type of satellite facility requires management of collection development and staffing including enlisting volunteers. Such operations demand at least some on-site inspection from time to time by the librarian if only for weeding of outdated materials and to ensure basic cleanliness of the facility. With some thought, labor, web know-how, and adroit diplomacy, a librarian with these satellite facilities could develop checkout procedures and a simple web-reference service using the intranet and public web presence in cooperation of with the hosting department.

Other Associated Services

As noted at the beginning of this chapter, in the results of an October 2009 informal survey and as shown in Chapter 3, Figure 3.1, the term "associated services" encompasses a broad range of programs and services. As librarians gain confidence in creating and marketing unique associated services, they can start considering developing similar services. In this section, some of the programs and services mentioned by respondents are examined in more depth.

Web Services Associated with Information Provision

ScanGrants (http://www.scangrants.com) is an example of a way that librarians can create a web service that can help raise the internal and public profile of their libraries. The downside of such services is that once launched, they require maintenance in technological quality control, staff time, and effort vis-à-vis updating the listings.

Launched in 2008, ScanGrants is a public service listing of grants and other funding types to support health research, programs, and scholarship. Designed to facilitate searches for funding sources to enhance individual and community health, the opportunities listed on ScanGrants may be of interest to virtually anyone associated with the health field: medical researchers, social workers, nurses, students, community-based health educators, academics, and others. ScanGrants has been described in several publications (Leman, 2008a,b; Leman, 2010b,c).

Originally developed as a tool for the staff of Samaritan Health Services, a health network in Corvallis, Oregon, and surrounding cities, it was quickly realized that ScanGrants would be of value to the wider biomedical community and general public, as very few free health care and clinical research-focused grant and scholarship listing services exist. ScanGrants lists grants and scholarship opportunities in more than 400 health categories, covering topics such as molecular genetics, leukemia, heart disease, and critical care nursing.

The creation of web services such as ScanGrants opens up opportunities for librarians in the areas of professional publication since one can write about such services in librarianship periodicals. Such projects are intellectually rewarding and can increase institutional reputation by linking to fields outside of the field of librarianship proper, such as the search engine industry and the

Due to the success of ScanGrants, Samaritan Health Services developed a new service called ResearchRaven (http://www.researchraven.com), which provides users with a broad web-based platform of resources, including a portal for finding professional conferences and calls for papers and presentations. These services are particularly important for graduate students and scientists at the young investigator level. ResearchRaven is an example of a service that draws upon content freely available on the World Wide Web. It aggregates the content and renders it subscribable and searchable, thereby saving time for the user. The discovery process is shortened. This is an example of librarians leveraging free content and free services such as FeedBurner to develop new services for new audiences. (Leman, 2010a,c) emerging movements of Open Science and Medicine 2.0. Moreover, such projects endow librarians with practical experience in website design, grantsmanship (given that such services are often grant-fueled themselves), public speaking, and marketing. The development of ScanGrants as a library web service fits well with what librarians often already do, assisting those looking for grants, scholarships, and science prizes.

Providing Business, Human Resources, and Insurance Information Services

As government policies demand that the health care sector control costs, librarians are increasingly called upon to conduct searches related to the topic of cost effectiveness and comparative effectiveness. As a result, health sciences librarians are expanding their professional skill sets to include the concepts of business intelligence, business analytics, and health economics to field questions on such matters from the administration, pharmacy, and marketing staff. While corporate librarians have done this for a while, it is new for medical librarians, who are setting up special interest groups on such topics as competitive intelligence in business.

Human resource information is another area in which librarians are often involved at their institutions. This can take the form of assisting patrons already employed by the institution who simply need help at a library computer locating online job announcements and filling out online forms on the institution's intranet pages. Assisting members of the public with filling out employment applications for the institution often causes the librarian to be the first contact of the job seeker.

Librarians can also assist employees and members of the public with obtaining information about scholarships or grants for continuing education. Helping people find scholarships is a useful public service and often creates long-lasting relationships with librarians as the seeker of scholarships progresses from seeker to student to health care worker and on up the professional ladder.

And just as health care institutions and students face financial pressures, so do average consumers. Librarians can, in conjunction with social workers and financial counselors, provide members of the public with basic guidance vis-à-vis the maze that is the medical insurance system today. This can entail something as simple as bookmarking, on public access computers, useful government and other websites on such topics as Medicare and other programs. Librarians often may find themselves liaising with other departments such as patient financial services and social services to ensure that the

patient and/or family member knows whom to talk to about insurance-related issues.

Facilitating the Health Care Institution's Marketing Program

Libraries can assist marketing departments in several ways. Libraries can serve as the host venue for special events, such as library-related events like an open house during National Medical Librarians Month or for hospital-sponsored events such as health screenings, health and safety fairs, or career fairs. Such duties, while they require staff time in terms of planning and cleanup, benefit libraries by ensuring that the name and location of the library are mentioned in employee newsletters, the local newspaper, etc. Such events can bring people to the library who might never have known about it or who knew about it but who had never visited it. Goodwill can be created between the marketing staff and library staff by co-sponsorship of these events.

Librarians often are early adopters of technologies and social media/social networking tools that marketing staff may either not know about or know about but have not received permission to adopt on an institutionwide basis. Librarians sometimes are the first to deploy such services as Twitter or Facebook. Success in such areas provides marketing staff with examples of such adoptions that they can use to persuade higher-ups of the value of new tools.

By developing new services that win kudos from such groups as the local Rotary chapter or local business technology groups, librarians enable marketers to build upon such public recognition for the institution as a whole. As an example, ScanGrants won a local award for business innovation and made the front page of the local newspaper; it had been nominated for the award by the marketing department.

Facilitating the Health Care Institution's Overall Internet Presence

Once a new web-based service is developed and wins awards, the announcement of the award is often put up on the web, thereby rendering the name of one's institution more search-engine friendly. Similarly, as one's service is adopted by other institutions the name of one's own institution is rendered search–engine friendly, given that the service often has appended to it wording such as, "A service of…." Web-services are often marketed via articles in trade publications and the scholarly press. Abstracts of these articles or the articles themselves can often be uploaded to the web. The health care institution's Internet presence is further strengthened.

Conclusion

This book has covered traditional and new management issues and services. Advocating for the provision and transfer of information is a goal for any library. As represented in this chapter, the librarian today can enter the information cycle at any point. The services developed may seem to be outside the usual preview of librarianship but many librarians are being asked to do them. By doing them well and thoroughly, they increase the presence of the library in the institution. By constantly scanning the environment in the health care setting of their library, librarians can seek out unmet or unknown needs and develop programs to meet them. Library customers may not even know there is a need because the technologies are so new. By keeping up with the professional literature and the literature of the library customers, librarians may be able to spot new trends and technologies and develop programs that in the past may not have seemed to be part of a library program. As the pace of change quickens, this perception and flexibility will be needed even more.

Acknowledgments

The Archives section author, Daniel Sokolow, is grateful to colleague Stephen Novak, Head of Archives and Special Collections at Columbia University's Health Sciences Library, for his insight on this issue of HIPAA-protected information and archival management.

References

Accreditation Council for Continuing Medical Education (ACCME). 2006a. "The ACCME's Essential Areas and Their Elements." Accessed October 1, 2010. http://www.accme.org/.

Accreditation Council for Continuing Medical Education (ACCME). 2006b. *The ACCME Standards for Commercial Support; Standards to Ensure Independence in CME Activities.* Accessed October 1, 2010. http://www.accme.org/.

Althouse, Benjamin M., Jevin D. West, Carl T. Bergstrom, and Theodore Bergstrom. 2009. "Differences in Impact Factor Across Fields and Over Time." *Journal of the American Society for Information Science and Technology* 60, no. 1 (January): 27–34.

Association of Research Libraries. 2009. *The Research Library's Role in Digital Repository Services.* Accessed June 14, 2010. http://www.arl.org/bm~doc/repository-services-report.pdf.

Barr, Nancy. 2004. "An Amazing Bookstore." *American Libraries* 35, no. 1 (January): 60–62.

Beard, Leslie, Kumanan Wilson, Dante Morra, and Jennifer Keelan. 2009. "A Survey of Health-Related Activities on Second Life." *Journal of Medical Internet Research* 11, no. 2: c17.

Bennett, Ed. 2010. "Hospital Social Network List." Found in Cache. Accessed November 30. http://ebennett .org/hsnl/.

Bergstrom, Carl. 2007. "Eigenfactor: Measuring the Value and Prestige of Scholarly Journals." *College & Research Libraries News* 68, no. 5 (May): 314–316.

Boyd, Robert. 2008. "Staffing the Commons: Job Analysis in the Context of an Information Commons." *Library Hi Tech* 26, no. 2: 232–243.

Brody, Howard. 2009. "Pharmaceutical Industry Financial Support for Medical Education: Benefit, or Undue Influence?" *Journal of Law Medicine & Ethics* 37, no. 3 (Fall): 451–460.

Campbell, Eric G., and Meredith Rosenthal. 2009. "Reform of Continuing Medical Education: Investments in Physician Human Capital." *JAMA: The Journal of the American Medical Association* 302, no. 16 (October 28): 1807–1808.

Chimonas Susan, Troyan A. Brennan, and David J. Rothman. 2007. "Physicians and Drug Representatives: Exploring the Dynamics of the Relationship." *Journal of General Internal Medicine* 22, no. 2 (February): 184–190.

Cornish, Jean K., and James C. Leist. 2006. "What Constitutes Commercial Bias Compared with the Personal Opinion of Experts?" *Journal of Continuing Education in the Health Professions* 26, no. 2 (Spring): 161–167.

Edwards, Jim. 2009. "14 Drug Companies Cited for Misleading Google Ads." BNet (April 7, 2009). Accessed September 9, 2010. http://www.bnet.com/blog/advertising-business/14-drug-companies-cited-for-misleading-google-ads/1044.

Ellison, Julie A., Charles H. Hennekens, Jing Wang, George D. Lundberg, and Destry Sulkes. 2009. "Low Rates of Reporting Commercial Bias by Physicians Following Online Continuing Medical Education Activities." *American Journal of Medicine* 122, no. 9 (September): 875–878.

Englander, Marlene S. 2003. "What Have You REALLY Written Lately? A Step-by-Step Guide to Tracking Institutional Publications." *Journal of Hospital Librarianship* 3, no. 3: 79–91.

Fitzpatrick, Roberta Bronson. 2007. "ISI Web of Knowledge: New Author Searching Capability and Reports Features." *Medical Reference Services Quarterly* 26, no. 4 (Winter): 65–74.

General Laws of Massachusetts. 2010. "Chapter 111N. Pharmaceutical and Medical Device Manufacturer Conduct; Section 6: Disclosure of data relating to provision of economic benefits valuing fifty dollars or greater." Accessed September 9. http://www.mass.gov/legis/laws/mgl/111n-6.htm.

Gluck, Jeannine C. 2004. "The Contribution of Hospital Library Services to Continuing Medical Education." *Journal of Continuing Education for Health Professionals* 24, no. 2 (Spring): 119–123

Gluck, Jeannine C., and Robin A. Hassig. 2001. "Raising the Bar: The Importance of Hospital Library Standards in the Continuing Medical Education Accreditation Process." *Bulletin of the Medical Library Association* 89, no. 3 (July): 272–276.

Goe, Leon C., Adriana M. Herrera, and William R. Mower. 1998. "Misrepresentation of Research Citations Among Medical School Faculty Applicants." *Academic Medicine* 73, no. 11 (November): 1183–1186.

Gomis, Melissa, Carole Gall, and Frances A. Brahmi. 2008. "Web-Based Citation Management Compared to EndNote: Options for Medical Sciences." *Medical Reference Services Quarterly* 27, no. 3 (Fall): 260–271.

Goold, Susan Door, and Eric G. Campbell. 2008. "Industry Support of Continuing Medical Education: Evidence and Arguments." *Hastings Center Report* 38, no. 6 (November–December): 34–37.

Gorbe, Betsy Barnett Chandler. 2005. "Toward the 'Great Good Place:' Should Libraries Have Coffee Shops?" MSLS Thesis, University of North Carolina at Chapel Hill, 45. Accessed July 10, 2010. http://etd.ils.unc.edu:8080/dspace/bitstream/1901/245/1/betsygorbe.pdf.

Greene, Jeremy A., and Scott H. Podolsky. 2009. "Keeping Modern in Medicine: Pharmaceutical Promotion and Physician Education in Postwar America." *Bulletin of the History of Medicine* 83, no. 2 (Summer): 331–377.

Harris, Cathryn. 2007. "Libraries with Lattes: The New Third Place." *Australasian Public Libraries and Information Services* 20, no. 4 (December): 145–152. Accessed July 10, 2010. http://www.thefreelibrary.com/Libraries+with+lattes%3A+the+new+third+place.-a0172010485.

Harris, Gardiner. 2009. "Pfizer Pays $2.3 Billion to Settle Marketing Case." *New York Times* (September 2). Accessed September 9, 2010. http://www.nytimes.com/2009/09/03/business/03health.html.

Harris, Gwyn. 2009. "Pharmaceutical Representatives Do Influence Physician Behavior." *Family Practice* 26, no. 3 (June): 169–170.

Hirsch, J. E. 2005. "An Index to Quantify an Individual's Scientific Research Output." *Proceedings of the National Academy of Sciences* 102, no. 46 (November 15): 16569–16572.

Hosansky, Tamar. 2009. "Accreditation Council for Continuing Medical Education Chief Executive Testifies at Senate Hearing." (July 7). Accessed September 9, 2010. http://www.accme.org/index.cfm/fa/news.detail/news_id/1572ba93-d8b0-4907-9315-096c6c699c42.cfm.

Koh, Gerald Choon-Huat, Hoon Eng Khoo, Mee Lian Wong, and David Koh. 2008. "The Effects of Problem-Based Learning During Medical School on Physician Competency: A Systematic Review." *CMAJ: Canadian Medical Association Journal* 178, no. 1 (January 1): 34–41.

Koopman, Ann, and Dan Kipnis. 2009. "Feeding the Fledgling Repository: Starting an Institutional Repository at an Academic Health Sciences Library." *Medical Reference Services Quarterly* 28, no. 2 (April/June): 111–122.

Lawrence, Sarah. 2007. "Access Anxiety: HIPAA and Historical Research." *Journal of the History of Medicine and Allied Sciences* 62, no. 4 (October): 422–460.

Leman, Hope. 2008a. "ScanGrants: A Case Study of the Creation of a Free Online Database of Current Grants, Scholarships, and Other Sources of Funding in the Health Sciences." *Journal of Electronic Resources in Medical Libraries* 5, no. 4 (December): 313–324.

Leman, Hope (sic Lehman). 2008b. "ScanGrants: A New Service for Libraries, A New Role for Librarians." *Computers in Libraries* 28, no. 8 (September): 20–23.

Leman, Hope. 2010a. "ResearchRaven: Its Value to Librarians." *Sci-Tech News* 64, no. 2 Article 5. Accessed July 10, 2010. http://jdc.jefferson.edu/scitechnews/vol64/iss2/5.

Leman, Hope. 2010b. "Promoting and Tracking the Use of Hospital Library Web Services by Outside Entities." *Medical Reference Services Quarterly* 29, no. 2 (April/June): 175–182.

Leman, Hope. 2010c. "That's So ResearchRaven (and ScanGrants): Tales from the Web Services Frontier." *Online* 34, no. 4 (July/August): 18–22.

Lombardo, Nancy T., Sharon E. Dennis, and Derek Cowan. 2007. "Streams of Consciousness: Streaming Video in Health Sciences Libraries." In *Medical Librarian 2.0: Use of Web 2.0 Technologies in Reference Services*, edited by M. Sandra Wood, 91–116. Binghamton, NY: The Haworth Information Press. (Also published as *Medical Reference Services Quarterly* 26, Supp. 1, 2007: 91–116).

Mazmanian, Paul E. 2009. "Commercial Support of Continuing Medical Education in the United States: The Politics of Doubt, the Value of Studies." *Journal of Continuing Education in the Health Professions* 29, no. 2 (Spring): 81–83.

Mello, Michelle M., David M. Studdert, and Troyen A. Brennan. 2009. "Shifting Terrain in the Regulation of Off-Label Promotion of Pharmaceuticals." *New England Journal of Medicine* 360, no. 15 (April 9): 1557–1566.

Millar, Laura A. 2010. *Archives: Principles and Practices*. New York: Neal-Schuman.

Mischke, K. L., B. Kruse-Losler, M. Hirtz, and U. Ehmer. 2004. "Internet-Capable Publication Database System." *International Journal of Computerized Dentistry* 7, no. 2 (April): 179–186.

Muallem, Miriam. 2007. "Hospital Libraries and Internet Point of Care—A Collaborative Approach." *Journal of Hospital Librarianship* 7, no. 3: 33–41.

National Institutes of Health. 2010. "National Institutes of Health Public Access." Accessed October 1. http://publicaccess.nih.gov/.

Neville, Alan J. 2009. "Problem-Based Learning and Medical Education Forty Years On. A Review of Its Effects on Knowledge and Clinical Performance." *Medical Principles and Practice: International Journal of the Kuwait University, Health Science Centre* 18, no. 1: 1–9.

O'Brien, Dorothy, Robin Davis, and Hope Leman. 2008. "How to Create a Simple Online Electronic Table of Contents Delivery Service: Medgrab as a Case Study." *Journal of Hospital Librarianship* 8, no. 1: 38–52.

Oldenburg, Ray. 1991. *The Great Good Place.* New York: Marlowe & Company.

Phillips, Sharon A., and Larry Weitkemper. 2000. "Managing Audiovisual Services." In *The Medical Library Association Guide to Managing Health Care Libraries*, edited by Ruth Holst and Sharon A. Phillips, 311–323. New York: Neal-Schuman.

PhRMA. 2010. "Code on Interactions with Healthcare Professionals." Accessed September 9. http://www.phrma.org/code_on_interactions_with_healthcare_professionals.

Piorun, Mary, and Lisa A. Palmer. 2008. "Digitizing Dissertations for an Institutional Repository: A Process and Cost Analysis." *Journal of the Medical Library Association: JMLA* 96, no. 3 (July): 223–229.

Price, David, Carol Havens, and Phillip Bellman. 2009. "Audience Assessment of Bias in Continuing Medical Education Programs." *Journal of Continuing Education in the Health Professions* 29, no. 1 (Winter): 76.

Reese, Terry, and Kyle Banerjee. 2008. *Building Digital Libraries: A How-To-Do-It Manual.* How-To-Do-It Manuals, no. 153. New York: Neal-Schuman.

Rethlefsen Melissa, Mary Piorun, and J. Dale Prince. 2009. "Teaching Web 2.0 Technologies Using Web 2.0 Technologies." *Journal of the Medical Library Association: JMLA* 97, no. 4 (October): 253–259.

Schneider, John A, Vineet Arora, Kristen Kasza, R. Van Harrison, and Holly Humphrey. 2006. "Residents' Perceptions Over Time of Pharmaceutical Industry Interactions and Gifts and the Effect of an Educational Intervention." *Academic Medicine* 81, no. 7 (July): 595–602.

Scoville, C. L., E. Diane Johnson, and Amanda L. McConnell. 2003. "When A. Rose Is Not A. Rose: The Vagaries of Author Searching." *Medical Reference Services Quarterly* 22, no. 4 (Winter): 1–11.

Smith, Aaron. 2006. "Life after Vioxx Is Good for Celebrex." *CNN Money* (September 21). Accessed November 29, 2010. http://money.cnn.com/2006/09/19/news/companies/celebrex/index.htm.

Society of American Archivists. 2005. "Code of Ethics for Archivists." Accessed October 1, 2010. http://archivists.org/governance/handbook/app_ethics.asp.

Sokolow, Daniel. 2004. "You Want Me to Do What? Medical Librarians and the Management of Archival Collections." *Journal of Hospital Librarianship* 4, no. 4: 31–50.

Steiner, Heidi M., and Robert P. Holley. 2009. "The Past, Present, and Possibilities of Commons in the Academic Library." *Reference Librarian* 50, no. 4 (October/December): 309–332.

Tanne, Janice Hopkins. 2009. "U.S. Senate Committee Investigates Conflicts of Interest in Industry Funded Medical Education." *BMJ* 339, (August 4): b3139.doi: 10.1136/bmj.b3139.

Theodorou, Mamas, Vasiliki Tsiantou, Andreas Pavlakis, Nikos Maniadakis, Vasilis Fragoulakis, Elpida Pavi, and John Kyriopoulos. 2009. "Factors Influencing Prescribing Behaviour of Physicians in Greece and Cyprus: Results from a Questionnaire Based Survey." *BMC Health Services Research* 20, no. 9: 150.

Thomson Reuters. 2010. *The Thomson Reuters Impact Factor.* Accessed November 29. http://thomsonreuters.com/products_services/science/free/essays/impact_factor/.

U.S. Department of Justice. 2004. "Warner-Lambert to Pay $430 Million to Resolve Criminal & Civil Health Care Liability Relating to Off-Label Promotion." Accessed September 9, 2010. http://www.justice.gov/opa/pr/2004/May/04_civ_322.htm.

University of Nottingham, U.K. 2010. *Directory of Open Access Repositories.* Accessed June 14. http://www.opendoar.org/index.html.

Weber Leonard J., and Michael G. Bissell. 2006. "There Is No Such Thing as Free Pizza." *Clinical Leadership & Management Review* 20, no. 6 (November 28): E8.

Winstein, Keith J., and David Armstrong. 2009. "Top Pain Scientist Fabricated Data in Studies, Hospital Says." *Wall Street Journal U.S. Edition* (March 11). Accessed November 29, 2010. http://online.wsj.com/article/SB123672510903888207.html.

16

Solo Librarians

Jerry Carlson

Look at the table of contents of this book and think of the chapters as the selections for a multiple-choice question: "Which chapter(s) do I need to focus on?" If you work in a university library or at the National Library of Medicine (NLM), you might mark just one chapter. In the two-thirds of hospital or corporate libraries that have two or more staff members, you can probably get by with five or six at most. For a solo librarian, however, the answer is "All of the above." You are the whole ball of wax. This chapter focuses on how to successfully use the knowledge in the previous chapters to provide the services health care providers and support staff need with the minimal staffing your library has. Time management and planning are crucial to meeting daily needs while at the same time looking to those of the future. Tapping into support services such as cataloging, interlibrary loan networks, and automation are also highly recommended. This chapter will also discuss staffing and coverage, promoting the library, and the librarian's professional development.

Characteristics of One-Person Libraries (OPLs)

In the 2000, 2004, and 2007 Medical Library Association (MLA) Benchmarking Surveys, fully a third of the respondents reported having 1.4 FTE or fewer (Medical Library Association, 2010). The actual proportion may be higher, as solo librarians are possibly less likely to have taken the time to answer the survey. And the number is growing; according to reports collected by MLA, 16 libraries were downsized to one-person since data collection began in October 2006 (Funk, personal communication, November 19, 2009). In some cases, one person is enough staff for a smaller institution, and even a larger one if supported by well-trained volunteers. The MLA Standards for Hospital Libraries recommend one library Full Time Equivalent (FTE) per 700 employees (Hospital Libraries Section Standards Committee, 2008). While this standard is based on an average library in the MLA Benchmarking Survey, many OPL situations do not meet this standard. This is a constant battle for OPLs. In the author's situation, where he alone, with a 0.5 FTE of volunteers, is serving over 5,000 employees, by the standards, there should be 6 librarians. But even under these circumstances, the author would say his co-workers are satisfied with his efforts.

One-person libraries (OPLs) vary greatly except in staffing. Some serve large teaching institutions with large collections and budgets. Others may be basement offices in rural hospitals, with only the most key reference books and journals. There may be no budget at all, beyond salary—just donations from the medical staff and clinical employees. At least one hospital in Colorado has a librarian without a library; she makes the rounds of the clinical floors with a laptop, serving their needs on the spot by tapping into electronic resources her hospital pays for in cooperation with the larger system to which the hospital belongs. Other OPLs serve drug, medical equipment, and health care database companies or professional associations.

Data from the largest group of small-staff libraries in the 2007 MLA Benchmarking Survey, those with 1.0-1.4 FTE, indicates that the median library spent $130,053 (including salaries) per year to make 1,000 books (including both print and online), 133 unique journal titles (also including both print and online), and three bibliographic databases available to patrons in 1,100 square feet of space. Median figures from all survey respondents were $193,707 in expenditures, 2,053 books, 319 journal titles, 5 databases, and 1,800 square feet, respectively (Medical Library Association, 2010).

Services provided run the gamut from a limited amount of basic literature searching and document delivery (especially if the librarian only works part time) to bibliographic instruction, ordering materials for other departments, and just about every associated service discussed in Chapter 15. Interestingly, of 16 respondents to a survey for that chapter on what associated services they provide, six identified themselves in a follow-up question as solo librarians—well in keeping with the proportion of OPLs reported previously (Leman, Hope, personal communication, November 11, 2009). But the goal of all OPLs is the same: to provide their organization with the knowledge it needs to care for current and future patients.

The library's place in the organization can be seen in two ways: reporting structure and service population. In the MLA Benchmarking Survey, 45 percent of librarians with 1.4 or fewer FTE had department director status (compared to 62 percent overall). The departments to which OPLs and all librarians report are compared in Figure 16.1. Eighty-six percent were separate departments with a specified budget and 14 percent were part of another department (Medical Library Association, 2010). Whether in a separate department or not, the solo librarian usually reports to a person who knows little about libraries, except as a user. Often, they have very little clinical or research experience and so have never even experienced the services of a health sciences library. Education and orientation of these supervisors, who often change, is very important.

But to whom the librarian reports administratively is less important than who the librarian serves: all medical staff; all clinical, research, and support staff; students doing internships or clinical rotations; visiting representatives from drug or other medical companies; patients and their families; and, if so defined in the library's mission, the general public. A recent cartoon comes to mind in which a character's boss can't understand why the

Figure 16.1. Reporting Structure of Health Sciences Libraries in Hospitals

Department	OPLs	All HSLs
Medical Staff/Medical Director/Medical Affairs	27%	20%
Administration (main)	20%	22%
Human Resources	9%	7%
Performance Improvement/Quality Management	7%	6%
Information Systems (IS/IT)	6%	6%
Medical Education	6%	11%
Institutional/Corporate Education	5%	7%
Nursing Services/Clinical Support Services/Clinical Affairs/Patient Care Services	5%	3%
Medical Records	3%	3%
Marketing or Public Relations	1%	1%
Other	10%	14%

Source: Medical Library Association, 2010. Data from the 2007 MLA Benchmarking Survey.

employee feels so overworked. On the wall is an organization chart (Figure 16.2), at the bottom of which is a single box that reports to every other box on the chart. That's the librarian's box.

Characteristics of Solo Librarians

Because of all this, the solo librarian needs to be independent and self-directed. The librarian needs to be able to handle both the hustle and bustle of multiple patrons lining up with requests and long stretches of loneliness. Departments in organizations often form mental silos. Silo thinking has no place for the health care librarian; the librarian must penetrate them daily, and sometimes serve as the tunnel to let the knowledge they contain flow freely between them. Flexibility and a love of variety are essential. Problem-solving and time management abilities, creativity, resourcefulness, and a sense of humor are necessary as well. The solo librarian must balance enough self-confidence to do the job and to take responsibility for library decisions with enough humility to seek help when needed and to do tasks that aren't in the job description. For example, unjamming printers and copiers comes to mind. In one library with three librarians and a technician, only the tech knew how to do that.

Librarians become solo librarians by a variety of paths. For new librarians, this may be their first experience. They can benefit from working at the full range of library tasks, definitely more tasks than they would have learned about in school. For their career path, they can identify those tasks in which they excel, should they want to apply for a more specialized position at a larger library.

Effective Solo Librarians Are:

- Independent
- Self-directed
- Comfortable in chaos
- Comfortable in solitude
- Silo breakers
- Flexible
- Variety lovers
- Problem solvers
- Time managers
- Creative
- Resourceful
- Self-confident
- Humble

Conversely, librarians in a multiperson setting may seek the greater variety of responsibility that an OPL position provides. Many librarians have spent their entire careers enjoying the challenges and rewards the OPL offers.

Rewards and Challenges

Indeed, there are rewards. As noted, solo librarians gain experience in all aspects of library work. They get both the thrill of the hunt found in public services and the joy of building a collection and laying the various pathways their patrons use to access the collection. Independence can be its own reward—to be the primary decision maker; to structure activities to suit ones own inclinations and preferences; to implement new services and policies almost effortlessly, without having to consult and educate other librarians, and as effortlessly to change them back should the patrons object.

The solo librarian is recognized by all and credited with the library's achievements, including the daily interlibrary loans. For the patrons, the librarian is the face of

---

Figure 16.2. Frank and Ernest: Where We Are in the Org Chart

Source: Thaves, 2009. Used with permission.

the worldwide library community. They know where to send their thank-you notes. Solo librarians have a direct connection with their patrons and their patron's work.

At the same time there are challenges. One may not get to do all that one wants to do, and so one needs to prioritize. Interruptions are endemic (for example, about halfway through writing the first paragraph of this chapter, a cardiologist came in with a request for ten articles for a presentation and a search for more on the same topic, then returned after five of the articles were downloaded with another question as to whether a current patient's heart condition could be related to his kidney disease). Besides the professional level requests, much of the work is purely clerical in nature. Vacation and meeting coverage is an eternal concern—or even getting away for lunch. For the latter, some librarians carry pagers.

Occupying a unique position in the organization, solo librarians may feel isolated. They may need to constantly remind patrons and the administration of the library's identity and value. And they must accept responsibility for all policies, services, and decisions. Even if the decision to cut the library budget was made far above, the librarian is the face of that budget.

A growing problem for OPLs, especially in a troubled economy, is greater vulnerability to being eliminated, due to the same forces that create OPLs in the first place: the apparent perception among many health care administrators that the library is just an expense, not an investment in enabling care providers to make decisions that ultimately lower the costs. Larger libraries can and do lose staff; if an OPL position gets eliminated, the whole library ceases to exist.

Planning for OPL Services

Planning services, policies, and procedures is necessary for all sizes of library; it is especially crucial for the OPL because all library work is the responsibility of that sole professional. Unfortunately, planning tends to fall to the bottom of the priority list in the face of patrons' wants and needs. Planning can be done in sections so that over time a whole plan is created.

Setting Goals and Objectives

Writing out the library's goals, and the objectives that lead to meeting those goals, will clarify the library's role for both the librarian and the patrons. Written goals are vital for explaining the library's needs as well as how the benefits of meeting those needs impact the needs of the

organization. The supervisors and managers who are in the position to most directly advocate for the library to the administration can better understand the workings and needs of a library if these goals are written and clearly explained. A graphic example can be seen in Figure 16.3. An enhanced, editable copy of this figure is available on the **accompanying CD-ROM**.

An outline of the library's goals is also extremely useful for giving volunteers a sense of their importance in providing library services. Many of the marketing, promotion, and outreach methods described in Chapter 3 can be used by solo librarians to determine what resources and services are most important to their patrons and potential patrons. Planning techniques from Chapters 3 and 6 can help identify the steps needed to provide those resources and services, avoid wasting time on tasks that don't address patron priorities, and draw reasonable limits to service, which patrons will learn, understand, and accept.

Basic library services include:

- finding information for patrons;
- providing access to resources owned or licensed by the library;
- providing access to resources owned or licensed by other libraries;
- acquiring new resources in accordance with established and changing patron needs;
- removing resources that no longer answer those needs;
- communicating with patrons;
- planning and evaluating library services and policies;
- documenting library activities, including usage statistics; and
- providing bibliographic instruction (especially important for an OPL—anything patrons can do for themselves leaves the librarian more time for what they can't do themselves).

Minimal activities needed to provide these services may include:

- telephone and e-mail reference services;
- online literature searches;
- interlibrary loan activities;
- photocopying or scanning library materials (this can be considered an additional, rather than minimal, service for patrons at the same physical location as the library);
- purchasing or licensing books, journals, audiovisual materials, and databases;

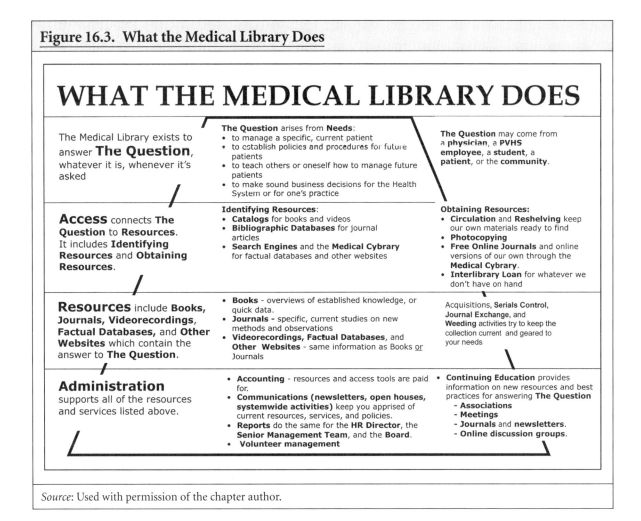

Figure 16.3. What the Medical Library Does

WHAT THE MEDICAL LIBRARY DOES

The Medical Library exists to answer **The Question**, whatever it is, whenever it's asked

The Question arises from **Needs**:
- to manage a specific, current patient
- to establish policies and procedures for future patients
- to teach others or oneself how to manage future patients
- to make sound business decisions for the Health System or for one's practice

The Question may come from a **physician**, a **PVHS employee**, a **student**, a **patient**, or the **community**.

Access connects **The Question** to **Resources**. It includes **Identifying Resources** and **Obtaining Resources**.

Identifying Resources:
- **Catalogs** for books and videos
- **Bibliographic Databases** for journal articles
- **Search Engines** and the **Medical Cybrary** for factual databases and other websites

Obtaining Resources:
- **Circulation** and **Reshelving** keep our own materials ready to find
- **Photocopying**
- **Free Online Journals** and online versions of our own through the **Medical Cybrary**.
- **Interlibrary Loan** for whatever we don't have on hand

Resources include **Books, Journals, Videorecordings, Factual Databases,** and **Other Websites** which contain the answer to **The Question**.

- **Books** - overviews of established knowledge, or quick data.
- **Journals -** specific, current studies on new methods and observations
- **Videorecordings, Factual Databases,** and **Other Websites** - same information as Books or Journals

Acquisitions, **Serials Control, Journal Exchange,** and **Weeding** activities try to keep the collection current and geared to your needs

Administration supports all of the resources and services listed above.

- **Accounting** - resources and access tools are paid for.
- **Communications (newsletters, open houses, systemwide activities)** keep you apprised of current resources, services, and policies.
- **Reports** do the same for the **HR Director**, the **Senior Management Team,** and the **Board**.
- **Volunteer management**

- **Continuing Education** provides information on new resources and best practices for answering **The Question**
  - Associations
  - Meetings
  - Journals and newsletters.
  - Online discussion groups.

Source: Used with permission of the chapter author.

- tracking materials that have been borrowed from the library;
- instructing patrons of policies, services, and resources; and
- creating the annual budget, then tracking expenditures.

If time, volunteer availability, and finances permit, additional activities may include:

- text messaging, and online live chat-based reference service;
- writing a library newsletter, a blog, or other communications;
- cataloging materials;
- creating a library webpage, with links to licensed and selected free online resources and to library policies and news; and
- consumer health information services and collection development.

Developing Policies and Procedures

The next step for the library manager is to create a policy and procedure manual. It establishes the limits of service for the patrons and serves as a position from which to negotiate if they feel they need to push the limits or a dispute arises. The latter is essential for training volunteers and vacation coverage and useful to the librarian for seldom-performed tasks. Portions of the manuals can be shared with patrons to educate them on circulation policies, library hours, service limits, and collection development policies. Both are necessary to orient consultants and, eventually, one's successor.

Setting Service Priorities

The solo librarian's limited time means that services may be limited, so clear service priorities must be set and communicated to patrons. The goals and priorities of the organization play an essential part in determining the library's priorities, as does input from the patrons and the library committee, if there is one.

At times patrons will request services that are beyond the librarian's ability to provide. In these cases, the librarian must tactfully explain this, and refer them to an information broker or university library that can provide the service. In this way the OPL maintains its image as a helpful resource, and perhaps wins that patron as a champion to increase staffing in order to expand services in the future.

Despite the development of service priorities, and with extensive education of patrons, demand can still exceed the supply of librarian time. Even at the risk of generating ill feelings, the librarian may need to place quotas on requests that an individual patron or department may make, such as a specific number of interlibrary loans per month.

Another tactic is to process only a limited number of articles from a large request per day, and to hold off on getting any loans that require a fee until the patron has had a chance to read those (the majority) available locally or loaned on a reciprocal basis (see Chapter 10), then decide if the others are still needed. Whatever limits are set, they need to be in the policy manual. They should also be negotiable for rare cases, e.g., for a grant request or research project, after which the patron's requests will dwindle to a reasonable level.

Time Management

The procedure manual should include a timetable of which tasks need to be done daily, weekly, monthly, or less frequently. Calendars, to-do lists, and online ticklers can help remind the library manager when deadlines are looming and to block out time to accomplish the task. Good time management skills are mandatory. Many books, articles, and workshops on the subject are available, some of them specific to librarians.

But the best laid plans of mice and librarians are subject to interruption; one mustn't forget that handling requests from patrons is the ultimate purpose of all library tasks. Technical services, planning, and evaluation take a backseat. The librarian never wants to appear too busy to be asked a question or to take a legitimate request. Patron requests for the patient upstairs have to take precedence over those for a future journal club. An important part of the reference interview is to ask exactly when a patron needs the search or article, just in case a more urgent request comes in, or to leave time for other work with a deadline.

On the other hand, some tasks do take long blocks of uninterrupted concentration and effort. It may be possible to curtail open hours for this purpose. The closed hours could be chosen based on factors such as times when experienced volunteers have front desk duty or simply to track in-person and telephone usage patterns and use the least busy times to close. In hospitals, shift change times (typically 3:00–3:30 pm) would likely fall into this category. Quicker, more routine tasks can be done in the more popular times, e.g., lunchtime. Those that require very little concentration or creative thought, e.g., filing or reshelving, might be saved for the late afternoon when fatigue typically sets in, or as a break from high-concentration work.

The telephone has been a source of interruption ever since Alexander Graham Bell interrupted Thomas Watson to help him with an acid spill. Many librarians use answering machines not only to take messages when they're away from the library, but also during high concentration work or while serving other patrons. Patrons may also be encouraged to use e-mail for less urgent requests. Either set of messages should be reviewed frequently and answered promptly, if for no other reason than to establish or negotiate a later deadline for the request.

Staffing and Coverage

While the solo librarian does most of the work in the OPL, additional help may be available to help with some library tasks. Sources of help include:

- volunteers,
- other employees under the same supervisor,
- job sharing arrangements with another department in the hospital,
- modified or light duty workers,
- temporary personnel,
- students, and
- other libraries.

Extra help with routine tasks can free the librarian for more professional level work or, as noted, high concentration tasks. Special projects assigned to students or more expert volunteers can enhance library services. Supplementary staff may also provide coverage for lunch, meetings, vacation, or sick leave.

Volunteers

Most hospitals and health systems have a corps of volunteers, with education levels and work experience ranging from high school students to retired PhDs or even MDs. As a general rule they are enthusiastic and willing to learn.

Volunteer programs are usually overseen by professional volunteer coordinators who work with the librarian to develop job descriptions; recruit volunteers who are able to meet the position's requirements; and serve as a resource regarding organizational and governmental restrictions or regulations regarding volunteer use (for example, dress code, operating some equipment), keeping records of hours worked, and conducting performance evaluations. Also, volunteers have to go through a basic orientation in hospitals as required by Joint Commission.

Much time and effort is needed to train volunteers, especially for the majority who lack library experience, and to determine which tasks fit them best, but this is an investment that should pay off greatly once they've established a routine and developed confidence in their abilities to perform their tasks. Some volunteers may be willing and able to perform only certain tasks: for example, the retiree who can only do clerical tasks; the student who quickly becomes bored with clerical work and wants something more challenging; or the physically weaker volunteer who can't handle heavy volumes. Others may be librarian material, with or without an MLS (volunteering can be a stepping stone to paid employment for library students and new graduates, especially with the experiences gained), able to take on all reference and document delivery functions. Interviewing a prospective volunteer can help to focus training, or determine that the volunteer would be better suited elsewhere in the organization and spare the librarian the investment altogether. A probationary period may also be desirable.

A few key points that should be included in volunteer training are:

- the library's service priorities;
- confidentiality of all transactions, especially those directly involving patients; and
- the boundary between pointing patrons to the resources that should answer their questions and volunteering knowledge or advice from their own education or experience.

One needs to be aware that as unpaid workers, volunteers have less incentive to be punctual or to show up at all. Even the most reliable may have restrictions on the time they can serve, are subject to illness, and take their own vacations.

But just as in a paid position, it is important to create written job descriptions for regular volunteer positions, describing the tasks to be done, the skills required, the time needed to complete them, and any physical requirements.

MANAGEMENT IN ACTION 16.1

Volunteer-Focused Online Procedure Manual

Organization: Poudre Valley Health System, a suburban community hospital and clinic system

Location: Fort Collins, Colorado

Description of Problem/Project: Librarian had written the Procedure Manual in a sequential outline format, which the volunteers found difficult to use because they needed to jump past steps not needed in most situations.

Impact On: Ability of volunteers and others to perform library functions

People Involved: Librarian, library volunteers, librarian's coworkers

Strategies for Success: One of the volunteers, a retired engineer, has experience in both process development and HTML program. He has been translating the outline, and flow charts hand-drawn by the Librarian, into a web-based "manual" in which each decision point has links to the next appropriate instruction for the situation. Both a new volunteer and a forgetful longstanding volunteer have successfully performed completed procedures, using the online manual. The Librarian has also pointed it out to coworkers who occasionally provide coverage, but has received no feedback from them.

Barriers Encountered: HTML programming is very time-intensive, especially when procedures change. The Librarian sometimes skips steps in flow charts because they are second nature for him. The Librarian could have done a better job of prioritizing procedures that all volunteers perform (e.g., interlibrary loan) over those that were easier to program because they were already in flow-chart format for patrons (e.g., PubMed searching).

Take Home Points: The Librarian should be open to feedback from the volunteers, and be ready to use their particular talents.

Contact Information: Jerry Carlson, Medical Librarian, Poudre Valley Health System, Fort Collins, Colorado. E-mail: gmc@pvhs.org.

Descriptions may be tailored to different levels of education and experience. Volunteers should also be directed to the policy and procedure manuals both in their training and in the course of their work, necessitating that these manuals are written clearly for use by nonlibrarians.

Basic tasks that volunteers frequently handle include:

- filing catalog cards or inputting online catalog records;
- checking in journals;
- shelving materials;

- copying or scanning articles for local patrons or interlibrary loan;

- compiling usage statistics for reports;

- inventorying the collection;

- conducting journal exchange activities;

- labeling new materials;

- recording circulation transactions and sending out overdue notices;

- answering the phone when the librarian is out or engaged in high-concentration work; and

- checking links on the library webpage.

Note that some of these tasks don't even require the volunteer to be physically in the library. For example, a volunteer doing receptionist work in a waiting room might label materials between queries or check-ins. Also, some tasks may be broken down into subtasks and split between volunteers, or done sequentially from shift to shift: Volunteer A just needs to leave a note to Volunteer B saying where he or she left off in the inventory, for example. Regularly scheduled meetings of all volunteers can reduce training time, and also provide them with an opportunity to air concerns and suggest improvements to library processes.

Reward and recognition are an important and enjoyable aspect of working with volunteers. Examples may include:

- taking all to lunch, or otherwise providing an opportunity to socialize, in addition to whatever the organization's volunteer program does;

- gifts for major gift-giving holidays, cards on their birthdays (the volunteer program should have these on file);

- souvenirs from vacations, especially to those who provided coverage (this goes for others who provide coverage as well); and

- their choice of vendor gifts from meetings.

One of the best rewards is to serve as a reference when they seek paid employment. The librarian may be losing a worker, but gaining a professional contact and demonstrating to the others that he or she cares about their needs. If it's a part-time or contract job, they may even stay or come back for temporary coverage.

One final note is to make sure that the library is getting a return on its investment of training time. Is the volunteer saving more time than is expended with ongoing reminders of what the librarian thought he or she had learned months or years ago?

Shared Employees

While the solo librarian often shares a department with nonlibrarians, these coworkers can be of some use to the library and its patrons. An administrative assistant might take care of ordering supplies or provide phone coverage. Others might unlock the library for self-service use in the librarian's absence, or answer basic directional questions. With clear instructions, they might even obtain documents for patrons using the library systems and interlibrary loan. If the librarian is able to return the favor by covering some of that person's functions from time to time, so much the better.

It is also conceivable that another department has a full-time employee with only a half-time workload. If that's the case, he or she might be able to give the library several hours of work a week. Take note that with any regular nonlibrary employees, especially in another department, their first loyalty is to their regular work, so extensive training may be out of the question, and use of them must be sparing.

One group of employees, modified or light duty workers, might be fully employed in the library if only temporarily. In many workers' compensation programs, employees who are injured on the job work for their benefits by doing less physically demanding work. Library work is perfect for this. Depending on the severity, and therefore the recovery time of the injury, extensive library training may prove worthwhile. They may even return as patrons.

Temporary Personnel

Another potential source of help, particularly for special projects, exceptionally busy periods, or vacation coverage, is a temporary employment agency. The organization may be willing to pay for temporary help since there is no long-term commitment to salary or benefits; the expense just needs to have been included in the library budget. Training time must be included in considering the budget, especially if the agency has no employees with previous library experience.

Students

Students from high schools, colleges, and graduate (especially library) programs can be among the most satisfying library helpers. The librarian may be creating a future colleague while providing the student with valuable experience. Typically students are members of a younger, more wired-in generation, and so they may have enough fresh perspective and technical savvy to teach the librarian something.

College students may be paid fully or in part through government or college assistance programs. Others may be required to perform so many hours of community service in order to receive their degree or diploma. Still others may simply volunteer for the experience, or to help them decide whether to pursue a library career.

Library programs generally offer internship opportunities and/or practicum courses to provide their students with actual library experience. Students can be assigned special projects the librarian hasn't had time for. The tasks assigned to volunteers can be useful to them for the experience, as well as professional-level reference services as appropriate. It's a nice synergy if a library task can double as a routine class assignment or even a thesis project.

Other Libraries

For extended absences, vacations, or multiday professional meetings, a solo librarian may form an agreement with another librarian to provide services for each other's patrons during these times. The National Network of Libraries of Medicine/MidContinental Region has instituted a formalized process for this, the MCR Reference Continuity Service Network (http://nnlm.gov/mcr/rsdd/continuity/index.html). But one can always make an informal agreement.

A final note about vacation and meeting coverage, whether by other employees, volunteers, temps, students, or other libraries: These people will have inadequate training, limited time, or their own customers. It is therefore imperative for the librarian to alert patrons that library services will be limited during that time, that they should contact the library only for direct patient care needs, and they should make all other requests in a timely manner before the librarian leaves or wait till he or she gets back. If at a professional meeting on work time, the solo librarian might want to bring a laptop with Internet access to keep in touch and do what can be done remotely (e.g., PubMed searches and DOCLINE requests); if sick or weather-bound at home, the same might be done with the home computer.

Support Services

Much of the more mundane work of the library can be outsourced to various agencies that can perform it much more efficiently and therefore less expensively than the solo librarian. Other services enable the OPL to ally with other libraries to share resources and other benefits. These services include automation, cataloging services, book and journal dealers, interlibrary loan and document delivery services, and library consortia.

Automation

Fifty-odd years into the computer age, it is a rare library indeed that has none of its functions automated. Decreasing costs and increasing capabilities put automation within the reach of even the least funded OPL. Computers can greatly increase the efficiency of the librarian, leaving more time for tasks that require more flexibility and imagination than a computer can muster. For example, it's much quicker to load a catalog record with multiple entry points than it is to file as many catalog cards.

It may be possible for the librarian to ally with a larger library to share a portion of their system; or to buy or license one of a number of low-cost basic systems designed specifically for small libraries, with modules for cataloging, circulation, serials control, and statistics. The system and its databases may be loaded on a server within the library's organization, or hosted on the Internet by a remote provider.

Automation also enables putting the library, or at least portions of it, at the point of care, creating greater efficiency for the patron. A library page on the organization's intranet can link patrons to every electronic resource and show them every physical source the library has to answer their questions. This is especially important if the library serves multiple facilities, whose employees and medical staff can't just pop into the library. E-mail and other e-communication services provide additional channels for patrons to send requests and for the librarian to quickly answer them.

> Automation represents a major investment for most one-person libraries. Decisions are too important to be made quickly and without adequate information. It's not unusual for the selection process to take 1-2 years or more between the initial decision to purchase a system and the signing of contracts. With this much invested in your decision, you'll want to be sure that the system you select will remain viable (though expecting it to remain so for more than 5-7 years is probably not realistic). With this in mind it's easy to understand why when automating it's a good idea to look ahead. (Berner and St. Clair, 1996: 230)

A good working relationship with the organization's information technology (IT) department employees is crucial. They are the ones who will be tending the server if the system is loaded locally, and maintaining the Internet connection if remote. They will probably have to determine that it won't interfere with any existing systems. But while they understand the larger world of computer automation, they might not grasp the special needs of library systems. The librarian must be able to clearly explain these needs to them. Conversely, the librarian must learn the IT department's protocols for purchasing new software, placing service calls, etc.

Once a system is installed, the librarian will be on the front line when patrons encounter problems. Troubleshooting training from the vendor and/or the IT department should be considered. Adequate time to set up hardware and install and test software must be included in the planning. There will be glitches, which really need to be corrected before the patrons see it. Once the system is operating normally, the librarian will need to be thoroughly familiar with its operations in order to help patrons learn how to use it. Time should be set aside for the purpose. More training from the vendor may shorten this process.

Cataloging Services

Nearly every health care-related book or other resource published can be found in the catalogs of the National Library of Medicine and the Library of Congress in a standardized format. Cataloging services such as Marcive and OCLC serve as conduits to incorporate these records into local library catalogs. Very few libraries need to do their own cataloging, other than a few specialized or locally or internally published books and materials (e.g., video recordings of CE programs). Typically, the service's price per record is much less than the cost in librarian time to do original cataloging.

Services provide records either as catalog cards or as electronic records. They can also provide spine labels and book cards. If the library has been purchasing cards from them, then converts to an automated system, the service may be able to provide a file of past purchases that can be readily uploaded to the new system. Caveat: Much time may be needed to remove records for discarded items if this has not been done all along. When subscribing to a service, the library creates a profile with its own classification preference, locations, and other local considerations. Locations, nonstandard call numbers (e.g., Planetree for consumer health materials), and local notes may be added when ordering records. In addition to providing records and labels, OCLC also incorporates them into its worldwide union catalog, with an option to lend the corresponding materials through interlibrary loan.

For keeping track of electronic journal holdings, it is useful to contract for a journal A-to-Z list service. After listing purchased resources with a vendor, as part of the service, they list all the open access titles. This increases the number of journals patrons can find. The next step is to update the service to include link resolver software that creates a more seamless connection between bibliographic databases and the listed holdings. For more on cataloging and listing services, see Chapter 8.

Book and Journal Dealers

Buying books and journals through centralized dealers can streamline the process, save money, and provide other benefits. Ordering journals through a subscription agent enables the librarian to avoid dealing with multiple individual publishers and renewal notices. All titles can be renewed once a year and paid on a single invoice (much to the pleasure of Accounts Payable departments, which may pay upwards of $80 per check they write). Claims for missing issues may also go through the agent; some maintain their own bank of excess journal issues in order to fill gaps more quickly. Agents can alert the librarian to changes in price, title, or publication schedule, and provide samples of titles under consideration. Automated check-in and claims programs may be available online, as well as reports of the library's holdings. As more and more print subscriptions include online access, the agent can inform the librarian on the process to activate that access. These services are provided for a fee, usually based on a small percentage of the total subscription price.

Book dealers carry titles from many publishers, freeing the librarian from the need to deal with many publishers directly. Most use their power of multiple purchases to negotiate discounts that they then pass on to the library. Many offer even deeper than usual discounts certain times of the year. Dealers can locate rare or out of print titles. Some have approval plans and some provide standing order plans for core title lists such as *Doody's Core Titles* (http://www.doody.com/dct/). Core title lists select what are the most important and current books in medical subjects selected by a group of subject experts. At least one dealer has its own online platform for electronic versions of key titles, at a price comparable to the print versions. Most allow libraries or purchasing departments to order online, by phone, or fax for delivery within a day or two.

Subscription agents expect a long-term relationship with the library, book dealers less so. Transferring multiple subscriptions to a new agent is very time-consuming, so it is important to find the agent whose fees and services best match the library's needs early on. Comparing services and soliciting input from colleagues can help prevent future dissatisfaction. Points to consider include these:

- Cost of service charges
- Titles and publishers available through the agent (One that specializes in health science journals is generally preferable.)
- Procedures and track record for claiming lost or damaged issues
- Procedures for ordering and claiming electronic journals
- Procedures for ordering new and renewing or cancelling existing subscriptions
- The organization's requirements for using vendors (Some organizations require a firm bid before ordering, which some agents can't provide.)
- Availability of online services for ordering new titles and/or placing claims

ILL and Document Delivery Services

With a limited budget, the typical OPL can only provide its patrons with a core selection of journals, which meet most of their needs; but patrons often need (or want) articles from beyond that core. So the library must turn to interlibrary loan or, in some circumstances, to commercial document delivery services. As noted in Chapter 10, DOCLINE provides powerful tools for locating and requesting medical journal articles, as does OCLC for books, audiovisual materials, and non-health care journal articles. Note that OCLC offers a lower-priced Group Access membership, which allows one to locate lenders and place requests online.

For even rarer materials, or if something is absolutely necessary to obtain while all potential lenders are closed for the night, the OPL or the patron may need to resort to the pay-per-view option for online journals, or to commercial document delivery services. Pay-per-view is generally available on the publisher's website; some aggregate services offer pay-per-view access to all the titles they sell. These services are generally expensive, entailing copying charges, copyright royalties, postage if mailed, and service fees. But it's conceivable that the solo librarian may find that the convenience of obtaining an article this way, with relatively little effort, outweighs the price.

Library Consortia

Local, statewide, and regional library consortia may provide reference, reciprocal interlibrary loan, and technical services to member libraries. Group discounts for OCLC or other databases, library supplies, and even computer hardware may be available. Union catalogs or serial lists of members' holdings might be produced to aid ILL. Consortia may also offer continuing education and opportunities for contact with other librarians.

Membership in a consortium usually requires an institutional or individual membership fee. Institutional fees may be uniform, or they may be scaled by library size. Some consortia include all types of libraries; others are more specialized. Member librarians may also be called upon to serve on committees for the consortium, help plan workshops or new programs, or even be elected as leaders. The solo librarian will need to balance the time commitment for this participation with the benefits of membership. If multiple consortia are present in the area, the librarian may need to compare and choose between them, selecting the one that best fits the library's needs.

Continuing Education

Every librarian needs to keep abreast of best practices for meeting patrons' information needs and of new developments in the health care and information technology environments. This is the purpose of continuing education. Ideally, the librarian should attend statewide, regional, and national meetings, where one can fully interact with trainers and colleagues presenting new ideas. To gain administrative support, one might point out that for nurses, as an example, it is more cost-effective to bring in one trainer to teach multiple nurses, but for a unique position like the librarian, it's cheaper to send that individual to multiple trainers. Also, remembering the isolation that solo librarians experience within the organization, it is a revitalizing opportunity to confer, converse, and consort with one's fellow librarians.

If getting away is impossible, or for topics that might not be covered at meetings, there are other options. MEDLIB-L and MLA chapter and section e-mail discussion lists (commonly called "listservs," after the trademarked name of a program for managing discussion lists) bring fresh ideas—and opportunities to share one's own ideas and experience—almost daily. Using RSS to read blogs is another way to keep up. Membership in MLA brings a journal and a newsletter full of still more ideas and research; its sections and chapters have their own communications. MLA, NN/LM, library schools, and other entities offer teleconferences and webcasts, some at low or no cost. Local journal clubs might meet face to face on a regular basis; others are conducted via e-mail. The MLA website (http://www.mlanet.org) contains many useful resources.

Advocacy

As noted earlier, OPLs are especially vulnerable to elimination, which makes advocacy for the library essential. Providing exceptional service is the first step; the powers that hold the purse strings need *to know* that the library's service is exceptional. The librarian should encourage patrons to tell them and send their comments up the line. Services the librarian can measure include tracking that requests are filled in time to meet the patrons' needs; asking if literature searches accurately addressed

the patrons' concerns and, if not, following up to get more details on what would; and tracking the impact of library services in terms of patient outcomes. The survey shown in Figure 16.4 is one way. An editable copy of Figure 16.4 is available on the **accompanying CD-ROM**.

Also see Chapter 6 for more evaluation ideas. Align these outcomes, and other benefits patrons identify, to the organization's goals and objectives. It is essential that the librarian extend services to administration and not be seen as serving only clinicians.

Some other ideas that can readily be implemented by solo librarians include:

- Joining committees to be seen throughout the organization. Research or Evidence-Based Practice committees and Institutional Review Boards are obvious matches. Patient safety is a growing concern in

---

Figure 16.4. Library Customer Service Survey

PVHS Medical Library Quick Customer Service Survey

Please complete and return survey AFTER reading and applying the article or search.

Service: ___ Literature Search   ___ Photocopy   ___ Interlibrary Loan

Quality:

Was the search/article **in time** to meet your needs?   __ Yes   __ No

Did the search **accurately** fit your needs?   __ Yes   __ No   __ N/A

Did it list: __ **too many**   __ **too few**   __ **the right amount of articles?**   __ N/A

Impact:

Why did you need the information?

___ To treat a specific current patient

___ To treat future patients (continuing education, policies/procedures)

Did the information lead you to (or to recommend that others):

(*check all that apply*)

___ change/validate the diagnosis?   ___ change/validate choice of tests?

___ change/validate choice of drugs?   ___ reduce length of hospital stay?

___ change/validate advice given to patients?   ___ avoid patient mortality?

___ avoid hospital-acquired infection?   ___ avoid surgery?

___ avoid additional tests or procedures?   ___ avoid additional outpatient visits?

___ save time?

___ None of the above

___ Other benefit? _____

Thank you!

Please return this form to the PVHS Medical Library at your earliest convenience.

MEDICAL LIBRARY
POUDRE VALLEY HEALTH SYSTEM
1024 LEMAY AVE
FORT COLLINS CO 80524

Source: Used with permission of the chapter author.

hospitals, with potential roles for librarians (Zipperer, 2004). Committees that are less obviously library related can introduce the librarian to employees who might not otherwise think of the library.

- Sitting down with physicians or senior management in the cafeteria to engage informally with staff.

- Finding out what continuing education is being offered in the organization, and offering to support it with bibliographies or to record it for those who are unable to attend.

- Forwarding announcements of new free online resources to those who are most likely to use them.

Conclusion

To conclude this chapter, I don't believe I can do better than to quote the first edition of this guide:

> During the course of a typical day, librarians in one-person libraries will be called upon to wear a variety of hats; they are catalogers, computer tech support providers, purchasing clerks, reference librarians, volunteer coordinators, and document delivery specialists. Switching hats can be fatiguing and stressful, but few solo librarians are bothered by boredom or becoming bogged down in routines. Each day offers new opportunities and new challenges.
>
> Certainly solo librarianship is not for everyone, but for those who are self-starters, the one-person library provides the possibility to define the library program and to organize the workday without the outside pressures and politics of larger libraries. Days are rarely boring. If the librarian grows tired of one task, there is almost always another one to turn to. While the absence of a staff means the solo librarian is responsible for accomplishing all the work, there are also no hassles with hiring employees and ongoing personnel issues.
>
> Often it is easier to develop satisfying professional relationships with library users in a one-professional setting. There is an opportunity to learn about patient care, medical research projects, and the ongoing business of health care. At the same time the librarian can also teach library users how to make the most of information technology and provide them with the tools for life-long professional learning.
>
> For some librarians, working in the one-person environment is simply a first step in a health sciences librarianship career as they seek challenges in larger organizations. For others, however, solo librarianship can be a satisfying and rewarding career.
>
> The choice lies firmly in the hands of the solo librarian. (Topper and Bensing, 2000: 189)

But I'll add something anyway: The story of Alexander Selkirk, a shipwrecked sailor, inspired not only Daniel Defoe's novel, *Robinson Crusoe*, but also these lines from William Cowper:

> *I AM monarch of all I survey;*
> *My right there is none to dispute;* (Cowper, 1782)

You, too, though you may feel isolated and without even the consolation of getting all your work done by Friday, are such a monarch. Take charge and rule well.

References

Berner, Andrew, and Guy St. Clair. 1996. *The Best of OPL II: Selected Readings from The One-Person Library 1989–1994.* Washington, DC: Special Libraries Association.

Cowper, William. 1782. "The Solitude of Alexander Selkirk." Bartleby.com. Accessed November 29, 2010. http://www.bartleby.com/106/160.html.

Hospital Libraries Section Standards Committee, Margaret Bandy, Jacqueline Donaldson Doyle, Anne Fladger, Katherine Stemmer Frumento, Linné Girouard, Sheila Hayes, and Diane Rourke. 2008. "Standards for Hospital Libraries 2007." *Journal of the Medical Library Association* 96, no. 2 (April): 162–169.

Medical Library Association. 2010. "Health Sciences Library Statistics and Benchmarking—2007 Benchmarking Survey." Chicago: Medical Library Association. Accessed April 17; data available to MLA member participants only, with information available online. http://www.mlanet.org/members/benchmark/.

Thaves, Bob. 2009. "Frank & Ernest." Comics.com, November 3. Accessed November 29, 2010. http://comics.com/frank&ernest/2009-11-03/.

Topper, Judith M., and Karen McNally Bensing. 2000 "The One-Person Library." In *The Medical Library Association Guide to Managing Health Care Libraries,* edited by Ruth Holst and Sharon A. Phillips, 177–190. Chicago and New York: Medical Library Association, Neal-Schuman Publishers.

Zipperer, Lorri. 2004. "Clinicians, Librarians and Patient Safety: Opportunities for Partnership." *Quality and Safety in Health Care* 13, no. 3 (June): 218–222.

Further Reading

Siess, Judith. *The New OPL Sourcebook : A Guide for Solo and Small Libraries,* Medford, NJ: Information Today, 2006.

Special Libraries Association, Solo Librarians Division. 2010. Accessed June 24. http://units.sla.org/division/dsol/.

About the Editors
and Chapter Authors

Margaret Moylan Bandy, MALS, DM/AHIP, FMLA, is Medical Librarian and Manager of Library and Media Services at Exempla Saint Joseph Hospital in Denver, Colorado, where she has worked since 1979. She served on the MLA Board of Directors from 2005–2008, was board liaison to the Task Force on Vital Pathways for Hospital Librarians, and contributed to the final report of the committee and the 2009 *Journal of the Medical Library Association*'s Vital Pathways Symposium. That endeavor was only one of Bandy's many efforts to advocate for librarians in health care settings. Most recently she collaborated in the development of the MLA Position Statement *Role of Health Sciences Librarians in Patient Safety*.

As part of the Vital Pathways project she worked closely with members of the Nursing and Allied Health Information Section of MLA to forge strong ties with the ANCC Magnet Recognition Program. As member of the MLA Board of Directors she encouraged the establishment of a representative to the annual Magnet Conference and with Melody Allison co-wrote the *Magnet Recognition Program Collaboration Proposal: The American Nurses Credentialing Center and the Medical Library Association White Paper*.

Bandy has served as an officer and committee member for many national, regional, and state associations including chair of the Midcontinental Chapter of the Medical Library Association (MCMLA), chair of the Consumer and Patient Health Information Section (CAPHIS) and chair of the Hospital Libraries Section Standards Committee. As chair of the HLS Standards Committee she led the revision of Standards for Hospital Libraries 2007. She was twice president of the Colorado Council of Medical Librarians (CCML) and as president

of CCML in 2003 she established the CCML Advocacy Committee to respond to the crisis facing hospital libraries in Colorado. That committee developed the "Myths and Truths about Library Services" materials that are on the MLA Vital Pathways website.

Considered a leader in the provision of patient and consumer health information, Bandy established the first hospital-based consumer health library in Denver, Colorado, in 1985. She wrote the chapter "Health Information for Patients and Consumers" in the 1st edition of the *Medical Library Association Guide to Managing Health Care Libraries* and participated in the development of the MLA/CAPHIS Policy Statement *The Librarian's Role in the Provision of Consumer Health Information and Patient Education*.

Bandy received an MALS from Dominican University, River Forest, Illinois, in 1972 and an MA in English from Loyola University, Chicago, Illinois, in 1976. She is a Distinguished Member of the Academy of Health Information Professionals of the Medical Library Association and was named a Fellow of the Medical Library Association in 2010. She has received a number of awards including the MLA Lois Ann Colaianni Award for Excellence and Achievement in Hospital Librarianship in 2002, the Hospital Libraries Section Scroll of Exemplary Service multiple years, the CCML Marla M. Graber Award for Excellence and Achievement in Health Sciences Librarianship in 2005 and the MCMLA Outstanding Achievement Award in 1991.

Rosalind Farnam Dudden, MLS, DM/AHIP, FMLA, is Library and Knowledge Services Director at National Jewish Health in Denver, Colorado. She has worked in a hospital library setting since 1971. A member of the Medical Library Association and the Colorado Council of Medical Librarians (CCML) since 1971, Dudden has been a leader in many of the technology and evaluation efforts of both groups. She has served in more than 60 elected or appointed offices at the national, chapter, and section and local levels. She is a Distinguished Member of the Academy of Health Information Professionals, a Fellow of the Medical Library Association, and a former member of the MLA board. She served as president of the MLA Hospital Libraries Section, the MLA Research Section, and CCML.

Committed to sharing the knowledge that she has gained throughout her career, she has taught more than 15 courses and presented many papers and posters. Some of her accomplishments over the years include work in standards, surveys, and technology. She was instrumental in the development of the 1984 edition of MLA's Hospital Library Standards during her tenure as chair of the Hospital Library Standards and Practices Committee. The committee also wrote a paper on the JCAHO standards that received MLA's Ida and George Eliot Prize in 1981. Dudden worked on the successful MLA Benchmarking Network Task Force and project since 1999, helping with the analysis of the 2002 and 2004 surveys. For her role in supporting the vision, development, and implementation on the Benchmarking Network, she received the MLA President's Award in 2003.

With CCML members, Dudden has worked on surveys of interlibrary loan activity form 1977 to 2007, a series of surveys designed to analyze usage patterns and promote balanced resource sharing. She and the survey committee members wrote a research article about the 1997 survey. For her work with these and other CCML efforts, she received CCML's Marla Graber Award for Excellence and Achievement in Health Sciences Librarianship in 2005.

With a career-long interest in technology and being a promoter of its use in libraries, Dudden worked on projects locally that promoted the use of e-mail for interlibrary loan as early as 1980 and was instrumental in expanding the shared integrated library system with a National Library of Medicine grant in 1991. For 13 years, she chaired the committee that produced the CCML *Journal Locator* as a computerized union list of serials starting in 1977, which ended in 2008. In the early 1980s she promoted MEDLINE searching and taught several courses that allowed CCML members to get access. For her work in collaborative technology projects through the years, she received the ISI/Frank Bradway Rogers Information Advancement Award from MLA in 1995. She created Denver's first hospital website in 1995, writing

or loading more than 300 pages, and was hospital webmaster until 2000. She also served as webmaster of both MLA's Hospital Libraries Section and the Consumer and Patient Health Information Section (CAPHIS). Her work contributed to the CAPHIS Top 100 Websites You Can Trust for consumers.

During her career she also received two awards from the Midcontinental Chapter of the Medical Library Association, the Barbara McDowell Award for Hospital Librarianship in 1988, and the Outstanding Achievement Award in 1995. The faculty at National Jewish awarded her the first Friend of the Faculty Award in 2002 and she was commended for dragging them kicking and screaming into the Internet age. In October 2004, Rosalind was awarded an NLM publications grant for two years to research and write the book *Using Benchmarking, Needs Assessment, Quality Improvement, Outcome Measurement, and Library Standards: A How-To-Do-It Manual* (A Medical Library Association Book) (Neal-Schuman, 2007). Rosalind's resume and CV can be found on the web at http://roz.dudden.com/

■   ■   ■

Alison Aldrich, MSI, MPH, is Technology Outreach Coordinator for the National Network of Libraries of Medicine, Pacific Northwest Region (NN/LM PNR) at the University of Washington Health Sciences Library in Seattle, Washington. She holds a Master of Science in Information degree from the University of Michigan and a Master of Public Health degree from Wright State University. Aldrich began her library career as a health sciences librarian at Wright State University in Dayton, Ohio. Her current work involves developing continuing education courses and other learning opportunities for librarians, promoting National Library of Medicine information resources, and outreach to unaffiliated health professionals.

Donna Beales, MLIS, is Librarian/Continuing Medical Education Coordinator for Lowell General Hospital, Lowell, Massachusetts. Prior to assuming her current position, Beales taught Directed Studies at the F.W. Parker Charter Essential School and was privileged to have many pedagogical discussions about the importance of libraries in lifelong learning with renowned educator Theodore "Ted" Sizer, founder of the Essential School movement. Beales holds multiple Scrolls of Exemplary Service from the Medical Library Association and currently sits on the editorial board of the *Journal of Hospital Librarianship*. Her past contributions related to

CME have appeared in *Medical Meetings* and the *Journal of Hospital Librarianship*.

Jerry Carlson, MS-LIS, DM/AHIP, is the sole librarian for Poudre Valley Health System, Fort Collins, Colorado, starting in 1989. From 1997–2000, he also managed a separate consumer health library. Professionally he has been active as a leader and committee member in the Hospital Libraries Section and Midcontinental Chapter of the Medical Library Association. His contributions to the Colorado Council of Medical Librarians, including serving as president, earned him the 2010 Marla Graber Award for Excellence and Achievement in Health Sciences Librarianship. Off the job, Carlson travels extensively, performs with several Cheyenne, Wyoming, choral and theater groups, and relaxes with his law librarian wife, Kathy, and their dachshunds Angel, Sadie, and Einstein.

Elizabeth Connor, MLS, DM/AHIP, is Associate Professor of Library Science and Science Liaison at the Daniel Library of The Citadel, the Military College of South Carolina in Charleston, South Carolina. She has worked as a community college librarian; a medical librarian at teaching hospitals and medical schools in three states (Maryland, Connecticut, and South Carolina) and two foreign countries (Kingdom of Saudi Arabia and Commonwealth of Dominica); and as an academic librarian. Connor's experience includes renovating and building library space and serving as the library consultant for several other projects. Recent publications include *A Guide to Developing End User Education Programs in Medical Libraries* (Routledge, 2005); *Planning, Renovating, Expanding, and Constructing Library Facilities in Hospitals, Academic Medical Centers, and Health Organizations* (Routledge, 2005); and *Evidence-Based Librarianship: Case Studies and Active Learning Exercises* (Neal-Schuman Publishers, 2007).

Jacqueline Donaldson Doyle, MS, AHIP, FMLA, is Head Librarian at the University of Arizona College of Medicine in Phoenix, Arizona, where she has had the pleasure and challenge of creating a team to develop and deliver a twenty-first-century library for a brand new medical campus. She has more than 30 years of library experience in clinical, academic, and public health settings and currently provides consultation services in library management and creation through her organization, JD3AZ. She has served as president of the Medical Library Association (MLA) and its chapter, the Medical Library Group of Southern California and Arizona (MLGSCA). Doyle has also served as president of the MLA Hospital

Libraries section and is a member of the Leadership and Management and Medical Informatics sections. She currently serves as the Phoenix liaison for the University of Arizona School of Information Resources and Library Science. Her professional interests are in library creation, collaboration, and networking and she has authored articles in the *Journal of the Medical Library Association*, *Medical Reference Services Quarterly*, and the *Journal of Hospital Librarianship*.

Marlene Saul Englander, MSLS, DM/AHIP, is Medical Librarian at the Cleveland Clinic Alumni Library, Cleveland, Ohio, and has more than 30 years experience in hospital, public health, and academic libraries. She has served in various leadership roles and on committees in the Medical Library Association and its sections and chapters and has been a frequent presenter at annual meetings. She has authored articles in the *Journal of Hospital Librarianship*, *HIMSS News*, and *National Network* on topics ranging from circuit librarianship to tracking institutional publications, and has co-authored cataloging chapters for other MLA publications. She currently is on the Editorial Board of the *Journal of Hospital Librarianship*. Englander received her BA from Indiana University and her MSLS from Case Western Reserve University. In her spare time, she is a flutist in a number of Cleveland-area ensembles.

Gretchen A. Hallerberg, MS, MSLS, DM/AHIP, is Director of the Cleveland Clinic Alumni Library, Cleveland, Ohio, starting in1981. She received bachelor's and master's degrees in biology before graduating from the Medical Librarianship program at Case Western Reserve University. She has worked in a variety of hospital and academic libraries, where a high point in her career was planning a new library six times the size of the old one. She has been a board member/officer of medical library and multi-type library organizations at the state and regional level, and is a Distinguished Member of the Academy of Health Information Professionals.

Craig C. Haynes, MS, DM/AHIP, is recently retired as Director, UC San Diego Medical Center Library, University of California, San Diego, California. He has more than 20 years of health care library management and collections experience. Though now retired, Mr. Haynes continues to serve on the faculty of the UC San Diego Physician Assessment and Clinical Education program (PACE) and provides training and consulting services to health professionals in Southern California. He is a past president of the Medical Library Group of Southern

California & Arizona (MLGSCA) and a former member of the Board of Directors of the Medical Library Association. Haynes's other publications include the monograph: *Ethnic Minority Health: A Selected, Annotated Bibliography* (Scarecrow Press, 1997) and several journal articles, mostly regarding the role of electronic knowledge-based systems in health care.

Barbara Jahn, BSPT, MHS, NHA, is Vice President of Operations, Exempla Saint Joseph Hospital, Denver, Colorado. Her career with Exempla Healthcare spans two decades. She earned her bachelor's degree in physical therapy from Northwestern University and after working for Saint Luke's Hospital in Phoenix, began her career at Exempla Saint Joseph Hospital as a physical therapist in 1985. She was quickly promoted to Director of Physical and Occupational Therapy and Neurodiagnostics and served in various leadership roles at both Exempla Saint Joseph Hospital and Exempla Lutheran Medical Center. Prior to her current position as Vice President of Operations, she was the Vice President of Performance and Clinical Excellence, and at one time served as the system director for Case Management at both hospitals. Currently she is responsible for Emergency Services, Imaging, Case Management, Lab/Pathology, the Pharmacy, Physical Medicine and Rehabilitation, Library & Media Services, and the Cancer Service Line. She also served as a Baldrige Examiner for two years. During Jahn's time at Exempla Saint Joseph Hospital, she has played an integral part in designing performance excellence functions that result in a culture of patient safety.

Dixie Alford Jones, MLS, DM/AHIP, is Associate Director of the Medical Library/Associate Professor of the Department of Medical Library Science at Louisiana State University Health Sciences Center, Shreveport, Louisiana. She has 35 years experience in health sciences libraries including nursing school, medical school, and hospital settings. She has served as president of both the Health Sciences Library Association of Louisiana and the South Central Chapter (SCC) of the Medical Library Association (MLA), and as a member of the MLA Board of Directors as well as its treasurer. She is a former chair of the MLA Hospital Libraries Section and the Louisiana Library Association's Subject Specialists Section. Dixie is currently a member of the editorial board of *Medical Reference Services Quarterly* and is co-editor of the Specialty of the House column for the *Journal of Hospital Librarianship*. Jones has been a Distinguished Member of the Academy of Health Information Professionals since 1990. Honors include receiving SCC's Distinguished Service

Award and selection as a Fellow of the National Library of Medicine's BioMedical Informatics Program.

Michele Klein-Fedyshin, BA, BSN, MSLS, RN, DM/AHIP, is clinical Reference Librarian; Faculty, University of Pittsburgh Library: Health Sciences Library System; Falk Library, University of Pittsburgh, Pittsburgh, Pennsylvania. Her present responsibilities include attending morning report with the Internal Medicine Department; Palliative Care Team membership; liaison to the Department of Psychiatry and Evidence-Based Practice Council at Western Psychiatric Institute & Clinic; and reference responsibilities such as systematic reviews. In addition, she is developing and will team-teach a distance learning course. Michele's previous positions include System Director of Library Services and Medical Photography in the Detroit Medical Center, and Manager of Library Services at Children's Hospital of Michigan. In 1996, Klein-Fedyshin received the Medical Library Association Award for Excellence and Achievement in Hospital Librarianship. She served on the Board of Regents of the National Library of Medicine from 1997–1999. She has numerous articles, grants, awards, and presentations among her accomplishments. She would like to acknowledge Peter J. Fedyshin, MD, as her constant consultant and Captain Micah J. Klein for his inspiration.

Michelle Kraft, MLS, DM/AHIP, is Senior Medical Librarian at the Cleveland Clinic Alumni Library, Cleveland, Ohio, and has more than 12 years experience in hospital libraries. She is an active member of the Medical Librarian Association serving on various committees, such as the Nominating Committee, Social Networking Task Force, National Program Committee, and she is currently the Chair-Elect of MLA's Medical Informatics Section. Kraft will begin her three-year term on the MLA Board in 2011. She has authored articles on library technologies in the *Journal of Hospital Librarianship*, *Medical Reference Services Quarterly*, and *Library Journal*. She is on the Editorial Board of *Medical Reference Services Quarterly* and is currently a member of the *New England Journal of Medicine* Library Advisory Board. Her professional interests are in the usage of social networking technologies within medicine and medical libraries and electronic resource usage.

Hope Leman, MLIS, is Research Information Technologist at the Center for Health Research and Quality, Samaritan Health Services, Corvallis, Oregon. She is a 2009 graduate of the master's program in library and information science of the University of Pittsburgh. Leman serves as the web administrator of the free online services, *ScanGrants* and *ResearchRaven*, which are designed to enable those in the health sciences to locate grants, fellowships, scholarships, and other sources of funding as well as to learn of venues in which to publish and otherwise disseminate the results of their research. Leman is particularly interested in the development of free online services by librarians and has written about such matters for such periodicals as *Medical Reference Services Quarterly*, the *Journal of Hospital Librarianship*, the *Journal of Electronic Resources in Medical Libraries, Computers in Libraries, Online*, and *Sci-Tech News*. She has served as chair of the Technology Committee of the Pacific Northwest Chapter of the Medical Library Association (PNC/MLA), as a member of the Professional Development Committee of the PNC/MLA, and as a member of the Medical Library Association's Technology Advisory Committee. Leman is a member of the MLA's Nursing and Allied Health Resources Section and Hospital Libraries Section. She began her career in health sciences librarianship as a library technical specialist at Murray Memorial Library at Good Samaritan Regional Medical Center, Corvallis, Oregon, working for Dorothy O'Brien (1943–2010), whom she would like to acknowledge as a model of a health sciences library manager who personified the skill, dedication and excellence that we all strive for in our field.

Susan Lessick, MLS, MA, DM/AHIP, is a consultant in Anaheim, California. In more than 25 years at the University of California, Irvine, she held a variety of positions in both hospital and academic settings, including Head of the Grunigen Medical Library, Acting Assistant University Librarian for Research and Instruction, and Special Associate for Copyright Education Planning at the University of California Office of the President. She was responsible for the management of traditional reference, virtual reference, instruction, and web services as well as interlibrary loan/document delivery and information technology. Throughout her career, Lessick has had a passion for research and developing new service models that employ information technology. She served as president of the Medical Library Group of Southern California and Arizona, Chair of the Hospital Library Section, and Chair of the Research Section. She received her MLS from University of California, Berkeley, and her MS from the University of California, Los Angeles. Susan was awarded the title Librarian Emeritus by the University of California, Irvine, in 2010.

Mary Fran Prottsman, MLN, AHIP, is the Associate Director, Collection Resources Division, of the Norris Medical Library at the University of Southern California in Los Angeles, California. She has managed financial plans for libraries of all sizes in private sector, U.S. Army, and Department of Veterans Affairs hospitals and medical centers in the southern United States and in Southern California as well as serving as the Department of Veterans Affairs Central Office Contracting Officer's Technical Representative for a national periodicals contract in Washington, DC. Prottsman has been an active member of MLA for more than 30 years and has enjoyed getting to know colleagues as she served on MLA's Nominating Committee, Books Panel, MLANET Editorial Board, Credentialing Committee, Mentoring Task Force, Vital Pathways Steering Committee, and Chair of the CE Grants Committee, Rittenhouse Jury, and the Award for Excellence & Achievement in Hospital Librarianship Jury. She has had the good fortune to serve as Chair of both Southern Chapter and MLA's Hospital Library Section and is currently the Chair-Elect of MLA's Collection Development Section.

Marian Simonson, MSLS, DM/AHIP, is Systems Medical Librarian at the Cleveland Clinic Alumni Library, Cleveland, Ohio. She has more than 27 years of experience in hospital libraries and has served on various committees of the Hospital Libraries Section of the Medical Library Association. She is a past co-editor of HLS' *National Network* and has written several articles for it as well. She is currently managing the library's computer and electronic resources at the Cleveland Clinic. In that role, her special interests are evaluating new products and streamlining access to e-resources for the library's customers.

Daniel Sokolow, MA, is both the Corporate Archivist and Multimedia Operations Manager for the North Shore-LIJ Health System in New York. He previously served as the Corporate Archivist for the McGraw-Hill Companies, and has held numerous other archival positions around the New York Metro area. A master's degree graduate of New York University's History and Archival Management programs, Daniel has managed every aspect of archival management including collection development, exhibit preparation, budgeting, and preservation. Sokolow's interest in technology has led to many additional responsibilities, including managing the e-Learning video portal for North Shore-LIJ. He lives on Long Island with his wife and three children.

Michele Spatz, MS, is a consultative services specialist for Planetree, an international non-profit organization dedicated to patient-centered and staff-supported health care. Michele is passionate about patient access to meaningful information, self-advocacy in the health care setting, and self-empowerment. Among other publications, she is author of *Answering Consumer Health Questions: The Medical Library Association Guide for Reference Librarians* (Neal-Schuman Publishers, 2008), and is former editor of the Charting Consumer Health column in the *Journal of Hospital Librarianship*. She has served as Chair of the Consumer and Patient Health Information Section (CAPHIS) of the Medical Library Association and was a member of the 2009 MLA Nominating Committee. A fellow of the National Library of Medicine's BioMedical Informatics Program, Spatz was awarded in 2010 the MLA Lois Ann Colaianni Award for Excellence and Achievement in Hospital Librarianship and the Outstanding Consumer Health Information Service Award from CAPHIS. She also served as President of the Oregon Health Sciences Library Association. Michele continues to teach two MLA CE courses on consumer health information. When not flying to her next assignment, Spatz lives in The Dalles, Oregon, with her husband Dan, dog Lucy, and cat Oreo. Inspired by their mother's profession, daughters Melissa and Kathryn are pursuing their own academic tracks into the medical field.

Lisa Traditi, MLS, DM/AHIP, is Head of Education at the Health Sciences Library at the University of Colorado Denver Anschutz Medical Campus (UCD-AMC), Denver, Colorado, starting in 1996. Previously she was a hospital librarian in the Denver area. Lisa leads a teaching team of 10 interdepartmental library staff and faculty in teaching hundreds of classes each year. Traditi is actively involved in the Medical Library Association (MLA) as a member of several sections and a former member of chapter council. She has served as president of both the Midcontinental Medical Library Association (MCMLA) and the Colorado Council of Medical Librarians (CCML). She has received the CCML Marla Graber Award for Excellence and Achievement in Health Sciences Librarianship and the MCMLA Bernice M. Hetzner Award for Excellence in Academic Health Science Librarianship. Lisa is the team leader for the librarian tutors at the Rocky Mountain Evidence-Based Healthcare Workshop, sponsored annually since 1999 by the University of Colorado Denver School of Public Health. Lisa contributed chapters to *Nursing Research Secrets* (Hanley & Belfus, 2003) and *Evidence Based Practice: An Implementation Guide for Healthcare Organizations* (Jones & Bartlett Publishers, 2010). In addition, Traditi was a 1999 fellow

of the National Library of Medicine's BioMedical Informatics Program and is a distinguished member of the Medical Library Association's Academy of Health Information Professionals.

Kay E. Wellik, MLS, DM/AHIP, is Director, Library Services, Mayo Clinic, Phoenix, Arizona, and Assistant Professor, Medical Informatics, College of Medicine, Mayo Clinic. She has served as Chair and Treasurer of MLA's Hospital Libraries Section. Ms. Wellik has been on the Nominating Committee, Continuing Education Committee, Academy of Health Information Professionals Credentialing Committee, National Program Committees, and was co-chair for the Local Arrangements for the MLA Annual Meeting in Phoenix. From 1995–1998, she served on the MLA Board of Directors and is a distinguished member of the Academy of Health Information Professionals. Kay is a member of several sections of the Medical Library Association and an active member of the Medical Library Group of Southern California/Arizona Chapter. She is on the editorial board for *Medical Reference Quarterly* and serves as Assistant Editor for *Journal of Hospital Librarianship*. Wellik holds a BS and MLS from San Jose State University, San Jose, California.

Lorri Zipperer, MA, is a cybrarian and the principal at Zipperer Project Management, Albuquerque, NM. She has been in the information field for more than two decades, over half of which have been focused on health care. She was a founding staff member of the National Patient Safety Foundation as the information project manager. Lorri currently works with clients to provide patient safety information, knowledge sharing, project management, and strategic development guidance. She was recognized with a 2005 Institute for Safe Medication Practices "Cheers" award for her work with librarians, libraries and their involvement in patient safety. She has initiated and published 2 national surveys of librarians on their role in patient safety work to map the evolution of that role over time. Zipperer's expertise was highlighted in the June 2009 Medical Library Association's *Role of Health Sciences Librarians in Patient Safety Position Statement.* Zipperer's knowledge management efforts focus on bringing multidisciplinary teams together to explore and enable effective knowledge transfer. She has collaborated with regional offices of the National Network of Libraries of Medicine to work with her colleagues in acute care environments to facilitate avenues for the development and implementation of knowledge-sharing initiatives.

Index

Page numbers followed by the letter "f" indicate figures; materials included on the companion CD-ROM are indicated by "CDch#." For main entries that include an overview or snapshot, for the reader's convenience, this topic appears first in the list of subentries.

3 Ds: disbelief, denial, and despair, 121
5 Ps of marketing, 54f
24/7 access, 231
30-day trial periods, 176
360Link, 169, 170, 247

A

a la carte selection, 143
A. T. Still Memorial Library (Kirksville, MO), 193
AAHSL (Association of Academic Health Sciences Libraries). *See* Association of Academic Health Sciences Libraries (AAHSL)
AAMC (Association of American Medical Colleges), 5, 6
Abels, Eileen G., 101
absences from one-person libraries, 381
Academy of Health Information Professionals (AHIP), 95
Access databases, 237
access options for users, 269
access restrictions (net nannies), 335
accessibility, ADA requirements, 195
ACCME (Accreditation Council for Continuing Medical Education), 346–347, 348
ACCME Standards for Commercial Support, 347
accountability
  budget focus on, 69
  for plan implementation, 51
Accountable Care Organizations (ACOs), 20, CDch2
accreditation, 6, 20–22, 119
Accreditation Council for Continuing Medical Education (ACCME), 346–347, 348
Accreditation Council for Graduate Medical Education (ACGME), 6, 263

ACGME (Accreditation Council for Graduate Medical Education), 6, 263
achievements recognition, 25–26
acid-free containers, 355
Ackoff, Russell, 302
ACOs (Accountable Care Organizations), 20, CDch2
acoustics, 191, 196
acquisitions
  electronic options, 139
  licensing and leasing, 136
  lists of, 57
  processes, 173–177
ACRL (American College and Research Libraries), 112, 262
ACRL (Association of College and Research Libraries). *See* Association of College and Research Libraries (ACRL)
action steps for plan implementation, 51, 52f
acute care, 14, 304
add-on budgets, 67
adjacencies within a building, 190
administrative leave, 91
administrative services, hospitals, 15
Adobe Captivate, 273, 360
adult learning principles, 266, 271
adverse events, identifying, 291
advertising, 84, 338
advisory committees, 41–42
advocacy
  administrative, 187
  of advisory committees, 41, 42
  for knowledge sharing, 313
  for one-person libraries, 384–385
aesthetically pleasing facilities, 189
Age Discrimination in Employment Act (1967), 82